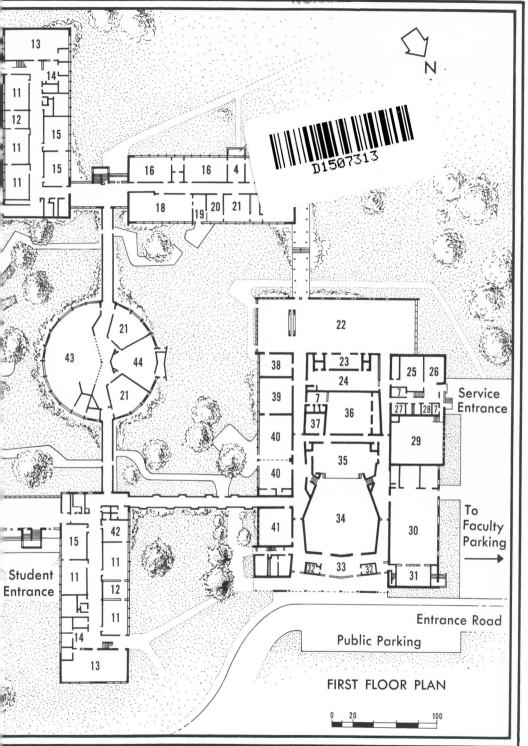

FIRST FLOOR PLAN

Newton South High School Floor Plan. Reprinted by permission of Newton School District, Newton, Massachusetts, and Architects Korslund, LeNormand, and Quann, Incorporated.

GLEN F. OVARD

Professor of Educational Administration
Brigham Young University
Provo, Utah

Administration of the Changing Secondary School

THE MACMILLAN COMPANY

COLLIER-MACMILLAN LIMITED
London

To Beverly for her patience
To Jacqueline, Kim, Ramona, David, and Roxann
for their impatience

Third Printing, 1969

Library of Congress catalog card number: 66–15027

THE MACMILLAN COMPANY
COLLIER-MACMILLAN CANADA, LTD., TORONTO, ONTARIO

Printed in the United States of America

Preface

We are living in a revolutionary period of time. Change and the need for change can be seen in all aspects of life. Long-established social values have been rejected. Moral values of past generations have been set aside. Science has replaced many aspects of religion. Man has been forced to adjust to the dynamic forces of revolution.

Education like other institutions has been affected by these changes. Never has society demanded so much of education. Not only must the educational institution adjust to these revolutionary social forces, but it must also provide each student with an education for individual excellence according to his abilities. At the same time, it must provide an education enabling him to master the science of space, to win the cooperation of fellow citizens, and to understand the processes of world peace.

Change toward the improvement of the individual and society must occur at all levels of education. Never has there been a more propitious time for educational change. Never has educational leadership of the highest order been at such a premium. The principal is the key person through whom educational change can occur. In a society of change, the principal must be an innovator of the new curricula, techniques, organizations, and administrative practices. To be effective in this role, he must organize his school and personnel for efficient instruction. He must administer his school with precision and finesse. Finally, he must evaluate all proposals for change. He should not desire change for its own sake, but he should constantly seek that which will promote a better school program for all concerned.

To accomplish these goals, the book has been organized in five major sections. The first section is concerned with "The Challenge of Leadership." The purposes of this section are to portray the principal as a leader of importance in educational improvements, to suggest guidelines and techniques through which his leadership can be improved, and to develop understanding about school administration as a profession. The nature of the leadership responsibilities are presented in chapters on the secondary school administrator, effective leadership, and the principalship as a profession.

The second and largest section of the book is "The Changing Instructional Programs." The principal should spend a major portion of his time in the areas of curriculum and instruction, so his role in curriculum improvement has been emphasized. The chapters are designed to assist him by providing the background for understanding the critical issues, the history and purpose of education, the curriculum pattern of schools, the organizational structure, the new curriculum programs, the need for experimentation.

The third major section is "The Administration of Student Affairs." Student personnel services, guidance and counseling services, the student activity program, and student discipline and control are discussed in this section.

The fourth section is designed to help the principal understand his role and function as related to business affairs, administration of the office, administration of auxiliary services, planning a secondary school, and school-community relations. Effective administration in these areas helps to create the desired atmosphere for learning and permits the principal to function more efficiently in his role as educational leader.

The final section of the book highlights the challenge to the principal as he looks to the future of education in this revolutionary time. For the principal of the future there are unlimited new educational frontiers to conquer.

The author hopes that this book will be a fundamental aid for the prospective school administrator and an in-service aid to the modern practitioner in their roles as secondary school administrators in our changing society.

To the extent that the purposes of this text are achieved, appreciation is expressed to my colleagues for their many suggestions, to my students for their critical reactions, to Lloyd C. Chilton, Jr., for his editorial advice, to William V. Layman for production, to Mrs. Karla Benson for her technical assistance, and to the authors, publishers, school administrators, boards of education, and architects for their permission to use reference and illustrative materials.

G. F. O.

Contents

List of Figures

List of Tables

PART I

Ours is a profession of great scope and difficulty.
Probably no other calling involves more complex
elements—social, human and technical.
Only persons of sound personality
and superior preparation should
enter this calling which successfully practiced
is as rewarding as it is demanding.

      —J. K. Norton, "Preparation Programs for Administrators,"
        School Executive, January 1956, p. 84.

THE CHALLENGE OF
LEADERSHIP

CHAPTER 1

The Secondary
School Administrator

"Principals are found everywhere—behind desks, at P.T.A. meetings, in halls, on stairways, on buses, in and out of classes, up and down between fourth floor storerooms and sub-first floor shop. School boards question them; supervisors watch them; teachers plague them; students alternately respect, fear and resent them; parents wonder at them and expect them to teach Johnny how to be a millionaire and still keep out of jail in sixty easy lessons."[1] The secondary school principal has been regarded as a warden, a boss, an autocrat, a will-o'-the-wisp, a slave driver, a good Joe, and occasionally a capable administrator. He sees himself as a person who is harried, tired, lonely, imposed on, Jack-of-all-trades, back patter, father confessor, office boy, and revolutionizer of the curriculum.

At any given time during the day, week, or year the principal may seem to be like any of the caricatures described. However, day in and day out he is a person intently interested in young people and their problems, constructively engaged in providing the best possible curriculum, and anxiously involved in organizing learning experiences for the young people of the community. Principals are indeed found everywhere. The education of youth in our modern changing society requires a versatile person. He must work harmoniously with students, teachers, nonteaching staff members, district personnel, and citizens. He is the responsible caretaker of the physical plant, which is frequently valued at several million dollars, and he runs a business operation of some magnitude. In all these activities he is the

[1] M. B. Scott, "What is a High School Principal?" *Clearing House*, September 1957, p. 30.

3

leader who can make the school the showplace of the nation. He can provide a learning environment that will produce makers of atom bombs, space travelers, entrepreneurs, and presidents. The principal's job is indeed interesting and varied and full of opportunity for the person who is stimulated by challenges. The principalship is a profession for those interested in organizing and administering all aspects of education that produce the attitudes, values, knowledge, and skills for the generations of the future.

Nature of Secondary School Administration

Leadership in school administration has been studied primarily from four main approaches: the man, the social setting, the tasks, and the process.[2] Each of these approaches has been emphasized at different times. Singly none of these approaches adequately describes the principalship and the nature of secondary school administration. By use of all these approaches, the principalship can be described fairly accurately. The following description and questions might be made about each approach:

1. The man approach emphasizes the man as the person, the principal as a personality. What personal qualities are necessary to be a principal? What skills must he possess? Can these qualities be developed?

2. The social setting emphasizes the complex social forces that affect the secondary school enterprise. How does the social setting affect education? How do these forces affect the man and his position? Are all school situations the same or is each one different—just as the principals are different?

3. The process approach emphasizes the dimensions of the administrator's actions or processes. What acts does he perform? What are the processes involved in secondary school administration? Are these acts common to all principals and school administrators?

4. The tasks approach emphasizes the specific jobs to be done. What does a principal need to know about organizing the school day, financial affairs, physical facilities, community relations? How does he work with faculty, staff, and students? What are his major functions?

Three of these approaches—the man, the social setting, and the tasks—are discussed in Chapter 1. The process of administration and general concepts of authority and responsibility are presented in Chapter 2. The principalship as a profession is discussed in Chapter 3.

---

[2] Donald J. Leu and Herbert C. Rudman, *Preparation Programs for School Administrators.* Seventh U.C.E.A. Career Development Seminar (East Lansing, Mich.: Michigan State University, 1963).

The "Man" and Effective Leadership

A Historical Review. In recent years a vast collection of material about leadership has been written. In areas of government, business, and education a central question has been, "What constitutes effective leadership?" Leadership effectiveness has run through the gauntlet of "Leaders are born" to "Leaders are products of their environment." The idea that men are born to be leaders through their social class was discarded long ago because the basic premise was incompatible with democracy. However, the search for leaders has continued as a necessary condition for the operation of our democracy.

Leaders have been analyzed for leadership traits in hopes that some universal traits might be found. Physical appearance, energy output, intelligence, and other personality traits have been analyzed.[3] In 1940, Bird surveyed the studies concerned with the trait approach. He discovered 79 traits, which were identified in 20 different studies. Only 5 per cent of these traits were common to four or more investigations.[4]

Gradually there developed a shift away from the trait approach to leadership typology,[5] biography,[6] motivation,[7] and behavior.[8] Researchers are presently spending most of their time in studying group dynamics and the leaders who evolve through the group process.[9]

---

[3] C. G. Browne and T. S. Cohn, *The Study of Leadership* (Illinois: Interstate Printers and Publishers, Inc., 1958). R. M. Stogdill, "Personal Factors Associated with Leadership," *Journal of Psychology*, 1958, pp. 37–71. Alvin W. Gouldner (ed.), *Studies in Leadership: Leadership and Democratic Action* (New York: Harper and Brothers, 1950), pp. 23–25.

[4] Charles Bird, *Social Psychology* (New York: Appleton-Century-Crofts, 1940), 564 pp.

[5] Fritz Redl, "Group Emotion and Leadership," *Psychiatry*, 1942.

[6] Lester G. Selegman, "The Study of Political Leadership," *The American Political Science Review*, December 1950.

[7] Carroll L. Shartle, "Studies in Naval Leadership, Part I," in Harold Guetzkow (ed.). *Groups, Leadership and Men* (Pittsburgh: Carnegie Press, 1951). Chester I. Bernard, *The Functions of an Executive* (Cambridge, Mass.: Harvard Press), 1938.

[8] Dorwin Cartwright and Alvin Zander (eds.), *Group Dynamics: Research and Theory*, 2nd ed. (Illinois: Row Peterson, 1960).

[9] Leland P. Bradford, Jack R. Gibb, and Kenneth D. Benne, *T-Group Theory and Laboratory Method* (New York: John Wiley & Sons, 1964). Warren G. Bennis, Kenneth D. Benne, and Robert Chin, *The Planning of Change* (New York: Holt, Rinehart and Winston, 1961). C. G. Browne and Thomas S. Cohn, *op. cit.* Murray G. Ross and Charles E. Hendry, *New Understandings of Leadership: A Survey and Application of Research* (New York: Association Press, 1957). Cartwright and Zander, *op. cit.* Thomas Gordon, *Group-Centered Leadership* (New York: Houghton Mifflin Co., 1955). Kenneth D. Benne and Bozidar Muntyan, *Human Relations in Curriculum Change* (New York: Dryden Press, 1951).

Effective Leadership and Personality. A study of effective leadership has indicated that leadership, per se, cannot be divorced from the person under discussion. The personal character traits are an important aspect of the functioning of a leader. However, the role of leaders and the specific situations in which the leaders are found indicate that a great many characteristics are needed. A specific situation may require one set of characteristics while another situation may call forth the opposite characteristics. Thus, we can say that the principalship does not require a special set of universal personality traits. The placement of a particular principal should be analyzed in terms of the situation and its needs and the type of personality required by the principal to meet the situation.

Personal Characteristics Desired of Principals. However, there does exist an image of what the modern-day principal should be like. Perhaps the image has been formed because the need for this type of a person is so frequent. The image has also been based on research studies that point out that certain characteristics tend to be generally desirable. Based on this popular image, the following personal characteristics are set forth as generally desirable qualifications for a principal:[10]

1. Intelligence. The principal should be above average in intelligence. By above average is meant that he should be at least as intelligent as the group with whom he works. It is generally accepted that he should rate somewhat higher in intelligence than the group. There is some indication, however, that if he excels the group by an extreme degree, his ideas are often not accepted. This condition is true though the ideas may be better than other alternatives.

2. Good Health. The principal should have good health. He needs to be sound in body and mind. The nature of his work is exacting in terms of mental and emotional strain and stress. Good physical and mental health are requisites for maximum effectiveness.

3. Self-Confidence. The many acts of initiative related to the faculty and staff, the superintendent, the students, and the members of the community require that he have confidence in himself and his ideas. When self-confidence is missing in an administrator, he ends up as a rubber stamp for persons or groups who do have confidence in themselves and their ideas.

4. Sociability. To function effectively in all the duties and responsibilities placed upon a principal, he must interact with many individuals and groups of people. To work effectively with all, the principal must be friendly, cheerful, genial, and sociable in his approach to people.

[10] Stogdill, *op. cit.*, pp. 35–71. Bird, *op. cit.* Gouldner, *op. cit.*, pp 23–25. Shartle, *op. cit.*

5. Consideration for Others. It is not enough to be friendly and sociable when one must work closely with other individuals for intensive and long periods of time. Many interpersonal problems arise. Every individual desires respect and consideration from his fellow human beings even though the idea he is espousing is not accepted or is wrong. Respect for human dignity requires considerateness on the part of leaders. Where illness, accident, or death of a family member is involved, a considerate principal can be most effective and create lasting good will by simple acts that show the person that the principal is concerned with his ideas, attitudes, and feelings. The effectiveness of an administrator could be shown by using the continuum for basic illustration. Refer to Figure 1.1.

Figure 1.1

Continuum of Concern for Opinion, Attitudes, and Feelings of Others

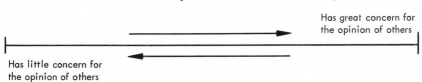

Has great concern for the opinion of others

Has little concern for the opinion of others

6. Professionally Minded. A principal should be positive in his approach to individuals and their problems. He should have a positive attitude toward the educational profession and toward the students, teachers, administrators, and other staff members in this profession. He must recognize the "good" for the profession and do what he can do to further it. Occasionally, he must face, with strength, opposition to the profession, its ideas, and its members.

7. Morally Strong. It is expected that a principal will exemplify high moral character. Adherence to standards of morality, honesty, and integrity are expected everywhere. Some of the other values of good or bad conduct will vary from one community to another and from one time period to another. However, a given community will expect the principal to uphold the values that are dominant in the community.

The Social Setting and Secondary School Administration

The Changing Society Affects Secondary School Administration. In order to understand the social setting of secondary school administration, one must understand that there are forces in our society that are producing vast changes. Some of these changes that affect our schools are the following: (1) the population explosion and the increasing enrollments, (2) the knowledge explosion and the increased demands in number and quality of curricular offering, (3) the increased value placed on education and the increased number of people from all social classes who desire more education and the increased emphasis on solutions for the problem of school dropouts, (4) the technological revolution with improved and changing methods of teaching, (5) the increase in leisure time for all segments of the population, (6) the stress on science and scientific discovery, and (7) the anxiety over world tensions, wars, and threats of wars. All these forces and many more affect the philosophy of the curriculum, the teaching-learning activities and the administration of the secondary schools. The externa-interna concept of the educational system in the social setting is provided by Downey in Figure 1.2.

Figure 1.2

A Concept of the Educational System in Its Setting—Interna and Externa

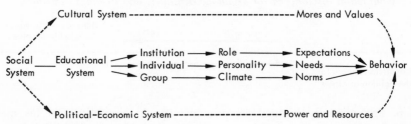

SOURCE: Lawrence W. Downey, "The Secondary School Principal," in Donald J. Leu and Herbert C. Rudman, *Preparation Programs for School Administrators, Common and Specialized Learnings*, p. 128. Copyright ©, 1963. Reprinted by permission of Michigan State University.

The social forces to be dealt with in one school may be quite different from those found in another school in another community.

Complexity in Secondary School Administration. All these forces of school administration can be found in school situations. Schools are different. A principal should recognize that every community or social setting is different, and as a result special problems and tasks arise. Many problems of a large high school are not present in a small high school, and the reverse is also true. Urban districts must solve different problems than rural schools. Rich and poor districts must find solutions to their own unique situations. Certain geographical, social, and cultural areas have conditions that are not present in other areas.

This complexity of problems in secondary school administration and the approaches to an analysis of secondary school administration can be demonstrated by examining the individual schools. Four examples of schools with different problems are presented for illustration and analysis. These examples are presented in a personalized, this-is-what-really-does-happen style. It is hoped that the student will visualize these situations as if he were the incumbent principal in such a position.

EXAMPLE ONE: URBAN HIGH SCHOOL

Richard Green was proud. He was proud to be the principal of Urban High School. The school had been built ten years before, and he had been principal of it for seven years. He was proud of the efficiency of his school. He had it well organized and staffed. He believed in the line and staff organization, and it seemed to be functioning well. In his mind and in the teachers handbook the line of authority went like this:

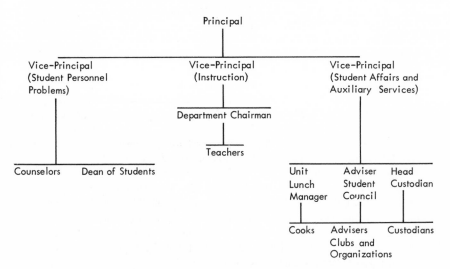

Mr. Green arrived at school at 8 A.M. every morning. An organization with 80 members required careful coordination. The school could function smoothly in his absence because he spent the time necessary to see that proper policies were made. However, Mr. Green knew that making policy was only one aspect of providing for an efficiently operated school. Interpreting the policies to the faculty, staff, and community was another problem. Handling abuses of and exceptions to the policies was still another aspect. As Mr. Green looked over his memorandum pad for the day, he mentally noted that he had a 10:30 A.M. appointment with the district administration to discuss items in the budget that he had submitted two weeks previously, a luncheon appointment with the Education Committee of the Chamber of Commerce, a 2:30 appointment with Jim Allen, Vice Principal responsible for Student Affairs, and at 4 P.M. he had his administrative staff meeting. Oh yes, tonight he was to give a speech at a Kiwanis meeting.

Mr. Green buzzed his secretary on the intercom. "Would you have George Lee (Vice Principal over Instruction) come in as soon as he arrives. I have a luncheon meeting with the Chamber of Commerce Education Committee today. I believe it would be well to duplicate the report I gave you yesterday. I think it would help us if they could see how well our students do on the various college entrance tests. Check with the vice principals to see if they have additional items to be placed on the agenda for the administrative staff meeting tonight, and send a memo to Jim Allen to give some thought to broadening the extracurricular program so we can encourage more students to participate. I'll discuss some ideas with him at 2:30."

Mr. Green began to go over his talk for Kiwanis, "What the Schools Are Doing to Meet the Space Age Challenge."

Mr. Lee came in at 8:40. "Sorry I couldn't get here sooner. I had to get a substitute teacher oriented with our procedure."

"Who is ill?" asked Mr. Green.

"Bill Richens is down with the flu. You know Bill, he teaches our five sections of geometry. I had to call four of the people on our substitute list before I could find a teacher."

"George, arranging for substitutes is getting to be a bigger problem every day," said Mr. Green. "Why not make the department chairmen responsible for the teachers in their department? It seems to me that this would have several advantages."

"How would we handle the payroll end of it?" asked George. "I am responsible to get the payroll to the district office each month."

"That's a problem all right," said Mr. Green. "Let's think it over. I believe something could be worked out. But that isn't what I wanted to see you about. I have a 10 A.M. appointment with the district administration about our budget. Apparently they have some questions about it. The total amount requested was 15 per cent higher than last year, and they are trying to keep it down. I am certain that they will ask us to trim the amount down. What items do we least need?"

Mr. Green and Mr. Lee reviewed the budget carefully and determined where the reductions could be made. Mr. Lee then said, "The Department chairmen report that the new absentee procedure that Mr. Vail (Vice Principal in charge of Student Personnel) is trying doesn't seem to be working. The teachers complain that it takes too much of their time to do the checking each period."

"Have they informed Mr. Vail of their objectives?" asked Mr. Green.

"No," said Mr. Lee. "They assumed that I was the one to whom they should report."

"I'm not so sure when it involves Mr. Vail's responsibility and policy. Let's talk it over with Mr. Vail and get the problem on the agenda for the administrative staff meeting tonight. Would you tell my secretary to include it on the agenda? I have an appointment at 2:30. Let's see if we can get together with Mr. Vail at 2:00 before staff meeting. Will you see if he is free at that time?"

Mr. Green buzzed his secretary and notified her that he was leaving for the district office and wouldn't be back until 2:00 P.M., and that she could reach him at the district office until 12:00 if he were needed.

EXAMPLE TWO: SMALL HIGH SCHOOL

John Little, principal of Small High School, was awakened at 7:00 A.M. by his ringing telephone. "Hello—yes. I'm sorry to hear that Bill is ill.

Has he a lesson plan at school that the substitute can use? No? Tell him not to worry—we'll work things out. Just get well. Thanks for calling. Good-by."

John Little knows that in this sparsely populated and isolated area finding a qualified substitute for Bill is a near impossibility. Bill teaches algebra, general math, physics (physics this year—chemistry next), geometry (geometry this year—advanced algebra and trigonometry next), and American history, and has one period free so he can handle the school lunch money during the lunch hour.

Mr. Little tried but was unsuccessful in finding a substitute, so he decided that he and other teachers would have to fill in.

Mr. Little arrived at school by 8:00 A.M., as was his custom. He had little enough time to take care of the administrative details even though he put in a 60-hour week. He had to teach five classes every day.

At 8:10 the agriculture teacher came into the office with fire in his eyes. "It isn't right! I tell you it isn't right! I won't teach here unless something is done about it!"

Mr. Little was disturbed at this reaction from one of his better teachers. Outwardly calm, he said, "What isn't right, Joe?"

"Do you know what that coach has done? Well, you know our state F.F.A. judging contest is this Saturday." Mr. Little nodded his head. "The state track meet is the same day. The coach told the boys that unless they participated in the track meet he wouldn't let them play football or basketball next year. He told the boys he would flunk them."

"How many of our boys are involved in both activities?" asked Mr. Little.

"I only have one boy who isn't involved. It isn't right for the coach to ruin our teams. What are you going to do about it?"

"I'll talk to him. Maybe we can get together and work something out. Meet me here after school tonight."

Miss Ellen, the school secretary, opened the door and said, "Mr. and Mrs. James are here to see you, and here is a list of things that the Junior Prom Committee needs to complete their decorations, and Mrs. Jones hopes you can visit her class today during fifth period. She has a special program today."

Mr. Little began to make out a purchase order but stopped and said, "Get the Junior Prom Chairman to come here and tell Mrs. Jones I'll be in as soon as I can get my class started."

He talked to Mr. and Mrs. James about their son, who sluffed school yesterday, solicited their support, and wrote out a slip admitting their son back to school.

As they left, the chairman of the Junior Prom Committee came in. The school bell rang as Mr. Little was explaining that the school had a policy which made it necessary for him to refuse to spend school money for a present for the adviser of the junior class. Miss Ellen put her head in the door and said, "There is a lot of confusion down the hall. Isn't Bill here today? His room is locked."

"No, he is ill. Unlock the door and tell them I'll be right down."

Mr. Little gave her the keys, completed the purchase order, and made out a late slip for the Junior Prom chairman. Then he went to his own class and gave them a reading assignment in the next chapter and told them that it was necessary for him to leave them and that he would discuss yesterday's work tomorrow. Then he went to Bill's class, quieted the bedlam, and spent five minutes finding out where they were in the text. He was just explaining the examples given in the text when Miss Ellen opened the door and said, "Pardon me, Mr. Little, but there is a salesman here from Audio Visual Incorporated. He wants to be at Valley High by noon. He would like to talk with you a minute and show you some new equipment."

So went Mr. Little's day—and the next—and the next.

Example Three: Rich High vs. Poor High School

Two young men were seated by each other at the state secondary school administrators' conference. The conference theme was "Improving Instruction in Secondary Schools." Mr. Moore and Mr. Less were principals of schools with a student population of 750. Both had the proper administrative certificate and held a master's degree in administration from State University.

After a few minutes of informal, get-acquainted conversation, Mr. Moore remarked, "I certainly think the theme of this conference is a good one. Improvement of instruction is the most important job of the principal."

"Yes," agreed Mr. Less. "It certainly is. I enjoyed the remarks of the keynote speaker. It seems to me that he hit the nail on the head when he said, 'The most important function of the administrator is to provide an environment conducive for holding good teachers in the systems.'"

"I think so, too," said Mr. Moore. "I'm working with the superintendent and board of education on a special project right now. We want to add swimming to the curriculum. The board has requested that some drawings be submitted. The teachers are really enthused about the idea. We told the faculty that they might use the pool during their free period each day and that every Wednesday from 4:00 to 6:30 would be reserved especially for faculty members and their partners."

"A swimming pool must be pretty expensive to build and to operate. Do you think your board will approve your request?" asked Mr. Less.

"Oh sure, I'm not worried about the pool," replied Mr. Moore. "I'm more concerned about the faculty dressing room, showers, and toilet facilities that we plan to build in connection with the swimming pool. We may have trouble here. Our superintendent has the president of the board with him today at this conference. I am certain the president of the board will be determined to do all he can to hold good teachers after attending this conference. The president carries a lot of weight on our board. He is the divisional manager of the oil company. Whenever he speaks, the whole community nods assent."

"I certainly would like to have a swimming pool added to our physical education facilities," said Mr. Less. "However, there isn't a chance in the world. We can't even get enough basketballs and other play equipment to take care of our present program. Our request for two new basketballs was turned down yesterday. Our library budget is the lowest in the state. We just can't seem to get the supplies the teachers need, and a free period for teachers is unthinkable."

"Doesn't the board support your school system?" inquired Mr. Moore.

"Oh, it isn't the board's fault. There just isn't any money available," said Mr. Less. "We are at the maximum mill levy for maintenance and operation. Most of our program is financed through state aid. Now, if the state really wants to improve instruction at our high school, the state should raise the equalization level so more money can be channeled to the poor schools."

"Oh, no," said Mr. Moore. "I would oppose this. Already our district is giving away too much of its money. If the state raised the level, we might not be able to give our teachers a raise next year. If we are going to keep our good teachers, we must have some financial flexibility so we can keep them happy."

"I agree that teachers need a raise. We lost half of our teachers this past year to districts that could pay more money. We did get a $100-a-year increase this year. The increase helped, but we still had to hire seven uncertificated teachers."

"We don't have any trouble attracting new teachers," said Mr. Moore. "We raised our minimum salary to $6,500 and our maximum to $10,000."

Mr. Less whistled. "Man, that's good! In fact, your beginning teachers make as much as I do. What do the principals get? Maybe I should see your superintendent."

Improvement of instruction involves different concepts for Mr. Moore and Mr. Less. Rich High School has $35,000 of assessed valuation behind every child. Poor High School has $150 behind each child. Mr. Moore's proposals for basic improvements are luxuries to Mr. Less. Mr. Moore is concerned about swimming pools. Mr. Less is concerned with helping teachers find new ways to utilize makeshift equipment.

Many of Mr. Less' problems—inadequate facilities, lack of qualified teachers, dearth of supplies and equipment, and low morale—are due to financial inadequacy never experienced by Mr. Moore.

EXAMPLE FOUR: TRANSIENT HIGH SCHOOL

Transient High School was located in a vegetable-and-fruit-growing area. It was a beautiful school, and the citizens of the area were justly proud. The Board of Education could meet the ordinary expenses of operating a school, and they were willing to pay the teachers and principal a better salary than many other schools in similar circumstances. However, the citizens were concerned because their principal and their teachers did not remain with them more than two or three years before moving to other areas.

Mr. Jones, a new principal of Transient High School, was at the school even though the school year had not yet commenced. He was carefully planning the schedule for next year. A careful review of his text in second-ary school administration pointed out that one of the first conditions for proper schedule making was to know the total enrollment and the enroll-ment of the school by grades. Mr. Jones knew what classes were required. He also knew that he had to start by determining the number of sections of each required subject that must be offered.

After thumbing through two file drawers of materials, Mr. Jones found the yearly statistical report. He copied the data on a piece of scratch paper.

	Total Enroll-ment	Average Daily Attendance
First term	601	504
Second term	710	308
Third term	805	350
Fourth term	1,202	479
Total enrollment	1,202	410

Mr. Jones then started to analyze the data. The more he looked, the more puzzled and bewildered he became. The highest average daily attend-ance figure was 504, yet the total enrollment reached 1,202. The fall average daily attendance was larger than the rest, yet enrollments kept going up. In desperation Mr. Jones phoned the superintendent. The super-intendent laughed at Mr. Jones's perplexing problem and invited the new principal to his office for his first orientation to an endless problem.

"In the first place," said Mr. Superintendent, "you are living in an agri-cultural area. Harvest season and planting season are the two big seasons. Much of the labor at these seasons of the year comes from migrant workers. The workers follow the crops from one place to another. When the harvest is over in our valley, the laborers move farther north. Does this explain your problem?"

"Well, yes," said Mr. Jones, "but it looks like I will need 16 teachers to handle the large enrollments. I believe you said there were ten hired and you were looking for three more."

"Thirteen is right," said Mr. Superintendent. "You might need 16 teachers for your peak period, but you would only need about ten for your low period. Since our basic state financial program is based on average daily attendance, we can hire only 13. During your highest attendance period we will see if someone in the community will assist us for a few months.

Mr. Jones took his problem back to his school and worked and worked. When he was satisfied that he had the best possible solution, he waited expectantly for registration.

On registration day 400 students enrolled. On each succeeding day addi-tional students enrolled. On Friday the enrollment had reached 501. Mr. Jones notified the faculty that they had reached the anticipated enrollment and that the teachers could settle down and hold school. That afternoon

35 students withdrew from school. Monday morning 50 new students enrolled, and on each succeeding day a few more students enrolled. It took Mr. Jones's mornings just to get students registered. Friday afternoon 25 students withdrew. The new week was a repeat of the previous week—new students, withdrawals, new students, withdrawals.

Mr. Jones could not find time to help the new teachers. Their morale was low. One teacher expressed the opinion of all when he said, "How can we teach school, when we can't even keep track of the students?" After the third week, a teacher quit. A housewife with two years of general college training was finally obtained to fill the vacancy.

After four weeks, a discouraged and frustrated Mr. Jones again put in a call to the superintendent. Mr. Superintendent again invited Mr. Jones to his office for a review of the facts of life and how to handle them at Transient High School.

The above examples highlight the degrees that can be found in school situations. A long list of different types of school could be enumerated in addition to those described, such as senior high schools, junior high schools, combination junior-senior high schools, vocational schools, night schools, combination junior-senior high schools, vocational schools, night dated schools. All these schools could be found in varying degrees of similarity or blends of different types in the many communities throughout America.

Elements Common to All Principalships

It is true that each community and each school will have some unique characteristics. This uniqueness brings the great diversity that can be found in secondary school administration. However, it is equally true that there are many elements that are common to all communities and to all schools. The students in all communities must be educated. A curriculum must be offered. The curriculum must change to meet the changing conditions of society. The needs of all American youth must be met. Classes, teachers, and students must be scheduled. Promoting effective teaching must be a continuous function. The principals must carry out the job requirements set forth by the board of education. They must be skilled in human relations. They must handle the day-to-day operational problems of business, school plant, and maintenance.

Many and varied are the principal's tasks. A major objective of this text is to help prospective and new principals become acquainted with these common areas and to aid them in the solution of the problems that arise. Therefore, a more definite understanding of the specific tasks to be performed is needed.

Tasks of Secondary School Principals

Great Number and Variety of Duties. One of the most common complaints of secondary school administrators is that they do not have enough time for the job. Stated more appropriately—the functions they regard to be most important are not being performed as they desire. There is often a conflict between how they do spend their time and how they think they should spend their time.

As one examines the number and variety of activities performed by the principal, it becomes easy to understand why a principal is sometimes regarded as a "Jack-of-all-trades" or as a person who does "something for everybody."

Total Time Spent on the Job. As one studies the multitude of duties required of the principal, it becomes obvious that the principalship is extremely demanding in terms of the time needed for the job. A successful principal cannot arrive and leave with the students or the teachers. A national study of the secondary school principals of the nation reveals that over 75 per cent of the principals spent 50 hours or more on the job, 45 per cent spent 50 to 59 hours, 23 per cent spent 60 to 69 hours, and 7 per cent spent 70 or more hours on the job. At the other extreme, only 7 per cent spent less than 40 hours per week. The median work week was 54 hours.[11] The school day and the school year are extended both ways for a principal. Based on a study of 500 Pennsylvania principals, a principal can expect to spend 521.66 hours a year extra time over the regular school day for others—more than 13 weeks, or about three and one-half months extra time.[12]

There is no standard that prescribes for a new principal the number of hours he will be required to spend each week. Each person is different in his work capacity and efficiency. Each position has its special requirements. However, there are numerous studies that show how he should distribute his time most effectively and what tasks are considered to be most important.

How the Principal Spends His Time. There have been a number of interesting studies reported in which the many duties are grouped into categories of related items, and the amount of time spent on each category has been determined. A study by Davis in 1921,[13] Billet in 1932,[14] and

[11] J. K. Hemphill, "Progress Report: A Study of the Secondary-School Principalship, Part II," *Bulletin of N.A.S.S.P.*, April 1964, p. 222.

[12] "The Study of the High School Principalship in Pennsylvania," *Bulletin of N.A.S.S.P.*, December 1953, p. 119.

[13] Adapted from H. C. Davis, "Duties of High School Principals," Part I, 20th Yearbook, North Central Association, 1921, pp. 49–69.

[14] "National Survey of Secondary Education," Bulletin No. 17, Monograph 11 (Washington, D.C.: U.S. Office of Education, 1932), p. 117.

Davis in 1953[15] indicated that although principals spend less time teaching than formerly, they are still spending too much of their time in routine administration and activities and not enough on curriculum. Davis' study revealed that 73 per cent of the week of the participating principals was given to activities falling within five major categories of administrative duties: namely, the organization, administration, and improvement of the instructional program; administrative routine; the organization, administration, and improvement of the guidance program; community relations; and the organization and administration of the school staff. In view of the considerable time given to them, these activities might be termed the "key duties" of secondary school principals. Three of these major categories—instruction, guidance, and the school staff—relate rather directly to the learning program of the school.[16]

A detailed breakdown of how the California principals spent their time is shown in Table 1.1 by size of schools. It can be seen that there is a direct relationship between the size of the school and the amount of time spent on curriculum and instruction. The principals of small schools spent more time teaching, while principals of larger schools spent more time in curriculum and instruction, guidance, and problems of the staff. The same general trend as to how time is spent is reported by Oregon principals.[17]

How Should a Principal Spend His Time?   The detailed examination of the duties of the secondary school principal reveals how the time of the principal is spent. But an examination of duties does not reveal how the principal's time should be divided. Practically all the studies on this topic indicate that the principal spends too much time on managerial and routine duties and not enough time on curriculum improvement. There is general agreement that the principal is the key person in the improvement of instruction. There is further agreement that improvement and supervision of the instructional program should be his major concern. Downey indicates that it is this phase of secondary school administration that makes the principal's tasks unique. He states:

> It is suggested that, in the case of the secondary school principalship, the order of priority that should be assigned to the various task areas *is exactly the reverse of the order in which they are listed above.* That is to say, finance and business management is the least crucial and calls for the lowest level of involvement; program developments and instructional leadership is the most crucial and calls for the highest level of specialized involve-

[15] H. Curtis Davis, "Where Does the Time Go?" *California Journal of Secondary Education*, October 1953, pp. 347–60.

[16] *Ibid.*, p. 349.

[17] Harold V. McAbee, "Time for the Job," *Bulletin of N.A.S.S.P.*, March 1958, p. 41.

TABLE 1.1 Per Cent of Hours Devoted to 15 Major Categories of Administrative Duties, Shown by Type of Duty and Size of School, by 324 California Secondary School Principals During One Week, March 16–20, 1953

Administrative Duties	SIZE OF SCHOOL				Total, Per Cent
	0–249 (50 Schools), Per Cent	250–749 (101 Schools), Per Cent	750–1,499 (110 Schools), Per Cent	1,500–3,900 (63 Schools), Per Cent	
1. Organization, administration, and improvement of the instructional program	22.91	24.80	27.33	30.95	26.56
2. Administrative routine	16.28	14.24	13.85	13.30	14.24
3. Organization, administration, and improvement of the guidance program	10.72	16.36	14.12	11.66	13.83
4. Community relations	7.63	8.69	10.21	11.15	9.53
5. Organization and administration of the school staff	4.63	7.50	10.43	9.86	8.53
6. Administration of the school plant	5.55	6.13	5.92	4.74	5.69
7. Board of education and administrative responsibilities	4.35	5.53	5.32	5.80	5.33
8. Business administration	6.42	6.26	4.21	3.62	5.08
9. Professional duties	3.68	3.39	3.00	2.98	3.07
10. Teaching	14.57	1.36	0.45	0.27	2.84
11. Planning the school year	0.58	1.97	1.90	2.50	1.84
12. Principal's personal business and misc.	1.29	1.98	1.93	1.64	1.79
13. Transportation	1.96	1.01	0.33	0.34	0.79
14. Relations with higher institutions	0.15	0.34	0.60	0.76	0.48
15. Principal's personal improvement	0.28	0.44	0.40	0.43	0.40
Total	100.00	100.00	100.00	100.00	100.00

Source: H. Curtis Davis, "Where Does the Time Go?" *California Journal of Secondary Education*, October 1953, p. 350. Reprinted by permission of *California Journal of Secondary Education*.

ment. In fact, I would contend that *it is primarily the unique aspects of the secondary school principal's tasks in program development and instructional leadership that makes his position a specialized one in educational administration.*[18]

A good example of how lay persons, teachers, and administrators regard this important function is found in a study at Lehigh University in Pennsylvania. Based on an analysis of about two thousand statements from these sources, the first three duties of the secondary school principal were: (1) leadership in the professional improvement of the staff; (2) improving classroom instruction; and (3) building and improving the curriculum.[19]

In the Oregon study the actual time spent by principals on their various duties is compared to the time both Oregon principals and national authorities thought they should spend on these duties. These data are presented in Table 1.2.

TABLE 1.2   Comparison of Time Spent with Principals and Authorities' Opinions As to How Time Should Be Spent in the Secondary Principalship

Categories of Duties	PERCENTAGE OF TIME		
	Authorities' Opinions N29	*Principal's Opinions* N204	*Actually Spent* N62
Office routine	9.7	12.9	22.5
Activity program	8.7	9.2	17.8
Teaching	3.1	5.9	13.0
Supervision of teachers and improvement of instruction	31.0	22.0	12.0
Pupil personnel	11.1	14.5	8.4
Public relations	9.7	6.7	5.6
Professional meetings	5.6	3.7	6.6
Administration of the plant	4.2	6.4	4.6
Superintendents' conferences	4.1	2.7	2.8
Business management	5.7	7.8	2.7
School board	2.1	3.2	2.2
Cafeteria	2.3	2.4	1.1
Transportation	2.8	2.6	.7

Source: Harold V. McAbee, "Time for the Job," *Bulletin of N.A.S.S.P.*, p. 41. Reprinted by permission from the *Bulletin of the National Association of Secondary-School Principals*, March 1958. Copyright: Washington, D.C.

[18] Lawrence W. Downey in Donald J. Leu and Herbert C. Rudman, *op. cit.*, p. 130.
[19] Pennsylvania Branch N.A.S.S.P., "The Study of the High School Principalship in Pennsylvania," *Bulletin of N.A.S.S.P.*, December 1953, p. 118.

A study of these data further indicates differences between how time should be spent and how it actually is spent. Office routine, activity program, and teaching took approximately twice as much time, 53 per cent, as the principals, 27 per cent, or authorities, 21.5 per cent, thought should be taken on these duties. Supervision and improvement of instruction received only 12 per cent of the principals' time, whereas, in contrast, the principals thought that 22 per cent of their time should be devoted to this area, while the authorities called for 31 per cent.

Summary

Leadership in secondary schools is the primary function of the school principal. A combination of the following approaches to the leadership functions best describes the secondary school administration as a profession: the man as a person; the social setting of the school, community, and society; the process or administrative actions; and the tasks to be accomplished.

A study of effective leadership and personality reveals that the diversified needs of the school situation do not require a universal personality or a special set of personality traits. However, the common school situations indicate that, generally speaking, the principal should be: above average in intelligence, in good health, self-confident, considerate of others, professionally minded, and morally strong.

The changing society has great effect on secondary schools. Some of these social forces affecting education are the population explosion, the knowledge explosion, the increased value placed on education, the technological revolution, the increased amount of leisure time, emphasis on science, and the anxiety over world tensions and conflicts. These forces, combined with many other unique problems in the various communities, have created diverse and complex social settings for secondary schools.

There are all types and degrees of secondary schools, such as urban, rural, junior high, senior high, consolidated, rich, poor, integrated, night, boarding, and private.

The tasks of the principal are many and varied, but there seems to be agreement that the unique task of the principal is the improvement of curriculum and instructional program. Some summary conclusions that can be made regarding the principal's duties and the manner in which he spends his time are: (1) the principal performs a wide variety of tasks; (2) the skills, training, and experience needed to perform the duties are extensive; (3) the nature of the response of the principal to the job situations determines whether the position is lonely or friendly, managerial or professional, autocratic or cooperative; (4) the total time spent on the job is probably well over 50 hours per week for principals; (5) certain duties, such as routine and student activity program, monopolize an excessive amount of time of the principal; (6) certain duties, such as supervision of teaching and improvement of instruction, are often neglected for other immediate and less important duties; (7) the manner in which a principal spends his time depends to some extent on the size of the school; principals of small schools spend more time in teaching; principals of larger schools spend proportionately more time on instruction; (8) the demands of time, variety of duties, and nature of the job require a professionally trained person whose personality can be adjusted to the many requirements that will be made of him; and (9) the gap between the desirable theory of how the principal should spend his time and the actual practice of how he does spend his time can be lessened or eliminated.

SUGGESTED PROJECTS AND ACTIVITIES

1. Debate: The man makes the job vs. the situation makes the man.
2. Arrange an appointment with one of the local secondary school principals. Discuss with him some of the following questions:
   a. What is your most important job as you see it?
   b. What is your most pressing problem?
   c. Which departments or areas of your school require more time than others?
   d. What things have you done this week that you believe have improved instruction?
   e. Which tasks do you find most disagreeable?
   f. Which tasks are most pleasant?
   g. What are some of the conditions in the community that affect your school and your administration of the school?
3. Survey secondary school administrators and list their varied duties.
4. Have each student describe the personality characteristics of his principal that most impressed him.
5. Role play the principal of each of the example schools presented in this chapter. Analyze the example from the approaches to secondary school administration described: the man, the social setting, and the tasks.

REVIEW AND DISCUSSION QUESTIONS

1. Why is it difficult to describe the qualities needed to be a successful secondary school administrator?

2. What are some factors that create diversity and complexity in any particular school?
3. How does a principal generally spend his time?
4. How should he spend his time?
5. What is the most important function of a principal?
6. What would you do to improve instruction if you were principal of a
   a. Small high school?
   b. Urban high school?
   c. Rich high school?
   d. Poor high school?
7. What are the main approaches used to describe secondary school administration as a profession?
8. Why should all these approaches be used together in this description rather than as separate approaches?
9. What are some of the elements common to all school administration?

SELECTED BIBLIOGRAPHY

Browne, C. G., and T. S. Cohn. *The Study of Leadership*. Illinois: Interstate Printers and Publishers, Inc., 1958.

Coleman, James S., "Social Change—Impact on Adolescent," *Bulletin of N.A.S.S.P.*, April 1965, pp. 11–15.

Conant, James B. "The Changing Educational Scene on Both Sides of the Atlantic," *Bulletin of N.A.S.S.P.*, March 1965, pp. 43–56.

Davis, H. Curtis. "Where Does the Time Go?" *California Journal of Secondary Education*, October 1953, pp. 341–60.

Fulbright, J. William. "Education and Public Policy," *Bulletin of N.A.S.S.P.*, March 1965, pp. 14–23.

Gardner, John W. "Innovation and Leadership in American Education," *Bulletin of N.A.S.S.P.*, March 1965, pp. 36–43.

Griffiths, Daniel E. *Administrative Theory*. New York: Appleton-Century-crofts, Inc., 1959.

Halpin, Andrew W. (ed.). *Administrative Theory in Education*. Chicago: Midwest Administrative Center, 1958.

Hemphill, J. K. "Progress Report: A Study of the Secondary School Principalship, Part II," *Bulletin of N.A.S.S.P.*, April 1964, pp. 215–33.

Kraft, Ivor. "The Coming Crisis in Secondary Education," *Bulletin of N.A.S.S.P.*, February 1965, pp. 5–45.

Leu, Donald J., and Herbert C. Rudman, *Preparation Programs for School Administrators*. U.C.E.A. Career Development Seminar. East Lansing, Michigan: Michigan State University, 1963.

McAbee, Harold V. "Time for the Job," *Bulletin of N.A.S.S.P.*, March 1958, pp. 39–44.

McCleary, Lloyd E., and Stephen P. Hencley. *Secondary School Administra-*

tion: Theoretical Bases of Professional Practice. New York: Dodd, Mead and Company, 1965.

McKay, Robert E. "The President's Program: A New Commitment to Quality and Equality in Education," *Phi Delta Kappan*, May 1965, pp. 427–29.

Norton, J. K. "Preparing Programs for Administrators," *School Executive*, January 1956, p. 84.

Richards, J. M. "Progress Report: A Study of the Secondary School Principalship," *Bulletin of N.A.S.S.P.*, April 1964, pp. 211–15.

Scott, M. B. "The Study of the High School Principalship in Pennsylvania," *Bulletin of N.A.S.S.P.*, December 1953, pp. 118–20.

————. "What Is a High School Principal?" *Clearing House*, September 1957, p. 30.

Smith, Mark C. "A Sober Look at the Administrators Responsibility Toward Change," *Bulletin of N.A.S.S.P.*, March 1964, pp. 39–45.

Snider, Glenn R. "Educational Leadership—An Analysis," *Bulletin N.A.S.S.P.*, April 1965, pp. 80–95.

"The Swing to Vocational Education," *Phi Delta Kappan*, April 1965, pp. 1–425. Complete issue on the social force of vocational education.

Trump, J. Lloyd, and Lois S. Karasik. *Focus on the Individual—A Leadership Responsibility*. Washington, D.C.: The National Association of Secondary School Principals, 1965.

Tyler, Ralph W. "Tasks Appropriate to the High School," *P.T.A. Magazine*, November 1964, pp. 22–24. Also reprinted in *Education Digest*, February 1965, pp. 19–21.

CHAPTER 2

Effective Leadership —
The Practical Process

It has been indicated that the study of secondary school administration involves knowledge about the man, the social setting, the tasks to be performed, and the administrative process. The personal characteristics, the social setting, and the specific tasks of the principal were discussed in Chapter 1.

This chapter is concerned with the authority and responsibility of the principal and the processes of administration by which specific acts are executed. Someone has said that "the principal has practically nothing to do except to decide what is to be done; to ask somebody to do it, to listen to reasons why it should not be done, why it should be done by someone else, or why it should be done in a different way; to follow up to see if the thing has been done; to discover that it has not; to inquire why; to listen to excuses from the person who should have done it; to follow up again to see if the thing has been done, only to discover that it has been done incorrectly; to point out how it should have been done; to conclude that as long as it has been done, it may as well be left as it is; to wonder if it is not time to get rid of a person who cannot do a thing right; to reflect that he probably has a wife and a large family; to consider how much simpler and better the thing would have been done if one had done it oneself in the first place; to reflect sadly that one could have done it right in 20 minutes, and, as things turned out, one has had to spend two days to find out why it has taken three weeks for somebody else to do it wrongly."

This statement indicates many of the specific acts involved in leadership.

The effectiveness of the principal's leadership is dependent on his ability to carry out these specific acts.

Authority and Responsibility and Effective Leadership

Two of the essentials in an adequate analysis of effective leadership are authority and responsibility. Authority without responsibility brings chaos. Responsibility without authority creates ineffectiveness.

Nature of Responsibility. Whenever human beings meet to work out common problems or to plan for their own improvement, organization of some type is indicated. This organization can be informal or formal; it can be verbal or written; but the transfer of a society's desires and needs into actualities requires some type of organization.

For organization to be effective, various members must do certain things. What they do must be predictable. Thus, the members find themselves responsible for carrying out certain acts. When the individuals do not perform the acts for which they have become responsible, the organization breaks down, the morale of members is affected, and the purposes for which the organization are created are thwarted.

The American people have always regarded education as a process that must be performed for the welfare of everyone; therefore, certain delimitations of responsibility have been made. The statement "The state is responsible for education" is often made. The state's responsibility came from the state constitution. The state constitution was approved by the people. By their acts the people made the state government responsible for education. The state in turn has delegated certain areas of responsibility to school districts and to the elected school board. The board of education has delegated some of this responsibility to the superintendent and through him to principals, teachers, and other staff members. Each person is delegated responsibility to carry out certain acts. Owing to the nature of the responsibility given to teachers, principals, and superintendents, these persons often become legally liable or accountable for their acts. When legal liability is indicated, legal responsibility has been delegated. Other acts performed by teachers, principals, and superintendents may involve psychological accountability. Although the person is not legally responsible, the group to which he belongs expects him to carry out the act. The individual becomes psychologically responsible to the group.

Responsibility, whether psychological or legal, is necessary for school systems to operate properly. The degree to which the purposes of education are achieved is dependent on the manner in which each person carries out the responsibility entrusted to him.

Nature of Authority. In clarifying some of the concepts about authority, it is well to understand that the word *authority* can be used in different ways. Some of the following definitions are associated with authority:[1] (1) legal or rightful power, a right to command or to act, to have jurisdiction; (2) power due to opinion or esteem, influence of character, station, mental or moral superiority; and (3) one claimed or appealed to, in support of opinions, actions, or measures. A further analysis of the definitions indicates that authority is primarily of two types: (1) legal and (2) psychological.[2] In actual practice these two aspects of authority are often combined.

Webster's Collegiate Dictionary has been used in the previous statement as an "authority" in the area of definition of words. In other words, psychological authority is ascribed by both the authors and the readers; therefore, the definitions become workable. Legal authority is the right or power to command or to act or to have jurisdiction based on law. The law describes and sets the boundaries of authority.

Legal Responsibility and Authority for the Operation of a School System. The United States Constitution did not list education as a function of the national government. The federal government, however, still has influence on education and educational programs. It is expected that effective citizenship and English will be taught. The Constitution sets forth the principle that church and state should be separate. Federal legislation has affected vocational education, school lunch programs, land grant colleges, scholarships, and research grants and general aid to education. The judicial branch has exercised its influence in behalf of individual rights and equality of opportunity in many areas including integration of schools.

The state sets up legal organizations known as school districts. Each school district has a board of trustees or a board of education. To this board of education (collectively, not individually) the state has given legal authority, rights, powers, and responsibilities. The board of education is free to act as a legal body within the educational sphere so long as it does not exceed the authority given to it. The local board of education thus becomes responsible for the education of the children within that district. With this responsibility are correlative powers or authorities. The local board of education can levy taxes, determine curriculum requirements, hire personnel to carry out its needs, and in general set its

---

[1] *Webster's New Collegiate Dictionary* (Springfield, Mass.: G. & C. Merriam Co., Publishers), p. 60.

[2] Some writers make this distinction as explicit and implied rather than legal and psychological.

own policies and procedures—provided there are no violations of the responsibility and authority delegated to it.

The functions that must be performed on a local level are many and varied. School board members are elected by lay citizens serving in the interests of their district. The board members do not possess the time or the special knowledge and skills necessary to operate large school system; therefore, the board of education selects an officer, a superintendent of schools, to operate the school system. This selection does not divorce the board of education from its responsibility or its authority. The members of the board of education are careful to select an individual to whom they can trustingly delegate responsibility and authority to perform acts for them. If in the opinion of the board of education this officer does not fulfill the responsibility placed on him or if he exercises his authority beyond his responsibility, he is relieved from his position.

As the number of students increases within the school systems, there develops a need for numerous school plants. The superintendent finds he cannot adequately carry out all the acts delegated to him by the board of education. He has more responsibility than he has time; therefore, with permission of the board of education he selects assistant officers, namely, supervisors and principals. To these assistants he delegates responsibilities. To see that these responsibilities are carried out he delegates authority. This delegation of responsibility and authority does not relieve the superintendent of his direct responsibility to the board of education. The delegation only makes it possible for him to function more efficiently. If in the superintendent's opinion the supervisor or principal has been negligent in his responsibility or in the use of his authority, the superintendent recommends to the board of education that a replacement should be made.

Teachers are then hired in each individual school. Under the jurisdiction of the principal, each teacher is given authority and responsibility in the areas of his preparation and skills. Figure 2.1 gives a graphic presentation of the government and structure of the schools in the United States. Figure 2.2 shows how this legal framework of delegated authority and responsibility extends from the board of education to the students.

Psychological Responsibility and Authority. Many of the responsibilities delegated to or assumed by the principal are psychological in nature. The principal is the prime mover in one of the most important institutions in the community. Whatever he says or does is regarded as significant in the eyes of the community. In the educational profession, the principal is regarded as the key person in the school. The teaching faculty and the nonprofessional staff look to him for leadership and direction. Psychologically they expect him to carry out many functions for and in their behalf. When he speaks he is supported by the prestige of the institution and of

Figure 2.1

Structural Framework of the Operation of Schools

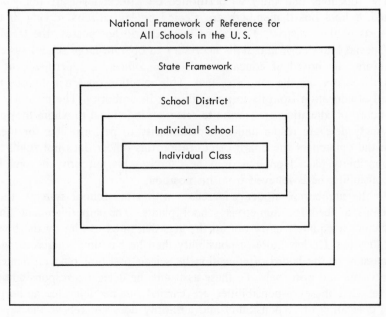

Figure 2.2

Legal Line of Authority and Responsibility

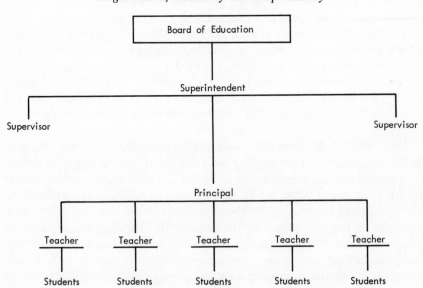

his office. The title of principal that he holds is a symbol of preferment that gives important status to all his official activities.

> There are attributes which society invests in the principal's job. They are not the delegations of power. They are the expectations of performance. The principal cannot always evade responsibility by saying, "The regulations demand that I do thus and so," or "I have distributed my responsibility among my colleagues, and it is their combined judgment that this is the proper course of action. . . . Both of these are legitimate at the right time. But the position of secondary school principal is dynamic as well as ministerial. As a professional educator, the principal has creative opportunities for which he will be respected and by which he will be judged.[3]

The members of his organization expect him to do certain things. When psychological responsibility is given, psychological authority must be assigned if the acts are to be successfully completed. For the group to expect a principal or for a principal to expect an individual or group to be responsible for something without also assigning him authority to act, is to make the person or group ineffective. Many problems are created in school systems owing to this seeming lack of consistency of delegating or assigning responsibility without authority.

Nature of Responsibilities and Authority Assigned to the Principal. The principal, then, is delegated certain legal and psychological responsibilities. He is delegated certain authority to carry out the responsibilities. Part of his responsibility is to the teachers who are assigned to his school. Part of his responsibility is to the students. His responsibility extends to the school curriculum and the implementation of the curriculum, to the school plant with its custodial and maintenance operations, to the school bus driver, to the programs of health and safety, and to all aspects of the functioning of the school and the school program.

The principal receives most of his responsibilities through rules and policies set forth by the board of education and through the superintendent. These policies should be in written form. In the absence of written policy the principal and the superintendent should have a very clear understanding of the duties and responsibilities placed upon the principal. Any policy procedure or role expectancy on the part of the board of education or superintendent that is not clearly understood by the principal will be the probable grounds for future misunderstandings. A clear concept of responsibility does not mean that all schools are expected to be duplicates of each other. Just the reverse is true. If each principal is designated as

---

[3] Rudyard K. Bent and Lloyd E. McCann, *Administration of Secondary Schools* (New York: McGraw-Hill Book Company, Inc., 1960), p. 27.

the responsible head of his school, one can expect to find wide variance in administrative practices—all of which can be acceptable by the super-intendent as being within the bounds of the principal's responsibility and authority. Therefore, the processes by which a principal uses his authority affect the quality of his leadership.

Acts of Leadership

It has been shown that effective leadership involves responsibility and authority. In addition, the administrator must act in terms of the specific problem situations that are presented to him. Some of these acts of leadership are planning, initiating, managing, delegating, coordinating, decision making, communicating, and evaluating.[4] In solving any particular problem, a principal might use one or several of these acts of leadership. Each of these acts of leadership is discussed below.

Planning. One point that became very clear in the chapter on "Duties of the Secondary School Administrator" is that the principal is faced with many problems. The problems must be solved and decisions must be made. Too often the principal finds himself involved in the solution of so many problems and in carrying out routine procedures that he does not take time to plan. An organization as complex as the school requires a great amount of time devoted to planning. Policies determined on the spur of the moment are usually ineffective. Further, they are often contradictory. Adequate planning is necessary for the preparation of the school year, faculty meeting, P.T.A., curriculum discussions, and all phases of admin-istration and the operation of the school. The Commission on Staff Relations in School Administration described planning as the attempt to control the future in the direction of the desired goals through decisions made on the basis of careful estimates of the probable consequences of possible courses of action.[5]

---

[4] Jack Culbertson, "Common and Specialized Content in Preparation of Admin-istrators," found in Donald J. Leu and Herbert C. Rudman, *Preparation Programs for School Administrators—Common and Specialized Learnings.* Seventh UCEA Career Development Seminar (East Lansing, Mich.: Michigan State University, 1963), pp. 34–60. This identifies the following processes: decision making, communi-cating, influencing, coordinating, and evaluating. Jesse B. Sears, *The Nature of Ad-ministrative Process* (New York: McGraw-Hill Book Company, Inc., 1950), pp. 31–37, lists the processes as planning, organization, direction, coordination, control, and personality.

[5] Commission on Staff Relations of the American Association of School Admin-istrators, *Staff Relations in School Administration*, Thirty-third Yearbook (Washing-ton, D.C.: The Association, 1955), p. 17.

Initiating. By definition, "initiate" means to introduce, to begin, or to commence. We are living in a dynamic society. There are social, economic, political, and scientific changes occurring almost daily. The changes occurring in our society should be reflected in our schools. Institutions, organizations, groups of people, and individuals tend to resist change because the status quo is usually quite comfortable. However, if our schools are to keep pace with the changes taking place in our society, change must occur. Someone must initiate this change. The principal is the key person in the individual school for initiating action. It should not be implied that all change is or should be initiated by the principal. The principal does not have a monopoly on good ideas and practices. However, regardless of the source of a good idea or practice, the idea cannot be developed adequately without some initiative on the part of the principal. If one looks back at the example of Small High School in Chapter 1, it can be seen that the principal will likely continue in his hectic routine forever unless he initiates some new ways to handle many of his recurring problems. The idea that "if you introduce something new, it will 'rock the ship' " may sometimes be true. However, no ship has ever arrived at its goal or destination unless there has been a little forward movement. The principal, by nature of his position, can and should be involved in acts of initiation.

Managing. The management functions of a principal are well known by those in the profession. Routines and procedures have to be developed and followed. The school should run smoothly. It has been said that ideal management is found when it looks as if the school runs by itself. The underlying thought behind a statement of this kind is that the problems have been reduced to routines and that policies are adequate and are being followed. The management act requires a great amount of time; in fact, a principal can spend his whole time and energy in this one phase of school administration. However, caution must be used, or the other aspects of administration will be neglected. A new principal will spend more time in management problems than he will after he has had several years of experience. Likewise, a principal in a new school will spend more time with acts of management than a principal of a school that has been in operation several years. Well-developed routines, policies, and procedures are the best techniques for efficient management. It will be recalled that the principal at Urban High School was concerned about policies and procedures. Efficient leadership demands that the schools be adequately managed. Routine policies and procedures should be determined as soon as possible so that the principal can spend more time in the improvement of instruction and other essential duties.

Delegating. The principles of responsibility and authority have been set forth in other sections of this chapter. The specific responsibilities of a principal were indicated. The responsibilities of a principal are frequently classified into three major categories: (1) duties that are mandatory, (2) duties that are discretionary, and (3) duties that can be delegated. A mandatory duty is one that must be performed; failure to do so is regarded as unprofessional conduct that warrants discipline or dismissal. Discretionary duties are those on which the principal may decide whether or not something should be done. Some discretionary duties may be required, but the principal determines how and when they need to be performed. Duties that can be delegated are those duties that the principal may assign to some other person. Both mandatory and discretionary duties can be delegated. There is more delegation of discretionary duties than there is of mandatory duties.

The act of delegation is an important act in effective leadership. The many duties of the principal indicate that unless delegation of responsibility is used, the principal will never get to the most important function of the school, i.e., improvement of instruction.

The principle of delegation requires that responsibility and authority are given to the person, group, or organization to whom a duty is delegated. Too often administrators want to delegate the dirty work and at the same time exercise control. A principal should not delegate with strings attached. If a principal delegates a duty, he should accept the decision of the person, group, or organization. The principal exercises his control by judging the person, group, or organization on his or their ability to make the right decisions.

Many of the time-consuming routine tasks can be delegated to a clerk or secretary. Traditionally, principals have been short-handed when it comes to office help. It is a parody on education that boards of education select one of their best teachers, require him to have several years of additional administrative schooling, and then tie him down with work that could be performed by a good responsible clerk who would need neither a teaching nor an administrative certificate. Principals should be persistent in showing to superintendents and boards of education the need for such clerical assistance.

Coordinating. The act of coordination is important in any complex organization. The school, with its many different curricula, departments, and services, requires some top-level coordination. The larger the school, the greater the need for coordination. Teachers are professional people, skilled in their fields and imbued with the idea that what they are doing is important. Therefore, it is not unusual to find a teacher of a department who desires to do an outstanding job. Such desires should be encouraged.

There are times, however, when the desire to improve one's own department or class conflicts with the desires of another teacher or department. The example at Small High School could be cited. One teacher had a state track meet, the other teacher had a state F.F.A. judging meet on the same day. Many of the same students were in both events. In order to solve the conflict, the principal had to act as a coordinator. He must try to bring harmony between the diverse elements.

Coordination is necessary in all programs and operations of the school if the principal is to provide effective leadership.

Decision Making. Many and varied are the decisions made by a principal. The first major decision, of course, is to be a principal. The second major decision involves the selection of the school district and school within which the principal will work. Many of the new principal's decisions have already been made when he arrives at the school. On taking office the administrator inherits a legacy of decisions made by his predecessors. He also has an inheritance of decisions made by other men throughout history, men such as Dewey, Barnard, Mann, Jefferson, Franklin, Herbart, Pestalozzi, Plato, and others. This legacy from the past has determined the present philosophy and operating policies of the school under consideration. A wise principal will try to understand all this legacy before he makes a decision to initiate change. However, changes will be needed. The principal will be pressured from many sides for changes. Decisions must be made.

There are two important aspects of decision making: (1) values and (2) knowledge and understanding. All decision making involves values. Downey states, "The persistent questions of purpose that constantly confront the secondary school administrator can only be answered in light of a comprehensive concept of the secondary phase of education and in light of a personalized philosophical mooring, a value orientation, a sense of purpose and direction."[6] When alternatives are given, they are weighed in terms of better or worse, good or bad, right or wrong. A principal should understand his own value system. He must have some conviction of what is good for the school, faculty, students, and community. In his own mind he should have a clear concept of the desirable that influences means, modes, and ends of action. The importance of values is clearly set forth in the pamphlet *Decision-Making and American Values in School Administration.*[7]

---

[6] Lawrence W. Downey, "The Secondary School Principal," in Donald J. Leu and Herbert C. Rudman, *op. cit.*, p. 132.

[7] Cooperative Program in Educational Administration, *Decision-Making and American Values in School Administration* (New York: Bureau of Publications, Teachers College, Columbia University, 1954), pp. 1–90.

The second major consideration in decision making is a knowledge and understanding of what is possible in a given situation.

> The whole history of the human race demonstrates that no generation can jump out of its skin, that no people can leap from barbarism to civilization, that no people can by act of will open the gates of Utopia. All decisions, therefore, must be made in the clear light of knowledge of existing forces and conditions. The primitive artisan may dream of a modern rifle, and the statesman may dream of one world founded on the principles of peace, justice, and equality for all men. But neither can realize his dream by ignoring the stubborn realities of his day and situation, the actual level of the practical arts in the one case, and the division of the world between tyranny and freedom in the other.[8]

The principal must know and understand his school, his community, and his American society. The more knowledge and understanding he has, the greater will be the number of his right decisions.

Evaluation.   Education as a process that is used to arrive at desirable ends must be evaluated periodically. Just as the work of students and teachers should be evaluated, the principal should be taking stock of his activities and responsibilities. He has been given jurisdiction over many persons and things. "Just how well am I doing?" should be an oft-repeated question the principal should ask himself. "What progress has been made in the improvement of instruction? Are the various curricula offerings and the departments involved harmoniously working together? How are my relations with the students, teachers, custodians, cooks, bus drivers? Am I meeting the expectations of the superintendent? What have I neglected? How can I do each of these jobs better?" These and many other questions could be the source of self-examination.

In addition to self-examination the principal should, on the proper occasions, talk over his problems with his superiors and ask for suggestions. Evaluation can come from within his school from students, teachers, and staff members. If a large-scale evaluation is needed, the Evaluative Criteria[9] could be used effectively. An effective leader must be concerned with growth and advancement. Only through some regular act of evaluation can the principal determine whether progress toward the desired end is being attained.

Communicating.   A principal might perform all the other specified acts of effective leadership in a very commendable way and still remain

[8] *Ibid.*, p. 10.
[9] National Study of Secondary School Evaluation, *Evaluative Criteria* (Washington, D.C.: 1960).

ineffective. Very adequate decisions might be made, a good plan for coordination might be worked out, itemized duties might be delegated and listed, but unless the principal adequately communicates with the individuals concerned, he will still be ineffective. The leader must be sure that there is effective communication between himself and other individuals involved. The principal makes many decisions when the involvement of everyone concerned would be either impractical or impossible. Other decisions might be made by a group when individual members are not present. The leader has responsibility to see that the information is passed on to those who are not present. Therefore, an effective administrator must communicate decision to those affected by the decision. The degree of effectiveness in communication could be represented in a continuum as indicated in Figure 2.3.

Figure 2.3

Continuum of Effectiveness in Communicating Decisions

Lets members affected by decisions find out about decisions by themselves

Carefully communicates with every person affected by the decision

A communication framework that gives the situations found in schools, the concepts to be described, and the communication process is shown in Table 2.1.

Methods of Operation for Effective Leadership

Use of Authority in a Democracy.   A theory that is very popular today is that leadership must be democratic to be effective. A dichotomy is often set forth; namely, a principal is either democratic or autocratic. Little attempt is made to define the meaning of the words *democratic* or *autocratic*. Staff participation in decision making is usually linked with democratic. Decision making by the principal without staff participation is often linked to autocratic behavior. Furthermore, a moral judgment is given each category. Democratic leadership is good. Autocratic leadership is bad.

When autocratic leadership is used to designate a person who makes a decision by himself, the assumption is often implied that the use of authority is undemocratic. Such thinking may lead to the conclusion that leadership and authority are incompatible in a democracy. However, the use of authority in a democratic society is not undemocratic.

A democratic school system, like a democratic government, must have someone responsible for the operation of the system. Where responsibility

TABLE 2.1 A Communications Framework*

Communication Situations Found in School Districts and Communities:	CONCEPTS TO DESCRIBE AND EXPLAIN COMMUNICATION PROCESSES					
	1. Communicator	2. Channel	3. Medium	4. Message	5. Communicatee	6. Effects
I. TWO-WAY ORAL A. Two person B. Small group	1. Purpose 2. Personality 3. Skills	1. Direction 2. Location 3. Efficiency	1. Audio 2. Visual 3. Audio visual	1. Content 2. Form	1. Personal factors 2. Situational factors	1. Message interpretation 2. Communicatee reaction 3. Communicatee modification
II. ONE-WAY ORAL A. Face-to-face audience B. Unseen audience (e.g., TV)	1. Purpose 2. Personality 3. Skills	1. Direction 2. Location 3. Efficiency	1. Audio 2. Visual 3. Audio visual	1. Content 2. Form	1. Personal factors 2. Situational factors	1. Message interpretation 2. Communicatee reaction 3. Communicatee modification
III. WRITTEN A. To an individual B. To a single public or group C. To multiple publics	1. Purpose 2. Personality 3. Skills	1. Direction 2. Location 3. Efficiency	1. Audio 2. Visual 3. Audio visual	1. Content 2. Form	1. Personal factors 2. Situational factors	1. Message interpretation 2. Communicatee reaction 3. Communicatee modification

*The framework is an abbreviation of a more elaborate one developed by the UCEA Task Force on "Communications." Members of the Task Force included William Roe, Sylvia Ciernick, Lloyd McCleary, S. J. Knezevich, Gordon McCloskey, John Ramseyer, Franklin Knower, William Monahan, and William Odell.

SOURCE: Donald J. Leu and Herbert C. Rudman, *Preparation Programs for School Administrators, Common and Specialized Learnings*, p. 40. Copyright © 1963. Seventh U.C.E.A. Career Development Seminar (East Lansing, Mich.: Michigan State University, 1963). Reprinted by permission of Michigan State University.

is assigned, authority to act must also be delegated. The authority to make decisions in the area of one's responsibility is not undemocratic, nor is it autocratic. The use of authority is necessary if the leader is to function in a democracy. The dichotomy of "democratic" or "autocratic" thus defined is unrealistic of the nature of administration and the essentials of effective leadership.

The Continuum of Administrative Operation. The principal is delegated authority to act in order to fulfill the responsibilities placed on him. However, he is not told how he should carry out these acts. The method of operation becomes part of his responsibility. If the method of operation disrupts the school, the program, or the staff, the principal will not measure up to his responsibilities. Both efficiency and morale are lowered. Thus the method of operation becomes a vital factor in the effectiveness of the school leader.

If one analyzes the many duties that must be performed by the principal, as indicated in Chapter 1, he soon reaches the conclusion that different duties may call forth different methods of operational techniques. Some practical situations are given below. It will be noted that the method of operation can vary greatly with the situation and size of school as well as with the inclination of the administrator. The examples of action taken are not intended to be inclusive. Many other alternatives could be listed.

SITUATION ONE

Friday morning as school commences, the cheerleaders request a short pep assembly prior to the game that is to be played on that day.

ALTERNATIVE OPERATIONAL METHODS

A. The principal gives immediate approval or disapproval.

B. The principal refers the cheerleaders to the vice-principal or adviser of student activities.

C. The principal suggests that they return for an answer later in the day (at some specified time) so that the principal can consult with (1) superintendent's office, (2) faculty or faculty committee, or (3) student body officers or adviser.

METHODS OF OBSERVATION AND SITUATION ONE

The practical action taken by the principal would depend on a number of conditions. Some of these conditions would be:

1. If the procedure used here is a regular procedure, established and recognized by the faculty and students, the principal could give immediate approval. The total faculty would consider it an affront to their time and person if they were invited in to discuss every minute decision.

2. Even though the procedure is a regular procedure, the principal might question the need for an assembly, or he might believe that this request is an afterthought that lacked careful preparation. Under these conditions he might refer the students back to the vice-principal or adviser in order to have assurance that the request should be honored. Under these conditions, the principal would not refer the decision to the total faculty for decision making.

3. If the school is new or under new administration and the policy procedure had not been determined or was not clear to the principal, he might well use this third alternative. He might even take an additional step and (at a regular faculty meeting) raise the question for faculty consideration. Action on a request of this type would affect the teachers and the teaching situation. Therefore, policy procedure could be discussed and adopted by the group. The principal could then exercise wisdom and judgment in the alternatives available to him when subsequent requests are made. The same procedure could be followed with the student council if it were recognized that a decision of this nature had been delegated to that body.

SITUATION TWO

The school furnace becomes inoperative on a cold day when students are in class.

ALTERNATIVE OPERATIONAL METHODS

A. The principal could consult with custodians and maintenance personnel regarding the amount of time needed to repair the furnace. He could hold students in class but permit them to get their coats and wraps as needed.

B. The principal might announce over loudspeaker that school is dismissed.

C. The principal could consult with superintendent and transportation supervisor to devise arrangements for a dismissal plan and expectancy of return to normal operation.

METHODS OF OPERATION AND SITUATION TWO

The practical action taken by the principal again depends on previous experiences with such matters as well as the degree of time needed to repair the furnace. The condition of the weather becomes a prime consideration. The alternative that would be selected would depend on the condition present.

1. If consultation with the custodian and maintenance repair personnel revealed that the furnace could be repaired in a short time period, the first alternative would seem most practical.

2. If the repair problem involved more serious implications and if a policy or procedure for emergency dismissal had already been established, the second alternative would be practical.

3. If no policy or procedure had been previously in operation or if the majority of the students were bussed to school, the third alternative would probably be followed. Both students and parents would need briefing.

It should be observed that in each of these situations the principal must make the decision. There is no need to call the faculty together for group discussion. Although the faculty is directly concerned in their teaching role with the action taken, they cannot add any great contribution to the effective solution of the problem. The superintendent and the transportation supervisor could aid in an effective solution. The faculty would not consider the principal autocratic for making this decision by himself. In fact, they would expect the principal to make the decision. The primary concern of the faculty would be that the decision reached was communicated to them so they would not be shivering in doubt as to what they should tell the students.

SITUATION THREE

Several teachers indicate that there are too many students, teachers, and organizational officers requesting that students be excused from classes. The teachers do not know whether the students should be excused or not.

ALTERNATE OPTIONAL METHODS

A. The principal could leave it to the discretion of the individual teacher to make the decision.

B. The principal could make the decision himself and thus set the policy.

C. The principal could refer the problem to the faculty for their consideration and decision.

METHODS OF OPERATION AND SITUATION THREE

1. The first alternative might be the most practical solution if policy and procedure had already been adopted and was being followed. The teachers might then be given the responsibility to make the decision. The principal might review the policy with the teachers involved to make certain that the teachers fully understood the policy and their freedom and responsibility in regard to the policy.

2. The second alternative might be used as a basis of operation until the faculty could jointly arrive at a solution. It might also be used if no agreement could be reached by the faculty regarding proper procedure.

3. The third alternative would generally be the most practical if policy had not already been made. It would also be the best alternative if the

teachers were raising questions about aspects of the policy presently in use. The faculty or the faculty's committee would want to be considered in this type of decision. As teachers who are holding class and thus being interrupted and as teachers making the requests for students to be excused in order to carry out their special programs, they are directly concerned with the adequateness of the solution. Both the effectiveness and morale of the teachers are involved. A superimposed mandate from above, even though adequate, would be rejected by many of the teachers. A policy decision by the principal would likely be considered autocratic behavior by some persons. The principal can give direction to a group discussion of this type. He can see that everyone is involved so that the final policy will more likely be accepted and practiced by all. And he can expedite discussion toward a more effective solution. However, in the final analysis, if a policy of this nature should be determined, the faculty ought to be involved in the decision. After the policy is made, the principal would see that it is carried out until it becomes evident that a revision is needed.

On the basis of the few examples given above, one can easily see that the principal might and does use many different methods in solving his leadership problems. Some of these problems are best decided by the administrator, some are best decided by the faculty, and some are best decided through joint action. The methods used in arriving at a decision might be placed on a continuum with independent decision on one end of the continuum and group decision on the other end. See Figure 2.4.

Figure 2.4

Continuum of Administrative Operation

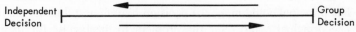

A particular method for solving a particular problem might be anywhere on this continuum. Its exact placement would depend on the nature of the problem, those affected, the kind of information needed to solve the problem effectively, the size of the group, the stability of the group, the interpersonal relations of the members of the group, the age of the school, and the time of year (winter, summer).

When to Use Independent Decision.   An administrator should decide an issue himself when some of the following conditions are more important than all other considerations:

1. When the administrator cannot share the responsibility with any other person or group, he is solely responsible for the decision. Examples that might fall in this category are: recommendations that a teacher be

transferred or not be given a contract for the next year, questions of morals and teacher effectiveness, and other problems that involve particular individuals.

2. When time is of greatest essence and the need for immediate action is necessary, independent decision becomes mandatory. Examples of this type might be: severe accidents to students or staff members and requests that do not permit time for group action made by the district office, staff members, public officials, parents, and students.

3. In carrying out policy that has already been defined and accepted by those responsible for making the policy, the principal often acts without further consideration. Examples of this type of operation might be: handling an unexcused absence or discipline problem, reporting teachers' absences from work, requisitioning supplies and equipment, handling school lunch money, and other managerial functions.

When to Involve the Group in Decision Making. An administrator should involve the group in making decisions when the following considerations are paramount:

1. When the principal holds the members of the group responsible for the action that takes place, the decision should be made by the group. Examples of this type of a problem might be: determining policy regarding excusing students from class, supervision of students during lunch hour, and reporting attendance.

2. When the morale of the group is seriously affected by the problem and its solution, the group should be involved in making the decisions. Some examples might be: methods to be used in supervision of instruction; interruptions of classes for announcements, excusing of students, and office business; and requests and demands made on teachers for supervision during noon hour, before and after school, and extracurricular activities.

3. When demands are made on the faculty by groups outside of the school organization which interfere with the normal teaching function, the group concerned should be involved in making the decision. Such demands might be made by community and state organizations for money drives and essay contests, and pressure might be made by businessmen to have information and material included in the curriculum.

4. When questions of practice that require a definition of the functions of public schools are raised, the group should assist in making the decisions. Such questions are: requests for students to conduct community and school fund-raising projects and the problem of whether the schools should be holding institutions for potential juvenile delinquents.

5. When "pooled knowledge" can bring about a more effective solution than individual decisions, the group should be consulted. A clear distinc-

tion should be made at this point between "pooled knowledge" and "pooled ignorance." An effective solution should be based on knowledge of facts and information. Members of a group should have something to contribute to the adequate solution of the problem. Group action otherwise is ineffective.

6. When a high degree of acceptance of a decision is desired, participation by individuals concerned makes them more likely to accept the decision and put the decision into operation.

Conclusion Regarding Method of Operation. Administrative leadership, as designated by the methods of operation used by the leader, rests on a continuum from independent decision to group decision. How much independent decision and how much group decision to use depends on many factors, as previously discussed. It is not just a technique that makes autocratic or democratic behavior. Autocratic or democratic behavior is a symbol applied to a leader or a process based on the way people feel about the leader and the procedures used to solve problems. The personality of the teachers also determines how they react to the method of operation of the leader. A study by Cornell[10] in four school systems indicated that individual teachers react differently to administrative decisions and operational relationships. Teachers who are rated high on the Minnesota Teacher Attitude Inventory will do a good job in the classroom regardless of the organizational environment. Teachers who are rated low on the scale do not change behavior with a change in the organizational structure. The more socially and emotionally mature persons tend to participate more in policy formulation. Some teachers need a concentrated type of administration; others do not. The above-average teachers in professional attitude are most affected by lack of participation in policy making and decisions. Teachers low in professional attitude are, on the average, as satisfied with their participation whether it was in an "administrator-centered" or a "teacher-centered" school system.

Group Dynamics and Effective Leadership

Importance of Group Dynamics. The study of leadership indicates that a knowledge of group dynamics and social psychology is most beneficial to an administrator. A major portion of a principal's time is spent in working with people, individually and in groups. Greater effectiveness can be achieved if a principal understands the group process and techniques for moving the group toward a goal. The study of group

[10] Francis G. Cornell, "Socially Perceptive Administration," *Phi Delta Kappan*, March 1955, p. 223.

dynamics is a subject for a course by itself. It should not be assumed that everything a principal should know about group dynamics can be included in this section. Only a summary of some of the more important principles can be given.

Why Group Decisions Are Effective. Group decisions are effective because they (1) improve the morale of those involved, (2) create greater acceptance to whatever decisions are reached, (3) improve the quality of the decisions, and (4) place maximum responsibility to carry out a decision at the operational level. Each of these points is expanded below.

The principal is working constantly with people. He can only achieve maximum efficiency when the human relations involved are at a satisfactory level. It is commonly accepted that morale develops proportionately to the extent that the group participates in decisions regarding policies affecting the group. It is also true that some teachers desire more participation than others.[11] The N.E.A. study[12] indicated that men teachers more than women teachers, and secondary teachers more than elementary teachers seemed to wish for greater responsibility in policy function. Research shows that when participatory processes have been employed, there are benefits that accrue to the institution and to the individual. Some of these benefits are (1) a greater general effort and attention on the part of employees; (2) a better understanding of organizational goals; (3) an improvement in creativity; (4) better communication; (5) a reduction in turnover, absenteeism, and tardiness; (6) a reduction in the number of grievances and matters of dissatisfaction; (7) a greater readiness to accept change; and (8) an improved quality of decisions made by those in responsible positions.[13] Satisfaction is increased and morale improves when participation is extended to those affected by a decision.

Greater acceptance of a decision takes place when the group participates in decision making.[14] As members participate, they have opportunity to get rid of aggressiveness, tensions, and fears. If the major consideration is acceptance, one should give people the right to accept their own ideas. They become committed to the decision because it is their decision.

---

[11] Cornell, *op. cit.*, p. 223.

[12] National Education Association, Research Division, "The Teacher Looks at Personnel Administration," *Research Bulletin*, December 1945, pp. 126–27.

[13] William B. Castetter, *Administering the School Personnel Program* (New York: The Macmillan Company, 1962), pp. 68–69. Harold E. Moore and Newell B. Walters, *Personnel Administration in Education* (New York: Harper and Brothers, 1955), p. 40.

[14] Dorwin Cartwright and Alvin Zander (eds.), *Group Dynamics: Research and Theory*, 2nd ed. (Illinois: Row Peterson Company, 1960), pp. 487–624. James A. Van Zwoll, *School Personnel Administration* (New York: Appleton-Century-Crofts, 1964), pp. 172–73. Castetter, *op. cit.*, p. 69.

Increased satisfaction within the group and the general acceptance of a decision do not necessarily bring a better decision as the end result. In fact, the decision could be a mediocre one. However, if one of the basic premises for using groups is followed, i.e., the members of the group are qualified by their knowledge and skills, the decision can be one of superior quality. Psychologists and sociologists have demonstrated that not all authority comes from status and that what a respected old-timer thinks may have more real force than what the boss orders. Principals should use devices that will extract the wisdom of the old-timer and the imagination and enthusiasm of the new teacher.[15] A leader cannot possibly evolve all of the good ideas that are needed to operate a school efficiently. If ideas are welcomed from the group, credit should be given to those making the contribution. If the ideas are placed into operating practice, there will never be an end to the ideas that will be available to the principal. However, the administrator should exercise wisdom in receiving and evaluating the ideas from the group. When the leader uses the proper techniques, he can be assured that accepted group decisions are decisions of quality.

When a solution to a problem is under consideration by a group, there is an underlying assumption that the group wants to solve the problem. A decision on policy and procedure does not solve a problem; it only produces a standardized procedure for handling the problem. In the end result, putting the decision into operation is the ultimate objective in either individual or group decision making. By sharing the right to make the decision, ". . . the administrator is not deprived of authority. He ceases to be either a rubber stamp or an autocrat, and becomes at once a participant and a leader in the formulation of educational policies. He simply uses his authority in the most effective way—he shares it with the staff."[16] This decentralization through group participation places maximum responsibility for carrying out the decision at the operational level.[17]

Function of the Status Leader. A major question in group dynamics revolves around the position of the status leader. In the school the status leader is the principal. If the principal allows the group to make a decision, what is his relationship with the group? Will his presence create an influence for better or worse decisions? The answer lies basically in what the status leader does in the group process. If he attempts to dictate or "tip

[15] John H. Fisher, "Towards a Sound Working Basis for Administrator and Staff," *Nations Schools, August* 1956, pp. 44–47.

[16] Van Miller, *Personnel Management in School Administration* (New York: World Book Company, 1955), p. 55.

[17] T. M. Stinnett and Albert J. Huggett, *Professional Problems of Teachers*, 2nd ed. (New York: The Macmillan Company, 1963), pp. 377–78.

his hand" in a certain direction, groups that are status-oriented will "follow the leader." If the leader stays away and exercises no influence, the group process can deteriorate from one democratically conceived to one autocratically controlled. There is no guarantee that individual teachers will not try to dominate and control in an autocratic manner a group left without a status leader. Koopman, Miel, and Misner indicate that "dependence on the thinking of the politician on a teaching staff or on the thinking of one or two cutthroat ringleaders among a teaching group is far from the course recommended here. Autocracy is autocracy whether it be practiced by an administrator, a teacher, a student, or a member of the community."[18] One of the major functions of the status leader is to protect the rights of the minority so they can freely express themselves. When minority rights are protected in this manner, studies show that a leader can upgrade the end result of a discussion without running the risk of downgrading the end product.[19] The quality of thinking in a democracy is thus dependent on the opportunities it affords minority opinions to be heard.

A second major function of the status leader at the initial stage is to structure the problem, to point out the implications of the problem, to define the responsibilities of the group and the limits of their authority and responsibility, and to indicate procedure that might be used to solve the problem. Thelen[20] points out that in the face of a status leader's withdrawal, the situation is unstructured, it is difficult to get any sense of a real problem, and there is no guidance in developing the procedure to be followed in finding the problem.

A third function of the status leader is to determine which group should be involved in the solution of the problem. Should the problem be turned to a standing committee or be presented to the total faculty, or should a new structure be created for handling the problem? Initiating structure is not regarded as nondemocratic; it is regarded as a fundamental characteristic of effective leadership.[21] A consideration of importance in initiating a new group structure would be the size of the group and the make-up of the group. The size of the group becomes an important consideration. As the size of the group increases, the agreement within the group decreases. Therefore, the group should be the smallest it is possible to have

[18] G. Robert Koopman, Alice Miel, and Paul J. Misner, *Democracy in School Administration* (New York: Appleton-Century-Crofts, Inc., 1943), p. 110.

[19] Cartwright and Zander, *op. cit.*, pp. 487–624.

[20] Herbert A. Thelen, "Resistance to Change of Teaching Methods," *Progressive Education*, May 1949, p. 209.

[21] Andrew W. Halpin, *The Leadership Behavior of School Superintendents.* School-Community Development Study Monograph, No. 4. (Ohio State University Press, 1956), p. 109. Hollis A. Moore, Jr., *Studies in School Administration* (Washington, D.C.: American Association School Administration, 1957), p. 52.

represented at the functional level of all of the socialization and achievement skills required for the particular problem at hand.[22] The group should include individuals who can make a contribution in the various roles needed for group effectiveness. Some of these roles are the encourager, harmonizer, compromiser, gatekeeper and expediter, standard setter, group observer and commentator, information giver, initiator, evaluator, and recorder.[23]

If any of these roles cannot be filled or if the role is not being fulfilled by a member of the group, the status leader can assume that role. In so doing he helps the group to be more effective. Assuming any given role as the need arises is a fourth function of the status leader.

A fifth function of the status leader is to put his status on the line in favor of the decision and to see that the decision is carried out. In other words, he effectively puts into operation the decision of the group.

On the basis of the functions presented above, it can be seen that the status leader does not cease to be an effective leader when problems are referred to the group for their discussion. The use of groups for decision making can enhance the effectiveness of the leader.

Sequence in Group Participation. A principal should be aware of some of the factors that are present as a group moves toward a goal. A knowledge of the inner operation of the group lets the leader know the progress that is being made toward the solution of the problem. An analysis of the interaction of a group indicates that groups tend to move from a relative emphasis on orientation to problems of evaluation, then to problems of control, and that, concurrent with these transitions, the relative frequency of both negative and positive reactions tends to increase and biases are produced.[24] A principal might find that a more detailed sequence involving group participation might be useful. The following sequence outlined by Moore and Walters is given as a guide:

1. Help the group identify the problem to be considered.

2. Determine the facts necessary to a solution of the problem, or a modification in present practice.

3. Locate the source of the facts and set up means of obtaining them.

4. Study the conditions that surround the solution such as people's feelings, precedent, and legal aspects.

[22] Kenneth D. Benne and Bozidar Muntyan, *Human Relation in Curriculum Change* (New York: Dryden Press, 1951), pp. 132–39. Herbert A. Thelen, "Principle of Least Group Size," *The School Review*, March 1949, p. 141, 147. Cartwright and Zander, *op. cit.*, pp. 507–17. Ralph Tyler, "Recent Research Sheds Light on School Staff Relationships," *Elementary School Journal*, May 1956, pp. 395–99.

[23] Benne and Muntyan, *op. cit.*, pp. 132–39.

[24] Cartwright and Zander, *op. cit.*, pp. 624–38.

5. Determine objectives and goals and secure necessary consensus to permit concerted action.

6. Consider the alternatives involved so that solution of one problem does not create others of equal magnitude.

7. Provide for evaluation of the process and keep lines open for the "next step."[25]

Malfunctioning of Group Participation. All that has been presented in this section on "Group Dynamics and Effective Leadership" has been aimed at helping the principal understand why groups can and should be used effectively. Perhaps a caution should be included at the conclusion of this section. Groups do not always function as idealized. If a group is not functioning properly, the problem may be more than the internal interaction of the group. Miller[26] indicates that malfunctioning in cooperative policy formulation can be expected if:

1. The administrator exercises line leadership instead of earned leadership.

2. The process is used without an understanding of the techniques involved.

3. Group members are not instructed in or do not know the boundaries of their responsibilities and authority. A group should be fully appraised of the known limitations. When authority accompanies responsibility, as it must, and the group understands the extent and nature of each, the framework within which to operate has been established.

4. Teacher participation is confined to matters of minor importance. A first-grade student knows when he is engaged in busywork. He often resents it, too.

5. Too many committees are elected or appointed. This retards the effectiveness of the development of unity of purpose.

6. No procedures are established to implement the policies formulated.

Summary

Effective leadership in the practical situation is the prime concern of the principal. However, one of the problems inherent in a study of leadership is that leadership has not been reduced to field of science. There is no one conclusion or factor that points to effective leadership. Leadership involves status positions and responsibility and authority. The principal

[25] Harold E. Moore and Newell B. Walters, *Personnel Administration in Education* (New York: Harper and Brothers, 1955), p. 45.
[26] Miller, *op. cit.*, pp. 69–70.

must understand his role relationship in the use of both legal and psychological authority.

Effective leadership involves the basic approach or processes used by the leader. Specific acts related to specific circumstances are part of a study of leadership. Some of these acts are planning, initiating, managing, delegating, coordinating, decision making, evaluating, and communicating.

Effective leadership is related directly to the method of operation of the principal. The typical use of "democratic" and "autocratic" has created false dichotomies in relationship to the principal's operating acts. The principal must decide when the group can best be used most effectively as compared to when he should make independent decisions. Guidelines for these decisions, as presented, aid the principal in formulating his methods of operation.

Since the principal will use the group frequently in the decision-making process, he should understand the process involved in group dynamics. Such an understanding should include a knowledge of why group decisions are effective, the functions of the status leader, the sequence in group participation, and the reasons why groups sometimes malfunction.

The "effective leader understands people and desires and is willing to use groups in decision-making in the problems which affect the group. The effective leader is one who delineates clearly the relationship between himself and the members of the group, and establishes well defined patterns of organization, channels of communication, and ways of getting the job done, but whose behavior at the same time reflects friendship, trust, respect and warmth of relationship between himself and the rest of the group."[27]

SUGGESTED PROJECTS AND ACTIVITIES

1. Assume that the principalship of a high school in the city in which you are now living is vacant. You are invited by the board and administrative officers to screen candidates for the position. Write a criteria list that you would use to make your selection.
2. Debate: Leadership is an art, not a science.
3. Have a panel consisting of a superintendent, a curriculum supervisor, a principal, a teacher, and a custodian discuss, "What makes an effective principal?"
4. Visit a faculty meeting. Analyze the meeting in terms of participation of the group, function of the status leader, and nature of the problems presented or worked on during the meeting.

[27] Hollis A. Moore, *op. cit.*, p. 52.

5. Invite the professor of social psychology to speak to the class on the subject, "What the principal needs to know when working with groups."

6. You be the judge by analyzing the following situation:

   The principal asks the faculty what they want to do about supervision during the noon hour. After some discussion, the faculty votes unanimously that they would assign everyone to supervision, alphabetically, on a day-by-day basis. The principal then says, "That just won't work. You will be too prone to forget. I will assign you to your post for a full week. Then everyone will remember his responsibility and we will get better supervision."

REVIEW AND DISCUSSION QUESTIONS

1. What have been some of the theories that have been advanced regarding effective leaders?
2. Why are responsibility and authority discussed as a unit in this chapter?
3. What is the difference between legal and psychological responsibility? Authority? Does a principal have more of one than the other?
4. What is the source of the principal's legal responsibility and authority? Does the teacher have legal responsibility? Authority?
5. Is the use of authority compatible with democracy? Why?
6. What is meant by the continuum of administrative decision making? How is this different from a discussion on autocracy vs. democracy?
7. Under what conditions does an administrator use independent decision?
8. Under what conditions does he use the group in making decisions?
9. What are some of the acts of leadership set forth in this chapter? Under what conditions does a principal use any particular act in carrying out his responsibilities?
10. What is the difference between a mandatory duty and a discretionary duty?
11. What are some conditions that should apply when one exercises the act of delegation?
12. How does the act of coordinating differ from the act of managing?
13. Why are group decisions effective?
14. Can a status person be effective in a group? Under what conditions?
15. What should an effective principal know about the interaction of a group? The make-up of effective groups? The proper size of a group?
16. Under what conditions can the malfunctioning of groups take place?

SELECTED BIBLIOGRAPHY

Bayles, Ernest E. *Democratic Educational Theory*. New York: Harper and Brothers, 1960.

Benne, Kenneth D., and Bozidar Muntyan. *Human Relations in Curriculum Change*. New York: Dryden Press, 1951.

Bennis, Warren G., Kenneth D. Benne, and Robert Chin. *The Planning of Change*. New York: Holt, Rinehart and Winston, 1961.

Bent, Rudyard K., and Lloyd E. McCann. *Administration of Secondary Schools*. New York: McGraw-Hill Book Company, Inc., 1960.

Brown, C. G., and T. S. Cohn. *The Study of Leadership*. Danville, Illinois: Interstate Printers and Publishers, Inc., 1958.

Cartwright, Dorwin, and Alvin Zander (eds.). *Group Dynamics: Research and Theory*, 2nd ed., Evanston, Illinois: Harper & Row, 1960.

Castetter, William B. *Administering the School Personnel Program*. New York: The Macmillan Company, 1962.

Cooperative Program in Educational Administration. *Decision-Making and American Values in School Administration*. New York: Teachers College, Columbia University, 1954.

Cronin, Joseph M. "The Principal's Role in Change," *Bulletin of N.A.S.S.P.*, May 1963, pp. 29–33.

Gardner, John W. "Innovation and Leadership in American Education," *Bulletin of N.A.S.S.P.*, March 1965, pp. 36–43.

Gillespie, R. L. "Evaluation: A New Approach," *Bulletin of N.A.S.S.P.*, October 1963, pp. 73–76.

Gouldner, Alvin W. (ed.). *Studies in Leadership: Leadership and Democratic Action*. New York: Harper and Brothers, 1950.

Griffiths, Daniel E. *Human Relations in School Administration*. New York: Appleton-Century-Crofts, Inc., 1956.

Haskew, L. D. "Leadership Is Personal," *Bulletin of N.A.S.S.P.*, April 1964, pp. 177–82.

Hodgkinson, Harold I. *Educational Decisions: A Casebook*. Englewood Cliffs, N.J.: Prentice-Hall, Inc., 1963.

Leavitt, Harold J. "Consequences of Executive Behavior," *Bulletin of N.A.S.S.P.*, April 1964, pp. 167–77.

Leu, Donald J., and Herbert C. Rudman. *Preparation Programs for School Administrators*. Seventh U.C.E.A. Career Development Seminar. East Lansing, Michigan: Michigan State University, 1963.

Lien, Ronald L. "Democratic Administrative Behavior," *Bulletin of N.A.S.S.P.*, March 1964, pp. 31–39.

McCleary, Lloyd E., and Stephen P. Hencley, *School Administration: Theoretical Bases of Professional Practice*. New York: Dodd, Mead and Company, 1965.

Matthews, Roderic D. "Evaluating the Evaluative Criteria," *Bulletin of N.A.S.S.P.*, April 1965, pp. 77–80.

Miller, Van. *Personnel Management in School Administration.* New York: World Book Company, 1955.

Moore, Hollis A. *Studies in School Administration.* Washington, D.C.: American Association of School Administrators, 1957.

Murray, Ross G., and Charles E. Henry. *New Understanding of Leadership: A Survey and Application of Research.* New York: Association Press, 1957.

Richards, J. M., and J. K. Hemphill. "Progress Report: A Study of the Secondary School Principalship," Parts I and II, *Bulletin of N.A.S.S.P.,* April 1964, pp. 211–33.

Sears, Jesse B. *The Nature of the Administrative Process.* New York: McGraw-Hill Book Company, Inc., 1950.

Stogdill, R. M. "Personal Factors Associated with Leadership," *Journal of Psychology,* 1958, pp. 37–71.

Trump, J. Lloyd, and Lois S. Karasik. *Focus on the Individual—A Leadership Responsibility.* Washington, D.C.: The National Association of Secondary School Principals, 1965.

Van Zwoll, James A. *School Personnel Administration.* New York: Appleton-Century-Crofts, 1964.

CHAPTER 3

The Principalship
as a Profession

The principal must be a versatile person to administer a school. It has been portrayed, through examples, that the principalship is not the same in all sections of the country and in all communities. There are large and small schools, rich and poor schools, stable and transient schools, and schools that are unique to individual communities all across the land. To adequately meet the many challenges that confront the principal, professional leadership of a high quality must be supplied.

But what of the principalship as a position, as a career, as a profession? It is the goal of this chapter to show that the principalship is, indeed, a profession to which a person can dedicate himself with satisfaction and success.

Becoming a Profession

Historical Development of the Principalship. As one views the principal today with his multitudinous duties, it is difficult to compare the current principalship with the first principalship. The Latin grammar school, dame schools, the sectarian religious schools, and early private schools were basically a one-man show: principal, teacher, custodian, and salesman. Frequently the person's duties also required him to be the minister or the substitute for the minister, custodian of the church, and sexton of the cemetery.

As the school increased in number of students, size, and reputation, additional teachers were added. With additional staff, a headmaster was selected. He taught his classes along with the other teachers but also served as chief disciplinarian and general master of the school. There was little need for a discussion on democratic school administration, for the headmaster was the boss. Gradually the headmaster became a full-fledged principal and assumed many of the duties he still has today. Released time was the next major development in the principalship. With released time came added responsibilities but greater opportunity for the principal to truly serve as an administrator rather than as a simple disciplinarian. Now that the principal had no direct responsibility for teaching, he was able to devote time to supervising, helping new teachers, and improving curriculum programs. Finally, the principalship has evolved as it is seen today—a principal, assistants, deans, departmental chairmen, clerical help, counselors, guidance personnel, and other staff members to carry out student personnel and auxiliary services. A typical secondary school principal is now a coordinator of all the multitudinous functions that must be performed. His functions are coordinating the efforts of all persons under him, integrating the school as a whole, keeping in touch with outside agencies, and devoting attention to professional improvements and progressive programs.

Desire for Profession Status. An occupational status symbol in our society is "profession." Everyone wants to be in a "profession." When high school students are surveyed for occupational choices, professional choices far outrank the percentage of the population that actually enters the professions. Most college graduates desire to achieve professional status.

The principalship is not a full-fledged profession in the same sense that one speaks of the profession of medicine or law. The principalship, as it exists today, is too young to have reached such status. There are still too many unresolved problems. Some of these problems are expressed in the case presented below:

You Will Never Have a Profession Until. . .

Mr. Nelson was pleased to have his good doctor friend stop by the school and come to his office. Their acquaintance spread over a period of three years, but this was the first time that Willis had visited him at school. His medical practice was too extensive for many daytime social visits.

After the normal greetings and small talk were over, Mr. Nelson remarked, "This is the first time I have seen you at school during the daytime. Special occasion?"

"Yes, I've got a complaint—not the legal kind—just a parent's vested interest in his daughter's future. I see in the newspaper that you are going to drop Latin from your curriculum. Why?"

Mr. Nelson explained the situation in detail and ended by saying that

Latin was a dead language with no use and that an additional modern language was to be added.

Willis spiritedly explained why Latin should still be in the curriculum and ended by saying, "The influential people in the city want it restored and I am speaking not just for me but for quite a group who believe it is anti-intellectual to drop it."

Mr. Nelson recognized that the group referred to were part of the basic power structure in the community. He desired their full cooperation and full support of the total school program; so he told Willis that he would, "reconsider and give it a little more thought."

The conversation then moved to Willis' schedule and the profession of medicine. Mr. Nelson indicated that the teachers belonged to a professional organization and that he belonged to the National Association of Secondary School Principals and the American Association of School Administrators and that these organizations were working for the improvement of the profession.

Willis said, "What profession?"

"The profession of school administration," replied Mr. Nelson.

"You don't have a profession and you never will have one," replied Willis. "When someone comes to me with a pain in their side, they don't tell me what's wrong or how to operate. You will never be a profession as long as people tell you what to teach and how to teach it."

Mr. Nelson began to wonder about the principalship. He had listened to his friend explain why he and the members of the community wanted Latin placed back in the curriculum; and then said that school administration would not be a profession as long as the principal listened to members of the community on such matters. The question should be asked, was the doctor right in his analysis? Must there be autonomy to be a profession? What is a profession?

Definition of a Profession. Abraham Flexner helped to clarify the profession status of the medical doctors. In 1915 he suggested the following identifying characteristics of a profession: (1) it is basically intellectual, carrying with it great personal responsibility; (2) it is learned, being based on great knowledge and not merely routine; (3) it is practical, rather than academic or theoretical; (4) its technique can be taught, this being the basis of professional education; (5) it is strongly organized internally; and (6) it is motivated by altruism, the professionals viewing themselves as working for some aspect of the good society.[1]

Fattu defined a profession in terms of characteristics. At a National Conference on Teacher Education and Professional Standards in 1961, he stated:

[1] Abraham Flexner, "Is Social Work a Profession?" in *Proceedings of the National Conference of Charities and Corrections* (Chicago: Hildmann Printing Co., 1915), pp. 576–90.

One distinguishes a professional from a non-professional person by the fact that the professional person knows "why" as well as "how." Unless here is a very close connection between the "why" and the "how" the "how" can easily become (or remain) a ritual with increasingly remote connection with reality, as in the case of the witch doctor. The professional person performs an essential public service by virtue of mastery over an extensive body of knowledge and skill, better than anyone who does not have such mastery. Mastery is determined by qualified peers. Such determination usually has a legal sanction through licensing. Licensing may rest upon examination, upon certification by the educational institution, or upon both. However, legal sanctions alone cannot give professional status, any more than a state legislature can repeal the facts of evolution. In the absence of professional competence, legislation becomes little more than empty mockery. . . . Licensing can be justified only if it is done to protect the public against quackery rather than to favor the profession.[2]

The Educational Policies Commission of the National Education Association has succinctly set forth six criteria in an adequate definition of a profession:

1. A profession is based on a body of specialized knowledge.
2. A profession seeks competence in its membership.
3. A profession serves the needs of its members.
4. A profession has ethical standards.
5. A profession influences public policy in its field.
6. A profession has group solidarity.[3]

On the basis of the criteria as set forth by the Educational Policies Commission, the profession of school administration is in a state of becoming. An analysis of these main points indicates much progress has been made toward a profession; yet there is much to be accomplished. A more detailed analysis of each of these criteria is presented below.

A Profession Is Based on a Body of Specialized Knowledge

A Profession for Principal, School Administrators, or Administrators? A basic question that influences the criteria of a specialized body of knowledge is whether there should be a profession of secondary school

[2] Nicholas Fattu, "A Profession Seeks to Guarantee the Competence of Its Members," in *Report of the NCTEPS Pennsylvania Conference* (Washington, D.C.: The National Education Association, 1962), pp. 99–108.

[3] Educational Policies Commission of the National Education Association of the United States and the American Association of School Administrators, *Professional Organizations in American Education* (Washington, D.C.: The Association, 1957), pp. 9-12.

principals, school administrators, or administrators in general. The question is not resolved to the satisfaction of all concerned. Agreement can be found that there will be an increasing number of specialist or staff positions that will require some of the same competencies.[4] There is also general agreement that the superintendent and the principal must have many of the same competencies.[5] There are some authorities who believe there is a generalized field of administration—governmental, private, and educational—to which all administrators could belong.[6]

Schutz indicated five basic functions that are common to all administrators: (1) creating conditions that enable people to function for accomplishment of organizational goals; (2) creating conditions that motivate; (3) providing guidance; (4) creating opportunities; and (5) creating conditions that bring personal satisfactions to personnel.[7] Griffiths asks, "Why not train an administrative class, the members of which would be interchangeable among organizations, or at least among those devoted to public service?"[8]

However, it is generally agreed among school administrators that school administrators should have teaching experience, and that they are recruited from the teacher ranks. While there are some bodies of knowledge common to all types of administration, particularly process functions, the linking of all administrators into one organization does not seem as practical as grouping school administrators together.

A Profession for School Administrators or Principals. The specialized bodies of knowledge for the principal-administrator are of two types: (1) knowledge common to both superintendent and principal as well as some other educational administrators, and (2) specialized knowledge primarily for the principal.

Hencley, in "Functional Interrelationships Within Administrative Performance System,"[9] indicates in a series of tables the suggested areas where the various educational administrators have responsibilities. In developing operational policies the principal had a major responsibility

[4] Van Miller, "Four Definitions of Your Job," *Overview*, 1960, p. 51.

[5] Hollis Moore, Jr., *Studies in School Administration* (Washington, D.C.: American Association of School Administrators, 1957), p. 30.

[6] Daniel E. Griffiths, *Administrative Theory* (New York: Appleton-Century-Crofts, Inc., 1959), p. 71. Van Miller, *op. cit.*, p. 51.

[7] William C Schutz, *Procedures for Identifying Persons with Potential for Public School Administrative Positions*, U.S. Office of Education Cooperative Research Project No. 677 (Berkeley, Calif.: University of California, 1961), pp. 16–19.

[8] Jack A. Culbertson and Stephen P. Hencley (eds.), *Preparing Administrators: New Perspectives* (Columbus, Ohio: University Council for Educational Administration, 1962), p. 96.

[9] Donald J. Leu and Herbert C. Rudman, *Preparation Programs for School Administrators—Common and Specialized Learnings.* Seventh UCEA Career Development Seminar (East Lansing, Mich.: Michigan State University, 1963), pp. 61–95.

in developing instruction and curriculum policies, pupil personnel policies, staff personnel policies, school plant and services policies, and community relations policies. He had a moderate responsibility in developing financial and business policies. The principal had direct supervisory responsibilities over all categories of instruction and curriculum development and pupil personnel except applying extreme measures for student irregularities and directing research and experimentation. There were many other areas where the principal had the responsibility of direct supervision or supervision and coordination.

Common and Specialized Bodies of Knowledge for Principals. In a general framework of processes of administration forces in the administrative setting and tasks of educational administration, Lawrence W. Downey, in "The Secondary School Principal,"[10] graphically portrays the areas of knowledge for a principal's background as shown in Figure 3.1.

Figure 3.1

The High School Principalship: Areas of Commonality, Areas of Emphasis, and Areas of Specialization

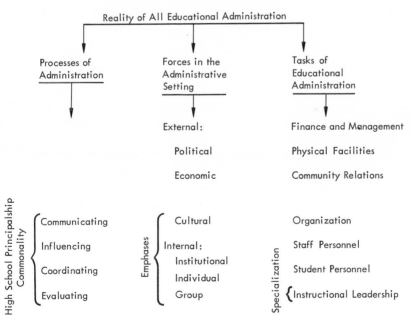

Source: Lawrence W. Downey, "The Secondary School Principal" as shown in Donald J. Leu and Herbert C. Rudman, *Preparation Programs for School Administrators—Common and Specialized Learnings*, p. 136. Copyright © 1963. Seventh U.C.E.A. Career Development Seminar. East Lansing, Michigan. Reprinted by permission of Office of Research and Publications, Michigan State University.

[10] *Ibid.*, p. 136.

In addition to the work of U.C.E.A. in defining the areas of specialized knowledge, the principals in a study sponsored by the N.A.S.S.P. have indicated specifically the areas of knowledge that a principal should have as a beginning principal, as shown in Table 3.1.

TABLE 3.1   Value of Course Work in Preparation for the Principalship

Course	Abso-lutely Essen-tial	Ex-tremely Valu-able	Quite Valu-able	Of Some Value	Little or No Value
Supervision of instruction	59	25	13	05	01
Personnel administration	48	34	13	04	01
Human relations	46	37	14	04	01
Curriculum	42	36	16	05	01
School organization	42	25	22	10	01
Administrative theory and practice	40	28	21	09	01
Psychology of learning	32	40	22	06	01
School law	32	30	24	12	02
School finance	31	27	25	15	02
History of education	16	13	32	40	10
Plant maintenance	08	24	36	28	04
Contemporary education	08	23	40	27	04
Research methods	07	22	33	28	09
Comparative education	06	19	36	34	04
Political science	05	14	34	38	11

SOURCE: J. K. Hemphill, "Progress Report: A Study of the Secondary School Principalship, Part II," *Bulletin of N.A.S.S.P.*, p. 227. Reprinted by permission from the *Bulletin of the National Association of Secondary School Principals*, April, 1964. Copyright: Washington, D.C.

On the basis of this study the bodies of knowledge deemed to be absolutely essential and extremely valuable to over 50 per cent of the principals are supervision of instruction, personnel administration, human relations, curriculum, school organization, administrative theory and practice, psychology of learning, school law, and school finance. Additional courses were deemed to be quite valuable and of some value.

The principalship can be defined as meeting the criteria for a specialized body of knowledge. There is still some question as to extent of field of administrators that should be included in the profession.

A Profession Seeks Competence in Its Members

The degree of competence that can be found in the profession can be seen by reviewing certification requirements, training and experience requirements, and special provisions for in-service development.

Certification Requirements. Every state has requirements for secondary school administration over and above those required of a classroom teacher, and each state maintains its own standards. Nearly all states require teaching experience plus additional university credit. A majority of states require a master's degree or its equivalent.

Because many states have specific requirements peculiar to themselves, a prospective school administrator should always have his credentials checked by the state in which he desires to practice. The regional accrediting associations also have standards for school administrators. The Northwest Association for Secondary and Higher Schools requires principals to have a master's degree, which includes 24 quarter hours of graduate work in education, or they must have completed 57 quarter hours in graduate work with 30 quarter hours in education. The North Central Association of Colleges and Secondary Schools requires a principal to hold a master's degree including at least 20 semester hours of graduate work in education with a major emphasis in administration and supervision. Two years of teaching experience are required. The Southern Association of Colleges and Secondary Schools requires that a major portion of one year of advanced study be in the areas of administration and supervision. The New England Association of Colleges and Secondary Schools and the Middle States Association of Colleges and Secondary Schools do not specify exact requirements, but the states within these associations do have specific requirements. The study on the secondary school principalship revealed that only 9 per cent hold less than a master's degree, as shown in Table 3.2.

TABLE 3.2   Highest Degree

Response	All Schools	LOCATION Cities	Rural
No college degree	00	00	01
Bachelor's (or equivalent)	09	07	15
Master's: education	35	25	40
Master's: other field	04	08	03
Master's: plus work	41	40	37
Master's: plus all doctor's course work	06	09	03
Doctor of Education	02	05	01
Doctor of Philosophy	01	05	00
Some other degree	01	01	00

Source: J. K. Hemphill, "Progress Report: A Study of the Secondary School Principalship, Part II," *Bulletin of N.A.S.S.P.*, p. 220. Reprinted by permission from the *Bulletin of the National Association of Secondary-School Principals*, April, 1964. Copyright: Washington, D.C.

The professional organizations to which teachers belong, the National Association of Secondary School Principals, and the American Association of School Administrators have all played an important role in improving the qualifications and requirements for positions in school administration. The American Association of School Administrators now has as part of its constitution an amendment that reads:

> Beginning on January 1, 1964, all new members of the American Association of School Administrators shall submit evidence of successful completion of two years graduate study in university programs designed to prepare school administrators and approved by an accreditation body endorsed by the executive committee of the A.A.S.A.

This requirement will markedly affect the future pattern of professional preparation for school administrators. Where a master's degree is quite common today for such a position, a doctor's degree or a specialist-in-education degree or its equivalent will be the most typical pattern for professional requirements. Principals who are desirous of moving upward in the profession should begin plans for improvement along the lines suggested by the American Association of School Administrators. It should be noted that in many of the large urban centers and especially in centers associated with a prominent university, many of the school principals already have a doctor's degree. Most of the new principals who are being hired in these areas have such a degree.

Training and Experience Background. Although most principals have a master's degree, the big question is still present, "Is it in the areas where the specialized bodies of knowledge have been indicated?" The N.A.S.S.P. study on the school principal indicates that 71 per cent of the principals in all schools were trained in the field of educational administration, 12 per cent were trained in secondary school education, while the remaining 17 per cent were trained in other fields. It was interesting to note that 75 per cent of the rural principals were trained in school administration, while only 49 per cent of the city principals had such training.[11]

Most principals have had some teaching experience prior to becoming administrators. The years of experience in teaching prior to the current position held by principals ranged from none to over 25 years. The median was about eight years. The median for principals of city schools was 13 years, which indicates that there is less opportunity for movement into a principalship in the city schools.[12]

In-service Development for Principals. There are several ways in which the prospective or practicing school administrator can improve his com-

[11] J. K. Hemphill, "Progress Report: A Study of The Secondary School Principalship," *Bulletin of N.A.S.S.P.*, April 1964, p. 220.
[12] *Ibid.*, p. 221.

petence in the field of school administration. The primary ways are through internships, workshops, conventions and conferences, and school visitations.

The internship has been used extensively in some major universities for years. Under these systems the student took classes part time and worked with a principal or superintendent part time. A partial salary was usually paid by the district, although occasionally the university also participated. For the school year 1964–65 a new program was initiated by the National Association of Secondary School Principals known as the Administrative Internship in Secondary School Improvement. Interns have been placed in schools where promising new practices and patterns of education have been introduced. The project is supported partly by the participating district and partly by funds from Fund for the Advancement of Education.[13]

The workshop is a practicable method of improving competence. A workshop theme or problem is selected. Principals and other individuals with knowledge to contribute are invited to work in an informal way with other principals. The key to a workshop is sharing of ideas and know-how.

Many new ideas, projects, and practices can be obtained at the national conventions and in state and regional conferences. Each year the National Association of Secondary School Principals holds its convention. The convention is the highlight of the principal's year. Some districts pay expenses for the principal to attend yearly or on a rotating basis. State conferences are usually held several times a year.

For practical information and on-the-spot observations and discussions, the school visitation is a practical way to increase competence. Visitation can be with schools in the district, state, or nation. In recent years internation visits have become rather commonplace. School visitation is frequently planned at the same time as the annual convention to make the most economical use of travel money.

A Profession Serves the Needs of Its Members

The phrase "needs of its members" is rather nebulous. It is defined here to mean the basic needs of welfare and professional growth. Professional growth has already been discussed under the section on competence except as it is linked directly with welfare. The principal must have a job, adequate salary, retirement benefits, opportunity for advancement, and status with his colleagues and in his community.

[13] National Association of Secondary School Principals, *N.A.S.S.P. Internship Project, News Report* (Washington, D.C.: The Association, Spring 1965), and *Focus on the Individual—A Leadership Responsibility* (Washington, D.C.: The Association, 1965), pp. 1–32. Also available as a filmstrip and record.

The Status of a Principal.   At the same time that the position of principalship was evolving from that of a teacher to a coordinating principal, the status of the principal was also experiencing interesting changes. Most of the early teacher-principals were hired in connection with some religious organization. A typical example was in the early Dutch colonies. In these colonies the Dutch West Indies Company had complete control of the government and the company appointed the schoolmaster and paid his salary. A house was provided for the schoolmaster, and school was maintained in the same building. The Dutch West Indies Company thus financed and equipped the school. The church looked out for the qualifications of the schoolmaster, including his piety and orthodoxy to the established religion. Although the Dutch West Indies Company was required to supply a teacher and pay his salary, the ruling church in Amsterdam selected and certified the schoolmasters for confidence, character, and doctrine. The schoolteachers were rated as minor officials of the church and served the church by carrying announcements, ringing the church bell, and, in the minister's absence, taking charge of services on the Sabbath. Some of the English governors of New York also continued the practice of licensing only schoolmasters who had been approved in the home country by the Church of England through the Agency of the Society for the Propagation of the Gospel in Foreign Parts. Under these arrangements, the teacher's pay was paid in part by the Society and in part by the community. In New England, the Puritans were convinced of the necessity of schools in order to keep Satan from leading the children astray. The teacher, of course, had to have the religious leader's stamp of approval.

As the population spread into the more isolated areas, the teacher was forced to move from town to town to teach his school. He lived and boarded at his pupils' homes for about a week at a time, first with one patron and then with another. Such a practice made the school money last a little longer. The wages were low—about equal to those of a good farmhand. The turnover was understandably high.

As the principalship evolved, the status of the principal improved, and he was often referred to as "the professor." He was considered a scholarly, cultured, and intellectual leader of the community. Today, economic conditions have improved markedly, and the principal is still regarded highly in his community. He is considered an authority, and the community involves him in many social and cultural activities.

Careers in Secondary School Administration.   Each year in the university and private educational placement bureaus across the nation, notices appear similar to the following job descriptions:

PRINCIPALS WANTED

Principal needed for a junior high school in Medine, New York. Master's degree and experience required. Salary $7,000-$9,000.

Principal: Sr. High School
Anton, Iowa
Application now being accepted for the Austin Senior High School. Qualifications: Administrator's certificate and five years' teaching and administrative position.
Salary open.

Position: Junior-Senior High School Principalship
Place: Cobin, Washington
Salary open
Requirements: Contact Placement Bureau or write
    Superintendent of Schools
    Cobin County School District
    Cobin, Washington

Openings are nearly always available for the person who wants to venture into the exciting experience of school administration. There are currently approximately 23,000 high schools and about 10,000 junior high schools in the United States. The number of high schools varies from about 1,200 in Texas to less than 50 in Rhode Island, Delaware, and Nevada.

Selecting a Position. A mistake that most aspirants make when the certification requirements are completed is to think that the job will automatically be right where the aspirant wants to live. Although such a windfall does happen, it is not typical. A quotation expressed at Stanford University is that the budding young administrator is willing to "go anywhere in the world between San Francisco and San Jose." A prospective principal in a university town is most likely to be surrounded with great numbers of candidates who have passed the legal requirements, but who are still teaching in the classroom because of lack of opportunity in the immediate area. A certificate of administration granted by any state will not create a job for a prospective candidate in his home town. Prospective administrators must go where the jobs are.

Most principals will begin their careers in small schools or as assistant principals. Conant's report on the *American High School Today* revealed that there were about 14,000 high schools with twelfth-grade enrollment of less than 100. Most of these smaller schools are in rural areas. Such a fact should not discourage a prospective principal. There are many advantages in a small school situation. A frequent quote is "there is no substitute for experience." Certainly a principal must go where he can gain experience, and the experiences in a small school are rich and rewarding. Whether the school is small or large, there are many common elements in the principalship. On the other hand, there are some unique experiences that can only be received in a small school. These experiences are invaluable for a principal's growth and development. In addition to the educational experiences, the principal in a small community is regarded as a figure of great importance. Everyone knows him, and he is soon involved in as many of the community's activities as his time and energy will permit. Seldom does any person in the community achieve a higher status and position of dignity and respect than does the school principal. Because of the high regard in which principals are held in a small community and because of the satisfaction that can be received through knowing all the individuals with whom they are working, many principals choose to remain in the small rural communities and exert their influence for good down through the years.

However, should a principal desire to advance to new and different problems, and most do, previous experience is a major determining factor in securing a position with more responsibility. Other factors being equal, a candidate who is currently serving as a principal is given extra consideration when an opening occurs. A typical pattern is for a principal to start in a small rural school and gradually move to schools with larger enrollments, increased number of faculty members, and increased responsibilities.

Although most openings occur in areas where small schools are prevalent, there are frequent openings in urban and suburban areas. Two types of candidates are usually considered for these openings: (1) the candidates who have had good experience and good records and who are principals in smaller schools, and (2) assistant principals, teachers, counselors, and other personnel within the school system who are qualified and desire the position. There are usually a large number of such applicants within the district. Many teachers secure their administrative certificate but do not desire to move from a particular locality. Districts that maintain a policy of promotion from within usually select such a person from their ranks. It is rather common practice to promote from within in city districts. When a vacancy is known to be occurring, the principal is often hand-picked and given training in anticipation of the opening. It should be remembered, however, that the number of such openings is much fewer than in rural areas and there are many more candidates seeking the position. Unless a district has already hand-picked the candidate or recognized the candidate through assignments in semiadministrative roles, most aspirants for an administrative position will usually find it to their advantage to seek a position where there is an opening rather than wait for such an opportunity to develop in an urban or suburban area.

The Assistant Principal. In addition to the principalship there are many assistant principals. Much has been and will be said about the principal, but little about the assistant principal. Since he is an assistant, one might conclude that everything said about the principal applies to his assistant. To a great extent this conclusion is true. Certainly he is to be regarded as a professional and a member in the profession. The new administrator frequently starts his professional career as an assistant and moves to a position of principal. There are many men and some women who desire to remain an assistant. The professional definition must include all assistants, not just those who are aspiring to principalships. Additional information is provided about the assignments of the assistant in Chapter 8.[14]

Economic Factors. Along with many other factors, aspirants for a position in school administration are interested in the economic considerations. A comparison with teachers' salaries reveals that the school principals receive substantially more than do classroom teachers. The amount of difference varies from district to district and state to state. It is not uncommon for the medium salary of a principal to be $1,500 to $2,000 higher than the medium salary for teachers. Assuming a total life potential of 25 years, the differential would amount to between $37,500 and $50,000. The executive committee of the National Association of Secondary School Principals has proposed a salary differential for principals and assistant principals on a ratio basis as shown in Table 3.3. The differential for assistant principals is from 30 to 65 per cent higher, and from 40 to 95 per cent higher for the principals. The administrator's ratio is based on the maximum teacher salary. Actual salaries change each year as the total district salary schedule changes; therefore, specific amounts are not provided here.

TABLE 3.3 Recommended Maximum Salaries for Secondary School Principals and Assistant Principals, Stated in Percentage Ratio Above Teachers' Maximum Salaries
(*Teachers' maximum salary with master's degree* = 1.00)

Suggested Size of Enrollment	*Principal*	*Assistant Principal*
A. Secondary schools under 500	1.60	
	1.40	
B. Secondary schools 500–1,000	1.80	1.50
	1.60	1.30
C. Secondary schools 1,000–2,500	1.95	1.65
	1.75	1.45

SOURCE: National Association of Secondary-School Principals. Approved by the Executive Committee, February 28, 1957. Reprinted by permission of the Association.

[14] Philip C. Wells, Robert H. Nelson, and Earl M. Johnsen, "The Assistant Secondary School Principal," *Bulletin of N.A.S.S.P.,* January 1965, p. 16.

Other Benefits.   In addition to the salary the principal has the other benefits accorded to educators. Retirement plans are in operation, many attached to or a part of the social security program. Hospitalization, medical plans, and group insurance plans are usually available through membership in the state education association. Some group insurance programs are also available through the national affiliations. Administrators may or may not have sick leave. Usually it is just assumed that they will do their job "even if it takes all summer," and it usually does.

A Profession Has Ethical Standards

A Code of Ethics for Administrators.   All criteria for a profession indicate the need for a code of ethical behavior. Such a code is the following code of ethics of the American Association of School Administrators.[15]

CODE OF ETHICS

PREAMBLE

Public education in America rests on firm commitments to the dignity and worth of each individual; to the pre-eminence of enlightenment and reason over force and coercion; and to government by the consent of the governed. Public schools prosper to the extent they merit the confidence of the people. In judging its schools, society is influenced to a considerable degree by the character and quality of their administration. To meet these challenges school administrators have an obligation to exercise professional leadership.

Society demands that any group that claims the rights, privileges, and status of a profession prove itself worthy through the establishment and maintenance of ethical policies governing the activities of its members. A professional society must demonstrate the capacity and willingness to regulate itself and to set appropriate guides for the ethical conduct of its members. Such obligations are met largely by practitioners through action in a professional society such as the American Association of School Administrators.

Every member of a profession carries a responsibility to act in a manner becoming a professional person. This implies that each school administrator has an inescapable obligation to abide by the ethical standards of his profession. The behavior of each is the concern of all. The conduct of any administrator influences the attitude of the public toward the profession and education in general.

These policies of ethical behavior are designed to inspire a quality of

---

[15] "Policies to Govern the Ethical Professional Behavior of School Administrators" (Washington, D.C.: American Association of School Administrators, 1962). Reprinted by permission.

behavior that reflects honor and dignity on the profession of school administration. They are not intended as inflexible rules nor unchangeable laws. They serve to measure the propriety of an administrator's behavior in his working relationships. They encourage and emphasize those positive attributes of professional conduct which characterize strong and effective administrative leadership.

The term administrator, as used herein, refers to those persons who, regardless of title, serve as chief school administrators.

Policy I. The Professional School Administrator Constantly Upholds the Honor and Dignity of His Profession in All His Actions and Relations with Pupils, Colleagues, School Board Members, and the Public.

The following examples illustrate but do not limit applications of this policy.

The professional school administrator:

A. is impartial in the execution of school policies and the enforcement of rules and regulations. It is a breach of ethics to give preferential consideration to any individual or group because of their special status or position in the school system or community.

B. recognizes and respects fully the worth and dignity of each individual in all administrative procedures and leadership actions.

C. demonstrates professional courtesy and ethical behavior by informing a colleague in another system of his intention to consider for employment personnel from that system.

D. never submits official and confidential letters of appraisal for teachers or others which knowingly contain erroneous information or which knowingly fail to include pertinent data.

E. never fails to recommend those worthy of recommendation.

F. is alert to safeguard the public and his profession from those who might degrade public education or school administration.

G. seeks no self-aggrandizement.

H. refrains from making unwarranted claims, from inappropriate advertising, and from misinterpreting facts about his school system to further his own professional status.

I. never makes derogatory statements about a colleague or a school system unless he is compelled to state his opinion under oath or in official relationships where his professional opinion is required.

J. exhibits ethical behavior by explaining and giving reasons to individuals affected by demotions or terminations of employment.

Policy II. The Professional School Administrator Obeys Local, State, and National Laws; Holds Himself to High Ethical and Moral Standards, and Gives Loyalty to His Country and to the Cause of Democracy and Liberty.

The following examples illustrate but do not limit applications of this policy:

A. A legal conviction for immorality, commission of a crime involving moral turpitude or other public offense of similar degree shall be sufficient grounds for expelling a school administrator from membership in the American Association of School Administrators.

B. Affiliation with organizations know to advocate the forcible overthrow of the government of the United States is evidence of unworthiness of public trust. A person who is so affiliated shall not be permitted to become or to continue as member of the American Association of School Administrators.

C. A professional school administrator, in common with other citizens, has a right and in many instances an obligation to express his opinion about the wisdom or justice of a given law. An opinion questioning a law, however, does not justify failure to fulfill the requirements of that law.

D. The ideals of his profession require a school administrator to resist ideological pressures that would contravene the fundamental principles of public education, or would pervert or weaken public schools, their educational program, or their personnel.

E. It is unethical to ignore or divert attention from laws which are incompatible with the best interests and purposes of the schools, as a way of avoiding controversy. Rather the professional school administrator will take the initiative to bring about the reconsideration, revision, or repeal of the statute.

F. The professional school administrator will not withhold evidence or knowingly shield law breakers.

Policy III. The Professional School Administrator Accepts the Responsibility Throughout His Career to Master and to Contribute to the Growing Body of Specialized Knowledge, Concepts, and Skills Which Characterize School Administration as a Profession.

The following examples illustrate but do not limit applications of this policy:

A. In addition to meeting the minimum standards required for legal certification in his state, the professional school administrator has a responsibility to satisfy the preparation standards recommended by his professional association, and has an obligation to work toward the adoption of these professional standards by the appropriate certification authorities in his state.

B. The school administrator has a professional obligation to attend conferences, seminars, and other learning activities which hold promise of contributing to his professional growth and development.

C. It is in keeping with the highest ideals of the profession for the administrator to support local, state, and national committees studying educational problems and to participate in such activities whenever and wherever possible, consistent with his obligations to his district.

D. The school administrator has a leadership responsibility for the professional growth of his associates which requires encouragement of their attendance at appropriate professional meetings and their participation in the work of local, state, and national committees and associations.

E. Concern for improving his profession, and for education generally, requires that the school administrator seek out promising educational practices and relevant research findings and that he share with others any significant practices and research from within his own institution.

F. The school administrator has a special obligation to contribute to the strengthening of his own state and national professional association.

Policy IV. The Professional School Administrator Strives to Provide the Finest Possible Educational Experiences and Opportunities to All Persons in the District.

The following examples illustrate but do not limit applications of this policy:

A. The school administrator will base differentiation of educational experiences on the differing needs and abilities of pupils, giving no preference to factors such as social status or other undemocratic or discriminating considerations.

B. A school administrator has an obligation to inform the board and the community of deficiencies in educational services or opportunities.

C. A school administrator resists all attempts by vested interests to infringe upon the school program as a means of promoting their selfish purposes.

D. A school administrator resists all attempts to exclude from consideration as teaching personnel members of any particular race or creed. He also resists pressures to employ teachers on the basis of the political, marital, or economic status of the applicant. The ability and fitness of the candidates for teaching positions are the sole criteria for selection.

E. A school administrator recognizes that the provisions of equal educational opportunities for all pupils may require greater or different resources for some than for others.

F. A school administrator is professionally obligated to assume clear, articulate, and forceful leadership in defining the role of the school in the community and pointing the way to achieve its functions.

Policy V. The Professional School Administrator Applying for a Position or Entering into Contractual Agreements Seeks to Preserve and Enhance the Prestige and Status of His Profession.

The following examples illustrate but do not limit applications of this policy:

A. A school administrator is morally committed to honor employment contracts. He shall refuse to enter into a new contractual agreement until termination of an existing contract is completed to the satisfaction of all concerned.

B. A school administrator does not apply for positions indiscriminately nor for any position held by an administrator whose termination of employment is not a matter of record.

C. Misrepresentations, use of political influence, pressure tactics, or undermining the professional status of a colleague are unethical practices and are inimical to his professional commitment.

D. Advertising, either to solicit new school positions or to offer professional consultation services, is inconsistent with the ideals of the profession of school administration.

E. A school administrator refrains from making disparaging comments about candidates competing for a position.

F. A school administrator refuses to accept a position in which established principles of professional school administration must be seriously compromised or abandoned.

G. A school administrator does not apply for or accept a position where a competent special professional investigating committee endorsed by the Association has declared working conditions unsatisfactory until such time as appropriate corrections in the situation have been made.

Policy VI. The Professional School Administrator Carries Out in Good Faith All Policies Duly Adopted by the Local Board and the Regulations of State Authorities and Renders Professional Service to the Best of His Ability.

The following examples illustrate but do not limit applications of this policy:

A. Adoption of policies not in conformity with the administrator's recommendations or beliefs is not just cause for refusal by the administrator to support and execute them.

B. It is improper for an administrator to refuse to work at his optimum level.

C. A school administrator has an obligation to support publicly the school board and the instructional staff if either is unjustly accused. He should not permit himself to become involved publicly in personal criticism of board or staff members. He should be at liberty, however, to discuss differences of opinion on professional matters.

D. If a situation develops whereby an administrator feels that to retain his position would necessitate that he violate what he and other members of the profession consider to be ethical conduct he should inform the board of the untenable position. In the event of his imminent dismissal the superintendent should request adequate reasons and if they are not forthcoming or if the situation is not resolved to his professional satisfaction he should report to the public.

Policy VII. The Professional School Administrator Honors the Public Trust of His Position Above Any Economic or Social Rewards.

The following examples illustrate but do not limit applications of this policy:

A. To resist, or to fail to support, clearly desirable approaches to improving and strengthening the schools is unbecoming to a professional person and unethical conduct on the part of a school administrator.

B. The school administrator has a commitment to his position of public trust to resist unethical demands by special interest or pressure groups. He refuses to allow strong and unscrupulous individuals to seize or exercise powers and responsibilities which are properly his own.

C. The rank, popularity, position, or social standing of any member of the school staff should never cause the professional school administrator to conceal, disregard, or seemingly condone unethical conduct. Any and all efforts to disregard, overlook, or cover up unethical practices should be vigorously resisted by a school administrator.

Policy VIII. The Professional School Administrator Does Not Permit Considerations of Private Gain nor Personal Economic Interest to Affect the Discharge of His Professional Responsibilities.

The following examples illustrate but do not limit applications of this policy:

A. A school administrator refuses to permit his relationship with vendors primarily interested in selling goods and services to influence his administration of the school system he serves.

B. It is improper for a school administrator to accept employment by any concern which publishes, manufactures, sells, or in any way deals in goods or services which are or may be expected to be purchased by the school system he serves.

C. It is improper for a school administrator to be engaged in private ventures if such endeavors cause him to give less than full-time concern to his school system.

D. This policy in no way precludes private investment of personal funds of the school administrator in ventures not influenced by his position in a given school system provided his own professional obligations are not neglected.

E. During the time of his employment the school administrator shall have no personal interest in, nor receive any personal gain or profit from, school supplies, equipment, books, or other educational materials or facilities procured, dispensed, or sold to or in the school system he serves.

F. It is a breach of public trust for a school administrator to use confidential information concerning school affairs (such as the knowledge of the selection of specific school sites) for personal profit or to divulge such information to others who might so profit.

G. It is inappropriate for a school administrator to utilize unpublished materials developed in line of duty by staff members in a school system in order to produce a publication for personal profit, without the expressed permission of all contributors.

H. A school administrator must be wary of using free consultative services from a commercial concern which may in effect be a skillful technique for promoting the sale of instructional or other materials in which that concern has a pecuniary interest.

I. A school administrator does not publicly endorse goods or services provided for schools by commercial organizations.

J. The school administrator should not recommend the appointment of immediate relatives to positions under his jurisdiction.

Policy IX. The Professional School Administrator Recognizes That the Public Schools Are the Public's Business and Seeks to Keep the Public Fully and Honestly Informed about Their Schools.

The following examples illustrate but do not limit applications of this policy:

A. A school administrator has an obligation to interpret to the community the work and activities of the school system, revealing its weaknesses as well as its strengths. It is unethical for a school administrator to present only the favorable facts to the patrons of the district.

B. A school administrator maintains confidences or qualified privileged communications entrusted to him in the course of executing the affairs of the public schools. These confidences shall be revealed only as the law or courts may require or when the welfare of the school system is at stake.

C. It is proper for a school administrator to discuss confidential information with the board of education meeting in executive session.

D. A school administrator considers that those with whom he deals are innocent of any disparaging accusations until valid evidence is presented to substantiate any charges made.

Overview. High Standards of Ethical Behavior for the Professional School Administrator Are Essential and Are Compatible with His Faith in the Power of Public Education and His Commitment to Leadership in the Preservation and Strengthening of the Public Schools.

The true sense of high calling comes to the superintendent of schools as he faces squarely such widely held beliefs as the following:

A. The effectiveness of the schools and their programs is inescapably the responsibility of the superintendent.

B. Every act, or every failure to act, of the superintendent has consequences in the schools and in the lives of people.

C. In many situations and to many people in a community the superintendent is the living symbol of their schools.

D. The public entrusts both the day-by-day well-being and the long-range welfare of its children and of its school system to the superintendent and board of education.

E. The ultimate test for a superintendent is the effort which he makes to improve the quality of learning opportunity for every child in the schools.

F. In the long run, what happens in and to the public schools of America happens to America.

A Profession Influences Public Policy in Its Field

In this area the National Association of Secondary School Principals and the American Association of School Administrators are very active. In addition to their own influence, they collectively unite with the National Education Association and other affiliates of the N.E.A. The greatest single attempt to influence public policy has been with the state and national legislatures in relationship to school legislation. The passage of a general federal aid to education bill was the outgrowth of years of combined work of all groups concerned.

The National Association of Secondary School Principals has been very active in influencing curriculum changes, organizational structure, and professional training through its committees and projects. The Association has cooperated with many other groups to accomplish these purposes.

The area of public policy is broad and continuous. Certainly much remains to be done to bring about all the changes needed in the profession. The changing nature of our society would also indicate that the profession will always have goals that will need implementation through national policy.

A Profession Has Group Solidarity

The criteria of group solidarity are difficult to evaluate. Certainly there are strengths and weaknesses. Part of the solidarity comes through the members' own organization, some through affiliation. The weaknesses are inherent in the areas of strength. Some of the evidences of solidarity or lack of it are given below:

Membership in the Professional Organizations. The two primary professional organizations for principals are the National Association of Secondary School Principals (N.A.S.S.P.) and the American Association of School Administrators (A.A.S.A.). Sixty-seven per cent of the principals belong to N.A.S.S.P., but only 16 per cent belong to A.A.S.A. (See Table 3.4.) This difference can be explained because the A.A.S.A. is primarily looked upon as the superintendents' association.

TABLE 3.4   Professional Activities of the Principal

Question:	Respond- ing "Yes"
Are you a member of N.A.S.S.P.?	67
Are you a member of A.A.S.A.?	16
Are you a member of your state's association of secondary school principals?	75
During the past two years have you:	
attended a statewide or national meeting of secondary school principals?	77
participated extensively in the activities of professional associations?	59
studied through higher educational institutions?	70
been involved in conducting research in education?	75
participated extensively in workshops or educational conferences?	59

SOURCE: J. K. Hemphill, "Progress Report: A Study of the Secondary School Principalship, Part II," *Bulletin of N.A.S.S.P.*, p. 226. Reprinted by permission from the *Bulletin of the National Association of Secondary-School Principals*, April, 1964. Copyright: Washington, D.C.

A further review of the table shows that the principal is active in his state association and participates in professional activities.

Most of the principals are also members of the National Education Association and the state and local associations. Such membership brings collective solidarity.

Other Groups and Organizations.   Still other groups and organizations are working for the development of school administration as a profession: National Conference of Professors of Educational Administration (N.C.P.E.A.); Cooperative Program in Educational Administration (C.P.E.A.); and the University Council on Educational Administration (U.C.E.A.).

The National Conference of Professors of Educational Administration (N.C.P.E.A.) was organized in 1947 to bring together the professors of school administration from across the country into one united group. The group has actively pushed for improvements in the profession of school administration. Although the principals cannot join, they receive the benefits of the organization's attempts to strengthen the profession.

The Cooperative Program in Educational Administration (C.P.E.A.) was organized in 1950 with a grant from W. K. Kellogg Foundation. The project was proposed by the A.A.S.A. to help make school administration a real profession. Studies of principals and superintendents were conducted from eight major university centers. Over 300 studies were made, which helped focus attention on many of the problems.

The University Council for Education Administration (U.C.E.A.) was organized in 1958 by 34 universities to ". . . promote, through inter-university cooperation, the improvement of the professional preparation of administrative personnel in the field of education." Because member institutions must have their graduate programs accredited by the National Council for Accreditation of Teacher Education (N.C.A.T.E.), U.C.E.A. exercises considerable influence in the preparation programs for school administrators.

Unresolved Problems

A profession that has "not yet arrived" has many problems to resolve, the resolution of which all groups mentioned herein are attempting to make. The facets of the problems as well as the solutions have not been found or acted upon with solidarity. Some of the problems have been alluded to in previous sections. Some of the problems needing further study are:

1. What is the profession as applied to public service?
2. Who should belong: administrators in general or school administrators or principals only?
3. Should school administrators separate themselves from teachers in the professional organization?
4. What is the general and specific nature of school administration?
5. To what extent should a public educational profession be autonomous and self-directing?
6. What is an appropriate code of ethics to which all groups in the defined profession can subscribe?
7. What areas and procedures are best for this profession in influencing public policy?
8. How can group solidarity be heightened when each group maintains its own organization and affiliations?

Summary

Secondary school administration is a field that presents many opportunities for prospective candidates. The principalship has been in existence for a long time and was one of the first administrative jobs associated with schools. The principalship has evolved through different stages from teacher, headmaster, teacher-principal, part-time administrator, and full-time administrator. During each of these periods, new responsibilities were added to the job. Currently the principal must perform multitudinous tasks that carry many major responsibilities. There are nearly 30,000 head administrative positions in secondary schools across the nation plus assistant positions. Approximately 20,000 of these are in the high school program. About 14,000 are in schools with twelfth-grade enrollments under one hundred students.

There are many different types of positions. The aspirant for a principalship might still find a principalship in any of the stages discussed under the evolution of the principalship. Most openings occur in small schools in rural communities. A prospective principal should plan to go where the jobs are rather than wait for the jobs to come to him. In a city system advancement is usually made from within.

A principal's economic position is better than that of a teacher. By and large, his medium salary is about $1,500 to $2,000 higher than the medium teacher's salary. The principal's salary is usually based on some type of ratio above the teacher's salary. The lifetime earnings of an average principal will be between $30,000 and $50,000 higher than those of an average teacher.

All states have certification requirements for school administrators, and many states require a master's degree, or its equivalent. Most states require several years of teaching experience as well as university course work. The certification requirements have been increasing over the years. The American Association of School Administrators has adopted a recent provision that two years of graduate work in an approved graduate program is a standard for membership in that association. Such a policy will greatly improve the professional qualifications of school administrators in the coming years.

In addition to the state requirements, the professional accreditation organizations generally have stipulations requiring advance work in school administration. A school administrator who truly plans to be a professional person should do all he can to improve his professional organization.

The principalship as a profession is in a "state of becoming" when judged against criteria for a profession as set forth by the Education Policy Commission. These criteria are: (1) a profession is based on a body of specified knowledge, (2) a profession seeks competence in its own members, (3) a profession serves its members, (4) a profession has ethical standards, (5) a profession influences public policy in its field, and (6) a profession has group solidarity.

SUGGESTED PROJECTS AND ACTIVITIES

1. Attend a meeting of the secondary school principals' association in your region or state. Determine the wide variety of schools represented and types of persons selected.

2. Make a study of the high schools in your state or in your immediate area and list their size and number of administrative positions. If the school is small, indicate the number of periods the principal is free to carry out administration.
3. Discuss with several principals their feelings about the future of the profession and what a young candidate should do to achieve success.
4. Invite the president of the secondary school principals' association of your state or some other officer to discuss with your class or group the professional developments in the area of secondary school principalships.
5. Write the state department of certification of your state and have the certification requirements for secondary school principals described. Check your own record against such requirements.
6. Review with principals in your area the economic conditions of the secondary school principals and find out what is being done to improve the economic status of the secondary school principalship.
7. Compare professional requirements of lawyers, medical doctors, and other such professions with those of the secondary school principal. In what ways are they similar and in what ways are they different?

REVIEW AND DISCUSSION QUESTIONS

1. In what ways were the job functions different in the five stages of evolution of the principalship?
2. In reviewing positions available today, are all these positions in keeping with the principalship as described today or are some principals still headmasters, part-time principals, etc.?
3. In what ways have the social and prestige factors of the secondary principalship changed over the years?
4. If small schools are consolidated, would the number of administrators be reduced? To what extent would assistant principals likely be needed?
5. How can the professional organizations and accreditation associations affect certification requirements for a secondary school principal?
6. What are the certification requirements for school administrators in your state?
7. Does college course work guarantee competence as a school administrator? If not, why such requirements?
8. How can the secondary school principalship be regarded as a profession?
9. What are the criteria for becoming a profession?

10. Why is the principalship as a profession described as in a "state of becoming"?
11. What are the unresolved problems in the attempt to become a profession?

SELECTED BIBLIOGRAPHY

American Association of School Administrators. *Professional Administrators for America's Schools*. Thirty-Eighth Yearbook. Washington, D.C.: The Association, 1960.

Austin, David B. "Tackling the Big Problems of Administrative and Supervisory Staffing." *Bulletin of N.A.S.S.P.*, April 1964, pp. 47–59.

Beach, Fred F. "Professionalization of Educational Administration," *School Life*, October 1959.

Culbertson, Jack A., and Stephen P. Hencley (eds.). *Preparing Administrators: New Perspectives*. Columbus, Ohio: University Council for Educational Administration, 1962.

Educational Policies Commission, *Professional Organizations in American Education*. Washington, D.C.: National Educational Association, 1957.

Flexner, Abraham. "Is Social Work a Profession?" in *Proceedings of the National Conference of Charities and Corrections*. Chicago: Hildmann Printing Company, 1915.

Griffiths, Daniel E. *Administrative Theory*. New York: Appleton-Century-Crofts, Inc., 1959.

Griffiths, Daniel E. (ed.). *Behavioral Science and Educational Administration*. Sixty-Third Yearbook, Part II. National Society for the Study of Education, Chicago: The University of Chicago Press, 1964.

Hemphill, J. K. "Progress Report: A Study of the Secondary School Principalship, Part II," *Bulletin of N.A.S.S.P.*, April 1965, pp. 217–30.

Hemphill, John K., Daniel E. Griffiths, and Norman Frederiksen. *Administrative Performance and Personality*. New York: Teachers College, Bureau of Publications, Columbia University, 1960.

Hodgkinson, Harold I. *Educational Decisions: A Casebook*. New Jersey: Prentice-Hall, Inc., 1963.

Leu, Donald J., and Herbert C. Rudman (eds.). *Preparation Programs for School Administrators—Common and Specialized Learnings*. Seventh U.C.E.A. Career Development Seminar. East Lansing, Michigan: Michigan State University, 1963.

McIntire, Kenneth E. *Recruiting and Selecting Leaders for Education*. Austin, Texas: University of Texas, 1956.

McPhie, Walter E., and Lucian B. Kinney. "Professional Autonomy in Education," *The Journal of Teacher Education*, Vol. 10, No. 3, September 1959, pp. 285–90.

Miller, Van. "Four Definitions of Your Job," *Overview*, 1960, p. 51.

Moore, Hollis, Jr. "Professional Status, Opinion Poll," *The Nation's Schools,* July 1958, p. 38.

———. *Studies in School Administration.* Washington, D.C.: American Association of School Administrators, 1957.

National Association of Secondary-School Principals. *Focus on the Individual— A Leadership Responsibility.* Washington, D.C.: The Association, 1965. Also available as a filmstrip and record.

———. *N.A.S.S.P. Internship Project, News Report.* Washington, D.C.: The Association, Spring 1965.

Richards, J. M. "Progress Report: A Study of the Secondary-School Principalship," *Bulletin of N.A.S.S.P.,* April 1965, pp. 211–17.

Schutz, William C. *Procedures for Identifying Persons with Potential for Public School Administrative Positions.* U.S. Office of Education, Cooperative Research Project No. 677. Berkeley, California: University of California, 1961.

Smith, R. A. "Maturity of Education as a Profession," *Journal of Teacher Education,* Vol. 8, September 1957, pp. 253–60.

University Council for Educational Administration. *Improving Preparatory Programs for Educational Administrators in the United States—Some Action Guides.* Committee Report. Columbus, Ohio: The Council, undated.

———. *Stimulation in Administrative Training.* Columbus, Ohio: The Council, 1960.

Wells, Philip C., Robert H. Nelson, and Earl M. Johnsen. "The Assistant Secondary School Principal," *Bulletin of N.A.S.S.P.,* January 1965, pp. 15–25.

PART II

*Three dimensions of school change need simultaneous
attention. Ignoring any of these three facets
inhibits the effectiveness of the other two.
These three dimensions are:
(1) selecting logical and sequential
curricular content; (2) using more
educational technology wisely and (3) paying
systematic attention to the institutional arrangements for learning.*
> —J LLOYD TRUMP, "Ingredients of Change," *Bulletin of
> N.A.S.S.P.*, May 1963, p. 12.

THE CHANGING
INSTRUCTIONAL
PROGRAMS

CHAPTER 4

Issues, History, and Purposes in Secondary Education

A principal who is without a knowledge of the historical development and purposes of secondary education is like a sailboat without a rudder—pushed to and fro with any prevailing wind. The boat moves but not toward a destination. At times the school wind blows from every direction and threatens to capsize the ship. Only the steady hand at the helm of a captain who knows where he has been and where he is going can keep her afloat—and then she takes water.

The principal is the captain. To keep the ship of education headed in the proper direction, he must know the direction the wind is blowing—the issues in American education—where he has been—the history of American education—and where he is going—the objectives of American education. Such is the task of this chapter.

Crucial Issues in American Education

A Revolutionary Period. We are living in what may prove to be the most epoch-making period of time. There is evidence all around that we are witnessing and participating in one of those tidal waves of human thought, emotion, and action that periodically sweep over the world and change the direction of human endeavor. This is a revolutionary period.

There is social and political upheaval. Long-accepted social values have been rejected and new ones have been adopted. Moral standards of our past generations have been set aside in theory and practice. Modern

83

science has disproved or supplanted many of the dogmas of religion. Man has ventured into the world beyond the world. The atom has been made to work for man—and against man! World governments have evolved to a point where "peaceful coexistence," though not a reality, is a necessity.

Anxieties of man have increased. Long-established beliefs and practices have been challenged, disproved and changed. Man, his society, and his institutions have been forced to adjust to the dynamic forces of revolution.

Education and Crucial Issues. Even in a revolutionary period, man must continue to strive for the good. Man must still search for happiness. Man must still educate his children. The institutions of our civilization are faced with the need to adjust to the new conditions. Education has been greatly affected by this period of turmoil.

Since 1950, the concern about and criticism of our public schools have multiplied, divided, and multiplied. Seldom have so many newspapers, magazines, journals, periodicals, and books featured education as the centerpiece of journalistic endeavor. Criticism has been positive and negative.[1] Yet underlying the totality of the writings is the evident need to analyze purposes and procedures in terms of philosophy and the changing society. The criticisms point out the problems of concern: who should get an education? For what purpose should they receive an education and how should the education be given? These and many more questions are being raised as society attempts to adjust to this revolutionary period.

Education is at the crossroads of human thought. Great decisions must be made in the next few years which will affect the total structure of American society. The crucial issues in education must be resolved. The nature of the resolution will affect generations to come. The resolution will be determined by the values held to be of highest worth in our society. School principals must understand the nature of these issues. They must understand that the problems are the ready-made occurrences of diverging philosophies. The principal must realize that only by a study of the issues as related to historical background and objectives for the future can effective solutions be attained.

Education: For Whom?

Education for All. Thomas Jefferson's statement, "If a nation expects to be free and ignorant in a state of civilization, it expects what never was and what never will be," has been a beacon light to American edu-

---

[1] Gordon Cawelti, "Replying to Our Critics on the Quality of Secondary Schools," *Bulletin of N.A.S.S.P.*, April 1964, pp. 130–41.

cation. The need for every citizen to be educated in our expanding concept of a democratic government has greatly challenged our educational system.

One fourth of the population of America is engaged in receiving an education in the public schools today.[2]

In addition to education of those who are presently enrolled in our schools, adequate preparation must be made for the future. The rate of population growth has increased markedly in the past two decades. Since 1954 the birth rate has surpassed four million each year. The Fund for the Advancement of Education dramatically indicated the problem of future enrollments in the following:

> On the morning of May 27, 1955, the population indicator in the main lobby of the Department of Commerce Building in Washington, D.C., registered 165,000,000—a figure which only ten years ago the Census Bureau believed would not be reached before the year 2000, if ever.
>
> Operating like the mileage indicator on an automobile speedometer, the population "clock" registers one birth every eight seconds, one death every 21 seconds, the arrival of one immigrant every two minutes, and the departure of one emigrant every 24 minutes—one net addition to the U.S. population every 12 seconds. In a very real sense, the steady ticking of this clock day in and day out dramatizes the magnitude of the task which confronts public and private education in the United States in the years ahead.[3]

Some states are having greater growth problems than others. The western states are especially increasing in population growth. The growth in California's schools dramatizes the problem of numbers: "It took California 90 years (1849–1940) to enroll one million pupils in its public schools, and 13 years (1940–1953) to enroll its second million pupils; it is estimated that within seven years (1953–1960), California will enroll its three-millionth pupil, and that within five years (1960–1965) California will enroll its four-millionth pupil."[4] Without doubt, the increasing number to be educated will tax the resources of the American people for many years to come.

Education for All Requires Special Programs. Implied in the above paragraphs is the basic concept that education is for all American youth. However, when one analyzes all American youth, one finds that they are not all the same. They are different in intelligence, abilities, interests,

---

[2] Paul Woodring, *A Fourth of a Nation* (New York: McGraw-Hill Book Company, Inc., 1957), p. 255.

[3] The Fund for the Advancement of Education, *Teachers for Tomorrow* (New York: The Fund, 1955), p. 7.

[4] *Ibid.*, p. 13.

values, cultural levels and backgrounds, and physical development. The Educational Policies Commission, in its statement on the goals of education,[5] recognized that students are different and that the differences must be reflected in the curriculum. Programs for the blind, the deaf, the slow learner, the gifted, and the handicapped have been included in the curriculum. Special rooms, special facilities, and special teachers are needed in many of these programs. Providing for *all* the nation's children with an education commensurate with their needs is a unique goal in educational thought.[6]

Education for All Not Accepted by Everyone.   There are critics who believe that education should be reserved for the gifted or the academic man. These critics believe that separate schools should be maintained for the college-bound student, with the remaining students needing only technical training or apprenticeship.

Many of these critics also regard the special education programs for the slow learner and the handicapped as unneeded. It is thought that society can benefit little from the contribution of these people. The expenditure of money is thought to be far in excess of the good that the society receives for these disbursements.

In addition, there are still other critics who question the validity of providing education for all on the basis of breaking down desirable social-class barriers. It is felt that education has long been the right of those people who have time and money. To provide education for the poor would threaten social-class standing and educate people out of their "proper station in life."

Some critics would deny education and educational opportunity on the basis of racial origin. Educational opportunity for the Negroes, historically, has been limited when compared to the opportunities of the Caucasians. There are extreme critics who would "keep the Negro in his place" by denying all educational opportunity. There are other critics who would grant the educational opportunity as long as "it is not with us." Providing equal educational opportunity for all American Negroes, Indians, and other ethnic and minority groups, as well as for the "disadvantaged," constitutes an educational frontier for the development of latent talent and manpower.

And finally, there are critics who pay lip service to the need for education for all, but who say, "the whole scheme is utopian and visionary and the country cannot afford it." The dollar, or the lack of it, becomes

---

[5] Educational Policies Commission, *Education for all American Youth* (Washington, D.C.: National Education Association, 1944), p. 421.
[6] James S. Coleman, "Social Change—Impact on the Adolescent," *Bulletin of N.A.S.S.P.*, April 1965, pp. 11–15.

the basic argument against education for all. These critics maintain that educational costs are high and will become prodigious as the number of students increases. Under a hierarchy of values of money first, some means must be found to reduce costs rather than increase the educational budget.

Solving the problem "education: for whom?" is critical for the principal. He needs a well-developed sense of values when planning his curriculum for all American youth.

Education: For What?

Our schools perpetuate the accepted value patterns in the culture. That is to say, the schools are organized to educate the youth into the accepted value patterns of the society. Education cannot be a neutral, aimless process. The principal must organize the schools for a purpose. If the purpose is not accomplished, formal education has failed.

Changes in Our Society Affect the School Curriculum. A problem that naturally arises during a period of vast changes is that the accepted value patterns are transformed. The apparent needs of the changing society require adjustment in the curriculum offering. Two problems immediately present themselves: (1) What are the specific needs of society, and (2) how should the curriculum be adjusted to meet these needs?

In a democratic society the needs of society are defined by the people and not by a controlling dictatorship. Thus any person may give his opinion regarding the nature of needs of society and the manner in which the schools should educate to realize these needs.[7] There is probably no area in which there is such a diverse opinion among the critics as in deciding "education: for what?" The increased criticism indicates the recognition of the need. Among the critics, there is no common agreement as to the type of education that is needed. Some areas of general concern, as seen by modern critics, are given below.

General Education. General education is the broad title given to cover the core of learning of all students. Basic fundamentals in elementary school, along with English, social studies, mathematics, science, physical education, and health in the secondary school, are usually part of this classification. However, a study in depth is not the major purpose of a general education. The program is based on minimum needs of all students and does not encompass the total curriculum offering. However,

[7] An example of great interest is given by Ivor Kraft, "The Coming Crisis in Secondary Education," *Bulletin of N.A.S.S.P.*, February 1965, pp. 5–45. Analysis and replies are given by 14 noted educators, pp. 45–108.

many critics say that these basic skills are not taught and frills have been introduced at the expense of the fundamentals. The "frills" are not usually defined. But all agree that the "fundamentals" must be taught. A good example of confusion of frills and fundamentals is presented below:

FUNDAMENTAL OR FRILL?

John Snow was the principal of Valley High School. The committee that had organized the White House Conference discussion had asked him to be chairman of the section entitled "What Our Schools Should Accomplish."

Mr. Snow called the meeting to order and said, "Our task as given to us is to discuss the question 'What Our Schools Should Accomplish.' I am sure you have some ideas; so let's get right to work. What should we be trying to accomplish in our schools?"

LAWYER: The trouble with education in general and with our high schools in particular is that there are too many frills. We need to get back to the fundamentals.

LAUNDRY OWNER: That's right. We could solve all our problems if we got rid of all the frills. [General nodding of heads.]

PRINCIPAL SNOW: I see there seems to be general agreement with what has been said; so let's start with this problem first. Let's talk about the frills and the fundamentals. If we can decide what is a frill, then we should know what our schools should accomplish. Now what is fundamental on the high school level?

LAWYER: We need to get rid of the frills and back to the old fundamentals. Every child should be required to take algebra, advanced algebra, geometry—both plane and solid—chemistry, physics, and calculus.

LAUNDRY OWNER: That's right. We need to get back to the fundamentals. Why, do you know that I have some of your students come to work for me, and they can't tell the difference between cotton, linen, nylon, Acrilan, Dacron. . .

HOUSEWIFE: Yes, we need to get back to the fundamentals. Every girl should be required to take homemaking or home living every year she is in school.

The conversation continued in this vein. All wanted to return to the fundamentals and to get rid of frills. Yet none seemed to recognize that one person's fundamentals were another person's frills.

A Liberal Education.   Those who parade the need for a liberal education are speaking in the traditional sense. Liberal is used to mean a variety of subjects from certain selected fields. It is not to be inferred that this liberal education is radical or "leftist." It is intended that the best in human thought of the cultural past is to be studied. The student disciplines his mind and his character from association with great books and great ideas.

The job of the school is very simple. Robert M. Hutchins indicates that "the elementary schools would be concerned with providing the tool courses of reading, writing, and reckoning, the secondary schools with developing proficiency in the use of these tools, and the college with using this skill to develop habits of clear and independent thinking, utilizing for materials the broad fields of human knowledge—the natural sciences, the humanities, and the social sciences."[8]

Hutchins further explains why a liberal education is necessary while a vocational education robs the individual and his country of the best of human accomplishment:

> . . . Nevertheless, vocational education is a fraud. It is a fraud on the individual and an even worse fraud on the country. It is a fraud on the individual because it deprives him of his rights as a free man. It purports to teach him how to do the work that will enable him to exist, but not to live. It aims no higher than a form of slavery, because it is training in its lowest form. It teaches him forms and routines, ignoring even the reasons for the forms and routines. The forms and routines may change, and in a country of rapidly advancing technology, such as the United States, they do change suddenly. The citizen who has only vocational training then is stranded, because he has not been given the means of adapting himself to the change.
>
> . . . If we are to live with any satisfaction, let alone, survive, we must achieve the means of solving our problems. The only means that is available is the power of the mind, and the only means of developing that power is liberal education.[9]

A Practical Education.   It should be obvious to the student that such strong, all-encompassing statements by Hutchins about the kind of education that is needed would be challenged. Proponents of vocational education or practical education make this challenge. Advocates of practical education do not deny that some liberal education is needed. It is believed that the required courses are designed to provide this training and that the general education that is part of the basic curriculum takes care of this need.

However, it is also believed that education is not just a matter of training the mind. Education is a social concern. All members of society must receive an education commensurate with their needs and abilities. Business and industry require high school graduates to offer some salable

---

[8] Robert M. Hutchins, " 'Liberal' vs. 'Practical' Education—The Debate of the Month," *The Rotarian*, 1946, pp. 14, 62–63 as reprinted in Winfield Scott and Clyde M. Hill, *Public Education Under Criticism* (Englewood Cliffs, N.J.: Prentice-Hall, Inc.), pp. 107–8.

[9] *Ibid.*, pp. 55–58.

skills in return for jobs.[10] Practical education must be included in the curriculum.

The history of American education clearly indicated the need for concern over the practical aspects of education. The early schools were known as Latin grammar schools. The basic curriculum was concerned with moral and liberal education. Subject matter centered around a study of the classics and the Bible. This education was not sufficient to meet the demanding and challenging needs of a society. Private schools began to offer practical subjects such as navigation, arithmetic, surveying, modern languages, and geography. The academy became the popular secondary school because Franklin and other leading citizens emphasized the need for practical education. The public high school and its curriculum further reflect this need.

It has become a universal practice for business and industry to require employees to be high school graduates and to offer some salable skills. The world of business is looking for young people who have combinations of specialized training and general education in advance of the high school.

The people have become convinced that education pays both economically and socially, and whether it be for good or ill, the evidence seems to support their conviction. In addition, only about 50 per cent of the students start college, and fewer finish it. Vocational and technical education help keep students in school as well as making them more productive when they graduate.

Education for Life Adjustment.   For a number of years an intellectual battle has been raging about life-adjustment courses in the public schools. Many of the earlier proponents of life-adjustment education used a progressive education rallying cry, "Education is life, not a preparation for life." Children and their problems became the central focus of attention. Subject matter was worked into the program that met the immediate needs of the youth. Life adjustment or "growth" in the most simple definition became the primary curriculum of the pragmatic progressivists.

However, as many of the social problems created by the depression and World War II began to be resolved, life-adjustment programs took on different aspects. Education again was concerned "with life" rather than "being life." Personal-adjustment courses and problems courses became more concerned with subject matter. Yet, many of the programs remained in schools, and many educators believe they should remain owing to the corrective influence on problem children that is attributed to these programs.

---

[10] Editors of U.S.A., *The Shape of Education for 1964* (Washington, D.C.: National School Public Relations Association, 1964), pp. 25–28.

Along with the curriculum changes, there developed a program for guidance counselors, psychologists, and, in larger districts, psychiatrists. The prime purpose of this new staff of school personnel was to help students adjust to themselves, other students, the school, and society. Proper selection of courses in keeping with abilities and interests along with long-range vocational guidance became important functions of school counselors.

Critics of life-adjustment programs argue that subject matter has been made a scapegoat for the problems of society and that the children are being schooled in "how to"—how to have a successful date, how to get along on the job or with the family, how to drive, how to be attractive, how to be happy. In short, according to the more constructive critics, adjustment to life has replaced the absorption of knowledge as the highest goal of a public school education.

An Education for Individual Excellence. The importance of the individual in our democratic society has been affirmed many times. The National Education Association states as the first principle of its Code of Ethics: "We measure success by the progress of each student toward achievement of his maximum potential. We therefore work to stimulate the spirit of inquiry, the acquisition of knowledge and understanding, and the thoughtful formulation of worthy goals. We recognize the importance of cooperative relationships with other community institutions, especially the home."[11]

Although educators have been concerned with every child, there have been many questions raised regarding the quality of education received by all of the children. Special concern has been expressed in regard to individual excellence.

It is believed by many that our schools lack a respect for excellence.

Our schools lack a healthy respect for excellence. Here, the critics' attacks strike home with the most impact. In its enormous task of schooling an entire populace, American education, perhaps more out of desperation than design, tends to slip into the role of a mere baby sitter. Weighed down by sheer numbers, the schools sometimes give more attention to their "custodial" function than to the job of education. They often view children as social ciphers, may look for what is normal rather than what is exceptional, and try, perhaps too hard, to make all children "average" and "happy."[12]

---

[11] The National Education Association, "The Code of Ethics of the Education Profession," adopted by the N.E.A. Representative Assembly, July 1963.

[12] C. Winfield Scott, Clyde M. Hill, and Robert W. Burns, *The Great Debate, Our Schools in Crisis* (Englewood Cliffs, N.J.: Prentice-Hall, Inc., 1959), p. 43.

A recent surge in programs for the gifted, in continuous progress, and in individualized instruction is indication that educators are aware of shortcomings in this area and are attempting to take corrective measures. However, the need for excellence applies to all students—the slow, the average, the above average, as well as the gifted.

An Education for Society. In addition to concern for the individual, education must be concerned with the needs and demands of our society. An education for present civilization must be concerned with social, political, religious, and scientific developments. Of great concern today is the need for international understanding and world peace. Curriculum adjustments must be made in offerings in foreign languages, current events, and cultural history.

Even more obvious in the struggle of national ideologies is the evident place of science and technology. Critics have blamed the American schools because Russia made some important "firsts" in space-age explorations. The schools became scapegoats for seemingly important deficiencies in our institutional programs. A new emphasis was placed on science education in the nation's schools.

The National Defense Act of 1958 recognized the need for improvement. Under Title III, financial assistance for strengthening science, mathematics, and modern foreign language instruction was made available to schools. Other portions of the National Defense Act provided money for vocational education: improvement in guidance, counseling, and testing, and in identifying and encouraging the able students.

Currently the social need is on integration and programs for the disadvantaged student. Also needed are programs for the dropout.[13]

The Principal's Key Position. The principal is the key leader of his school and must take all the conflicting elements and build a sound curriculum program. To give him some basis for right decision making, he should know some of the history, major events, and objectives that have shaped American education. Only by such a study can he have insight into the changing society and its effect on the secondary school. A few of these important events are reviewed hereafter.

Historical Development of Secondary Schools

The Latin Grammar School. Colonial secondary education may be characterized by describing the Latin grammar school. As early as 1635

[13] Adam Clayton Powell, "The Role of Education in the War on Poverty," *Bulletin of N.A.S.S.P.*, March 1965, pp. 56–69. Gardner A. Swensen, "Early School Leavers," *Bulletin of N.A.S.S.P.*, October 1963, pp. 26–27.

the citizens of Boston established the Boston Latin School. This school was supported by money from public lands and by bequests. It was patterned after the Latin grammar schools of England, which prepared students for Oxford and Cambridge.

Pupils preparing for the ministry and other leadership positions entered the school at the early age of seven or eight and remained in the school until age 15. The curriculum was primarily a study of the classics in Latin and Greek combined with an understanding of Puritan theology and morality. The major purpose of the school was to prepare students to meet the entrance requirements at Harvard.

The Latin grammar school, which began in Boston, spread to other areas. By 1647, the Massachusetts legislature passed the Old Deluder Act which required a grammar school to be established when a community had 100 families. A penalty was set for those communities that did not do this. The purpose of the school was to instruct youth so they would be able to enter the university.

New England was not the only place where the Latin grammar school was established. This type of school was virtually the only type of secondary education found in the colonies until about 1720.

The Development of the Academy.   The Latin grammar school served a useful purpose in training men for the clergy and for some state positions. However, the curriculum was not flexible enough to meet the needs produced by a changing society. Some of the conditions that brought about the decline of the Latin grammar school and the corollary growth of the academies were: (1) the need for training programs for the clergy declined because there were more applicants than there were positions; (2) the revolution and the growth of democracy demanded that more people be educated, to take part in civic and everyday affairs; (3) expanding trade brought about a greater need for a knowledge of navigation and modern languages; (4) the increase in free enterprise and commerce increased the need for practical arithmetic; and (5) the westward migration placed a high premium on surveying and other practical courses.

The first attempt to solve these problems came in the form of the private schools. Some of these schools started as early as 1720 and were often called public schools because any student could enroll—provided he could pay the fee. These private schools depended on advertising in order to keep their doors open. An advertisement of such a school is given below so that the student may examine the character and curricula of the schools.

JOHN WALTON OFFERS TO TEACH MANY SUBJECTS IN NEW YORK, 1723

There is a School in New York, in the Broad Street, near the exchange where Mr. John Walton, late of Yale-Colledge, Teacheth Reading, Writing, Arethmatick, whole Numbers and Fractions, Vulgar and Decimal. The

Mariners Art, Plain and Mercators Way; Also Geometry, Surveying, the Latin Tongue, and Greek and Hebrew Grammars, Ethicks, Theoretick, Logick, Natural Philosophy and Metaphysicks, all or any of them for a Reasonable Price. The School for the first of October till the first of March will be tended in the Evening. If any Gentlemen in the Country are disposed to send their Sons to the said School, if they apply themselves to the Master he will immediately procure suitable Entertainment for them, very cheap. Also if any Young Gentlemen of the City will please to come in the Evening and make some Tryal of the Liberal Arts, they may have opportunity of Learning the same Things which are commonly taught in Colledges.[14]

Although these private schools were functional and practical for certain groups, the Latin grammar school was still the major type of secondary education until the establishment of the academies. Secondary education as it is known today was not provided for all children, nor was it deemed important that all children be educated to the level of the Latin grammar school.

The private schools were a partial answer to the changing society. However, they were too restrictive in their own sphere and thus did not develop as did the academies.

Benjamin Franklin, who frequently is given credit for the academy movement in America, recognized that private schools were serving a useful function. He also recognized that the Latin grammar school was not flexible enough to promote the curricular needs of the times. In 1749, in his *Proposals for the Education of Youth in Pennsylvania,* he advocated a school in which French, Spanish, German, English grammar, rhetoric, literature, history, and sciences, along with the classical languages, would be taught. Franklin was a practical man. Just writing of the need for an academy was not sufficient. He formed one.

The need for the type of curriculum offered by the academy was so great that academies began to appear all over the land.

The academies were financed primarily by tuition, endowments, and town levies. The trustees had control of the purpose for which the academy existed as well as the curriculum and instructional staff. The academies were more flexible than the Latin grammar school. Many of the original academies are still operating today.

In addition to the great stimulation the academy movement had in getting male members of society involved in education, girls were permitted, and at times even encouraged, to participate. However, most of the early instruction for girls was for the development of home skills and

---

[14] Edward W. Knight and Clinton L. Hall, *Readings in American Education* (New York: Appleton-Century-Crofts, 1951), pp. 41–44.

social graces. In 1792, Mary Wollstonecroft took up the pen on behalf of rights for women and advocated ". . . that to improve both sexes they ought, not only in private families, but in public schools, to be educated together."[15] Gradually, women were admitted to the same academy although classes were often held separately. Finally coeducation became an established practice in the academies.

The academy was the dominant secondary school for over 100 years. In fact, it was still the predominant form of educational institution until the close of the nineteenth century. The major contributions of the academies were: (1) they developed the idea that education on a secondary level was for the common man; (2) secondary education was needed for those not furthering their education at a university; (3) they extended the course of study into useful and practical subjects; (4) they introduced and developed educational programs for girls; and (5) they made secondary education so popular that they prepared the way for the public secondary school of today.

Free Public High Schools.   The first free high school was established as the English Classical School of Boston in 1821. In 1824 the name was changed to English High School to make clear that it was not preparing students for college entrance in the classical languages. This school was successful and gained recognition. The Massachusetts law of 1827 required a school of like character in every town of more than 500 families. Thus the credit for initiating free public high schools as well as the Latin grammar school can be given to the city of Boston and the state of Massachusetts.

The high school program began to spread, for it was a natural upward extension of the free common schools. Conflict arose between academies and high schools. As the state began to assume more of the responsibilities for education, the free public high schools, as part of the common school program, began to have ascendency over the academies.

In the various states there have been many court cases that affected the right of the high schools to be maintained and operated through taxation. In 1872, the Kalamazoo case of the state of Michigan set the precedent for most of the decisions regarding the right of public schools to exist and be supported through public taxation. The growth of the number of high schools has been phenomenal since this date.

Although the public high school was free, not everyone attended. The importance of a high school education was not widely accepted. Problems that arose during World War I and the realization of the need for in-

---

[15] Mary Wollstonecroft, *A Vindication of the Rights of Woman* as printed in Knight and Hall, *op. cit.,* p. 703.

creased knowledge as a result of the war gave a major impetus to high school training. The technological advances during the 1920's and the great depression during the 1930's created a strong new feeling that children needed to have a high school education. Such attitudes were made into laws. By 1940, the free public high school not only existed, but every child was expected to be enrolled unless an exception was granted through established legal agencies. Since that date the emphasis has continued to be focused on the dropout—the one fourth of America's youth who do not graduate. Many states have greatly reduced the dropout rate, but it is still a problem in the nation.[16]

Organization and Curriculum in Retrospect

Early Organization. The organization of the first English high school in Boston set a pattern that was widely duplicated. Some of the organizational structure and curriculum still exists in our present schools.

As this early age the curriculum of the high school, like that of the academy, was centered around the practical courses rather than the classical. The high school did, however, operate a program for those who desired to go on to the university. The main difference between the academy and the public high school lay primarily in differences in control and tuition charges. The academies were controlled by a private board of directors, while the high school elected board members from the communities. The academy charged tuition, while the public high school was free.

Committee of Ten. Because there was no centralized agency that set forth a standardized program, the curriculum and organization of the public high school grew increasingly diversified. Some colleges and states began to take steps to bring about some standardization. In 1892 the National Education Association appointed a committee to study the scope and function of secondary schools in order to solve some of these problems. This committee was largely dominated by university personnel. The recommendations of the committee set forth four separate curricula, namely, classical Latin, scientific, modern languages, and English. The goal was "four years of strong and effective mental training." Practical courses were not considered as part of the curriculum. Secondary schools generally opposed the recommendations of the Committee of Ten,[17] while

---

[16] Kenneth B. Hoyt, "Guidance and Dropouts," *Education*, December 1964, pp. 228–33. Reprinted in *Education Digest*, March 1965, pp. 12–15.

[17] *Report of the Committee of Ten on Secondary School Studies*, Bulletin 205 (Washington, D.C.: U.S. Bureau of Education, 1893).

universities tended to favor the recommendations. However, the curriculum of the high school was to become primarily college preparatory as a result of this report and subsequent studies.

Committee on College Entrance Requirements. In 1895 the National Education Association appointed a second committee—Committee on College Entrance Requirements. This committee recommended a six-year secondary school program beginning with grade seven, a limited amount of free electives, sequential courses in science, acceleration of gifted students, and acceptance for credit by universities of any course taught four times a week for one year. These recommendations were more universally acceptable to the high schools than those of the Committee of Ten.

Carnegie Foundation for Advancement of Teaching. In 1906, the Carnegie Foundation for the Advancement of Teaching[18] accepted the reports mentioned above as a starting place and then evaluated each course of study and placed unit values—one or one half—on each course. This standardized measurement became known as the Carnegie Unit System.

Committee of Nine on the Articulation of High School and College. The Committee of Nine on the Articulation of High School and College,[19] appointed in 1910, defined a well-planned high school course as follows:

Every high school course should include at least three units of English, one unit of social science (including history), and one unit of natural science.

Every high school course should include the completion of two majors of three units each and one minor of two units, and one of the majors should be English.

The requirements in mathematics and in foreign languages should not exceed two units of mathematics and two units of one language other than English.

Of the total fifteen units, not less than eleven units should consist of English, foreign language, mathematics, social science (including history), natural science, or other work conducted by recitation or home study. The other four units should be left as a margin to be used for additional academic work and any other kind of work that the best interests of the student appear to require.

In place of either two units of mathematics or two units of a foreign language, the substitution under proper supervision should be allowed of a

---

[18] *First Annual Report of the President* (New York: Carnegie Foundation for the Advancement of Teaching, 1906), pp. 37–39.

[19] "Committee of Nine on the Articulation of High School and College," *Proceedings of the N.E.A.*, 1911, pp. 559–67.

second unit of social science (including history) and a second unit of natural science.

In other words, there should be allowed under proper supervision the selection of four units from the following:

(1) Two units of one foreign language.
(2) Two units of mathematics.
(3) Two units of a second unit of social science and a second unit of natural science.

This report brought about the standardization sought by the Committee of Ten and set the general pattern for graduation from high school. The pattern of the school curriculum was still strongly college preparatory, although the emphasis placed on the classics by the Committee of Ten had diminished somewhat.

Eight-Year Study.   Protests against this type of curriculum began during the 1930's and gathered momentum under the progressive education movement. The great social problems of the day brought encouragement to schools to study the community and spend more time on personal and social problems. More students from all social classes came to school. About 10 per cent of the graduating classes entered college, and secondary school personnel began to rebel against the college preparatory program. The number of vocational and other practical courses was increased. Courses to train the mind began to receive less emphasis, and those courses having more immediate utilization qualities were emphasized.

In 1942 the results of the monumental Eight-Year Study were released.[20] Students from 30 representative secondary schools were permitted to take the new-curricula program. Greater freedom of election of classes was permitted. These students were compared with students taking the traditional program. Each student was paired with another person of as nearly equal social and economic background, age, sex, I.Q. score, type of school and community, individual interests, and future plans as it was possible to arrange.

On the basis of the results of this study, it was not difficult to conclude that: (1) the graduates from the 30 experimental schools were not handicapped in college work; (2) departure from the traditional program did not detract from a student's readiness for the responsibilities of college; and (3) the students from the schools with the greatest curricular revisions did distinctly better than the students with whom they were compared.[21]

The recommendations of this study, which are given below, are almost

[20] Wilfred M. Aiken, *The Story of the Eight-Year Study.* Adventures in American Education, Vol. I (New York: Harper and Brothers, 1942).
[21] *Ibid.*, pp. 118, 119, 122, 124.

a complete reversal of those proposed by the Committee of Ten. These recommendations were:[22]

First, until the purposes of general education in the liberal arts college are clearly defined and plainly stated, subject and unit prescriptions and entrance examinations that prescribe the content or organization of the secondary school curriculum should be discontinued.

Second, the knowledges, skills, habits, and qualities of mind and character essential as preparation for college work should be ascertained by colleges and schools cooperatively.

Third, a plan of admission should be adopted which provides the college with needed information concerning candidates, but which does not prescribe the content or organization of the secondary school curriculum.

Conant Report on the American High School. Although this study did not revolutionize the traditional curriculum, it did justify the inclusion of many practical courses and brought some change. The high school became more diversified in meeting the needs of all the students. A new name, the comprehensive high school, was coined to describe this new school with its revised program.

During the 1950's, there developed an increased national interest in education. At both the elementary and secondary levels, public education was subjected to severe criticism. In the midst of this confusion, Russia sent a satellite into space. The schools were promptly blamed because the United States was not the first to orbit the earth. The criticism intensified, and in the midst of this confusion a report by James B. Conant entitled *The American High School Today*[23] was published. This study, which had been financed by the Carnegie Corporation, reaffirmed both the faith in and the need for the comprehensive high school. However, recommendations to meet the increased need for quality education were also presented. A subsequent report by Conant, *Education in the Junior High School Years,*[24] was published in 1960. This report supplemented the one on the senior high school. Details of these reports are given in Chapter 5.

Commission on Experimental Study of the Utilization of the Staff. The National Association of Secondary School Principals released a report in 1959 the effect of which will be felt for decades to come. The report by J. Lloyd Trump was entitled, *Images of the Future—A New Approach to*

[22] *Ibid.*, p. 125.
[23] James B. Conant, *The American High School Today* (New York: McGraw-Hill Book Company, Inc., 1959).
[24] James B. Conant, *Education in the Junior High School Years* (Princeton, N.J.: Educational Testing Service, 1960).

the Secondary Schools.[25] This report called for a complete reorganization of secondary education. The details and effect of this study are presented in Chapter 5.

Aims and Objectives of Secondary Education

The Need for Guiding Principles. The administration of a secondary school should be regarded as a positive venture. Education has long been viewed as an institution that educates the young into the accepted value patterns of the culture. Hitler knew he had to control the institutions of education, which were responsible for the promotion of attitudes, values, knowledge, and understanding of the society. Today, the Communists are well aware that the training of youth must be controlled if the communist doctrine is to triumph. *Sovietskaia Pedagogika,* the official organ of the Academy of Pedagogical Science, states: "The ideological training of our youth is above all political," and "we must not forget for a moment that every science is party science," and "teaching cannot be divorced from the politics of party and state," and "workers in pedagogical science must first of all study stubbornly, persistently, and consistently the science of sciences—the Marxist-Leninist theory," and they "must become bold and militant propagandists of the great Communist ideas of educating the new man."[26]

It is not the purpose of this chapter to set forth the idea that American education or American educators must become bold, militant propagandists in educating the American youth to some super race or utopian concept of a new world order. However, it should be understood that American secondary education is not an aimless enterprise blown hither and yon by the whims of any administrator, public official, or partisan group.

Education as a process is neutral and as such can produce Stalins, Hitlers, Lincolns, and Gandhi, but education sponsored by a community, state, or nation cannot be neutral. The very purpose for which the schools are organized in a given society calls forth commitments. Inherent in any educational enterprise is a commitment toward some general and/or specific goal. The crucial phase in education for a democracy or a dictatorship is the selection of the aims and objectives.

Seven Cardinal Principles of Education. It has been shown that public secondary education received a rather slow start in the United States.

[25] J. Lloyd Trump, *Images of the Future—A New Approach to the Secondary Schools.* Commission on the Experimental Study of the Utilization of the Staff in the Secondary School, N.A.S.S.P., 1959.

[26] *Sovietskaia Pedagogika,* No. 10–11, October-November 1946, pp. 3–8.

The direction of the educative enterprise developed quite slowly. However, after the national committees began to set forth their now famous reports, new direction and unification toward common ends became more universal.

In 1918 a famous report by the Commission on Reorganization of Secondary Education, known as the "Cardinal Principles of Secondary Education," was published. This report reviewed, among other ideas, the need for reorganization of secondary schools, the goals of education in a democracy, the role of secondary education in achieving these objectives, and the need for relating the curriculum to these objectives. This report first made clear the purpose of education in a democracy by stating: "The purpose of a democracy is so to organized society that each member may develop his personality primarily through activities designed for the well-being of his fellow members and of society as a whole. . . . Consequently, education in a democracy, both within and without the school, should develop in each individual the knowledge, interests, ideals, habits, and powers whereby he will find his place and use that place to shape both himself and society toward ever nobler ends."[27]

After examination of the activities of an individual in American democracy, this study reported that a sound program of secondary education needed to provide for functions involved in home membership, vocational work, and citizenship. Further, effective citizenship required that education should provide for worthy use of leisure, good health, soundness in English and mathematics, and development of ethical character. The commission then set forth the following principles of education, which are commonly known as the Seven Cardinal Principles of Secondary Education:

1. Health.
2. Command of fundamental process.
3. Worthy home membership.
4. Vocation.
5. Citizenship.
6. Worthy use of leisure.
7. Ethical character.

The Ten Imperative Needs of Youth. The Seven Cardinal Principles became the basic statement of objectives from 1918 until World War II. In 1942, the Educational Policies Commission, a commission approved by the National Education Association and the American Association of School Administrators, began to work on policies for postwar education.

Education for All American Youth was published by this commission in 1944. A major emphasis in this report is that (1) education is for *all*

[27] Commission on the Reorganization of Secondary Education, *Cardinal Principles of Secondary Education*, Bulletin 35 (Washington, D.C.: U.S. Bureau of Education, 1918), p. 9.

American Youth and (2) every member to be educated is different. Eight categories of significant educational differences were enumerated. These differences are as follows:

1. Differences in *intelligence and aptitude* will exist, regardless of modifications in the environments of individuals. While certain portions of these differences are inherited, even these cannot be predicted from parentage. These differences require different educational procedures, content, and standards of speed and achievement.

2. Differences in *occupational interests* and outlooks are both desirable and necessary. They require guidance to match abilities against the requirements of the job, desires against opportunities. They require curriculum adjustments that provide the necessary preparation for thorough workmanship in all occupations. They require administrative arrangements that will remove or minimize undemocratic "social status" distinctions among occupational fields and their corresponding educations.

3. There are differences in *availability of educational facilities*, differences caused either by location of residence or family economic status. The elimination of these differences is an entirely practicable matter of administration and finance, involving the proper organization and location of schools, and the provision of transportation and student-maintenance facilities, of state and federal equalization funds, and of public or private scholarship funds.

4. There are differences in *types of communities* in which youth reside. Insofar as these differences are educationally significant, they can be met by a guidance program providing information and outlooks which transcend community barriers, and by curriculums which are adjusted to the needs and opportunities of diverse communities.

5. There are differences of opportunity resulting from differences in *social and economic status*, often aggravated by differences in *race*. The removal of such inequalities is a difficult matter, often requiring basic social and economic changes in the community. Yet, even so, these differences can be measurably reduced by wise educational leadership and administration, and by the objective study of community problems in schools.

6. There are differences in *parental attitudes and cultural backgrounds*. In many cases, cultural differences can be utilized for valuable education purposes. In other cases, where differences give rise to conflict or jeopardize the proper development of children and youth, the undesirable effects may be minimized through a program of home visitation and parent education.

7. There are differences in *personal and avocational interests*. Within reasonable bounds, these differences may well be encouraged by a broad curriculum with opportunities for some selection of studies.

8. There are, finally, differences in *mental health, emotional stability, and physical well-being*. Extreme disabilities must be compensated for in special schools and classes. Other temporary or less serious deviations from

normal health may be met by appropriate adjustments in curriculum and regimen and by remedial health instruction and school health services.[28]

It was recognized that youth are different. Further, the principal must reflect these differences in the curriculum. It is also true that youth have qualities that are common to all. These common qualities were enumerated.

The report then set forth a plan of education for two imaginary American communities, which were called Farmville and American City. Finally, the Commission issued its statement on educational needs, or a summary of ten "imperative educational needs of youth." These are:

1. All youth need to develop salable skills and those understandings and attitudes that make the worker an intelligent and productive participant in economic life. To this end, most youth need supervised work experience as well as education in the skills and knowledge of their occupations.

2. All youth need to develop and maintain good health and physical fitness.

3. All youth need to understand the rights and duties of the citizen of a democratic society, and to be diligent and competent in the performance of their obligations as members of the community and citizens of the state and nation.

4. All youth need to understand the significance of the family for the individual and society and the conditions conducive to successful family life.

5. All youth need to know how to purchase and use goods and services intelligently, understanding both the values received by the consumer and the economic consequences of their acts.

6. All youth need to understand the methods of science, the influence of science on human life, and the main scientific facts concerning the nature of the world and of man.

7. All youth need opportunities to develop their capacities to appreciate beauty in literature, art, music, and nature.

8. All youth need to be able to use their leisure time well and to budget it wisely, balancing activities that yield satisfactions to the individual with those that are socially useful.

9. All youth need to develop respect for other persons, to grow in their insight into ethical values and principles, and to be able to live and work cooperatively with others.

10. All youth need to grow in their ability to think rationally, to express their thoughts clearly, and to read and listen with understanding.[29]

[28] Educational Policies Commission, *Education for All American Youth* (Washington, D.C.: National Education Association, 1944), pp. 15–16. Reprinted by permission of the National Education Association.
[29] *Ibid.*, pp. 225–26.

Many principals looked upon the "ten imperative needs of youth" as ushering in a new era in secondary education. Many schools changed their curriculum and their methodology.

The White House Conference on Education. At midcentury, President Eisenhower called for a White House Conference on Education. The conference reviewed many aspects of education. One phase of this conference was entitled "What Should Our Schools Accomplish?" This educational conference was unique in its scope. Local districts throughout the United States organized conferences and held public meetings in which lay citizens discussed the vital phases. Delegates from the local areas were then sent to the state to discuss the issues on a state level. State delegates then met at Washington.

All 53 states and territories took part in the program, with more than 3,500 local, county, regional, and state conferences being held prior to the White House Conference in Washington on November 28 to December 1, 1955. More than a half million Americans were involved in these conferences.

Adam S. Bennion and William Carr summarized the conclusions of the 2,000 laymen and professional educators at the national conference. Some of the philosophy and objectives accepted in this report are presented below.

It is the consensus of these groups that the schools should continue to develop:

1. The fundamental skills of communication—reading, writing, spelling, as well as other elements of effective oral and written expression; the arithmetical and mathematical skills, including problem solving. While schools are doing the best job in their history in teaching these skills, continuous improvement is desirable and necessary.

2. Appreciation for our democratic heritage.

3. Civic rights and responsibilities and knowledge of American institutions.

4. Respect and appreciation for human values and for the beliefs of others.

5. Ability to think and evaluate constructively and creatively.

6. Effective work habits and self-discipline.

7. Social competency as a contributing member of his family and community.

8. Ethical behavior based on a sense of moral and spiritual values.

9. Intellectual curiosity and eagerness for life-long learning.

10. Esthetic appreciation and self-expression in the arts.

11. Physical and mental health.

12. Wise use of time, including constructive leisure pursuits.

13. Understanding of the physical world and man's relation to it as represented through basic knowledge of the sciences.

14. An awareness of our relationships with the world community.[30]

To achieve these goals for every child the schools must have an effective program of guidance and counseling in preparation for the world of work.

It will be noted that no attempt was made to push these ideas as a new statement of objectives for America's schools. In fact, the report said that the "schools should continue to develop. . ." that which they were doing. However, the number of objectives was enlarged to 14. Some new elements were included. The significance of the White House Conference was: (1) it reaffirmed previous statements of objectives that are important in our democracy, (2) it adapted these objectives to the changing conditions of the day, (3) emphasis was placed on the needs of "every child," and (4) a diversified program to meet the objectives was required.

President's Commission on National Goals.   In 1960 the President's Commission on National Goals made its report. Its introduction reads, "The paramount goal of the United States was set long ago. It is to guard the rights of the individual, to ensure his development, and to enlarge his opportunity." In keeping with this general goal, the specific goals for education were stated: "The development of the individual and the nation demands that education at every level and in every discipline be strengthened and its effectiveness enhanced. . . . There must be more and better teachers, enlarged facilities, and changes in curricula and methods. . . . Above all, schooling should fit the varying capacities of individuals; every student should be stimulated to work to his utmost; authentic concern for excellence is imperative."[31]

Recent Developments.   Many social changes and technological advancements have been made by our society since the White House Conference report was issued in 1955. The effect of these changes on schools and school curricula has been of extreme importance. Many states and local districts have increased graduation requirements in mathematics, science, and languages. Emphasis has been placed on "gifted programs." Experimental programs in large and small group instruction, improved staff utilization, television teaching, and many other programs have been introduced. A major revision in the whole area of secondary education

[30] The reports of the chairman as given in Washington, D.C., November 28 to December 1, 1955.

[31] The Representative Assembly, *Goals for Americans. The Report of the President's Commission on National Goals* (Englewood Cliffs, N.J.: Prentice-Hall, Inc., 1960), pp. 1, 6–7.

seems imminent. These programs and organizational structures will be discussed in the following chapter.

Throughout all these changes and experiments the need for new objectives has not been indicated. There has been an emphasis placed on certain objectives such as "ability to think and evaluate constructively and creatively." In 1961 the Educational Policies Commission set forth a new statement *The Central Purpose of American Education.*[32] In this statement the ability to think was identified as the central purpose of education and it was emphasized that every student's rational powers must be recognized as centrally important. "Effective work habits and self-discipline" and "understanding of the physical world and man's relation to it as represented through basic knowledge of the sciences" have also been emphasized. However, these changes in the curriculum seem to be based on emphasizing certain objectives rather than on discarding old and creating new objectives.

Summary

This chapter has been concerned with the antecedents of our present-day secondary schools. There have been four major types of schools: the Latin grammar, the private schools, the academies, and the free public high school. Each of these types of schools was developed because of the changing needs in our society. The curriculum of the Latin grammar school was primarily classical (Latin and Greek). The purpose was to prepare students for the university and later for theological and governmental positions. The private schools were organized to meet specific needs not fulfilled by the Latin grammar school. Practical classes in arithmetic, navigation, surveying, and modern languages were the primary concern. The academies were introduced to provide for both specific practical needs and general preparation. Along with mathematics, English grammar, literature, history, and sciences, the modern language courses were stressed. Classical learning was also available for those who desired it. The public high school started in the same curricular vein as the academy, but the high school was free to all. Gradually this free public high school, a natural extension of the free common schools, became the dominant school throughout the land.

A number of national reports have brought some unity in general purpose, organization, and curricular matters.

The aims and objectives for public high schools have been set forth

---

[32] Educational Policies Commission, National Education Association, *The Central Purpose of American Education* (Washington, D.C.: The Association, 1961).

in five separate national reports: (1) the Seven Cardinal Principles, (2) Ten Imperative Needs of Youth, (3) "What Our Schools Should Accomplish" (White House Conference), (4) the President's Commission on National Goals, and (5) the Central Purpose of American Education. Principals should be familiar with these reports because of the great influence these statements of aims and objectives have and will continue to have on secondary education.

SUGGESTED PROJECTS AND ACTIVITIES

1. Study and review the history of a high school in your area.
2. Invite the principal of a private school to class to discuss the history and need for a private school.
3. Prepare a comparative chart that gives the four major types of schools discussed in this chapter. Compare each school on such features as purpose, organization, curriculum, support, length of time in existence, why it was begun, and what have been the major contributions.
4. Debate: Liberal vs. practical education.
5. Discuss the materials presented in this chapter based on the following:
   "My interest in thinking about the process of change grows from a very real skepticism as to the good that results when small groups of people decide what schools ought to be like and then work very hard to get them to become that way. I would be more sympathetic to a different process, one which involves working intimately with people in schools in attempts to find out what kind of schools they want and then doing everything possible to facilitate study and research to bring about these conditions."—Stephen M. Corey quoted in *Factors Affecting the Improvement of Secondary Education,* p. 5.
6. Have student reports on some of the criticisms of our schools. For a good selection of these criticisms refer to Section II of C. Winfield Scott and Clyde M. Hill, *Public Education Under Criticism,* pp. 17–104.
7. Debate: Secondary education should be an intermediate stage on the way to citizenship. Its goals should be preparation for higher education.
8. Conduct an on-the-spot survey on the question "What should be the primary purpose of public secondary education." Compare opinions of (1) lay citizens interviewed at random on the streets, (2) secondary education professors, and (3) professors of some of the academic disciplines in the university.
9. Show the film *A Desk for Billie,* National Education Association.

REVIEW AND DISCUSSION QUESTIONS

1. What was the Latin grammar school like in purpose, organization, curriculum, and support?
2. What factors led to the development of the early private schools and later of the academies?
3. How did the curriculum of the private schools differ from that of the Latin grammar schools?
4. Describe the academy in regard to purposes, organization, curriculum, and support. How was the academy different from the Latin grammar school?
5. What was the major contribution of the academy?
6. When and where was the first free public high school started? What conditions brought about the establishment of the free public high school in the very state that first initiated the Latin grammar school?
7. What are some of the issues in American education?
8. In tracing the growth of the public high school, what periods of time seemed to evidence the greatest increases? Why?
9. What was the importance of the Kalamazoo case to the free public high school?
10. What were the contributions and effect upon secondary education of the following?
    a. Committee of Ten.
    b. Committee on College Entrance Requirements.
    c. Committee of Nine on the Articulation of High School and College.
    d. Aiken's Eight-Year Study.
11. What were some of the organizational features of the first high school? How do these features compare with those of the schools of today?
12. Why does a principal need a knowledge of the past history of secondary education?
13. In what way can education be neutral? If education can be neutral, what is the importance of aims and objectives?
14. What are the Seven Cardinal Principles? The Ten Imperative Needs of Youth? The Aims of the White House Conference? The Goals for Americans?
15. In what ways are these statements of objectives similar? In what ways are they different?
16. In what way do the social, economic, and scientific changes in our society affect our statement of purposes?
17. Why is it important for a principal of a secondary school to have a knowledge of the aims and objectives of secondary education?

SELECTED BIBLIOGRAPHY

Aiken, Wilfred M. *The Eight-year Study*. Adventures in American Education, Vol. 1. New York: Harper and Brothers, 1942.

Alexander, William M., and J. Galen Saylor. *Modern Secondary Education*. New York: Rinehart and Company, Inc., 1959.

Cawelti, Gordon. "Replying to Our Critics on the Quality of Secondary Schools," *Bulletin of N.A.S.S.P.*, April 1964, pp. 130–41.

Coleman, James S. "Social Change—Impact on the Adolescent," *Bulletin of N.A.S.S.P.*, April 1965, pp. 11–15.

Commission on the Reorganization of Secondary Education. *Cardinal Principles of Secondary Education*, Bulletin 35. Washington, D.C.: Bureau of Education, 1918.

Committee for the White House Conference on Education. *Report of the Committee for the White House Conference on Education*. Washington, D.C.: U.S. Government Printing, 1955.

Conant, James B. *The American High School Today*. New York: McGraw-Hill Book Company, Inc., 1959.

———. *Education in the Junior High School Years*. Princeton, N.J.: Educational Testing Service. 1960.

Educational Policies Commission. *The Central Purpose of American Education*. Washington, D.C.: The Commission, 1961.

———. *Education for All American Youth*. Washington, D.C.: National Education Association, 1944.

French, William Marshall. *American Secondary Education*. New York: The Odyssey Press, 1959.

Good, H. G. *A History of American Education*, 2nd ed. New York: The Macmillan Company, 1962.

Hoyt, Kenneth B. "Guidance and Dropouts," *Education*, December 1964, pp. 228–33. Reprinted in *Education Digest*, March 1965, pp. 12–15.

Knight, Edgar W., and Clifton L. Hall. *Readings in American Educational History*. New York: Appleton-Century-Crofts, 1951.

Meyer, Adolph E. *An Educational History of the American People*. New York: McGraw-Hill Book Company, Inc., 1957.

Powell, Adam Clayton. "The Role of Education in the War on Poverty," *Bulletin of N.A.S.S.P.*, March 1965, pp. 56–69.

Representative Assembly. *Goals for Americans*. The Report of the President's Commission on National Goals. Englewood Cliffs, N.J.: Prentice-Hall, Inc., 1960.

Swensen, Gardner A. "Early School Leavers," *Bulletin of N.A.S.S.P.*, October 1963, pp. 26–27.

Trump, J. Lloyd. *Images of the Future—A New Approach to the Secondary Schools*. Commission on the Experimental Study of the Utilization of the Staff in the Secondary School. N.A.S.S.P., 1959.

CHAPTER 5

Curricular Programs and Organizational Structure

In an age when satellites orbit the earth, Telstar brings instant, world-wide communication, and scientists plan their trip to the moon, the principal and teachers are often asked, "What's new in education?"

If the teachers and principal must dig their heads, scratch their backs, and play for time to find an answer, they are in a rut and need to be launched into orbit.

The answer is easy. There is a revolution in education now under way across the nation, a revolution in which long-established practices in school organization, school buildings, curriculum, teaching methods, and teaching equipment and materials are being questioned and changed.

To explain these new developments more fully, a review of curricular offerings and the organizational structure is presented.

Curricular Programs of Secondary Schools

Social Forces Affecting the Curriculum. The general revolution in education has not been limited to a philosophical level involving the purpose of the secondary schools. The upheaval has moved from philosophy to curriculum and from curriculum to organization. Within the changing society certain social forces are changing the organizational structure and patterns. The result of the social forces is to try and move new programs into the curriculum. The process of moving out curriculum content to make room for the new is just as critical. This favorite statement applies:

110

"Changing the curriculum is like moving a graveyard, even the dead have friends." Therefore, the principal is caught on the horns of a dilemma—the need to move new content into the curriculum as a result of the changing forces in society, and the resistance to the withdrawal of anything outdated. But the insistence arising from the social forces and the need for new curriculum force the principal to evaluate and restructure his curriculum. Our curricular programs are now in need of such an evaluation.

The social forces are usually exerted through organizations of people and our social institutions. These social forces have been grouped into four principal categories: the influences of various governmental agencies, quasi-legal forces, professional organizations, and special-interest groups.[1] Some of the forces affecting the curriculum are indicated below:

1. The governmental forces include the federal, state, and local governments. Their influence is both direct and indirect. The federal government in the promotion of the general welfare does not have the right to control the state governments and the educational programs therein. There is no national organization on curriculum. However, over the years the federal government has influenced the curriculum through legislation that has made money and services available to the states for educational purposes. Table 5.1 shows the major federal activities in education that have profoundly affected education in the United States.[2]

The U.S. Supreme Court has made interpretations that have established rights regarding private schools, places of religious training in public schools, integration of races, rights of individuals against forced patriotism through flag salute, compulsory attendance laws, and many others.

The U.S. Office of Education is becoming more influential in all phases of education. The fact that funds appropriated to it for distribution have been increased will automatically increase its influence. Vocational and other programs for the disadvantaged will be emphasized. Research funds will improve curriculum programs generally.

The National Science Foundation, Economic Opportunity (War on Poverty) Office, and many other governmental agencies have substantial influence on curriculum programs.

The state governments through their constitutions have control over the education within the state. The state legislature enacts laws on finance, some curriculum requirements, and occasionally course content. The state board of education passes other acts and policies that are binding to the state, such as graduation requirements, approval of course of study, and selection of textbooks. The state department of public instruction

---

[1] James W. Thornton, Jr., and John R. Wright (eds.), *Secondary School Curriculum* (Columbus, Ohio: Charles E. Merrill Books, 1963), p. 146.

[2] For further discussion see Percy E. Burrup, *The Teacher and the Public School System* (New York: Harper and Brothers, 1960), pp. 142–43.

TABLE 5.1   Major Federal Activities in Education

Activity	Year	Provisions and Purposes
Federal Land Grants	1785 1787	Section 16 of each township—encouragement of education. After 1850 also gave Section 36. Three states received Sections 16, 36, 2, 32
Morrill Act	1862	30,000 acres of land per Congressman —encourage teaching of agriculture, mechanics. Provided for establishment of colleges of agriculture; required military training
U.S. Office of Education	1867	Beginning of the Office of Education with its various departments
Smith-Hughes Act	1917	Funds—to stimulate teaching of agriculture and home economics in secondary schools
Civilian Conservation Corps (CCC)	1933	Funds and education—provide work, relief and restoration of depleted natural resources
Public Works Administration (PWA)	1933	Funds—to stimulate local spending and to help build school buildings
National Youth Administration (NYA)	1935	Funds—to provide aid for needy youth, both in and out of school
Works Progress Administration (WPA)	1935	Funds—to encourage economic recovery after the depression of the early 1930's
George-Deen Act	1936	Funds—to provide vocational education in distributive education subjects
The Lanham Act	1941	Funds—to assist local districts that had federal defense activities
GI Bill of Rights	1947	Funds—to provide educational benefits for World War II veterans. Later, Korean Conflict veterans were included

TABLE 5.1 (Continued)

Activity	Year	Provisions and Purposes
Public Laws 815 and 874	1950	Funds—to discharge financial responsibility of federal government to communities affected by federal activities and to provide for a nationwide survey of school plant needs
National Science Foundation	1950	Funds—improvement science education
Public Law 597	1956	Funds—for a five-year program for states for library services in rural areas
National Defense Education Act	1958	Funds—student loans; improve teaching of science, mathematics, and foreign languages; improve college teaching; improve guidance and testing services; foster research in use of communication media; improve vocational education; improve statistical services of state education agencies
Elementary-Secondary Education Act	1965	Funds—general aid to education, vocational programs for the disadvantaged, research, improved state education agencies

administers the total state school system, develops courses of study, and provides leadership and general supervision for the various curriculum programs. The attorney general provides legal opinions, and the court interprets school laws within the state.

The local board of education is a legal arm of educational affairs. It may and does regulate graduation requirements beyond those prescribed by the state, provide finances for books and supplies, and set other policies affecting the curriculum.

2. Professional organizations and associations have great influence on the curriculum of schools. The most important of these associations is the accrediting association. The purpose of these associations is to upgrade quality in the schools by setting forth standards. At times these standards are interpreted as maximums instead of minimums. Some associations currently have standards regarding the number and length of periods. The

standard comes in conflict with other forces that are bringing a modified schedule.

There are multitudes of professional affiliations that exert influence on policy and curriculum. The National Education Association with all its affiliates perhaps is most influential. The National Association of Secondary-School Principals has long been the guiding association for the principals of the country. The Association's interest is not confined to administrative matters. Curriculum receives considerable attention.[3]

The universities and colleges affect the curriculum through entrance requirements and special requirements for entrance into the various colleges of the university. For example, the amount and type of mathematics and science offered in the secondary school may be structured to meet the college requirements. The N.E.A. Research Division found that four years of English, more than two years each of mathematics and science, more than two and a half years of social studies, and two years of foreign language and physical education appear to be typical requirements of college preparatory programs.[4]

The teachers' organizations are becoming more influential in school affairs. The competition for recognition between the National Education Association and the American Federation of Teachers has made each become more militant in its demands, and principals have frequently modified the curriculum to meet these demands. The extracurricular phase of the program has been one area that has been seriously affected in some schools.

3. Foundations and publishers have been influential in affecting the curriculum. The commercial publisher has always tended to mold the curriculum because what is to be taught is so vitally affected by what is available. In many respects publishing houses have held down curriculum changes. This action is not by design, for most publishing houses want to be current. However, as private enterprises, they must realize a profit from their activities. The profit comes in publishing in areas where the market is established or can readily be established. Those who are innovating find it difficult to get experimental materials published. The availability of materials affects the continuance of the program.

[3] The *Bulletin of the National Association of Secondary-School Principals* has always carried curriculum articles. Some complete issues have been devoted to special curriculum areas, such as "The Coming Crisis in Secondary Education," February 1965; "What's Happening in English," February 1964; "A Look at Acceleration and Enrichment," December 1963; "Secondary-School Curricular Areas," November 1963; "Health, Physical Education and Recreation," May 1960; and "Patterns of Curriculum Practices," February 1960.

[4] National Education Association Research Division, *High-School Diplomas and Graduation Requirements.* Research Memo 1959–27 (Washington, D.C.: The Association, December 1959), p. 15.

In recent years, the philanthropic foundations have filled this gap to some extent. The Ford Foundation supplied the money for the staff utilization projects described later in the section on organization. Carnegie, Rockefeller, Russell Sage and many other foundations have provided the money that has made innovation and changes possible and practical.

4. Special-interest groups have always influenced curriculum programs. There is no end to these groups. The National Association of Secondary School Principals has found it necessary to limit and publish every year a list of approved contests and activities sponsored by such groups. The approved list is still approximately five single-spaced pages. The groups most active are the patriotic and civic clubs and organizations, religious organizations, and business and economic groups. Individuals with vested interests are also active in trying to have the school promote their own private cause.

Since education has now become a major instrument in the economic, social, and political advancement of nations, it is little wonder that the basic forces described above affect the curriculum of the secondary school in America.

Basic Principles for Curriculum Organization. Anderson and Gruhn, in their book *Principles and Practices of Secondary Education,* indicate that the following basic principles apply to curriculum organization: (1) the curriculum should be organized in such a manner that it facilitates the student's seeing relationships among experiences in different subjects and activities during the school day; (2) the curriculum should be experimental and varied for individual goals and needs; (3) the curriculum should be organized around problems to facilitate learning of attitudes, appreciations, skills, and understandings for a democratic society; (4) the program of studies should provide for common learnings for all pupils as part of their general education and specialized learnings to develop diversified and unique interests and abilities; (5) the total curriculum in the school day should be organized to give each student maximum experiences; and (6) the curriculum should be organized to provide good articulation in learning experiences from one level to another.[5]

Diverse Curriculum Offering Needed. The need for different types of curricular offering is based on two premises: one, the needs of the students, and two, the needs of society. The needs of society make it mandatory that every student have certain learnings. These learnings are placed in the school curriculum as required courses. The needs of the

[5] Vernon E. Anderson and William T. Gruhn, *Principles and Practices of Secondary Education* (New York: The Ronald Press Company, 1962), pp. 142–46.

students call for a diversified program. A wide range of elective courses is basic to meeting the needs of individual students.

The diversity of the high school curriculum can be seen in the extensive listing of courses available. It has been jokingly stated that a student can find a range of courses from fly tying to calculus in the same school. It takes nine pages in the *Biennial Survey of Education in the United States* to list the courses offered in the secondary schools. A complete list of these courses would be superfluous. Therefore, only those courses more commonly offered are listed in Table 5.2.

TABLE 5.2   Typical Required and Elective Courses in Secondary Schools

Grade	Required	Credit	Electives
7	English (language arts)	1	
	Arithmetic	1	
	Social studies	1	
	Science	1	
	Physical education	½	
	Art		These courses are often required part time during the year. Some schools make them elective
	Music		
	Industrial arts or home economics		
			Club activities
8	English (language arts)	1	
	Arithmetic	1	
	Science	1	
	Social studies (U.S. history)	1	
	Physical education	½	
	Art		Required part time during the year. Some schools make them optional
	Music		
	Industrial arts or home economics		
			Club activities
9	English I	1	
	Algebra or general math	1	Algebra or general math
	Social studies	1	
	Science	1	Foreign language
	Physical education	½	Industrial arts
			Home economics
			Music
			Art
			Speech

TABLE 5.2   (Continued)

Grade	Required	Credit	Electives
10	English II	1	Algebra, geometry, mathematics,
	Social studies[a] (world		industrial arts, home eco-
	history)	1	nomics, music: instrumental
	Biology	1	and vocal, art, speech, foreign
	Physical education	½	language, typing
11	English III	1	Algebra I or II, geometry, chem-
	Social studies (U.S.		istry, physics, foreign lan-
	history)	1	guage, speech, debate and dra-
	Physical education[b]	½	matic art, music: instrumental
	Mathematics or science		and vocal, typing, shorthand
	electives[c]	1	I, bookkeeping, home living,
			industrial art, trades and in-
			dustry
12	English IV or foreign		Algebra I or II, geometry, trigo-
	language or speech	1	nometry, physics, chemistry,
	Social studies[a] (Am.	1	geology, art, speech, debate,
	problems)		foreign language, music: in-
	Physical education[b]	½	strumental and vocal, typing,
	Mathematics or science		shorthand I or II, bookkeep-
	electives[c]	1	ing I or II, home living, indus-
			trial arts, trades and industry

[a] Social studies is often required two out of three years of the senior high school.
[b] Physical education is usually required two out of three years in the senior high school. Some states require it every year.
[c] Mathematics and science is a general requirement for graduation. Two units are common requirements.

Conant's Curriculum Recommendation.   There have been many recommendations for curriculum improvement by groups such as those
discussed under the social forces affecting curriculum. Conant's study
and report *The American High School Today* is more objective. A few
of his recommendations for grades 9 through 12 are given below:

1. Requirements for graduation for all students would be four years of
English, three or four years of social studies—including two years of history (one of which should be American history) and a senior course in
American problems or American government—one year of mathematics
in the ninth grade (algebra or general mathematics), and at least one year
of science in the ninth or tenth grade, which might well be biology or

general physical science. At least seven other courses, not including physical education, would be required.

2. Diversified programs which lead to the development of marketable skills should be offered. These programs would include typing, stenography, use of clinical machines, home economics, distributive education, vocational agriculture, and trade and industrial programs (3-hour programs).

3. Remedial reading programs should be provided for students in the ninth grade who only read at the sixth grade level. A developmental reading program designed to facilitate reading speed and comprehension should be part of the school program.

4. For the academically gifted students special elective programs should be planned. Such a program might include the following minimum requirements: four years of mathematics, four years of one foreign language (some may wish to take two foreign languages), three years of science, four years of English and three years of social studies. At least fifteen hours of homework should be required each week.

5. The school board should offer a third and fourth year of a foreign language no matter how few students are enrolled.

6. All students should take some science (biology or physical science). Two types of chemistry courses should be offered—one in which an algebra grade of C is mandatory, the other of easier requirements. Regular physics should be offered in the twelfth grade. A practical physics course should also be given for students with average ability.

7. Twelfth grade American problems or government should be required. Students should be grouped heterogeneously. Current problems facing American Democracy should be discussed and understood.[6]

New Curriculum Programs.   There are many new curriculum programs in the various districts throughout the United States. These are significant in that they have influence on general educational improvement. If the schools are publicized or visited, they may have local, state, or national influence.

There are a number of significant curriculum studies of national significance that are effecting changes across the nation. Some of these programs are economic education sponsored by the Joint Council on Economic Education, civic education projects, audiolingual approach to foreign language, science teaching improvement program sponsored by the American Association for the Advancement of Science, the Biological Science Curriculum Study sponsored by the American Institute of Biological Sciences and National Science Foundation, the Chemical Bond Approach Project sponsored by the Crown-Zellerbach Foundation and the National Science Foundation, the Chemical Education Material Study

[6] James B. Conant, *The American High School Today* (New York: McGraw-Hill Book Company, 1959), pp. 47–75.

sponsored by the National Science Foundation, the Physical Science Study Committee sponsored by the Massachusetts Institute of Technology and the National Science Foundation, School Mathematics Study Group sponsored by the National Science Foundation, Illinois Mathematics Curriculum Committee, Ball State Mathematics, Greater Cleveland Mathematics, and the President's Council on Physical Fitness.[7]

In addition to these programs, the Manpower and Education Act and the Economic Opportunity Act have introduced many new programs in the vocational and technical fields and for disadvantaged students.

Organization and Structure of Secondary Schools

National Influence on Education. One principle of American school organization that is unique is the absence of a national system of education. Unlike most European nations, the American schools are neither controlled nor organized on a federal basis. There are some who may desire such organization, and there are some strong arguments for a national system. However, the development of our democratic way of life has been toward a more diversified system. The constitution did not delegate education to the federal government; so, whether by default or design, the states became responsible for education. This does not mean that the federal government is without influence. In fact, the federal aid to education legislation, along with interpretations of the Supreme Court, indicates a trend in the direction of increased federal influence in education.

State and Local District Organization. Education has traditionally been defined as a state function. The state has maintained direct control of the schools through the state laws, the state departments of education, and the local school districts. The laws of the states are not the same, and as a result, the general pattern of organization varies from state to state. Hawaii has only one school district, while some states have several thousand school districts. Whereas Utah has only one type of school district, California has elementary, high school, unified, and junior college school districts. Students of secondary school age can be found in all these districts except the junior college district.

Each school district has the responsibility of organizing its schools. The specific patterns commonly used are discussed under the heading "Organizational Patterns Within the School District." But regardless of the pattern

---

[7] A good summary of these programs can be found in Leonard W. Clark, Raymond L. Klein, and John B. Burks, *The American Secondary School Curriculum* (New York: The Macmillan Company, 1965).

used, the individual school is organized as a unit by itself with a principal responsible for the functioning of the unit. Figure 5.1 shows how the local secondary school fits into the total picture of organization of schools.

Figure 5.1

*Authority and Organizational Pattern from the State Framework
to the Local School*

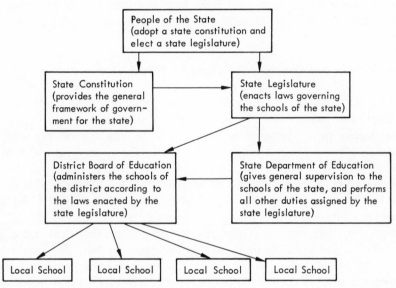

Organizational Patterns Within the School District. There have been many organizational patterns advocated throughout the nation. Of these organizational patterns, only three of the most common will be discussed for their implications in administration of the secondary schools. These three prominent patterns are the 8–4, the 6–3–3, and the 6–6.

1. In the 8–4 organizational pattern, grades kindergarten through eight are housed in one plant and are considered as elementary grades, and grades 9 through 12 are considered to be the high school grades. The 8–4 plan of organization has been very widely used throughout America.

The following arguments are often given in support of the 8–4 organization as compared to the 6–3–3 organization: (a) The junior high school takes one year away from the high school program. Colleges are interested in student records from grades 9 to 12, and guidance counselors cannot evaluate the college potential of students in only three years. (b) Good teachers trained for junior high school teaching are hard to find. As a result, school systems must rely on teachers trained either for elementary school or for high school. (c) Students under the program have to make an adjustment not only from elementary to junior high school, but also from junior high school to senior high school. (d) It is more expensive to operate the 6–3–3 program. (e) Rural one-room schools need the financial benefit derived from keeping grades seven and eight. (f) Better discipline can be maintained in an elementary program than in a junior high school. (g) Students "grow up" too soon.

2. The 6–3–3 plan of organization places grades kindergarten through six in the elementary school, grades seven, eight, and nine in the junior high school, and grades 10, 11, and 12 in the senior high school. Both the junior high school and the senior high school are considered to be part of the secondary schools. Thus under the 6–3–3 plan, secondary school administrators have a choice of two levels of schools that they can administer. Each level has its own objectives and curriculum. Obviously, the program for grades seven and eight under a 6–3–3 pattern will be markedly different from curricula programs organized under the 8–4 plan.

The following arguments are given in support of a 6–3–3 organization: (a) The junior high school meets the needs of early adolescents better than any other plan of school organization. (b) It provides a more varied curriculum and provides opportunities for students to choose electives on the basis of their interests and abilities. (c) It lends itself to grouping in accordance with ability, so that subject matter can be presented more effectively. (d) It makes it possible to establish effective health and physical educational programs geared to the needs of this age group. (e) It makes it possible to organize special education programs for mentally retarded, emotionally disturbed, and socially maladjusted students. (f) It permits a gradual transition from the one-teacher system of the elementary school to the departmentalization of the senior high school. (g) Rural students have an opportunity to participate in activities that are not available to them in small schools.

3. The 6–6 plan of organization frequently is found where enrollments do not justify a separate junior high school. Under this program grades 7 through 12 are housed in one building, and all grades are considered to be part of the high school organization. The students of junior high age are able to participate in the wider curriculum advantages as indicated under the 6–3–3 organization. However, the problem of "growing up too soon" is often cited as a disadvantage.

Rural, City, and Consolidated Schools. In addition to the general types of district organization discussed above, the organization of schools is further complicated by geography and demography. Where the population is sparse, the small rural school develops. The one-room school is well known on the elementary level, but less well known is the number of schools on a secondary level that are too small in size to offer an adequate curriculum. Over 70 per cent of the public high schools have less than 100 students enrolled in the twelfth-grade class.

In Chapter 1, the Small High School was given as an extreme example of a small school. However, there are Small High Schools in every state in the union. Most of these schools are in the rural areas. Some of the major problems of the rural secondary school are (1) curriculum is inadequate, (2) there are too few teachers, (3) the principal must teach part or full time, and (4) administrative help is often nonexistent.

The city school is characterized by large enrollments from the urban and suburban population. The mode of living is based on the technical and industrial society. The principal of the urban high school is generally a person with considerable educational training. A doctor's degree in school administration is not uncommon. The principal has an administrative staff of vice principals, deans, department chairmen, counselors, and clerks that far exceeds the total staff of most rural schools.

Major problems of the large city school are (1) coordinating curricular offering, (2) securing cooperation between departments, (3) determining policy and encouraging the staff to carry out procedures involved in a large-scale business operation, (4) solving problems of overcrowded classrooms, (5) solving safety problems created by the excessive traffic resulting from the number of cars, and (6) providing opportunity for a greater number of students to share leadership responsibilities and to participate in extracurricular activities.

In its organization the consolidated school is somewhere between the rural school and the large city school. The consolidated school usually has a full-time principal and a full-time clerk. When the school reaches a student population of about 500, a part-time vice-principal is generally added to the staff. Other administrative officers are added as size increases. The curriculum is usually greatly improved over that of the rural schools in both quality and quantity. A major problem is bus transportation. Most of the students are transported by buses owned and operated by the district. The consolidated district may vary in size from a few square miles to several thousand square miles. Obviously a major problem for the principal arises from transportation. Students are confined to buses for long periods of time each day, and handling the discipline problems due to these long and tedious rides is a vexing problem for principals. Another problem arises because some buses make two "runs." Busloads of students are thus deposited at the school at early morning hours while the bus returns for a second load of students. Supervision is necessary during the lunch hour as well as before and after school.

Aside from the bus problem, the principal of a consolidated school generally has a combination of the problems presented in large city schools and small rural schools.

Trend Toward Larger Units. In the organizational pattern of schools, one trend stands out above all others. There is a definite trend toward larger units of operation. This trend is true on a district, county, and regional basis. At the same time large city schools are attempting to find ways to keep the larger unit but get more informality by subdividing into smaller units. The House Plan and other new patterns are presented later.

Just as the districts are combining to make large operating units, so are the schools within the district consolidating. Two or more small high schools are merged into one large high school. This consolidation makes it possible to provide an enriched curriculum offering for the students, and a better administrative operational unit is created. The people of the area profit from consolidation through (1) an improved educational curriculum and (2) a more efficient and effective expenditure of the tax dollar.

In his book *The American High School,* James B. Conant recommended that wherever possible, the small high school should be eliminated. Graduating classes should have a minimum of 100 students if the needs of the students and of society are to be met and a school of smaller size could only offer the desirable and needed program at exorbitant expense.[8]

Conant reports that there are approximately 4,000 high schools with graduating classes of 100 or more students, while there are 17,000 high schools with graduating classes of less than 100. Of the million and a half high school students, approximately 1 million attend 4,000 high schools. This means that 500,000 students are scattered among 17,000 high schools. Conant concluded that the 17,000 high schools should be reduced to 5,000. The total number of high schools needed would be 9,000 instead of 21,000.[9] Such a plan for reorganization would greatly improve the educational structure.

Organization Within Schools. The curriculum organization that is most commonly found in secondary schools is the traditional departmentalized, subject-oriented curriculum. The academic curriculum is divided into departments, i.e., English, social studies, science, math, etc. Each department has its own course offering. With few exceptions these courses are given an equal time period in the curriculum. The typical school day is arranged into a six-, seven-, or eight-period day. Students generally work out their own schedules. Grouping comes in the elective courses on the basis of the students' interests.

Other types of curriculum organization involve core and block-time programs. These programs are usually formed by organizing learning

[8] James B. Conant, *op. cit.*, p. 38.
[9] *Ibid.*, pp. 80–81.

experiences from two or more subjects into units. Students are scheduled into these classes for two- or three-hour blocks of time. The most common combination of subjects is English and social studies. Mathematics and science are sometimes grouped together. The core program is found frequently in the junior high school.

The following reasons have been advanced for organizing core and block-time programs in both the junior high and senior high schools:

1. The longer block of time permits the teacher and the student to pursue a learning situation with fewer stops, breaks, and changes.

2. The unit and problems approaches to teaching can be used more effectively.

3. Integration of subject matter is enhanced. Such integration is more like the true life situations, which call for integration rather than segregated and compartmentalized materials.

4. Teaching and learning activities can be improved. Greater variety of activities can be introduced such as construction, map work, creative writing, and other project-type activities. Provisions for individual differences can be more easily planned.

5. Teachers can help students with their individual needs when they have longer blocks of time to work with the students. A more effective guidance program can be realized.

6. The student can make the transition better from the single-teacher elementary school to the separate-teacher-for-each-subject high school program.

The problems encountered in organizing and administering these programs are: (1) teachers are generally trained on the subject-departmentalized programs, (2) textbooks, especially on the senior high level, have not been adequately developed, (3) many teachers are not convinced that the programs have merit, (4) scheduling problems arise in scheduling two or more teachers to teach in these programs, and (5) material work centers are not available in most schools.

Studies Designed to Improve Secondary Education

The American High School Today.   The comprehensive high school is uniquely American. Under one administration all the children from the community are brought together to be educated. The average, the slow, and the gifted; the rich and the poor; children from the lower social class and children from the middle and upper classes are all instructed in the ways of democracy. With such a variety of needs to be met, it is little wonder that problems exist. American education has been, is now, and will continue to be criticized for its deficiencies.

The study by Conant came at an appropriate time. Many of the fears of "a deficient education" were allayed. The report vindicated the need for and the accomplishments of the comprehensive high school. However, the report also made recommendations to strengthen and improve the organizational structure of secondary education in America. These recommendations are of vital concern to the principal as he looks to the improvement of the curricula and organization of his school. These recommendations are as follows: (1) Every student should have a planned individualized program based on his needs. This program would permit the flexibility that is needed but often not found under the track systems. (2) In the required courses and those elective courses in which a wide range of ability would be present, the students should be grouped according to ability subject by subject. (At least three levels would be needed.) (3) The school day should be organized so that there will be at least six periods in addition to physical education and driver's education. Under a seven- or eight-period day, laboratory classes and industrial arts classes should be scheduled for double periods.[10]

Commission on the Experimental Study of the Utilization of the Staff. At the time Conant was making his study, other studies were sponsored by the National Association of Secondary-School Principals and financed by the Ford Foundation. These studies were under the direction of a staff of educators appointed by N.A.S.S.P. and entitled Commission on the Experimental Study of the Utilization of the Staff in the Secondary School. The purpose of these studies was to experiment to see how the staff might be used more efficiently and effectively. Quality education was the key word and the goal to be obtained through experimentation, organization, structure, and utilization of the staff. The official reports are found in the *Bulletin of the National Association of Secondary School Principals.*[11] Based on these studies, *Images of the Future, A New Approach to the Secondary Schools*[12] was published. The purpose of the proposals presented was to stimulate imaginative research and developments aimed at improving organization and staffing in secondary schools.

On the basis of the experimental studies, it was proposed that the secondary school of the future would be different in several respects from those of today. These differences are itemized with appropriate explanatory information below:

1. The school would no longer be organized in the traditional standard classes, daily schedules, and departmentalized instruction. The school would

[10] *Ibid.*, pp. 1–76.
[11] National Association of Secondary-School Principals, *Bulletin of N.A.S.S.P.* The Association, January 1958, 1959, 1960, 1961, 1962. Complete January issues devoted to these studies.
[12] J. Lloyd Trump, *Images of the Future*, Commission on Experimental Study of the Utilization of the Staff in Secondary Schools, 1959.

be organized around three types of activities: (1) large-group instruction (100 or more students), (2) small-group discussion (12 to 15 students), and (3) individual study. Figure 5.2 indicates how this type of instruction would be organized, the functions performed in each, the facilities needed, and the approximate time devoted to each type of instruction.

2. The class schedule would also be changed. The future class schedule would call for students to be in class groups only 18 hours a week instead of 30. Twelve of the eighteen hours would be in large-group instruction and six hours would be in small-group discussion. The student would spend about 12 hours in individualized study. Blocks of time would be utilized to a greater advantage. This type of organization would lend itself to teaching the student to study, think, and solve problems on his own.

3. The instructional staff would consist of (1) professional teachers—teacher specialists and general teachers (one professional for each 40 students), (2) instructional assistants (hours per week served by assistants would be about 20 times the number of professional teachers in the school), (3) clerks (hours per week served by the clerks would be about ten times the number of professional teachers in the school), (4) general aids (hours per week served by assistants would be about five times the number of professional teachers in the school), (5) community consultants, and (6) staff specialists. Trump gives a breakdown of the instructional staff based on a 400-pupil school.[13]

Many other reports and recommendations regarding the school of the future have been given. However, the proposals given here are basic to the organization and administration of the future school. Certainly the proposals have been imaginative and stimulating. Experimental programs in secondary schools have been greatly stimulated as a result of these staff utilization studies.

New Organizational Patterns

Ability Grouping and Phase Programs. Organizing the curriculum to take care of the wide range in abilities has long been a problem. Terman's studies of gifted children in the 1920's were an early approach to this problem. However, with the emphasis of the Conant study, staff utilization studies, and other independent experimental studies, new approaches are being made to meet individual differences. The advent of space exploration has also brought about a change in the attitude of the public in regard to ability grouping and curriculum organization.

Organization of the curriculum into tracks and levels or phases is receiving attention. In many high schools, a three-phase program is used:

[13] *Ibid.*, pp. 5–27.

Figure 5.2

Organization of Instruction in the Secondary School of the Future

ORGANIZATION OF INSTRUCTION

Teaching-Learning Experiences:

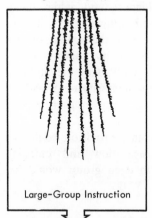

Large-Group Instruction

Small-Group Discussion

Individual Study

Introduction	Group examination	Read
Motivation	of terms and con-	
Explanation	cepts and solution	Listen to records and tapes
Planning	of problems	
Group Study		View, Question, Analyze,
Enrichment	Reach areas of	Think
Generalization	agreement and	
Evaluation	disagreement	Experiment, Examine
		Investigate, Consider Evidence
PLACE	Improve inter-	
	personal relations	Write, Create, Memorize,
Auditorium, little theater,		Record, Make
cafeteria, study hall,	PLACE	
classrooms joined via		Visit
television or remodeling,	Conference room,	
other large room	classroom	Self-appraise
about 40 per cent	about 20 per cent	PLACE

Library, laboratories, workshops, project and materials centers, museums — inside or outside the school plant

about 40 per cent

SOURCE: J. Lloyd Trump, *Images of the Future*, p. 9. Reprinted by permission from the National Association of Secondary-School Principals, 1959. Copyright: Washington, D.C.

a slow-learning group, an average group, and a rapid-learning group. Larger schools can further diversify. The old track organization is also used, which divides students into college preparatory, general education, and vocational. Currently, the emphasis is placed primarily on the areas in which a student will profit most according to his ability.

Phasing by levels is based primarily on intelligence and achievement tests and teacher recommendations. The increased knowledge of intelligence tests has (1) demonstrated more convincingly the extent of individual differences and (2) made it possible to classify children more accurately on the basis of native ability. Also, as a result of the findings in these fields, there has come the realization of the necessity of providing differentiated courses of study for the pupils progressing in each of the levels.

In a secondary school of 1,000 to 2,000 students, provision could be made for five levels—gifted, above average, average, slow, and remedial or special. A suggested percentage of students in each group would be as follows:

Gifted	1 to 3 per cent
Above average	10 to 20 per cent
Average	54 to 78 per cent
Slow	10 to 20 per cent
Special	1 to 3 per cent

School systems of 500-to-1,000-student enrollment usually will have three levels or phases. An adjustment involving at least two levels would seem to be feasible even in a small school having only four or five teachers.

A multiple-level plan calls for a differentiated course of study in both content and method. The development of such courses is one of the most urgent needs in education today.

Small-School Study Projects. Although the desirability of eliminating small schools has been discussed, the possibility of complete elimination is highly unlikely. If for no other reasons than isolation and distance between communities, the small secondary schools will remain for many years.

Two basic research projects have been carried forth on a broad-scope basis. These are the Catskill Area Project in Small School Design (CAP) and the Rocky Mountain Area Project for Small High Schools (RMAP).

The Rocky Mountain Area Project for Small Schools has used (1) multiple-class teaching—two or more classes under the same instructor at the same time, (2) small-group techniques—different abilities and backgrounds handled in a single session; and (3) large-group, ungraded structure with certain subject areas such as mathematics or English. Team teaching, independent study, rotating schedules, and special seminars are a few of the features of these programs.

The Catskill Area Project in Small School Design has emphasized various flexible schedules, supervised correspondence courses not offered in the curriculum, and multiple classes in the same room with a single teacher, along with other combination features.

Both these projects have been extremely successful in upgrading the quality of the curriculum and the instructional techniques in small schools.

Ungraded School. "The most serious of the many problems confronting education today is what to do about the grade. The dilemma is a formidable one. The grade has become anthropologized, historized, psychologized, and polarized into the process of learning. The graded organization is like an ice tray guaranteed to freeze into rigidity everything that is put into it. Iconoclasts have condemned it as 'a cage for every age.' "[14] Unlike most curriculum reforms, which attempt to make the reform fit the current organization, the ungraded school restructures the organization.

The ungraded school is based on the needs of the individual students rather than on the age of the students. The students are grouped according to their stage of learning. The stage of learning should be distinguished from intelligence-level groupings because rate of learning is based on achievement rather than potential. The nongraded school is an organization that makes arrangements for the student to pursue any course in which he is interested, and has the ability to achieve, without regard to either grade level or sequence.[15]

The need to unlock the grade lockstep was set forth by J. Lloyd Trump:

> In tomorrow's schools, the points of entry to and exit from elementary, secondary, and higher schools will be determined by each student's mental and emotional maturity—his readiness to move on—and by his capacity for organized instruction. This will require *professional decision.* Today's school settles entrance to and exit from school by *clerical* decisions; date of birth and number of credits are the determining factors.
>
> The curriculum will be divided into stages or steps not identified as years or grades, and without any fixed number. The rate of progress through school will be determined by the student's previous achievements and by his capacity to take the next step. His readiness to move on, again, will be gauged by a professional decision and not by a test, a grade, or a unit of

---

[14] B. Frank Brown, *The Nongraded High School* (Englewood Cliffs, N.J.: Prentice-Hall, Inc., 1963), p. 27. B. Frank Brown, principal of Melbourne High School, is credited with establishing the first ungraded high school.

[15] *Ibid.,* p. 43.

credit. That professional decision will answer this question: Has the student assimilated as much skill, knowledge, and understanding in the present stage as can reasonably be expected of him?

Such individual progress will be at different rates of speed in different subject areas, or different skills, or even at different times in the student's life.[16]

Melbourne High School's nongraded structure is centered around five cycles or phases of learning based on skills. The phases are organized as follows:

Phase 1 Subjects are designed for students who need special assistance in small classes.

Phase 2 Subjects are designed for students who need more emphasis on the basic skills.

Phase 3 Material is designed for students with average ability in the subject matter.

Phase 4 Subject matter is designed for capable students desiring education in depth.

Phase 5 Challenging courses are available to students with exceptional ability who are willing to assume responsibility for their own learning and go far beyond the normal high school level.[17]

The ungraded school is a new type of organizational structure that allows student growth and development unhampered by grade barriers.

Continuous Progress School and Individualized Instruction.[18]   The Continuous Progress Plan at the Brigham Young University Laboratory School is another unique attempt to organize the students for better instructional programs. The emphasis is almost totally on the individual and his growth and achievement. Under this organization the curriculum has been reorganized so that students can progress through it at their own individual rate. The counseling department plays a very vital role in aiding this program. Student conferences are held with the student, counselor, and parents. On the basis of intelligence and achievement tests, past grades, and teacher judgments, the students are given two achievement goals: (1) a quantity achievement, such as an amount equal to a regular course, one half a course, a course and one half, or any other rate of achievement goal; and (2) a quality achievement—work to be com-

---

[16] J. Lloyd Trump and Dorsey Baynham, *Focus on Change—Guide to Better Schools* (Chicago: Rand McNally and Company, 1961), pp. 55–57.

[17] B. Frank Brown, *op. cit.*, p. 50.

[18] The Continuous Progress School is at the Brigham Young University Laboratory School, Provo, Utah.

pleted at the 60–70–80–90 per cent level before moving to the next curriculum unit or sequence.

The students spend most of their time in independent study using self-instructional material. The material is both commercially published materials and school-developed guides and other materials. The independent study time is augmented by frequent small group conferences with students who are on the same unit at that time. Because students progress at different rates, the grouping is flexible. When a student determines that he is ready to pass an area of work, he goes to a testing area for evaluation purposes.

Large- and Small-Group Organization. Large-group organization saves time and personnel. All learning activities that can be given to a large group as easily as to one person might be considered suitable for large-group instruction. The basic purposes of large-group instruction are to motivate, disseminate, and assign. The more students spread out along the learning continuum, the less need there is for large-group instruction.

The small group is the ideal organizational pattern where the activities are primarily for student discussion with each other. The school facilities must provide for these small-group informal arrangements. The teacher's role is one of a consultant-catalyst-analyzer-evaluator.

Combination of New Patterns. Many of the secondary school principals have seen the merit of one or all of the new organizational patterns, but because of caution, lack of preparation of the staff, citizen resistance, or other reasons have elected to try the new organizational structure on a limited basis. The traditional organization is mixed with an ungraded English class. Independent study is provided for the gifted. Programmed mathematics materials are used while other classes use standard texts. These combinations indicate a general acceptance of the newer organizational structures, but also indicate that changes come slowly in education. There are even more schools that have not initiated change.

School-Within-a-School and House Plan. Two other types of organization have developed primarily in the large urban centers. These organizational patterns have evolved to solve problems in the large secondary schools. The problems to be solved were the impersonality of large schools for both the student and the teacher, the administrative red tape—who is responsible to whom, the need for more individualized guidance and programs of instruction, and decentralization of administration.

The school-within-a-school was organized so that each grade level had a separate wing of the school and separate administrators, faculty, and guidance personnel. The gym, shops, library, and other special facilities were shared. Other facilities were separate.

The house plan has the same basic goals. However, in organization a house is a unit in which all grade levels are usually represented. The house more closely resembles a typical secondary school of about 500 students in organization and administration. However, the advantages are that all the highly specialized programs along with the special facilities can be provided for a student body of 1,500 to 2,000 students.

The Principal's Role in Change

The Principal Is a Leader. One of the themes in Chapter 1 and throughout this book is that the principal should spend more time on the improvement of instruction in his school. It was further indicated in Chapter 2 that the principal is the responsible agent in the school and that leadership is his primary function. The history, aims and objectives, present organization of schools, and curriculum content have been presented. Now what about experimentation and innovations? What about meeting the needs of the changing society? Change is inevitable. Curriculum change should also be inevitable. However, too often the changes in schools do not follow the changes in our society. The following fable illustrates this point.

RIP VAN WINKLE'S SON

Young Rip wanted to beat his father's record of twenty years' sleep, so in 1905 he entered a fur-lined cave in the Adirondacks. He awoke in 1955, arose, walked to the door of the cave, stepped out and stretched. Being hungry, he thought of his old home down the hill in the town.

He walked to the old gravel road. Lo and behold, the old road was no longer. There was a double ribbon of solid stone. He stepped on it to try it. As he did, a great machine with two glass eyes, pink in color, came up the rock road at him at 50 miles an hour. He jumped to safety behind a bush. Others came! Black, brown, red, yellow and green.

"Methinks the cornfield is a safe place for me." He ran across the hills to the nearest cornfield, entered it and crouched down to hide. Soon a great snorting animal with one iron wheel and two great back wheels came down the row at him. It wasn't husking corn, it was eating up the cornfield whole.

He thought, "I'm not safe here," and bolted for the highest peak for safety from such elements. He caught his breath and settled down to rest and plan his future actions. As he pondered, five big arrows came at him out of the sky, with the speed of light. He flattened himself, and as they went by, he was scared by the most unholy noise. As he lay there, they came at him from the opposite direction and, lo, they were gone before he heard them.

"Now where can I be safe?" He spied the little old red schoolhouse down the mountainside and fled to it as fast as he could go. As he hid inside for safety, he sighed to himself, "I'll be safe here! There've been no changes here in the last 50 years!"[19]

Again it is emphasized that the principal is a leader. Curriculum change in keeping with the changing needs of society should be one of his primary concerns.

Evaluation of the Programs. One basic act of leadership explored in Chapter 2 was that of evaluation. No other phase of the work of the principal is as important as the instructional program. Basic to the improvement of any good ongoing program is evaluation. Evaluation of the aims and objectives of the courses, evaluation of the content designed to meet the objectives, and evaluation of the procedures to teach the content are fundamental problems of the principal. The best instrument that has been devised to aid the teachers, the principals, and the community to appraise their program is *Evaluative Criteria.*[20] First published in 1940, it was revised in 1950 and again in 1960. An instrument recently developed for evaluation of junior highs is *Junior High School Evaluative Criteria.*[21] Every principal should be acquainted with these instruments.

Basic Principles of Changing Organizational Patterns. In this changing educational climate, where imagination and creativity are allowed free rein, schools and staffs within schools have been organized into new and different patterns, such as school-within-a-school, house plan, ungraded schools, continuous progress schools, large-group instruction, small-group instruction, team teaching, and independent study. Combinations of these new patterns can be found. Some schools have tried to incorporate all the newer organizational patterns. As a principal contemplates change, certain guidelines may be useful. Some of these principles are as follows:

1. The principal should initiate change for a purpose and not just for the sake of change. He might ask, "What do I really desire to accomplish? What are my goals? What type of organizational pattern will achieve the best results?" When the problem to be solved is clearly understood, changes can be made to solve the problem. The public seldom criticizes an innovation if a solution of a problem of concern to all is being sought.

[19] First printed by Kenosha, Wisconsin, Board of Education.
[20] *Evaluative Criteria* (Washington: Cooperative Study of Secondary School Standards, 1960).
[21] *Junior High School Evaluative Criteria* (Salt Lake City, Utah: State Department of Public Instruction, 1960), 491 pp.

2. The principal should involve in the planning all personnel who will be affected by the new organizational pattern. A principal will have new problems to solve when he moves to a new pattern; fighting his staff should not be one of the problems. This basic principle was discussed in the chapter on leadership.

3. The new organization pattern should be flexible. Setting too rigid a pattern makes it difficult to adjust to new problems and to shift to new emphases when needed. A pattern without plans for adjustment is too rigid to be successful. The end result is usually a return to the previous organizational pattern.

4. The new pattern adopted should be simple in scope and design. Overcomplication discourages staff members who must make it work.

5. The personnel, facilities, equipment, and supplies needed for the success of the new organizational pattern should either be present, promised, or adaptable. Team teaching cannot succeed if the teachers concerned refuse to share ideas and work together. Large-group instruction requires special facilities or means to adapt auditoriums, gymnasiums, and cafeterias.

6. The principal should have the support of the superintendent and other interested district personnel before initiating the project. If special funding, budgets, or services are required, the principal should clear all of these in advance.

7. Finally, the principal should be prepared to solve problems. Innovation "rocks the boat" until appropriate solutions are found to the new challenging problems. The principal and his staff must also be flexible.

Summary

The two most important responsibilities of the principal are the organization of the school and the organization and administration of the curriculum. Under the laws of the land the state is responsible for education. The state through the legislature has organized a department of public instruction to supervise the educational functions. The legislature has created local school districts to carry out the functions of education. The principal of a local school comes under the organizational division of the district. The size of the school district is increasing, as is the size of the high school. Through consolidation, both efficiency and effectiveness in learning have been improved. There are still too many small high schools in many states.

Within the school district, the district can organize its schools as is deemed appropriate to the needs of that communal area. Many patterns of organization can be found. The three most common plans are the 8–4, the 6–3–3, and the 6–6.

Experimentation in school organization has resulted in many new structures: nongraded school, continuous progress, large and small groups, independent study, school-within-a-school, and the house plan. The criticism of our schools has been centered around the curriculum. The common core courses to meet the needs of society become the required classes. The electives meet the individual needs. In addition, the need for ability grouping, track systems, levels and phasing, and some system of individualized program planning is indicated.

The principal must be concerned with the nature and quality of the curriculum. Evaluation thus becomes necessary. The *Evaluative Criteria* and the *Junior High School Evaluative Criteria* are instruments to aid in this evaluative process.

Significant studies have been made on the secondary school. James B. Conant's study of the comprehensive high school listed specific recommendations for an improved secondary education. The studies on staff utilization culminating in a report by J. Lloyd Trump suggested a vast reorganization of secondary schools. The small-school study projects have aided the small high schools. These reports were concerned with improving the quality of secondary education—a principle of supreme importance to dedicated high school principals.

Finally, the principal's role in curriculum change is that of a leader. Unless the principal is concerned with and continually strives to improve the curriculum, very little change occurs.

SUGGESTED PROJECTS AND ACTIVITIES

1. Discuss the effect of organization on curriculum and curriculum on organization.
2. Visit schools that are organized in a 6–6, 6–3–3, and 8–4 manner. How does the organization affect the curriculum? Make a chart showing the curricular offering at each grade level in each type of organizational plan.
3. Interview the principals of each type of school listed in number 2 above. List the major problems of the principal. How many problems are common with all organizational plans? How many problems are inherent in each type of organization?
4. Visit a nongraded school or a continuous progress school or prepare a report that shows how they are different from the traditional school.
5. Visit some new curriculum programs. Discuss the essential differences from the traditional programs with the teachers.
6. Obtain a list of the curricular offering of the largest high school of your state and the smallest high school of your state. Compare both the courses that are required and those that are elective.

7. Determine the course requirements for graduation from high schools in your state.
8. Take a section of the *Evaluative Criteria* to the nearest high school and evaluate that program.
9. Show the film *And No Bells Ring,* National Association of Secondary-School Principals film. This film dramatizes Trump's plan of organizing the future school.
10. Debate: The high school diploma should indicate completion of requirements according to ability and should not signify a standard of achievement.

REVIEW AND DISCUSSION QUESTIONS

1. In what way is the American school system different from most of the European schools?
2. Why are districts increasing in size? How is this possible?
3. Why is the local school placed under the jurisdiction of the district rather than the state department?
4. What are some of the advantages of the small rural high school, the consolidated high school, and the urban high school? What are some of the disadvantages?
5. How is an ungraded school organized?
6. What is meant by 6–6, 8–4, and 6–3–3 plans of organization?
7. What are the advantages and disadvantages of each kind of organization?
8. What is meant by "continuous progress plan"?
9. What are some principles for curriculum organization?
10. Why is it wrong to assume that all students should reach the same standard achievement?
11. What are the advantages and disadvantages of ability grouping, track programs, phases, individualized placement programs, and heterogeneous grouping?
12. What are some characteristics of the core, block, unified, and fused programs? What are the advantages? What are the disadvantages?
13. What were some of the specific recommendations of Conant's report? How do these recommendations agree or disagree with current practice today?
14. What were the recommendations of the Commission for the Utilization of the Staff? How have these recommendations changed the organizational structure of the secondary school?

SELECTED BIBLIOGRAPHY

Alberty, Harold B., and Elsie J. Alberty. *Reorganizing the High School Curriculum*, 3rd ed. New York: The Macmillan Co., 1962.

Alexander, William M., and J. Galen Saylor. *Modern Secondary Education.* New York: Rinehart and Company, Inc., 1959.

Anderson, Vernon E., and William T. Gruhn. *Principles and Practices of Secondary Education.* New York: The Ronald Press, 1962.

Arbolino, Jack N. "The Advanced Placement Program," *Bulletin of N.A.S.S.P.*, April 1964, pp. 136–41.

Brown, B. Frank. *The Nongraded High School.* Englewood Cliffs, N.J.: Prentice-Hall, Inc., 1963.

Brown, Kenneth E. "Which Mathematics Program?" *Bulletin of N.A.S.S.P.*, April 1964, pp. 105–13.

Bush, Robert N., and Dwight W. Allen. *A New Design for High School Education.* New York: McGraw-Hill Book Company, 1964.

Clark, Leonard H., Raymond L. Klein, and John B. Burks. *The American Secondary Curriculum.* New York: The Macmillan Company, 1965.

Conant, James B. *The American High School Today.* New York: McGraw-Hill Book Company, 1959.

———. *Shaping Educational Policy.* New York: McGraw-Hill Book Company, 1964.

Cronin, Joseph M. "The Principal's Role in Change," *Bulletin of N.A.S.S.P.*, May 1963, pp. 29–33.

Douglass, Harl (ed.). *The High School Curriculum.* Third Edition. New York: The Ronald Press Company, 1964.

Fraser, Dorothy McClure. "The Changing Scene in the Social Studies," *Audiovisual Instruction*, December 1964, pp. 662–65. Reprinted in *Education Digest*, March 1965, pp. 43–46.

Gardner, John W. "Innovation and Leadership in American Education," *Bulletin of N.A.S.S.P.*, March 1965, pp. 36–43.

Kraft, Ivor. "The Coming Crisis in Secondary Education," *Bulletin of N.A.S.S.P.*, February 1965, pp. 5–45.

Mildenberger, Kenneth W. "The Expanded N.D.E.A. Institute Program," *Bulletin of N.A.S.S.P.*, March 1965, pp. 285–92.

National Society for the Study of Education. *Individualizing Instruction.* 61st Yearbook, Part I. Chicago: University of Chicago Press, 1962.

Oliver, Albert I. *Curriculum Improvement.* New York: Dodd, Mead and Company, 1965.

Reed, Wayne O. "The Federal Government and Education," *Bulletin of N.A.S.S.P.*, March 1965, pp. 151–57.

Sand, Ole, and Richard I. Miller. "Curricular Innovations," *Bulletin of N.A.S.S.P.*, May 1963, pp. 120–44.

Saylor, Galen. "What Changes in School Organization Will Produce Better Learning Opportunities for Individual Students?" *Bulletin of N.A.S.S.P.*, September 1962, pp. 102–9.

Scott, C. Winfield, and Clyde M. Hill. *Public Education Under Criticism*. New York: Prentice-Hall, Inc., 1954, p. 414.

Smith, Frederick R. and R. Bruce McQuigg. *Secondary Schools Today: Readings for Educators*. Boston: Houghton Mifflin Company, 1965.

Stimson, Paul, and Paul Petrich. "How Can Students Best Be Grouped for Teaching and Learning?" *Bulletin of N.A.S.S.P.*, September 1962, pp. 78–91.

Stoddard, Alexander J. *Schools for Tomorrow: An Educator's Blueprint*. Fund for the Advancement of Education, 1957, pp. 1–60.

Thompkins, Ellsworth. "Individual Differences in the 1960's—Their Implications for School Administrators," *Bulletin of N.A.S.S.P.*, April 1962, pp. 1–7.

Thornton, James W., Jr., and John R. Wright. *Secondary School Curriculum*. Columbus, Ohio: Charles E. Merrill Books, Inc., 1963.

Trump, J. Lloyd. *Images of the Future*. Washington, D.C.: Commission on the Experimental Study of Utilization of the Staff, N.A.S.S.P., 1959.

Trump, J. Lloyd, and Dorsey Baynham. *Focus on Change—Guide to Better Schools*. Chicago: Rand McNally and Co., 1961.

"A 'Trump Plan' School—Four Years Later," *School Management*, October 1964, pp. 56–60, 112–17. Reprinted in *Education Digest*, January 1965, pp. 13–16.

CHAPTER 6

The Annual Cycle — Beginning and Ending the School Year

Beginning the School Year

The success of every venture in life is greatly enhanced by getting off to a good start. Each fall the principal should examine his track shoes and get into condition for the big race. Getting the school off to a good start requires the same detailed planning and execution that is necessary for a successful track meet. To be a winner, the principal must be prepared for all events, contenders, and conditions.

This chapter is concerned with the practical aspects of secondary school administration. Getting the school off to a good start is necessary for a successful school year. Some specific helps are provided to aid the principal in this endeavor.

Orienting the New Principal

Be Prepared. The motto "Be Prepared" is especially appropriate for the new principal. The first impressions made by the principal are often lasting ones. Therefore, the principal must demonstrate that he is and can be the titular head of the school. The principal has been through the university, has received training in school administration, and usually has had teaching experience. However, if he cannot get the school off to a good start, the confidence level of the teachers, students, community, and district office is lowered.

The best way for the principal to assure himself that the school will get off to a good start is to plan. Planning was one of the acts of leadership discussed in Chapter 2. At no other time during a school year is this act of leadership more important. Plans well conceived can be executed with finesse. Planning takes time, and the principal should be at school long enough in advance to see that there is sufficient time to do all that should be done. The exact amount of time needed will depend on the previous experience of the principal, the size of the school, and the state of the planning when the previous principal left the job. Some districts require the principal to be on the job a week, two weeks, or a month prior to the opening of school. When the principal accepts the job, he should investigate present conditions and determine how much time he will need to get the school ready. But he should allow time for the unexpected!

Orientation Features for the Principal.   The orientation of the principal should begin prior to signing a contract and will continue through the complete school year. Every phase of operation will be new to the principal, including preparing the final reports at the end of the school year. Each task, each problem, and each solution will provide the experience needed for the complete orientation. However, there are aspects of the orientation that are fundamental before getting acquainted with the specifics of the job. These general orientation features include getting acquainted with (1) the community; (2) the district organization, superintendent, and staff; and (3) the school to which the principal has been assigned.

A Knowledge of the Community Needed.   A knowledge of the community is very helpful to the principal. It is especially important that he understand the value structure and the power structure. The value system is the hierarchy of objects or situations with relative degrees of worth to the people. The power structure refers to the arrangement of authority in the community. If the principal does not understand the customs and traditions of the community and the relative values assigned to various objects, it is easy to make mistakes and thus antagonize members in a community because sacred codes have been violated.

It would be extremely helpful to the principal if he made a community analysis as one of his first get-acquainted acts. The following items are given as a suggested pattern for such an analysis:

1. *General impression.* This would orient the reader to the type of community and the general impression given to the observer.
2. *Demographic characteristics.* Population statistics, trends, composition, and characteristics would be noted under this heading.

3. *Ecological pattern.* The community's geographical limits, the spatial distribution of people, and the location of buildings and service institutions are important in community analysis.

4. *Historical backgrounds.* This refers not to the chronological description of the conventional historian, but rather to the life-history analysis used by sociologists and anthropologists. Growth cycles and significant developmental events in the community's past are brought to attention.

5. *Life activities.* Life activities refer to the behaviors engaged in by the people largely within the pattern of institutional structure. They include such factors as (a) making a living, (b) home and family life, (c) health and physical well-being, (d) training the young, (e) spending leisure time, (f) getting information, (g) religious behavior, (h) politics, law and order, (i) social class, and (j) the world outside.

6. *Value system.* Every community has a system of values, which, in total effect, represents a hierarchy of objects having different degrees of worth to the people. The people believe these objects help to satisfy human desires.

7. *Power system.* Every community has a system of power relations arranged in a hierarchy. Power is the ability to dominate or to compel action. The power system is of crucial importance to the school.

8. *Impact of regional and national culture.* No community is a self-contained cultural unit; there are countless ways in which regional subculture and the national culture fuse with the culture of the local community.

9. *Community "characters."* While not an integral part of community analysis, the local "characters" are an interesting aspect for describing one's community. We are referring here to colorful local personalities who, because of dramatic, unusual, or deviant personal behavior patterns, attract attention. They become a part of the living lore of community behavior.

10. *Miscellaneous.* There are other special characteristics of communities that should be included in a community analysis.[1]

After the principal has made this analysis, he will be acquainted with the community, its leaders, and its expectations.

Interview with the Superintendent. As part of the employment interview and in succeeding meetings with the superintendent, the principal should gather information about the district. Some of the following questions could serve as a guide for district orientation:

a. What type of organization is present? Is it a unified district or strictly secondary? What is the internal organizational structure (6–3–3 or 8–4 or other)?

b. How is the staff organized?

[1] Wilbur B. Brookover, *A Sociology of Education*, (New York: American Book Company, 1955), p. 374.

c. To whom is the principal directly responsible?

d. Are the bus drivers, cooks, and custodians as well as the teachers responsible directly to the principal or are they responsible to the district supervisor?

e. How does the district handle the budget business affairs as they affect each school? Does the school have a budget? What are the procedures for ordering and receiving equipment and supplies?

f. What supervisory help is available?

g. What are the specific responsibilities of the district staff as they affect the principal and his school?

School Orientation. In addition to the community and the district, the principal must be oriented to his school. There are a number of things he should know before he begins his work. Some things he will want to do are:

a. Tour the school to learn what the general plant is like. How is it oriented? Where are the specific facilities as related to the administrative offices?

b. Meet the custodians and arrange for a detailed inspection of the plant.

c. Investigate the special features that are included in the plant, such as school lunch facilities.

d. Investigate the size of classrooms, shops, gyms, etc., for the purpose of determining schedules.

Starting the New Job

Getting Acquainted with the Job. With the general orientation behind him, the principal can concentrate on his new assignment. The first phase is a get-acquainted phase. Like the general orientation, a knowledge of certain things in advance will save time and help him do a better job.

1. The principal should learn his duties as given in the district handbook of policies and procedures. If such a book is not available, he should obtain in writing the responsibilities assigned to him by the superintendent and board of education.

2. He should review the handbook of the school. Such a handbook states the school policies and procedures and gives other pertinent information about the school. If such a handbook is not available, the principal should review faculty minutes and talk to teachers and staff members about the policies and procedures. The creation of such a handbook should be part of the plans for the year if one has not been made.

3. A "snooping" tour of the administrative offices is a must. The type and location of office equipment should be noted. The principal should

know "what is filed where." He must get acquainted with all the facilities in the office.

4. A meeting with the school secretary should be arranged if she is not presently at the school. Arrangements should be made for the secretary to spend all or part of the day at the offices to take care of the secretarial and clerical phase of getting the school started. The principal should review with the secretary the little things that create an efficient organization. The secretary can instruct the principal in the use of the intercommunication system between offices and throughout the school, methods used in filing, and unfinished work. Many of the administrative procedures of the school can be provided by the secretary. Thus routine can be quickly learned. If a secretary has not been hired, this should be discussed with the superintendent immediately. If the secretary is new, it is doubly important that she be on the job early so that she may also learn her responsibilities.

5. The principal should review the year-end reports submitted by his predecessor. These reports are the quickest way the principal can determine the present status of affairs in the operation of his job.

Where to Start. Obviously if a principal has done all the things that have been mentioned previously, he has already started his job. Getting to the specifics of operation of the job is now important. One of the best places to begin is correspondence. An accumulation of summer correspondence will confront the principal. Some of these letters will be in urgent need of a reply. Others will be business letters and letters of information. Each of these letters will add insight to the nature of the work. A few hours of dictation will usually handle this problem.

After the letters are completed, he can check on the supply orders and purchase order forms and other matters that have accumulated during the summer. Equipment items delivered during the summer can be routed to the proper rooms. With these perfunctory tasks completed, with a clean desk, and with a sense of real achievement, the principal is ready to start some real work.

Inspect the Building and Grounds. Inspection of the building and grounds should come early on the principal's schedule. In fact, this duty would normally be attended to prior to or during the time a principal is building the registration schedule. Building the schedule requires a knowledge of size of room and number of students who can occupy the room. Therefore, a brief inspection becomes mandatory. However, the principal is far more concerned with the building than just counting the student stations. The building has to be ready for occupancy when school starts. Not only must floors be cleaned and polished, but desks often need resurfacing, and the walls occasionally need a new coat of paint. Heating and ventilating systems should be operating properly, as should the bell system. The fire extinguishers and general safety conditions should be checked.

In general, this inspection provides a wonderful opportunity to learn the details of the buildings. It is also an excellent time to become acquainted with the custodial staff. A compliment to them for work well done at this early date will help extend the quality of maintenance care throughout the school year.

Scheduling and Registration

Scheduling of Classes. One of the most important tasks in getting school started is building a class schedule. Fortunate indeed is the new principal who finds the schedule completed when he arrives. If such is the case, the principal's job becomes one of review rather than construction. In either event, the principal should review the schedules for prior years. This review will serve as a good guide for the present schedule. Building the schedule requires considerable information and technical knowledge; therefore, the details are presented in the following chapter.

Assignment of Teachers. Once the schedule has been determined, the next step is to assign the teachers. A new principal may find this a relatively easy job if there have been no changes in either the schedule or his staff. However, it is now typical to find that some teachers have vacated their position. Another teacher on the staff may be waiting to take over some of these classes but not all of them. Through a combination of circumstances, usually a number of changes in assignment are needed.

A problem confronting many principals is that of the assignment of athletic coaches to academic work. In many schools the program of athletics is too large for one coach. Yet the number of physical education courses is not sufficient for two full-time coaches. Right or wrong, the value decision is usually made to retain two coaches. When this decision is made, the usual principles for assignment of teachers should apply. Many schools have solved this practical problem by hiring a coach who has specialized in an academic area but who has participated in athletics in the university program.

Another group of assignment problems in small schools comes from the specialized areas such as music and art. Should the district hire a music teacher and assign him part time to social studies or some other academic area, or should the school hire an academic teacher and limp through a music program? These decisions can be made only by the principal and the superintendent as they assess all the values important to the community and the students.

Registering Students

Registration Requires Planning. Registration can be one of the biggest headaches of a principal or it can be just another event in the school. Planning makes the difference. Registration traditionally has taken place in the fall of the year and officially opened the school year. In recent years there has been an increased emphasis placed on spring registration. If a spring registration procedure is used, the problems in the fall registration are primarily limited to transfer students and students who can justify the need for a change in registration.

The traditional manner of handling registration is to have students divide into grades and go to rooms where advisers are present. A copy of the schedule along with a list of required subjects and optional subjects is given to the student. Other registration procedure is set forth. The advisers sign or approve the registration. The student's registration is then tallied on a master list of classes. When a given class is filled, the advisers are so notified. After the classes are tallied, the student then pays student-body fees and locker fees and purchases books and supplies (in districts where these items are not furnished). Students then go to a shortened but full-day schedule.

In larger schools, the registration often takes several days or evenings. Each grade is registered on a different day. The procedure described above is used. Transfer students may be registered on these evenings too. The principal and counselors can usually spend more time with the transfer student and his parents when separate registration days are used for each grade.

Advantages of a Spring Registration. Registration of students should begin early enough in the spring so that all students can be registered prior to the ending of school. The principal can then work on scheduling and assignment of students and teachers at the close of the school and during the summer. The principal will delegate as much of his responsibility to the registrar and counselors as is justifiable with their positions. Spring registration is certainly an activity well worth the principal's time and effort. Registration in the spring has several important advantages. These advantages are: (1) Students can carefully plan their program with the school counselors. (2) A longer time period can be used. Registration can be individualized. Parents can even be invited to school to participate in the planning. (3) The summer can be used to make adjustments in load and to work out special problems. (4) The opening of school can commence with little or no interference. Students can be assigned to class sections and notified of their completed registration. Figure 6.1 is a sample student registration form. Figure 6.2 is a "key sort" registration form used by many schools. Students are also registered with data processing equipment.

Figure 6.1

Student Registration Form

STUDENT REGISTRATION FORM

Name ______________________ Class ________

Address ____________________ Locker Number ______

Period	Class	Days	Room	Teacher

Figure 6.2

Key Sort Registration Card

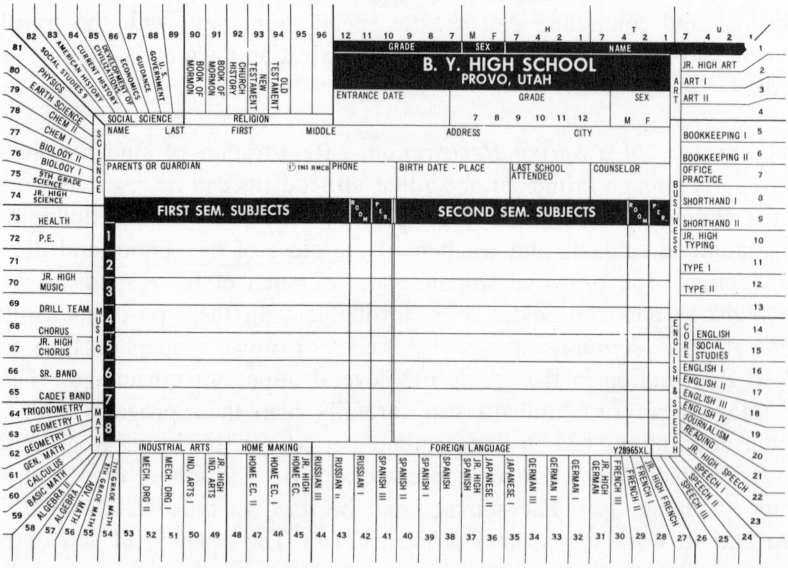

SOURCE: Brigham Young High School, Provo, Utah. Reprinted by permission of Brigham Young High School and Royal McBee Corporation.

Beginning Operations

There will be many problems arise the first day of school. New students to register, student schedules to change, distribution of books and supplies, assignment of lockers, etc. Teachers will also have unexpected problems. At the end of the first day the principal may desire to hold a short faculty meeting. The faculty meeting should be designed to solve problems not readily adjusted during the day. If registration is well planned, there may be few problems. All teachers may then be excused. Those teachers with special problems can then receive help from the principal. The principal should not prolong discussion and hold teachers for a long period of time. Teachers have first day adjustment problems of their own and should be allowed to work on their own materials and problems in peace and quiet.

During the first few days the principal will find it necessary to make many adjustments in the pupils' programs, balancing class size and adjusting room equipment and supplies. In addition, the principal should establish the procedure of student accounting. New teachers will need extra help in the process of reporting students who are absent. The principal must spend extra time with new teachers until habit routines are established.

Another problem involves getting the students enrolled in school who are not registered. Some of these students are still working on their summer job and plan to report "in a few days." Others have no intention of registering until they are forced in by the school attendance officer. The principal should report these students to the district attendance officers. If students get several weeks behind in the classes and are then forced into school, they seldom make a satisfactory adjustment.

After the school has been in operation long enough to establish routines, then fire drill practices should be called, the activity calendar for the year should be scheduled, and other policy matters of school operation should be discussed with students and teachers.

The School Year

With the school year safely launched, the principal is ready to look at the total school year. Schedules for supervision, extracurricular activities, intramural programs, club meetings, lunch hour dismissal, and curriculum improvement can be made. Improvement of instruction through aid to the teachers can be initiated. Guidance services can be coordinated. Policy and procedures can be clarified and improved. Many of the Chapters in this text are part of the principal's responsibilities for the ongoing school year. Therefore, these items will not be discussed in this chapter. However, there are many special problems associated with the closing of the school year that need special consideration.

Ending the School Year

The last few days of school are hectic, to say the least. The principal must get grades out for everyone, pay honor to students who may or may not deserve the award, wipe eyes and noses before and after graduation while awarding student diplomas, and keep the city together after graduation exercises. The teacher, who is sitting on his suitcase with hand outstretched for his final check, must be kept unruffled while the principal gives the teacher's reports, roll books, and statistical data the third degree. And when the last teacher is gone, the principal can say, "At last, everyone is checked out. Now I can go to work."

The activities related to the closing of the school year are of such vital importance that the principal is obligated to plan for them several months in advance of the closing date. Closing the school at the end of the year requires the full cooperation of all faculty and nonteaching personnel. The entire personnel is involved in some phase of these culminating activities. The principal will receive help and directives from the superintendent's office. A checklist of items for which the district is holding the principal accountable is usually provided. The checklist and directives are very helpful to the principal but do not constitute all of his year-end duties. The teachers should understand that they are not allowed to leave the school until all reports and final requirements are in to the principal. The principal is not released until his summation report is received by the superintendent. The importance of winding up the school year right cannot be too strongly emphasized.

Slowdown Activity Schedule.   During the spring of the year the school is bombarded with the many activities that take place in school and at district and regional meets. These activities involve track meets, baseball, F.F.A. judging contests, music activities, commercial contests, speech and drama meets, journalistic conferences, and many others. It is of particular importance to the principal that he understand the full load of activities that comes in the spring. The principal must schedule activities so they will be ended prior to the last week or two of school. The last few weeks should be regarded as a slowdown period—a period when students can concentrate on the completion of their academic programs and teachers can begin their work of ending the school year. There will be requests for all types of assemblies and special meetings. The principal should be cognizant that these requests will come, and he should channel them to sources whereby the requests can be handled without disruption of classes.

Final Tests and Report Cards. As part of each school year, the final tests are regarded by students as their culminating endeavors, and the report card is regarded as the achievement status symbol for the year's work. Report cards are discussed in detail in the chapter on evaluating student progress. An anachronism exists for the teacher in that he is expected to hold school and to carry out the teaching processes until the last day. In most cases final examinations are not given until the last few days. At the same time, the teacher must be completing the final grades so they can be placed on the student's report cards for distribution on the last day. Obviously, the principal must plan and coordinate these activities so that teachers are not giving their final examinations and determining grades too early; yet at the same time, the arrangements must be flexible enough so that grades can be placed on the proper cards in time for the final day. Traditions within a school usually have established this practice. A new principal should be slow to change these traditions. After a year in the school, the new principal will be in a better position to make recommendations for the improvement of these practices.

Grades, Credit, and Transcripts. In addition to the report cards, the final grades and credit to be given must be placed on the permanent record card of each student. This responsibility is frequently given to each teacher. The teacher must usually go through all the permanent record cards of all the students and have the grades and credit entered on the permanent record. At a special grade-level meeting these permanent record cards should be reviewed by the teachers. Where an omission is noted, a teacher should supply the necessary information to complete the required permanent record.

The principal must also prepare many transcripts of credit for graduating students who plan to attend colleges and universities throughout the land. Some students will request that copies of their transcripts be sent to a number of different schools. An orderly procedure should be established by which the secretary prepares the transcripts and forwards them to the principal for his signature.

Promotion and Retention. At the same meeting in which the grade-level teachers are checking for omissions in the grades and credits of students, promotions or retentions should be considered. At the senior high level, class failure usually affects only the one class as any class can be repeated as needed. Grade-level retention is not usually followed. At the junior high level, promotion is frequently by grade; therefore, retention is a problem. There are many factors that should be considered when a student is officially retained in a given grade level. The decision should involve all the teachers who know the student and who have had the student in their classes. Once the teachers in the grade-level faculty meeting have given their judgment, the principal should follow through to arrange a parent-teacher conference. Such a conference should not come as a surprise to the parents if the school has supplied them with reporting data during the school year. However, the principal must still be aware of the feelings and desires of the parents as well as the considered judgment of the school. There are times in which the teachers should be invited to a conference with the parents. The school policy should always be in the best interest of the student and for his growth and development

Honors Program.   At the close of the school year, usually the last day of school, special assembly programs are called by the principal and the student-body officers to pay honor to students whose achievements deserve special recognition.

These honor programs must be coordinated and handled efficiently in order to keep the attention of all students who are not directly involved at any given moment and to assure the proper dignity in the presentations. The principal must arrange the awards to be given from the student council, faculty, P.T.A., community organizations, and universities into an integrated program. The following are some of the specific awards and honors that should be considered at this time:

1. Letter awards for performance of extracurricular activities.
2. Honor achievements or scholarship awards given by the high school.
3. University scholarships.
4. Special recognition awards, such as outstanding student community worker.
5. Parent-Teachers' Association scholarships and awards.
6. Tributes to retiring teachers.

Graduation.   Graduation is the event long looked for and too seldom planned by the senior group. The graduation usually is in two major segments: a graduation program and a social following the program.

The graduation program should pay honor to the students and should end in their official graduation with the presentation of the proper diploma from the state. The graduation programs are usually of two basic types. The first type of program is prepared primarily by the administration of the school and the school district. This type of program usually involves addresses by a guest speaker, valedictorian, and salutatorian as well as remarks by the principal and a member of the board of education. The diplomas are then presented. The second type of program is planned and developed by the students. A program of this nature can be a series of talks by students, or it can be a production as dramatic as one of the school plays in which all members of the class are in some way involved in speaking, acting, singing, and other means of participation. At the conclusion of this type of program the class is officially presented by the principal to the board of education, and a few formal remarks are made and the diplomas are presented. The principal's responsibility is the same for either type of program. He must plan and supervise the program. The principal has fewer problems with the first type of program. Aside from the arrangement of the speakers and the detailed manner in which each member of the class will be presented and receive his diploma, his planning time is not greatly involved. In the second type of activity, the principal has the additional obligation to assign staff members, to work out detailed programs, to schedule rehearsal practices, and to coordinate all the production efforts, which usually involve the same members of the staff as would be involved in a school play production. Both types of programs can be uplifting and beneficial to the students and community. The degree to which these programs are successful depends to a significant extent on the quality of advance planning.

The second phase of graduation is the graduation social following the formal program. In most schools a school dance to which students, parents, and interested community members are invited is held. Such a dance must be well supervised and carefully planned. There is always the danger that some highly elated, recently graduated students will believe they have license to conduct themselves in a manner that would not be permitted at other school affairs. The problem is reduced if the senior class members are given adequate counsel prior to these graduation exercises and socials.

The greatest problems usually arise, not at the dance, but with the events that follow the dance. In some communities it is assumed that the graduating class or at least members of it will be involved in all-night activities of one type or another. Generally the school is in no position to supervise or control the various activities that take place after the dance, and many problems arise. The principal should clearly understand where his responsibility begins and ends, and he should make it clear to the teachers and parents where the school's responsibility begins and ends. If the school is not sponsoring an all-night activity, the parents should be notified that the school activity ends at the time of the social, and the school is not responsible nor does it encourage activities other than the social planned by the school. On the other hand, if the school should decide on activities that run until the early hours of the morning, the school should provide adequate supervision. Generally speaking, a guideline for the principal to follow would be to plan no activities in which the principal cannot be in complete control, as he is expected to assume the responsibility for the actions of the students.

Checking Out Teachers

The teachers and the principal recognize how the pressure of the last few weeks of the school year builds levels of expectancy and tensions within the student. The student is, of course, most anxious that school should end and usually displays exuberance when the final day occurs. What the student does not know, but the principal does, is that the teacher is equally as anxious to get away from school as the student. The closing of school is a major event for the teacher, and for some, the pressure mounts until it reaches a climax. The teacher has been building up for this event for some months by aiding with the spring registration, the spring budget, honor assemblies, and other such activities. As the final week of school draws near, there are some members of the faculty who have their suitcases and their golf bags packed and are anxiously sitting in their vacation cars. The principal must make it clear to the teachers that school must be held and that they must maintain effective control of all students until students are dismissed on the final day. Since tests are given in the last few days, special types of activities should be planned following the tests. These might involve oral tests and quizzes, special summary reports, or other activities. These activities should be planned far enough in advance so the students will recognize that these activities are a part of and can affect the final disposition of their grades. Teachers who plan in this manner have few problems and are able to complete effectively the work required. It is the teacher who is not forewarned and who does not plan who does not know how to handle the class during these last few days. The principal should work with new teachers and teachers who may have been special problems in previous years to see that these unwarranted events do not occur. In large schools, the assistant principals and departmental chairman can be assigned administrative responsibilities for check-out day.

Several weeks prior to the ending of school, the principal should provide the teacher with a bulletin giving adequate instructions and a checklist of items for which each teacher will be responsible. The check-out day for teachers should be firmly established as part of their year's contract, and teachers should understand that check-out time does not take place prior to this date. Unless the principal maintains a firm policy, many teachers in the school will be ready to check out the same afternoon that the students leave, even though all the closing activities have not been completed. Once a teacher is away from the school, it is nearly impossible to get the detail work done. The principal then finds himself in the position of doing the teacher's work in a less efficient way than the teacher could have done it prior to his leaving the school. The checklist and instructions to the faculty members will contain information about some of the following items:

1. *Report Cards.* Instructions will include when report cards may be marked, where the files will be maintained during this period, the date of distribution to the students, and any other special instructions that will assist the teacher in reporting procedure.

2. *Permanent Record Card.* In addition to report cards, the teacher has a responsibility to transfer both the grade and the credit received to the student's composite card. This card, when completed, is used by the secretary to transfer the information to the permanent record file of each student. The teachers should know where the composite cards will be maintained, whether the faculty members can take the card to the room or must complete it at its central location, and the time of the special grade-level conference when the student's records will be checked and any omissions will be cleared.

3. *Roll Books.* The roll book is the official record of the students' achievements. Any question that arises on the report card or permanent record card by student or parent will eventually be checked out in the teacher's roll book. It is most important that this roll book be accurate and readable. Teachers should be instructed that all marks should be in ink, pencil marks should be properly erased, every grade given should be substantiated with basic data, the credit given should be in keeping with the grade, the title of the class, the text used, and other vital data necessary for reference. If the student has failed, sufficient justification must also be in the roll books so that in later years the principal can refer to the book if needed to find out why the student failed. Such questions do arise and are invariably embarrassing if the grade cannot be substantiated and explained from the roll book.

4. *Statistical and Financial Reports.* Not all teachers are involved with statistical and financial reports. For those teachers who must keep records for state financing based on average daily attendance or total enrollment or for advisers who must turn in financial reports to the principal, uniform instructions should be given for the completion of these reports.

5. *Inventory.* The inventory would normally include an inventory form or forms along with instructions as to the type of items to be inventoried. A definition of the supply and equipment items should be provided.

6. *Requisitions.* Since the teachers assisted in preparing the budget at an earlier date, the requisition of items for the next school year is a formality that can be delegated to the business operations of the school. However, the checking-out period is the best time for the principal and the teachers to review the budget items and to order items that are needed and approved for the next school year. In accordance with district policy, these requisition forms can then be held at the school, turned in to the district, or given to the vendor with the proper instructions to fill the orders at the beginning of the new fiscal year.

7. *Textbook Inventory.* Where books are checked out to teachers who are responsible for a grade level and the books are furnished to students on a deposit or a no-cost basis, teachers are usually involved in receiving the books from the student, checking them, assessing any fine or penalty that may be needed, and storing the books. A summary of the number of books and their condition and location should be turned in to the principal. As part of the textbook inventory, the number of replacement copies needed should be indicated.

8. *Curriculum Report.* Each teacher should summarize a report on his curriculum for each course taught. The curriculum report should include a description of the program, the accomplishments of the year, the goals for next year, and the planned improvements to reach these goals. The curriculum report is one report that teachers could be preparing several weeks prior to the ending of school, and it need only be turned in at the check-out time.

9. *Evaluation of Administrative Procedures and School Policy and Recommendations for Improvement.* The principal should encourage all members of the staff to make recommendations regarding improvements of the administrative procedures, policies of the school, and the over-all climate of the school. Teachers should be assured that this evaluation, even though points may become personal, is requested only as an improvement report and that the principal desires such a report for self-improvement. An evaluation of this nature can be of great assistance to a principal for improvements that can be made in his own administration and in the administration of the total school program.

10. *Repair Requests.* Each teacher will know better than any other person the repairs that may be necessary in their physical facilities. These repairs should be itemized by rooms with adequate descriptions. The principal uses these requests to organize the work of the custodians during the summer.

11. *Keys.* As the last item the principal will request the keys from the teacher. The keys must be properly stored until the next school year. Some teachers who have summer programs and others who are known to live in the community and who will enter the school plant for curriculum planning should be allowed to retain their keys. Teachers who leave the community and have no intention of performing curriculum work during the summer should leave their keys at the school. The teacher who comes only occasionally to school can be accommodated through the school custodian.

12. *Payroll and Summer Address.* The teacher should understand that his final check is in the hands of the principal. The check is to be distributed at the time of completion of all the above items on check-out day. At this time the principal will request the teacher to sign a summer payroll address. This address is used both by the district office and by the principal for subsequent communications.

Checking Out Nonteaching Personnel

Besides the reports and information obtained from the teachers, the principal must also check out nonteaching personnel—school lunch workers, bus drivers, custodians, the school nurse, counselors, and other personnel. In each of the nonteaching areas, the reports required are somewhat similar to those required from the teachers. The school lunch director must submit an inventory of the equipment and supplies and must turn in a financial report and an annual school lunch report. These reports are usually reviewed by the principal and forwarded to the district school lunch supervisor.

The transportation report is one that can involve more detail than even the school lunch report unless it is organized at the beginning. School transportation is often a factor in state-support finance programs. The following transportation data are usually needed for the financial report: the student's name, his address, the number of miles he is transported one way and round trip, and the days he attended school. There are many ways in which this data can be obtained. The bus driver might keep a record, and this record would become the acceptable report. The school might keep the record for the report. One pattern often used as a double check, especially when the average daily attendance is computed as part of the state financial transportation formula, is to have the average daily attendance checked against the bus driver's report on the student. A procedure sometimes of great benefit is to have the bus driver review the accumulated student lists by grades for transportation in the same manner that the teachers would review these lists in determining the final grade and credit. This list might actually be a worksheet that has on it all these data including the names of students, both withdrawals and late entries, and the total possible days of attendance and the actual days attended. Such a composite list can be used by both teachers and bus drivers, as well as other interested individuals. Where the principal is held responsible for some phase of the transportation report, he must provide a release for the bus driver to the district office and district bus supervisor. The district bus supervisor will then know that the bus driver has completed his responsibilities to the school.

The school custodian does not usually check out in the same way that teachers, bus drivers, and cooks do at the end of the school year. The custodian is usually hired on a full-year salary. However, since the principal must turn in an annual report, the school year usually ends at the same time for the custodian as it does for other members of the staff. The principal is especially concerned with the care and upkeep of the school plant, and he will request the custodian to submit in detail a complete list of all repair and remodeling items that are needed. This report, along with repair reports from the teachers, will be compiled by the principal as part of his annual report. The custodian will also report on other problems involving building and grounds. The principal, working with the district building and grounds supervisor, will organize the summer work for the custodians.

The school nurse and other personnel involved in the high school health program would also complete a final report, which would show the activities, referrals, immunizations, etc., that have been completed during the year. As in the other areas, recommendations for improvement should be encouraged.

The counseling and guidance department of the school will have several reports that are unique to its area and that are usually turned in directly to the district personnel department. The principal, of course, signs and approves these reports. Since the federal government has supplied money through the National Defense Education Act and this money has been augmented through state funds, the reports required are usually on a state basis. Information required might involve dropouts, marriages, releases, enlistment in armed forces, information on the educable and mentally retarded classes, remedial reading, and other such programs encouraged by the state department through the district office.

The Principal's Annual Report

All the reports that have been discussed previously are preparatory for the principal in preparation of his final annual report. The principal's annual report can be a single report or it may be issued as several separate reports. The annual report supplies each district superintendent, members of the board of education, and the community with vital information that is needed for their understanding of the year's activity. The reports should be carefully prepared by the principal and used to the full advantage of the school. The report should provide information of two types: (1) accomplishments of the past year and (2) information for planning the following school year. The policy and instructions from the district office will determine the amount of detail to be included. The items discussed briefly below are generally regarded as basic to the principal's report:

1. *Curriculum and Instruction Data.* The principal should carefully summarize the curriculum accomplishments from the reports given by the teachers. Special attention should be given to new curriculum areas, outstanding achievements, special recognitions, and awards given to the school during the past year. Anticipated plans for the next school year should be itemized. Such plans should especially include details on experimental programs and other programs that are on a trial basis during the school year.

2. *Statistical Information.* In this category the principal should summarize the total enrollment for the school year, the average daily attendance, percentage of average daily attendance, dropouts, data involving marriage of students in school, awards given to students such as scholarships, number of students anticipating enrollment in college, and other such data of value to the district and the public generally.

3. *Financial Report.* The financial report should summarize the district budget for the high school including a breakdown of budget categories with expenditures and any balance or deficit that may be present at the end of the school year. A detailed financial report of the student activity program should also be provided. Details of this report are discussed in the chapter on school business administration.

4. *Recommendations for Improvement in the School Plant Facilities.* This report would be a summary of the items suggested by the teachers and the custodians supplemented by items deemed important by the principal. Normally the principal would place these items in a priority listing.

5. *Inventory.*   A school inventory would be included in a section of the annual report. The inventory would be a composite of all inventories prepared by the teaching and nonteaching personnel.

Other reports that might be part of the principal's annual report but could be submitted as separate entities would include recommendations regarding staff, the school history, the school scrapbook, a file folder of requisitions for the next school year, and a summary of names and summer addresses of all staff members. The annual report can sometimes be extremely detailed and include every affair of the school.[2]

The comprehensive annual report can be used to the greatest advantage if the report is placed in a form that will be most helpful to the superintendent in the preparation of his annual report to the board of education. Even if an annual report is not required by the district office, its value is sufficient that the principal should prepare such a report for purposes of evaluation, planning, and publicity.

Planning Ahead

The annual report should serve as a blueprint for the principal for the year ahead. The report should summarize the past year's accomplishments and should keynote the following year's needs and expectations. Since the principal does not leave the school until several weeks after the teachers leave, and sometimes does not ever check out, his summer time should be spent in planning the next school year. The steps for such planning have already been suggested. The principal should then implement his planning by completing the following items: (1) replacement of staff members, (2) ordering of equipment and supplies, (3) improvement of building and grounds, (4) registration and placement of students and teachers, (5) summer school registration and instruction, and (6) opening of the next school year. In all these areas the principal should use his time to advantage so that the following year will be even better than the one just completed.

Summary

The principal of a school is initially faced with "getting the school off to a good start." This phase of the principal's work requires detailed and advanced planning. The amount of time required depends on the work left by the principal's predecessor. The principal is often judged on the basis of these initial phases of the school program.

The new principal needs an orientation to the community, the district

[2] Lester W. Anderson, and Lauren A. Van Dyke, *Secondary School Administration* (Boston: Houghton Mifflin Company, 1963), pp. 543–45.

organization, the district personnel, and the school to which he is assigned. The orientation begins during the employment interview and continues throughout the year. A sociological analysis of the community is helpful. Interviews with the superintendent and district personnel help the principal to understand the school philosophy and current practices. The principal should get acquainted with his job by reviewing his duties as set forth in the district rules and regulations; studying the handbook for teachers; examining office equipment, records, and administrative facilities; interviewing the secretary and custodians; and examining the reports of his predecessor.

Once the principal has become acquainted in a general sense, he is ready to begin on specifics. Handling correspondence, inspecting the building and grounds, and scheduling classes are some of his early responsibilities.

Registration is held in both spring and fall. In the fall just prior to the opening of school or on the first day of school is the traditional time of registering. Spring registrations are most effective. Advantages of spring registration are found in improved guidance and program planning, longer periods of time to adjust the student problems and smooth out the registration problems, and the opportunity to begin the school year with a minimum of confusion.

With the commencement of school there are a number of problems to be solved such as adjustment of the class load and overloaded classrooms and provision of the teachers with supplies and materials. After a routine is established, fire drills, assemblies, scheduling of activities, supervision, club meeting times, etc., can be introduced. The principal can then begin to work more consistently on long-range improvement projects.

Winding the school up right is as important to the principal as getting the school off to a good start. The principal is responsible for seeing that an array of reports are available at the end of the year. He must carefully plan the concluding weeks of school. Such planning should include a proper scheduling of school activities to cause the least amount of interference with the school day. Other pertinent items are scheduling final tests and examinations, working with the teachers to complete report cards, disposing of promotions and retentions of students, and planning the graduation program and social activities.

The principal must also check out teachers at the close of the school year. Bulletins should be issued to the teachers indicating their responsibilities and giving adequate instructions for the preparation of all reports. A checklist should be provided for both the teacher and principal. When the teacher has completed all of the items on the checklist, and during the proper check-out time, the principal should receive the teacher's keys and summer address and officially release the teacher from the year's work.

In addition to receiving year-end reports from the teaching personnel, the principal must also check out nonteaching personnel such as the school lunch workers, bus drivers, custodians, nurses, and counselors. In each of these areas, special reports for the school district and the state are usually required. The principal must review the reports and certify them for accuracy.

The principal's annual report is a summary report of all reports previously mentioned. The principal's annual report is used by the superintendent in the preparation of his annual report to the board of education. The principal's annual report is basically composed of two parts: (1) a review of the statistical data, curriculum program, and accomplishments during the current year, and (2) the plans for the year ahead. Such plans usually consider the need for district participation and improvement of the high school program.

Once the annual report has been completed, the principal should then spend his time planning ahead and looking forward to the next school year. He should follow through on the following items: replacement of staff members, ordering of equipment and supplies, improvement of buildings and grounds, summer school program, registration and scheduling of students and teachers, and details for opening the school year.

SUGGESTED PROJECTS AND ACTIVITIES

1. Make up a checklist of the items that should be completed prior to the opening of school. Is this a workable list? How much time will be needed to complete the list?
2. Assume you are to be hired as principal in a community unknown to you. Make a list of the things you will want to know.
3. Using the community analysis guide presented in this chapter, analyze the community in which your university is located.
4. Sociodramatize or role-dramatize a superintendent-principal interview. What does each one want to know?
5. Refer again to Chapter 1 and the example of Transient High School. If you were the principal, what would you or could you do to smooth out the registration problems?
6. Find out how the schools near you register students. Have a student visit each school and report the different procedures used. Advantages and disadvantages should be given.
7. Visit a school involved in actual registration. Observe the organization and planning needed to provide a smooth operation.
8. Collect from the district office a checklist of items required of school principals to be completed prior to their completion of the school year.

9. Collect from a school a checklist of items to be completed by teachers as part of the requirements for ending the school year.
10. Debate: Students should not be given social promotions and a greater percentage of students should be retained.
11. Review a principal's annual report. Discuss areas of strength and weaknesses.

REVIEW AND DISCUSSION QUESTIONS

1. Discuss the statement "Plans well conceived can be executed with finesse," as related to planning for the opening of school.
2. How much time should a new principal expect to take in making certain that he is ready for school to commence?
3. When should the orientation of a principal commence? The orientation of a new teacher?
4. What are three main areas of concern in orienting a new principal?
5. What is meant by a community analysis? What is included in such an analysis?
6. What are some things a principal might do to become better acquainted with his job?
7. Why should the principal conduct a detailed study of the building and grounds? What items might be included in this inspection?
8. Describe the traditional registration procedure. How does this differ from a spring registration?
9. What are some of the special problems that a principal might be confronted with during the first day? The first week? Thereafter?
10. Why is planning so essential prior to and during the first phase of school operation?
11. Why is it difficult for teachers to complete the final report cards for distribution at the last day of school?
12. What are the differences and uses of the data required in (1) the report card, (2) a permanent record card, and (3) the teacher's roll book?
13. When should a student be promoted or retained?
14. Should high schools be involved in all-night graduation programs or socials that last until early-morning hours? If so, on what basis?
15. Why must teachers be checked out? If they are professional people, why shouldn't they leave as soon as they believe that they have completed their work satisfactorily?
16. What is the purpose of such reports as: inventory, textbook requests, and building repairs?
17. Why should the principal prepare a curriculum report that sum-

marizes the program, accomplishments, goals, and planned improvements for the next school year?

18. Which would be most effective, a short annual report or a long, inclusive report. Would it be better to have several separate reports rather than one big report?
19. Who is responsible for planning the summer school program?
20. When should the opening of the school year be planned?

SELECTED BIBLIOGRAPHY

American Association of School Administrators. *Off to a Good Start: Teacher Orientation*. Washington, D.C.: A.A.S.A., May 1956, pp. 1–24.

Anderson, Lester W., and Lauren D. Van Dyke. *Secondary School Administration*. Boston: Houghton Mifflin Company, 1963.

Ayars, Albert L. *Administering the People's Schools*. New York: McGraw-Hill Book Company, Inc., 1957, pp. 107–50.

Brookover, Wilbur B., and David Gottlieb. *A Sociology of Education*, 2nd ed. New York: American Book Company, 1964.

Burrup, Percy E. *Modern High School Administration*. New York: Harper and Brothers, 1961.

Cronin, Joseph M. "The Care and Treatment of First-Year Teachers," *Bulletin of N.A.S.S.P.*, October 1961, pp. 159–62.

Elsbree, Willard S., and E. Edmund Reutter, Jr. *Staff Personnel in the Public Schools*. Englewood Cliffs, N.J.,: Prentice-Hall, Inc., 1954.

"High School Graduates," *School Life*, August 1964, p. 7.

Jacobson, Paul V., William C. Reavis, and James D. Logsdon. *Effective School Principal*. Englewood Cliffs, N. J.: Prentice-Hall, 1960.

Miller, Dan (ed.). *Providing and Improving Administrative Leadership for America's Schools*. Fourth Report of the National Conference of Professors of School Administration. New York: Bureau of Publications, Teachers College, Columbia University, 1951.

CHAPTER 7

Schedule Making

Schedule making is a vital function of the principal. The principal, through careful or careless planning of the schedule, can affect instruction, curriculum, and learning to a far greater extent than he can through any other one-phase operation. It has been said that "the typical secondary-school schedule today is like a hand-tooled piece of furniture. It shows careful planning and work; all joints are tight and well fitted; there is evidence of the polish and design which result from a pride in craftsmanship. The daily schedule is truly a work of art, and the secondary school administrator an artisan. With precision he manipulates numbers of people through time and space, with the hope that learning will occur."[1]

The importance of scheduling is further emphasized in our changing high schools where experimentation and innovations are so prevalent. The implementation and success of the programs in team teaching, staff utilization, individual instruction, large- and small-group instruction, and curriculum improvement hinge on scheduling practices and techniques. The complexity of the task is dependent on the size of the school, number and types of programs, and background of the administrator.

In an early attempt to commit the complex task of master scheduling to the technology of a computer, the program requests for 1,500 students were fed into the machine. Amazingly, over 1,490 separate individual programs resulted. Since this first attempt, many years of research have

[1] Robert H. Johnson and M. Delbert Lobb, "The Transformation of the Sacred Secondary School Schedule," *California Journal of Secondary Education*, February 1960, p. 96.

been devoted to computer scheduling. Given the right type of information, it is now possible to schedule large high schools in a matter of minutes. However, most new principals do not have a computer available and must do their scheduling through the conventional techniques. Even those who do have computers must make the human decisions that are basic for accurate computer programming. Therefore, the principal must understand the basic information required to build a good schedule whether it is done by traditional methods, data processing, or computers. Because of the signal importance of this duty, this chapter is entirely devoted to details of schedule making. The basic information required, traditional scheduling techniques, as well as modern flexible scheduling practices are presented.

Gathering Preliminary Information

Need for Information.   Scheduling of classes is such an important duty that the principal cannot afford to go about it in a haphazard manner. Guesswork—even good guessing—is not compatible with the importance of this duty. The process of scheduling is technical. Specific information is required. Information is needed about the knowledge of the total curricular offering, required and elective classes, number of students to be enrolled, number and length of class periods, minimum and maximum class size, room capacities, number of students desiring each elective subject and qualifications and desires of the faculty.

Curricular Offering.   The first thing a principal must know is the curricular offering of his school. What classes should be offered? The answer to this question can best be determined by reviewing the schedules for previous years and by preregistration of students. In essence, the question must be answered on each grade level. Some subjects can be taken by students in a number of grades, for example, speech, physics, and typing. Other subjects are only offered on a particular grade level: physical education 7, homemaking 9, industrial arts 8, etc. The principal must know what students want to take and what they must take to meet state and local requirements.

A principal can find out what a student must take, i.e., what is required. States and districts have requirements for graduation. Elective classes are based on the students' choices. Students have to be given information about course offerings if they are to choose wisely. New course suggestions or offerings should be carefully explained.

Number and Length of Class Periods.   Once the curriculum is tentatively determined, the principal must know how many periods he will have during the school day. He also must know the length of the periods. The length of periods will vary from school to school and may range in traditional schools from 40 to 70 minutes. Some special classes may be even shorter or longer. In some of the experimental programs the class period is based on modules of 15, 20, or 30 minutes. A given course might require any number of modules. Subjects that require a block of time of one and one-half, two, or even three hours can be found in many comprehensive high schools. Where a class period extends over a period of 55 to 60 minutes, there are few classes that require a double period. When class periods are shorter, double periods in certain subjects are often needed, such as in vocational, science, and language classes.

A study of 938 high schools, or 97 per cent of the high schools in Illinois, Iowa, Minnesota, Missouri, and Wisconsin, revealed seven different types of schedules ranging from five periods a day of approximately 70 minutes with each class meeting four times a week, to 11 periods a day with an average of 50 minutes. Schools using 10 and 11 periods were on double sessions. The most popular number of periods was six (40 per cent of the schools), then seven (30 per cent of the schools), and then eight (22 per cent of the schools). The remaining 8 per cent used either a five-period schedule or more than eight periods. The length of the periods was related to the number of periods a day. The typical six-period day had periods of 55 minutes; seven-period day, 50 minutes; eight-period day, 45 minutes; and nine-period day, 40 minutes.[2]

Some advantages given for the typical 50-to-60-minute class period are:

1. It provides time for "learning by doing" rather than just lecture recitation.

2. Student growth and improvement of behavior can be observed and directed through longer time periods.

3. Problem-solving and critical-thinking approaches can be utilized more advantageously.

4. Study time can be supervised by teachers trained in the field under consideration.

5. Field trips can be taken without disrupting other class schedules.

The primary advantage of the shortened period in a traditional school is that students have a greater selection among classes and can take more elective classes.

The amount of time between classes and for lunch must also be determined. Three to five minutes between classes is typical. Schools built on a "campus plan" require more time between periods than do compact schools. The amount of time needed for school lunch and homeroom or

---

[2] A. W. Sturges, "Scheduling Practices in Midwestern Secondary Schools," *Bulletin of N.A.S.S.P.*, April 1962, pp. 43–50.

activity period must be arranged. The time for lunch period will depend on the size and location of the school. If the students go home for lunch, a full hour is often needed. If students eat at school, 30 minutes or less is sufficient. If the size of the school makes a double lunch period desirable (two 30-minute lunch periods), alternating the lunch period and the activity period, club meetings and homeroom can be successfully scheduled. Since most high schools provide a portion of the school day for these activities, combining a 30-minute lunch period and a 30-minute activity period on an alternating basis is a good workable plan. A common plan is to have two days for clubs, two days for homeroom, and one day for assembly. In large high schools three or more lunch periods must be scheduled to accommodate the number of students in the facilities available. A standard three-lunch-period schedule is 11:40 to 12:10, 12:10 to 12:40, 12:40 to 1:10. A five-wave lunch schedule became necessary in a large Seattle high school. The schedule was as follows:[3]

Lunch Schedule		4th-Period Class Groups	
1st lunch	11:40–12:10	12:10	1:10
2nd lunch	11:55–12:25	11:40–11:55	12:25–1:10
3rd lunch	12:10–12:40	11:40–12:10	12:40–1:10
4th lunch	12:25–12:55	11:40–12:25	12:55–1:10
5th lunch	12:40– 1:10	11:40	12:40

1st lunch—30 minutes and then to class for 55 minutes

2nd lunch—to class for 15 minutes; to lunch for 30 minutes and to class for 45 minutes

3rd lunch—to class for 30 minutes; to lunch for 30 minutes and then to class for 30 minutes

4th lunch—to class for 45 minutes; to lunch for 30 minutes and back to class for 15 minutes

5th lunch—to class for 55 minutes; then to lunch for 30 minutes

A new principal should generally use the same number of classes and time sequence as were used the previous year unless there is some demonstrated need for altering this schedule.

Number of Students. An adequate schedule cannot be made unless there is some indication of the number of students to be registered on each grade level.

There are several sources that are helpful when computing the estimated class enrollments.

1. District Enrollment Figures. The districts keep records of total en-

[3] John C. Maxey, "A New Idea on Lunch Period Scheduling—The Five Wave Plan," *Bulletin of N.A.S.S.P.*, April 1962, pp. 43–50.

rollments and average daily attendance. If the district shows 350 students enrolled in the sixth grade at the close of the school year, it is assumed that these students will be the group to plan for in the seventh grade. However, the principal must subtract the number of retentions from this total number of students. It is also helpful to look at a five-year enrollment history. A comparison of the enrollments of the previous sixth grade with the enrollment in the seventh grade should be made. An average for the previous three to five years would normally be used to determine the dropout or in-migration factor. It is assumed that if district conditions remain about the same, this average can be added or subtracted from the current sixth-grade enrollment. A formula for making this calculation would be:

$$\text{Estimated Seventh-Grade Enrollment} = \begin{array}{l}\text{Sixth Grade Enrollment} \pm \text{ average difference of} \\ \text{progression from sixth to seventh grade over a three-} \\ \text{to five-year period}\end{array}$$

This basic formula can be adapted for use at all grade levels.

2. Specific School Information. In large districts where there are more than one junior high school and more than one senior high school, the district's total figures are not helpful in determining estimated enrollments. Enrollments in the schools that feed into the junior high school or senior high school must be used. Enrollments for grades six, seven, and eight become the basis for anticipated enrollment in grades seven, eight, and nine. Table 7.1 gives the estimated enrollments based on the feeder schools.

TABLE 7.1 Estimated Enrollments Based on "Feeder Schools" for Lincoln Junior High School

Name of School and Grade Involved	6	7	8
Roosevelt K-6	25	0	0
Franklin K-6	50	0	0
Hoover K-6	90	0	0
McKinley K-6	100	0	0
Wilson K-7	0	50	0
Central K-8	0	0	35
Lincoln Junior High		265	315
Total number of students	265	315	350

Class-Size Policy. After the enrollments are determined, class-size policy becomes a factor for consideration. How many students should be taught in any particular subject? What is the desirable number? Each district will have different policies based on the philosophy and the financial ability of the district. Where such policy is left to the principal, the principal should consult teachers, superintendents, and other interested personnel. The traditional assumptions are that academic classes of English, history, mathematics, and science should enroll about 25 to 35 pupils. Typing, physical education, chorus, and band can handle double this number. Industrial arts, art, and home economics tend to limit enrollment to a maximum of 24. These figures are not intended to be a standard for new principals. The principal will have to determine this policy from conditions within his district. Some factors that affect the policy on class size are: philosophy about class size and teacher effectiveness, capacity of classrooms, special facilities in classrooms, teachers' feelings, financial ability, and instructional experimentation programs, such as staff utilization projects.

Room and Building Capacity. The principal must know the capacity of each room. This information can be obtained as part of the building inspection discussed in an earlier section. The principal should know the maximum capacity of the room as well as the desirable capacity. The desirable capacity is the number that the principal will try to maintain as the class size. The maximum capacity is that number at which there is "no room for one more even though the cause may be just." The room assignment schedule shown in Figure 7.1 shows how the room capacity is used in aiding the principal to assign rooms to the various subjects and teachers.

Figure 7.1

Room Assignment Schedule

Room	Absolute Capacity	Desirable Capacity	Subject and Teacher by Periods:						
			1	2	3	4	5	6	7
1									
2									
3									
4									

Estimating the Number of Class Sections Needed. Estimating the number of class sections involves two categories: required classes and elective classes.

1. Required Classes. The number of required classes is easy to estimate once the principal has the estimated enrollments by grades. If the

class is required on that grade level, the procedure is to divide the previously determined class-size policy into the estimated enrollment.

Example A:
Class in seventh-grade mathematics
Estimated enrollment in seventh grade is 605
Class-size policy, 30 students per class
Computation: 605 ÷ 30 = 20 sections
Example B:
Eleventh-grade American history
Estimated enrollment is 109
Class-size policy, 30 students per class
Computation: 109 ÷ 30 = 3.6 sections

In Example B it will be noted that 3.6 sections are needed. Since there is no such thing as six tenths of a class or six tenths of a teacher, an administrative decision is required. The classes in American history will have to be increased to 36 students in three sections, or the number of sections will have to be increased to four. Class size would then be 25. The decision will rest primarily on availability of classrooms and financial considerations. Since this same problem will exist in a required English class on the same grade level, the increase in sections would require the time of an individual teacher two periods of the day. If the rooms are available, the decision is usually determined by available finances. Another solution available to the principal is to reduce the number of elective classes by two.

2. Elective Classes. Elective classes and classes that are required—but not on any particular grade level—create problems that are not solved so easily. How many students will register for speech I, speech II, algebra II, and art? How many sections of algebra I and consumer mathematics are needed? There are two sources of information to help the principal:

a. Review of Previous Years' Enrollments. If a consistent pattern in registration can be found and if there are no changes in requirements, the previous records can be used as the basis for schedule making.

b. Preregistration. A more exact method, and one that brings adjustment to meet changing desires and needs of students and society, is preregistration. After proper counseling, students indicate which classes they are going to take based on an anticipated curricular offering. A preliminary registration form is shown in Figure 7.2. These preregistrations are then tallied on a master list. The number of students who would take an elective class can then be estimated with some degree of accuracy. Class-size policy for that subject is then considered. From this point, the number of sections is determined in the same manner as with required subjects.

Figure 7.2

Preliminary Registration Form

PRELIMINARY REGISTRATION FORM

Name _____ Phone _____ Present Grade ___

Address _____ Check: Boy ___ Girl ___

Period	Studies Desired Next Year
1	
2	
3	
4	
5	
6	
7	

Selections approved by:

Parent _____

Counselor _____

Registrar _____

After the tabulations have been completed, it can be observed that some classes may not have sufficient enrollment to justify the time of a teacher. Such classes may be removed from the schedule. Students should

TABLE 7.2 Tentative Summary of Class Sections and Teacher Assignment

Subject	Total Class Registration	Sections Needed	Teacher Assignment	
Social studies	167	5	Swensen	5
World history	62	2	Halley	2
American history 11	180	6	Halley	3
			Jones	3
American problems 12	54	2	Jones	2
Physics	48	2	Griffith	2
Chemistry	60	2	Griffith	2
Algebra I	130	4	Peterson	4
	. . .	. . .	. . .	
Total students	3,054	150	25 teachers	

be notified of this action so they may substitute other courses. The principal should prepare a summary sheet of the sections needed. At a glance, he can check to see if all the students are registered, how many teachers will be needed, and how to assign his staff. Table 7.2 is a section of a tentative summary sheet for determining number and assignment of teachers.

Traditional Schedule Making

Mosaic or Individual Method. The mosaic or the individual method of schedule making is used by most principals. The individual class sections are placed on a master schedule one at a time at the place where the principal believes there will be the fewest pupil conflicts. This pattern is continued until all sections are on the master schedule. A principal who has worked on the same basic schedule for several years will know the problem areas and will adjust the schedule accordingly. The greatest conflict to the pupils will arise from one-section classes and double-period classes. Therefore, a good practice is to start with the classes that have only one section or double periods. Then the classes with two sections are added. Another practice often used is to start with seniors, then juniors, sophomores, and freshman.

Conflict Sheet. A more exact method of eliminating conflicts is to build a conflict sheet. A principal can teach a clerk or paraprofessional the procedure. The conflict sheet lists subjects that will conflict if placed in the same period. Only one-section classes need to be plotted. Each student's preliminary registration is checked and one-section classes are plotted on a tentative schedule. A separate conflict sheet is used. The principal can see which one-section classes will conflict with other one-section classes. He can then shift the classes on the schedule so that the conflicting classes will be at different periods. A section of a conflict sheet is shown in Figure 7.3.

Mechanical conflict aids can be developed. The registration card can have numbers around the outside of the card. A hole is punched above the number. Each class on the schedule is given a number. The registration card is notched on each number that corresponds with the number assigned on the class schedule. On the basis of the conflict schedule shown in Figure 7.3, the following numbers might be assigned: physics, 1; algebra II, 2; chemistry, 3; Spanish II, 4; speech II, 5; art II, 6; chorus, 7; and band, 8. All registration cards are placed on a tray. A needle is put through number one. All students registered for physics drop out. Then the cards of physics students are taken, the needle is put through algebra II,

Figure 7.3
Conflict Sheet

	Physics	Algebra II	Chemistry	Spanish II	Speech II	Art II	Chorus	Band
Physics		THL II		III				
Algebra II			THL				I	II
Chemistry								
Spanish II					III		II	I
Speech II							I	
Art II							I	I
Chorus								THL THL
Band								

which is number 2, and all students who have a conflict between physics and algebra II drop out. This process can be repeated for the other one-section classes. The advantage of such a mechanical system is that both the student's name and his registration card with needed data are immediately available when smoothing out registration conflicts.

In many school districts it has proved practical to register students with machine-punched cards, as do most universities.[4]

The Block Method.   The block method of scheduling is used very frequently in the junior high schools. It can also be used in high schools to a limited extent. In this plan, students are assigned to a section or block. Each student remains in this section or block as he follows his program through the day. Table 7.3 is a simplified section of a seventh-grade schedule in which the block method of registration is used. It can be seen that conflicts can be completely eliminated with this system. How-

[4] "Case For and Against Machine Techniques for School Scheduling," *Bulletin of N.A.S.S.P.*, April 1959, pp. 195–98.

TABLE 7.3   Block Method of Scheduling Seventh-Grade Classes

Class	PERIOD STUDENTS IN BLOCK CLASSES WILL TAKE COURSE OFFERING				
	Block A	*Block B*	*Block C*	*Block D*	*Block G*
English	1	2	3	4	7
Arithmetic	2	3	4	5	1
Science	3	4	5	6	2
Social studies	4	5	6	7	3
Home economics (girls)	5	6	7	1	4
Industrial arts (boys)	5	6	7	1	4
Music (½ year—alternate)	6	7	1	2	5
Art (½ year—alternate)	6	7	1	2	5
Physical education	7	1	2	3	6

ever, the application works primarily with the required classes. When elective classes are available, the individual or mosaic method is more practical.

Scheduling for the Excess Students

Excess Students. When the population of a school district increases rapidly, a school principal must plan for an excess number of students. The normal school facilities under the normal school schedule will not take care of the increased number of students. Such conditions are sometimes temporary while a new school is constructed. At other times the condition becomes permanent. In either event the principal must find some way to house the excess students. Some of the practices that have been used are given below.

Overload the Building Facilities. Through the use of portable seats all available space within the classroom is used for student seating. Such a practice decreases the functional use of the room for nearly all activities but lecture discussion. Cafeterias, auditoriums, music rooms, and all special facilities are used whenever possible.

Double Sessions. Another solution is to have double sessions. One half of the students go to school from 8 to 12 A.M. and the other half attend from 12 to 4 P.M. The facilities thus accommodate double the normal amount. Class periods are frequently shortened to 40 minutes. All studying is done at home. Among the problems presented by this plan are: students receive little supervised study, bus transportation is more complicated, students have too much free time, teachers must work extra hours or share facilities with a whole new administration and teaching staff, and time for proper custodial care is reduced.

Extended School Day. Some school principals solve the excess-number-of-students problem by extending the school day.[5] School classes start earlier and go later. The number of periods is increased from six or seven to 10 or 11. Some students start as early as seven o'clock in the morning, and leave by one, two, or three o'clock in the afternoon. Others arrive at later hours but stay in school until five or six o'clock in the evening. The lunch schedule extends over several periods. Homeroom and activity periods are planned in the morning and afternoon so all students can be involved. Some disadvantages of this type of schedule involve bus transportation, supervision of students throughout activity and lunch periods while other classes are in session, and assignment of teachers. Both the administrative personnel and the teachers can be "worked to death" unless clear-cut policies regarding load and assignment are followed.

Platoon System. Another method is to block students into sections or platoons. This method was discussed under the block method of scheduling. Students are blocked in activity classes as well as required subjects. Creative activity blocks alternate with content blocks. Some schools report that this plan can increase the facilities up to one quarter of the capacity.

Multiple Load and Balance. Under a "multiple load and balance"[6] plan all available space is used except the visual-aid room and the cafeteria. The over-all capacity of the building is determined by the following computations: the library is to house 10 per cent of its capacity, the physical education class is to be held at 55 students, home economics and shops are to be held to their statutory limits, and the classroom is to be computed at $30 \times$ number of rooms $\times$ 1.2. Classes are arranged for library experiences. By planning to send four classes into the library for planned experience, extending the school day by one period, and using the building to capacity, the school capacity may be increased by 35 per cent.

Flexible Scheduling

Flexible Class Schedules. As a result of desires to change school programs consistent with the changing needs of our society, the many

[5] Samuel Forsheit, "The Extended Session Schedule," *Bulletin of N.A.S.S.P.*, September 1959, pp. 166–69.

[6] H. James Green, "Housing the Excess," *Bulletin of N.A.S.S.P.*, March 1960, pp. 85–86.

new experimental programs have been initiated. The traditional schedules are not adequate for most programs of team teaching, individualized study, television teaching, and large- and small-group instruction. Schedules must be made to fit the new programs and procedures. Flexible scheduling can make better use of the professional competencies of teachers and provide improved learning experiences for students.

Examples of Flexible Scheduling. A basic question might be asked, "How can a principal make the schedule more flexible?" Some examples will illustrate how flexible scheduling can be achieved:

Some schools have organized the school day into blocks or modules 15 to 30 minutes in length. Instead of the present six 55-minute periods, there are eighteen 20-minute periods. Classes or time in laboratories, libraries, and the like involve two, three, five, or whatever number of modules is desired. Other schools achieve flexibility by scheduling classes for two hours one day, one the next, and two hours the third. All sorts of similar modifications are made. The use of a "floating" period makes it possible for a student to have longer class periods for more subjects. Classes meet four days per week. Still other schools have added two periods in the day when larger-than-usual or smaller-than-usual groups can be assembled without disturbing other classes. One variation is to have no classes at all scheduled on a given day. The schedule on those days permits field trips, longer amounts of time in laboratories and libraries, meetings of special groups, and other types of activities. Scheduling similar sections of a given subject the same period permits team teaching with regroupings of students as needed. So does back-to-back scheduling involving two sections of students taking the same two subjects with the same two teachers.[7] Three or more groups may be scheduled in this manner for greater flexibility. Even greater flexibility can be achieved if some adaptation of staff and program reorganization, as suggested in the staff utilization studies[8] or *Images of the Future,*[9] is made. Electronic scheduling is desirable for this adaptation, and greater variations in the use of time, space, and personnel are possible. Acceptance of the point of view that facilities should be used more hours and days per week makes flexible scheduling even easier.

From these and other examples the following types of flexible scheduling may be found:

1. Class Addition and Exchange. At any given time or on a regular basis, a class may be scheduled with an extra period. All classes may

[7] J. Lloyd Trump, "Flexible Class Schedules," *California Journal of Secondary Education,* February 1960, p. 95.

[8] *Bulletin of the N.A.S.S.P.,* January 1962; January 1961; January 1960.

[9] J. Lloyd Trump, *Images of the Future.* Commission on the Experimental Study of the Utilization of the Staff in the Secondary Schools (Washington, D.C.: National Education Association, 1959), p. 12.

be shortened to allow for the extra period at any given time, or a regular schedule may be maintained in which each period is doubled in time once each week. Such a schedule can be made by shortening all other periods or by omitting a different period each day on a rotating basis.

2. Block Scheduling. Block scheduling has been practiced in junior high schools for years. A large block of time is given core, block, or unified curriculum programs. Adaptations would allow for blocking on any period if alternate days of the week were given to the periods requiring an extended time.

3. Laboratory Period Scheduling. Students who register for certain classes must also register for a laboratory period following the regular class. This class often becomes a two-hour block on alternating days. Independent study is frequently planned when the laboratory is not in session.

4. Rotation of Periods. A rotating period is designed to provide changes in the length of periods or to allow additional curriculum programs into the schedule by rotation and omission of other periods. The many variations of this pattern are limited only by the administrator's imagination. Some rotating variations are sequence rotation, displaced rotation, compressed rotation, expanded rotation, variable period length, and combination of these patterns.[10] An example of a rotating schedule that releases students and gives the teacher blocks of time that are periodically longer or shorter is shown in Table 7.4.

TABLE 7.4   Rotating Schedule

	Mon.	Tues.	Wed.	Thurs.	Fri.	Mon.	Total length of period
8:00– 8:20	1	2	3	4	5	6	20 minutes
8:25– 9:45	2	3	4	5	6	7	80 minutes
9:50–10:30	3	4	5	6	7	1	40 minutes
10:35–11:45	4	5	6	7	1	2	70 minutes
Lunch	—	—	—	—	—	—	—
12:30– 1:00	5	6	7	1	2	3	30 minutes
1:05– 2:55	6	7	1	2	3	4	110 minutes
3:00– 3:40	7	1	2	3	4	5	40 minutes
3:40– 4:00	8	8	8	8	8	8	20 minutes

Daily Demand Scheduling. There are some principals who desire complete flexibility, i.e., the opportunity to change the schedule daily as needed. Under this type of schedule a new master schedule and new

---

[10] Robert N. Bush and Dwight W. Allen, *A New Design for High School Education Assuming a Flexible Schedule* (New York: McGraw-Hill Book Company, 1964), pp. 88–117.

student schedules are made each day. Flexibility for program needs, teacher needs, and student desires is at a maximum. Such a program is described briefly below:

1. All computer scheduling will be initiated by Daily Request Forms either from the teacher or the administrative personnel. Student requests must be channeled through the individual teacher involved and be reflected in that teacher's request.

2. The scheduling will be done two days in advance. For example: Teacher requests received during school hours on Monday (day 1) will be scheduled during the evening and returned to the students to give them opportunity to make their selection of electives on Tuesday morning (day 2). This schedule will be processed and returned as the completed student daily schedule on Wednesday (day 3). The student will, therefore, know one day in advance what his schedule will be and can prepare accordingly.

3. The school day will begin at 8:00 a.m. and be divided into periods of time called "modules." Each module will be 20 minutes in length. The school day can be extended to any limit desired by students and staff.

4. Students will be grouped and report to the same teacher in the same room during Module 1 each day to work out their schedules and accomplish the "daily chores" necessary in every school.

5. All students will be scheduled and accounted for during every module of the day. An accurate system of student accounting will make it possible to locate any student at any given time with a minimum of effort and without confusion.

6. Scheduling requests may be made for any grouping of students from one individual to the entire student body or any combination(s) of students that may be desired.[11]

Team Teaching and Scheduling

Examples of team teaching can now be found in all subject areas and in many different organizational patterns. Scheduling for team teaching must be tailored for each unique program. However, basic to most team approaches are the following patterns: large groups, intermediate-size groups, small groups, independent study, and a joint conference time for the teachers. An example of a schedule where team teaching was practiced in a small school was that used at the Roosevelt High School. The entire class (125 pupils) was scheduled as one large group. The information from this schedule is given below:[12]

[11] Brigham Young University Laboratory School, Provo, Utah. Adapted for Computer Scheduling from the Brookhurst Junior High School flexible-schedule program.

[12] Matthew F. Noal, "The Need for and Effect of Schedule Modification in Walquist, Roosevelt, and Hurrican High Schools," *California Journal of Secondary Education*, February 1960, pp. 109–10.

The modified Roosevelt High School schedule reveals the application of the teaching-team technique in a small school. The entire eighth grade (125 pupils) was included in one large group. Four teachers were assigned three periods of the school day for the project. One period was used as a group planning and preparation period. Through a redeployment of teachers and a versatile grouping of pupils based upon needs, interests, and abilities, special competencies were made available to more pupils. And thus a better utilization of teacher time was actually accomplished.

The school faculty set up the following goals:

1. A revised school schedule providing a two-period block of time and a common consultation and activity period.

2. Better utilization of teacher time through additional periods for preparation of special services.

3. Increased teacher competencies through the utilization of a teacher's major skills for the benefit of the maximum number of pupils.

4. Better instruction through increased interest and additional time for preparation.

5. Enlarged and more skillful use of instructional material and equipment.

The organization pattern of the schedule follows:

Period	Monday	Tuesday	Wednesday	Thursday	Friday
1					
2					
3	Conference of Four Teachers				

A large high school of 1,800 students in Pennsylvania involves team teaching in English, history, and mathematics in a four-period block of time. The large-group instructional period can be in each of these subject areas, or it can be designated as an independent study group. A one-day schedule in which history is scheduled in the large group is shown in Figure 7.4.

Television and Scheduling

The use of television has aided in the development of large-group instruction. Extremely large, and often unused, areas of the school, such as the auditorium, can be utilized with open- and closed-circuit television. Better instruction as well as economics in finance can be realized. Miami

Figure 7.4

Examples of Large-Group Instruction Schedules

Period	Diagram 1			Period	Diagram 2
1	Large-Group History Lecture (90 pupils)			1	Large-Group English Instruction (Theme Writing — 90 pupils)
2	English Section 1	Study Section 2	Mathematics Section 3	2	Large-Group Testing (Mathematics — 90 pupils)
3	English Section 2	Study Section 3	Mathematics Section 1	3	Large-Group History Lecture (90 pupils)
4	English Section 3	Study Section 1	Mathematics Section 2	4	Common Study Hall (90 pupils — 3 teachers)

SOURCE: Edward Tracy and Carl H. Peterson, "The Easton, Pennsylvania, Team-Teaching Program," *Bulletin of N.A.S.S.P.*, pp. 145–55. Reprinted by permission from the *Bulletin of the National Association of Secondary-School Principals*, January, 1962. Copyright: Washington, D.C.

Jackson High School in Florida estimates a savings in teaching personnel of 3.8 teachers for each 1,350 students. Throughout Dade County the use of educational television along with an extended school day schedule has saved an estimated 12 million dollars over a five-year period.[13] How to schedule classes in order to gain the benefit of these facilities is shown in Weber High School:

We started scheduling all sophomore biology students for two sections, first and second periods and all juniors in U.S. history the same periods. This way the 400 in each section could use the same number of classrooms alternately with the auditorium on alternating days—one day in the auditorium for large-group instruction lesson via TV, and the next day in small groups of twenty-five to thirty for more personalized instruction with the teacher, giving time for questions and answers on the previous day's TV lesson.

Using this pattern, we scheduled through a seven-period day, five days a week—sophomore English in two sections against one section of health and one of eugenics; two sections of junior English against one section of American problems and one section of world history; and one section of senior English against a second section of world history.

In a school that was constructed to house 1,400 students, we are now handling over 2,100 students, utilizing a heretofore little-used 720-seat auditorium, but more important than this, it was done without destroying

[13] Loran L. Sheeley, "Improve Instruction—Educational Television in Miami, Florida," *Bulletin of N.A.S.S.P.*, January 1962, pp. 209–12.

the quality of education. To the contrary it is giving better instruction and our students are doing as well, or in many cases better than in the traditional situation.

The credit for this can go partially to the impact that TV has on boys and girls, more to the longer hours of preparation and better teaching of our teachers, and much to the cooperation of the students to make it work in a difficult situation.[14]

Data Processing and Computer Scheduling

Data Processing.   Many of the steps involved in registration and scheduling can be handled fast and efficiently through the use of automatic data processing. The first use of the equipment is to produce a registration card for each student from the student master card file. The name and code number of each course requested are written on the card, and holes are punched by a key punch operator or by a reproducer that has a mark-sensing attachment. A mark sense registration card is shown in Figure 7.5.

Figure 7.5

Mark Sense Card

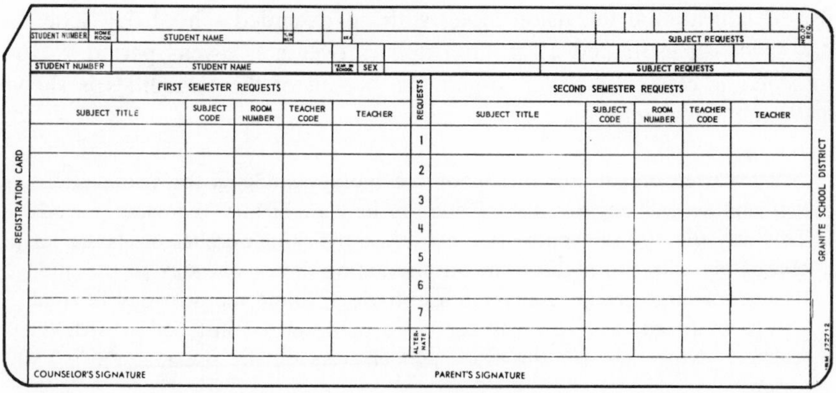

SOURCE: Granite School District, Salt Lake City, Utah. Reprinted by permission.

The registration cards are sorted to determine the number of student requests for each subject. Dividing the desired class size into each subject total will provide the number of class sections needed. The number of students can also be tallied by subject to provide data for conflict sheets. The course-requirements tally and the conflict sheet can then be used to assist in preparing the master class schedule. Once the master schedule is

[14] John A. Larsen, "Television and Schedule Revision in Utah," *California Journal of Secondary Education*, February 1960, p. 125.

made, machine procedures are available that provide sectioning of pupils and printing of individual class schedules and class rosters.[15]

Computer Scheduling. The daily demand schedule and other types of flexible schedules are receiving impetus through the use of computers. Some principals look askance at these new procedures and question the surrender of years of judgment to a machine. Some mistakes are usually part of any new experiment; computer scheduling is no exception. The following is taken from *Education U.S.A.*

CONFUSION ON THE COMPUTER

The Automated Age turned things upside down at Myers Park High School in Charlotte, N.C., on opening day. To simplify procedures, school officials decided to make class assignments for the 1,500 pupils with data-processing equipment. The results: One girl received a monotonous schedule with several lunch periods; another had only one lunch period, but it was at 8:45 a.m.; a student who had flunked French I three times found a friend in the machine—it advanced him to French IV; and another student almost got away with a restful semester—three study halls. School officials hastened to explain that the mistakes were due to "human error" at the school in preparing the data.

At the University of Texas researchers expect to be able to feed the statements a person makes into a computer and get back a written description of the individual's personality and how he can be expected to behave in certain situations. Just to be on the safe side, the researchers say psychologists will be around to give the computer analysis "the leavening of human wisdom."[16]

Aside from the interesting errors—made by human beings—computer scheduling is here to stay. Computer programs for a master schedule called "class" (class loading and student scheduling) have been developed by two school districts in Ohio. The programs and instructions are available through the I.B.M. Corporation and can be used with an I.B.M. 7070 computer. The Stanford University School Scheduling System project is expanding the number of schools served by their computer service each year.[17] One school of 2,000 students was scheduled in 15 minutes. With computer scheduling the teachers in the schools decide the ways in which they would like to teach their classes. They specify the staff to be assigned, course structure, length of class periods, size of classes, rooms and special

[15] James W. Whitlock, *Automatic Data Processing in Education* (New York: The Macmillan Company, 1964), pp. 48–65.

[16] "Confusion on the Computer," *Education U.S.A.* Washington, D.C., October 11, 1962.

[17] Robert N. Bush, "Decision for the Principal: Hand or Computer Scheduling," *Bulletin of the N.A.S.S.P.*, April 1964, pp. 141–46.

facilities to be used, and the number of sections. At the same time, counselors or other qualified persons prepare the course requests for each of the students.

These data, along with the student's name and general school information, are placed on cards. The cards are then placed in a computer. The vast number of "pieces of information" puts this task beyond the capacities of human beings. The result—tables showing who has been assigned to teach what, when, and where, and the names of the students in each class.[18]

Once the machine has processed these cards, it has become a storehouse of information. It could produce lists of student schedules, teacher schedules, room assignments, etc.

Summary

Scheduling of classes becomes one of the major tasks of a principal. Good schedules improve the course offering and improve the quality of the curriculum program. The education of the students is affected directly by the general provisions of the schedule and by the arrangement of the classes in the schedule. In order to build a good schedule the principal needs a considerable amount of preliminary information. Some of the information needed to build a good schedule is (1) the past curricular offerings, (2) the required and elective classes, (3) the number and length of class periods, (4) the number of students, (5) the class-size policy, (6) room and building capacity, and (7) the number of sections for each subject.

The traditional methods of making the schedule have been the mosaic or individual method and the block method. Under the mosaic or individual plan each subject is placed one at a time on a master sheet. Classes are arranged during periods in which conflicts are not "built into the schedule." A conflict sheet is used to provide the knowledge needed to avoid conflicts. Students then are registered according to their choice of subjects. In the block plan, students are assigned to a certain group. This group goes through the day together. Each group is assigned to classes. This plan is very effective in junior high scheduling. It is less adaptable to senior high where the choice of elective subjects is greater.

A problem confronting many principals is that of providing for an excess number of students. This problem exists temporarily for some principals while new buildings are under construction. For other principals the problem is a permanent one. Principals have at least partly solved this problem by methods involving overloading facilities, double sessions,

---

[18] Bush and Allen, *op. cit.*, p. 88–117.

extended school day, platoon systems, and "multiple load and balance."

In the past few years there have been many experimental programs involving team teaching, television teaching, large- and small-group instruction, and individualized study. These experimental programs have created the need for a flexible schedule. The types of schedules are geared to the particular experimental program, but basic to all of them is the need for flexibility from the traditional scheduling procedures. In recent years, the computer has been programmed for flexible scheduling purposes.

SUGGESTED PROJECTS AND ACTIVITIES

1. Visit a high school in your area. Obtain all the preliminary information indicated in this chapter. Lay out a master sheet with the number of periods across the top and the number of staff members on the left side, as indicated below. Construct a schedule, using the mosaic method, for this high school. (Remember to start with one-section classes first.) Present your schedule to the class for evaluation.

	Period							
Teachers	1	2	3	4	5	6	7	8

2. Assume you are principal of a junior high school. The following classes are required:

Seventh Grade	*Eighth Grade*	*Ninth Grade*
English 7	English 8	English 9
Arithmetic 7	Arithmetic 8	Algebra 9 or cons. math 9
Science 7	Science 8	(sections divided)
Social studies 7	Social studies 8	Physical education 9
Art 7	Art 8	Home ec. or ind. arts 9
Ind. arts or home ec. 7	Ind. arts or home ec. 8	Social studies 9
Physical education 7	Physical education 8	Music 9
Music 7	Music 8	Arts and crafts 9

In addition to the required class, you desire that every pupil attend a homeroom period and an activities period. The enrollments are as follows: seventh grade, 120 students; eighth grade, 90 students; ninth grade, 150 students. Ninety students desire algebra 9 and

60 students desire consumer mathematics 9. Assume a desirable class load of 30 students per teacher. The students eat lunch at school. Work out a schedule. Present your schedule to the class for evaluation.

3. You are principal of a senior high school. Compute the dropout factor or the in-migration factor for grades 10, 11, and 12 from the following enrollment data.

	9	10	11	12
1956	300			
1957	350	293		
1958	402	357	285	
1959	375	408	345	280
1960	380	375	412	330
1961	390	385	365	400

4. The classroom and building capacity of your school is computed at 1,500 students, on a six-period day. The enrollment has increased to 2,000 students. Based on an average of 30 students per teacher, compute the number of periods that would be needed to handle the excess students. Draw up an outline giving the number of periods, lunch times, and number of students who would be enrolled each period of the day.

5. Visit a computer and data-processing center. Discuss with the personnel the procedures that might be used in scheduling classes with computers and other data-processing equipment.

REVIEW AND DISCUSSION QUESTIONS

1. Why is schedule building a vital duty of the principal?
2. What preliminary data must be gathered before the principal begins constructing the schedule?
3. What type of information is needed to estimate the number of class sections?
4. How does a principal know how many students can be registered in each classroom?
5. Who determines class-size policy? Number and length of periods? Required and elective classes on each grade level?
6. Describe the mosaic or individual method of schedule making. The block plan. How do they differ?
7. When would a principal use the mosaic plan? The block plan?
8. What is a conflict sheet? How is one built? How is it used?
9. What plans have principals used to house the excess number of students? Describe each of these plans.

10. Discuss the need for flexible schedules and experimental programs in secondary education.
11. Give some examples of how scheduling might be done for team teaching, television teaching, large- and small-group instruction.
12. What is the job of the principal in schedule making?
13. How is the Daily Demand Schedule different from the rotating schedule?
14. Why does the use of data processing and the computer hold such great promise for the principal?

SELECTED BIBLIOGRAPHY

Allen, Dwight W. "First Steps in Developing a More Flexible Schedule," *Bulletin of N.A.S.S.P.*, May 1962, pp. 34–36.

Anderson, G. Ernest. "How to Schedule With a Computer," *Nation's Schools* April 1965 pp. 80–82.

Baker, W. "Streamlined Individualized Programming by Hand-Punch Cards," *Bulletin of N.A.S.S.P.*, December 1959, pp. 160–67.

Bulletin of N.A.S.S.P., January, 1959, 1960, 1961, 1962. Complete issues.

Bush, Robert N., and Dwight W. Allen. *A New Design for High School Education Assuming a Flexible Schedule.* New York: McGraw-Hill Book Company, 1964, pp. 1–197.

Bush, Robert N. "Decision for the Principal: Hand or Computer Scheduling?" *Bulletin of N.A.S.S.P.*, April 1964, pp. 141–46.

———. "Flexible Scheduling for What?" *Journal of Secondary Education*, October 1961, pp. 346–53.

———. "The Problem of a Flexible Schedule," *Educational Leadership*, January 1961, pp. 205–8.

Bush, Robert N., Dwight W. Allen, *et al.* "Flexible Scheduling," *Bulletin of N.A.S.S.P.*, May 1963, pp. 73–119.

California Journal of Secondary Education, February 1960. Complete issue.

"Case for and Against Machine Techniques in Scheduling," *Bulletin of N.A.S.S.P.*, April 1959, pp. 195–98.

Forsheit, Samuel. "Extended Session Schedule." *Bulletin of N.A.S.S.P.*, September 1959, pp. 166–68.

Greene, H. James. "Housing the Excess," *Bulletin of N.A.S.S.P.*, March 1960, pp. 85–86.

Morry, Michael A. "Scheduling Two Schools in One Building," *Bulletin of N.A.S.S.P.*, March 1964, pp. 99–104.

Robb, H. H. "Flexibility? Try a Module," *The Clearing House*, May 1962, p. 550.

Robinson, E. D. "New Look at Scheduling in the Small School," *Bulletin of N.A.S.S.P.*, March 1960, pp. 50–52.

"Team Teaching and Scheduling," *Bulletin of N.A.S.S.P.*, January 1960, pp. 79–93.

Trump, J. Lloyd. *Images of the Future.* Commission on the Experimental Study of the Utilization of the Staff in the Secondary School, N.A.S.S.P., 1959, pp. 1–30.

Wallace, Charles E. "Flexible Scheduling for the School Year," *Journal of Secondary Education*, March 1962, pp. 132–35.

Whitlock, James W. *Automatic Data Processing in Education.* New York: The Macmillan Company, 1964.

Yerby, Robert M. "Flexible Scheduling: Some Critical Questions and an Experiment," *Journal of Secondary Education*, March 1962, pp. 197–200.

CHAPTER 8

Organization, Administration, and Utilization of the Staff

The educational revolution that is occurring all over the United States and in foreign countries is affecting personnel administration in the selection, organization, and utilization of school staff members. The principal of the secondary school is in an enviable position—right in the center of all the activity.

At no period in educational history has the principal been provided with such a wide opportunity for experimentation in personnel administration. The extensive research and experimentation by the Commission on the Experimental Study of the Utilization of the Staff in the Secondary School,[1] culminating in *Images of the Future,*[2] *Focus on Change—Guide to Better Schools,*[3] and *And No Bells Ring,*[4] have created revolutions in organization and staffing patterns. Nongraded schools, continuous progress instruction, individual instruction, team teaching, and flexible scheduling are a few of the observable results. The principal should be actively involved in these new approaches to school organization and personnel administration.

---

[1] National Association of Secondary-School Principals, *Bulletin of N.A.S.S.P.,* January, 1962, 1961, 1960, 1959, 1958. The complete issues are reports of these projects.

[2] J. Lloyd Trump, *Images of the Future* (Washington, D.C.: National Association of Secondary-School Principals), 1959.

[3] J. Lloyd Trump and Baynham Dorsey, *Focus on Change—Guide to Better Schools* (Chicago: Rand McNally and Co., 1961).

[4] *And No Bells Ring.* 58 min., Parts I and II, 16 mm. sound film, b & w (Washington, D.C.: National Association of Secondary-School Principals).

Selection of Staff Members

Determining Needs.   Each year the principal must determine the staff needs of the school. He must know the anticipated enrollment and the number of sections of required and elective classes. He must know the number of replacements for teachers who have left his school. The method of determining the number of teachers needed from these data has been provided in previous chapters on registration and scheduling. The exact number of teachers allocated to a school is influenced by the philosophy and wealth of the district and the state school finance formulas. Also affecting the type and qualification of the new staff members will be the type of organization that is placed into operation. On the basis of the known number of vacancies for specific assignments, the principal is then ready to "look the field over."

Who Selects Personnel.   The boards of education actually hire the teacher, but for practical purposes they act through their agent, the superintendent. The superintendent recommends candidates to the board of education. In some districts the superintendent makes the selection without consulting building principals. In large school systems, the personnel director may be given this responsibility. If selection is to be made without involving the principal, the principal must furnish the district detailed descriptions of his needs.

Because of the unique combinations and specialized needs of secondary schools, the principals are usually involved in a cooperative selection of staff members along with district personnel. In large schools department chairmen and occasionally teacher committees may be involved.[5] It is highly recommended that the principal have an active part in the selection of his teachers.

In team teaching programs it is often wise to involve other members of the team along with the principal and district personnel officer in the selection of teachers to replace vacancies on a team.

Availability of Teachers and Sources of Supply.   For the past two decades there has been a shortage of qualified teachers throughout the United States. The National Education Association estimated a shortage of 134,000 teachers in 1962.[6] At the same time the report indicated that the total number of college graduates in all fields was only 106,000. The

---

[5] Charles W. Mintzer, "A Plan for the Selection of New Staff Members," *Bulletin of N.A.S.S.P.*, October 1951, pp. 63–64.

[6] Research Division, National Education Association, *Teacher Supply and Demand in Public Schools, 1962* (Washington, D.C.: The Association, 1962), p. 21.

report shows the areas of need as follows: 19,000 teachers were needed for replacement purposes, 35,000 to fill new openings due to increasing enrollments, 30,000 to relieve overcrowding, 25,000 to provide special educational services, and 25,000 to replace the unprepared. The principals cannot satisfy all their needs with highly qualified personnel for many years in the future. However, the general picture should improve during the next decade because the colleges are now being swamped with students.

Although the general picture reveals a shortage, there are some areas, such as social studies, where shortages do not exist. The secondary schools situated in or near a university usually can be highly selective in their recruitment practices. This condition exists owing to the cultural advantages of a university, to the number of students pursuing higher degrees on a part-time basis, and to the availability of women teachers who are supporting their husbands who are still in school. Districts that have unusually high salary schedules are also able to attract enough candidates so that a selective system can be used.

The primary source of supply for new teachers is the teacher placement bureau associated with a teacher training institution. About 62 per cent of all teachers hired are new and are hired through the teacher placement offices.[7] Other sources of supply are teachers who left to assume home duties but are now available and persons who became certificated but entered other fields. The principal will know many of these individuals. Some he may desire to recruit on a permanent basis—others he may wish to employ as part-time aides, clerks, or home readers for themes, papers, and tests.

Selecting the Teachers.　All states have teacher certification standards. However, the standards vary from state to state. Even within a state, teacher training programs can be very different and still meet basic state requirements. Further, the prospective teachers are of diverse ability, personality, and readiness for teaching. The principal's task is to match job needs against personal qualifications and prospect against prospect. He should have one question foremost in his mind, "Who is the best candidate for this position?"

To answer this question he will review completed application forms, credentials from teacher placement bureaus, letters of reference, tests, transcript of credits, and subject specialties. He may even call the previous principal or superintendent. An analysis of these data against the requirements for the position will eliminate many candidates.

The remaining candidates should be observed in a teaching situation whenever possible and invited to make an appointment for a personal

---

[7] *Ibid.*, p. 22.

interview with the principal and district personnel. The manner in which the interview is conducted and the information obtained can be most helpful in making the final decision. The principal can probe for strengths and weaknesses, determine personality characteristics, and assess the desires of the candidates to be a success. Most interviewing procedures are of the pleasant, get-acquainted type. A few districts regard the interview as a potential testing situation where the candidate is assessed under pressure. Such an interview usually involves three phases: (1) exploratory, (2) attack or "grill," and (3) decompress or unwind.[8] Whether the interview is best conducted as exploratory or in depth under pressure is debatable. But in any interview both parties should provide and obtain the necessary information.

Orientation of New Teachers

Need for Orientation.   The first days at school are the most difficult for new teachers. There are so many things that the teacher does not know about the community, the school plant, the children, fellow teachers, instructional materials, and operational procedures. Principals and experienced teachers settle into a routine and tend to forget the difficulty of first-year adjustment. A new teacher—like all teachers—wants to succeed. Many of the mistakes and embarrassing situations in which new teachers find themselves could be eliminated through proper orientation procedures.

Orientation Begins with Application and Hiring.   The orientation procedures should begin at the time a teacher makes application to the district. The first phase of orientation is at the district level, where the prospect is acquainted with the general information about the school system. Once a contract is signed, the district should provide the new teacher with copies of the district handbook on policies and procedures. Addresses—current, summer, and permanent—should be obtained. Payroll forms should be completed. Salary conditions including deductions should be explained.

The new teacher should next report to the school of his assignment, where the principal can provide information about the school, a copy of the school handbook, and policies and procedures. The principal should obtain personnel data for future reference and for purposes of assignment to committees and other student activities. The current, summer,

---

[8] "The Teacher Selection Interview," *School Management*, December 1964, pp. 35–37. Reprinted in *The Education Digest*, March 1965, pp. 35–38.

and permanent addresses should also be made available to the principal. The principal should give the new teacher a tour of the school, especially of the area assigned to the teacher. Curriculum guides, textbooks, and other specific aids for advanced planning should be given to the teacher. The teachers begin at this moment to prepare for their assignments and are much more easily adjusted to the teaching situation when school commences.

Areas of Concern for New Teachers. The school systems have found that new teachers have questions and are concerned about the following:

1. *The terms and conditions of employment* including the teaching assignment, certification, health services, sick leave, salary, pay days, working hours, extra assignments, retirement benefits and inservice training requirements.
2. *The new community*—living accommodations, social, cultural, and recreational activities, church facilities, customs and taboos affecting teachers, the people and their clubs and organizations, and the attitude of the community toward the school.
3. *The school system*—its facilities, staff help for teachers, availability of materials for use in teaching, and its general philosophy, practices, and operating procedures.
4. *The administrative staff*—the educational viewpoint of the superintendent, how the principal works with teachers, the assistance given by supervisors and other special personnel.
5. *The school*—its physical arrangements, its facilities and equipment for teaching, rules and regulations, requirements concerning records and reports, its personnel and staff and their arrangements for helping the new teacher.
6. *The teachers*—their professional organizations, the clubs to which they belong, their social and recreational activities, and their community responsibilities.[9]

Specific Help Needed and Ways of Providing for It. The specific problems to be solved through orientation will vary with each school district. One of the best ways to get at these unique problems is to ask teachers who have recently come into the school district about the things that caused them concern. Another method is to record the type of questions and information requested of the principal during the early period of orientation and during the first year.

The American Association of School Administrators has identified some

[9] American Association of School Administrators, *Off to a Good Start: Teacher Orientation* (Washington, D.C.: The Association, 1956), pp. 5–6. Reprinted by permission of the American Association of School Administrators.

of the kinds of help needed and ways of providing for it. These are given below:

Understanding Terms and Conditions of Employment

1. Include full description of job with announcement of vacancy and application forms.

2. Take time for complete and honest discussion of job during interview.

3. Give full explanation of salary, certification, benefits, assignment (as nearly as can be determined), and other terms of employment at time contract is offered.

4. Review regulations governing rights, privileges, and restrictions at time of reporting and later as questions arise.

Becoming Acquainted with the Community

1. Enclose description of community with announcements and application forms.

2. Take time for more information and questions during interview.

3. Arrange for visit to community before hiring or between employment and reporting time.

4. Acquaint teacher with facilities for transportation, banking, shopping, and medical, dental, and other personal services.

5. Prepare and put in teachers' hands listings of housing, with descriptive information.

6. Arrange tours of the community to become acquainted with its business, cultural, educational activities, for personal reasons and for teaching background.

7. See that invitations are extended to attend and take part in civic, religious, social, cultural, and recreational activities.

8. Enlist the help of organizations in arranging special events for introducing new teachers.

Getting to Know School System, Its People and Its Organization

1. Provide information about organization of school system at time application is made and during interviews.

2. Furnish copies of rules and regulations, statements about policies, philosophy, and practices. (A number of school systems incorporate this and other information into a handbook for distribution.)

3. Describe help available, such as teaching materials, supervisory assistance, and special services.

4. Place copies of courses of study, textbook lists, and similar materials in hands of incoming teacher.

5. Put new teacher on mailing list for all bulletins, newsletters, and other publications sent to teachers.

6. Arrange for correspondence by superintendent, principal, supervisors, and fellow teachers prior to reporting.

7. See that new teachers meet and talk with superintendent.

8. Schedule conferences with supervisors and other staff personnel responsible for services to teachers prior to opening of school.

Learning About the School to Which Assigned

1. Take teacher on tour of building for becoming acquainted with layout and facilities.

2. Arrange meetings with building principal to learn about obtaining supplies and equipment, keeping records and making reports, handling problems of classroom management and organization, and the other details of school operation.

3. Assign an experienced teacher as a personal counselor and adviser.

4. See that there is time for getting acquainted with other members of the faculty and staff.

5. Allot time to work professionally with faculty in meetings before school opens.

6. Acquaint the new teacher with her professional organizations.

Adjusting to the Teaching Job

1. Set aside time of principal and supervisors to help in planning work, locating sources of material, handling problems of classroom organization and management, making pupil evaluations, and preparing reports.

2. Make time freely available for talking over problems as they arise in private conferences with principal, supervisors, and others, as often as either party feels the need.

3. Assist the new teacher in getting to know pupils and parents.

4. Arrange opportunities for viewing demonstrations and observing experienced teachers at work.

5. Schedule meetings of new teachers for discussion of their own special problems.

6. See that the new teacher is given a reasonable and fair teaching load, commensurate with her training, skills, and experience.

7. Provide opportunities for continuing and expanding professional preparation begun in the college, by offering inservice education activities especially designed to help new teachers.[10]

Orientation and Preschool Workshops and Institutes. As part of the orientation plan the teachers should be on the job for several days to a week prior to the opening of school. Some of this time can be spent in district orientation. The major portion of the time should be spent in the individual schools. Books, supplies, and other teaching materials should be issued to teachers; lesson plans prepared; instructions on registration assignments given; policy for school operation reviewed and changed where needed. Special instructions can be given to new teachers.

In addition to the general orientation, many districts schedule a day or a half-day institute and workshop. The institute is designed to get teachers back into the "teaching frame of reference." The institute is

[10] *Ibid.*, pp. 11–15.

often used to begin the in-service educational program sponsored in the district.

The Principal's Role in Orientation.   A good orientation program should be district-wide. But there are many facets of the program that can only be carried out effectively by the school principal. The principal sets the climate in which the day-to-day teaching job is done. He is responsible for the organization and operational procedures of the school. Acquainting teachers with their work, the school procedures, and the consideration for the teachers' general well-being is the principal's responsibility. The principal's goal of improvement of instruction can be greatly advanced by a good orientation program sponsored and supported by the administration. Since the principal cannot possibly answer all questions when the answers are needed, the teaching staff should be involved in planning and carrying out orientation procedure. Assignment of new teachers to regular faculty members as part of a "buddy system" is helpful. The following new-teacher-orientation checklist will aid the principal in more adequately carrying out his responsibilities in a consistent manner.

New-Teacher-Orientation Form and Checklist

1. Personal information and schedule:
   Name_____ Address_____
   Major_____ Minor_____ Phone:_____
   Schedule:
   1. _____   4. _____
   2. _____   5. _____
   3. _____   6. _____
   Extracurricular assignment_____
2. When the new teacher has signed his contract, and prior to opening institute, he should:
   a. Receive a copy of the school district policies and procedures—teacher and student sections
   b. Receive letters from supervisor and principal
   c. Report to principal with completed copy of a personal data form
   d. Receive his teaching schedule
   e. Receive teaching materials, textbooks, workbooks, and a list of audio-visual equipment
   f. Receive a copy of teacher and student handbooks
   g. Plan summer appointments for discussion and planning
3. At the beginning institute he should:
   a. Meet with district staff
      (1) Be introduced to the administration and new teachers
      (2) Review the district facilities

New-Teacher-Orienation Form and Checklist (Continued)

      (3) Review professional organizations

      (4) Review credit union and other service organizations

      (5) Meet with supervisor and principals

          (a) Slide-sound story or other orientation to the secondary schools in the district

          (b) Instructions by supervisor and principal

  b. Meet in assigned school with his principal

      (1) Review school policies and regulations

      (2) Review curriculum schedule

      (3) Review reports that will be required during year

      (4) Be given special assignments

      (5) Be assigned to a staff member (buddy system)

4. During the school year he should:

  a. Receive classroom visits

  b. Have private consultations

  c. Be community oriented

  d. Be evaluated for improvement purposes

Organization of the Staff

Organizing Administrative Personnel. Basic to all organizations is some form of division of responsibility and authority among administrative personnel. "Who is responsible to whom?" is often questioned in large school systems. The terms *line* and *staff* are used to clarify concepts of responsibility and authority. Line authority is the direct authority delegated by appropriate officials. It is the official "chain of command." In the school system line authority goes from the board of education to the superintendent, to the principal, to the teachers, and to the student. However, most school systems need additional personnel to carry out the multitudinous functions, such as assistants, directors, and supervisors. These supplementary personnel are called staff personnel. They work with the school in the area of their responsibility. The principal works and cooperates with them, but they do not carry official authority over him.

Within the school there are also line and staff personnel. In small schools line authority is from principal to teacher. In large school systems assistant principals and departmental chairmen may be given line responsibilities and authority, as shown in Figure 8.1. Where line authority is not delegated to them, they become staff members. Other staff members are nurses, counselors, attendance officers, social workers, and other personnel who work with students and teachers.

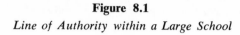

Figure 8.1

Line of Authority within a Large School

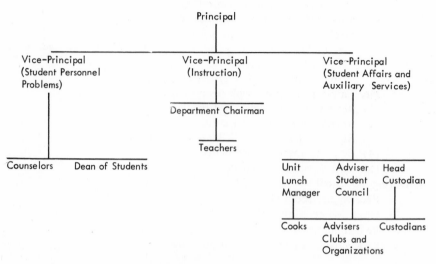

The Principal's Role in Staff Organization. The job of the principal has been discussed in Chapter 1 and throughout this book. As related to organizing the staff, his job is to see that responsibilities are delegated and that all members work as a team toward a common purpose. He may delegate responsibilities and authority to line and staff personnel as he believes to be in the interest of the school. Among the duties that he retains are (1) selecting assistants, departmental chairmen, coordinators, teachers, and other personnel; (2) evaluating and rating staff members where required; (3) building the schedule; (4) assigning teachers; (5) doing in-service work with teachers for improved teaching techniques; and (6) directing innovations, experiments, and research.

The method or plan by which the principal hopes to effect the best organization of his staff is determined largely by the size of staff and his philosophy about new approaches to education. In small schools he works directly with the teachers. In large schools he frequently works through his assigned staff members. Regardless of the size of school, he should utilize the strengths of all personnel to the best advantage. Further discussion is presented on this topic under the section "Utilization of the Staff."

The Assistant Principal. The assistant principal is the professional administrator next in authority to the principal. The larger and more complex the school, the greater the need for assistants. In a small high school the assistant may be a full-time teacher who assumes responsibilities in the absence of the principal. In the large high schools, the assistant may be a highly specialized administrator who is assigned one phase of administrative activity, such as curriculum, student personnel, or student affairs. (See Figure 8.1.)

The duties assigned to the assistant principal have traditionally been those the principal felt least qualified to handle or those he preferred not to handle. Student discipline and attendance are usually always assigned to an assistant. Other duties frequently assigned are other pupil personnel functions, student activities, and clerical functions.[11]

As schools innovate and move to new approaches in curriculum, organization, and teaching methods, the role of the assistant principal also seems to change. As the school takes on a "new look," supervision, scheduling, and curriculum planning are being added to the list of responsibilities.[12]

The number of assistant principals in each school is most often based on a ratio to the number of students. The ratio varies from district to district and from state to state, but it has been reduced from one assistant to about 2,000 students to one assistant to 500 to 850 students.[13] However, the many added responsibilities, functions, and changes in the modern schools require more and improved leadership. At the secondary school level a half-time assistant principal should be added when the number of students approaches 200 to 300, and a full-time assistant should be added when the number reaches 500 to 700. In schools where extensive experimentation and innovation are taking place, additional administrative staff is required to permit the principal to handle the many new problems and to allow time to show the many visitors through the program.

The Departmental Chairman. The department is organized to improve curriculum programs and teaching techniques and to coordinate activities within the curriculum area. Since the principal cannot be highly qualified in all subject areas, he appoints an appropriate chairman. Some of the duties of a departmental chairman are those concerning: (1) new programs and innovations within the subject field; (2) in-service education of teachers within the field; (3) development of courses of study; (4) coordination with other departments; (5) investigation of new textbooks,

---

[11] E. Dale Davis and John Moore, "The Assistant Principal in the Junior High School," *Bulletin of N.A.S.S.P.*, January 1965, pp. 1–4. Melvin Michaels, "The Role of the Assistant Principal," *Bulletin of N.A.S.S.P.*, January 1965, pp. 5–11.

[12] Philip C. Wells, Robert H. Nelson, and Earl M. Johnsen, "The Assistant Secondary School Principal," *Bulletin of N.A.S.S.P.*, January 1965, pp. 15–25. T. Marcus Gillespie, "The Assistant Principal: Status, Duties, and Responsibilities," *Bulletin of N.A.S.S.P.*, December 1961, pp. 59–68.

[13] *Ibid.*, p. 18.

curriculum materials, and audiovisual aids; (6) recommendation of assignment of teachers; (7) organization and planning of departmental meetings; (8) examination and evaluation of standards and measurements within the department; (9) aid for new teachers to become adjusted; and (10) supervision of the instruction within the department.

Too frequently the departmental chairman is simply a glorified teacher. However, in our rapidly changing society with its increased demands for specialization, the departmental head should be superior in teaching skills and in curriculum development and, above all else, a dynamic, creative administrator.

Other Coordinate Administrators. Under the principal and assistant principal are other administrators, such as the dean of boys, dean of girls, activity coordinator, and other responsible administrators. The principal delegates responsibility and authority to each of them at the level at which they are working. Each has authority in his area of responsibility over teachers and students, but at the same time must work with them to be effective in his role. Each school may assign and describe the responsibilities to meet the unique needs of the school's organizational structure and curricular programs.

Committees. To effectively carry out supervision assignments, planning sessions, study assignments, and other responsibilities, the principal forms committees. Committees should not be created unless cooperative and representative effort can produce effective decisions or an improvement in faculty morale. (See Chapter 2 and the discussion of when to use the group.) Some job functions may require certain standing committees; other committees should be formed to handle special problems. Out of a committee study have developed many general faculty projects of significance to the school. Many of the current innovations started through small group discussion, study, and promotion.

Faculty Meetings. The faculty meeting is one of the most important meetings through which a principal can communicate with his staff on items of business on development of policy and the improvement of instruction. The faculty meeting is the one meeting in which the principal can seek unity from all members for common problems. Wallazz B. Eaton stated, "All groups when they organize have underlying motives for their existence. The group endeavor is the fulfillment of common objectives and is the base for existence."[14]

[14] Wallazz B. Eaton, "Democratic Organization—Myth or Reality?" *Bulletin of N.A.S.S.P.*, October 1961, pp. 66–78.

The faculty meeting is the responsibility of the principal. There are three major areas for his consideration: (1) scheduling the meeting, (2) planning the meeting, and (3) conducting the meeting.

In scheduling the meeting the principal should find physical facilities that will handle his total faculty in whatever type of discussions are given. When the faculty is not too big, it is wise to have everyone seated around a common table. The date and time of the faculty meeting vary greatly. Generally speaking, Mondays and Fridays are ruled out as possible days —Friday because of activities and Monday because of the need to organize the week's work. Tuesday, Wednesday, and Thursday are the most common days for faculty meeting, with Tuesday being the most popular. The time of the meeting may be the early morning, after school, or the evening. The principal should let the faculty help set the time of the meeting. The principal's main concern should be to determine when all faculty members can be present. A meeting immediately following the school day has many conflicts with teachers and advisers who conduct athletics and other activity programs. The length of the meeting will depend to some extent on the purposes for holding the meeting. A business meeting should be shorter than a curriculum improvement meeting. Generally speaking, faculty meetings held before school are held weekly for one hour only. The frequency of the meetings helps to overcome the shortness of the meeting. Faculty meetings held after school or in the evening should have a specific time limitation, so teachers will not develop the feeling that faculty meetings last all night.

The old adage that "if one fails to prepare, he prepares to fail" holds true with faculty meetings. The success or failure of the meeting is usually determined by the kind and amount of planning that precede the actual meetings. Successful faculty meetings have some of the following characteristics:

1. The problems under discussion must be of interest to the majority of the teachers.

2. A cooperative approach to the solution of the problems should be planned.

3. Every member should be expected to attend every meeting for maximum effectiveness.

4. The meeting should be scheduled in advance.

5. The agenda should be prepared in advance, with faculty members being able to place items on the agenda or to have representation on the faculty agenda committee.

6. Every staff member should have a clear understanding of the school program and how his individual contribution fits into the total program.

7. The faculty meeting must be long enough to accomplish the work but short enough to keep morale high.

The principal would normally call the general faculty meeting to order and conduct the business. As problems are discussed, the principal should recognize that domination often destroys effectiveness. The principal should recognize that teachers generally take a rather dim view toward their faculty meetings. The teachers' feelings of satisfaction and accomplishment are different from those of the principal, and more negative attitudes are expressed in principal-centered interaction than in faculty-centered interaction.[15] The principal is encouraged to study the suggestions in Chapter 2 under the heading of "Group Dynamics and Effective Leadership."

The principal should arrange for his secretary or some member of the faculty to make a permanent record of each meeting. The importance of this record is indicated by Wiles.

> A permanent record should be kept over every meeting which includes the names of the group, date, meeting place, members present, members absent, problems discussed, suggestions made, decisions reached, responsibilities accepted or assigned and plans for the next meeting. The record is essential for securing continuity of planning and avoiding waste of time through repetition. The planning committee of the faculty can use it as the basis for determining the phases of the program that need greater attention and the faculty meeting agenda committee will find the record a source of guidance in assigning items priority at the next meeting.[16]

The general purposes of the faculty meeting are sometimes classified under the categories general administration, improvement of instruction, and development of rapport with staff members. Brubaker lists the following four basic types of meetings:

1. *Curriculum or Subject-Centered Meetings:*
    Attention is given to a specific area of the school's educational program. A department or sub-division is responsible for the program. Members of departments plan and conduct the meeting, emphasizing goals and activities of their department.
    Serves to acquaint faculty with aspects of the educational program which they have probably not seen before.
    Gives teachers an appreciation for the educational program beyond their own classroom.

---

[15] Arthur Blumberg, "A Comparison of Teacher and Principal Attitudes Toward Faculty Meetings," *Bulletin of N.A.S.S.P.*, March 1964, pp. 45–55. Edmund Amidon and Arthur Blumberg, "School Faculty Meetings: The Teacher's Point of View," *Bulletin of N.A.S.S.P.*, September 1962, pp. 66–72.

[16] Kimball Wiles, *Supervision for Better Schools* (Englewood Cliffs, N.J.: Prentice-Hall, 1955), p. 165.

2. *Administrative Meetings*:
   Devoted to analysis, evaluation and formation of school policy.
   Here there is need for careful application of group processes and democratic principles of administration. Development of policies and procedure should be accomplished with the help of those who will execute and use the policies.
   Should be directed and chaired by the principal—his leadership should be in evidence throughout the process of establishing policies. Provision for free exchange and expression of ideas and suggestions is essential.

3. *Informational Meetings*:
   Largely to disseminate information which is too involved or complex for use of bulletins and other written media, e.g. held at the first of the school year when much information and data is passed to the faculty.

4. *In-service Training Meetings*:
   Devoted to the purpose of enhancing and increasing a faculty's goal, e.g. the topic of legal liability of teachers may be presented and discussed or lesson plans analyzed, discussed and prepared as a sample.[17]

Teacher Handbook. If the principal is to secure some semblance of unity in philosophy, organization, and interpretation of the various rules and regulations and in attitude toward such provisions, he should plan to publish a handbook for teachers. Handbooks are available in an infinite number of styles and varieties. The handbook can be a loose-leaf binder with inserts or a printed bound volume. Generally speaking, it is more economical to have a handbook in which pages can be added or replaced. Such a provision will allow the handbook to be kept up to date as new policies are adopted or changes made. If the handbook is bound, it is usually necessary to reprint the handbook every year or two to keep the book up to date. The handbook might include some of the following categories:

Board of education rules and regulations
    A. District government
    B. District administration
    C. District staff services
    D. School faculty services
    E. Student regulations
High school policies and procedures
    A. Student Accounting
    B. Purchasing procedures

[17] Lowell K. Brubaker, "New Vistas in Principal-Faculty Relationships—Through Faculty Meetings," *Bulletin of N.A.S.S.P.*, December 1962, p. 55.

    C. Student activities

    D. Care of school property

    E. Evaluation and reporting

    F. Supervision

    G. Substitution

    H. Transportation

    I. Fire and health regulations

    J. Other

Philosophy and history of the school

Financial

    A. District-approved high school budget

    B. Student activity budget

    C. Purchasing procedures

    D. High school accounts

General high school administration

    A. Job descriptions

    B. High school calendar

    C. Faculty assignments

    D. Supervisory assignments such as, school lunch, school dances, halls

Literature of interest

The teacher's handbook should be organized for the most functional use; therefore, faculty members should help structure the book as well as approve the items to be placed within it. The principal should never assume that the "handbook in hand" will automatically bring unity. Only when the policies are read and understood will they be followed. The principal should constantly work with the faculty members to improve their understanding of the contents of the book. New faculty members should receive a copy of the handbook at the time they sign the contract, so they may have an opportunity to become acquainted with its contents prior to the busy opening days of school.

Substitute Teachers. The principal frequently gets the "telephone blues" between 6:00 and 8:30 A.M. A telephone call at this time usually means that someone on the faculty is ill and that a substitute teacher must be provided. Teachers should not be in school when they are ill, and the principal should make every effort to let them know that he appreciates the call, that he will miss them in school, and that he wishes them a speedy recovery. Such an attitude will greatly improve the morale of the teacher; however, it will not solve the principal's immediate staffing problem. He must make arrangements for a substitute so the instructional process can be carried forth with as much success as possible. The principal cannot afford to spend his time doing substitute work, nor can he afford the time to solve the problems that are created as a result of the mishandling of classes when the regular teacher is not present. William B.

Castetter listed the following guidelines, which are helpful to the principal in maintaining instructional standards during the absence of regular personnel.

1. Formulation of a specific plan to be followed in administration of personnel replacements.

2. Specifications for personnel replacements.

3. A permanent, specialized corps of replacements to meet minimum district needs, to be composed of highly competent personnel, deliberately selected and trained to deal with special problems of substitution. A salary advantage is suggested because of the exacting nature of the assignment.

4. A second group of temporary teachers to be employed seasonally when the replacements cannot be filled by the permanent corps suggested above. This group to be recruited and selected on the basis of criteria designed to employ personnel able to perform in this capacity.

5. Responsibilities for carrying out the details of the replacement plan are clearly defined. This includes administrative responsibility for development, assignment, and full utilization of permanent corps of replacements, as well as recruitment, selection, orientation, supervision, and appraisal of temporary personnel.

6. Preparation of a handbook for temporary employees which will routinize the procedures to be followed and which will help to clarify and minimize the problems usually encountered.

7. Advance planning in each building unit by the principal and regular staff regarding the preparation of plan books to be followed in the event of absence. The matter is important since the continuity of education by the replacement depends upon clear instructions.

8. Continuous appraisal of the replacement plan. Records of the daily, monthly, and yearly absence rates are necessary to enable administrations to determine, for example, the feasibility and cost of employing permanent replacements. Many other aspects of the plan must be appraised, such as the reasons for absence, the predictable need for temporary personnel, and the effects of whatever plan is employed upon the quality of instruction.[18]

Utilization of the Staff

Assignment of Teachers. One of the responsibilities that requires special attention of the principal is the assignment of staff to their teaching responsibilities. The principal must give careful study to the teachers' background of teaching, professional qualifications, and interests in making the assignments. The assignments must also further programs of team teaching, individualized instruction, large- and small-group instruction, and other experimental innovations.

[18] William B. Castetter, *Administering the School Personnel Program* (New York: The Macmillan Company, 1962), pp. 314–19.

The following principles are given to aid the principal in making his staff assignments:

1. Team teaching involves the cooperative planning of two or more faculty members; therefore, assignments between teachers must be coordinated. Teachers who are involved in team teaching and special programs should be assigned first before other assignments are made.

2. Teachers who have extended periods of service in the school should be assigned to the subject or subjects to which they were previously assigned, unless there is evidence that they would be more effective or happier with another assignment for which they are academically prepared.

3. Teachers should be assigned in their area of specialization and training. This principle applies wherever possible. In an extremely small school teachers may have to teach outside their area of specialization. Where such teaching is necessary, the teachers should be placed according to their major field first, minor field second, and interest level third. In schools with a graduating class of at least 100 students, practically every teacher can teach in the area of his major specialization.

4. Teacher interest and desires should be considered but not at the exclusion of the major field of preparation.

5. New teachers should be assigned early. They will find it more difficult to adjust because of their lack of experience. Too frequently the new teacher gets all the leftovers. The teacher thus assigned is placed under a double handicap—lack of experience and no preparation for multiple assignments.

6. When teachers are hired, they should be hired according to their specialization to fill the special requirements of the school.

7. Teachers should be assigned duplicate sections of a subject whenever possible. The amount of time needed for preparation is thus reduced.

8. The teacher should be notified in the spring or early summer of his tentative assignment. However, the notification should include the recognition of the need for some possible last-minute adjustments. A teacher who had been teaching junior high mathematics and science for 30 years received notice of his assignment and protested to the new principal. In his 30 years of service the teacher had never taught in the area of his major specialization, which was social studies. The first year he had just filled an opening in mathematics and science. Each year thereafter he had been assigned on the basis of the prior year. Obviously this type of protest should be recognized and adjustments made whenever possible.

9. The teaching load should be spread as evenly as possible. When the principal computes the teaching load, extra class assignments should be included. The teaching load of new teachers should be lighter than that of the more experienced teachers.

Teacher Load. Along with the assignment of teachers, the principal must also consider teacher load. Although faculty members have different capacities for work, the principal should know the load of each teacher in order to maintain some equity in assignments. The factors used in determining teacher load are:

1. The number of sections taught daily (or weekly).
2. The number of pupils taught.
3. The number of different preparations required.
4. The amount of time required for co-operations: study halls, activities, etc.
5. The length of the class period.
6. The nature of the subject taught and the consequent amount of time required for preparation, for marking papers and notebooks, and for arranging equipment, apparatus, and materials.
7. The personnel of the pupils taught: tractability and range of individual differences in ability, factors very difficult to measure.
8. The age and maturity of the pupils taught and the consequent character of the subject matter.[19]

The Douglass formula is one formula that takes these factors into consideration. The formula is presented here to aid principals in equalizing teaching load. The justification, application of the formula to special-type classes, and examples can be found elsewhere.[20]

$$TL = SGC \left[CP - \frac{Dup}{10} + \frac{NP - 25\,CP}{100} \right] \left[\frac{PL + 50}{100} \right] + .6PC \left[\frac{PL + 50}{100} \right]$$

TL = units of teaching load per week.

SGC = subject coefficient used for giving relative weights to classes in different subject fields.

CP = class periods spent in classroom per week.

Dup = number of class periods spent per week in classroom, teaching classes for which the preparation is very similar to that for some other section, not including the original section.

NP = number of pupils in classes per week.

PC = number of class periods spent per week in supervision of the study hall, student activities, teachers' meetings, committee work, assistance in administrative or supervisory work, and other cooperations.

PL = gross length of class periods, in minutes.

[19] Harl R. Douglass, *Modern Administration of Secondary Schools* (New York: Ginn and Company, 1963), p. 79. Reprinted through the courtesy of Blaisdell Publishing Company, a division of Ginn and Company.

[20] Harl R. Douglass, "The 1950 Revision of the High School Teaching Load Formula," pp. 18–20. Reprinted by permission from the *Bulletin of the National Association of Secondary-School Principals*, May 1, 1951. Copyright: Washington, D.C.

TABLE 8.1 **Subject Grade Coefficients for Use in the Teaching-Load Formula**

Grade Level	7 and 8	9	10, 11, 12
English	1.0	1.1	1.1
Art	1.0	.9	1.0
Home economics	1.0	1.0	1.1
Music	.9	1.0	1.0
Mathematics	1.0	1.0	1.0
Agriculture	—	—	1.3
Industrial arts	.9	.9	1.0
Physical education	.8	.9	.9
Health	.9	1.1	1.2
Commerce	1.0	1.0	1.0
Social studies	1.0	1.0	1.0
Foreign language	1.0	1.0	1.0
Science	1.0	1.1	1.1

SOURCE: Harl R. Douglass, "The 1950 Revision of the High School Teaching Load Formula," *Bulletin of N.A.S.S.P.*, pp. 18–20. Reprinted by permission from the *Bulletin of the National Association of Secondary-School Principals*, May, 1951. Copyright: Washington, D.C.

Challenging Traditional Utilization Patterns. In the traditional school, where periods are neatly segmented—six or seven a day—and the day is carefully regulated by the same length of periods, students move from class to class by clockwork with the help of the bell. The organizational pattern is to assign one teacher per class, load the class to 25 to 30 students, assign the teacher according to his background and interest, and let the school year go by on a fixed, regular schedule.

Many of the traditional assumptions for such a pattern are now being challenged. Some of these assumptions are: (1) the optimum-size class for educational learning is 25 to 30 students, (2) one teacher should be responsible for a subject or class, (3) students always learn best in teacher-directed classrooms, (4) students attending a class every day for 40 to 50 minutes provides optimum learning, and (5) the quality of learning can be measured by prescriptive, quantity standards.

Experimental Studies in Staff Utilization. The need for change in traditional programs of staff utilization became evident as a result of three factors: (1) the intense criticism of education from public-spirited citizens, (2) the genuine recognition by professionals that quality improvements were needed, and (3) the shortage of teachers to meet existing needs.

The Commission on the Experimental Study of the Utilization of the Staff in the Secondary School was created by the Executive Committee of the National Association of Secondary-School Principals "to institute nationwide pursuit of improved education despite the shortage of teachers."[21] Invitations were issued to high schools all over the country to submit proposals for experimentation, which would be supported in part by a fund grant from Ford Foundation. No attempt was made to structure the experiments; the committee was searching for new techniques, variations of current techniques, and better utilization of the professional competencies of teachers. The end result was an explosion of new ideas, experiments, and innovations. Detailed reports of the studies can be found in the January issue of the *Bulletin of the National Association of Secondary-School Principals* for the years 1958, 1959, 1960, 1961, and 1962. (Other official publications were cited in the introduction to this chapter.)

Probably the greatest benefit of these studies was not the individual projects themselves, as significant as these were, but the long-lasting attitude created toward innovation and change.[22]

New Designs for Staff Utilization. As a result of all these separate studies, several patterns emerged. As pointed out in an earlier chapter, the school will be organized to provide large-group instruction, small-group instruction, and independent study. Some schools put the emphasis on the large-group organization as the basis for change, while others place the emphasis on individualized instruction.

The instructional staff consists of master teachers, general professional teachers, teacher assistants, paraprofessional clerks, aides, materials mediasts, community consultants, and staff specialists. In the improved utilization of these personnel, different combinations of grouping and use can be effected. Organization is not enough. Teachers must learn new instructional roles.

Team Teaching. Team teaching is a cooperative activity in which each person does what he is most able to do in the instructional system.[23] In this role a teacher recognizes that a colleague, film, programed materials, consultant, or student may perform some part of the teaching process better than one teacher. Strengths of teachers are utilized. Cooperation between members of the team is a necessary element of success. The principal must consider compatibility as one criterion for assignment. Teacher assistants and paraprofessionals will be part of the team to do clerical work, prepare audiovisual aids, read papers, record student progress, organize groups, and assist the teachers when necessary.

[21] Trump, *Focus on Change, op. cit.*, p. 19.

[22] The complete *Bulletin of N.A.S.S.P.*, May 1963, is concerned with the changing secondary schools, the nature of change, and examples of change in schools.

[23] David W. Beggs, III (ed.), *Team Teachings, Bold New Venture* (Indianapolis, Indiana: Unified College Press, 1964). Judson T. Shaplin and Henry F. Olds, Jr. (eds.), *Team Teaching* (New York: Harper and Row, 1964).

Large- and Small-Group Instruction. Large-group·instruction is best used for motivation, dissemination, and assignment·purposes. The teacher lectures, presents, demonstrates, shows films, and gives tests to students. The principal can save staff time by having teachers make only one presentation, as shown in Figure 8.2, to cover material best presented, as

Figure 8.2

Large-Group Instruction

SOURCE: Used with permission of Iron County School District, Cedar City, Utah.

indicated above, instead of making five or six separate presentations. The time thus saved can be used by the teacher for preparation of more effective presentations and for more profitable instruction in small groups.

Small-group instruction requires new roles for teachers. Students must be taught how to communicate with each other. The teacher is a consultant who helps the student by correcting errors, pointing up problems, clarifying issues, and recommending sources and methods that lead to solutions. Most teachers have trouble in this role, and principals must be prepared to help them understand and improve their techniques in working with small groups.

Independent Study. Under the new organizational patterns, independent study is one of the important parts of the student learning process. The teacher's role is a simple one of displacement, i.e., teach the student to be resourceful and independent to the point that the teacher is not needed, as shown in Figure 8.3. Consultant's help should be available to students to give them direction as required. Many schools currently are

Figure 8.3
Independent Research

SOURCE: Iron County School District, Cedar City, Utah. Reprinted by permission.

operating programs based primarily on independent study.[24] Other schools
have placed large blocks of time open to students for independent study.
Figure 8.4 shows one school's plan for independent study areas and the
utilization of these areas. Discipline problems are usually increased if
students are not prepared for such a change. Self-motivation is fundamental
to successful independent study programs. The principal may desire to
assign paraprofessionals to keep order until students have accepted full
responsibility with their new freedom.

Summary

The educational revolution has affected positively the selection, orientation, organization, and utilization of the staff. Teachers must be selected
on the basis of need, and the principal should be involved in this selection

[24] Two good examples of such schools are the Continuous Progress Programs at
the Brigham Young Laboratory School, Provo, Utah, and Theodore High School,
Theodore, Alabama.

Figure 8.4

Independent Study

SOURCE: Iron County School District, Cedar City, Utah. Reprinted by permission.

process. To find the right teacher for each assignment involves a careful search for candidates and an effective data-gathering and screening process. Interviews should be held with candidates who pass the screening tests.

Once a contract is extended to the teacher, orientation procedure should commence. The district should provide copies of the rules and regulations, salary and deduction information, and information about the school system. The principal should provide the teacher a handbook, schedules, assignments, curriculum guides, and textbooks. Orientation procedures should be planned for the whole year.

The principal must organize his staff for effective instruction. Line and staff positions should be designated. Responsibilities of assistant principals, departmental chairmen, directors, deans, counselors, and committee chairmen should be in writing and should be reviewed with the faculty. The principal is responsible for selecting staff members, evaluating and rating the staff, building the schedule, assigning the teachers, providing and stimulating in-service work, and directing experimentation and innovation.

Faculty meetings are held to effectively operate the school. Teachers generally hold a dim view of faculty meetings; yet the principals find them necessary. Successful faculty meetings must be carefully planned. The principal should allow and encourage teacher-centered meetings rather than principal-centered meetings.

The faculty handbook is another device by which the principal communicates policies and procedures to the staff. The handbook should be organized for functional use. The teachers should help plan as well as change items in the handbook.

A major assignment of the principal is to assign the staff for the most effective utilization. Assignments should be based on principles rather than whims and wishes of the principal or teacher. The load of the teacher should be calculated and adjusted to the best interests of the teachers and the school.

Recent experiments and innovations in schools have created new patterns of staff utilization. Large- and small-group instruction, independent study, continuous progress education, and nongraded schools have changed the type of personnel needed for effective instruction. Many instructional staffs now consist of master teachers, professional teachers, teacher assistants, paraprofessionals, clerks, aides, materials mediasts, consultants, and staff specialists.

SUGGESTED PROJECTS AND ACTIVITIES

1. Invite a personnel director from a school district to discuss the steps taken in his district prior to offering contracts to a candidate.
2. Visit the teacher placement bureau on campus. Have the director explain the record-keeping and operational phase of his office.
3. Role-play a principal-prospective-teacher interview.
4. Interview new teachers and develop a program of teacher orientation based on the needs of new teachers.
5. Visit a large and a small high school. Discuss the differences in organization. Draw diagrams of line and staff relationships.
6. Invite a department chairmen to discuss his responsibilities and relationships to other departments and administrative officers.
7. Make a collection of teacher handbooks and review the items contained therein.

8. Attend a faculty meeting and discuss with the principal the various types of meetings he holds.
9. Using the Douglass formula, calculate the load of the teachers in a secondary school.
10. Spend a day visiting a school that is experimenting in the utilization of the staff. Describe the differences as compared to a traditional school.

REVIEW AND DISCUSSION QUESTIONS

1. What is an educational revolution? Is there one in process? What direction is it taking?
2. How does the principal know the qualifications he desires in a prospective candidate?
3. Why should the principal be involved in selecting the teachers for his school?
4. What is the purpose of a teacher orientation program? What should be included?
5. What is the purpose of preschool institutes and workshops? How could they be improved?
6. What is the principal's role in a teacher orientation program?
7. What is the difference between "line" and "staff" assignments?
8. What are the principal's responsibilities as related to staff organization?
9. How are the assistant principal's duties changing in the new programs?
10. What would you do as a principal to make all your faculty members want to be present at faculty meetings?
11. How could substitute teaching be improved?
12. What are some of the principles for making teacher assignments?
13. What factors should be considered in determining teacher load?
14. How have staff utilization projects affected selection, organization, assignment, and utilization of teachers?
15. What are the goals in large- and small-group and independent study patterns?

SELECTED BIBLIOGRAPHY

Austin, D. B. "Tackling the Big Problem of Administrative and Supervisory Staffing," *Bulletin of N.A.S.S.P.*, April 1964, pp. 47–59.
Begg, David W., III (ed.). *Team Teaching, Bold New Venture*. Indianapolis, Indiana: Unified College Press, 1964.
Bennis, Warren G., Kenneth D. Benne, and Robert Chin. *The Planning of Change*. New York: Holt, Rinehart and Winston, 1961.

Blumberg, Arthur, and Edmund Amidon. "A Comparison of Teacher and Principal Attitudes Towards Faculty Meetings," *Bulletin of N.A.S.S.P.*, March 1964, pp. 45–55.

Brubaker, Lowell, K. "New Vistas in Principal-Faculty Relationships—Through Faculty Meetings," *Bulletin of N.A.S.S.P.*, December 1962.

Castetter, William B. *Administering the School Personnel Program*. New York: The Macmillan Company, 1962.

Davis, E. Dale, and John Moore. "The Assistant Principal in the Junior High School," *Bulletin of N.A.S.S.P.*, January 1965, pp. 1–4.

Fawcett, Claude W. *School Personnel Administration*. New York: The Macmillan Company, 1964.

Gillespie, T. Marcus. "The Assistant Principal: Status, Duties, and Responsibilities," *Bulletin of N.A.S.S.P.*, December 1961, pp. 59–68.

Habbe, Stephen. *Recruiting and Selecting Employees. Studies in Personnel Policy*. No. 144, National Industrial Conference Board. New York: The Board, 1954.

Heffernan, Helen. "Induction of New Teachers," *California Journal of Elementary Education*, August 1957, pp. 54–64.

National Education Association, Research Division. *Teacher Supply and Demand in Public Schools*, 1962. Washington, D.C.: The Association, 1962.

National Association of Secondary-School Principals. "Changing Secondary Schools, Part I Nature of Change, Part II Some Examples of Change," *Bulletin of N.A.S.S.P.*, May 1963, pp. 1–162. (Complete issue devoted to this topic.)

———. *Design for Leadership*. Washington, D.C.: The Association, 1964.

Pitruzzello, P. R. "Staff Utilization: Implications for Administrators," *National Catholic Educational Association, Bulletin*, August 1964, pp. 280–84.

Shaplin, Judson T., and Henry F. Olds, Jr. (eds.). *Team Teaching*. New York: Harper and Row, 1964.

Spriegel, W. R., and V. A. James. "Trends in Recruitment and Selection Practices," *Personnel*, November-December 1958, pp. 42–48.

"The Teacher-Selection Interview," *School Management*, December 1964, pp. 35–37. Also reprinted in *Education Digest*, March 1965, pp. 35–38.

Trump, J. Lloyd. *Images of the Future*. Washington, D.C.: National Association of Secondary-School Principals, 1959.

———. "What Is Team Teaching?" *Education*, February 1965, pp. 327–32.

Trump, J. Lloyd, and Dorsey Baynham. *Focus on Change—Guide to Better Schools*. Chicago: Rand McNally and Co., 1961.

Trump, J. Lloyd, and Lois Karasik. *Focus on the Individual—A Leadership Responsibility*. Washington, D.C.: National Association of Secondary-School Principals, 1965.

Wells, Philip C., Robert H. Nelson, and Earl M. Johnsen. "The Assistant Secondary School Principal," *Bulletin of N.A.S.S.P.*, January 1965, pp. 15–25.

CHAPTER 9

Implementing Effective Instruction

The curriculum of the secondary schools has been discussed in a previous chapter. Also discussed have been many details relating to starting the school year efficiently and effectively. Once school is under way and the beginning operational problems have been smoothed out, the principal can concentrate on the most important task, that of implementing effective instruction. Of course, everything that a principal does in a school is in some measure for this purpose. School lunch, bussing students, effective discipline, guidance services—all programs within the school are in some way related to the instructional program. However, in this chapter the emphasis will be placed on the teacher, the teacher's role in improving instruction, morale, supervision, and ways the principal can effectively work with the teacher to improve the instructional program.

Improving Staff Morale

Definition. Morale is a term used to describe the extent to which an individual has actually identified his own personal hopes, desires, and ambitions with the goals of the organization for which he works. High morale indicates the individual's willingness to stay with the organization, to exert the maximum effort, to complete the work assigned to him, to develop skills, attitudes, and knowledge so that he can be of greater service to the organization, and to study the problems of the organization and help the organization accomplish its goals. Low morale indicates the

214

individual's reluctance to stay with the organization, to exert maximum influence to complete tasks assigned, and to work for the improvement of the organization.[1]

In the school setting, high morale is achieved when the administrators and teaching and nonteaching personnel desire to remain with the school over a period of years, put forth maximum effort in the tasks assigned to them, and are willing to work toward the solution of problems within the school. Low morale is characterized by obstructive or noncontributory behavior. The American Association of School Administrators states:

> . . . Morale is a disposition on the part of persons engaged in an enterprise to behave in ways which contribute to the purposes for which the enterprise exists. When this disposition is strong, morale is said to be high. It manifests itself in a tendency to subordinate personal considerations to the purposes of the enterprise, to work as a member of a team for the accomplishment of common goals, and to derive satisfaction from achievements of the organization. When the disposition toward the achievement of common purposes is weak, morale is said to be low. Low morale is characterized by behavior that is obstructive or noncontributory to the common purposes, by failure to derive personal satisfaction from group achievement, and by a tendency to elevate personal interests above the purposes of the enterprise.[2]

Benefits of High Morale.   Most morale studies have been conducted in industry and then related to other types of organizations, such as education, on the assumption that "people are people," "organizations are organizations," and "techniques are techniques." Most authorities in educational administration and supervision believe there is enough similarity that transfer of many basic principles can be made. However, there have been enough educational studies to show that teacher morale and educational achievement are related. Where morale is high, teaching and student achievement are good, and teacher-principal relationships are good.[3] Some of the more specific findings and interesting implications as a result of high morale were summarized by Suehr as:

---

[1] Claude W. Fawcett, *School Personnel Administration* (New York: The Macmillan Company, 1964), p. 115.

[2] American Association of School Administrators, *Staff Relations in School Administration*, Thirty-Third Yearbook (Washington, D.C.: National Education Association, 1955), p. 15.

[3] Claude W. Fawcett, *op. cit.*, pp. 115–28. Lester W. Anderson, "Teacher Morales and Student Achievement," *Journal of Educational Research*, May 1953, pp. 693–98. John H. Suehr, "New Vistas in Principal-Faculty Relationships—Teacher Morale," *Bulletin of N.A.S.S.P.*, September 1962, pp. 58–62. Frederick L. Redefer, "Factors That Affect School Morale," *The Nation's Schools*, February 1959, pp. 59–62.

a. A greater personal effort and attention on the part of employees. Wouldn't you like to have all your teachers willingly and accurately complete every administrative detail on time?

b. A reduction in turnover, absenteeism, and tardiness. I am sure we would all be for this. In my study of teacher morale, the low-morale teachers missed much more school than did the high-morale teachers.

c. A reduction in the number of grievances. In a well-run school there shouldn't be many grievances, but there should still be a grievance procedure.

d. An improved quality of decisions made by those in responsible positions. Whether this comes before or after high morale is difficult to determine, but we do know it is a necessary constituent.

e. A greater readiness to accept change. This quality is greatly needed by teachers and principals, if we are going to accept the challenge present now and in the years ahead. Secondary schools actually have changed very little in the last sixty years.[4]

The last point, "readiness to accept change," is most significant when one considers the many changes and innovations that are waiting for the principal and staff who have initiative and have demonstrated practical, on-the-job teamwork.

Factors Affecting Morale

There are two main categories of factors that affect the morale of the staff—material factors and human factors. Both are important and each has a place. More emphasis for improvement has been given to the material factors; yet the human factors are probably more significant in a long-range program of morale improvement.

Material Factors Affecting Morale. Some of the material factors affecting morale related to working conditions are salary, sick leave, medical and hospitalization insurance, retirement programs, facilities, equipment, and supplies. Improvement in the material factors is the major concern of the professional organizations to which the staff belongs. The principal should encourage teachers in their organizational goals, and positive practices should be used to improve these material factors.

The economic factor should be a major concern to the principal. One of the goals of high morale indicated above was maximum performance of the tasks assigned. A teacher who cannot support his family at a satisfactory level cannot be positive in his work. In fact, he frequently

[4] John H. Suehr, *op. cit.*, p. 62.

"moonlights" after school and takes a summer job based on economic considerations rather than professional growth and advancement. The greatest waste of manpower in the United States today is the teachers of the nation who are trained at a high professional level but are forced to clerk in grocery stores and do other tasks unrelated to their professional training. Principals who can remedy this situation can channel the total productive energies of their staffs toward school improvement. Both morale and instruction cannot help but be improved markedly.

Related to the economic factors are those involving personal health. Sick leave provisions are most essential for sound teaching and good morale. A teacher who has no sick leave provisions cannot afford a deduction in salary; so he comes to school ill. The teacher, the children, and the school are all affected negatively. Sick leave provisions allow the teacher to recover at home. The health objectives of the school are promoted and the physical and mental health of the teacher are improved. A school district should allow a minimum of ten sick days per year. Some districts allow these days to accumulate. Such action discourages a few unprincipled teachers from "taking the ten days they have coming." More forward-looking districts have unlimited sick leave. Teachers appreciate this positive, forward-looking program and treat it like a life insurance policy—"wonderful to have but I hope I never use it." Districts with unlimited sick leave seldom find an abuse, and many report fewer days absent for illness than when the ten-day provision was in effect.

Along with sick leave, some districts have programs of medical and hospital care and retirement programs. These programs are usually supported by both the teacher and the district. However, in recent years many districts have been paying full costs of such programs.

Other material factors affecting morale are facilities, equipment, and supplies. Most teachers want to do an outstanding job. Many are limited by these physical and material factors. The principal should do all he can to help create and provide the ideal teaching climate within the limits set by the board of education. A discussion on budgeting, obtaining equipment, and communications relating to this process is given in detail in Chapter 14.

Human Factors Affecting Morale. The importance of the human factors affecting morale have long been recognized in business. The most significant early studies on human factors were the Western Electric Company studies at its Hawthorne Works. The "Hawthorne effect" is a byword for evaluating research that has not overcome the influence of the human factors of morale on production or achievement. In these studies changes were made in the physical conditions to improve productivity. A control group was maintained, which worked under less favorable conditions. The unexpected result was that both groups increased production and the experimental group remained high even after normal conditions were restored. A conclusion that had not been anticipated in the beginning was made; i.e., when interest and special attention are shown to employees, the employees feel important, morale is improved, and production increases.[5]

The principal is in a key position to influence the human factors of morale. He can select individuals for certain roles, change attitudes of staff members, change the nature of their relationship with him and with other staff members, and generate interpersonal hostility and distrust or interest, confidence, and trust. Leavitt indicated the importance and stages of understanding of the human factors of morale when he said:

> Again, we have learned a good deal in just the past 20 years or so, about the human dials in organizations. First, we learned the obvious; that feelings and attitudes are generated by administrative acts whether we intend to generate them or not. Then we learned that those feelings and attitudes influenced work behavior. We were naïve about it at first. We thought happy people worked better than unhappy ones. Then we discovered that happiness wasn't a single unitary phenomenon anyway. And we also learned that possibly it [happiness] could yield no work at all, or work directed in the opposite direction from what the administrator wanted. So we moved from the notion that the administrator ought to make his people happy to the more realistic notion that the administrator ought to make work interesting, challenging, exciting. We moved also to the realization that one path to a challenging environment was an open environment, one with a high degree of mutual trust and mutual confidence. One path to such an environment is widespread involvement in decision making and planning, and therefore widespread use of groups as well as individuals. Hence the development in recent years of programs within organizations and outside them for equipping administrators with skills in setting up and leading groups, and skills in diagnosing and responding to what used to look like irrelevant human needs.[6]

When analyzed, the human elements affecting morale that should be given attention in the school framework are personality traits of both teachers and administrators, physical and mental health, grievance procedures, sensitivity training, and involvement in decisions affecting staff members.

All these human factors are important. Involvement in decision making was discussed in detail in Chapter 2. Personality conflicts have always

---

[5] F. J. Roethlisberger and W. J. Dickson, *Management and the Worker* (Cambridge, Mass.: Harvard University Press, 1943).

[6] Harold J. Leavitt, "Consequences of Executive Behavior," *Bulletin of N.A.S.S.P.*, April 1964, pp. 167–76.

been recognized as causes of low morale; teachers and administrators might be matched scientifically on the basis of personality tests. At least the extremes might be kept apart.

"Sensitivity" training attempts to better acquaint teachers and principals with themselves and other individuals. Jersild, in *When Teachers Face Themselves,* stated, "The ghost of old hurts, the souls of agonies of an earlier day, live on in many of our children at school—and in the colleagues with whom we work, and in ourselves. And it is to the extent that each of us has the courage to look into the haunted house within himself where these ghosts reside that we can gain some insight into the way the lives of others are ravaged by anxiety."[7]

A training program that shows what teachers think of principals and what principals think about individual staff members might also be profitable. However, harm can be done if sufficient time is not allowed for the "breakdown" sessions to go through complete cycles so that adjustments in personality can take place.

Morale and Grievance Committees. Principals generally have reservations about formulating a grievance committee. A principal aware of the importance of human relations on morale will maintain an "open-door" policy. Teachers with courage can "tell a principal off" or talk about their problems. However, even a principal who is noted for his empathy for his staff is only fooling himself if he thinks all the gripes and problems seriously affecting morale are brought to him.

The benefits of a grievance procedure are: (1) human problems can be brought to light where they can be seen for what they are, (2) problems are found and corrected before becoming serious to the individuals concerned, (3) the procedures used to solve the problem teach members techniques in human relations, (4) the procedures can serve as a check and balance on the principal if he becomes arbitrary and capricious, and (5) problems and gripes that would have remained active on a horizontal staff level are allowed to move vertically to line officers where the sources of cooperation, authority, and group discussion are marshalled toward effective solutions.

Perhaps the most important value to be gained from all the studies on morale is that the principal must learn more about the teachers individually and as a group. He must understand their background, the roles they perform as a teacher, the sources of conflict and strain, how they regard each other, and how they visualize the principal's role. The next section provides much of this basic information.

[7] Arthur T. Jersild, *When Teachers Face Themselves* (New York: Bureau of Publications, Teachers College, Columbia, 1955), p. 55.

Understanding the Teacher

If the principal is to be effective in his goal to improve the instructional program, he must have an understanding of the teacher and the teacher's role, and he must be effective in working with the teacher.

How a Teacher Spends His Time. An extensive study on the teaching assignment of secondary public school teachers was conducted by the Research Division of the National Education Association.[8] A summary of the survey, as shown in Table 9.1, indicates the following results: Secondary school teachers, on the average, taught 26 periods per week, and these averaged 55 minutes in length. The average number of pupils per class was 27, and the average number of different pupils taught was 156. More than half the teachers had at least one conference or preparation period each day, but 21.4 per cent had definite assignments every day in the week.

Ninety-three percent of the teachers in secondary schools devoted more than half of their time to a single curriculum field; about 2 per cent divided their time equally between two fields; the remainder taught various combinations of fields. English, social studies, science, and mathematics were taught full time or more than half the time by 55.0 per cent of the teachers.

The average working week of the teacher was 45 hours, 54 minutes, as shown in Figure 9.1. In addition to 23.6 hours of class instruction, secondary school teachers worked an average of 13.3 hours on correcting papers, preparing materials, giving individual help to pupils, and conferring with parents. Teachers were assigned additional miscellaneous duties, which required nine hours per week for such assignments as study halls, monitorial duties, records and report cards, athletic coaching, club sponsoring, official meetings, and administrative assignments.

According to some educators, the teaching load of teachers has increased in recent years owing to the extension of school services and increased enrollments. The National Education Association conducted a study on the secondary teacher's load in 1950 similar to the study in 1960. A comparison of the two studies indicates that the teacher actually spent two hours per week less time in school-related activities in 1960.[9]

Background of the Teacher. When a person speaks of a salesman, administrator, public official, secretary, or teacher, popular images or

[8] National Education Association, *The American Public School Teacher.* Research Monograph 1963 M2 (Washington, D.C.: The Association, April 1963), p. 8. Used with permission of National Education Association, Research Division.

[9] National Education Association, "Teaching Load in 1950," *Research Bulletin,* NEA Research Division, February 1963, p. 19.

TABLE 9.1 Differences in Certain Aspects of Teaching Load, Secondary School Teachers, by Type of School and Curriculum Field

Aspects of Teaching Load	All secondary school teachers[a]	Junior high school teachers	Senior high school teachers	Teachers of skill-centered curriculum fields[b]	Teachers of book-centered curriculum fields[c]
1	2	3	4	5	6
CLASS SIZE					
Mean size of classes taught—number of pupils	26.6	29.9	25.0	25.1	27.3
Per cent with mean class of fewer than 20	17.8%	6.2%	22.7%	33.7%	10.2%
Per cent with mean class of 35 or more	10.0%	16.5%	6.1%	13.2%	8.4%
PUPILS TAUGHT					
Average number of pupils in classes taught	155.8	183.3	137.9	155.6	155.9
Per cent teaching fewer than 100	16.6%	7.2%	21.4%	31.7%	9.4%
Per cent teaching 200 or more	16.9%	29.6%	9.3%	20.3%	15.2%
PUPIL PERIODS PER WEEK					
Average number of pupil periods	684.0	786.5	632.3	642.0	704.2
Per cent having fewer than 500	19.9%	7.5%	25.4%	35.0%	12.7%
Per cent having 900 or more	14.7%	26.2%	9.4%	16.0%	14.1%
CONFERENCE PERIODS					
Per cent having none	21.4%	16.5%	22.6%	23.9%	19.8%
Per cent having 5	57.6%	59.6%	58.9%	53.8%	59.7%
Per cent having 10 or more	6.8%	4.7%	8.0%	10.3%	5.0%

TABLE 9.1 (Continued)

Aspects of Teaching Load	All secondary school teachers[a]	Junior high school teachers	Senior high school teachers	Teachers of skill-centered curriculum fields[b]	Teachers of book-centered curriculum fields[c]
1	*2*	*3*	*4*	*5*	*6*
HOURS PER WEEK FOR CLASS INSTRUCTION					
Average number of hours	23.6[d]	23.8	23.2	23.3	23.6
Per cent of teachers giving 30 hours or more	4.6%	4.4%	4.7%	6.0%	3.9%
HOURS PER WEEK FOR OUT-OF-CLASS INSTRUCTIONAL DUTIES					
Average number of hours	13.3[d]	12.5	14.1	11.4	14.1
Per cent giving 20 hours or more	19.1%	14.9%	23.9%	11.3%	23.1%
HOURS PER WEEK FOR MISCELLANEOUS ASSIGNMENTS					
Average number of hours	9.0[d]	8.0	9.3	9.2	8.9
Per cent giving 15 hours or more	14.1%	9.4%	16.0%	16.8%	12.9%
HOURS PER WEEK FOR ALL DUTIES REPORTED					
Average number of hours	45.9[d]	44.6	46.8	44.2	46.7
Per cent giving 55 hours or more	15.3%	14.0%	18.1%	10.8%	17.9%
NUMBER OF TEACHERS[e]	781	286	371	261	472

[a] Includes teachers in junior-senior-high combinations, not included in columns 3 and 4, and excludes elementary-secondary combinations.
[b] Comprises agriculture, art, business, health and physical education, industrial and vocational arts, music, and driver education.
[c] Comprises teachers of English, foreign languages, core, mathematics, and science.
[d] Figures shown are for 757 teachers reporting the time given on all three types of activities—class instruction, out-of-class instructional duties, and miscellaneous assignments.
[e] Number in sample; each question was answered by slightly fewer than 100 per cent of the possible total.

SOURCE: National Education Association Research Division, "The American Public School Teacher." Research Monographed 1963 M2. Reprinted by

Figure 9.1

How the High School Teacher Divides the Week
(Average work week of 45 hours, 54 minutes)

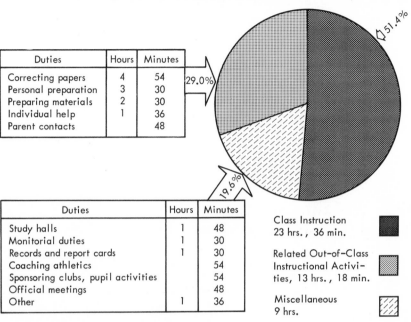

Duties	Hours	Minutes
Correcting papers	4	54
Personal preparation	3	30
Preparing materials	2	30
Individual help	1	36
Parent contacts		48

Duties	Hours	Minutes
Study halls	1	48
Monitorial duties	1	30
Records and report cards	1	30
Coaching athletics		54
Sponsoring clubs, pupil activities		54
Official meetings		48
Other	1	36

Class Instruction
23 hrs., 36 min.

Related Out-of-Class
Instructional Activi-
ties, 13 hrs., 18 min.

Miscellaneous
9 hrs.

SOURCE: National Education Association, *The American Public School Teacher*. Research Monograph 1963 M2 (Washington, D.C.: The Association, April 1963), p. 55. Reprinted by permission.

stereotypes are formed in the mind of the listener. Not all people hold exactly the same image of a teacher; yet there are popular images expressed in art, cartoons, literature, television, and other means of communication.

Some of the common popular images of the teacher are:

1. The teacher is incompetent. The teacher teaches because he cannot work elsewhere. "Those who can, do; those who can't, teach; and those who can't teach, teach teachers."

3. The teacher is inhuman, stern, dignified, reserved, emotionless. The teacher is "the warden," "the great stoneface."

3. The teacher is a frustrated, middle-aged, single female.

4. The teacher is of "white-collar, middle-class origin."

Although the popular image of the teacher is interesting and in some respects true, the principal should know the facts about the teacher—his background, his work, and his attitudes and values. Just as the popular concept of the principal, as presented in Chapter 1, is misleading, so is the typical stereotype of the teacher.

The following information should help the principal to better understand the teacher:

1. There is a heterogeneity of social backgrounds. It is no longer safe to assume that teachers are of predominantly white-collar origin. Teachers represent in substantial number all but the extremes at the upper and lower ends of the socioeconomic range.

Moreover, a large proportion of teachers are upwardly mobile persons. Many have moved from lower-middle to upper-middle status, and many have moved from upper-lower to lower-middle class.[10] McGuire and White, in a study of school personnel in Texas, state: "Teaching as a profession appears to involve upward social mobility for at least 40 per cent of those who enter the field. Only one in five, however, come from upper-lower-class family backgrounds. Some of the lower-status origin apparently achieve an upper-middle-class way of life; others although upward mobile, attain only a lower-middle status in their community. . . . About three of every four of the persons in education seem to follow an upper-middle-class pattern of living and more than a third come from such family backgrounds."[11]

2. Based upon studies and analysis, Terrien suggested that the following personality characteristics tended to be associated with teachers:

    a. Not strongly motivated to enter the occupation.

    b. Not strongly motivated toward advancement.

    c. Somewhat, though not generally, dissatisfied with the occupation.

    d. Inclined to accept the status quo with uneasy grace, making little effort for change. . . .

    e. Likely to be cooperative and helpful—as in the case of granting interviews.

    f. Adept at school work.

    g. Somewhat likely to grow authoritarian over time.

    h. More inclined to follow than to lead.

    i. More likely to be conservative than to be liberal, though not bigoted.

    j. Rather prone to think of teachers as different from other occupational groups—a condition which leads to stereotyping.

    k. Lack of aggression.

    l. A strong sense of service.

    m. Considerable optimism, and a determination to make the best—emotionally—of a situation, if female, and rather generalized pessimism, if male.[12]

[10] Robert J. Havighurst and Bernice L. Neugarten, *Society and Education*, 2nd ed. (Boston: Allyn and Bacon, Inc., 1962), p. 456.

[11] Carson McGuire and George D. White, "Social Origins of Teachers—Some Facts from the Southwest," *The Teacher's Role in American Society*, sixteenth yearbook (John Dewey Society, 1957), pp. 362–63.

[12] Frederic W. Terrien, "The Behavior System and Occupational Type Associated with Teaching." Unpublished doctoral dissertation. New Haven, Conn.: Yale University Library, pp. 402–3.

Role of the Teacher and Sources of Conflict. The principal will gain further insight into understanding the teacher if he considers the role definitions as defined by the California Council on Teacher Education. Over a five-year period the California Council on Teacher Education coordinated a statewide program of study and research, which resulted in defining the following roles of the teacher:

A Director of Learning. This is the most widely recognized role.

A Counselor and Guidance Worker. It is generally recognized today that, to the degree that the school has a counseling program, it is carried on largely by the teachers, and primarily in the classroom.

A Mediator of the Culture. Our civilization and culture depends on the effectiveness of our schools.

A Member of the School Community. In curriculum building, participating in the school government, extracurricular activities, and so on, the teacher is sharing in the responsibilities of the school program.

A Liaison Between School and Community. As a member of the community the teacher has a responsibility to interpret the educational program to the public.

A Member of the Profession. As a member of an organized profession, a teacher is responsible in leadership in building the educational program needed in our society and safe-guarding the quality of membership and welfare of the members of the profession.[13]

Bidwell indicates that (1) when the teacher's role expectation of the administrator and his actions are the same as perceived by the teacher, the teacher expresses satisfaction with the teaching situation, (2) when the expected role and practice are divergent, the teacher is dissatisfied with the teaching situation, and (3) the level of teaching satisfaction is dependent on convergence or divergence of expectations and perception of their fulfillment and is independent of the nature of expectations.[14]

Robert N. Bush, in his book *The Teacher-Pupil Relationship,* reported three main types of teachers: Type A, the academic teacher; Type B, the counseling teacher; and Type C, the creative teacher.

He suggests that in the teacher-pupil relationship the principal might consider matching students to teachers by types. To Type A teacher, the academic teacher, might be assigned the academic-type student. To Type B, the counseling teacher, might be assigned the emotional-type student, and to Type C, the creative teacher, might be assigned the creative student.[15]

[13] Lucien B. Kinney, *Measure of a Good Teacher* (Stanford, Calif.: California Teachers Association, 1952), pp. 9–10.

[14] Charles E. Bidwell, "The Administrative Role and Satisfaction in Teaching," *The Journal of Educational Sociology,* September 1955, pp. 42–43.

[15] Robert N. Bush, *The Teacher-Pupil Relationship* (Englewood Cliffs, N.J.: Prentice-Hall, Inc., 1954), p. 197.

Bush further indicates that "effective educational leadership will be promoted by increasing the teacher's knowledge of individual differences of his students, providing such knowledge is attended by an objective attitude toward, and insight into, human belief. Teachers should possess in-the-head-knowledge about each pupil in their classroom in these fields: (1) health, (2) abilities, aptitudes, competency, interests, (3) ambitions, purposes, desires, (4) special blocks or strains or stresses (5) cultural backgrounds, including home situation."[16]

There are three major aspects of the high school organization as shown in the Wabash study, relevant to the teacher's role. They are (1) the formal organization of the school, which prescribes learning achievements, (2) the system or student organizations often called extracurricular, and (3) the network of interpersonal relationships defined by the friendship choices (informal system). The study indicates that in the performance of the teacher's role there are several sources of strain:

1. By the virtue of adult status, personal orientation to knowledge, and as custodian of the institutionally prescribed tasks, the teacher tends to seek performances from the student that are higher than the adolescent group will set for itself. There results an incompatibility in the learning output norms.

2. The teacher wants to give awards or grades on the basis of achievement (standards). The community ascribe success (better grades) to those in high socio-economic groups. The conflict of these values creates conflict.

3. Conflict arises between the community's demands for standards based on competition and the philosophy of education that the teacher is obligated to help all students. The teacher feels that he fails if he doesn't help all students achieve.

4. Discipline is a source of strain. The duty of a teacher is to maintain control or order both as a condition for learning and as a sign of competency by the administration, teachers and students. Conflict results between this expectation and the informal group (student contact). There is close interaction between the teacher and the students. Talking, whispering, horseplay are accepted until such disturbance reaches a point of challenge to authority. The greater the support the principal gives the teacher's role of authority, the more likely the formal institutional role of the teacher will be used as a basis of classroom control. The less willing the principal is to support the teacher's institutional authority, the more likely that the teacher will absorb the conflict in his classroom role, and the more likely he will be to resort to personalized leadership, and face a situation of conflict. When teachers are unsupported, the personality of a teacher is exposed. The balance of power is shifted to the students.[17]

[16] *Ibid.*, p. 97.

[17] C. Wayne Gordan, "The Role of the Teacher in the Social Structure of the High School," *The Journal of Educational Sociology*, September 1955, pp. 21–29. Chapter 13, on discipline and student control, gives suggestions for both teacher and principal.

Getzels and Guba also indicated that there are three major areas of strain for a teacher because of conflicting role requirements. The first area of strain is the socioeconomic. The community demands that a teacher live by respectable, middle-class living standards but refuses to pay him on that level. Second, he is a responsible citizen, but moral and other values of the community are higher for him than for other adults. Third, he is an expert in his field; yet he is told what to teach and how to do it by administrators and members of the public alike.

As has been indicated, the socioeconomic area is a major source of strain. Much has been written over the years about the salaries of teachers. Numerous studies have been made to show that teachers basically are underpaid in relationship to other persons of equal training. The principal should be interested in improving the economic status of the teachers and should work with them and their associations to achieve this very important goal.

Information on current salaries compared to other groups is available to teachers, and since it changes every year, these comparisons will not be given here. Gradually the teaching profession is improving its comparative standing in relationship to other nonprofessional workers.

Another major source of strain is the lack of status of teachers. One reason why the status of teachers suffers is because of the intangibility of the product. Terrien indicates that

> the work of professionals is more tangible. If a man is ill, he can go to a doctor, and the doctor will cure him. If a man is in trouble, he can go to a lawyer, and the lawyer will extricate him—but if a man is stupid, and he goes to a teacher, the teacher can do little for him. The teacher offers no product which can be called up and delivered by his own efforts without assistance from others. His work always depends upon cooperation and the hard labor of the person who comes to him. Thus, the credit for the successful use of the teacher's product is rarely given to the teacher, but is instead seized by the user. An examination is passed, not because of the teacher who imparted the necessary information, but in spite of the teacher.[18]

However, there are still many people in society who look at the teacher as an ideal and expect the teacher to be a perfect example for the youth to emulate. Since these people see the teacher in this role, they expect the teacher to be the sanctioning agents for the young, the guardians of morals, the arbiters of conduct. It is in this status that they are remembered by all adults from their own childhood. In truth, teachers constitute a kind of conscience in society, and their status is that of the conscience—

[18] Frederic W. Terrien, "The Occupational Roles of Teachers," *The Journal of Educational Sociology*, September 1955, pp. 19–20.

recognized as fundamentally important, but neglected as much as possible.[19]

A Code of Ethics for Teachers. Many problems are created in a school situation between teachers and students, teachers and fellow teachers, and teachers and administrators. Most of these problems could be avoided if teachers and administrators were completely aware of and followed the Code of Ethics adopted by the National Education Association and by most state education associations. The code is given in its entirety in the Appendix to provide the principal with the ethical base for many decisions affecting relationships with teachers.

The Teacher Looks at the Principal. Teachers look at principals in terms of the teacher's personality. Every teacher has certain expectations of what a principal should do and be. The principal also looks at his job as he thinks it should be, and as he thinks teachers think it should be. The new principal desires the teachers to recognize his new authoritative position, but he wants them to regard him as being in empathy with the teachers. At the same time, the principal wants to take on the role behavior that is consistent with his expectations of that position. Conflicts sometimes become evident in these discrepancies. The position of the principal in the hierarchical structure is sometimes a disruptive rather than a cohesive force in teacher-administrator relationships. Teachers assert that there must be greater equality in salary if teaching, administration, and counseling are to be regarded as equal though different functions, rather than different levels of educational endeavor. However, popular prestige holds the principal of the school to be more important, higher in ability, wisdom, and rank than his employees. Specialization has caused members of each area to be preoccupied with their own development—and consequently they lose the ability and desire to understand the purposes and activities of other areas and to see their relationships to the whole. The problem of value also pulls teachers and principals apart. Teachers are concerned about conditions that directly affect their work with pupils: curriculum, books, materials, load, equipment, and freedom to teach as they wish. The administrator must be able to smooth out friction points, between departments, teachers, teacher-students, and parents. In this exposed position, the administrator develops habit patterns of caution, delay, compromise, and finesse. The teachers want immediate changes. The administrator often wants compromise.[20]

Teachers expect administrators to show leadership, to develop a sound

---

[19] *Ibid.*, p. 20.
[20] Bush, *op. cit.*, pp. 146–48.

school program, to facilitate instruction, and to contribute to the highest morale for all teachers. Teachers believe that these goals could be accomplished if the administrator would:

Spend more time and energy on the program of the school and less on the board of education.

Concentrate on learning rather than running a bank or department store.

Have a philosophy of education and know how to achieve its aims.

Understand that true leadership is not a matter of status but competence.

Understand that teachers need to help plan—like to have a consensus.

Realize that teachers like to know what the problems are.

Not sacrifice his integrity on the altar of public relations.

Show more interest in the real value of teachers' work rather than superficial "doctored" progress reports.

Act as a counselor so teachers can present their problems to him without fear of recrimination.

Establish rapport that discourages phoneyness and encourages honest self evaluation.

Stimulate teachers to do better and recognize the teacher's contributions.

Provide needful information through faculty meetings rather than by publishing bulletins.

Develop inservice training but not insist there is only one way to teach.

Understand that teachers expect proper orientation to the school, its program and goals.

Understand that teachers expect to be supplied with necessary equipment and attractive environment.

Make morale a year round concern; not a one-a-year party.

Recognize teacher opinion, his work, his ideas and consult with him when decisions affect him.

Discourage cliques and encourage group harmony.

Set aside time for consultation and encourage teachers to come in.

Provide opportunity for advancement and better salary.[21]

Supervising Instruction

Supervision: A Principal's Primary Responsibility. One of the principal's primary tasks is the improvement of the curriculum program. Correlated with this assignment is the need to improve and make more effective the instruction within the school. Swearingen indicates that ". . . supervision focuses upon the improvement of instruction. It is concerned with the continuous redefinition of goals, with the wider realization of the human dynamic for learning and for cooperative effort, and with the

---

[21] Modified from Richard M. Bossone, "What Teachers Expect of Their Administrators," *California Journal of Secondary Education*, February 1957, pp. 71–73.

nurturing of a creative approach to the problems of teaching and learning."[22] A good supervisor is thought of as a helper, adviser, resource person, coordinator, consultant, and leader. A principal may not be able to serve adequately in all these roles to all teachers, but he can do much more than is generally being done.

In Chapter 1 it was indicated that the total amount of time that a principal should spend in the curriculum and instructional work was about 31 per cent, according to authorities in the field of secondary school administration, while the principals believe that 22 per cent of their time should be spent in this area; but the studies revealed that principals were spending only 12 per cent of their time for the improvement of curriculum and instructional programs. Davis made a study of how the California secondary school principals actually distribute their time within the curriculum and instructional phase of their responsibilities.[23] Table 9.2 shows the distributions of time devoted to working with individuals, staff members, groups, classroom visitations, and in-service programs. Table 9.3 shows the percentage of hours devoted to the instructional improvement activities as shown by the size of the schools. It will be noted that the larger the school system, the more time the principal is able to devote to the curriculum and instructional activities and that the time spent in each category is actually increased with the increase in the size of the school.

Discovering Needs.   If the principal is to improve instruction, he must first establish areas where improvement is needed in the curriculum or in the instructional techniques. There are many ways by which the principal might identify these needs. Swearingen suggests the following:

Analyze a learning situation
Search for appropriate materials
Listen to teachers talk
Ask the teachers directly
Search records
Work with professional organizations
Engage in action research
Evaluate the program with the faculty.[24]

Instituting Change and the Principal's Role.   The principal should realize that there is a close interrelationship between curriculum develop-

[22] Mildred E. Swearingen, *Supervision of Instruction: Foundations and Dimensions* (Boston: Allyn and Bacon, Inc., 1962), p. 1.

[23] H. Curtis Davis, "Where Does the Time Go?" *California Journal of Secondary Education*, October 1953, pp. 347–60.

[24] M. E. Swearingen, *op. cit.*, p. 139.

TABLE 9.2 Distributions of Time Devoted to (A) Working with Individual School Staff Members on Curriculum Problems, (B) Working with Groups of Staff Members on Curriculum Problems, (C) Classroom Visitation and Supervision, and (D) In-service Training Programs by 324 California Secondary School Principals During the Week of March 16–20, 1953

Hours Per Week	(A) WORKING WITH INDIVIDUALS		(B) WORKING WITH GROUPS		(C) CLASSROOM VISITATION AND SUPERVISION		(D) INTER-SERVICE TRAINING PROGRAM	
	No. of Principals	Per Cent of Principals	No. of Principals	Per Cent of Principals	No. of Principals	Per Cent of Principals	No. of Principals	Per Cent of Principals
0	31	9.57	192	59.25	81	24.00	154	47.53
¼–2	182	56.17	95	29.34	150	46.31	136	42.29
2½–4	77	23.77	33	10.18	50	15.43	22	6.79
4¼–6	26	8.02	3	0.92	34	10.49	2	0.62
6¼–8	4	1.23	1	0.31	5	1.54	3	0.92
8¼–10	1	0.31	0	0.00	4	1.23	4	1.23
10¼–12	1	0.31	0	0.00	0	0.00	2	0.62
Above 12	2	0.62	0	0.00	0	0.00	0	0.00
Total	324	100.00	324	100.00	324	100.00	324	100.00

SOURCE: H. Curtis Davis, "Where Does the Time Go?" *California Journal of Secondary Education*, October 1953. Reprinted by permission.

TABLE 9.3 Per Cent of Hours Devoted to Instruction Improvement Activities, Shown by Type of Duty and Size of School, by 324 California Secondary School Principals During One Week, March 16–20, 1953

Administrative Duties	SIZE OF SCHOOL				
	0–249 (50 Schools) Per Cent	250–749 (101 Schools) Per Cent	750–1,499 (110 Schools) Per Cent	1,500–3,900 (63 Schools) Per Cent	Total Per Cent
1. Curriculum					
A. Principal working alone	0.21	0.12	0.40	0.43	0.29
B. With individuals within the school	2.17	3.54	4.24	6.19	4.08
C. With groups within the school	0.70	1.21	1.42	2.19	1.39
D. With persons outside the school	0.81	1.42	1.54	1.18	1.32
2. Cocurricular	12.65	12.62	12.53	12.19	12.51
3. Classroom visitation and supervision					
A. Direct classroom supervision	3.43	3.11	3.59	4.41	3.58
B. Other supervision of students	1.53	1.40	1.80	0.97	1.47
4. In-service training program	1.41	1.38	1.81	3.39	1.92
Total	22.91	24.80	27.33	30.95	26.56

SOURCE: H. Curtis Davis, "Where Does the Time Go?" *California Journal of Secondary Education,* October 1953. Reprinted by permission.

ment, improvement of instruction, professional growth, and personal development. Curriculum change is primarily social in nature, since curriculum change requires change in the human being. Curriculum development is closely allied to the teacher's personalities. Change is a great source of anxiety for most individuals, and teachers are no exception. The teacher in a rut seldom recognizes the depth of the rut. It is easier to bring about change with a person who is constantly improving himself than with a person who is in an established rut. The principal should use positive approaches in initiating change and should secure the cooperation of all teachers. At the lowest level of improvement, the positive approach requires a principal to look for actions to be praised, supported, and reinforced. Such recognition provides additional incentive to do better, and no defense mechanisms are aroused in the teacher. The question might be asked, "But how does one get out of a rut or help others out of a rut?" The following suggestions can be used from a positive approach to help teachers recognize the need for change:

1. Read the professional books in the field. The principal has an obligation to see that these professional periodicals are available.

2. Attend state and national conventions in the curriculum areas. The principal's responsibility is to make funds available for such attendance and encourage teachers to participate.

3. Attend university classes and workshops. A principal's responsibility is to encourage such participation prior to such classes and to listen to the teacher talk about the new ideas after participation.

4. Become personally involved in the profession. The principal's responsibility is to have faculty members placed on district and state curriculum committees and to encourage faculty members to speak before clubs and other organizations.

5. Discuss new ideas. The principal's responsibility is to create an atmosphere for free and open discussion and to serve as a catalyst for such discussions.

6. Participate in experimentation. The principal's responsibility is to aid the teacher in planning, conducting, and evaluating an experiment. The principal should assure the teacher that experimentation is important whether the results are positive or negative.

7. Get help from consultants. The principal's responsibility is to recognize needs and to make available district, state, and university consultants.

Supervision: A Two-Way Street. It should be recognized, however, that improvement is a two-way proposition. The principal can initiate it, supervisors can assist, but the teachers must actively participate in it. Teachers expect the principal and supervisors to have some of the following qualities: sincerity, tactfulness, positive approach to criticism, sense of humor, kindliness, self-control, tolerance, and approachableness. Supervisors, on the other hand, sometimes find teachers who are not cooperative. Peckham classified undesirable teachers as the Monday-through-Friday teacher who belongs to the "Thank God for Friday club"; the self-satisfied teacher who knows all the answers; the teacher who demands all the time —the clinging vine; the turncoat—or hypocrite; the no-observation-in-this-class teacher—who will not teach while the principal or supervisors are present; and the you-will-have-to-show-me teacher.[25]

Supporting the Teacher.   An area of great concern to most teachers is the degree to which the principal gives them support in actions they must take or have taken. The importance of such backing improves the over-all morale of the school and in general makes the teachers more effective in their class presentations. The following case illustrates the need for supporting the teachers in their decisions:

Student Locker Cleanup

It was customary to hold a student locker cleanup at a specified time during the last week of school. Past experience showed that students were especially careless, neglectful, and wantonly messy or sloppy in performing this task. Papers and books had been torn to bits and scattered in the halls.

At the regular faculty meeting immediately preceding the locker cleanup, the principal expressed great concern regarding student behavior and the need for supervision during the locker cleanup period. He requested each teacher to station himself in the hall adjacent to his classroom to supervise and "police" the area during the cleanup. Student behavior that "got out of hand" was to be reported to the principal for disciplinary action.

At the appointed time, the locker cleanup proceeded. As usual, the litter began to accumulate on the floor rather than in wastecans that had been provided. Most teachers did not bother to check the halls because experiences in the past indicated to them that they would have little administrative backing in their "police" duties.

A teacher obediently followed the request of the principal and tried to maintain control, but one rebellious student refused to conform to the teacher's suggestions. The teacher reported the student to the principal for disciplinary action. The principal said that he would act immediately.

On the following day, the student involved came to the teacher who had reported him and stated, "The principal said you wanted to see me."

The principal had contacted the student and sent him to see the teacher to settle the matter.

[25] Dorothy Reed Peckham, "Tribulations of a Supervisor," *Educational Leadership,* December 1948, pp. 158–60.

The importance of supporting teachers in their roles is demonstrated in this case. If the principal had consistently supported the teachers in the past in diciplinary action, all teachers would probably have aided in supervision of the cleanup. The students would have used wastecans and the problems would not have occurred. In this situation the teacher who tried to follow through with the principal's suggestion was penalized twice —once in the imposition of his time to supervise the activity, and once by the necessity to institute and carry out a penalty that should have been the principal's concern. Obviously, at the next cleanup season one more teacher will not be present in the halls.

Teachers always feel the need for the supporting influence of the principal. New teachers may not understand their full responsibilities and how situations should be handled. The principal should be especially concerned in his support. He must give suggestions to teachers and make corrections as needed; however, as a professional person he should treat teachers courteously at the time of correction. He should not criticize or reprimand a teacher in front of the students.

In-service Programs. One of the most effective ways to bring about curriculum development and instructional improvement is through organized in-service programs within the school. Many districts have a district-wide in-service program each year. Other districts leave such programs to the individual school. Some of the more effective programs are those in which the district sets a standard of in-service development, provides time in the schedule for such development, and then permits the individual schools to determine the scope of the projects. Under this arrangement, the teachers have time allotted as part of their schedule for professional growth and development. Seldom does a negative attitude arise regarding potential changes. In-service programs are most effective if the principal approaches the problem through effective use of group dynamics.

Administrator Ethics in Personnel Matters. Because this chapter is concerned primarily with the teacher and the principal working together to provide effective instruction, the principal should consider carefully the matter of ethics in personnel matters. The following statement of administrator ethics was prepared and endorsed by California Association of School Administrators, California Association of Secondary School Administrators, California Elementary School Administrators' Association, and Personnel Standards Commission of the California Teachers' Association and the State Council of Education. (The complete code is in the Appendix. Only this portion on the supervisor is provided here.)

In the supervision and leadership of his staff . . .

1. He assumes responsibility for the success of all employees, realizing that failure of an employee is at least partially an administrative failure— in selection, in supervision, or in assignment.

2. He makes sure that observed weaknesses are called to the attention of the employee, and that assistance toward their correction is extended.

3. He reports no negative criticism of any employee to the board without having discussed this criticism with the employee involved.

4. He informs the board about the good performance and contributions of employees.

5. He is alert to opportunities to further the advancement of each employee.

6. He values the professional suggestions and criticisms of staff members, according to each the recognition to which he is entitled as a fellow professional in the field of education.

7. He provides opportunity for employees to discuss their problems or complaints freely with him and assists in the cooperative development of systematic channels for reporting and discussing employee grievances and suggestions.[26]

Evaluating Instruction

Purposes of Evaluation. The primary purposes of evaluations are to provide a review of what has been accomplished and to give direction for future instruction. Fawcett indicates that,

Evaluation of personnel in an organization is essential to the accomplishment of its goals. If the personnel employed fail to have the skills, attitudes, and knowledge essential to the accomplishment of its goals, the organization will not succeed. . . . Skill can be lost; knowledge is not permanent. Changes in goals require different skills, new attitudes, and different knowledge. Personnel changes in any organization. Employment of a new person may force reassignments of responsibilities to those who are already employed. Employees with indispensable skills, attitudes, and knowledge retire, die, and resign. The organization must survive these changes, and there must always be the capability of reaching goals despite changes. The inventory function of evaluation is indispensable to the planning and operation of an organization.[27]

---

[26] California Association of School Administrators, California Association of Secondary School Administrators, California Elementary School Administrators' Association, and Personnel Standards Commission of the California Teachers' Association and the State Council of Education, *Administrator Ethics in Personnel Matters.* (California: The Associations, April 1956). Reprinted by permission of the California Teachers' Association.

[27] Claude W. Fawcett, *op. cit.,* p. 55.

Although evaluation is used frequently at the end of an activity, it is not a terminal act. Evaluation, like learning, should be a continuous process. It should lead to further learning—and better teaching.

Evaluation of the Teacher.   Considerable controversy can be found when questions of evaluating teacher competency are raised.[28] There are some educators who maintain that teacher effectiveness cannot be appraised because the effect of the teaching being observed can only be measured in the behavioral pattern of the student years in the future. Others maintain that there are many aspects of teacher competency that can be measured and that not only can measurement take place, but also comparison of the teacher with himself and with other teachers can be made.

For all practical intent the principal must assume that teacher evaluation can be made, for it is part of his responsibilities. At the end of the year, he usually is required to turn in to the district officials some type of evaluation on teacher effectiveness. On new and probationary teachers these evaluation reports may be required several times during the year. Three factors are important: (1) the skills of the principal in making evaluative judgment, (2) the readiness of the teacher to be evaluated, and (3) the instrument or criteria used in making the judgments.

The principal should have background in at least two subject fields and several years of teaching. As principal he should have opportunity to visit all types of teachers and see all types of teaching techniques. He can approach the task with some degree of objectivity. In addition to general observations that a principal gradually receives over the weeks, months, and years, he should observe the teacher's classes, using some teacher-approved rating scale, and hold conferences with the teachers. Critical to his effectiveness are his attitude and communication skills when working with the teachers. The conference should be a two-way reaction of goals, attempted techniques, and success in meeting the goals. Observations of teaching strengths should be discussed first, and then problems should be raised which lead to suggestions for improvement. A teacher should not be told, "You did this wrong, . . ." but he should be led to a discussion of needed improvement; for example, "I noticed that this happened . . . . What were you trying to accomplish?" or "I noticed that the boys over in the corner seemed to have difficulty controlling their behavior today, what was the trouble with them? . . ."

If a redirection in teacher behavior is indicated as a result of the evaluation, the teacher must know that the behavior is in need of change.

[28] National Education Association, Research Division, "Teachers, Administrators, and Evaluation," *N.E.A. Research Bulletin*. Washington, D.C.: The Association, December 1964, pp. 108–11. Reprinted in *Education Digest*, April 1965), pp. 22–24.

If the correct behavior is known and accepted by the teacher, and the teacher has identified his own hopes and desires with the goals of the school organization (high morale), the teacher will be motivated to change. If the needed changes are numerous, seem impossible of accomplishment, or impair other activities or values held by the teacher, or if the teacher has not identified personal goals with the organizational goals (low morale), termination of employment may be considered by the teacher and/or the principal.

Assuming that the teacher desires to improve, the basic task ahead is the redirection of behavior. The principal should help the teacher attack the problem piece by piece so that improvements can be seen. "Redirection of behavior, then, is dependent upon the administractor's skill in programming the changes in behavior that seem desirable. This is made easier if the administrator has done a proper job of identifying successions of skill development among the desirable behaviors. He and the teacher can then concentrate on the next most difficult skill, the next most desirable attitude, and the next most desirable block of knowledge. The true enormity of the total progress to be made is then reduced to shorter range goals."[29]

Merit Rating for Salary Purposes. Merit rating is even more controversial than simple teacher evaluation. Merit rating is teacher evaluation linked with salary increases. In a system of merit pay it is not enough to locate "good teachers"; "better" and "best" teachers must be identified. The classroom teachers' organizations have opposed merit rating on the basis that rating devices for salary purposes are impractical and inadvisable. Boards of education have tended to favor merit rating, and many districts have such programs.

The basic arguments for and against merit rating are given below:

Pros—
1. Teachers should be paid for what they are worth and for quality of the work done.
2. Merit rating provides incentive for wanting to improve.
3. Merit rating will tend to draw and hold "superior" teachers.
4. The present system tends to give security to incompetents and poor teachers.
5. Relating salary to competence will promote morale in teachers.
6. The community is more willing to pay for education when better teaching is developed.

Cons—
1. Measurement is not accurate—too subjective.
2. It takes time which could better be used to improve teaching.

[29] Claude W. Fawcett, *op. cit.*, p. 63.

3. It reduces staff morale, working relationships.

4. Limitations on numbers who can be promoted cause differences between outstanding teachers, and also causes younger teachers to wait for openings in quotas.

5. It too frequently stereotypes teachers to standards, thus discouraging creative teaching.

6. It tends to worsen working conditions (tensions, worry, and strain at rating periods).

7. Teacher training institutions should weed out their incompetents before they become teachers.

8. Emphasis should be on developing all teachers to become better rather than rewarding or punishing a few.[30]

An analysis of the many arguments for and against indicate that the principle of merit is quite widely accepted but the practice is condemned. There are four major concerns: (1) Can an instrument be devised that will measure the quality of teaching performance? (2) What factors should be included? (3) How and by whom should merit rating measures be administered? (4) What will be the harmful effects on teacher morale and thus teacher efficiency? The advocates of merit rating quickly point out that there are also plenty of problems and inequities in the present system of equal pay for unequal work.[31]

As a result of the controversy, the principal should recognize that for a merit rating for salary purposes to be successful, he should (1) develop a valid definition or description of good teaching, (2) develop a fair and practical procedure of appraisal, (3) develop a constructive relationship between the appraisal system and the salary system, and (4) secure the cooperation and participation of teachers in development of the program.

Summary

Improving teacher morale is most effective in improving instruction because high morale is correlated with efficient teaching and satisfactory learning. The factors affecting morale of the staff are material and human. The material factors affecting morale are salary, sick leave, medical and hospitalization insurance, retirement provisions, facilities, equipment, and supplies. Some of the human factors affecting teaching morale are personality characteristics, physical and mental health, grievance procedures, sensitivity training, and involvement in making decisions.

[30] Glen F. Ovard, "Teachers Merit Rating," *The American School Board Journal*, October 1959, p. 37.

[31] Margaret Bennett, "A Matter of Merit," *Phi Delta Kappan*, January 1965, pp. 225–26. Bernarr S. Furse, "Merit Pay Is Feasible and—Sometimes—Desirable," *Phi Delta Kappan*, January 1961, pp. 143–47.

If the principal is to be effective in the goal of improving instruction, he must have an understanding of the teacher's background and the teacher's role. The social and psychological backgrounds of a teacher should be understood. Teachers are generally well respected in their communities and participate in social organizations; however, there are a number of factors that create conflict and strain for the teachers. These factors are the intangibility of the educational product, the socioeconomic conditions, the high moral expectancies (double standard) of a teacher, and conflict between teacher and student and teacher and administrator. A code of ethics gives the teacher guidelines to aid him in avoiding conflict.

Supervision of the instructional program is important in implementing instruction. According to authorities, the principal should be spending approximately 31 per cent of his time in this field. Principals believe that they should be spending 22 per cent but actually are spending only 12 per cent of their time in the area of curriculum and instruction. By working with the teachers, the principal should rededicate himself to this task.

The secondary school teacher averages 45 hours and 54 minutes per week in carrying out his duties. This is divided between class instruction, related out-of-class instructional activities, and miscellaneous activities.

In working with the teacher for the improvement of instruction, the principal might well review the principles discussed in Chapter 2 under "Group Dynamics and Effective Leadership." Human relations is a key factor in the improvement of instruction. Teachers get into ruts and resist change. The principal should create opportunities whereby the teacher desires improvement. Suggestions that can be given for such encouragement are: attendance at state and national conventions, attendance at university courses and workshops, personal involvement in professional circles, professional reading, participation in experimentation, discussions with the principal and other faculty members, and talks with consultants.

Evaluation of instruction is also a principal's responsibility. The evaluation gives the teacher and principal a review of accomplishments and a guide for improvement. Teacher evaluation linked with salary adjustments is known as merit rating. Merit rating is controversial; yet it can be approached in such a way as to eliminate many of the problems.

SUGGESTED PROJECTS AND ACTIVITIES

1. Working with a school principal, conduct a morale survey of his staff. Analyze why some teachers have high morale while others do not.
2. Review the table on how a secondary school teacher spends his time. Is the activity program indicated?

3. Analyze and discuss the code of ethics for teachers. How can the code of ethics be used to improve morale?
4. Examine various in-service education projects. What elements are contained in the in-service program that have aided in the success or failure of such a program.
5. Review the case presented on supporting the teacher. Role-play the possible ways each situation could have been handled.
6. Prepare a report on the subject "Resistance to Change" and adapt it to curriculum work.
7. Invite a supervisor to class or visit a district supervisor and have him discuss his job.
8. Go with a district supervisor to make classroom visitations. Review procedures that are used from the point of entering a school to the final point of making suggestions for teacher improvements.
9. Visit a school system that operates a merit pay. Review the operating procedures. Develop a policy and procedures for instituting a merit system.

REVIEW AND DISCUSSION QUESTIONS

1. Why are curriculum development and instructional improvement considered to be the most important duties of a secondary school principal?
2. If the principal is to be effective in the improvement of these programs, what is the most important consideration for this effectiveness?
3. In what ways does morale affect effectiveness?
4. What are some of the background characteristics associated with teachers?
5. What are the teacher's roles and how are these different from the administrative roles?
6. What are the primary sources of conflict for the teacher?
7. Could teacher and pupils be matched—based on certain characteristics, as suggested by Bush?
8. How is the teacher affected by the intangibility of the educational product?
9. In what way can a teacher be considered the conscience of a society?
10. Why should teachers subscribe and adhere to a code of ethics?
11. How can a principal support a teacher when the teacher has broken school policies or regulations in the very act for which they desire support?
12. How can teachers be encouraged to get out of a rut when they are not aware they are in one?

13. How can a principal evaluate a teacher from an administrative role and still be effective in producing desirable changes?

SELECTED BIBLIOGRAPHY

Austin, D. B. "Tackling the Big Problem of Administrative and Supervisory Staffing," *Bulletin of N.A.S.S.P.*, April 1964, pp. 47–59.

Bennett, Margaret. "A Matter of Merit," *Phi Delta Kappan*, January 1965, pp. 225–26.

Bossone, Richard M. "What Teachers Expect of Their Administrators," *California Journal of Secondary Education*, February 1957, pp. 70–73.

Castetter, William B. *Administering the School Personnel Program*. New York: The Macmillan Company, 1962.

Douglass, Harl R., Richard K. Bent, and Charles W. Boardman. *Democratic Supervision in Secondary Schools*. Boston: Houghton Mifflin Company, 1961.

Fawcett, Claude W. *School Personnel Administration*. New York: The Macmillan Company, 1964.

Furse, Bernarr S. "Merit Pay Is Feasible and—Sometimes—Desirable," *Phi Delta Kappan*, January 1961, pp. 143–47.

Hammock, Robert C., and Ralph S. Owings. *Supervising Instruction in Secondary Schools*. New York: McGraw-Hill Book Company, 1955.

Leavitt, Harold J. "Consequences of Executive Behavior," *Bulletin of N.A.S.S.P.*, April 1964, pp. 167–76.

Lien, Ronald L. "Democratic Administrative Behavior," *Bulletin of N.A.S.S.P.*, March 1964, pp. 31–38.

Manlove, Donald C. "The Principal's Role in Improving Instruction," *Bulletin of N.A.S.S.P.*, December 1962, pp. 1–5.

National Education Association Research Division, *The American Public School Teacher*, 1960–61 Research Monograph 1963–M2. Washington, D.C.: NEA Research Division, April 1963.

———. "Teacher, Administrators, and Evaluation," *N.E.A. Research Bulletin*, December 1964, pp. 108–11.

———. "Why Few School Systems Use Merit Rating," *N.E.A. Research Bulletin*, May 1961, pp. 61–63.

Ovard, Glen F. "Teachers Merit Rating," *The American School Board Journal*, October 1959, p. 37.

Swearingen, M. E. *Supervision of Instruction: Foundations and Dimensions*. Boston: Allyn and Bacon, Inc., 1962.

Weir, Edward C. "Some Thoughts on Evaluation," *Bulletin of N.A.S.S.P.*, December 1962, pp. 23–29.

Wiles, Kimball. *Supervision for Better Schools*. Englewood Cliffs, N.J.: Prentice-Hall, Inc., 1955.

Van Zwoll, James A. *School Personnel Administration*. New York: Appleton-Century-Crofts, 1964.

PART III

*The focal point of efficient school administration should
always be located nearest to those vital purposes
for which the public school exists. This means
the boys and girls. Every act of teaching
and every aspect of the organizing, administering, and
supervising functions should contribute directly to
the end that the boys and girls in each stage of
their development receive a full measure of attention.*
—WILLIAM A. YEAGER. *Administration and the Pupil.*
New York: Harper and Brothers, 1949, p. 21.

THE ADMINISTRATION
OF
STUDENT AFFAIRS

CHAPTER 10

Student Personnel Services

Schools are for students and the educational program should be designed for them! If boys and girls are to receive a full measure of attention at each stage of their development, the schools must provide a full range of student personnel services. The emergence of student personnel functions in the secondary schools has been slow but gradual.[1] However, in this day of widespread educational change and increased focus on the individual, each school must reassess its practices and provide more and better services. Modern technology should be used to update many practices. New programs and record-keeping forms, such as the Cooperative Plan for Guidance and Admission, might well be instituted. National attention on the dropout along with federal financial assistance for such potential students emphasizes the need for creative, new approaches.

The principal is the director of these services in his school. Generally speaking, the following areas are placed under his direction: school attendance and its related problems; orientation, admission, classification, and assignment of students to an educational program; evaluation and reports on pupil's progress; supervision of programs for the exceptional students such as remedial reading and special education; supervision of student discipline; guidance and counseling programs; health and safety programs; and the personal, social, and emotional adjustment of students.[2]

---

[1] Charles R. Keller, "Schools Are Students—And Teachers Like Miss Eleanor Parker," *Bulletin of N.A.S.S.P.*, March 1965, pp. 259–67.

[2] A theoretical discussion on social forces that have brought forth the need for these services may be found in Lloyd E. McCleary and Stephen P. Hencley, *Secondary School Administration: Theoretical Bases of Profession Practice* (New York: Dodd, Mead and Company, Inc., 1965), pp. 240–57.

The principal, of course, cannot manage all these functions without assistance; and to the extent to which he is able, he delegates responsibility in the pupil personnel area to assistants, counselors, nurses, and other personnel.

This chapter covers only a portion of the total student personnel services. The following chapter on guidance and counseling and a portion of the chapter on administration of auxiliary services both discuss a part of these important services. This chapter will be concerned primarily with the admission, orientation, and classification of students, student accounting, student achievement, and evaluation and reports of student progress.

Orientation and Admission of New Students

Admission Policies. Students have not always had the rich opportunity of educational advancement that they have today. Admission of students to secondary schools was a great concern in years gone by. However, with the increased emphasis on mass education and laws supporting public education, such as manpower and education, "War on Poverty," and general federal aid to education, all adolescent children who can profit in any manner from instruction should be provided with a full opportunity for an education. Therefore, admission to the changing high school is primarily a matter of assessment and placement of students in the appropriate program and of record keeping to determine whether all the potential students actually are in school. There is very little selective procedure. Today's admission requirements allow entrance to any person of secondary school age, usually from 12 to 18 or 19, who can profit by the opportunities afforded him and who will not, because of physical, mental, or social handicaps, become a menace to other students. Of course, the records, information, transcripts, residence, and other data about the student must be secured from previously attended schools. The student may be placed in special programs, but seldom is a student excluded from attending a public secondary school. Only in private schools is the policy of selectivity in effect. In these schools, admission may still be on the basis of examination, ability to pay, parental tradition and influence, promises of success, and other such specific requirements as may be set by the school.

Classification and Assignment of Students. During the 1920's and early 1930's much progress was made in the field of educational placement of students according to their individual needs. During the late-1930-and-early-1940 period more emphasis was placed on the social well-being and problems involving the social order than on the individual. In the current decade the pendulum has swung once again to a greater emphasis on the individual differences of students and on the recognition that to meet these individual differences special programs and individual placements are necessary. Therefore, measuring students' abilities and achievements and placing them in situations where the greatest growth will occur are major concerns today.

A trend toward nongraded high schools[3] is one recent effort to more effectively group students according to their need. Not only are students "phased" according to ability and achievement, but also they are allowed to develop their creative and discovery potentialities. Another unique program in which student ability and potential are used to determine individual standards of achievement is the continuous progress program. The student and his parents meet with counselors. An expectancy rate of the total course content to be completed, one-half year, three-quarters year, one year, one and one-half years, etc., as well as quality standards of 70, 80, or 90 per cent, are set. Each student has his own placement and achievement expectancies.[4] The special vocational, scientific, and dramatic arts high schools of New York City are attempts citywide to more adequately group students on the basis of individual needs. There are still obvious program gaps as shown by the extensive dropout problem. The schools must provide assignments within a broader and more diversified program for all students.[5]

Orientation of New Students. The principal has the major responsibility for the initial adjustments of students to a new school situation. Orientation is needed at two times: (1) when students leave the elementary school and enter a secondary school, and (2) when students are transferring from the junior high school to the senior high school. At both these times the principals must be concerned about student adjustment to new facilities, teachers, and educational programs.

The transition from the elementary grades, which have a self-contained type of educational program, to the departmentalization found in most secondary schools is especially difficult. Attempts to smooth this transition have resulted in the establishment of core curricula or broad field subjects

---

[3] A good coverage of such a program may be found in the book by that title. B. Frank Brown, *The Nongraded High School* (Englewood Cliffs, N.J.: Prentice-Hall, Inc., 1963).

[4] Jack V. Edling *et al.*, *Four Studies in Programmed Instruction* (New York: Fund for the Advancement of Education, 1964), pp. 66–94.

[5] L. G. Hall, "A Gap in Our High School Program," *Bulletin of N.A.S.S.P.*, September 1963, pp. 32–39. "Phases of Guidance in the Secondary School," *Bulletin of N.A.S.S.P.*, November 1961, pp. 1–196. Robert J. Havighurst, "The Educationally Difficult Student—What the Schools Can Do," *Bulletin of N.A.S.S.P.*, March 1965, pp. 110–27.

in which students are registered with a single teacher for a large block of time, usually from two to three hours. It is believed that programs with some larger blocks of time make the transition between the elementary and secondary school much easier for the student. The principal, however, must also be concerned that the curricula in these broad course areas are satisfactory and that the educational program is not sacrificed simply for adjustment. Another procedure often used at both levels is for some student organization such as Boys League or Girls League to have individual members assigned as big brothers or big sisters to certain students or groups of students. A third effective procedure is to assign students to homeroom teachers who will be sympathetic and understanding of the students' problems and who can give the special attention that is needed by new students. A fourth procedure often used is a special visitation or get-acquainted day when students are brought to their new school and given a brief orientation.

In addition to the needs of the students who enter new schools in large blocks, the transfer students who may arrive at any grade level and at any time during the school year from other schools within the district, state, nation, or world need an orientation program. These students usually require special individualized attention in the understanding of school procedure and policy. Part of the students' information can be given to them at the time of their registration, but some program of continuous orientation is also needed.

Student Handbook. One means of providing all students with an orientation to the school's philosophy, history, and policies is the student handbook. The student handbook serves as an orientation tool and provides useful information that all students need during the course of the year. It can also be used by parents and community citizens who have a desire to know certain fundamental facts about the school.

One very important function of the student handbook is to explain the many policies that have been established for the effective control of the total school program. These policies have usually been developed as the needs arose and have become part of the tradition of the school. The policies should be placed in writing and explained to both students and parents. The student handbook might well include information on some of the following areas of school policy; proper dress at school, arrival time at school, procedures for being excused from school, appointments during school time, absentee procedure, truancy, tardiness, lockers, lost-and-found articles, bicycles, student insurance, parties, bus service, telephone use, cheating, visitor permissions, care of school property, student behavior, and smoking and drinking.

In addition to the items involving school policy, other informational items can be given in a school handbook. Such information is very helpful and profitable to the students. Information that is frequently found in student handbooks includes the following:

A brief history of the school
Curriculum requirements
Requirements for graduation
Fees
Calendar of school events
Student organizations
Bus service
School lunch
Dismissal program
Fire drills and evacuation procedures
Requirements for physical examinations
Summer programs
Library service
Clubs and organizations
Sample report card and explanation of reporting procedure
Description of courses offered
Program-of-studies planning sheet
Names and addresses of faculty and students

Student handbooks are produced in many forms and shapes. The most simple is a duplicated handbook stapled together; the most complex, a type-set, printed publication. Most commonly the books are small enough to fit in the pocket.

Student Accounting

Compulsory School Attendance. The principal, in cooperation with the central office, must have some system of student accounting because each state has adopted compulsory attendance laws. The procedure of handling compulsory attendance laws varies from district to district. Compulsory school attendance of every student of school age is necessary in our democratic way of life. Education is necessary for both the well-being of the individual and the well-being of the state. Compulsory school attendance is based on the premise that a law requiring every student to be in school is good for the student as well as the state. However, the accomplishment of the goals of democracy is placed above the desires of individual students. Although the age for compulsory attendance varies among the states, all states have compulsory education laws. The following trends relating to compulsory attendance laws are observable:

1. Both the time and the number of years in which students are required to be in school are increasing.

2. The parents as well as the student are held responsible for compliance with the education law.

3. Compulsory attendance laws are being tightened to provide for greater continuity in school attendance.

4. A gradual shift is being made from penalties for violations to preventive measures for students who fail to observe the laws.

There are some exceptions in which public school attendance is not required. Attendance in private schools is one major exception. Although the law requires students to be in school, it does not require that the student must be in a public school. This question was brought to the courts, and the Supreme Court ruled that no state had the authority to require students to attend public schools exclusively.[6] Where instruction is provided in private schools, the private school must show that the education given is substantially equal to that ordered by the state. Legal age limits must be adhered to, and certain scholastic achievements and graduation requirements must be maintained.

The only other way a student may legally be excused from attendance at public school is to receive such permission from the board of education. Often the principal must make such a recommendation to the board of education on behalf of the student. The state usually specifies the reasons for which a board of education may release a student from school. Probably the most common exceptions granted by the states are for mental incapacity, moral baseness, incorrigible behavior, and maintenance of a family.

The School Census.   If the student is to be in school on a compulsory basis, the first obligation of the school system is to know the whereabouts of all the students. One procedure used to determine where all students are within a school system is to have a school census. The school census serves other important purposes, such as determining the nature and scope of other educational services it must provide, aiding the school in the adequate planning of the school building, and determining the number of children who will be starting school in any given grade. The school census is required in most of the states and is usually taken annually. The census is based on a careful house-to-house canvass, with a separate census card being completed for each family. Names of the children and other data required are recorded on the card. A typical census card is shown in Figure 10.1.

The administrative procedure of taking a census may be handled in

---

[6] Pierce vs. Society of the Sisters of Holy Names of Jesus and Mary, 268 U.S. 510, 45 S. Ct. 571, 69 L. Ed. 1070, 39 A.L.R. 468.

Figure 10.1

School Census Card

◇Surname of Children									
SCHOOL CENSUS Area_____ Block No._____ District_____									
Name of Responsible Parent or Guardian			Street Address, Zone and Town					Relationship	
1 List all children who are under age 18 on Oct. 31 (List by age-oldest first)	2 Sex M-F	3 Age Oct. 31	4 Birth Date Mo. Day Yr.	5 Handi-capped (Enter code no.)	6 Grade Now In	7 School Now Attending	8 School Last Attended	9 Reason not in any School (code no.)	10 Name, address of other school child attends, not main-tained by district

Code Numbers for Reasons for Not Enrolling in Any School
1. Over 16, completed 8th grade, enters employment, attends school for 144 hours (school requirement may be met at home)
2. Over 16, supports mother or invalid father, enters employ-ment, attends school for 144 hours (may be taught at home)
3. Has completed the work of a senior high school.
4. Is taught adequately at home.
5. Physical or mental condition makes attendance inexpedient or impracticable (Board may require physician's certificate)
6. No class is available within 2 1/2 miles of home or place of employment, and no free transportation is provided.
7. Adequate education provided in connection with employment.
8. Over 16 and cannot profit from school attendance.
9. Illegally not enrolled.
10. Married.
11. Armed Forces.

Code Numbers for Handicapped Children (All Ages)
These children may or may not be enrolled in school.
A. Physical health impairment of major consequence (rheumatic fever, polio, etc.)
B. Motor handicaps (cerebral palsy, arthritis, etc.)
C. Intellectual disabilities (low mental maturity, brain damage, pre-natal malformations, etc.)
D. Seeing handicaps (cataracts, damaged retina, etc.)
E. Hearing handicaps (eardrum, nerve damage, etc.)

Form F-9 -- Rev. 1958

SOURCE: Utah State Department of Public Instruction. Reprinted by permission.

many different ways. In some school systems the teachers are organized by districts and are required to take the census, while in other school systems nonteaching personnel are hired to take the census. Unless a district maintains a staff to take the census, the enumeration, recording, tabulating, and compiling of the reports must be done through the pupil personnel division. The high school usually is responsible for a certain portion of the school district. And the principal and his staff must organize, enumerate, and tabulate the results for the area assigned to his school.

It must be remembered that the census only locates the students; it does not bring them to school; therefore, some procedure must be devised not only by which students can be located but also by which their regis-tration can be checked. The job of actually getting students to school when they do not desire to attend is primarily a function of an attendance officer at the district level. The principal must work in cooperation with the attendance officer so that both will know when the student has arrived in school. Once the student is registered, the major responsibility for accounting for his attendance lies with the principal.

The Daily Class Schedule. As part of the student's registration, he will complete a form that indicates his name, address, telephone number;

the name, address, and telephone number of his parents; and the daily class schedule showing the subject, room, and teacher. This form is usually called the daily class schedule and is shown in Figure 10.2.

Figure 10.2

Daily Class Schedule

Last Name	First Name	Middle Name	Home Room	Class	Date of Birth
Address	Phone Number	Church Preference	Enrolled Date		Locker Number

DAILY CLASS SCHEDULE — FIRST SEMESTER				DAILY CLASS SCHEDULE — SECOND SEMESTER			
Period	Subject	Room	Teacher	Period	Subject	Room	Teacher
1				1			
2				2			
3				3			
4				4			
5				5			
6				6			

Name of Parent _____

If not residing with parent, name of person responsible in case of emergency _____

Address of Parent _____   Address _____ Phone _____

Phone Number _____ Parent's Occupation _____ Relationship _____

The daily class schedule is filed alphabetically. It is used constantly to find students during the school day.

Accounting for Students' Absences.   When an absence occurs, it is important that it be recorded in some consistent manner whereby a cumulative record on the student may be maintained. Each individual teacher should maintain such a record in his roll book as part of the accounting procedure. In some schools individual teacher records are sufficient; however, in most schools today, master cumulative attendance records of all students are maintained. Such an attendance record is shown in Figure 10.3.

When an absence occurs, its cause must be ascertained. On the basis of the cause, the principal can plan what action should be taken. The school and the board of education determine the legitimacy of the absence. The board of education's policies governing attendance procedures should be in writing. The principal and those who work with the attendance policy must administer the district policy but should be given allowances to cover individual circumstances. The attendance policy should be adequately communicated to teachers, pupils, parents, and the community in general.

When a student returns to school following an absence, the school

Figure 10.3

Attendance Record

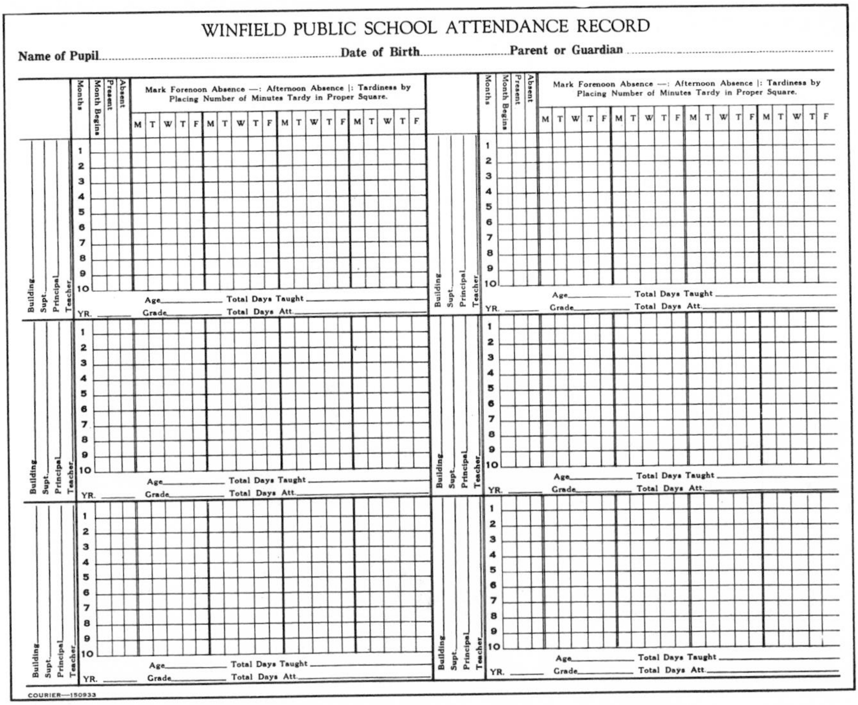
WINFIELD PUBLIC SCHOOL ATTENDANCE RECORD

Name of Pupil.......... Date of Birth.......... Parent or Guardian..........

Months | Month Begins | Present | Absent

Mark Forenoon Absence —: Afternoon Absence |: Tardiness by Placing Number of Minutes Tardy in Proper Square.

M T W T F M T W T F M T W T F M T W T F

1 2 3 4 5 6 7 8 9 10

Building | Supt. | Principal | Teacher

YR. ______ Age______ Grade______ Total Days Taught ______ Total Days Att. ______

COURIER—150933

SOURCE: Winfield Public Schools, Winfield, Kansas. Reprinted by permission.

must decide whether to classify the absence as excusable or unexcusable. Some system of marking should be used to designate both categories. Each absence, as recorded on the public school attendance record, should be designated by this marking system.

Unexcused Absences. Since the school must designate whether an absence is excused or unexcused, some system must be devised whereby the principal may obtain this information. Workable techniques used to gain this information are as follows: (1) telephone calls on the day of the absence, (2) written notes from home signed by parents stating the cause of the absence, (3) statements signed by the students in which the student on his honor indicates the reason for the absence, and (4) a periodic letter sent to the home advising the parents of absences from school and requesting parents to contact the school if such absences do not agree with their knowledge of the student's whereabouts. If it is determined that the student is absent without justifiable excuse, the principal must work with the student to help him see the educational value of school and the importance of regular attendance. Teachers are notified of the reasons for absences so they may know how to deal with the students in their individual classes. Sometimes schools find it necessary to impose penalties on those students who consistently choose to be absent without excuse. The penalties vary from social disapproval, at one end of the continuum, to discounting a student's grade or denial of a school award at the end of the year, at the other end of the continuum.

In addition to students who are absent all day without excuse, the principal frequently must handle the problem of unexcused absences during the day. A procedure commonly used in most schools to keep track of students during the day is as follows:

During the first period of the day, all teachers fill out an absentee form, which is collected by secretaries from the office. (See Figure 10.4.)

Figure 10.4

Absentee List

ABSENTEE LIST			
Teacher _____		Date _____	
Name		Period	Class
1.			
2.			
3.			
4.			
5.			
6.			
7.			
8.			
9.			
10.			
11.			
12.			
13.			
14.			
15.			
16.			

The office then compiles a complete alphabetical master list of all students who are absent during the day. During the subsequent periods the teachers check absences during their periods and verify on the master list whether the student was absent during the first period. If the student was present, it is assumed that the student is absent from this teacher's class only. The student's name is then listed and the period shown for which he is absent.

At the end of the day this second absentee list is picked up by the office and another list is made that shows names of students who were absent during any given period during the day. Opposite these names will appear the reason for the absence during the period, such as illness, dental appointment, doctor's appointment, called home by parents, etc. Students not thus accounted for are considered unexcused unless properly cleared the following morning.

It is obvious that this system calls for a complete check-in and check-out system. If a student arrives late to school or must leave for any given reason, most schools require the student to report to the office at this time. The central office must serve as the clearinghouse for students who have been absent without excuse. Teachers must be notified when such absence occurs.

Tardiness. Tardiness is also a problem for teachers and principals. Unless some system is used to keep it in check, it can become a major problem. Therefore, most schools require students to be in class promptly on time. Unless the school has a uniform policy, each teacher is left to work out his problem by himself. Since every department is different, some flexibility, even under a uniform policy, is necessary. The school should have some system whereby students who are detained legitimately by the office or by other teachers may report late to a subsequent class without penalty. A tardy excuse is usually used for this purpose. See Figure 10.5.

Figure 10.5

Admission Excuse

```
                    ADMISSION EXCUSE

     Admit _____

            Absence ☐        Tardiness     ☐

            Excused ☐        Not Excused ☐

     Remarks:

     Date _____ Signed _____
```

Some suggestions for teachers in handling the late problem were given by individual teachers as a result of a conference on the tardiness problem.[7] Some of these suggestions are as follows:

[7] Glen F. Ovard, "Suggestions for New Teachers in Handling the 'Late Problem,'" *Bulletin of N.A.S.S.P.*, September 1959, pp. 144–46.

1. Teachers holding students for consultation, teachers' work, intramurals, or other teacher-approved activity should provide the next class instructor with an excuse for the student.

2. When a student has three unexcused tardy marks in a given class, the teacher should lower the mark one grade unless this is waived by the teacher for special guidance purpose.

3. Continued excessive tardiness should be reported to the committee on attendance.

4. Teachers should not ask students to perform errands for them unless it is an emergency. A proper pass should be given the student if such emergency arises.

5. Teachers should not excuse students to go to their lockers for books and supplies. It is better to be near the door when the student enters and send him to his locker before class starts. If teachers stand by their doors prior to bell time and close the doors as the bell rings, students will realize that teachers are starting classes on time.

6. Start classes immediately when the bell rings. Do not answer individual questions until the whole class is under control and work commenced.

7. Assume always that arriving on time is necessary.

8. Activity that would be a handicap to the student if missed should be planned frequently for the beginning of the class.

Evaluating Student Achievement

Tests. The evaluation of student achievement begins in the classroom and is initiated by the teacher. The teacher has two major purposes for evaluation: (1) to see how well the materials have been taught, and (2) to see how well the materials have been learned. The test is one device used for these measurements. The principal should understand that in most courses, the criteria used for evaluation vary greatly with the subject matter as well as the philosophy of the teacher. Mathematics teachers use different criteria than do art teachers. Physical education teachers use different criteria than do business teachers. Industrial arts teachers use different criteria than social studies teachers. The actual tests, based on these criteria, will also vary. The tests may be objective, subjective, skill development, project skills, etc.

A basic policy question that principals in most schools must resolve is: "Should the student be compared with himself, or compared with the other members of the class, or compared with some outside standard of measurement?" If a student is to be measured against himself, the school must have a system or some source of data that describes the students, their abilities, achievements, rate of growth, and other such information. On the basis of such initial data, the teachers can then give tests that will measure the advancement the students are making relative to their abilities and limitations. The expectancy level is thus regulated by the students' abilities and limitation levels. Grades are given to the students according to the degree to which they achieve as compared to their ability.

When students are compared with other members in the class, a basic assumption is made that the class is a normal class with a wide range of abilities and limitations. The school expects the student to succeed at a rate different from the rates of other students in the class. The school further expects that there will be a normal distribution of scores on any given test. The degree to which there is not a normal distribution would indicate that either the class is not a typical class or the test given was not a good, typical, or representative test. The grades that are given on the examination are based on a certain percentage of students who fall in the probable distribution ranges. Some schools have modified the normal distribution curve at the lower end to allow for individual effort. Under such a modification, failures are seldom given if students have been working up to their ability level.

The third type of evaluation calls for a comparison of the students with some outside standard. An example of an outside standard is the percentage system in which the number of points possible is divided into the number of points scored. The standard is set at 90 to 100, A; 80 to 90, B; 70 to 80, C; 60 to 70, D; and below 60, failing. Another outside standard might be a fixed rate of speed, such as words per minute as is often found in typing and shorthand classes. Students who can perform at a given skill level are graded accordingly. The skill level, such as 120 words per minute, becomes the outside standard.

As teachers prepare their courses of study, the principal should assist them in consideration of evaluation standards. Some teachers believe that they have personally failed unless they fail a certain portion of the students enrolled in their class. Other teachers want to give all students the top grade. A great difference exists between individual teachers. The principal must work with the teachers to try and smooth out the obvious irregularities. The smoothing-out process usually ends up in some type of generalized school policy regarding grading procedure. An important point for the principal to remember is that the grading criteria, test scores, and other data used in evaluation by the schoolteacher should always be entered in the teacher's roll book.

Grades. Teachers generally accept the process of student evaluation and the data-collecting devices recommended because they are anxious to assess the growth and development of the student. However, when it is necessary to categorically state a student's achievement record in comparison with himself, other students, or some outside standard, the teacher generally prefers not to make such comparisons. Whether teachers are right or wrong in their preferences seems to make little difference because the parents expect some type of quantitative and qualitative report on the student's progress. Since parents desire to know how well a student has performed, the teacher is required to give a grade. The principal must make plans to adopt a policy to see that a grading procedure is followed in his school.

The grading system most often used over the years has been a system that gives five categories of comparison. Either a letter grade or a numerical grade is used to designate the comparative rating as follows:

Letter Grade	Numerical Grade	Definition
A	1	Superior
B	2	Above average
C	3	Average
D	4	Below average
F	5	Failing

Some school systems have tried to refine the five-point classification by assigning to each letter grade a plus or a minus for every letter above F; thus a total of 13 categories is created.

Recording and Reporting Student Achievement

The principal is the key person in the school in determining policy and procedures relating to recording and reporting student achievement. The school grades are used for informing students, parents, employers, colleges, and universities about the achievement of the student, for promoting students, for counseling the student, and for providing basic vocational data about the student. Because of the high degree of importance attached to recording and reporting student achievement, various types of systems are presented here to help the principal in this phase of policy determination.[8]

Letters and Parent-Teacher Conferences. Far too frequently, teachers wait until a given reporting period to make a progress report to parents. When a student is not performing in a satisfactory manner, some system of reporting earlier than the set reporting period is needed. The student, parent, and principal should be apprised of the situation. A teacher can quickly notify the student because of his constant contact within the classroom situation. However, there is no assurance that a student will carry the message home. In fact, at the high school level, the message most likely will not reach home. The first knowledge that a parent generally has that the student is performing unsatisfactorily is the report card at the scheduled reporting period. By this time, one quarter of the year has

[8] A more detailed description of general principles, practices, and cautions may be found in: Sterling Callahan, *Successful Teaching in Secondary Schools* (Chicago: Scott, Foresman and Company, 1966).

Figure 10.6

Notice to Parents of Student's Unsatisfactory Work

NOTICE TO PARENTS OF STUDENT'S UNSATISFACTORY WORK

Student _____ Class (circle) 7 8 9 10 11 12

Subject _____ Present Grade _____ Date _____

Areas of Greatest Weakness

1.	Daily work	____	5.	Notebook work	____
2.	Quizzes	____	6.	Written work	____
3.	Class discussion	____	7.	Homework	____
4.	Oral work	____	8.	Laboratory work	____

Reasons for Unsatisfactory Work

1.	Reading difficulty	____	7.	Poor written work	____
2.	Fails to follow directions	____	8.	Fails to hand in assignments	____
3.	Inattentive in class	____	9.	Poor work habits	____
4.	Does not volunteer	____	10.	Too frequent absence	____
5.	Does not ask questions in class	____	11.	Failure to do make-up work	____
6.	Antagonistic attitude	____	12.	Other (see comments below)	____

_____ I have had a conference with the student concerning his unsatisfactory work.
_____ I have scheduled a conference with the student.
_____ Student is aware of his unsatisfactory work.
_____ Student fails to keep appointments concerning his unsatisfactory work.
_____ Student does not come in for special help when it is offered.
_____ Student has not asked for special help.

Comments:

_____

_____

_____

_____

Please call the school if you wish an appointment with the teacher or counselor. The teacher is available for conference during the periods checked below. The counselor is available throughout the day upon appointment.

Period 1,	8:00 — 8:45 A.M.
Period 2,	9:00 — 9:45
Period 3,	10:00 — 10:45
Period 4,	11:00 — 11:45
Period 5,	1:00 — 1:45 P.M.
Period 6,	2:00 — 3:15
Period 7,	3:30 — 4:15

_____
Teacher

_____
Counselor

passed and much vital information necessary for the further progress of the student has been missed in the class. Parents are usually unhappy at this point. Their expressions of unhappiness are leveled at both the teacher and the principal. Therefore, the principal should encourage teachers to notify parents of unsatisfactory performance. Notification to parents may be through a telephone call, a letter, or a request for a parent-teacher conference. A notice to parents of unsatisfactory work is shown in Figure 10.6. Regardless of the procedure used, the primary purpose is to communicate the problem to the parents and solicit their cooperation in a solution. A school should maintain a record when such contacts have been made.

Report Cards.   The report card is the traditional device for reporting student achievement to parents. Although the purpose is basically the same everywhere, report cards are found in all styles, shapes, and descriptions. The report card must reflect the over-all grading philosophy of the school and must provide sufficient information to explain to the parents the system of grading used.

Samples of report cards, which express various philosophies as well as various styles, are presented below with commentary:

1. A simple academic report card is shown in Figure 10.7. This card

Figure 10.7

Academic Report Card

| Grade _____ JUNIOR HIGH SCHOOL   School year 19__ – 19__ | | | | | | | | | | | | |
| Report of _____ | | | | | | | | | | | | |

SUBJECT	First Quarter		Second Quarter		Third Quarter		Fourth Quarter		FINAL			TEACHER
	Absences	Grade	Absences	Grade	Absences	Grade	Absences	Grade	Absences	Grade	Credit	
_____												
_____												
_____												
_____												
_____												
_____												
_____												
_____												

| Principal _____ | Homeroom Teacher _____ |

is one of the simplest and is used in many secondary schools throughout
the United States. The basic data shown are the absences from school,
a general citizenship grade, and a subject matter grade.

2. An achievement and adjustment report is shown in Figure 10.8. This
report card is very brief but shows both grades received and achievement
in relation to capabilities and adjustment to the school situation.

Figure 10.8

Achievement and Adjustment Card

Student's Name		Address				Grade	
ATTENDANCE RECORD		First Term	Second Term	Third Term	Fourth Term	TOTAL	
Days Belonging							
Days Present							
Days Absent							
SCHOOL CITIZENSHIP							
SUBJECTS:						Final Mark	Credit

A-Exceptional. B-Above average. C-Average. D-Below average (Passing). E-Not passing

3. A speedy, sensitized report card is shown in Figure 10.9. An interesting feature of this report card is that it is in duplicate and the paper
is the carbonized type. Typical data are presented. The teacher spends
less time preparing the card. The explanation for the numerical letters is
given on the reverse side.

4. A Key Sort report card is shown in Figure 10.10. This report card
combines scholarship and citizenship information, but does it within the
McBee Key Sort system for speed and efficiency. Carbon copies are also
made from this report.[9]

5. A scholarship and ability report card is shown in Figure 10.11. This
report card is used to show scholarship and whether this scholarship is
consistent with ability. A global citizenship rating with detailed citizenship
criteria is also presented.

[9] Also see Howard Dalman, "What Are Some New Trends in Reporting Student
Growth and Achievement to Parents?" *Bulletin of N.A.S.S.P.*, April 1960, pp. 148–49.

Figure 10.9

Sensitized Report Card

Report Card
BRIGHAM YOUNG UNIVERSITY HIGH SCHOOL
Provo, Utah
Phone FR 4-1211 — Extensions 2721, 2722

Last Name .... First Name .... Class .... Homeroom Teacher ....

........Marking Period   Date........   Final Grade........   Credit Earned........

Hour	Subject	Grade	Absent	Tardy	Teacher
		A B C D F I 1 2 3 4 5 6 7 8	School Excused .... Other .... Total		

Letter and number explanation on other side.

Remarks:

☐ Parent-Teacher Conference is advised. Please call for appointment.

System of Marking

The primary aim of the Brigham Young University High School is the attainment of fundamental concepts, habits, skills, attitudes and appreciations which are necessary for personal success and acceptable American citizenship. This report card summarizes for one subject the achievment of these goals.

Letter Grade

The letter grade indicates the level of attainment as compared to other students in the group. It is based on class paricipation, tests, quality of projects, and assignments completed.

An I (incomplete) indicates that essential work has not been completed. If work is not satisfactorily accomplished within three weeks, the grade automatically becomes an F (failure).

Number Grade

The number grade reports the student's achievement in relation to his capabilities and adjustment to the school situation and is to be interpreted as follows:—

1. Expected progress is being made.
2. Shows definite improvement.
3. Performance is below the level of ability.
4. Study time is unwisely used.
5. Attitude inhibits efficient learning.
6. Does not function effectively in a group.
7. Fails to work well when on his own.
8. Class attendance is irregular.

C 38-39 2600 5-64 36573

SOURCE: Brigham Young University Laboratory School, Provo, Utah. Reprinted by permission.

Figure 10.10

Key Sort Report Card

B O Y | 1 7 4 2 1 | 7 8 9 10 11 12 | 7 4 2 1 | 7 4 2 1 | 7 4 2 1 | 4 2 1

ADVISOR | GRADE | STUDENT (H T U) | SUFFIX

WINFIELD JUNIOR & SENIOR HIGH SCHOOL
WINFIELD, KANSAS

YEAR 19____ 19____

CITIZENSHIP RATING: +-OUTSTANDING; BLANK-SATISFACTORY; U-UNSATISFACTORY

GRADE EXPLANATION: A-EXCELLENT; B-ABOVE AVERAGE; C-AVERAGE; D-BELOW AVERAGE; F-FAILING; I-INCOMPLETE

	CITIZENSHIP RATING	1	2	3	4	5	6
SOCIAL	IS CONSIDERATE OF OTHERS						
	PRACTICES SELF-CONTROL						
	IS CAREFUL WITH PROPERTY						
	RESPECTS AUTHORITY						
	ACCEPTS RESPONSIBILITY						
WORK HABITS	USES TIME TO ADVANTAGE						
	CONTRIBUTES TO CLASS						
	FOLLOWS DIRECTIONS						
	COMPLETES ASSIGNMENTS						
	THINKS AND WORKS INDEPENDENTLY						

	SCHOLARSHIP								ATTENDANCE					
									ABSENCES					
	1	2	3	SEM.	4	5	6	SEM.	1	2	3	4	5	6
CLASS GRADE														

STUDENT'S NAME | CODE | CLASS

SUBJECT | CODE | INSTRUCTOR | CODE | PERIOD

INSTRUCTOR'S COMMENTS: REPORT TO PARENTS

Z68043X

INSTRUCTOR (U T) | PERIOD (0 1 2 3 4 5 6) | SUBJECT (U T H)

SOURCE: Winfield Public Schools, Winfield, Kansas. Reprinted by permission of Winfield High School and Royal McBee Corporation.

Figure 10.11

Scholarship Compared to Ability Report Card

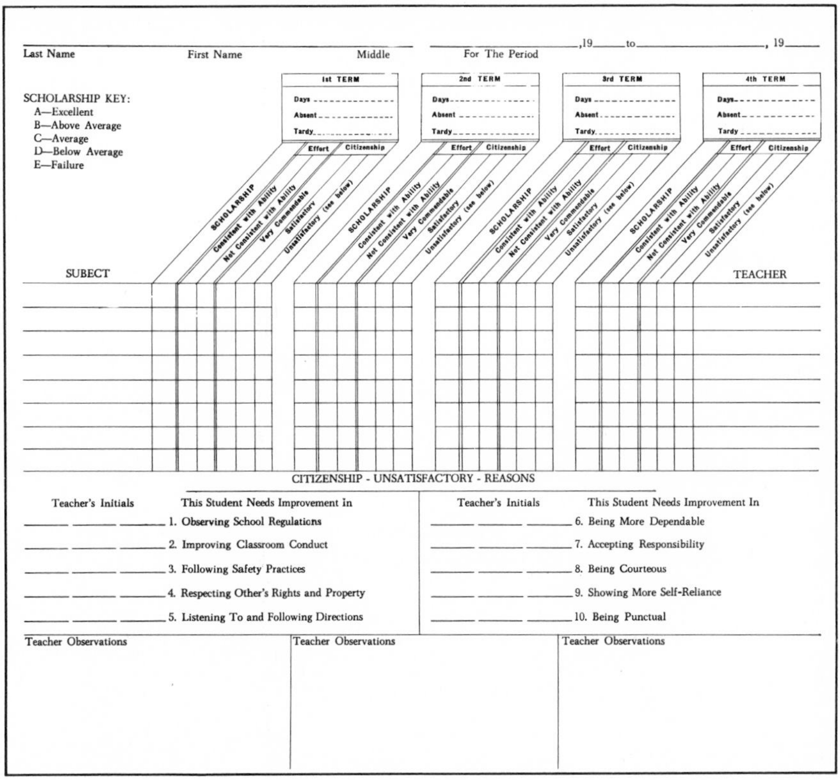

| Last Name | First Name | Middle | For The Period ,19___ to___ , 19___ |

SCHOLARSHIP KEY:
A—Excellent
B—Above Average
C—Average
D—Below Average
E—Failure

1st TERM — Days___ Absent___ Tardy___ — Effort / Citizenship

2nd TERM — Days___ Absent___ Tardy___ — Effort / Citizenship

3rd TERM — Days___ Absent___ Tardy___ — Effort / Citizenship

4th TERM — Days___ Absent___ Tardy___ — Effort / Citizenship

SCHOLARSHIP — Consistent with Ability — Not Consistent with Ability — Very Commendable — Satisfactory — Unsatisfactory (see below)

SUBJECT .... TEACHER

CITIZENSHIP - UNSATISFACTORY - REASONS

Teacher's Initials	This Student Needs Improvement In	Teacher's Initials	This Student Needs Improvement In
___ ___ ___	1. Observing School Regulations	___ ___ ___	6. Being More Dependable
___ ___ ___	2. Improving Classroom Conduct	___ ___ ___	7. Accepting Responsibility
___ ___ ___	3. Following Safety Practices	___ ___ ___	8. Being Courteous
___ ___ ___	4. Respecting Other's Rights and Property	___ ___ ___	9. Showing More Self-Reliance
___ ___ ___	5. Listening To and Following Directions	___ ___ ___	10. Being Punctual

Teacher Observations | Teacher Observations | Teacher Observations

Permanent Records for Transcripts

In addition to the report card, the principal is responsible for maintaining a permanent record.

Permanent Record Cards. The permanent record contains the information about the student that the school desires to retain on a permanent basis. The record is maintained at the school indefinitely and is always available when requests for information about the student are made. The data that appear on the permanent record vary with the individual school and usually depend on the amount of information that is kept on another record called the cumulative record. The cumulative record is used more by the counseling system, and the permanent record is used more by the administration. As long as both records are available, the material on the permanent record need not contain much more information than the basic data, such as the name, dates attended, final marks and credit in a subject area, the date of graduation, and date of entry or transfer. The purposes of the information in the cumulative folder are discussed in the chapter on guidance and counseling services.

The permanent record is kept in the principal's office and should not leave that office for any purpose, for it is the summation of the student's academic achievement. For daily use the record should be kept in a fireproof cabinet, while all records that are not in use should be kept in a fireproof vault. There are numerous types of permanent record reports. The Comprehensive Student Report, described hereafter under Cooperative Plan for Guidance and Admission, is one type of permanent record card that provides other copies for use by the counselors and for transcripts to universities. The National Association of Secondary-School Principals has also developed a permanent record card, size 5 × 8, which is used in many schools. See Figure 10.12.

Figure 10.12

Permanent Record

PERMANENT RECORD

School City

Last Name First Name Middle Name Sex Race Birthplace Month Day Year

Entered from Date Age Class Curriculum Adviser

Parent or Guardian Occupation Nationality Address Telephone No.

EXTRA CLASS ACTIVITIES

Date	Activity	Honors or Offices	Pts. Crs.

INTELLIGENCE-TEST RECORD

Date	Name of Test	Form	Score	%-ile Rank	MA	CA	IQ

ACHIEVEMENT-TEST RECORD

Date	Name of Test	Form	Score	Class Norm.	%-ile Rank	Subject Age

Was Graduated Date Rank No. in Class

Left Date Reason

ATTENDANCE RECORD

Semester	1	2	3	4	5	6	7	8	9	10	Totals
Days Present											
Days Absent											
Times Tardy											

PERSONALITY RECORD

Symbols: (1) High; (2) Above Av.; (3) Av.; (4) Below Av.; (5) Low

	1st yr.	2nd yr.	3rd yr.	4th yr.	5th yr.	Summary
Motivation						
Industry						
Initiative						
Influence & Leadership						
Concern for Others						
Responsibility						
Integrity						
Emotional Stability						

General Health

Significant Limitations

Home conditions Parents Living No. Brothers No. Sisters

Vocational Preferences

College or Position Date

Credits Sent to Date

Standard size, 5" x 8"; flexible cardboard.

SOURCE: National Association of Secondary-School Principals. Reprinted by permission of the National Association of Secondary-School Principals. Copyright: Washington, D.C.

The principal has the responsibility to protect and safeguard these records. In addition to storing the records in the vault and other fireproof files, he should have the records microfilmed for permanent storage. When students transfer to other schools or enter a college, a copy of the student's record is made and sent to the school concerned.

The principal's responsibility with regard to the permanent card is to select the system used; to administer the system; to see that all appropriate data are placed on the card; to protect the record from solicitors and curiosity seekers; and to supply the data required by colleges, universities, employers, and other groups or organizations that have a legitimate use for the information. The principal can delegate the mechanics of the operation to the secretary.

Cooperative Plan for Guidance and Admission. The Cooperative Plan for Guidance and Admission (C.P.G.A.) has developed a unique and comprehensive transcript service and record-keeping system. By means of a computer, the C.P.G.A. is able to store, summarize, retrieve, and communicate meaningful and comprehensive information about students in a quantity and quality unknown before to the educational community. The final result of this computer processing—the Comprehensive Student Record—may be one of the most significant contributions in recent history in school-to-college and school-to-employer, as well as faculty member, communications. The system was started in Georgia. Demonstration pilot systems in five states were then made with over 114 high schools and over 10,000 students involved in the pilot project. The program is now available through Educational Testing Service[10] to any school that desires to participate.

The C.P.G.A. student record is on two sides of an 8½ × 11 form, which looks like a test answer sheet and is entitled Student Profile Record. (See Figure 10.13.) The Student Profile Record is the input document used for central processing. It requires about six to ten minutes of clerical preparation. The computer assimilates all this information about the student, processes it, computes usual descriptive statistics, and prepares a document that combines the student record and the results of the calculations. The output document is the "Comprehensive Student Report" (Figure 10.14). The school does not need to spend further time on rank, class calculations, grade point average, or other kinds of arithmetic. These are all completed in the computer center. The comprehensive student report is prepared in multiples of five and returned to the school. Studies indicate that the actual time spent in maintaining a school record is reduced by more than two thirds under the C.P.G.A. system.

[10] Student Profile Record and Comprehensive Student Record, reprinted by permission of the Educational Testing Service.

Figure 10.13

Cooperative Student Profile Record

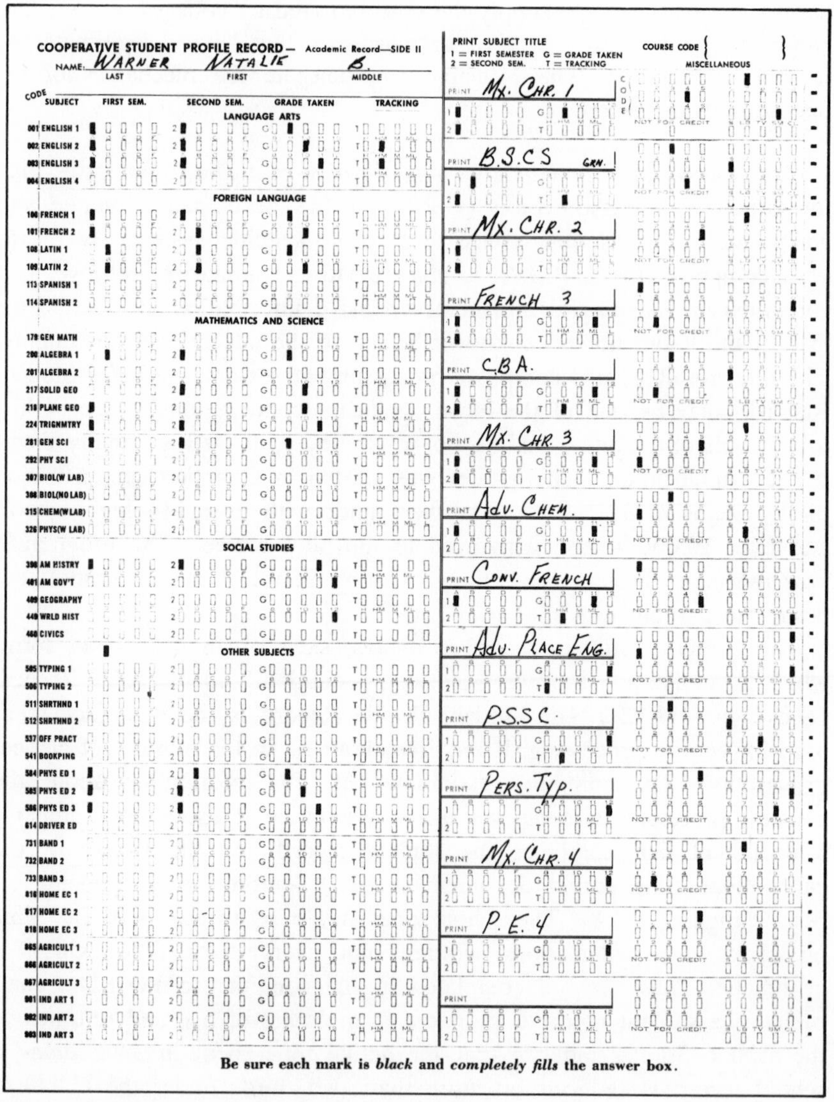
COOPERATIVE STUDENT PROFILE RECORD— Academic Record—SIDE II

NAME: WARNER NATALIE B.

LAST FIRST MIDDLE

CODE	SUBJECT	FIRST SEM.	SECOND SEM.	GRADE TAKEN	TRACKING
	LANGUAGE ARTS				
001	ENGLISH 1				
002	ENGLISH 2				
003	ENGLISH 3				
004	ENGLISH 4				
	FOREIGN LANGUAGE				
100	FRENCH 1				
101	FRENCH 2				
108	LATIN 1				
109	LATIN 2				
113	SPANISH 1				
114	SPANISH 2				
	MATHEMATICS AND SCIENCE				
178	GEN MATH				
200	ALGEBRA 1				
201	ALGEBRA 2				
217	SOLID GEO				
218	PLANE GEO				
224	TRIGNMTRY				
281	GEN SCI				
292	PHY SCI				
307	BIOL(W LAB)				
308	BIOL(NO LAB)				
315	CHEM(W LAB)				
326	PHYS(W LAB)				
	SOCIAL STUDIES				
398	AM HISTRY				
401	AM GOV'T				
409	GEOGRAPHY				
440	WRLD HIST				
460	CIVICS				
	OTHER SUBJECTS				
505	TYPING 1				
506	TYPING 2				
511	SHRTHND 1				
512	SHRTHND 2				
537	OFF PRACT				
541	BOOKPING				
584	PHYS ED 1				
585	PHYS ED 2				
586	PHYS ED 3				
614	DRIVER ED				
731	BAND 1				
732	BAND 2				
733	BAND 3				
816	HOME EC 1				
817	HOME EC 2				
818	HOME EC 3				
865	AGRICULT 1				
866	AGRICULT 2				
867	AGRICULT 3				
901	IND ART 1				
902	IND ART 2				
903	IND ART 3				

PRINT SUBJECT TITLE
1 = FIRST SEMESTER G = GRADE TAKEN
2 = SECOND SEM. T = TRACKING

COURSE CODE

MISCELLANEOUS

PRINT Mx. CHR. 1
PRINT B.S.C.S GRN.
PRINT Mx. CHR. 2
PRINT FRENCH 3
PRINT C.B.A.
PRINT Mx. CHR. 3
PRINT Adv. CHEM.
PRINT CONV. FRENCH
PRINT Adv. PLACE ENG.
PRINT P.S.S.C.
PRINT PERS. TYP.
PRINT Mx. CHR. 4
PRINT P.E. 4
PRINT

NOT FOR CREDIT

Be sure each mark is *black* and *completely fills* the answer box.

SOURCE: Cooperative Student Profile Record. Reprinted by permission of the Educational Testing Service.

Figure 10.13 (Continued)

STUDENT PROFILE RECORD Personal Record—SIDE I

PERSONAL CHARACTERISTICS

MOTIVATION
INDUSTRY
INITIATIVE
INFLUENCE-LEAD
CONCERN-OTHERS
RESPONSIBILITY
INTEGRITY
EMO. STABILITY

HONORS & AWARDS YES

NAT'L. HONOR SOCIETY
LETTER CLUB
SCHOL. SEMI FINALIST
NATIONAL AWARD
STATE AWARD
SCHOOL HONORS
LOCAL AWARD
OTHER

HEALTH SUMMARY ABSENCE SUMMARY TARDINESS SUMMARY

FRESHMAN
SOPHOMORE
JUNIOR

HOURS PER WEEK WORK RECORD OCCUPATIONAL CODE

CURRICULUM

ACADEMIC
AGRICULTURE
COMMERCIAL
GENERAL

TRADE
MUSIC or ART
HOME EC.
OTHER

General Clerk
Payroll Clerk
Cafeteria Cashier
Baby Sitting
Reporter

Social Club
Debating Club
St. Council Board
Journalism
Future Teachers

EXTRA CURRICULAR ACTIVITIES

RATING PARTICIPATED & NOT RATED ACTIVITY CODE

TEST NAME	TEST CODE	GRADE TAKEN	TYPE OF LOCAL SCORE	TEST NORM SCORE	SUB-SCORES						
D.A.T.	290	9	14		95	95	90	85	60	85	80
S.C.A.T.	632	9	14	G	96- / 99	99- / 99b	82- / 83	79- / 80	65		
S.T.E.P.	641	9	14	H	82- / 80	83- / 84	78- / 80				
Coop. Ag.	239	9	24		95						
Otis & S(Gm)	571	10	15		125						
P.S.A.T.	600	11	16	K	62	65					
N.M.S.Q.T.	550	11	90	L	23	25	27	15	19	22	

SCHOOL NAME Rocky Hill H. S. Charlotte, N.C.

STUDENT NAME WARNER NATALIE B.

STUDENT'S STATE OF BIRTH GA.

STUDENT'S DATE OF BIRTH 8 / 6 / 48

PARENT OR GUARDIAN'S NAME WARNER WILLIAM

COLLEGE BOARD SCHOOL CODE NO. 110170

MOTHER'S MAIDEN NAME EVERETT

SEX MALE FEMALE

PHYSICAL DISABILITY YES

Be sure each mark is *black* and *completely fills* the answer box.

Cooperative Plan for Guidance and Admission
Copyright © 1963 - Educational Testing Service

Figure 10.14

Comprehensive Student Report

COMPREHENSIVE STUDENT REPORT

STUDENT INFORMATION

NAME: WARNER, NATALIE B

SEX	BIRTH DATE	STATE OF BIRTH
F	8/ 6/48	GA

PARENT OR GUARDIAN: WARNER, WILLIAM

CURRICULUM	HEALTH FR	SO	JR	SR	PHYSICAL DISABILITY
ACADEMIC	0	0	0		

DAYS ABSENT FR	SO	JR	SR	DAYS TARDY FR	SO	JR	SR
5	2	3		0	0	1	

ACADEMIC SUMMARY

RANK IN CLASS DATA	POINTS	UNITS	AVERAGE	RANK	GROUP SIZE	% ILE STANDING
COMPLETE CLASS:	72.3+	19	= 3.80	4	IN 430	= 99
ACADEMIC GROUP: (ACADEMIC COURSES ONLY)	60.5+	16	= 3.78	4	IN 260	= 99
COMPLETE CLASS WEIGHTED:	77.3+	19	= 4.07	3	IN 430	= 99

COMPOSITE TEST: PRELIMINARY SCHOL APT T

VERBAL TEST SCORE	MATH TEST SCORE	CONVERTED VERBAL COURSE SCORE	CONVERTED MATH/SCIENCE COURSE SCORE	CONVERTED ALL COURSE SCORE	VERBAL COMPOSITE	MATH/SCIENCE COMPOSITE	ALL COURSE COMPOSITE
62	65	71	71	74	64	66	67

SCHOOL INFORMATION

SCHOOL NAME: ROCKY HILL H S

LOCATION: ATLANTA, GA

CLASS PD (MIN)	MEETING/WEEK	WEEKS/YEAR	MEANING OF GRADES: PASSING	HONORS	COL REC	D	C	B	A
55	5	36	70	90	87	70	79	87	95

CEEB SCHOOL NUMBER	CLASS SIZE	GRAD. YEAR	UNITS REQ.	SCHOOL ACCREDITED BY
110170	430	64	18	STATE, REGION

OTHER SECONDARY SCHOOLS ATTENDED	DATE LEFT

ACADEMIC RECORD

AREA	AVERAGE
LANG ART	4.0
FOR LANG	3.5
MATH	3.8
SCIENCE	3.9
SOC STUD	4.0

VERBAL COURSE AVG. 3.7

MATH/SCIENCE COURSE AVG. 3.8

GRADE 9

SUBJECT	1	2	UNIT	GROUP	MISC.
ENGLISH 1	A	A	1		
FRENCH 1	A	A	1		
LATIN 1	B	B	1		
ALGEBRA 1	B	A	1		
GEN SCI 1	A	A	1		
PHYS ED 1	A	B	.50		
MIX CHOR1	A	A	.50		

UNITS TOWARD GRADUATION 6 — GRADE 9 AVERAGE 3.7

GRADE 10

SUBJECT	1	2	UNIT	GROUP	MISC.
ENGLISH 2	A	A	1	HM	
FRENCH 2	A	B	1		
LATIN 2	B	B	1		
PLN GEOM	A		.50		
SLD GEOM		A	.50		
BSCS GRN	B	A	1	HM	
PHYS ED 2	A	A	.50		
MIX CHOR2	A	A	.50		

UNITS TOWARD GRADUATION 6 — GRADE 10 AVERAGE 3.7

GRADE 11

SUBJECT	1	2	UNIT	GROUP	MISC
ENGLISH 3	A	A	1	HM	
FRENCH 3	A	A	1		
FREN CONV	A		.50	HM	CL
TRIGNMTRY	A	A	1		
CHM BND A	A	A	1	HM	
ADV CHEM	A		.50	HM	CL
AM HIST 1	A	A	1		
PHYS ED 3	A	A	.50		
MIX CHOR3	A	A	.50		

UNITS TOWARD GRADUATION 7 — GRADE 11 AVERAGE 4.0

OTHER GRADES

GRADE	SUBJECT	1	2	UNIT	GROUP	MISC.
12	CBAP ENGL				H	
12	PHYS SSC				HM	
12	AM GOVT 1					
12	WLD HIST1					
12	PHYS ED 4					
12	MIX CHOR4					
12	PERS TYPE					

UNITS TOWARD GRADUATION — OTHER GRADE AVERAGE

TEST RECORD

GRADE	TEST INFORMATION	GRADE	TEST INFORMATION
9	DIFFERENTIAL APTITUDE NRM:GRD 9 SCOR:% ILE SCHOL 95 , VERB 95 NUMER 90 , ABST 85 SPACE 60 , MECHL 85 CLERL 45 , L-SPL 85 L-SEN 80		SCIEN 82-95, MATH 86-95
9	SCH&COLL ABIL TST LVL3 NRM:GRD 9 SCOR:% BND VERB 96-99, QUANT 99-00 TOTAL 99-99	9	CO-OP ACH H S MATH Z NRM: 1 YR ST SCOR:% ILE E ALG 95
9	SEQNT TST ED PROG LVL3 NRM:GRD 9 SCOR:% BND READ 92-00, WRITE 83-94 LISTN 73-90, SOC S 89-95	10	OTIS QCK-SCR M A GAMMA NRM:GRD 10 SCOR:I Q SCORE 125
		11	PRELIMNARY SCHOL APT T NRM:GRD 11 SCOR:STAND VERB 62 MATH 65
		11	NATIONL MERIT SCHOL QT NRM:COLLEG SCOR:STAND ENGL 23 MATH 25 SOC S 27 N SCI 15 WORD 19 TOTAL 22

EXTRA-CURRICULAR

ACTIVITY	FR	SO	JR	SR
SOCIAL CLUB		3		
DEBATNG CLB		3	2	
STD COUN BD			2	
JOURNLM CLB	3	3	2	
FUT TEACHRS			2	

WORK RECORD

JOB	FR SUM	FR TERM	SO SUM	SO TERM	JR SUM	JR TERM	SR SUM	SR TERM
CLERCL OCC				1				
CLERCL OCC			17					
ACCT&BOOKP						9		
NURSEMAID	9	1	1	1	9	1		
WRITING								

PERSONAL RECORD	FR	SO	JR	SR
MOTIVATION	1	1	1	
INDUSTRY	1	1	1	
INITIATIVE	1	1	1	
INFLUENCE-LEAD	1	1	1	
CONCERN-OTHERS	1	1	1	
RESPONSIBILITY	1	1	1	
INTEGRITY	1	1	1	
EMOTIONAL STABILITY	1	1	1	

HONORS AND AWARDS

NATL HONOR SOC
LETTER CLUB

John Barr — Prin. — Sept. 3 1963
SIGNATURE — TITLE — DATE

COOPERATIVE PLAN FOR GUIDANCE AND ADMISSION

SOURCE: Comprehensive Student Report. Reprinted by permission of the Educational Testing Service.

Figure 10.14 (Continued)

P R I N C I P A L' s   R E C O M M E N D A T I O N

Natalie's interest and ability levels are high in many areas, particularly in biography, marine biology, and foreign languages. At present, she is considering careers in journalism and as a teacher of English or foreign languages.

When her father was killed in an auto accident during Natalie's first year of high school, the chances of attending college for the four Warner children seemed dim. Since that time, her mother has obtained a position with the Family Service Group and with her help and scholarship aid, Natalie should be able to meet her expenses.

At present, Northwestern is Natalie's only choice of college. Her high school faculty feels that she should be able to maintain a high level of scholarship there. It is a pleasure to recommend this serious, wholesome, and unspoiled child who has such a serious desire to continue her education.

9/3/63 — *Ethel Thomas* — College Counselor
Date — Signature — Title

SPECIAL SYMBOLS

*	Information insufficient for reporting and computing purposes. Grades and units not included in computations or averages. If an improper composite test entry is coded, summary composites have not been developed.
#	Information improperly coded or insufficient for reporting purposes. Computations of averages or composites are not affected. If "grade taken" information is not available, grade level average only will be affected.
&	Additional information not reported due to space or code limitations. Supplementary information should be added by the high school. For courses coded as "other," grade points and units are not included in area averages or academic group calculations.

Colleges have action to take in completion of this Report one year after its receipt. At that time, colleges are to send a transcript of student progress to the Secondary School for completion of its records.

STUDENT INFORMATION

Code #	Days Tardy and Days Absent
0	None
1	One
2	Two
3	3-4
5	5-7
8	8-11
12	12-16
17	17-21
22	22-26
27	27 or more

HEALTH

Code #	Illness Interfered with Studies
0	Not at all
1	To slight degree
2	To moderate degree
3	To appreciable degree
4	To serious detriment of progress.

SCHOOL INFORMATION

Meaning of Grades — The number printed below any grade letter is the lowest grade possible for receipt of that letter grade. **Col. Rec.**—The minimum alphabetic grade for college recommendation. **Grad. Year**—The expected year of graduation. **Units Req.**—The total number of Carnegie Units required for graduation.

ACADEMIC SUMMARY

All Academic Averages are based on assigned values of A=4, B=3, C=2, D=1, and F=0. Rank in Class and Percentile Standing are based on the student's course average (grade points divided by units earned) compared to the course averages of his classmates for each of the separate classifications. Complete class data are based on the total class for all courses taken. Academic group calculations are presented only for those students in the academic curriculum and are based on academic courses only. Complete class-weighted data include all students and all courses. The calculations assign one additional value (A=5, B=4, etc.) for courses tracked as high and high-middle and one less value (A=3, B=2, etc.) for course tracked as middle-low or low-Composite test notes the testing program employed at a school from which composites have been computed.

Converted Verbal Course Score, Converted Math/Science Course Score, and Converted All Course Score place each of these in-school averages on a scale to which composite test scores can be conveniently transposed. After the appropriate test sub-scores are transposed to this scale, the converted course scores are adjusted by one half the difference in means between class distributions of the course scores and the test scores. From these components, the following composites are developed:

$$\text{Verbal Composite} = \frac{\text{Transposed Verbal Test Score} + \text{Adj. Verbal Course Score}}{2}$$

$$\text{Math/Science Composite} = \frac{\text{Transposed Math Test Score} + \text{Adj. Math/Science Course Score}}{2}$$

$$\text{All Course Composite} = \frac{2\,\text{Trans. Verbal Test Score} + 2\,\text{Trans. Math Test Score} + 3\,\text{Adjusted All Course Score}}{6}$$

All composites reflect relative measures of student ability and should not be regarded as direct predictions of college freshman grades. Technical details with regard to adjustments, conversions, transpositions, composites and other computations may be found in the publication "Interpretations from Comprehensive Student Reports"—ETS, 1963.

ACADEMIC RECORD

Field Averages are computed from final grades awarded in all courses taken in separate fields of Language Arts, Foreign Language, Mathematics, Science, and Social Studies. The Verbal Course Average is calculated from final grades in all courses in Language Arts, Foreign Language, and Social Studies. The Math/Science Course Average is calculated from final grades in all courses in Mathematics and Science.

GROUPING

A notation will appear in this space only if students in that course were homogeneously grouped.

Code	Tracking Group	Definition
H	High Group	Advanced Placement (CEEB)
HM	High-Middle Group	Content geared to the above average or superior learner
M	Middle Group	Middle Group
ML	Middle-Low Group	Content adjusted to accomodate a low average learner
L	Low Group	Remedial

MISC.

This column takes note of the following information.

Code	Definition
S	Summer Course
LB	Laboratory Course
TV	Television Course
SM	Seminar Course
CL	Course on College Campus

OTHER GRADES

The "Other Grades" column may include course work from the 8th and/or 12th grade. The column entitled **GRADE** will note the specific grade in which the subject was taken.

TEST RECORD

GR-Grade Taken	%ILE-Percentile
NRM-Denotes the test norm group	IQ-Intelligence Quotient
SCOR-The type of score reported	GRD P-Grade Placement
%BND-Percentile Band	RAW S-Raw Score
STAND-Standard Score	STA 9-Stanine

EXTRA-CURRICULAR ACTIVITIES

Student Performance is rated on the following five point scale.

Code #	Activity
1	President, captain, editor, or group leader doing a high quality job.
2	Other elected officers, appointed officer, a letter man effecting his responsibilities.
3	An effectively contributing 'participant or varsity member.
4	Member of Junior-Varsity or general participant.
X	A disinterested and uncooperative member.
‖	Student participated but was not rated.

WORK RECORD

The work record is divided into Summer and Term classifications for each of the four school years.

Code #	Hours Worked/Week
1	1-8
9	9-16
17	17-24
25	25-32
33	33 ‡

PERSONAL RECORD

Personal characteristics are rated on a scale one through five, one being the highest possible rating, five the lowest. The characteristics are those on the Personality Record of the National Association of Secondary School Principals. Schools are instructed to average three independent ratings for each trait.

Summary

The emergence of student personnel functions in the secondary school has been slow. Today student personnel services are many and varied. Generally speaking, the following services are included: school attendance and its related problems; orientation; admission; classification and assignment of students to the educational program; evaluation and reports of pupil progress; provision for individual differences; supervision of student discipline; guidance and counseling problems; health and safety problems; and the personal, social, and emotional adjustments of students. The principal is the director of all these services in his school, but he delegates to assistants, counselors, and other personnel many of the responsibilities in the student-personnel area.

The initial functions of the student personnel office are to admit students into school, to classify and assign students to the proper program that best suits their individual needs, and to orient students to the new school and the new school program. The student handbook is one tool used in orientation.

Once the student is officially enrolled and oriented, the next major function in personnel work falls in the area of student accounting. Some phases of student accounting actually take place prior to the time students enter school, such as the school census. The state requires students to attend schools, and enforcing compulsory school attendance is another phase of student personnel work. The school district, welfare agencies, and courts are frequently involved in a joint effort to secure the attendance of all students at school. A record of the student's attendance is kept up by teachers in the central office. The principal is charged with the responsibilities of securing, developing, and enforcing attendance policies. In carrying out his responsibilities, the principal must develop a system that accounts for students who are in school, who are out of school, and who enter or leave school officially or unofficially during the school day. Along with actual attendance in class is the problem of tardiness to school and to classes. If the school has no uniform policy, teachers are left to work out this problem themselves.

Another major function of the pupil personnel service is to evaluate, record, and report student achievement. Teacher tests have the primary purpose of evaluating progress in any given subject area. The tests should effectively measure the objectives to be accomplished within the course work. Criteria must be determined for grading policies, and each subject may require different criteria. The grades themselves are usually determined from the policy and philosophy set by the school. Grades are usually based on the comparison of the student with himself, or comparison of the student with other students, or comparison of the student with some outside standard. The school adopts a uniform reporting system so that information can be provided to parents and guardians. No two districts will have the same reporting system, and frequently no two schools within a district will have the same system. Report cards generally reflect one or more of the following: student achievement, student effort, student ability, citizenship factors, and reasons for positive or negative performance. Final grades and credit are entered on permanent record cards. The permanent record card is retained indefinitely in the school and is used to supply data to colleges, universities, employers, and other organizations that have justifiable reasons for requiring the information.

The principal is the administrator over all of these services but can delegate much of the responsibility to his secretaries and other personnel. His primary role is to determine the type of system to be used and to see that the records and information are current and permanently available.

SUGGESTED PROJECTS AND ACTIVITIES

1. Collect from a school or a school district the forms that are used to account for student attendance.
2. Prepare an orientation program or plan to be used from the time students leave the preceding school until the time of their satisfactory adjustment in the secondary school.
3. Invite a district personnel administrator to explain the functions of his office as they relate to the success of the personnel functions at the secondary school level.
4. Research the compulsory attendance law of your state and provide a report for the class.
5. Visit a school and find out from a teacher the procedures that are used in handling the problem of tardiness.
6. Collect samples of report cards that are used in your state.
7. Make a list of all the different types of data that can be found on a permanent record card.

REVIEW AND DISCUSSION QUESTIONS

1. What should be the role of the principal as the director of student personnel services?
2. Why should students be classified and assigned to varying educational programs?

3. What information would be most helpful to you in your orientation to a new school?
4. Discuss the purposes that could be served through a student handbook.
5. Why should school attendance be compulsory in a democratic governmental system?
6. What are the values to be gained from an annual school census?
7. What are the causes for nonattendance in school and the most likely solutions?
8. Why should the school be so minutely concerned about the whereabouts of students during the day and during assigned school hours?
9. Why fight student absence and tardiness problems?
10. Which suggestions on handling the late problem appeal most to you? Why?
11. Should the school adopt a uniform policy on handling tardiness or should the policy be left flexible for departments or classes?
12. Why cannot the principal lay down a hard and fast rule regarding the type of tests to be given in class and the criteria on which grades will be determined?
13. To what extent can a policy about a school grading system be descriptive?
14. What are the purposes to be served by a report card and what type of report card best serves these purposes?
15. What are the functions to be served by the permanent record card?

SELECTED BIBLIOGRAPHY

Anderson, Lester W., and Lauren A. Van Dyke. *Secondary School Administration*. Boston: Houghton Mifflin Co., 1963, pp. 428–64.

Bollenbacher, Jones. "Student Records and Reports—Elementary and Secondary," *Encyclopedia of Educational Research*, 3rd ed. New York: The Macmillan Company, 1960, pp. 1437–42.

Brown, Edwin John, and Arthur Thomas Phelps. *Managing the Classroom*. New York: The Ronald Press Co., 1961, pp. 97–113.

California State Department of Education. *Evaluating Pupil Progress*. Volume XVI, No. 6, 1952.

Callahan, Sterling. *Successful Teaching in Secondary Schools*. Chicago: Scott, Foresman and Company, 1966.

Elicker, Paul E. "Record Forms for Secondary Schools," *Bulletin of N.A.S.S.P.*, November 1947, pp. 39–48.

Keller, Charles R. "Schools Are Students—And Teachers Like Miss Eleanor Parker," *Bulletin of N.A.S.S.P.*, March 1965, pp. 259–67.

Litwack, Lawrence, June E. Holmes, and Jane S. O'Hern. *Critical Issues in Student Personnel Work: A Problems Casebook*. Chicago: Rand McNally and Company, 1965, p. 105.

McCleary, Lloyd E., and Stephen P. Hencley. *Secondary School Administration: Theoretical Bases of Professional Practice.* New York: Dodd, Mead and Company, Inc., 1965, pp. 240–57.

National Society for the Study of Education. *Personnel Servicing Education,* 58th Yearbook. Chicago: University of Chicago Press, 1958.

Whitlock, James W. *Automatic Data Processing in Education.* New York: The Macmillan Company, 1964.

Zeran, Franklin R., and Anthony C. Riccio. *Organization and Administration of Guidance Services.* Chicago: Rand McNally and Company, 1962.

CHAPTER 11

Guidance and Counseling Services

The key to the guidance and counseling services is the student. All services are organized for his needs. Nowhere in the school is greater recognition given to the importance of each individual than in this area. Wrenn keynoted the importance of each student when he said, "I will respect the integrity of each individual with whom I deal. I will accord to him the same right to self-determination that I want for myself. I will respect as something sacred the personality rights of each person and will not attempt to manipulate him or meddle in his life."[1]

To guide the growth of children in desirable directions is a basic purpose of education. However, as the social institutions have grown more complex, a group of functions known as guidance and counseling functions has emerged as part of the total student personnel services. The services to the student are related to his educational, personal, social, and vocational adjustment. The core of a good guidance program lies in the human relationships in the classroom and throughout the school. Guidance is a function in which every teacher, counselor, and administrator participate daily. The administrator, aside from being a participant in the guidance services, also must organize the total school guidance and counseling program and see that it is administered properly. Therefore, he must have a knowledge of the program and the functions that are to be performed by the counselors if he is to be an effective organizer and administrator.

[1] C. G. Wrenn, "The Ethics of Counseling," *Educational Psychology Measurement*, 1952, pp. 161–77.

Definition and Scope of Guidance Services

Definition of Guidance Services. Guidance is a misused term imputed to mean just about anything. Therefore, it is more functional to discuss the guidance program within its total scope. When this is done, the guidance program can be defined as educational services that exist for the pupil in the school and involve the participation of the entire school staff, with specialized leadership being provided by counselors and other specialists. The Educational Policies Commission has described the guidance program as ". . . no mechanical process, whereby counselors and teachers sort out boys and girls as a grading machine sorts apples—this one to stay on the form, and that one to work in an airplane factory, this one to be a teacher, and that one to run the local garage. Guidance is rather the high art of helping boys and girls plan their own actions wisely, in full light of all of the facts that can be mustered about themselves and about the world in which they will work and live. Guidance is not the work of a few specialists. It is rather services from the entire school staff, which requires some people with special knowledge and skills, but enlists the cooperation of all."[2]

The Scope of Guidance Services. The scope of the guidance and counseling services falls into two major categories: services pertaining to students and services pertaining to teachers and the school in general.

The most important of these functions is to serve the students. Smith, in his book *Principles and Practices of the Guidance Program,* defines six individual services for students. They are as follows:

1. Preparation and use of an individual inventory for each student in the school.
2. Preparation and use of informational sources to meet the needs of each student.
3. Counseling services for all students in the school.
4. Planning and assisting with systematic follow-up studies.
5. Planning and assisting with placement for pupils.
6. Conducting case conferences and assisting teachers to make case studies of individual students.[3]

The second major function of the guidance program is to provide services pertaining to staff members and the school in general. Some of

[2] Educational Policies Commission of the National Education Association and the American Association of School Administrators, *Education for All American Youth* (Washington, D.C.: 1944), pp. 39–40.

[3] Glenn E. Smith, *Principles and Practices of the Guidance Program* (New York: The Macmillan Company, 1951), pp. 8–11.

these services are to assist teachers to secure and utilize information related to the respective subject fields, to organize and conduct in-service training related to the guidance program for administrators and teachers, to conduct follow-up studies and community surveys and make the results available, and to carry out research services as needed to provide information relating to the development and the improvement of the program.

Organization of the Guidance Program

Basic Principles.   The principal is responsible for the organizing of the guidance program in his school; therefore, he should understand certain basic principles. Some of these basic, guiding principles for organizing a guidance program are given below:

1. It should be inherent. The program should be based on the needs, purposes, and interests of the students in the school. A superimposed organization from some other school district will not be as effective as one tailored to each unique school.

2. It should be planned to serve all students in the school. In some schools, programs have been organized for the slow learner, or the gifted, or the emotionally disturbed, or the "disadvantaged." The principal must recognize his responsibility to all students and their inherent needs.

3. It should be continuous in nature. The program should be planned for the full year, not for segments of the year. Even during the summer, some counseling and guidance help should be available.

4. It should involve all school personnel. The dichotomies of group guidance versus individual counseling, teacher versus counselor should be omitted. The program should be planned, all personnel being made part of it, with special definitions given to make role relationships for specialists functional.

5. It should be operated from policies and procedures that have been approved by the staff. The principal should take the lead along with the guidance committee and counselors in arriving at these policies and procedures.

6. It should provide for all services generally accepted to be part of this program by the school, the school district, and the community.

7. It should be flexible to allow for adjustments and changes. Even the policy and procedures should be subject to change when conditions indicate that change is desirable.

Organizational Pattern.   On the basis of the basic principles previously stated, it cannot be assumed that there is a "best" organizational pattern for every school. Certainly each school must allow that which is unique to affect the organizational pattern. Some schools may require an emphasis on vocational programs and others on college preparatory. Large schools will require more structure than small schools. Some schools may have a complete staff of specialists, while others may have them available through the district. Still other schools may have no specialists.

Common elements may also be found in schools. Generally some school-wide committee is organized under the direction of the principal to provide school-wide direction to the guidance program. Such a committee is frequently called the guidance committee. In organizing such a committee the principal should plan to have representation from all broad areas of his school. The specific personnel for such a committee should be selected as a result of their demonstrated interest in and concern for students and their needs. The members of the committee might well include the principal or vice-principal over student personnel problems, director of guidance where one is established, the counselors or their representative, the faculty members, and other members at large as the unique needs of a school may indicate to be appropriate.

The policy and procedures used to operate the program would be developed by this committee and submitted to the faculty for their adoption. The principal would aid the committee in establishing role relationships, functions, referral procedures, and forms to be used.

Role of the Administration and Staff in the Guidance and Counseling Program

Role of the Principal. As in all other matters, the principal is the central figure in developing or improving guidance services in his school. He will delegate specific responsibilities to assistant principals, counselors, teachers, and others. The principal should provide general support and administrative leadership to the total program. He serves as the liaison officer between the school and the district. He requests budgets and services the program in the same way that he does other departments in the school. He organizes the program and aids in the selection of counselors and other staff members. He helps develop policies and procedures for the operation of the program within the school. In a small school, the principal may also serve as the chairman of the department. He provides and schedules time, personnel, and facilities. He serves as a catalyst in the implementation of the program.[4]

It is important that the principal recognize the wide diversity that the term *guidance* has meant to teachers in the past, because this recognition will lead him to define more closely the role and function of the staff members. The definition should be in writing and become a part of the

[4] J. E. Nunley, "Initiating A Guidance Program," *Clearing House*, January 1963, pp. 269–71.

total job description of all guidance personnel. If the role definitions are in writing, much of the confusion can be eliminated and a greater solidarity toward a common program can be developed.

The Role of the Teachers. The classroom teachers have a coordinate responsibility with the counselors in that the students meet the teachers each day. The students' problems become the teachers' problems as well as the counselors'. The classroom teacher should individualize instruction to provide for the abilities and limitations of all students. The teacher should aid the students in making wholesome adjustments. Specifically the classroom teacher will do some of the following:

> Learn interests, abilities, characteristics, needs, and backgrounds of pupils.
> Learn problems and frustrations faced by pupils.
> Learn of future plans or lack of them.
> Reorganize his teaching in the light of information gathered through the above items.
> Refer to the counselor problems that the teacher cannot help the pupil see or solve.
> Teach subject matter to individuals rather than to a "class."
> Check on individual progress and aid where special aid is needed.
> Use guidance resources available.
> Help students toward a better adjustment whenever possible.

Role of Counselors. The counselor should have better rapport with students than all other persons in the school. The counselor works directly with the student to help him solve as many of his educational and adjustment problems as possible. The counselor works with the teacher and the principal in providing information and assisting them in the understanding of children. The principal should aid the staff to understand the responsibilities of the counselor. The following list of specific duties of counselors is helpful in providing information about the counselor's role, the responsibilities he carries, and the service he can perform:

Educational Counseling
> Coordinate orientation of beginning students to the school situation.
> Interpret objectives and opportunities of the school to pupils, parents, and teachers.
> Assist pupils in selecting subjects and making out courses of study.
> Assist pupils in determining long-term educational plans as early as possible.
> Make program changes when necessary to aid the student in his school adjustment.

Advise pupils of educational opportunities and requirements beyond the high school level.

Secure and organize pertinent data about the student.

Be responsible for administering tests given for guidance purposes, collecting test data, and interpreting the results to parents, student, and teacher.

Be responsible for the accurate recording of standardized test scores in cumulative records.

Supervise the preparation and maintenance of the cumulative guidance records for each counselee.

Maintain an adequate file of educational guidance material.

Recommend and assist in transferring students to other schools.

Provide information on military programs: college ROTC, reserve forces, service academies, and compulsory military training requirements.

Provide information regarding college entrance requirements, scholarships, and entrance tests.

Identify pupils with special problems needing specialized help and assistance.

Keep principal informed concerning major findings from testing program and significant trends.

Vocational Counseling

Assist the student to clarify his occupational aims and his educational plans, giving due consideration to his abilities, aptitudes, interests, personality, economic and social environment.

Maintain an occupational file and vocational counseling materials for students and teachers.

Administer vocational interest and aptitude tests at appropriate grade levels and record and disseminate information to those concerned.

Assist counselees in regard to job placement.

Conduct follow-up studies of counselees who have left school.

Personal and Social Counseling

Help the student arrive at a satisfactory solution to his personal problems.

Help the student understand and accept himself as a person.

Help the student understand others and his relationship to them and make adequate social adjustments.

Conduct teacher, parent, and pupil conferences to help solve school adjustment problems.

Inform teachers about the problems and difficulties that individual students face and help teachers gain insight and understanding through a discussion and appraisal of the pertinent data.

Make necessary reports for social agencies.

Carry on liaison work between school, home, and community referral agencies.

Services to Teachers

Assist teachers to understand the objectives and purposes of the guidance program through discussions at faculty meetings, conferences, and discussions of individual student problems.

Route materials to teachers that will help them understand young people and their problems.

Distribute to teachers helpful guidance materials.

Assist teachers in using group work as an adjustive process.

Assist teachers in the wise use of tests and other information-gathering devices.

Administration of Guidance and Counseling Services

Individual Inventory Services. The purpose of the individual inventory service is to discover information through which students can learn about themselves and to help students, teachers, and administrators aid the student in a better educational, social, and personal adjustment. To adequately aid in the performance of individual inventory services the principal must make arrangements for collecting, testing, and recording information that can be used for this purpose. The following types of data are needed to adequately understand the student.

1. Individual capacities and achievements.
2. Home environment information.
3. Personal data.
4. Scholastic information.
5. Health data.
6. Interest inventories.
7. Vocational interests and work experiences.
8. Follow-up information.
9. Anecdotal data.
10. School attendance patterns.

It is obvious that if an inventory system is to be successful, a systematic procedure for obtaining information must be organized. It is also obvious that the data obtained must be systematically recorded in a handy, usable manner. (A more complete discussion of some of these areas is found in the chapter on student personnel services.)

The cumulative folder is most frequently used for this purpose. Although some schools attempt to keep permanent record data, as described in the chapter on personnel services, most school systems have adopted a cumulative record folder, which makes it possible to maintain all data needed about a student. The simplest form of the cumulative folder is a file folder with the student's name, in which all test data, health information, anecdotal records, and other materials are inserted. Another type of record of similar pattern but different design is the envelope-style folder into which materials are inserted. A style that is becoming standard is one that has basic data printed on the cover of a file folder. Anecdotal material can then simply be dropped in the file. A good example of this style folder is shown in Figure 11.1 The printing is on the back half of the file folder with the front part left blank.

In addition to selecting the type of record system to be used, the principal must also set policies and procedures for collecting and recording the information, housing the records, and providing for their use. The counselors will usually be charged with the responsibility of collecting and recording appropriate data. The records must be stored in a fireproof vault. They should be microfilmed and an official copy preserved for emergency purposes.

Tests and Testing. The growth of standardized testing programs in schools has been phenomenal, and students now take objective-type tests of regular academic programs. Most of these objective-type tests are standardized on a national basis to assess reading skill and comprehension, intelligence, personality, scholastic aptitude, subject matter achievement, academic placement, and college entrance potential. The data gained from these tests have been most beneficial and helpful, especially when they are used properly and placed in the hands of personnel who understand testing and can interpret tests properly.[5] However, the excessive use of standardized tests has created some problems. Critics point out that we are becoming slaves to testing, and that we place greater validity on test scores than the present state of development warrants. If used properly, the tests are invaluable aids in the understanding of students.

In addition to the tests that are given by the school, there are a great many external tests—tests sponsored by outside agencies—which are given to students during school hours and after school hours. These external tests are frequently used for college or employment placement. The principal must be aware of the extensive use of these tests and try to protect students, the school, and the community in both the administration and the interpretation of the results. The following problems have been raised in regard to the external tests.

1. There is multiplicity of external tests.
2. External tests create undue pressure on both students and the home.
3. External tests tend to prescribe the individual student's preparation.
4. External tests affect the school's image in the community.

[5] W. Wesley Tennyson, Donald H. Blocker, and Ralph H. Johnson, "Student Personnel Records: A Vital Look But a Concern of the Public," *Personnel and Guidance Journal,* May 1964, pp. 888–94.

Figure 11.1
Cumulative Folder

ADDRESS (2311)
& TELEPHONE (2320)

ADDRESS
& TELEPHONE

| LAST NAME (1010) | FIRST | MIDDLE |

ADDRESS
& TELEPHONE

ADDRESS
& TELEPHONE

SEX: MALE ☐   FEMALE ☐

DATE OF BIRTH (1050)

BIRTH CERTIFICATE (1060): YES ☐ NO ☐

PLACE OF BIRTH:

CITIZEN (1110): YES ☐ NO ☐

HEAD OF HOUSEHOLD (1070)	NAME (2310-2210)	BIRTHPLACE (1080)	EDUCATION (2140-2240)	OCCUPATION (2150-2250)	RESIDENCE ADDRESS (2310)	CITIZEN (2140-2240)	RACE (1040)	DECEASED
FATHER						YES ☐ NO ☐		
MOTHER						YES ☐ NO ☐		
MALE GUARDIAN						YES ☐ NO ☐		
FEMALE GUARDIAN						YES ☐ NO ☐		

MARITAL STATUS OF PARENTS: LIVING TOGETHER _____ SEPARATED _____ DIVORCED _____ REMARRIED: FATHER _____ MOTHER _____ HUSBAND'S NAME _____

CHILD LIVES WITH: _____

LANGUAGE OF HOME (2350) _____

CHURCH (1120) PREFERENCE

BROTHERS AND SISTERS (2340): LIST NAMES AND YEAR OF BIRTH _____

SCHOOL HEALTH RECORD (3010)

	K	1	2	3	4	5	6	7	8	9	10	11	12
GRADE													
DATE													
HEIGHT													
WEIGHT													
VISION RIGHT													
VISION LEFT													
HEARING RIGHT													
HEARING LEFT													
HEALTH EXAM (3080)													
DENTAL													
DISABILITY (3020)													
RESTRICTIONS (3110)													

IMMUNIZATIONS (3070)

TYPE	DATE	DATE	DATE
DIPHTHERIA			
TETANUS			
SMALL POX			
TUBERCULIN			

ENTRY RECORD (5000)

DATE	GRADE	REASON	RECEIVED FROM

WITHDRAWAL RECORD (5330)

DATE	GRADE	AGE	REASON	TRANSFERRED TO (5530)

CODE (5330):

W1 Transferred
W2 Graduated
W3 Released for early admission to a university
*W5 Released because of physical disability
*W6 Excused because of mental disability
*W7 Released to enter employment to support family
*W8 Enlisted in the armed forces
*W9 Left school because of marriage or pregnancy
*W10 Became 18 years of age but had insufficient credit for graduation
*W11 Released because of incorrigibility (habitual truant, vicious, immoral, ungovernable)
*W12 Consistent failure to achieve in regular school work
*W13 Committed to a correctional institution
*W14 Other

OTHER SIGNIFICANT PERMANENT DATA

A SUPPLEMENTARY FOLDER SHOULD CONTAIN THE FOLLOWING:

1. Autobiography—family background.
2. Health history—physical examination data.
3. Anecdotal items—short descriptions of observed behavior without interpretation.
4. Participation in co-curricular activities.
5. Work experience.
6. Interview notes with students and parents.
7. Correspondence with the home.
8. Referrals to the principal or correctional or helpful agencies.
9. Information relating to educational and vocational plans.
10. Teacher evaluations of school progress —grades, comments, etc.
11. Information on retentions.
12. Standardized tests.
13. Pertinent samples of school work.

INSTRUCTIONS

CODE: N= NOTHING SIGNIFICANT   V= SATISFACTORY OR OBSERVATIONS BELOW

OBSERVATIONS AND COMMENTS (3030):

GENERAL INSTRUCTIONS: Refer to Manual of Instruction for Pupil Accounting in Utah School Districts for specific instructions. The Code Number on this form refers to the Manual. Fill in all information. Use proper ink for machine reproduction. SPECIFIC INSTRUCTIONS: Elementary School Record: Opposite instructional setting, indicate the types of special education programs (speech or hearing therapy, remedial, special classes). Secondary School Record: Record the amount of credit earned when the student discontinues school for any reason. Record the total number of students in the school's senior class in the space "Number in 12th grade." Achievement Tests: This section can be used to office test labels, to record annual test scores (grade placement or percentile), and/or to make a test profile using standard scores (rol or grade placements (gpl). Multifactor Tests—Scholastic Aptitude Tests: PR refers to percentiles. SC refers to row or standard scores. SC—chronological age. MA—mental age. ID—intelligence quotient. School Health Record: Permanent information should be recorded. Withdrawal Record: Original reason, enter the appropriate code number. The addition of an asterisk—W5 through W14—signifies the withdrawal is considered a dropout. W1 through W4 are never considered dropouts.

RECORD OF TRANSCRIPT (5000-6173)

DATE	TO WHOM SENT	REASON

SIGNATURE _____ POSITION _____ DATE _____

FORM GS-40   UTAH STUDENT PERMANENT RECORD

SOURCE: Utah State Department of Public Instruction, Salt Lake City, Utah. Reproduced by permission.

Figure 11.1 (Continued)

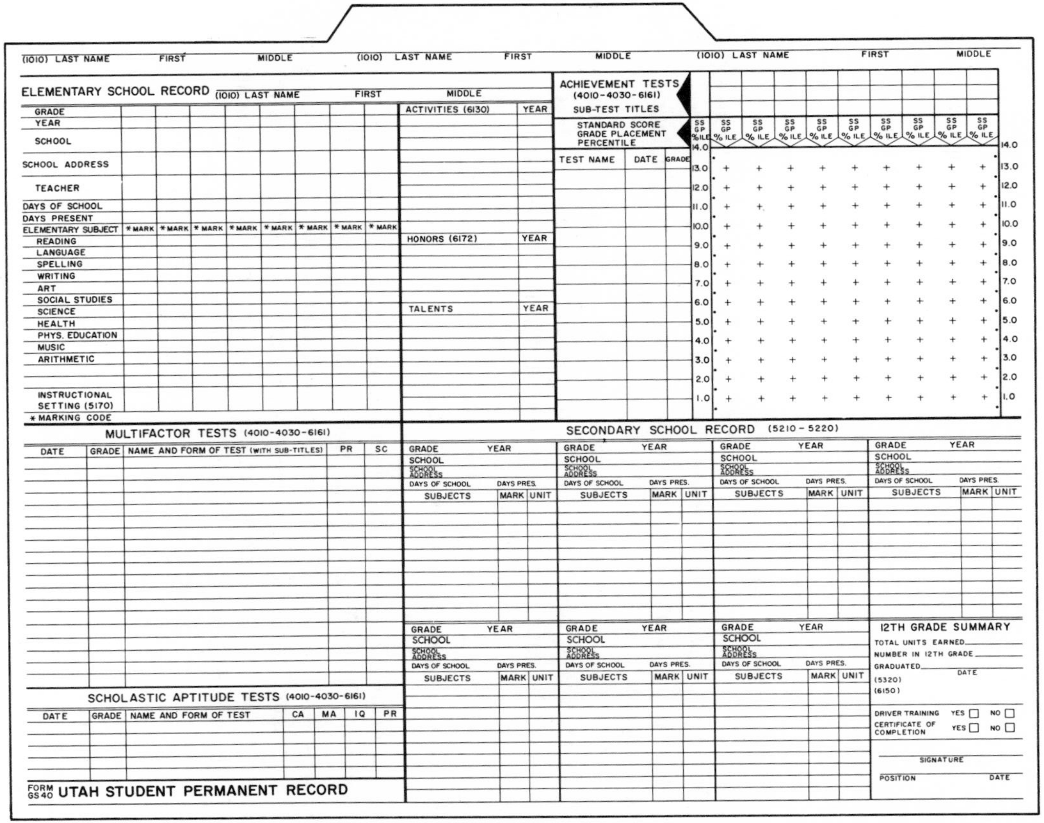

(1010) LAST NAME FIRST MIDDLE (1010) LAST NAME FIRST MIDDLE (1010) LAST NAME FIRST MIDDLE

ELEMENTARY SCHOOL RECORD (1010) LAST NAME FIRST MIDDLE

GRADE
YEAR
SCHOOL
SCHOOL ADDRESS
TEACHER
DAYS OF SCHOOL
DAYS PRESENT
ELEMENTARY SUBJECT *MARK *MARK *MARK *MARK *MARK *MARK *MARK *MARK
READING
LANGUAGE
SPELLING
WRITING
ART
SOCIAL STUDIES
SCIENCE
HEALTH
PHYS. EDUCATION
MUSIC
ARITHMETIC
INSTRUCTIONAL SETTING (5170)
*MARKING CODE

ACTIVITIES (6130) YEAR
HONORS (6172) YEAR
TALENTS YEAR

ACHIEVEMENT TESTS (4010-4030-6161)
SUB-TEST TITLES
STANDARD SCORE
GRADE PLACEMENT
PERCENTILE
SS GP %ILE
TEST NAME DATE GRADE
14.0 13.0 12.0 11.0 10.0 9.0 8.0 7.0 6.0 5.0 4.0 3.0 2.0 1.0

MULTIFACTOR TESTS (4010-4030-6161)
DATE GRADE NAME AND FORM OF TEST (WITH SUB-TITLES) PR SC

SCHOLASTIC APTITUDE TESTS (4010-4030-6161)
DATE GRADE NAME AND FORM OF TEST CA MA IQ PR

SECONDARY SCHOOL RECORD (5210 - 5220)
GRADE YEAR
SCHOOL
SCHOOL ADDRESS
DAYS OF SCHOOL DAYS PRES.
SUBJECTS MARK UNIT

12TH GRADE SUMMARY
TOTAL UNITS EARNED
NUMBER IN 12TH GRADE
GRADUATED DATE
(5320)
(6150)
DRIVER TRAINING YES ☐ NO ☐
CERTIFICATE OF COMPLETION YES ☐ NO ☐
SIGNATURE
POSITION DATE

FORM GS40 UTAH STUDENT PERMANENT RECORD

The following guidelines from *Testing, Testing, Testing,* sponsored by the National Association of Secondary School Principals, may be used to aid the school principal in his understanding and use of external tests: (1) that school officials, administrators, and teachers refrain from using the scores made by their students on a single national test as the measure of the quality of their educational program; (2) that school teachers, administrators, and other professional personnel become more knowledgeable in the field of measurement and evaluation; that they learn what tests can do and what tests cannot do; (3) that all individuals or organizations having access to test scores refrain from publicly using them to compare students, schools, or states; and that the use of test scores for publicity purposes by test makers, test publishers, school administrators, or others be regarded as an unprofessional practice; and (4) that all external tests be given outside of regular class time, at a time convenient for the students and faculty involved, and that the school should refuse to participate in nationally sponsored tests unless those tests can be demonstrated to have value commensurate with the effort, money, time, and emotional strain involved.[6]

All tests that are given must be stored and protected. Since the purpose of the tests is to help the student, the principal, counselors, teachers, and other staff personnel must have access to the test results. However, harm can be done to the student if these tests are misused. The principal should work with the counselors and teachers and develop a policy that will bring about maximum but proper use.

Information Service. The information service is self-explanatory by definition. One purpose of the service is to supply the student with information about himself, about the school, and about society in general. The student handbook has already been described as a good informational device by which the student can become acquainted with the school. The handbook serves as an excellent orientation guide. The principal usually refers the publication of the handbook to the guidance and counseling staff. A second major purpose of the information service is to aid the student in the understanding of himself. This understanding comes primarily through counseling situations in which the counselor interprets test data and other social and personality information that are useful to the student. A third, and probably the most used, service is to provide occupational information for the students. The counselor must know accurate sources for occupational materials. There are many government, as well as private, agencies that publish these materials. The principal must arrange for adequate budget so needed information will be readily available. The

[6] American Association of School Administrators, Council of Chief State School Officers, National Association of Secondary-School Principals, *Testing, Testing, Testing* (Washington, D.C.: The Association).

counselor and principal should consider the following questions when selecting the materials: Is adequate, pertinent personal information contained in the publication? Is the information prepared and issued by a reputable agency or individual? Are the facts presented relatively free of bias? Is the language level appropriate for pupils? Are recent facts contained in the publication? Can the cost of materials be justified? Are printed materials easily readable? Does the publication suggest other sources of information?

In the dissemination of information, the counselor and teachers work closely together. The counselors normally organize the program, secure the information, and prepare it for the teachers. The teachers, through their homeroom organizations or classroom activities, disseminate the information through the group processes. In addition to the group instruction, individuals may secure this information and discuss it with the counselor. The principal should coordinate the work of the counselor and the librarian in establishing a good library file that can be used for both personal and occupational purposes. The principal, counselor, and librarian should decide where these materials should be kept and who should be the trustee of the materials. Generally it is assumed that these materials can best be housed in the library as long as the counselor and students know of their availability.

Counseling Services. The counseling service is the heart of the guidance program. The counselor is the person who meets the students face to face and aids them in their personal, social, and educational adjustment problems. Acceptance of the counseling service is directly correlated with the attitude of the principal regarding these services. Through a guidance committee and the faculty, a school philosophy about guidance and counseling should be developed.[7] In faculty meetings, conferences, and community groups, the principal should explain the services and the benefits that can be derived from these services.

The principal can aid the counselor if he provides teachers with in-service materials that will help them understand the type of problems that should be referred to the counselor.[8] The counselors cannot fulfill their complete role if discipline problems are sent to them.[9] Some typical problems that might be referred are presented in the descriptions below:

Jack is one of the brightest boys in the English class, with an I.Q. of 140. His immediate interest, however, is airplanes, and during English class

[7] Paul Nash, "Some Notes Toward a Philosophy of School Counseling," *Personnel and Guidance Journal*, November 1964, pp. 243–48.

[8] George Esper, "Characteristics of Junior High School Students Who Seek Counseling," *Personnel and Guidance Journal*, January 1964, pp. 468–73.

[9] Norman S. Gilbert, "When the Counselor Is a Disciplinarian," *Personnel and Guidance Journal*, January 1965, pp. 485–91.

periods he spends his time drawing excellent designs of planes instead of attending to class activities. His written work is hastily done and is usually turned in late; his recitation is often poor because of his lack of attention to questions and class discussion; and his performance on various tests is about average. The teacher asks, "How can I get him to do quality work in English?"

Susan is in an algebra class—not because she has an aptitude for or an interest in algebra, but because her parents want her to attend a college where algebra is a prerequisite for entrance. Despite a great deal of home study, considerable tutoring by her mother, who was a former mathematics teacher, careful attention to class activities, a wholesome attitude toward study, and a determined effort to master the work, her performance on daily exercises and tests falls in the lowest tenth of her class. The class is an average class. What should the teacher do?

Bill is somewhat handicapped in scholastic aptitude in science and mathematics, but he is anxious to master these subjects sufficiently to be admitted to the radio division of the Air Force. He puts forth his best effort in laboratory exercises but is slow and frequently makes errors. By virtue of "burning considerable midnight oil" his written work is of excellent quality and is submitted on time. Due to an inadequate background and aptitude for science, however, his performance on tests and class recitations is slightly below average. How can Bill be helped?

Bud is the oldest of eight children of poor parents. He is compelled to work after school and on Saturdays in order to help support the family. Consequently he has neither the time nor the proper environment to do essential home study. He manifests an excellent attitude toward his teacher. He is more attentive and uses his time during history classes better than anyone else in his class. However, because he has insufficient time for outside reading, his achievement on tests falls in the lowest tenth of his class.

Ethics and Counseling. Frequently principals and teachers, who misunderstand the purpose of the counselor and the functions he performs, request the counselor to provide information or to act in a way that would be harmful to both the student and the counselor.[10] Therefore, it is important that the principal and teachers understand that the counselor operates under the Code of Ethics of the American Psychological Association. The following problems tend to illustrate the need for such a code:

Problem 1: The school is having difficulty with 12-year-old John Jones and a case conference has been called for Friday. At lunch it happens that most of the case conference participants, plus other teachers, are

---

[10] Charles M. Clark, "Confidentiality and the School Counselor," *Personnel and Guidance Journal*, January 1965, pp. 482–84.

eating together in the cafeteria. The teachers begin talking over the case of John Jones and also begin directing questions of confidential information about John to the counselor. Should the counselor participate?

The Code states: "Information obtained in a clinical or consulting relationship should be discussed only in professional settings and with professional persons clearly concerned with the case."

Solution: The counselor may diplomatically state that he has information that may be helpful but the details are in the office and he will present this on Friday. When he provides information, he will not do so to impress or to please. He will withhold the content of the interviews but not the needs of the boy as revealed by the interviews. Unless he seeks permission from John, he will not relate the fact that John feels inferior to other boys and needs support and praise. If Miss Gossip (one of John's teachers) is present, the counselor is to give caution on professional use *only* of the information and he himself must act accordingly.

Problem 2: A case conference has been held with Tim Powers as the client. He has been referred to the juvenile court and must pass all classes (he has the ability according to the tests) or attend the reformatory. One day the boy visits the counselor and wants to drop out of school. Because of information gained in the case conference, the counselor wants Tim to stay in school. Tim says, "Mrs. English Teacher told me that I must earn a score of 75 on weekly papers or fail. She gave me 70. It's not fair. If I don't pass there is no need to come back to school. Look at that paper. Do you think this is fair?"

The possible solutions seem to be (a) to look over the paper and determine if the grade is fair, (b) to go directly to the teacher and question her, (c) to appeal to the teacher to be more charitable, or (d) to appeal to the principal to urge the teacher to change.

The Code states that psychologists may serve most effectively when their relationships with other professional workers are characterized by understanding, respect, and mutual support. Psychologists should keep relationships on a mature level and free from petty actions demeaning to themselves and to the profession. A psychologist should not attempt to gain favor by making personal comparisons damaging to colleagues, nor should he belittle the services of ethical professional workers.

Solutions:
a. Counselor should not act as a judge.
b. Counselor should not re-evaluate the exam paper.
c. Counselor should not condemn the teacher.
d. Counselor should not uphold the teacher against Tim.
e. Counselor should apply counseling competence to Tim's problems.

However, if the teacher is mentally ill or grossly inadequate, the Code states that the need for good interprofessional relationship does not prohibit evaluation of the work of other professional persons when such appraisal will clearly serve in the welfare of the counselor, nor should it discourage exposure of incompetence or of unethical conduct.

Problem 3: The principal asks the counselor to test Ronald and explain in the case conference why he is an underachiever. The counselor cannot determine the cause, but the principal presses for the solution.

The Code states that the use of the clinical or consulting relationship primarily for profit, for power or prestige, or for other personal gratification is unethical.

Solution: The counselor resists temptations and is honest. He recommends referral.

Determining the Number of Counselors.   Since the heart of the guidance program rests with the counselors, it is important that an adequate staff of counselors be available. Most schools have one or more; however, in small schools the number of students may prohibit the possibility of such service. In larger schools the number of school counselors should be available at a ratio of about 300 to 400 students to each full-time counselor. The Northwest Accrediting Association recommends one counselor for each 400 students in secondary schools. The North Central Accrediting Association recommends one counselor for each 300 students in large schools. Conant, in his book *The American High School Today,*[11] recommended one full-time counselor for every 250 to 300 students.

Placement Services.   The placement service is both educational and vocational in nature. It focuses on the student and his needs. In its initial phase the placement service requires a study of an individual inventory data of the student and the adequate placement in the educational curriculum that best suits the individual needs. The counselor helps the student plan and adjust his educational program as he changes his vocational goals and as he progresses upward in the curriculum. At the senior high school level, the student is encouraged to begin some specialization toward a vocational line or preparatory programs for entrance into colleges and universities. The school counselor assists the student in making these decisions. Upon completion of high school, some students must be recommended to universities for their next educational sequence, while other students should be placed in job situations or other vocational-type training programs.

As a preliminary preparation for actual job placements, the counselors, through the guidance program, should have oriented the student into the

---

[11] James B. Conant, *The American High School Today* (New York: McGraw-Hill Book Company, Inc., 1959).

world of work and have supplied information in regard to the occupational fields. The student should be given an opportunity to analyze his abilities and limitations and to check these against possible occupational choices. The culminating phase is the actual placement of the student on the job and follow-up surveys to find out what and how the student is doing.

The principal and the counselor should work closely and cooperatively with community agencies. In addition to the final job placement, students are always looking for summer work. Many students desire work after school, and through the cooperative endeavors of the school and the community, these students can ordinarily be placed in their vocational choices.

Follow-up Service. The follow-up service of the guidance and counseling program is designed to secure basic information that is important for evaluating and planning the many phases of the school program. The information is secured from students who have graduated, students who have transferred to other school systems, and students who have dropped out of school. The high school dropouts have long been a source of great concern. Approximately one fourth of the students who enter the ninth grade do not graduate. A comparative study of dropouts by states, as shown in Table 11.1, shows the number of ninth-grade students in 1958–59

TABLE 11.1 **The Number of Ninth Graders in 1958–59 Compared with the Number of High School Graduates Four Years Later, Public Schools, by State**[a]

State	Ninth Graders 1958–59	High School Graduates 1961–62	Per Cent Graduating
Total U.S. (50 states)	2,415,309	1,682,609	69.7
Alabama	51,860	30,455	58.7
Alaska	2,266	1,424	69.8
Arizona	19,009	12,499	65.8
Arkansas	30,576	19,328	63.2
California	201,721[b]	166,500	82.5
Colorado	24,581	17,367	70.7
Connecticut	29,944[b]	21,941	73.3
Delaware	5,630	4,026	71.5
Florida	6,039	42,882	64.9
Georgia	63,458	36,014	56.8
Hawaii	9,418	7,793	82.7
Idaho	11,851	8,722	73.6
Illinois	118,189	82,739	70.0
Indiana	67,575	46,825	69.3
Iowa	38,030	30,081	79.1
Kansas	31,398	24,715[c]	78.7

TABLE 11.1 (Continued)

State	Ninth Graders 1958-59	High School Graduates 1961-62	Per Cent Graduating
Kentucky	41,524	23,759	57.2
Louisiana	48,004	28,492	59.4
Maine	12,966	8,655	66.8
Maryland	40,190	26,438	65.8
Massachusetts	62,719[b]	45,826	73.1
Michigan	96,147	75,323	78.3
Minnesota	47,977	38,340	79.9
Mississippi	36,474	22,094	60.6
Missouri	55,921	40,174[c]	71.8
Montana	10,115	7,413	73.3
Nebraska	18,619	14,469	77.7
Nevada	4,173	2,638	63.2
New Hampshire	7,282	4,896	67.2
New Jersey	72,210	50,977	70.6
New Mexico	15,205	8,971	59.0
New York	195,278	131,741	67.5
North Carolina	81,342	48,068	59.1
North Dakota	9,782	7,604	77.7
Ohio	122,055	86,681	71.0
Oklahoma	39,347	27,052	68.8
Oregon	26,780	20,127	75.2
Pennsylvania	140,151	103,037	73.5
Rhode Island	9,010[d]	6,448	71.6
South Carolina	39,878	23,929	60.0
South Dakota	10,141	8,186	80.7
Tennessee	57,164	33,701	59.0
Texas	137,872	86,518	62.8
Utah	15,674	12,130	77.4
Vermont	4,810	3,315	68.9
Virginia	54,843	34,232	62.4
Washington	41,525	33,223	80.0
West Virginia	32,587	19,527	59.9
Wisconsin[e]	50,741[b]	41,401	81.6
Wyoming	5,258	3,913	74.4

[a] This table was compiled by the Office of Education. The first two columns of figures are not completely comparable, owing to interstate migrations and transfers to or from nonpublic schools.
[b] Enrollment not cumulative, but as of a specific date.
[c] Estimated by the state.
[d] Partly estimated by the Office of Education.
[e] Excludes vocational schools not operated as part of the regular school system.

Source: Leonard M. Miller, "The Dropout: Schools Search for Clues to His Problems," *School Life*, May 1963, pp. 5-8, 30-33. Reprinted by permission of the U.S. Office of Education.

compared with the number of high school graduates four years later, in 1962–63. A careful review, state by state, shows that the dropout ratio is as high as 43 per cent, while the state with the best ratio still has a dropout factor of 13 per cent. The dropout problem is one of national concern, and many efforts are being made nationwide to find ways to overcome this problem. One major purpose of the follow-up service is to try and determine the reason for dropouts and what should be done to correct the problem. The second major purpose is to aid the school in planning a more adequate curriculum and guidance program. The principal should give direction to these studies so that appropriate data will be available to aid in decisions about the types of programs to be initiated.

Some of the specific objectives of the follow-up study are as follows:

1. To determine the holding power of the school.
2. To discover grade levels at which most dropouts occur.
3. To seek information that will provide clues for identifying potential dropouts.
4. To learn why pupils leave school before graduation.
5. To determine the mobility of former pupils.
6. To determine the percentage of dropouts and graduates who seek further training after leaving school and whether the secondary schools should provide training of the kinds pupils seek later.
7. To determine the percentage of former pupils who enter employment immediately after leaving school.
8. To evaluate the effectiveness of the school's placement activities.
9. To discover employment opportunities for young workers in the local community.
10. To discover the barriers to employment and occupational adjustment encountered by former pupils.
11. To obtain the opinions of former pupils concerning the efficiency of the guidance program.
12. To obtain opinions concerning needed modifications of the curriculum in light of the experiences of former pupils.
13. To compare the occupational stability and adjustment of graduates and dropouts.
14. To compare the occupational interests of pupils with those expressed by them before leaving school.
15. To identify former pupils who need further counseling to aid them in making more adequate personal, educational, or occupational adjustments.
16. To identify former pupils for whom the school might offer additional education, training, or other needed services.[12]

[12] Smith, *op. cit.*, pp. 309–10.

To gather the information desired and to satisfy the objectives, some type of questionnaire or data sheet must be devised and mailed to all graduates and dropouts in the classes under consideration. The follow-up card of the National Association of Secondary-School Principals, as shown in Figure 11.2, is one such device.

A questionnaire is often used to secure the factual data from the former students. The typical questionnaire is shown in the appendix.

Summary

The counseling and guidance program consists of six primary services: (1) the individual inventory service, (2) the information service, (3) the counseling service, (4) the placement service, (5) the follow-up service, and (6) the case conference service.

Because the word *guidance* has been used for many and varied functions, it is important that the guidance service program be defined and placed in writing. This written definition will help to unify teachers in their thinking and help give direction to the program. The role of the principal is primarily one of providing administrative leadership and organizational patterns for the program. The principal also secures physical facilities, materials, and supplies to make the program effective. He has a positive attitude toward the program and aids in the in-service training of teachers in the use of the guidance services. The teacher works with the counselor and is the right arm of the counseling service. The teacher meets the students daily and thus has opportunity for many contacts. He can refer individuals he cannot help to the counselor. He may receive information about students to help in their personal, social, and educational adjustment.

The individual inventory service is designed to provide information about the student. A cumulative folder is used to record and store information about the student. The information service is designed to secure and provide students with information about educational opportunities, personal and social problems, and vocational information. The counseling service is the heart of the guidance and counseling program. The counselor meets with students, face to face, and assists them with adjustment problems relating to personal, social, educational, and vocational needs. In this relationship the counselor must observe a code of ethics if he is to be effective in his position. The placement service is designed to help students by placing them in educational programs best suited to their abilities and interests, to help them find summer employment, and to recommend them to colleges and universities best suited to their interests, talents, and desires. The follow-up service is the evaluation phase of the school program.

EMPLOYMENT

	1	3	5		1	3	5		1	2	3	4	5	6	7	8		1	2	3	4	5	6	7
		A				B					COUNSELING										PLACEMENT				

(11)-(12) HOW SECURED — 1 3 5
(13) MARITAL STATUS — 1 3 5
(14) WITH WHOM LIVING — 1 3 5
(15) EXPECTED OCCUPATION — 1 3 5
(16) WHEN DECIDED — 1 3 5
(17) WITH WHOM TALKED — 1 3 5
(22) REASON FOR LEAVING SCHOOL — 1 3 5

NAME AND ADDRESS OF EMPLOYER	KIND OF BUSINESS	NAME OF JOB	INCLUSIVE DATES	WAGES	REASON LEFT

COUNSELING AND PLACEMENT

EMPLOYMENT AGENCIES

DATE OF FOLLOW-UP (1) (3) (5)

DATE	SOURCE OF CONTACT	ABOUT WHAT	RECOMMENDATIONS MADE	RESULT OF CONTACT	COUNSELOR

F — 1 3 5
E — 1 3 5
D — 1 3 5
C — 1 3 5

SOURCE: National Association of Secondary-School Principals. Reprinted by permission from the National Association of Secondary-School Principals. Copyright: Washington, D.C.

Figure 11.2 (Continued)

FORM DD

FOLLOW-UP RECORD CARD

NATIONAL ASSOCIATION OF SECONDARY SCHOOL PRINCIPALS

Questionnaires are formulated and records maintained on students in selected graduating classes. Reasons for dropouts, places of employment, curriculum programs most helpful, and other data that would help the school better evaluate its program and make it more effective are secured.

SUGGESTED PROJECTS AND ACTIVITIES

1. Outline a high school guidance and counseling program to see if all six services are included in the program. Write a report indicating improvements needed.
2. Obtain a cumulative folder from a high school and review the data in the folder.
3. Evaluate the individual inventory service to see if all functions of the inventory service are being performed in the high school interview.
4. Through reading, prepare a bibliography listing sources of vocational materials that would be useful in an informational service.
5. Analyze the duties of a high school counselor and classify the duties performed.
6. Study the code of ethics for counselors and role-play the cases presented.
7. Prepare a report on the current interest in the dropout problem in the nation and discuss what efforts are currently being made to decrease the dropout rate.

REVIEW AND DISCUSSION QUESTIONS

1. What is the difference between the individual inventory service and information service?
2. What precautions should be taken to safeguard the cumulative folders and why are such safeguards necessary?
3. Is the suggested ratio of counselors to students—1 to every 300 to 400—feasible and practical?
4. Considering the six services that are performed in the guidance and counseling program, what type of educational program would be suited for development of a school counselor?
5. Why should the principal define the role of the administration to teachers and the counselor as related to the guidance program?
6. In your opinion do counselors have a moral obligation that is not covered in the code of ethics?
7. Why should the school organize a placement service when most communities have available a very fine employment security office designed to take care of the vocational placement?

8. What are the purposes to be served by follow-up study on dropouts?
9. Considering that approximately one fourth of the students drop out before they graduate from high school, what curriculum programs might be instituted that would have a greater holding power?

SELECTED BIBLIOGRAPHY

American Association of School Administrators, Council of Three-State School Officers, National Association of Secondary-School Principals. *Testing, Testing, Testing.* Washington, D.C.: The Association.

Andrew, Dean C., and Roy DeVerl Willey. *Administration and Organization of the Guidance Program.* New York: Harper and Brothers, 1958.

Arbuckle, Dugald S. *Pupil Personnel Services in American Schools.* Boston: Allyn and Bacon, Inc., 1962.

Blocker, Donald H. "Issues in Counseling: Elusive and Illusional," *Personnel and Guidance Journal,* April 1965, pp. 796–800.

Clark, Charles M. "Confidentiality and the School Counselor," *Personnel and Guidance Journal,* January 1965, pp. 482–84.

Esper, George. "Characteristics of Junior High School Students Who Seek Counseling," *Personnel and Guidance Journal,* January 1964, pp. 468–73.

Gilbert, Norman S. "When the Counselor Is a Disciplinarian," *Personnel and Guidance Journal,* January 1965, pp. 485–91.

Glanz, Edward C. *Foundations and Principles of Guidance.* Boston: Allyn and Bacon, Inc., 1964.

Hatch, Raymond N., and Buford Stefflre. *Administration of Guidance Services.* Englewood Cliffs, N.J.: Prentice-Hall, Inc., 1958.

Humphrys, J. A., A. E. Traxler, and R. D. North. *Guidance Services.* Chicago: Science Research Associates, 1960.

Miller, Carroll H. *Foundations of Guidance.* New York: Harper & Row, 1961.

Miller, Leonard M. "The Dropout: Schools Search for Clues to His Problem," *School Life,* May 1963, pp. 5–8, 30–33.

Nash, Paul. "Some Notes Toward a Philosophy of School Counseling," *Personnel and Guidance Journal,* November 1964, pp. 243–48.

National Association of Secondary-School Principals. "Administering Guidance in the Secondary Schools," *Bulletin of N.A.S.S.P.,* November 1954, pp. 1–236. (The entire bulletin is devoted to this phase of guidance.)

————. "Aspects of Guidance and Counseling," *Bulletin of N.A.S.S.P.,* September 1963, pp. 1–136. (The entire bulletin is devoted to this phase of guidance.)

————. "Guidance Practices in the Secondary School," *Bulletin of N.A.S.S.P.,* November 1962, pp. 1–148. (The entire bulletin is devoted to this phase of guidance.)

————. "Guidance Procedures in the Secondary School," *Bulletin of N.A.S.S.P.,* May 1961, pp. 1–274. (The entire bulletin is devoted to this phase of guidance.)

————. "Phases of Guidance in the Secondary Schools," *Bulletin of N.A.S.S.P.,*

November 1961, pp. 1–200. (The entire bulletin is devoted to this phase of guidance.)

Powell, Adam Clayton. "The Role of Education in the War Against Poverty," *Bulletin of N.A.S.S.P.*, March 1965, pp. 56–59.

Tennyson, W. Wesley, Donald H. Blocker, and Ralph H. Johnson. "Student Personnel Records: A Vital Look But a Concern of the Public," *Personnel and Guidance Journal*, May 1964, pp. 888–94.

Wrenn, C. G. "The Ethics of Counseling," *Educational Psychology Measurements*, 1952, pp. 161–71.

Zeran, Franklin R., and Anthony C. Riccio. *Organization and Administration of Guidance Services*. Chicago: Rand McNally and Company, 1962.

CHAPTER 12

Student Activity Programs

A principal directing the student activity program is like a manager of a three-ring circus. He gets the circus to town, arranges the big tent, advertises, sells tickets, assigns duties, supervises the activities, and occasionally performs. In the ring to the left, he tries to hold classes and keep teachers happy by juggling students and schedules. In the ring to the right, he rides his favorite hobbyhorse with one foot on district policy and the other foot on the high school regulations. In the center ring, athletic teams show their agility, actors perform, and the music plays on—while all around the rings the public is waiting, demanding, hissing, booing, and occasionally applauding.

Such a description of the activity program reveals the variety of responsibilities attached to management of the program. Over the years the student activity program has been under criticism for many and various reasons. This criticism has increased in recent years owing to the current emphasis placed on the academic curriculum. However, as one reviews the student activities and sees the extent to which student activities are a part of the high school, there is little doubt that student activities are here to stay. The principal is the central figure in this program, and a considerable portion of his time is spent in planning and administering the activity program.

The names by which the activity program has been called have changed with a changing philosophy of education. The values of the program, from a curriculum-in-action viewpoint and from the viewpoint of fulfilling the needs of adolescence, are essential. The principal should build on these values. He should design, plan, organize, and administer the separate phases of the student activity program so they will be kept in balance and in harmony with the total objectives of the school. To this end, the principal dedicates his time and energy.

Background of Student Activity Program

Historical Background. The inception of the secondary school in America, the Latin grammar school, was based on serious preparation for Harvard University. With its nonflexible curriculum, other needs such as surveying, modern language, bookkeeping, and navigation were fulfilled by private schools. Gradually the general needs for a more practical curriculum created the academies and finally the free public high school. However, through all of this period the program was basically centered around academic needs. Leisure-time activities and especially activities for recreation or play were never considered as part of the curriculum program. In fact, in the early history, these activities were denied and regarded as evil. As social thought changed, the activities were no longer considered evil, but they were still not accepted as part of education. To meet the needs of youth, programs of activities were gradually organized by students and youth groups. The organization and programs were conducted after school and were not considered to be in the school program. Neither the school nor the faculty had any responsibility. Gradually, the school did permit these activities to exist and in many places give official permission—as long as they did not interfere with the students' academic studies. This period of permission or toleration existed until about the end of the first quarter of the twentieth century.

Although ancient Athens and Sparta incorporated athletics, public speaking, music, and dancing as part of the essential curriculum, the schools across the United States did not seriously recognize student activities as they are now known as valuable school programs until after about 1925. After this time the school sponsored them and provided a certain amount of faculty supervision. The values to be gained were publicized, and gradually the student activities became widely accepted across the nation. Schools not only recognized these activities in their school program as extra programs, but also provided facilities such as fields and gymnasiums. Equipment and materials were supplied. Finally, the daily schedule was adjusted for their inclusion into the school day.

The activity program now has the approval of students, administrators, parents, board members, and the public in general. In many schools the program has become such an integral part of the school that the activities are scheduled during class time in the same manner as any other subject. In other schools, the activity program may still be considered as extracurricular, but the program is given a high priority in the scheduling of events.

Athletic events are of such great interest in some communities that this program tends to be the center of community activity. There is some evidence that in many of our schools, another period is evolving— one of exploitation. "The tail is wagging the dog" is often used to express this new relationship between student activities and academic subject areas.

Also, in some schools, the student activity program is being exploited by the school, coaches, and community for their own individual advancement and recognition.[1]

In recapitulation, it has been shown that the activity program has had five major periods. Not all schools are at the same place in their positions within these periods. These periods are as follows: (1) denial of the student activity program, (2) toleration of the student activity program, (3) recognition of the student activity program, (4) wide acceptance of the activity program, and (5) exploitation of the student activity program.

Names Used to Describe the Student Activity Program. In the historical development of the student activity program there have been many names used to describe the program. Some of these names are in current usage. The following terms have been used: extraclass activities, social activities, extracurricular activities, cocurricular activities, the activity curriculum, informal curriculum, campus activities, noncurriculum activities, associative activities, group activities, third curriculum, and student activities.

The names most frequently found in usage today are: student activities, extracurricular activities, extraclass activities, and cocurricular activities. In this chapter these activities will be known as the student activity program or student activities.

Major Types of Student Activities. The new principal will be greatly startled by the number of student activities that are part of his total school program. He will soon learn that he could spend all of his time in this one area. No two schools may have the exact activities nor will they have the same number of activities. The variety can only be exceeded by the imagination of students and faculty members. Robert W. Frederick, in his book *The Third Curriculum,* classifies student activities and provides

[1] William R. Reed, "Intercollegiate and Interschool Athletics—Assessing the Accomplishments and Problems," *Bulletin of N.A.S.S.P.*, April 1964, pp. 271–80.

a detailed list of over 250 types of activities that may be found in secondary schools.[2] A few of the major student activities are listed below:

1. Student government.
2. Class organizations.
3. Homerooms.
4. Musical activities—bands, chorus, etc.
5. Speech and dramatic activities.
6. School publications.
7. Clubs and service organizations.
8. Scholastic and honor societies.
9. Athletics and intramurals.
10. Assemblies.
11. Social activities.
12. Cooperative sponsored organizations.

Purposes and Objectives of Student Activities

With such a large list of possible student activities, it is crucial that the principal be concerned with the purposes and objectives of the student activity program so the program can be kept in balance. There have been many lists of objectives prepared by interested individuals writing in the area of student activities. The list by Ellsworth Tompkins classified the outcomes into three useful groups:

Individual Outcomes:
1. Using leisure time constructively.
2. Developing personality.
3. Enriching personality.
4. Achieving self-realization for good purpose.
5. Developing personal initiative and responsibility.
6. Learning how to conduct and participate in a meeting.
7. Affording opportunity for self-appraisal by the individual.

Social Outcomes:
1. Providing mental and physical recreation.
2. Gaining practice working with others.
3. Developing democratic group responsibility.
4. Learning to practice good human relationships.
5. Understanding group processes.
6. Furthering good pupil-teacher relationships.
7. Increasing one's social contacts.

Civic and Ethical Outcomes:
1. Establishing bonds of understanding between pupils regardless of race, creed, religion, economic status and ability.

[2] Robert W. Frederick, *The Third Curriculum* (New York: Appleton-Century-Crofts, Inc., 1959), pp. 429–33.

2. Implementing the unifying process essential to the support of American ideals.

3. Interpreting and diversifying the curriculum.

4. Helping youth to like school.[3]

Principles for a Student Activity Program

Principles for a Good Student Activity Program.   With the objectives established, the principal is ready to consider the underlying principles for the inclusion of any particular activity in the program. He is constantly receiving requests from students, teachers, and outside agencies who desire such inclusions. The following principles, as given by Miller, Moyer, and Patrick in their book *Planning Student Activities,* are suggested:

A. General Principles

1. The pupil should be regarded as a citizen of his school.

2. A constructive program is essential.

3. All students, teachers, and administrative personnel should contribute to the promotion of the program.

4. Cooperation (team work) is basic.

5. Activities tend to flourish in a democratic study.

6. Few, if any, restrictions should be placed on participation.

7. Pupil participation has natural limitations.

8. Guidance, individual and group, must be emphasized.

9. The process is more important than the product.

10. The program should be predicated upon the purposes for which our schools exist.

11. The program should take into account the special or unique needs of a particular school.

12. To insure maximum attention to the needs and interests of all pupils, a comprehensive and well balanced program must be provided.

13. Authority must be commensurate with delegated responsibility.

14. The program must be evaluated with special reference to its contribution to the accepted education values of the school and the efficiency with which the several activities are carried through.

B. Principles Related to the Total Instructional Program

1. Cocurricular activities should furnish a rich source of motivation for class instruction.

2. Classroom instruction should furnish a rich source of motivation for cocurricular activities.

3. Cocurricular activities must be considered as an integral part of the total instructional program rather than as extra or as an independent program.

[3] Ellsworth Tompkins, *Extraclass Activities for All Pupils* (Washington, D.C.: Federal Security Agency, Office of Education, 1950), p. 3.

C. Principles Related to Adult Leadership

1. The degree of success of the program depends, to a large extent, upon the intelligent and whole-hearted leadership from faculty advisers.

2. The teacher must remember that he is primarily an adviser and counselor.

3. The adviser must be held accountable for the results achieved by the activity for which he has assumed responsibility.

4. Consultants may be used as needed when available, but responsibility for the consequences must be assumed by the school adviser.

5. Even though teachers should accept their full share of the responsibility for the whole program, they must not be exploited.

D. Principles Related to Administration and Supervision

1. The administration must demonstrate a favorable attitude toward this phase of the school's program.

2. Whenever possible, activities should be scheduled on school time.

3. In planning assignments of instructional responsibilities for teachers, the administrator should include both curricular and cocurricular activities in his assignment.

4. Essential facilities must be provided insofar as it is possible to do so.

5. Adequate financial support must be forthcoming.

6. All finances should be handled in a business-like manner and must be carefully supervised.

7. Activities should receive continuous democratic supervision from the school officials responsible for the total instructional program.

8. The cocurriculum must be thought of as an integral part of the total instructional program of the school.

9. Provision should be made for the objective evaluation of the activities program.

10. Community support, not domination, should be encouraged.

11. It must be clearly understood by all that the principal is the responsible head of the school.[4]

Principles Governing Membership. Once a particular activity is permitted in the program, certain fundamental principles regarding membership participation should be planned. The need for membership guidelines is presented in the case below:

GIRLS' PEP CLUB EXCLUSIVE

Miss Parley had reviewed the procedure that had been adopted many years previously for election of girls into the Pep Club. The procedure called for the election of six members to the Pep Club from the ninth grade. Miss Parley was the ninth-grade adviser.

[4] Franklin A. Miller, James H. Moyer, and Robert B. Patrick, *Planning Student Activities* (Englewood Cliffs, N.J.: Prentice-Hall, Inc., 1961), pp. 21–32. © Copyright Prentice-Hall, Inc., 1961. Published with permission of Prentice-Hall, Inc.

The bell rang, which was the signal for all the ninth-grade students to meet in her room for the election. The meeting was called to order by the president of the Girls' Pep Club. Twenty girls were nominated by the class, and a popular ballot was conducted. The actual counting of the ballots was to be done by the Girls' Pep Club officers under Miss Parley's supervision. The girls who were elected had to be approved by the total membership of the Girls' Pep Club, and then the membership committee had to be notified which girls were elected.

The following day six fortunate girls were notified. Many of their friends as well as many other girls who desired to be in the Pep Club were not admitted. The tears flowed freely and many girls were upset—some became sick. That afternoon, evening, and the following day both the principal and Miss Parley were deluged with calls from unhappy parents who wanted their daughters admitted to the Pep Club. The principal and Miss Parley sat down together to discuss some of the basic problems. Some of these problems were: Why was the Girls' Pep Club so exclusive? What factors should be considered for membership? Was popular vote the right procedure to use for this particular type of activity? Should membership be broadened? Should criteria be developed so that students would automatically be permitted into the club upon their completion?

The principal and Miss Parley decided that during the year they would make a detailed evaluation of the club and its activities to determine how it might be organized to be more representative of the school.

This example is typical of many problems presented to the principal as related to membership. Membership criteria and procedures for entrance are both critical to the proper functioning of clubs and organizations. The principal should see that criteria and procedures are established that qualify students for membership. Douglass indicated the following as being some of the more important principles governing membership:

1. *There should be complete democracy in the means of determining membership.* Membership should not be dependent upon the preference of members or leaders of cliques.

2. *Membership should be determined on the basis of the pupil's interest and ability in the work of the organization, in accordance with the objective rules of the organization.* If the organization does not stand ready to accept all candidates, there should be set up objective means of selecting candidates, such as tryouts conducted by faculty advisers, order of seniority of pupils, or formal application.

3. *Membership should be restricted to pupils in good standing.* No school organization should admit to membership or to participation in its activity any person not a bona-fide member of the student body. All members should be boys and girls subject to the discipline of the school. Outsiders almost invariably constitute unusual and unnecessary problems difficult to handle.

4. *Membership should be regulated by rules which prevent monopoly of activities by the more able or popular pupils.* Regulations should be provided and enforced that will make it impossible for a small number of pupils to enjoy a large share of the opportunities for training in the activities of the school to the exclusion of those more in need of such training. Means of administration of such regulations have just been outlined and discussed.

5. *Membership should not depend upon any degree of scholarship beyond passing marks.* It has been shown that participation in activities (with the possible exception of certain types of athletics—notably football) has little or no effect upon the quality of work done by participants on their regular, conventional studies. In perhaps a majority of instances the pupil who is not capable of or interested in such studies will profit relatively more by participation in activities than the normal or superior pupil; in fact, many inferior pupils will profit very little from attendance in school except by means of activities.

6. *Membership should not be subject to severance in the interests of the highly specialized training of a selected few.* This principle is violated in almost every organization or activity which engages in interscholastic competition. Coaches or sponsors of such activities are prone to place a good showing of a picked team above the educational value of the activity. Pupils of lesser promise are frequently forced to discontinue. This practice is indicative of a perverted concept of values and should give way to a regime which makes provision for those who need the training most and are willing to acquire it, as well as for those who are most gifted or who have already reached a high degree of training.[5]

Dangers in the Student Activity Program. Because of the great interest that has been expressed in recent years in the student activity program, the principal must be aware that there are certain problems and dangers. The most important danger is that a disproportionate amount of time can be spent with the student activity program. In truth, the tail can indeed wag the dog.

A second problem is the trend toward large group spectator sports and activities in which students participate only as observers. As the quality of the programs improves, there is a tendency to select only the best students for participation. All others are sidelined.

Such selection of top participants automatically leads to a third problem —hero worship. Sports writers have a tendency to glorify the boy carrying the ball, while other members of the team seldom receive credit. Student growth and development are the primary purpose of the activity. The

[5] Harl R. Douglass, *Modern Administration of Secondary Schools*, 2nd ed. (New York: Blaisdell Publishing Co., 1963), pp. 214–15. © Copyright Ginn and Company, 1963. Reprinted through the courtesy of Blaisdell Publishing Company, a division of Ginn and Company.

game is not for the coach's win-loss record, the school's reputation, or the parent's ego satisfaction.

A fourth major danger is that all the activities become competitive in nature, and only competitive events are considered valuable.

A fifth danger, similar to the last, is that the interschool athletics will have a tendency to dominate and in many cases displace all other similar activities. Interscholastic athletics may do away with the intramural program unless constant observation and direction are provided.

A sixth major danger is that community groups begin to place pressure on the school personnel. During a winning season, a coach may receive anything he desires, and a suggestion to downtown groups is enough to bring its realization. On the other hand, a losing season works in reverse, and the downtown group puts pressure on the principal for the release of the coach regardless of the quality of sportsmanship, education, and other value that the coach may contribute to the school. Athletics is not the only area affected by such community pressures.

A seventh danger is imitation of universities and other status-type organizations. The goals of the high school are forgotten in the search for sophistication.

Finally, a danger of which the principal should constantly be aware is the extent to which his faculty members are involved in the supervision of extracurricular activities. The teachers' loads should be evaluated with extracurricular activities included. Frequently a faculty member spends most of his time on student activities at the expense of his academic responsibilities. The principal is likewise affected and his time must also be considered and guarded.

Administration of the Activity Program

Delegation of Responsibility.   Next to office routine the principal spends the largest percentage of his time on the student activity program. Approximately 18 per cent of the principal's time is spent on these programs. In contrast to the amount of time spent, the principals indicated that they should only spend about 9 per cent, while authorities thought that principals should only spend about 8 per cent of their time in these activities. The principals spend two times as much of their total time in the student activity program as they believe should be spent. If asked why, the answer would be very clear and straightforward. The programs require that much time. One principal expressed it this way, "I could mismanage all of the school funds and years might go by and I would never be questioned, but if I mismanaged one basketball ticket I would be run out of town tomorrow." Since the program does require excessive time, it is the responsibility of the principal to find effective ways of delegating many of the duties relating to the program.

The first person to whom he should make delegation is the assistant principal, when there is an assistant principal in the school. Second, he should delegate responsibility to activity coordinators or to the teachers. Third, he should carefully control the activity program to keep it in balance. Too many activities may be the cause of the excessive time expenditure. Fourth, he should seek additional clerical help to alleviate some of the excessive load of this program. The coordinator of student activities, whether he be an assistant principal or a teacher, could handle most of the detail that is entailed in each student activity. The principal could then serve as an administrative director of the program.

Administrative Control. Many reasons have already been cited that would indicate why the principal must be in control of the student activity program. For effective control, criteria should be established and screening take place prior to granting permission for new clubs or organizations to exist. Every club should have a constitution, which states the purpose of the organization, objectives, membership qualifications, and other procedure. The constitution should be approved by the student council, faculty adviser, and principal. Appropriate bylaws should also be approved. Each organization should submit to the principal through the coordinator of student activities the yearly program for that organization. At this point, the principal should check the proposed yearly program against the constitution of the organization and against the school's aims and objectives. By making this check, he can keep the activities of each organization within the defined objectives. Activities that are planned but are considered undesirable by the principal can be eliminated and proper substitutes made.

If the student council is properly organized, the principal might use it as the coordinating agent for controlling these groups. The student council would have the primary responsibility for securing the constitutions, bylaws, applications, and programs; checking them as to their fitness; and making recommendations to the principal. Scheduling of student events and activities could be coordinated through the student council.

Every principal has had the experience, at some time during his career, of receiving a report that an unauthorized club exists in his school. In most cases, these clubs do not exist at all; yet the public is convinced that they do exist and are sponsored by the school. These unauthorized clubs are usually clubs that are organized outside the school. The principal cannot keep groups of students from organizing in their own homes or neighborhood for whatever purpose they desire; however, he must insist that they do not carry on activities within the school. Further, he can prohibit them from participation in extracurricular activities.[6] If the principal has well-established criteria for admission of clubs and a reasonable check on the control of these clubs, unfounded rumors can be quickly stopped.

Financing School Activities.   The student activity program, like all curriculum areas, requires financing for its success. Seldom does a school district underwrite the school's activity program. Since the program has traditionally been an extracurricular program, with the emphasis on *extra,* the program has been financed by the high school rather than from the operating budget of the district. Student activity fees may be charged, but these fees seldom carry the total program. The principal thus must promote a fund-raising operation. As a result of these fund-raising drives, sale of tickets, etc., high schools of approximately 700 students have been known to have a general surplus activity account of over $20,000. Surplus funds should be wisely invested.

To make the activity program solvent, the yearly operating budget must be determined, the source of finances must be examined, and expenditure procedures must be initiated. The funds come primarily from student-body fees, sale of tickets, money-making projects, contributions, and sale of advertisements in student publications. The detailed procedures of financing student-body activities and the expenditure of student funds are discussed in the chapter on the administration of business affairs.

Supervision of Student Activities.   Because of the nature of student activities, careful supervision is required. The principal will be at most activities, but he cannot be with all groups at all times during planning and preparation for the activity. Since supervision is necessary, the principal must assign teachers to be advisers for the various student activities. The careful scheduling of the activities during the school day makes it possible to give more careful supervision and to involve all faculty members who are needed. Whether the activity is scheduled in the day or at night, the principal should not allow activities without the direct supervision of a faculty member in their planning and performance.

The adviser should not take from the students their right of leadership; yet a good adviser must inform students of school policies and not permit deviation from such policies. Within the framework of the defined regulations, the adviser may allow leeway for the exercise of student initiative and leadership.

In addition to the faculty supervision, there are many events in which

---

[6] E. C. Bolmeier, "Legal Aspects of Curriculum and the Extracurriculum," *Bulletin of N.A.S.S.P.*, March 1965, pp. 128–42.

the principal will desire to have representatives from the community present, such as the local police force. Whenever student dances, ball games, and night activities are held, it is well to inform the local police and provide them with an open invitation to be present. Where problems are anticipated, attendance by the police should be requested, for their presence prevents many problems.

Extra Pay for Activity Supervision. In recent years there has been considerable activity on the part of teachers' organizations to increase salaries and working conditions. One condition that has been severely criticized is the excessive demands made on teacher time for supervision of student activities.[7] Some teachers' organizations have been successful in securing extra pay for these assignments. The extra compensation is given for two types of supervision: (1) athletic coaches, publication advisers, speech and drama advisers, and advisers of similar types of activities; and (2) supervision of night games and dances, hall supervision, and other after-school activities.

When extra pay for activity supervision is given, it should be clearly understood that the compensation is for work beyond that expected from the professional service for which the person already receives a salary. Approximately 75 per cent of the districts currently provide some compensation for these extra services. However, each district varies as to the degree of coverage and the amount to be given.[8]

Patron Supervision. Some districts have attempted to solve the problem of extra pay for supervision of activities by releasing the teachers from their responsibilities. Under these conditions, school patrons are invited to assume these responsibilities. Although many lay citizens provide commendable service, the quality of supervision is usually lower than that of professionally trained teachers, who know how to handle the youth. The principal must spend more time in organizing, instructing, and assisting these nonprofessionals in carrying out their responsibilities.

Scheduling Activities. The principal must plan and schedule activities in the same way he does other classes. The constant unscheduled interruption of classes creates confusion and discord among students and faculty members. The activities should be planned in advance, cleared with the activity coordinator, and approved by the principal. Announce-

---

[7] Charles I. Brown and Thomas G. Edwards, "Extraclass Activities of Social Studies Teachers," *Bulletin of N.A.S.S.P.*, March 1962, pp. 183–89. Monte S. Norton, "Extra Duties for Teachers," *Bulletin of N.A.S.S.P.*, December 1961, pp. 105–12.

[8] *Extra Pay for Extra Work* (New London, Conn.: Arthur C. Crofts Publication, March 1961), p. 1.

ment of the activity should be made several days and preferably a week in advance. In fact, most of the activities can be planned early in the fall for the total school year.

Many schools must schedule all activities during the school day because students are transported by buses that make several trips for different schools. Activity periods by necessity become part of the school day. The principal must devise a schedule that permits practices as well as performances during the regular day. A few possible schedules that may be used are (1) lengthened noon hour to permit rehearsals, intramurals, (2) shortened periods of ten minutes each on activity day to permit an additional period to be added, (3) omission of classes on a rotating basis —first period one week, second period the next week, etc., or (4) a combination of the above.

In the junior high schools that have club programs once a week, the selected activity schedule can be in motion in the same way it can be for a football game or a student assembly. Usually the shortened period system is used on club day.

Encouraging Participation. One of the most persistent unresolved problems is how to get all students involved in student activities. If the values derived from participation are justified, the advantages should be extended to all students. The principal must strive to have a sufficient number of activities for all students, and he must develop a system of accounting so he can tell which students are and are not involved in the activity program. Too frequently the well-adjusted student is involved in many activities, while the shy or problem student is never considered. An intramural activity program for both boys and girls is one good way to encourage participation by all students. Details of an extensive intramural program are discussed in subsequent sections. Other programs that provide for wide participation should be encouraged by the principal.

The principal should provide a bulletin board that can be used to advertise all activities. The student council should be given responsibility for the care of the bulletin board. Special announcements over the public address system may also be used to stimulate interest in coming activities.

High School Activities Association

Each of the states has a high school activities association. This activities association has as its primary purpose the central control of the activities that take place within the state—to keep them within bounds and to constantly improve them. The high school activities association within the state operates within the framework of an approved constitution and approved bylaws. All member high schools have the opportunity to be represented in both legislative and executive functions. The major sections of a typical high-school-activities-association constitution are name; purposes; membership; organization; legislative council; board of directors; funds, fees, and expenses; the executive secretary-treasurer; meetings; miscellaneous; and elections.

Typical bylaws of such an organization describe some of the following: eligibility of players, 19-year age rule, semester attendance rule, sports season rule, rules against playing on teams of higher institutions, amateur rule, scholastic regulations, transfer rule, undue influence rule, graduates' ineligibility, physical examination requirements, exchange of eligibility lists, protests and penalties, breach of contract, defacement of school property, unsportsmanlike conduct, schedule, awards, postseason and preseason contests, who may coach, and eligibility of out-of-season athletic activities.

The efforts of the associations to improve and control the student activities in the various member schools have been very effective. If the associations did nothing more than solve the squabbles that always exist over eligibility, they would be doing monumental work. However, the association coordinates all state activities, schedules state meets, and conducts state contests.

A new principal should be very familiar with the constitution and bylaws of his high school activities association and should follow these bylaws in setting policies within his own school. The athletic, speech, drama, music, and other activities within his region, district, and school are governed by the policies of this association. Although each state has its own activity association there are common elements in the constitution and bylaws of all the states. Because the principal must be acquainted with these bylaws, which govern large portions of his activity program, a sample constitution and bylaws are provided in the Appendix for reference purposes.

Student Government

Student Council. It is common practice in secondary schools to permit the students to have some governmental organization. The students elect officers to represent them, and these officers conduct activities and other matters for the general welfare of the total student body. The student council is the organization that usually represents all the students. The organizational patterns of the student councils vary with the size of schools. Generally speaking, there is a president, vice-president, secretary, and treasurer. Beyond these four positions, the philosophy of the various schools and school size are major factors in determining the other positions needed. Additional officers sometimes included are: chief of police, class presidents, homeroom presidents, yearbook editor, school newspaper editor, cheerleader, and activity manager.

The objectives of a student council are well presented by the National Association of Student Councils in *A Handbook for Student Councils*. These objectives are as follows:

1. To allow students to participate in or manage extracurricular affairs.
2. To develop student responsibility, initiative, leadership and school pride.
3. To promote the welfare of the school through proper student, faculty relationship.
4. To promote citizenship training.
5. To promote general welfare.
6. To aid in the internal administration of the school.
7. To provide for pupil expression.
8. To furnish a working model of government.[9]

The student council is an effective representative of the students. If the principal works closely with them, many of the problems of discipline and control as well as many projects for the over-all improvement of the school can be launched and carried forth. Aside from the benefits that the school derives from such an organization, the student council also is an excellent training ground for responsible citizens and responsible leaders. The council should be organized to reflect, as closely as possible, the actual operation of the society in general. The student council should have real problems to solve and be given authority and responsibility to solve these problems. As long as the student council operates within the policies that are determined, the organization is most effective.[10]

Membership in the student council is normally determined by the provisions of the high school constitution. Similarly, the qualifications for membership are usually given. Generally, a student council member should have the following qualifications: (1) he should be a member of the school, (2) he should be a good citizen within the school, (3) he should be able to represent his fellow students and have their respect, (4) he should be able to work with other students, and (5) he should have qualities for leadership.

[9] National Association of Student Councils, *A Handbook for Student Councils* (Washington, D.C.: National Association of Secondary-School Principals, 1950), p. 14.

[10] Willard J. Morgan, "Increasing the Effectiveness of Student Councils," *School Activities*, April 1964, pp. 233–35.

Principal's Role with the Student Council. The principal's responsibility to the student council varies in proportion to the size of the school. In a large school the principal will meet with the student council long enough for them to get acquainted and to introduce advisers and other individuals who will be working more closely with the student council. The principal will discuss the student council's responsibility in relationship to the total school and will explain the area of its jurisdiction. The actual operation of the council can then be turned over to the assistant principal and advisers to the student council. The principal should be consulted when important decisions are pending. In smaller schools the principal may be the only adviser to the student council. He must work with them directly as an adviser, attend their meetings, supervise their activities, and in general plan and encourage them in their duties. Figure 12.1 shows

Figure 12.1

Student Government Line of Authority

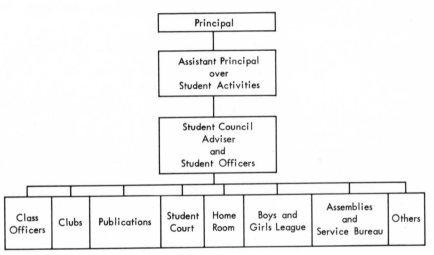

how a student council might be organized to carry out its responsibility with other student organizations. The principal has the additional responsibility of scheduling the student council meetings so that all members may be properly represented, to provide proper facilities for the council's activities, to provide the equipment and supplies needed, to select an adviser interested in student activities, and to show a continued interest in the student council activities.

Homeroom. The homeroom organizational pattern is somewhat similar to that of the student council, but on a classroom basis. The basic objectives of the homeroom are (1) to promote citizenship training by giving more students opportunity in student government, (2) to facilitate the dissemination of information prepared through the guidance and counseling services, and (3) to carry out other activities as needed.

The homeroom organization functions with varying degrees of effectiveness, depending on the responsibility that is entrusted to the organization and the interest of the faculty adviser. The principal must arrange the schedule for the homeroom period. Frequently a portion of the first-period class is used as needed. A second scheduling practice is to schedule a special homeroom class once or twice a week. The adviser is responsible for the agenda and the planning of the meeting, and he works in cooperation with the homeroom officers who conduct the meeting.

The homeroom is frequently used as an arm of the guidance services. The homeroom teacher is expected to know his students better than other teachers, to work with them closely on guidance problems, and to make referrals on students as needed.

Class Organization. The class organization is patterned after the student council. The class organization represents the total student body at a given grade level. Officers are elected and activities planned. These activities usually include a yearly assembly, a dance or other social, and intramurals or interclass competition. All business and administrative detail pertaining to a given age group is usually channeled through a class organization. Each class should have an adviser or advisers to assist in the planning and guidance of the class officers. Periodically, class officers should meet with the student council to aid the student council in carrying out worthy projects.

Assemblies and Service Bureau. The school assembly program can be one of the unifying forces in the high school. The degree of unity is dependent on the quality of the planning. On the other hand, a school assembly can be very disruptive if the quality of the assembly is poor. One way to guarantee a high-quality assembly is to require all assemblies to be approved in advance. The approval can be given through the adviser. However, a higher-quality assembly can usually be presented if the assembly must be cleared before a group organized for such a purpose.[11] In some schools an organization known as the service bureau exists. The purposes and functions of a service bureau are to supervise all assemblies originating within the school and maintain a record of all student talent; to supervise the presentation of all assemblies, approve the script, see to all necessary stage work, and review and approve all assemblies prior

[11] Arthur C. Hearn, "Are School Assembly Programs Missing the Boat?" *School Activities,* May 1964, p. 274.

to their final presentation; and to be responsible for seeing that all groups presenting entertainment meet the standards and requirements of the adopted assembly code.

The service bureau might consist of the student-body vice-president, who acts as chairman of the service bureau; the vice-president of each class; and the vice-presidents of the boys' and girls' leagues. A member of the faculty, appointed by the principal, serves as adviser. Community organizations frequently call on the service bureau to furnish programs and special numbers.

In order to keep assemblies on a high plane, some regulations are necessary. The principal may desire to have the service bureau along with the student council develop an assembly code. In addition to serving as a judge over the quality of assemblies, the service bureau may also act as a consultant for the improvement of the assemblies. Items from typical assembly codes are presented below:

1. The assembly must appear before the service bureau no less than four days before presentation. A copy of the script must be given to the service bureau the day before the official review.

2. The presentation must be free of coarse, rude, vulgar expressions and of any suggestive material of an immoral nature. The program should *not* contain:

a. References to any student or teacher that reflect upon their character, unless agreed to by the individual concerned.

b. Material that invades the private life and habits of any student or teacher.

c. Costumes, pictures, or properties that tend to degrade any participant or embarrass the audience.

d. The use of any object or substance that may damage the stage, floor, cyclorama, curtains, or electrical fixtures.

3. Nothing may be pinned, taped, or glued to cyclorama or curtains. Directors and advisers should discuss staging problems with stage crew manager *before* putting up a set.

4. Separate lists of staging and lighting needs should be given to the service bureau in advance of rehearsals.

5. Advisers should instruct assembly participants not to hang on or pull curtains or lines. All permanent stage equipment is the sole responsibility of the stage and light crews.

6. Each group presenting an assembly is responsible for cleaning the stage and dressing rooms after each performance.

7. Where any doubt exists concerning the script, stage, properties, or lights, the service bureau should be contacted before any action is taken.

In addition to guaranteeing the quality of assemblies, the principal has the responsibility of selecting sponsors, scheduling the assembly for the least disruption of school time, and taking care of any total school business that might be best handled in an assembly. He should encourage the service bureau or other organized groups to evaluate and to work for the constant improvement of the assemblies.

Student Publications.   A school may have any number of publications, but the most common are the school newspaper and the school yearbook. The school newspaper is under the direction of a student editor and student reporters. An adviser who is competent in journalism is selected. Whenever possible, those participating in the production of the school newspaper should register for a class in journalism. The actual writing and publication of the paper can be done as part of a classroom project. Students may receive credit for such a class as they would for other subjects. The basic style of the paper will be determined by the background and the experience of the adviser. The printing will depend on the available finances and equipment. A typical small high school newspaper is published on a mimeograph or offset machine. The operation of the machine is part of the students' experiences. At the other extreme, school newspapers are published by regular printing firms with students submitting copy and aiding in typesetting and printing processes. When the local newspaper prints the school paper, arrangements can often be made to have the school paper inserted into every copy of the local paper. Under this arrangement, every home subscribing to the local newspaper receives the school newspaper. Such a practice can be a useful public relations device. However, where practiced, the editors and advisers of the newspaper have an even greater responsibility to improve the quality of the publication.

Because student newspapers usually carry some columns that are interesting "talk or gossip" columns, it is very important that some policy be established to disallow items that are derogatory or hurtful to fellow students.

The student yearbook or annual has many of the same problems as discussed in relationship to the student newspaper. However, the primary purpose of the annual is to present in graphic as well as in written form the events and the important functions of the school. It is well for the adviser to have some knowledge of photography, make-up, and general publication procedures.[12] There are several problems connected with a school annual. The annual is costly, frequently *too* costly. It does not include all grade levels. It is not planned as a total artistic production. Johnston and Faunce have given suggestions for management of the school annual that tend to reduce the effect of these limitations. These suggestions are as follows:

[12] Mabel Robrock, "Yearbook Trends," *Scholastic Editor*, January 1965, pp. 14–16.

1. Costs can be reduced by careful planning. As a last resort, a June issue of the school paper or magazine can be devoted to the senior class record and serve as a low-cost annual. This device is not entirely satisfactory, however, for achieving the purposes of the annual. Offset printing can produce a highly satisfactory yearbook at low cost. Competitive bidding can cut the engraving and printing costs if a printed annual is desired. A reasonable budget, carefully planned and rigidly adhered to, will help.

2. The yearbook can be planned by the whole school through representation on the advisory board, and built up in original fashion around some appropriate local theme. Pictures and other decor can be developed on this central theme.

3. The annual can devote space to all students and all activities, thus enhancing the general appeal of the book. The test of the success of an annual lies in its appeal to the average reader, who makes its publication possible by his support.

4. The faculty adviser's schedule should be so arranged as to allow sufficient time for supervision of this task. If a yearbook is important to have, it is important to schedule time for guidance of the project.

5. The yearbook should be a student product, with every piece of copy, photography, and layout the work of students. The same should be true of business and circulation work. Engravers, printers, and photographers can help with advice, but the actual decision and the real planning must be in the hands of students under the guidance of a competent, interested sponsor.

6. Plans should be made to get the kind of photographs which tell an action story. Informal pictures in a natural action setting are much more interesting than portraits. Individuals and groups should be presented in their characteristic settings: the principal at his desk, the biology class on a field trip, the football team lined up for the big game.

7. There is an excellent opportunity for educational planning in presenting the various activities in such a way as to interpret the spirit and life of the school. The Grosse Pointe (Michigan) View Pointe, for example, carries on its cover an artistic photograph of some feature of the school— the clock tower framed by trees, the flagpole seen through the columns of the school entrance, a winter view of the school, three graduates in uniform with the school as background. The book then has eighteen pages of vivid photographs of students and faculty at work and play, arranged under suitable captions, and with accompanying interpretation and comment.

8. In illustrating and describing the educational activities of the year, the annual incidentally can help the parents to understand better the total program of the school. It can be a potent public relations instrument, without diverting it from its major function of providing a souvenir record for students.[13]

---

[13] Edgar C. Johnston and Roland C. Faunce, *Student Activities in Secondary Schools.* Copyright 1952, The Ronald Press Company, pp. 181–88, Reprinted by permission of The Ronald Press Company.

The student yearbook is usually financed from the subscriptions of students, activity fees budgeted through the student council, the sale of advertising space, and subsidies from the board of education.

Class-Related Activities

Music.   Music activities were among the first to become part of the student activity program. The concert and marching bands, orchestras, student ensembles, choirs, and operettas have tended to be the core of the music program. Since most of these activities have their corollary in class instruction, the basic instruction is usually given in class work with some time outside of class taken for rehearsals. The presentations are made in the evening or on scheduled assembly, activity, and contest days. The advisers for these activities are the music instructors. Most of the actual events are organized by the adviser. The principal's responsibility is primarily one of scheduling and arranging facilities. However, when a large regional meet is held, the principal's responsibility increases to include other functions, such as total program organization, scheduling, facilities, rehearsal areas, housing, and many other related activities. In communities where students must stay overnight to participate in the event, large numbers of students require housing in the homes in the community. The principal's responsibilities are then increased to include student housing, transportation, arrangement for meals, concessions, and other similar services. In addition to these major items, the principal must always provide for minor first-aid emergencies.

The music program is under the direction of the high school activity association, and general rules and regulations pertaining to travel and outside-of-state participation apply.

Speech and Dramatic Arts.   Speech and dramatic arts include forensics, oratory, debating, extemporaneous speaking, discussions, readings, plays, pantomimes, and other dramatic performances. Like the music activities, the speech and drama activities are generally a part of the classroom program. The speech and drama teachers serve as the advisers, and these activities are under their direction. The principal can rely on the advisers to plan and carry forth the activities. The principal's duties are similar to those discussed in the music program.

Subject-Oriented Clubs.   There are many clubs organized in schools which provide additional experiences for students in a given subject area, such as a biological science club or social studies club. The Thespian Organization is one such group, organized on a national basis, which accomplishes these purposes. A written set of goals and objectives, a planned yearly program, and an adviser who is interested in carrying forth a program are essentials. These clubs usually function efficiently as long as the advisers maintain their interest. A change in advisers sometimes spells the death of these club programs. The principal's primary responsibility is to see that the club is within the philosophy of the total student activity program and see that the advisers provide adequate supervision.

Future Farmers of America and Future Homemakers of America. These two organizations are related to the agricultural and the home economics programs within the school. The organizations are national in scope, with national and state organization and local functioning chapters. Officers are elected to carry out the objectives of the program. Both organizations, but particularly the Future Farmers of America, conduct a wide variety of activities at the state and national level. The advisers of these two organizations usually are the agriculture teacher and the home economics teacher.

Clubs and Other Organizations

As was indicated at the beginning of the chapter, there are many approved clubs and organizations that are allowed within a school because they promote some of the basic objectives of the school. Such clubs or organizations may be: boys' and girls' league organizations, boys' and girls' pep clubs, honor societies, and social and service organizations. Each club has its own set of officers and functions within the framework of its own constitution, bylaws, and program. The principal should see that adequate instructions and policies are set for the organizations. The following policies for advisers, taken from bylaws of many schools on club organization, initiations, and handling of student money, may be helpful:

1. Advisers are responsible to the principal for the actions of their club or organization. The adviser should approve all the activities in advance. It is not assumed that the adviser will do the planning or the work; however, he will give suggestions, correct when plans may be contrary to school policies, and be in attendance at all meetings and rehearsals of the organization—including officers' planning meetings.

2. Advisers should check with the principal if they are in question regarding a club activity and school regulations.

3. Every club must be under the direction of the school and conform to school regulations.

4. A constitution and bylaws must be approved and be on file with the principal and student council.

5. As soon after the opening of school as possible, and before any club activity takes place, a list of officers and a plan of the activities for the school year must be on file and be approved by the principal and student council.

6. Club activities are to be evaluated at the end of the school year and periodically, if desirable, by the organizations and student council.

7. The student council shall be the coordinating agent for clubs and organizations.

8. Provision should be made in each constitution for the removal from the club of students who do not conform to the standards of the organizations.

9. Clubs may be declared "nonfunctioning" or completely removed from the school if they act contrary to school policies or if they cease to have planned activities.

10. All initiations are to be constructive in nature. No hazing, feeding, etc., are to be allowed. Initiations are to be confined to one day before and after school. No initiations of any type are to be held during school hours.

11. Advisers should check with the school treasurer at the beginning of each school year to see if the club or organization has money on the school accounts. Advisers must submit the "purchasing request" to the principal for approval and obtain a purchase order before any purchase is made. They should plan activities with the officers so that purchasing requests are submitted several days in advance of need. This makes for more efficiency in planning office work. All money should be counted by the treasurer in the presence of the adviser. Money should be sealed in a container and locked in a safe until properly counted.

Competitive Athletics

Values and Principles. Competitive athletics are regarded as fundamental to school activity programs. The history of such events can be traced prior to the Olympic games of ancient Greece. Emphasis on the development of the human body and the values to be gained from competition is ever-present. However, it will be recalled, from the section regarding the dangers of the student activity program, that the tail sometimes wags the dog. If there is one area in the student activity program that can easily get out of bounds, it is that of interscholastic athletics. The principal should be aware of the values of the program and make these values his primary objectives.[14] A widely accepted set of objectives for

[14] William R. Reed, *op. cit.*, pp. 271–80.

school athletics is the "Cardinal Athletic Principles," taken from the *Journal of Health and Physical Education.*

To be of maximum effectiveness, the athletic program will:

1. Be closely coordinated with the general instructional program and properly articulated with the other departments of the school.

2. Be such that the number of students accommodated and the educational aims achieved justify the use of tax funds for its support and also warrant the use of other sources of income.

3. Provided, that the time and attention which is given to the collection of such funds is not such as to interfere with the efficiency of the athletic program or of any other departments of the school.

4. Confine the school athletic activity to events which are sponsored and supervised by the proper school authorities so that any exploitation or improper use of prestige built up by school teams or members of such teams may be avoided.

5. Be planned in such a way as to result in opportunity for many individuals to explore a wide variety of sports and to set reasonable season limits for each listed sport.

6. Be controlled in such a way as to avoid the elements of professionalism and commercialism which tend to grow up in connection with widely publicized "bowl" contest, barnstorming trips, and interstate or intersectional contests which require excessive travel expense or loss of school time or which are claimed to be justified by educational travel values.

7. Be kept free from the type of contest which involves a gathering of so-called "all-stars" from different schools to participate in contest which may be used as a gathering place for representatives of certain colleges or professional organizations who are interested in soliciting athletic talent for their teams.

8. Include educative exercises to reach all non-participating students and community followers of the school teams in order to insure a proper understanding and appreciation of the sports skills and of the need for adherence to principles of game ethics.

9. Encourage a balanced program of intramural activity in grades below the ninth to make it unnecessary to sponsor contests of a championship nature in these grades.

10. Engender respect for the rules and policies under which the school conducts its program.[15]

At the junior high school level there is considerable controversy over interschool athletics. The traditional theoretical position is that interschool athletics should be left to the high school and that intramurals should be promoted at the junior high school level. In practice, however, there are many junior high schools that do have interschool competition. If a school

---

[15] *Journal of Health and Physical Education,* September 1947, pp. 435, 557–58. Used with permission of American Association of Health, Education and Recreation.

system does have such a practice, the program should be structured on the needs of the participants, with emphasis on health, safety, sportsmanship, leadership development, fellowship, and teamwork. The program should be "child-centered" not "school-centered."[16]

Principal's Responsibility.   The principal will be faced with many difficult problems in the interscholastic athletic program. Regardless of the amount of time he spends, these problems will always be present. However, the principal can rest assured that unless he accepts certain responsibilities, he will create problems that will be far greater than the normal operational headaches. In this regard the principal should make every effort to hire or have hired good responsible coaches who recognize that athletics is only part of the school program, who are willing to assume other teaching responsibilities, and who are known through their own participation as good sports. He must spend time with the coach to let the coach know the expectations of the principal, the areas in which the principal gives unqualified support, and the areas in which the principal expects the coach to give his unqualified support. The principal should insist that the coach follow the High School Activities Association's rules and policies and that he be ethical in his dealings with students, teachers, and officials. Eligibility lists should be submitted to the competing schools. Eligibility policies within the schools should be enforced. The principal should organize all athletic contests so that details of sale of tickets, seating, officiating, and general control have been planned and well executed. He should institute a sportsmanship program as part of the interscholastic athletic program to constantly upgrade the quality of sportsmanship displayed by the athletes, the students, and the public during the contests. Arrangements for adequate insurance for all participants of athletic contests should be made. The principal should arrange for supervision 'for all trips and games away from home. Finally, the principal should set up a system of financial accounting so that all funds received and dispersed are carefully controlled and accepted accounting procedures are used.

Evaluating the Interscholastic Athletic Program.   The principal should continually evaluate the athletic program in his school. The following criteria, as given by Miller, Moyer, and Patrick in their book *Planning Student Activities,* might be used in this evaluation:

1. Do all pupils have equal opportunity to share in the athletic program of the school?

[16] James W. Jordan (ed.), "Interscholastic Athletics—Yes or No?" *Bulletin of N.A.S.S.P.*, October 1963, pp. 5–6.

2. Are athletics an educative experience of the same quality as experiences in other curriculums?

3. Is the athletic program geared to the different needs, abilities, desires, age levels, and sex of the pupils?

4. Are those who will guide students in this curriculum truly teachers, in the same sense as those who guide youth in science or social studies, for example?

5. Since all athletics should be educative experiences, are they financed by the school taxes? Are the amounts received for athletics proportionate to the number of students served?

6. Are sources of income other than tax funds used only when it can be clearly demonstrated that the activity that brings in the funds is primarily an educative activity?

7. Are all athletic activities initiated because they are educational experiences that most efficiently meet the educational objectives of the school, and are the athletic experiences always terminated when the law of diminishing returns, in its relation to the youth involved, begins to operate?

8. Is the athletic policy of the school formulated, administered, controlled, and evaluated by the same criteria as the other cocurricular activities of the school?

9. Does the school succeed in placing athletic events and athletes and their teachers on the same social, financial, emotional, and educational plane as other co-curricular activities that entail equal numbers of participants, equal intelligence, and equal time?

10. Is your school a member of local, regional, state, and national athletic associations? Is your school actively participating in improving the effectiveness of these organizations in serving the best interests of youth?[17]

Intramurals

The intramural program can be an excellent student activity program. Much of the sting that arises from being left off an interscholastic athletic team can be taken away through participation in a good intramural program. However, the program should not be designed simply to handle students who could not make the athletic team. This program should be broad and planned for the inclusion of all students. Many activities besides athletics should be included in the program. Such activities can include all physical education activities from academic subject fields, class activities, and programs and activities sponsored by honor societies, clubs, student council, and homerooms. Broadly conceived, the program need only be limited by the creative imagination of student leaders, advisers, and principals.

If the program is to be a success, the principal must give it his encourage-

[17] Miller, Moyer and Patrick, *op. cit.*, pp. 351–52.

ment and support. Time must be scheduled for the activities. Where bus transportation is no problem, before and after school are suitable times. Where bus transportation is a problem, an extended noon hour usually must be scheduled. The extended noon hour is often limited to an early dismissal of participants for preparation purposes. An example of the well-planned intramural program is given in the Appendix.

Evaluation of Student Activities

Because the student activity must be under constant surveillance, it is important that the total program of student activities be evaluated periodically.

Besides the need for general evaluation, the increased emphasis on academics in the curriculum leaves less time for student activities. The whole program of activities should be evaluated in terms of the new demands in the space age.[18] The following criteria might be used in this evaluation: Is the activity providing optimum educational value, satisfying student needs, meeting socially acceptable standards, promoting democratic ideals, providing carry-over values, and being economical to the student and school.[19]

This evaluation should take place at several levels. First, the officers and advisers of the sponsoring organization should examine each activity as to its success or failure. Recommendations regarding improvement or deletion should be noted for subsequent officers. Second, the student council or activity council should evaluate all the activities of each organization to guarantee that planned activities are consistent with the objectives of the organization and the school. Finally, the principal should evaluate each activity and each organization to keep a proper balance within the total school. He should strive for participation of all students and, at the same time, improved quality of each program.

Summary

The student activity program is one of the principal's major responsibilities, and next to the time spent in administering the office this activity consumes the largest portion of the principal's time. Approximately one

[18] Elmer R. Pohl, "A Student Council for the Space Age," *School Activities*, April 1964, pp. 237–39. William C. Craig, "How Practical Is the Intellectual Movement?" *School Activities*, December 1963, pp. 114–16.

[19] Adolph Unruh, "Improving Extra-class Activities," *School Activities*, January 1964, pp. 141–43.

fifth of his time is spent on organizing and administering the student activity program.

The program of student activities has evolved through various stages: (1) denial of activities, (2) toleration of activities, (3) recognition of activities, (4) acceptance of activities, and (5) in some cases, exploitation of student activities. The scope of the student activity program includes student government, extracurricular activities related to classroom instruction, and organizations not directly related to classroom activity. Carefully defined objectives and purposes are needed. If the program is to be successful, it should operate from a well-defined and established set of principles. In addition to the general principles some policy regarding membership and participation in the activities must be formulated. There are some dangers in the program, such as emphasis on spectator sports, emphasis on heroes or outstanding players, overemphasis on competition and winning, the effect of pressures, and the lack of a complete program for all students.

The principal must learn to delegate responsibilities to vice-principals, coordinators of student activities, coaches, and advisers. The delegation does not relieve him of his responsibilities in scheduling the time of the events, making facilities available, and providing general supervision. The principal should be in control of the student activity program and should insist that each group or organization be approved, that a constitution and bylaws be available, and that the year's activities be approved in advance. Unauthorized clubs should not be allowed in the school, nor should activities that have not been authorized be permitted. The principal should become acquainted with the High School Activities Association, its rules, policies, and procedures, and he should instruct his coaches and advisers accordingly. He should provide constant supervision for all functions. The financing of student activities should be carefully controlled. Budgets and disbursements should be approved and audits held.

The students are represented in student government through the student council, class organizations, homeroom organizations, and other representative student groups. Each of these groups and organizations should have an adviser, and their programs should be planned so that students receive the maximum training in representative democratic government. Students should be given real problems to solve and should be given the responsibility and authority to solve the problems.

There are many clubs and organizations that are extracurricular in nature but are associated directly with classroom activity. Some of these programs are music, speech and drama, commercial clubs, Future Farmers of America, Future Homemakers of America, and academic clubs and societies. These groups usually have as their adviser the faculty member who is responsible for teaching similar course work in the curriculum.

Other clubs and organizations exist within the school that are not related directly to instructional programs, such as pep clubs, leagues, and service organizations. It should be a matter of policy that all clubs and organizations have student leaders, appropriate advisers, and planned and approved programs.

Competitive athletics is a major activity in the student activity program, and the principal will spend much time supervising in this activity area. He should be aware of both the values to be gained from such activities and the pitfalls and dangers that arise. He must work closely with his coaches and constantly try to improve the organization.

The intramural program is most valuable and should not be confined to athletic events but should include many other activities. The program should have a broad base with activities available to all students with all types of interests.

Finally, the student activity program should be periodically evaluated and improvements made. The evaluation should be done by the officers of the sponsoring organization, the student council, and the principal.

SUGGESTED PROJECTS AND ACTIVITIES

1. Secure from your state high school activities association a copy of their handbook. Read it and discuss any areas or questions that are raised.
2. Attend a meeting of the high school activities association at a regional or state level to find areas that are being discussed and to discern care taken to control the high school student activities.
3. Secure a teacher's handbook that is in use in a high school and review the information and policies used to administer the student activity programs.
4. Debate: The tail wagging the dog should be cut off.
5. Report to the school on the day of a football or basketball game or other large group activity and assist in planning the details and carrying out all the responsibilities from the initial point of organization of the day to banking the money after the activity is completed.
6. Develop your own list of criteria that you believe desirable for the establishment, direction, and control of the student activity program within the high school that you will administer.
7. Have a principal come to class and discuss what he considers to be the most important problem a principal must solve in relationship to the student activity program.
8. Lay out a plan whereby the student activities can be more closely related to curriculum instruction.

9. Visit a school with a good intramural program. Analyze the program for its strength and weaknesses.

REVIEW AND DISCUSSION QUESTIONS

1. What is meant by exploitation in the student program?
2. What are the evolutionary periods that have been ascribed to the student activities program?
3. Of the purposes and objectives listed, which ones have the greatest meaning for the school program and which ones have the least?
4. What are some of the guiding principles for a good activity program?
5. What should be some of the governing principles as related to membership in student organizations?
6. What dangers can be found in the student activity programs and which one do you believe to be the most important?
7. How can a principal effectively delegate responsibilities in the student activities program if he is (a) principal of a large high school, (b) principal of a medium-sized high school, and (c) principal of a small high school?
8. Why is it important that the principal maintain control of the student activity program? What would be the results if he released complete control to the student, the advisers, or some other organization?
9. What values can be served by having student organizations turn in a list of their planned activities of the year at the commencement of the year rather than having activities approved during the year as they are needed?
10. What financial provisions should be followed in the budgeting and distribution of student funds?
11. What are the functions performed by the high school activities association?
12. What problems might well be turned over to a student council?
13. What organizational procedures should be used to coordinate the efforts of clubs, classes, homerooms, organizations, and other student programs?
14. How do clubs and organizations that are related to class activities differ from the clubs and organizations that are not part of the classroom instruction? Give examples of each type.
15. What are the distinguishing differences between competitive athletics, interschool athletics, intramurals, and intermurals?
16. Is the program of interscholastic athletics "getting out of hand"?
17. What are the principal's responsibilities as related to the interscholastic athletic program?

18. How can the principal best organize a good, sound intramural program?

SELECTED BIBLIOGRAPHY

Bolmeier, E. C. "Legal Aspects of Curriculum and the Extracurriculum," *Bulletin of N.A.S.S.P.*, March 1965, pp. 128–42.

Brown, Charles I., and Thomas G. Edwards. "Extraclass Activities of Social Studies Teachers," *Bulletin of N.A.S.S.P.*, March 1962, pp. 183–89.

Coleman, James S. "Social Change—Impact on the Adolescent," *Bulletin of N.A.S.S.P.*, April 1965, pp. 11–15.

Craig, William L. "How Practical Is the Intellectual Movement?" *School Activities*, December 1963, pp. 114–16.

Douglass, Harl R. *Modern Administration of Secondary Schools*, 2nd ed. New York: Ginn and Co., 1963.

Educational Policies Commission. *School Athletics*. Washington, D.C.: National Education Association, 1954.

Frederick, Robert W. *The Third Curriculum*. New York: Appleton-Century-Crofts, Inc., 1959.

Hearn, Arthur C. "Are Student Assembly Programs 'Missing the Boat'?" *School Activities*, May 1964, p. 274.

Johnston, Edgar Grant, and Roland C. Faunce. *Student Activities in Secondary Schools*. New York: The Ronald Press Company, 1952.

Jordan, James W. (ed.). "Interscholastic Athletics—Yes or No?" *Bulletin of N.A.S.S.P.*, October 1963, pp. 5–6.

———. "Non-athletic Activities Program," *Bulletin of N.A.S.S.P.*, October 1963, pp. 20–22.

Kilzer, L. R., H. H. Stephenson, and H. O. Nordberg. *Allied Activities in the Secondary School*. New York: Harper and Brothers, 1956.

McKown, Harry Charles. *Extra-curricular Activities*. New York: The Macmillan Company, 1952.

Miller, Franklin A., James H. Moyer, and Robert B. Patrick. *Planning Student Activities*. Englewood Cliffs, N.J.: Prentice-Hall, Inc., 1961.

Morgan, Willard J. "Increasing Effectiveness of Student Councils," *School Activities*, April 1964, pp. 233–35.

National Association of Secondary-School Principals. "Student Activities in the Secondary School," *Bulletin of N.A.S.S.P.*, January 1944. (The entire bulletin is devoted to this phase of student activities.)

———. "Vitalizing Student Activities in the Secondary School," *Bulletin of N.A.S.S.P.*, February 1952. (The entire bulletin is devoted to this phase of student activities.)

National Association of Student Councils. *The Handbook for Student Council*. Washington, D.C.: National Association of Secondary-School Principals, 1950.

Norton, Monte S. "Extra Duties for Teachers," *Bulletin of N.A.S.S.P.*, December 1961, pp. 105–12.

Pohl, Elmer R. "A Student Council for the Space Age," *School Activities*, April 1964, pp. 237–39.

Reed, William R. "Intercollegiate and Interschool Athletics—Assessing the Accomplishments and Problems," *Bulletin of N.A.S.S.P.*, April 1964, pp. 271–80.

Robrock, Mabel. "Yearbook Trends," *Scholastic Editor*, January 1965, pp. 14–16.

United States Office of Education. *Financial Accounting for Student Activities.* Washington, D.C.: U.S. Department of Health, Education, and Welfare, 1959.

Unruh, Adolph. "Improving Extraclass Activities," *School Activities*, January 1964, pp. 141–43.

Zeigler, Earle F. "A Philosophical Analysis of Amateurism, Semiprofessionalism, and Professionalism in Competitive Sports," *School Activities*, March 1964, pp. 199–203.

CHAPTER 13

Discipline and Student Control

No one questions that the principal is responsible for his school. But there seems to be serious question regarding who is responsible for the students. Parents, guardians, teachers, principals, district personnel, social workers, policemen, and juvenile judges all get into the act. But few thinking persons will deny that parents have the major responsibility for teaching discipline and that schools and their officers and other community organizations and agencies must supplement the role of parents. But if parents fail in their teaching, as some do, how far can a teacher or principal go in acting for and in behalf of parents?

When students arrive at school, they come under the principal's jurisdiction. To what extent should he promote or curtail their freedom in order to maintain adherence to policies and procedures that are in the best interest of other students and the school? The answers to these and other questions are presented in this chapter.

School Spirit, Morale, and Discipline

School spirit, student morale, and good discipline are closely linked together in the promotion of good citizens. Seldom will any of these three items be found in isolation in a secondary school. Sound citizenship training requires that students be provided opportunity to exercise self-control, to solve school problems, and to promote the welfare of the school.

Dictatorial action, whether by government officials, principals, teachers, or student leaders, breeds contempt for authority and lowers morale of all concerned. Under such government, the students resist attempts to improve themselves or their school. In fact, there are those students who will actively search for ways of undermining, and creating discord and rebellion under oppressive rule.

The principal and teachers should set an example of self-control and internal discipline in their classes and throughout the school generally. The positive approaches to education, prevention, and solution of problems should become the standard. Faith in the desire and ability of students to do the right and socially accepted thing will do much to create trust, build self-confidence, and improve morale.

The positive approach does not mean that students are provided license or unrestricted freedom to do as they please. Restrictions with freedom are a necessary part of the positive theory of effective discipline.

Theory for Effective Discipline

It's a Free Country, Ain't It?

It was Carl Brown's largest class that gave him trouble. The four previous social studies classes were a joy to teach, but this fifth one was impossible. Besides having 45 students in the small room, he had a group of boys who were problems in every class. Bill was the ringleader.

Mr. Brown was discussing the freedoms guaranteed by the Constitution. Bill and his group were at it again. For the third time Mr. Brown stopped and requested Bill to stop talking, but to no avail. Then Mr. Brown said, "Bill, you stop talking or leave the room."

In the silence that followed Bill said, "I can talk if I want to. It's a free country, ain't it?"

Mr. Brown again told Bill he must stop talking or leave the room. Bill's nasty reply was, "Yeah! You and who else are going to make me?"

Mr. Brown went to get the principal. When he came back, Bill was gone. Later that night Mr. Brown began to analyze the incident. What should he have done? Bill does live in a free society. Can or should he force Bill to remain quiet? What is the relationship between discipline and freedom?

Discipline and Freedom.   In our society and in our schools the individual citizen is granted certain inalienable rights, among them life, liberty, and the pursuit of happiness. These three statements have been translated into constitutional freedoms that allow to each individual citizen the freedom to speak as he pleases and the freedom of self-movement and self-direction. Frequently, a minority interpret freedom to mean that they can do as they please and that no one should call them to task for their actions. In a society, freedom of the individual must be considered along with his relationship with society; therefore, a person's freedom must be defined not only in terms of the individual person but also in terms of the social structure in which the individual must live. It is true that ultimate choice rests with the individual, but the individual must be accountable for his actions.

Freedom and Responsibility. In a society, freedom is linked invariably with responsibility. A person has freedom to act and choose but he must accept the responsibility and the consequences of his actions. A student has the freedom to speak out in class or to disrupt class, but he also has responsibilities involved in being a student. These responsibilities extend to his parents, his fellow classmates, his teacher, his state, and the community that has made his education possible. The student who said, "It's a free country, ain't it?" is recognizing his freedom without accepting the responsibilities that are part of the freedom. A purpose of society is to make every individual responsible with his freedom. Freedom used with responsibility creates a self-disciplined person.

The *Dictionary of Education* lists four definitions of discipline that apply to the student. They are as follows:

1. The process or result of directing or subordinating immediate wishes, impulses, desires or interests for the sake of an ideal or for the purpose of gaining more effective, dependable action.
2. Persistent, active, and self-directed pursuit of some selected course of action, even in the face of obstacles or distractions.
3. Direct authoritative control of pupil behavior through punishments and/or rewards.
4. Negatively, any restraint of impulses, frequently through distasteful or painful means.[1]

A student who is self-disciplined recognizes his freedom and responsibility and is in effect defining his freedom in a self-directed pursuit of some course of action in the face of obstacles or distractions. In this process he must subordinate immediate wishes, impulses, and desires for the sake of the goal or purpose for which he is striving.

Freedom, Responsibility, and Restrictions. Although the goal of 100 percent attainment of self-direction for all individuals is desirable, it must be recognized that human beings are not perfect. The student forgets or occasionally believes some other goals to be more important than ones that would be more desirable from a group maintenance viewpoint. There

[1] Carter V. Good (ed.), *Dictionary of Education* (New York: McGraw-Hill Book Company, Inc., 1959), pp. 176–77.

are also a few individuals in every group who have a tendency to be irresponsible or who believe that their freedom allows them to do anything they please without responsibility. In a society it becomes necessary to set up restrictions for the control of such behavior. Restrictions should not be looked upon as only negative controls. Restrictions that are placed in keeping with the responsibility needed grant to the individual more freedom and as such become rewards. Restrictions that are set and regiment a group beyond the responsibility needed take away freedom unduly.

In a classroom, as in society in general, restrictions are necessary. These restrictions are the policies, rules, and regulations of the school. If a principal's attendance policy is too rigid and is not in keeping with the responsibility needed in handling secondary school students, the students, parents, and teachers rebel. Rebellion is the typical manner of expression when restrictions take away more freedom than is justified with the responsibility required in the situation. If a teacher exercises complete domination of a class and restrictions are too severe, the teacher generally has an excess number of discipline problems that eventually find their way to the principal's office. Restrictions must be in keeping with the responsibility needed in the given situation.

Freedom, Responsibility, Restrictions, Rewards, and Penalties. Whenever restrictions are levied to govern the behavior of a group, rewards and penalties are necessary to support the restrictions. Most of the students are responsible and desire to promote their own self-discipline. Both the teacher and the principal should support this attitude through social recognition and approval. Compliments on good behavior, a clean building, work well done, etc., are typical methods of expressing approval. Good behavior is thus reinforced by social reward or approval. There are some individuals who forget or who are completely irresponsible and refuse to conform in any way to society's expectations. For these individuals a penalty is assessed or social disapproval expressed to bring conformity to the accepted social pattern.

Promoting the Positive Approach to Discipline

Prevention and Self-Control. As leader of his school, the principal must take the lead in promoting the positive approach to discipline. To do this he must be aware of the factors and practices that aid in developing good behavior patterns in schools. Lawrence E. Vredevoe, in his "Third Report on a Study of Students and School Discipline in the United States and Other Countries," indicated that practices that students and teachers believe to be most successful in developing good teacher-student relationships do not differ in size, location, or composition of the student body. In the schools selected as representative of the best citizenship and teacher-student relationships, these practices seemed to be common: (1) There was an understanding and apparent recognition of the purposes and values of the standards and rules in force by faculty and students. (2) Emphasis was placed on self-discipline by teachers and students. (3) Good citizenship and conduct were characteristic of the faculty as well as the student body. Courtesy, consideration, respect, professional dress and manner, and good speech were practiced by the faculty members. (4) Standards and rules were subject to review and change, but were enforced until changed by due process. (5) The emphasis in treatment of all discipline cases was on the individual involved and not the act. This represents a significant change in law enforcement in our democracy in the past 50 years. Today society is more concerned with the transgressor than the crime. (6) Students could expect fair but certain reprimand or punishment for violation of rules and standards. Teachers were confident that their colleagues were also trying to cooperate in maintaining standards. (7) The punishments meted out were fitted to the individual rather than the transgression. (8) Faculty and students cooperated in establishing, maintaining, and revising rules and standards. (9) The program was challenging to all groups.[2]

The kind of discipline to work for in a democracy is self-discipline. Such discipline begins at the earliest years with external authority imposed by parents and teachers and is gradually relaxed as the student finishes the secondary school. From a sociological and psychological base, discipline is a learning process whereby the individual progressively learns to develop habits of self-control and recognizes his own responsibility to society. Although there are the 3 to 5 per cent on whom corrective measures must be used, the general emphasis in schools should be on the prevention of misconduct and education toward self-control.[3] McPhie indicates that methods of preventing problems of control can be divided into two categories: (1) things that should be done, and (2) things that should be avoided. The following things should be done: use personal experience as a guide in identifying students as discipline problems, talk informally with the students at the beginning of the year about classroom procedures and expectations, permit students to sit where they choose,

---

[2] Lawrence E. Vredevoe, "School Discipline—Third Report on a Study of Students and School Discipline in the United States and Other Countries," *Bulletin of N.A.S.S.P.*, March 1965, pp. 215–26.

[3] Herman J. Bowman, "A Review of Discipline," *Bulletin of N.A.S.S.P.*, September 1959, pp. 147–55. Peter F. Olivia, "High School Discipline in American Society," *Bulletin of N.A.S.S.P.*, January 1956, pp. 1–55. "Discipline in the Public Schools," *N.E.A. Research Bulletin*, December 1957, p. 152.

learn the students' names early, begin lessons promptly, be enthusiastic, provide each student with an opportunity for success, admit error, make assignments reasonable and clear, occasionally do something nice for your students, and, above all else, be alert. The following things should be avoided: don't try to buy popularity, don't be a comedian, don't talk through noise, don't enter into arguments, and don't do things for students that they can do for themselves.[4]

Helping the Teacher Take a Positive Approach to Discipline. Many disciplinary problems are caused initially by the behavior reaction of teachers and principals. Discipline problems can be created while someone is trying to solve problems. It is sometimes helpful to remember that many discipline problems can be solved through preventive correction by the teacher instead of a control penalty on the student. The better the teacher is in his preparation, teaching technique, personality, etc., the less likely are student control problems to arise. The following suggestions by Brown and Phelps, in their book *Managing the Classroom,* show how both a poor teacher and a good teacher handle the same type of problems.

Teaching Skill

Poor Teachers	*Good Teachers*
Makes vague assignments or no assignments at all. Pupil doesn't know for certain what he is to do, so does nothing on his assignment. Undesirable activity often results.	Makes a clear and definite assignment. The pupil knows what is expected of him and does it. No time for undesirable activity.
Makes an assignment which is impossible for the child to accomplish. Pupil gives up as he sees no chance of succeeding, does something else —possibly undesirable.	Gears assignments to time allowed and to ability of students. Realizes that learning is tied to a successful completion of an act studiously attempted.
Speaks in a rasping, quarrelsome tone of voice indicating irritation. Talks too much, nags, scolds.	Controls and modulates voice. Remembers that nagging (symbolic drive) diminishes a teacher's effectiveness.
Fails to get attention of every person in his class before proceeding with oral work. Is sometimes competing	Gets attention pleasantly (if possible), but gets attention of every pupil before proceeding with oral work.

[4] Walter E. McPhie, "Discipline Problems: An Educational Malignancy," *Bulletin of N.A.S.S.P.*, December 1961, pp. 82–91.

Teaching Skill (Continued)

Poor Teachers	Good Teachers
with students for attention. Respect for teacher lost. Control weakened.	There must never be any doubt in any pupil's mind as to who is in charge of the classroom.
Pays inadequate attention to classroom logistics (movement of students, handling supplies, student seating, etc.). Because pupils have not been instructed specifically they fail to respond specifically. Confusion leads to disorder, which in turn leads to reprimands and ill-feeling.	Is definite in setting up classroom routines. Allows no exception to occur until routines are established. Since the routine is definite and clear, the child has little reason for deviation. The child who deviates is definitely wrong and all the children know it.
Pays insufficient attention to the physical conditions of the room. Pupil discomfort causes restlessness, which in turn forces the teacher into some form of disciplinary action.	Notes physical conditions, (heat, light, ventilation) frequently, as these tend to vary with outside conditions during the day. The physically comfortable child gives less trouble.
Does not recognize, or if he does recognize, does not compliment an unusually fine effort on a student's part. Student feels effort was unappreciated, makes less effort on later assignments; may show resentment by unsocial activity.	Recognizes and shows appreciation for honest effort. Feels that failure to commend unusually fine work by a student is bad manners on the teacher's part. Student is inspired to further and better efforts; is not likely to make trouble in class.
Is sarcastic in his criticisms. Hurts pupil's sensibilities. Pupils show resentment by being (in turn) ungracious.	Criticizes constructively; shows consideration of pupil's feelings. Always gives a child a chance to "save face."
Is inconsistent. Scolds a pupil for what has been condoned in another. Pupils will forgive anything in a teacher except what they consider to be injustice.	Is consistent although he may not always be right. Pupils recognize fairness in attitude of the teacher. Not inclined to feel resentfulness—one of principal causes of pupil behavior problems.
Sloughs off reasonable questions or gives a facetious answer. A reasonable (to the child) question is	Listens seriously to a reasonable question, but if time is limited suggests the question be brought up again.

Teaching Skill (Continued)

Poor Teachers	Good Teachers
treated as triviality. Pupil feels snubbed, shows resentment through undesirable behavior.	Pupil pleased, feels important; therefore not inclined to resentfulness.
Plays favorites. Lets it be known when he dislikes a child. Child reacts much as would an adult.	Plays no favorites. Goes out of his way to alleviate a hurt which he may have unintentionally given.
Stops a student curtly when student is seriously discussing or reporting on an assignment. Gives impression that discussion is trivial.	Encourages discussion but controls a situation which is wandering or getting out of hand. Treats children as he would colleagues in same situation.
Disparagingly criticises community social groups, forgetting pupils' parents may be members of groups. Pupils tell parents. Child may be advised by parents to "tell that teacher off." Result: discipline problem.	Avoids comments or discussions which tend to reflect in a derogatory way on any group or individuals. Teacher remembers that he is serving all of the community.[5]

Causes of Pupil Offenses. The specific causes of student offenses related to specific instances are many and varied, but most discipline problems can be attributed to a few fundamental reasons. Some of these are as follows: lack of general training and development, lack of interest in course work, poor teaching, poor school organization, unsatisfactory home conditions, lack of social adjustment, bad associates, physical defects, lack of responsibility, adjustment to adolesence.

Although books could be written about the various causes of discipline problems, adjustment to adolescence affects every student in the school. Part of the school's task is to teach youth some of the responsibilities of growing up. The adjustment to both adolescence and adulthood involves certain developmental tasks, as indicated by Havighurst.

1. Learning new and satisfactory relationships with age mates of both sexes.
2. Learning acceptable masculine or feminine roles in society.

[5] Edwin John Brown and Arthur Thomas Phelps, *Managing the Classroom—The Teacher's Part in School Administration*, 2nd ed., pp. 121–23 (New York: Copyright © 1961, The Ronald Press Company). Reprinted by permission.

3. Learning to accept the student's own physique and bodily characteristics, and to use and care for his body effectively.

4. Establishing personal and emotional independence from parents and other adults.

5. Acquiring a measure of economic independence.

6. Choosing an occupation and preparing for it.

7. Preparing for the responsibilities of marriage and family life.

8. Preparing for effective life as a citizen.

9. Accepting and acquiring desirable standards of social behavior.

10. Acquiring a philosophy of life, with accompanying sets of ethical, aesthetic, religious, and other standards of values.[6]

The principal must certainly understand adolescent growth and behavior to effectively administer disciplinary action within the school. To know what is normal behavior will assist the principal greatly in understanding the type of solution that should be given for any particular type of problem. An example of this basic principle is given in the illustration that follows.

"DON'T YOU KNOW IT'S WRONG TO STEAL?"

Mr. James had a problem. For weeks reports had been coming to him of the theft of girls' clothing in the girls' physical education dressing room. Although he had worked with the problem he had not been able to solve it. The physical facilities did not lend themselves to adequate control. In this building the only girls' rest room facilities were located in the same general area as the lockers and dressing rooms. There were no separate dividers. Neither the dressing rooms nor the rest room could be locked during the activity period. In addition, the girls' lockers were very small in size, about one foot square. The current dress vogue was large flowing dresses with hoop skirts. Since the girls were unable to get their clothing in the lockers, they simply threw them over the lockers during their physical educational period. Because the dressing room was not separate from the rest room, any girl within the school had access to the clothing. Repeatedly, sweaters, underclothing, and other articles had been reported missing. Mr. James finally worked out a system in which not only the physical education teacher, but also the home economics teacher and other women teachers were involved in periodically checking these facilities to see if they could catch a person in the act. A few days later the home economics teacher found Betty stealing an article of girl's apparel, and Betty was brought to Mr. James. Mr. James talked to Betty for some minutes in a general sense and then said, "Betty, don't you know it's wrong to steal?"

Betty replied indignantly with flashing eyes, "Mr. James! Of course I know it's wrong to steal."

"Then why did you take these articles?"

---

[6] Robert J. Havighurst, *Human Development and Education* (New York: Longmans, Green and Co., Inc., 1953), Chaps. 9, 10, and 11.

Again Betty replied indignantly, "Mr. James, do you know how important it is for a girl of 16 to have all of the fine clothes that other girls have?"

Mr. James was caught on the horns of the adolescent's need for social approval and society's need for moral integrity and the protection of private property.

What should Mr. James do with Betty? What correction should be given? The following are some alternatives:

1. Turn Betty over to the police.
2. Let Betty go on the assumption that it was not really her fault.
3. Have Betty return all the lost articles, with no further punishment given.
4. Report her to her parents and have them supply missing items or make proper adjustment.
5. Give her a good lecture on moral honesty.
6. Refer her family to the social welfare institution.

In his solution, Mr. James must deal with two types of problems. The first is a control of behavior. He cannot sanction Betty's actions on the basis that she needed these things for group approval even though the reason may have been sufficient for Betty. Second, he must try to find some way in which Betty can achieve her needs for group acceptance, or he will never solve the problem. Teaching responsibility in relationship to freedom would require that Betty must find some other approved method of securing group approval, especially as related to dress behavior. At the same time, the correction must in some way be educative in nature so that cause and effect can be brought together and controlled.

The Principal Administers Discipline

Sources of Discipline Problems. The school is a society in which the students and teachers interact with each other for a common purpose. Freedom exists but with it comes great responsibility, and as in all societies, there is need for restrictions. These restrictions are usually defined in the student handbook and become part of the rules and regulations governing the school. Rewards and penalties must be associated with the restrictions to be effective. The over-all purpose within the school is to have all students do that which is recognized to be socially good through self-discipline and motivation. As has been pointed out, not all students will react this way. Therefore, the principal becomes involved in discipline problems. These problems come from two major sources. The first source is the total operational milieu of the school. There are many situations before school, after school, in the halls and lunchroom, etc., in which the principal must make corrections. The secondary primary source of problems is notification by other individuals—students, faculty, or non-teaching personnel. Solutions to these problems may have been attempted by the person making the referral. Problem students are usually referred to the principal. The principal is in the position of the responsible agent in the school and must determine and administer policy restrictions and corrections.

Fixing Responsibility in Disciplinary Situations.   The school shares with the parents and the community in general responsibility for disciplinary action. Not all situations requiring discipline by the principal occur at school. The total extent of school responsibility begins at the time the students leave for school and extends until students arrive at home. Some of the specific areas of concern are given below.

1. Transportation to and from school in bus, in automobile, or on foot. If misbehavior occurs on the school bus, it is assumed that the problem comes under the direction of the principal. The bus driver refers this disciplinary problem to the principal in the same manner that teachers would refer such cases when they need help. On the other hand, if a student is walking to school, a principal cannot be held responsible for all the things that a student does. But if a larger student should get into a fight with a smaller one, it would usually be expected that the principal would become involved in the situation. If students who are passing on their way to school throw balloons full of water, eggs, or other such objects at students walking to school, the principal would take a major disciplinary role in the situation. Violations at school, before and after school, and during the noon hour are of primary concern to the principal. Such violations can be on the outside of the building as well as on the inside of the building. These problems can involve automobiles, damage or breakage of school equipment or facilities, or personal insults or injuries to other students or faculty members.

2. Extracurricular activities such as athletic contests, parades, concerts, parties, dances, and other school socials.

3. Class activities under the direction of a classroom teacher, such as debates, field trips, excursions.

4. Assemblies, rallies, and other total school meetings.

5. General personal dress and conduct and maintenance of desirable standards.

6. Boy-girl relationships such as holding hands, dating, and types of dances.

The principal must recognize that he is not the sole disciplinarian in a community. Some situations extend beyond his own primary responsibility, including some instances that take place in school. There are situations that take place in the community that do become his primary responsibility. School authorities and civil authorities sometimes become confused as to who is responsible. The following situations took place in a community but were not part of the school program:

Boys Beat Up Cheerleaders

Two rival schools played a football game, which attracted both students and alumni. No incident occurred before, after, or during the game on the immediate school grounds. But several hours later, several miles away, some boys from one of the schools stopped their car and beat up some cheerleaders from the other school. The boys were not identified immediately. Whether they were students, alumni, or other members of the community was not definite; yet it was assumed by everyone that they were students of the opposing school.

The principal obviously has a major responsibility in determining who the assailants were and what the disciplinary action should be.

Summer Home Vandalized

About 20 minutes' drive from an urban community was a summer home area. One Sunday morning the newspapers came out with some major headlines that read, "Students of Hilltop High School Vandalize Summer Home." The article indicated that $3,000 worth of damage had been done to a summer home. The students had been arrested. No names of students were given, but the article indicated that the students were students of Hilltop High School.

The principal's responsibility in this situation is a supplementary responsibility.

Circumstances such as these are constantly presenting themselves to a principal. Certainly the principal cannot be the community's scapegoat. On the other hand, he is responsible not only for disciplining students while they are at a school but also for helping teach students self-direction and self-control. He cannot completely escape criticism for actions that may be completely unrelated to the school objectives and functions. The principal must know when to assume a major responsibility or a minor responsibility and when to refer situations to other appropriate community agencies.

Effective Use of Student Organizations. Frequently a principal finds it necessary to call the whole school to task regarding conduct in assembly, sportsmanship at athletic events, and behavior at a visiting school. Principals can, and, of course, do, call mass assemblies in which these types of items are discussed. However, the principal will often find it more effective to work in smaller groups and to utilize the student-body officers, homerooms, and student organizations. The student council or other student organizations can be very effective in assisting the principal in preventing and correcting undesirable situations. Programs of prevention and correction that are discussed and developed by student-body officers and then carried to students through homeroom discussions or other discussions are usually far more effective and have greater influence at the adolescent level than a mass meeting in which the principal discusses the need for correction.

Principles for Correction

Since the principal will find it necessary to make corrections and issue penalties at least for the 3 to 5 per cent who will not accept responsibility, the following principles for corrections and penalties are suggested.

1. The correction or penalty should be educative in nature. The primary purpose of correction is to bring about a self-disciplined person— one who observes the restriction because it is the best thing to do. The penalty should be educative and bring to the attention of the person his responsibility.

2. The penalty should be in keeping with the violation of the restriction. For example, a teacher or principal should not assign a student a 500-word theme for every misdemeanor. Such an assignment is not in keeping with most violations and only serves to undermine the English teacher across the hall. It is far better to have the student who has violated a restriction on chewing gum clean up the seats of the desks and remove all gum than it is to require him to write a 500-word theme on "I Will Not Chew Gum."

3. The correction should be administered as soon as possible after the misdemeanor. If a student has violated a basic school policy and then is allowed to continue for several days without being contacted, his behavior, in the meantime, may have changed; and he will be very indignant at being called to task for the misdemeanor. If the student misbehaves in a teacher's classroom, it is well for the teacher to say, "John, will you please stop talking?" If the teacher believes that drawing attention to the act would be inappropriate at a given time, she should simply say, "John, I would like to talk to you after class." Then, at the close of class, when the teacher discusses John's problem, John will make the association with the time in which the misdemeanor occurred.

4. The penalty should bring about acceptable behavior. Even though a penalty should be educative in nature, there are times in which the penalty must first bring control. Neither a teacher nor a principal can

permit students to abuse them in public without losing respect and over-all control. Both the principal and the teacher may need to take immediate action in order to gain control of a situation. A control penalty is required. When a teacher asks a student to leave the classroom and report to the principal, the teacher is exercising a control penalty. In our society the supreme control penalty is placing an individual in prison for a crime. However, it should be remembered that even in prison the educative aspect of the penalty is not overlooked. The attempt to make the inmates responsible is the primary goal of the reform program within the prison. Likewise, the student who tells the teacher that he will not be quiet must have some type of control penalty placed upon him before an educative penalty can be placed into effect. Such a control penalty is exercised for the benefit of the rest of the students so the students may continue in their activities in a normal manner.

5. The penalty should be one that the teacher wants to carry out, i.e., a penalty believed to be right and just after careful consideration.

6. The penalty should be one that the teacher or principal can carry out. For example, a teacher cannot suspend a student from school. Suspension is a principal's responsibility. A principal cannot expel a student from school, for the denial of the right to attend school rests with the board of education.

Samples of Effective Penalties. As has been indicated, penalties must be educative in nature but must also provide control factors where needed. At no time should the educative factor be forgotten. There are times in which the control penalty must be exercised first so the educative penalty can be allowed to be placed into effect. Examples of effective penalties are given below:

Violation	*Penalty*
Placing chewing gum under the seat of a chair	Have student clean off bottoms of the chairs
Painting swastikas on public property	Cleaning and restoring property and learning about the Hitler movement
Writing on walls in classrooms, halls, and rest rooms	Cleaning walls and restoring property
Breaking windows	Paying for and helping to install windows
Talking between two students	Move students into separate areas of the room

Violation	*Penalty*
Defiance of teacher's corrective suggestions	Remove student from the room with instructions as to where to go and the next action required
Incorrigible behavior	Take the student to the principal
Stealing	Restoration of the article to the person offended

The penalty should be in keeping with the violation and should be as educative as possible. The penalty should vary with both the nature of the offense and the number of times the student has been corrected. On a first offense, the penalty may simply be social disapproval or a word of disapproval. A second offense might require "a talk on the rug." A third violation might involve a control aspect as each violation becomes exceedingly more troublesome. With each violation there is usually need to take different and more forceful action.[7]

Corporal Punishment

Laws Regarding Corporal Punishment. Both teachers and principals are faced with the basic legal question regarding the use of corporal punishment. The use of corporal punishment is not a new issue in our society, for it has been discussed pro and con over the centuries. Certainly the use of corporal punishment has been an established practice in schools. In the early history of our nation, there were periods of time in which "beating the devil out of students" was regarded not only as proper discipline but as good for souls that were basically evil. Such a philosophy is not generally held today. Corporal punishment is looked upon with general disfavor. However, there are a few students in every school who do not respond to educative-type penalties, nor do they respond to simple minor control-type penalties. It becomes futile to continue to say to an incorrigible child, "Please be quiet," when he has already demonstrated that he not only won't be quiet but that he is ready to beat the teacher.

The actual use of corporal punishment is questioned from both a legal and a moral basis. Legally, the corporal punishment is permitted in some states. In other states, it is not permitted. If corporal punishment is not permitted, the teachers and principals who use corporal punishment are

---

[7] Lee R. Williamson, "An Analysis of Discipline Practices in Selected Junior High Schools of Texas," *Bulletin of N.A.S.S.P.*, February 1962, pp. 429–32. Walter M. Jackson, "Discipline in a Large Junior High School," *Bulletin of N.A.S.S.P.*, October 1963, pp. 55–58.

automatically in violation of the law and become personally responsible before the courts for their actions. Where corporal punishment is permitted, it is only a permissive type of law and not mandatory legislation. If a teacher or principal resorts to corporal punishment in a state that has permissive legislation, the teacher may still be held liable in the courts for the use of such punishment. Any parent may sue a teacher and bring him into court. Generally speaking, the courts have interpreted that the teacher or principal has the same rights and responsibilities that a prudent parent would have under the same circumstances. The language of the courts is usually expressed as *in loco parentis,* which means that the teacher or principal stands in the place of the parent. Every court case must be judged in relationship to the events surrounding it. According to Robert R. Hamilton, one of the leading authorities of the laws as they affect schools, the following conditions are considered by the courts in corporal punishment cases:

> . . . From the purely legal point of view, even in states in which corporal punishment is permitted, a teacher who resorts to it assumes substantial legal risks. He is bound, under the law, at least to:
> 1. Act from good motives, and not from anger or malice.
> 2. Inflict only moderate punishment.
> 3. Determine what the punishment is in proportion to the gravity of the offense.
> 4. Convince himself that the contemplated punishment is not excessive, taking into account the age, sex, size and physical strength of the pupil to be punished.
> 5. Assume the responsibility that the rule he seeks to enforce is reasonable.[8]

One can only hypothesize how a court will act. The actual decision cannot be made until all the facts and value judgments are presented. Harold H. Punke provides an excellent review of corporal punishment in the public school in which cases and decisions are provided. These cases are presented under the following headings: general authority of teachers to administer corporal punishment, what constitutes moderate and excessive punishment? penalties for administering excessive punishment, use of force, considering past behavior in judging current punishment, punishment for action off the school premises, who may administer punishment? assault by pupils or parents on teachers and social philosophy, and corporal punishment.[9]

[8] Robert R. Hamilton, *Legal Rights and Liabilities of Teachers* (Laramie, Wyo.: Laramie Printers, Inc., 1956), p. 36.
[9] Harold H. Punke, "Corporal Punishment in the Public Schools," *Bulletin of N.A.S.S.P.*, September 1959, pp. 118–38.

Because the placement of responsibility is still questionable when corporal punishment is used, it is generally in the best interest of the teacher and the principal never to get involved in the administration of corporal punishment. However, even under a general policy under which the principal will do all in his power to find other means, there still may be circumstances in which the principal is forced to use corporal punishment.

The Principal's Responsibility. The principal's responsibilities as related to corporal punishment are (1) to determine whether in his state it is legal or illegal to use corporal punishment, and (2) to convey this information and instructions to the teachers. If corporal punishment is legal within the state, the principal should instruct his teachers regarding the dangers involved if it is used, the relationship and decisions of the courts as related to corporal punishment, and the conditions under which a teacher would normally be held liable for the use of such punishment. As far as possible, both teachers and principals should find other satisfactory penalties that will accomplish the same result as corporal punishment.

Suspension and Expulsion from School

In most school systems only a principal is given the right by the board of education to suspend a student from school, and only the board of education has the right to deny the privilege of attending school to a student. Suspension from school is a temporary act, a control-type penalty that is placed on the student to remove him from the school situation long enough for him to think seriously about the importance of education. The board grants to the principal the right of suspension; however, it does not extend this privilege to the teachers. Teachers usually only have the right to suspend students from their classrooms. A teacher should never administer a control-type penalty by saying, "Leave my classroom and don't ever come back." The teachers are not in control of the total school program, and circumstances may arise in which the student must be admitted back into that class. A teacher has no authority to tell a student that he will "kick him out of school." Only the principal has such authority. Normally, a suspension penalty is given to a student when the principal believes that it is in the best interest of the school or the student to have the student denied the opportunity to be in school pending a satisfactory adjustment between the principal, the student, and his parents. Seldom will a principal suspend a student from the school without contacting the parent and requesting a conference. The result of the conference should end in promises of cooperation from the parents and the student.

The principal must recognize that he is dealing with many different types of students. If the student already has placed a high positive value on education, suspension can be very effective. On the other hand, if the principal is working with a student who is trying to get out of school and whose nonattendance at school is very frequent, and the parents really desire the student to be released from school to work on the farm or to help make family money, suspension from school is not usually an effective penalty. In effect, suspension becomes a reward to this type of student. The principal must judge when a suspension penalty will be effective.

Expulsion from school can only be administered by the board of education, since the board alone holds the right to deny a student the privilege of attending school. Expulsion from school usually follows many other types of penalties including suspension from school. A recommendation for expulsion should not be held lightly for it denies the student the opportunity for an education. Usually, however, the student who requires this type of penalty has reached a point where the principal believes the student can no longer profit from school instruction. Some students may be regarded as incorrigible. Expulsion from school might even accompany or precede court action concerning incorrigible behavior.

Procedures involving both suspension and expulsion will usually be formulated at the district office and will become a part of the policies that are handed down to the principal. If such a policy does not exist, it usually must be developed at the school level. Such policies would usually require the following conditions: (1) the teachers and principals present evidence that the school personnel have consistently tried to solve the problem through some other type of correction; (2) the actions taken by the school are verified in writing or documented; (3) the parents are informed immediately of such action; (4) the superintendent's office is notified of such action (both parents and the superintendent's office should be notified by telephone with written correspondence to follow as a matter of record); (5) students and their parents are informed of readmittance policies; (6) the results of the conference and the agreement reached are placed in writing and signed by the student and parent; and (7) faculty members are informed of all action taken with students and parents.

Working with Parents with Grievances

Quite frequently, when principals have administered penalties to students, the principals can expect reaction from students and parents. In many cases the parents see only one side of the problem as it is presented to them by the child. At other times the parents are unhappy with a teacher for disciplinary action that the teacher has exercised upon the student. In both circumstances the parents usually call at the school. The principal is the person who must handle the situation. An analysis of the following case might prove helpful to the principal in his guidelines for handling such situations:

IRATE BROTHER

Ben was a ninth-grade student who disliked school. He was achieving at a very low level, and his achievement was greatly affected by his attendance pattern. He was out of school almost as often as he was in school. The principal had contacted the mother on numerous occasions and had written letters to the home about the absence pattern. The father had passed away some years previously, and the mother worked as a cook in a restaurant and was seldom home. She indicated to the principal that she hoped that he could do something with her son because she had no control over him. Ben's older brother had had a similar pattern when he was in school and had served a period in both a juvenile home and a state corrective institution. He was now living in the same community but not in the same household. Ben also had the habit of becoming very ill about every other day and requesting permission to go home. The principal had excused him on numerous occasions but had found in checking the home that Ben never reached home and occasionally ended up in a beer hall. After one such occurrence, the principal had denied Ben an excuse to go home because of his illness. The principal had also told him that this pattern was not to continue any longer or some serious corrective procedures would need to be taken, including the possibility of referral to the juvenile court. On the following day the principal heard a very loud, boisterous voice in the outer office. He opened the door to find out what was going on and saw a man shaking his fist in the secretary's face, demanding to see the principal and making loud statements about what he was going to do. The principal stepped out to take over the situation and said, "I'm the principal; may I help you?"

The man, bigger than the principal, shook his fist in the principal's face and in a loud voice said, "I'm going to beat the hell out of you!"

The principal, calm on the outside, but greatly concerned on the inside, for he could see that the person could do it, said, "Won't you come in and we'll discuss it." He led the man into his office. All the time the man was shaking his fist in the principal's face. The secretary and other clerks were obviously very shaken by the occurrence and were not sure whether they should call the police.

In the office the man said, "I'm Ben's brother, and I'm going to beat the hell out of you!"

The principal held out his open hand and said, "I'm pleased to meet you. Won't you sit down?"

The man ignored the principal's hand and, half standing and half sitting, continued to tell the principal, "Quit picking on my brother or else I'll beat the hell out of you."

The principal said, "Well, obviously your brother has been talking to you. What has he told you about the situation?"

The brother spilled out a story of abuse, discrimination, and unjust treatment. By this time the man had worked off most of his anger and the principal could see that he could now discuss the situation more sensibly. He stated, "I am sure that you have cause to be concerned, but obviously you have only had an opportunity to hear what Ben has had to tell you. Would you like to know more about the situation?" The man indicated that he would; so the principal then began to explain all the things he had done—the many contacts he had had with the mother, the many conversations he had had with the student, the excuses he had given the student for illness with the student later being found in the beer halls, and other such instances. He finished his narration by telling the brother that the day before he had told Ben that unless he straightened up and took care of these problems, it would be necessary for the principal to refer Ben to the juvenile court.

The brother, who had a chip on his shoulder from his own experience, had been misled by hearing only one side of the story. He further recognized from his own experiences some of the factors that had led to his bad experiences, and his younger brother obviously was following in his footsteps. As he left the principal's office, he said, "What you've done is right; and if Ben doesn't give you his cooperation, you let me know and I'll beat the hell out of him!"

This example, although involving a threat to the principal, is not unusual. The principal must be able to cope with irritated parents. The following guidelines may be helpful when handling irate parents:

1. Be calm. Do not get excited or show anger even though abused unjustly. There may be a place for a principal to surrender to righteous indignation, but the opening of a conference with an irate parent is not the place.

2. Hear the parent out. Allow the parent to say what he has on his mind. Catharsis, alone, will help solve many problems.

3. Explain the circumstances as you understand and know them. If the parent comes to you about a situation in class that has not been brought to your attention, explain to the parent that you, too, are concerned about the problem, that you are sure there are other circumstances, and that you will investigate the problem and will contact the parent.

4. Assure the parent of your interest in the child and that your action and judgment, and the teacher's action and judgment, were taken in the interests of the child even though they may not seem to be that way to the student or parent.

5. Where a mistake was made and correction was administered in a period of anger by a teacher or principal, it is sometimes best to apologize and say, "This incident happened. I had hoped that it would not happen,

but the circumstances were such that it took place." However, an apology is not made for action or penalties that are administered under careful consideration and judgment.

6. When you believe you are right, be kind but firm even though parents may not be completely satisfied with the solution or the penalty you have administered.

7. Ask for their suggestions about handling future situations with their children.

8. Support the teacher. Do not correct him in front of the parents; make such corrections in an individual conference with him. Justify your action and the action taken by the teacher.

9. Solicit the cooperation of the parents.

10. Work out an agreement whereby in future situations there might be mutual communication before the problem reaches the crisis stage.

11. Show by action that you are attempting to administer penalties fairly and justly on the basis of the individual circumstances, and that these circumstances are affected by previous violations of the person involved.

12. As the parent leaves, have him leave feeling as good as he can about the teacher, the principal, and the school.

13. Make a written note of the incident, including conclusions and agreements reached, for use if future problems arise.

Summary

The principal shares with parents, guardians, teachers, district personnel, social workers, policemen, and juvenile judges the responsibility for teacher self-control and administering discipline to youth. The schools should supplement the role of parents and other agencies when these other agencies have a major responsibility in providing both teaching and corrective measures. The school has the major responsibility when the violation takes place within the framework of the school's program. It is important for the principal to understand the theory of effective discipline as well as the practical aspects of administration of discipline.

A student, like other citizens in the community, has freedom, but the freedom is tempered by the responsibility that is involved in any given situation. In a free society restrictions are necessary to define the limits of both freedom and responsibility. Because there are people who forget, or who place other values ahead of society's accepted values, or who are completely unwilling to accept responsibility, it is necessary to have penalties. Corrections should first be educative in nature to bring about self-discipline. But there are times when a penalty must be issued for control purposes. The principal should administer penalties that are in keeping with the nature of the violation; they should be administered as soon after the violation as possible. The penalty should be one that the principal feels just and at the same time one that can be successfully imposed.

The principal has responsibility for student discipline from the time the student leaves for school until he arrives back home.

In solving disciplinary problems, the principal should effectively use the student council and other student groups.

Although corporal punishment has been in schools as long as schools have existed, the use of corporal punishment today is still a serious matter for the principal. Some states permit corporal punishment; other states do not. States that permit corporal punishment do not make it mandatory. The teacher and principal are still liable for their actions. The courts have generally interpreted that a principal or a teacher has the same rights and responsibilities that a prudent parent would have under the same circumstances, and that the teacher and principal stand in place of the parent. As far as possible, both the teachers and the principals should find other satisfactory penalties that will accomplish the same result as corporal punishment.

Only the principal may suspend a student from school, while expulsion is a right reserved to the board of education.

When the principal is dealing with an irate parent, he should remember to be calm, to hear the parent out, to explain the circumstances as he understands them, to show the parents his interest in the child, to stand on principle if no error is present, to ask for parent suggestions, and to support the teachers.

SUGGESTED PROJECTS AND ACTIVITIES

1. Review the case "It's a Free Country, Ain't It?" Discuss the case from the viewpoints of the teacher, the principal, and the student. How might the principal and teacher handle the situation differently?
2. Have a panel of teachers discuss what they expect from their principals in regard to support in discipline situations.
3. Invite a juvenile court judge or a social worker to discuss effective discipline as seen by the juvenile court.
4. Role-play the case presentation "Don't You Know It's Wrong to Steal?" with different members of the class acting as the principal. The emphasis should be on the solution to the problem.
5. Have a principal discuss the type of discipline problems that he has handled in a given day, where the discipline problem occurred, and whether the school has a major or minor responsibility in the solution of the problem.

6. In your state find out if corporal punishment is prohibited or permitted. Report on the general attitude of a school district on the use of corporal punishment.

7. Secure records from the court regarding juveniles who have been referred to the court by the school. Check out the nature of the referral and the adjustment of the student to the school situation.

REVIEW AND DISCUSSION QUESTIONS

1. Why should freedom be defined as more than simply the right to choose?
2. Who should define the responsibility needed in any given social contact?
3. How can adherence to restrictions give a person more freedom?
4. How can too great a restriction take away freedom?
5. If self-discipline is a goal, why should penalties be exercised?
6. What are some suggested principles when one administers penalties?
7. Why is a 500-word theme for every misdemeanor a poor penalty?
8. When one reviews the causes for pupil offenses, which cause seems to be most important?
9. Why is moralization of a principle usually an ineffective penalty?
10. In the case study "Don't You Know It's Wrong to Steal?" what should be the solution to Betty's and the principal's problem?
11. What are some helps that can be given to a teacher in preventing discipline problems?
12. How can the principal most effectively use the student organizations in solving a discipline problem?
13. Why is it undesirable for a principal or a teacher to use corporal punishment?
14. Why should the right to suspend a student from school not be given to every teacher and the right to expel students not be given to every principal?
15. What is the principal's responsibility to teachers as related to the use of corporal punishment?
16. What are some effective techniques a principal might use in conferences with irate parents?

SELECTED BIBLIOGRAPHY

Addicott, Irwin O. *Constructive Classroom Control.* San Francisco: Howard Chandler, Publisher, 1958.

Bowman, Herman J. "A Review of Discipline," *Bulletin of N.A.S.S.P.*, September 1959, pp. 147–55.

Brown, Edwin John, and Arthur Thomas Phelps. *Managing the Classroom— The Teacher's Part in School Administration.* New York: The Ronald Press Company, 1961.

"Discipline," *School Management*, March 1965, pp. 80–84.

"Discipline in the Public Schools," *N.E.A. Research Bulletin*, December 1957, p. 152.

Duncan, John W. "Motivation and the Academically Troubled Student," *Bulletin of N.A.S.S.P.*, January 1965, pp. 92–97.

Hamilton, Robert R. *Legal Rights and Liabilities of Teachers.* Laramie, Wyo.: Laramie Printers, Co., Inc., 1956.

Havighurst, Robert J. *Human Development and Education.* New York: Longmans, Green and Co., Inc., 1953.

Jackson, Walter M. "Discipline in a Large Junior High School," *Bulletin of N.A.S.S.P.*, October 1963, pp. 55–58.

McPhie, Walter E. "Discipline Problems: An Educational Malignancy," *Bulletin of N.A.S.S.P.*, December 1961, pp. 82–91.

Punke, Harold H. "Corporal Punishment in the Public Schools," *Bulletin of N.A.S.S.P.*, September 1959, pp. 118–38.

Sheviakov, George D., and Fritz Redl. *Discipline for Today's Children and Youth.* Washington, D.C.: Association for Supervision and Curriculum Development, National Education Association, 1956.

Vredevoe, Lawrence E. "Effects of Desegregation on Discipline," *Education Digest*, April 1965, pp. 12–16.

———. "School Discipline—Third Report on a Study of Students and School Discipline in the United States and Other Countries," *Bulletin of N.A.S.S.P.*, March 1965, pp. 215–26.

Williamson, Lee R. "An Analysis of Discipline Practices in Selected Junior High Schools of Texas," *Bulletin of N.A.S.S.P.*, February 1962, pp. 429–32.

PART IV

The school administrator . . . must find the personal resources to exercise significant educational leadership in a wide variety of tasks. To his school board, to his faculty, and to his community he must present continuing evidence of his educational statesmanship and professional skill in conducting the total affairs of the school system. In no area of his activities will he find a greater degree of community surveillance and critical evaluation of his work than in his day-to-day conduct of the business activities of the school.

—FREDERICK W. HILL and JAMES W. COLMEY. *School Business Administration in the Smaller Community.* Minneapolis: T. S. Denison and Company, Inc., 1964, p. 13.

THE ADMINISTRATION
OF
AUXILIARY SERVICES

CHAPTER 14

Administration of
Business Affairs

An interesting discovery of prospective school administrators as well as of interested lay citizens is that education is big business. When one considers the amount of money spent for buildings, maintenance, salaries, supplies and equipment, bus service, school lunch, etc., education becomes a major business enterprise. With the exception of large cities, education is often the biggest single enterprise in most communities.

Although it is agreed by school administrators that business functions are and should be secondary to the prime purpose of improving curriculum and instruction, business functions have increased markedly in recent years. The knowledge and techniques needed to be a successful school business manager have multiplied. The principal cannot shirk his responsibilities in this area without that knowledge becoming generally known, nor can he be haphazard in his business procedure, for his job and reputation depend on exactness in this field.

The principal can delegate much of this responsibility, but the effectiveness of this delegation comes only after the principal has demonstrated his knowledge and capabilities in handling the problems that inevitably arise. This chapter attempts to recognize the practical phase of business administration.

Determining the Budget

The board of education and the superintendent are responsible for all phases of the business operation of a district. One of the major re-

357

sponsibilities of the superintendent is to plan and have approved a budget for each year. This budget becomes the operating plan for school expenditures. The budget year is usually a fiscal year from July 1 to June 30. The school year easily falls within this time period.

Budget Determined from Educational Program. The budget should be determined from the needs of the educational program. Because the principal of each school is in the best position to know what educational programs require finance, the superintendent usually involves the principal in budget determination. The principal in similar manner requests the assistance of the teachers and departmental chairmen.

Budget Divisions. To properly assist in the preparation of the district budget, the principal must be acquainted with the basic budget categories. The U.S. Office of Education recommends the following divisions:

A. Current Expenditures—those expenses for the daily operation of the school, consisting of:

　1. Administration—the costs of the affairs of the school that are system-wide.

　2. Instruction—those activities which deal with the teaching of students or improving the quality of teaching.

　3. Attendance Services—those activities which promote and improve children and youth's school attendance.

　4. Health Services—services (not instruction) in the inspection and treatment of physical and mental health.

　5. Pupil Transportation Services—those activities related to conveying pupils to and from school.

　6. Operation—housekeeping activities concerned with keeping the physical plant open and usable.

　7. Maintenance—activities concerned with keeping the grounds, buildings, and equipment at their original condition of use (repairs and replacements).

　8. Fixed Charges—expenditures of a generally recurrent nature.

　9. Food Services—activities for the purpose of preparing and serving food.

　10. Student Body Activities—direct and personal services for pupils that are managed or operated by the student body.

　11. Community Services—those provided by the school district for the community as a whole.

B. Capital Outlay—includes money spent for new sites, new buildings, and new equipment.

C. Debt Service—includes money spent for retiring a debt—both principal and interest.[1]

---

[1] Paul F. Reason and Alpheus L. White, *Financial Accounting for Local and State School Systems* (Washington, D.C.: U.S. Office of Education, 1957).

The principal must summarize his needs in the appropriate budget divisions as set forth in his district.

Involving the Staff in Budget Determination. In Chapter 2, the principal was given some guidelines regarding when to use independent decision making and when to involve the group in decision making. One major criterion set forth for group decision making involved the degree to which the group was to be affected by the decision. There are few decisions made that affect the kind and quality of teaching as significantly as do decisions regarding the kind and amount of supplies and equipment that are needed. The supplies and equipment can only be obtained if they have been planned as part of the regular budget. Teachers should play a major role in budget determination.

Some teachers are anxious to help—so anxious, in fact, that they can find uses in their department for the total budget allocated to the school. Other teachers do not realize the importance of a budget or have not been taught how to ask for money. The case presented below shows two extremes; yet the teachers involved were given the same instructions and the same opportunities to secure supplies and equipment for the improvement of their educational program.

A Budget Request

Principal Benson wanted to involve his faculty in budget determination. He carefully reviewed with the superintendent what was expected of him as principal. The superintendent remarked, "Of course, money is limited—but we want our principals to let us know what they need. You should be realistic, but if you need money for special programs, request it. Plan your program and then put on the dollar sign. We will go with you as far as we can. You might have priorities determined so that the ax can be used judiciously if cutting is necessary—and it always is . . ."

Mr. Benson went back to his school and prepared some forms that had space for the teacher's name and the following headings: program, supplies and equipment needed, and cost. In faculty meeting he discussed the needs and the procedures and asked the teachers to "carefully lay out your educational needs from a long-range point of view and then indicate specific equipment and supplies needed together with the purchasing price of such items. Turn-in date will be January 31, three weeks from today."

A reminder was placed in the faculty mailboxes a week before and again the day before the turn-in date.

On February 1, Mr. Benson began to review the budget requests. He found all varieties and all extremes, but the greatest extremes were found on the budget forms of Mr. Request and Mr. Satisfied. He reviewed them carefully.

Mr. Request was an industrial arts teacher who knew where he was going and what he wanted. Not only had he filled out the required form, but he had attached six single-spaced pages of supply and equipment items needed. The total came to over $8,000. Mr. Benson knew that the amount requested was as much as the whole school was allocated the previous year. Mr. Request taught only four sections with 25 students per section. "Only 100 students and $8,000. Wow!"

Mr. Benson turned to the next form. Mr. Satisfied wrote on his form, "The English teachers had a conference and decided to turn in only one request. We would like what we received last year."

Mr. Benson looked at last year's English Department budget—$150. "Every student in school takes English and they only need $150. They certainly have no program, no plan, and no money. . ."

From the example above, we see not only the variation in teachers' requests but also elements of planning and caution for a school principal. The principal should involve his staff in budget determination.

There are many procedures that a principal could use to involve his teachers in preparing the budget. The principal should help the teachers answer the following basic questions:

1. What is the desirable educational program?
2. What is needed to carry out the program?
3. What will it cost?

In arriving at the answers to these questions, the principal will involve his department chairmen as coordinators of budget areas. The department chairman will work with the teachers assigned to his department. The principal should give aid to the chairman as needed. In the example cited, the principal should hold a conference with the English chairman and discuss the program and needs. The English chairman obviously should be encouraged to make specific requests. The chairman of the industrial arts should help the teacher who made such a large request understand the total budget program. Certainly the teacher who has planned in advance should be commended while he is also developing understanding of the financial limitations.

When each departmental budget has been collected, the principal will then compile the total budget for the school and submit it to the district office.

After the budget requests from all of the schools have been compiled by the superintendent's staff, it will usually be found that the total amount requested is far greater than the superintendent can ever hope to obtain. Some "judicious pruning" is required. A wise principal should anticipate such an obstacle and should be prepared to both defend and prune his requests. In the involvement of the faculty, they should also have been prepared for such a probability. Departmental items have been listed by priority. However, the principal should not arbitrarily make cuts in each budget. A safe guideline for a principal to follow would be: When the faculty members are involved in preparing the budget, they should also be involved in the cutbacks that are needed. If the chairman, members of the faculty, and other staff members are involved in determining the items to be omitted, morale will remain high even when budget pruning is required.

Purchasing Equipment and Supplies

Centralized or Decentralized Systems. Once the budget has been approved by the board of education, the mechanics of purchasing can be set in motion. Specific procedures will vary from district to district. The new principal will be wise to learn the district's procedures as one of his first assignments. Having learned the procedures, the principal can maintain control and at the same time turn the mechanics over to a secretary or clerk.

There are two basic organizational plans as related to purchasing: (1) centralized and (2) decentralized. In a centralized system, the district does the purchasing for all schools. In a decentralized system each school purchases the items that have been approved in the budget, pays the bills, and requests reimbursement from the district office. The centralized system of purchasing and accounting is the most widely used and has the advantages of providing greater purchasing power, more qualified personnel, and a more efficient business operation. The big disadvantage is that communication from the teacher to the district is difficult to maintain, and the teachers too often do not know the disposition of their requests. Under the decentralized system most of the advantages of the centralized system are lost, and the principal must spend more time in business operations. However, there is better communication between the teacher and principal concerning the status of a request.

Purchasing Procedure. In most systems the process of purchasing requires action by three individuals: the teacher or department chairman, the principal, and the superintendent or his appointee.

An adequate purchasing procedure will provide a process whereby the items needed by the teacher will be ordered, received, and delivered to the teacher and appropriate payments made. The purchasing process will also provide some means whereby each of these individuals is aware of the status of the request item. For example, the teacher desires to know if the item was approved by the principal and ordered by the district. The principal desires to know if the item has been ordered. When an item is sent directly to a school, the district desires to know that the item has been received by the school prior to the payment of the invoice. Finally, the principal and teacher should know the exact price of the item, which can only be known after the invoice is received by the district.

The following procedure is proposed as a typical plan whereby both purchasing and communication can be handled simultaneously:

1. The teacher or department initiates a request for an item; the data shown in Figure 14.1, Request for a High School Purchase Order or District Requisition, are provided. This form can be used in smaller systems that do not have centralized accounting with budget numbers simply by modifying the form to show the name of the account to be

Figure 14.1

Request for a High School Purchase Order or District Requisition

REQUEST FOR A HIGH SCHOOL PURCHASE ORDER OR DISTRICT REQUISITION
(Request must be approved by the principal before purchase order can be issued)

High School Funds	District Budget
Club or Department _____ Please check: ____ Purchased from club or departmental funds ____ Sold to students with art, shop, or photography cards ____ Ordered to be sold through bookstore ____ Make Check payable to: _____ Name For services rendered or materials received (Do not check if above have been checked)	Department _____ Budget number _____ Note: District will not order materials without budget number and price. If exact price is not known, please estimate as closely as possible.

Order from: _____   Address: _____

Quantity	Catalogue Number	Article and Description	Price Each	Total Price

ACTION TAKEN
(To be filled in by office and returned to advisor)

Date _____   Signature of Adviser _____

Principal's Approval _____ Purchase Order or Requisition Number _____

Issued to: _____ Date _____

(Please retain this form for your files)

charged. The same form can be used for all requests even though the equipment and supplies may be ordered from the district while the high school activity accounts are maintained at the school.

2. The principal approves the item as being approved in the budget. The secretary or clerk then takes the data needed from the Request for a High School Purchase Order or District Requisition and places the data on a high school purchase order if the high school does its own purchasing from that account or on a district requisition if the item is to be charged

Figure 14.2

District Requisition

REQUISITION Name of School		REQUISITION NUMBER _____ Purchase Order Date _____ Purchase Order Number _____		
Quantity	Item		Actual Cost	Estimated Cost

Suggested Source of Purchase:

Name _____ Date _____

Street _____ Account To Be Charged _____

City and State _____ Signature for Department _____

against the district-approved budget. The estimated amount of the purchase is always indicated so that the amount can be encumbered. The Request for a High School Purchase Order or District Requisition is then returned to the teacher. The teacher knows the item has been ordered.

3. The district requisition is usually in triplicate and in three different colors. See Figure 14.2. The principal keeps one copy and forwards two copies to the district. On the basis of previous acceptance of bids, quotation, and price lists from various vendors, the district issues a purchase order, as shown in Figure 14.3.

Figure 14.3

District Purchase Order

PURCHASE ORDER		
Name of School		
Date _____		Purchase Order Number _____
To:	Ship To: Name of School Department Address Via:	
Quantity	Description	
Requisition Account	By:	Name of School By:

4. Upon the receipt of an invoice the district checks to see that the merchandise was received and delivered to the school and thus to the teacher. The exact price is placed on two copies of the requisition, and one copy is returned to the school.

5. The principal posts the return copy and returns his original to the teacher or the department with the exact price shown.

There may be many modifications of this procedure. A step-by-step analysis is shown in Figure 14.4.

The Time to Order Equipment and Supplies. The time to order equipment and supplies is before they are needed. Yet, a common mistake made by teachers and principals is to delay until the items are needed. As can be concluded from the discussion on purchasing procedures, purchasing takes time. The budget is set for the school year ahead, but some teachers want to begin spending in April and May for the year about to be completed.

The best time for the principal to order equipment and supplies is in the late spring or early summer with an understanding with the vendor that the items and invoices are to arrive after July 1 and prior to the opening of school. Such a plan has several advantages: (1) the materials are available when school opens; (2) the materials can be used throughout the year; (3) the vendors can take advantage of the slack seasons and can often provide a savings to the district; and (4) the district has plenty of time to compile orders and receive the best price through careful bidding and quantity purchasing.

Receiving and Storing Equipment and Supplies. A school district that has a centralized purchasing department usually maintains a district warehouse for receiving and storing supplies and equipment. A competent staff is hired to see that materials are not only received and stored properly, but also distributed to the appropriate schools. The district usually stores large quantities of consumable supplies, and such supplies are often purchased in carload quantities. The principal requisitions these consumable supplies in much the same manner as described earlier. The district simply fills the orders and indicates the prices on the appropriate requisition.

Frequently pieces of equipment are ordered for a given school. To save the district money in distribution costs, the districts request that the items be shipped directly to the school. The high school must have a plan as well as facilities for receiving equipment and supplies. The principal, through his custodian or secretary, must check to see if the goods received are as ordered and if any damage has been made in shipping. Any damage or discrepancy should be noted on the invoices.

Figure 14.4

Tracking down a Purchase Request

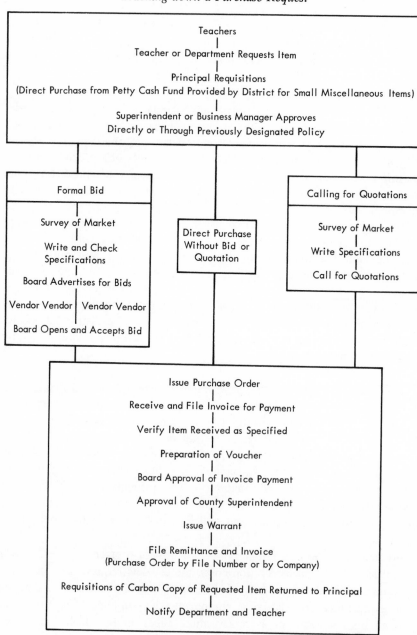

Teachers

Teacher or Department Requests Item

Principal Requisitions
(Direct Purchase from Petty Cash Fund Provided by District for Small Miscellaneous Items)

Superintendent or Business Manager Approves
Directly or Through Previously Designated Policy

Formal Bid

Survey of Market

Write and Check
Specifications

Board Advertises for Bids

Vendor Vendor   Vendor Vendor

Board Opens and Accepts Bid

Direct Purchase
Without Bid or
Quotation

Calling for Quotations

Survey of Market

Write Specifications

Call for Quotations

Issue Purchase Order

Receive and File Invoice for Payment

Verify Item Received as Specified

Preparation of Voucher

Board Approval of Invoice Payment

Approval of County Superintendent

Issue Warrant

File Remittance and Invoice
(Purchase Order by File Number or by Company)

Requisitions of Carbon Copy of Requested Item Returned to Principal

Notify Department and Teacher

Inventories for Equipment, Books, and Supplies

Keeping an Inventory. A school inventory provides valuable information needed by both principals and teachers. An inventory can be used for the following:

1. To let the principal know at a glance what equipment is in the school.
2. To aid in the development of the budget.
3. To assist in establishing values in case of fire.
4. To help avoid theft or loss.

A plan commonly used requires each teacher to submit to the school principal a complete list of all equipment, supplies, art treasures, and other materials in his room at the close of the school year. Another method is to maintain a continuing inventory. Such a system requires a clerk to make an entry for all supplies and equipment when delivered. When an item is lost or discarded, it is deducted from the inventory list. Such an inventory may be kept on individual cards with the equipment numbered the same as the card, or a composite sheet may be kept. A typical inventory form is shown in Figure 14.5. Regardless of the type of inventory

Figure 14.5

Equipment and Supplies Inventory

EQUIPMENT AND SUPPLIES INVENTORY Name of School								
Article	Number Last Inventory	Number Discarded	Number Added	Total Number	Cost Per Item	Date of Purchase	Date of Inventory	Present Value

kept, the principal should make at least one check each year to ascertain that all equipment listed is in the building. Any loss discovered should be reported to the district office immediately.

Textbook Inventory. Textbooks are generally listed as separate items from equipment and supplies in an inventory. Textbooks may be furnished free by the district, rented to the student by the district or the school, or owned by the student.

Regardless of the source of supply, book inventories must be maintained. See Figure 14.6. The useful life of a book is normally four to five years.

Figure 14.6
Book Inventory

BOOK INVENTORY Name of School			
Title of Book	Lost	Unfit	Number End of Year

If books are rented or provided free, students are generally held responsible for loss or damage. Proper storage for texts must be provided during the summer months. If a central book room is not available, the inventory should show the storage area.

The School Bookstore

The school bookstore is an institution of long standing and great controversy. The initial purpose of the bookstore was to provide student-owned textbooks and a few supplies. Gradually the items to be sold increased as the needs increased. Currently bookstores are the vendors of textbooks, papers, art and poster boards, pens, inks, erasers, paperback books, physical education clothing, student rings, graduation announcements and gowns, candy, and many other commodities.

There are several advantages in maintaining a bookstore. First, the bookstore is convenient for students and teachers. Second, the school year usually ends with a surplus in the bookstore account, which can often be used at the discretion of the principal for improvements within the school. Third, the bookstore can be a source of true, practical education for students majoring in accounting, business procedures, and distributive education. Too often, this last and most important function is the most neglected.

The disadvantages of the bookstore come from criticism of downtown businessmen who claim the "school is taxing us to compete against us." A second disadvantage is the amount of time spent by the principal and clerk to operate the store. If the bookstore is seen primarily as a source of service to students and a curriculum resource to teachers, the bookstore can be more easily justified. Some schools prefer to use vending machines rather than to bother with a bookstore.

Financing the Student Activity Program

Financing Student Activities—A Major Problem. It has already been shown that a major portion of the principal's time is spent in the student activity program. The business phase of this program is no small matter. It is not uncommon for high schools to have accounts ranging from $10,000 to $75,000. Davis estimated that student activity funds in Los Angeles public schools would reach $7 million.[2] In some school districts these funds are handled and controlled by the district in the same manner as educational supplies. However, owing to the convenience and the need for easy access to funds for both depositing and purchasing, these funds are generally banked in the name of the school and as such come under the direct jurisdiction of the principal. A central treasurer for the school should be bonded and given the responsibility to receive and disburse all activity funds.[3] In recent years some school districts have turned these functions over to the district office owing to legal problems.[4]

Budgeting and Purchasing for Student Activities. The same principles as given for the district budget and purchasing apply to financing student activities. The advisers should help the student officers in preparing the budget by developing an activity plan, listing materials and services needed and the costs involved. The total estimated receipts from all sources

[2] Clifford M. Davis, "Supervision and Control of Student Body Finances," *Proceedings of Association of School Business Officials*, 43rd Convention, October, 1957, pp. 210–15.

[3] Stephen J. Knezevich and John Guy Fowlkes, *Business Management of Local School Systems* (New York: Harper and Brothers, 1960), p. 3.

[4] R. R. Hamilton, "The Legal Status, Control and Use of Athletic and Other Extracurricular Funds," *The Bi-Weekly School Law Letter*, September 1953, pp. 57–60.

including the sale of tickets, dues, gate receipts, guarantees, other money-earning projects, board allocations, and unused balances from the previous year should be reviewed and allocations made.

At the conclusion of each budget year all surpluses should be transferred to a general fund and all accounts cleared. The only exceptions to this policy should be for such accounts as a class account in which the class is saving for a school gift or senior trip. These accounts are generally known as "clearing accounts" and should not be included in the activity budget.

All purchases should be made by purchase order and should be initiated by the adviser. Refer to Figure 14.1.

Handling Receipts and Disbursements.   There is no place in financial accounting where more misunderstandings can arise than in the area of receiving money. The procedures should be carefully stated and understood by all who handle student activity money. Occasionally, a good, honest principal loses his good name and his job because he was not exacting in money matters. The following suggestions should prove helpful to all students, teachers, clerks, bookkeepers, and principals:

1. Where possible, tickets should be numbered and recorded. Gate receipts should be checked against tickets issued.

2. Where tickets are not issued, the money should be counted by more than one person and receipts issued by the treasurer. Figure 14.7 shows a sample receipt.

Figure 14.7

Official Receipt

OFFICIAL RECEIPT		
Name of School		

Number _____

Received from _____

Source of Income _____

Fund	Account	Amount

Signature _____

Date _____   Title _____

3. Money should be banked daily. Where night activities are held, a night depository should be used.

4. With the exception of a petty cash fund, which is used for payment of small items and for which proper records are kept, all payments should be made by checks issued by the treasurer after the invoice has been approved by the adviser. See Figure 14.8. Additional protection is given

Figure 14.8

Voucher

VOUCHER

Name of School

Number ______ Date ______

Pay to ______

Amount $ ______

From Fund ______

Purposes: Purchase Order ______ Attached

Invoice ______

Describe purpose briefly

The goods or services mentioned above were received and payment is approved.

Authorized Student ______ Faculty Adviser ______

PAID

Date ______ Check Number ______

Authorized Signature ______

by having a dual signature—the treasurer's and the principal's. Checks should be numbered and entered into an appropriate ledger.

5. At the end of each month the bank statements and books should be reconciled and a monthly report sent to each adviser. Such a report form is shown in Figure 14.9. The report should be simple, with the understanding that an adviser of any organization may request a detailed description of the status of his account at any time.

Figure 14.9

Monthly Financial Report

		MONTHLY FINANCIAL REPORT		
		For Month of _____		
Account	Balance End of Preceding Month	Receipts	Disbursements	Balance End of Month
Totals				

6. A year-end report should be submitted to the principal, and an annual audit should be made of all school funds.

7. Personnel handling money should be properly bonded.

U.S. Office of Education Handbook. The U.S. Office of Education has a handbook, *Financial Accounting for School Activities,* that should be available to all principals and in which the following policies are recommended:

1. The general administration of school activity fund accounting should be governed by rules and regulations prescribed by the board of education of the school district.

2. The board of education should designate a person (usually the superintendent) to implement all policies and rules pertaining to the supervision and administration of funds in schools under his jurisdiction.

3. One person should be designated (usually the principal) to be responsible for funds in each individual school.

4. Expenditures for school activities should be carefully planned with the resources of the activity, which would make the use of a budget control of receipts and expenditures desirable and sometimes necessary.

5. Persons handling the school funds should be bonded through the regular school district procedures, and the bond should be in an amount sufficient for adequate protection of the funds of the school.

6. An annual audit should be made of all school activity funds by trained and recognized auditors.

7. Regular financial reports should be made to the administrative head of the school and to the board of education.[5]

Making Business Management a Curriculum Project

Too often the principal gets involved in business and managerial details to the point where all his time is thus consumed. The details of business management become so numerous that the only escape is to appoint and delegate responsibility. In his desire to achieve efficiency, the principal should not overlook the curriculum and teaching possibilities inherent in the business operations. Some high schools have excellent distributive and vocational education programs in which students have released time to learn business operations and selling. These same schools too often have the principal, faculty member, or secretary manage and operate the bookstore without any student involvement. The same premise is true in the total business operation. The teacher's time could best be spent in teaching students the business operations and providing them with opportunities for practical application and supervision. The principal should always be alert to ways in which more effective curriculum programs and instructional procedures can be implemented within his school.

Summary

The business management of a school is a continuing responsibility of a school principal throughout the school year. Education is big business.

---

[5] U.S. Office of Education, *Financial Accounting for School Activities.* (Washington, D.C.: Government Printing Office, 1959), pp. 51–52.

The principal must account for the wise management of large sums of money. Mismanagement may result in loss of reputation and position.

The principal has two primary budgets to handle. The district budget is primarily for equipment and supplies needed to carry out the instructional program. The high school activity budget and funds are used to carry out the extracurricular activity programs.

Both the district budget and the high school activity budget should be determined from the program desired; equipment, supplies, and services needed to carry out the program; and the cost of such items. The faculty and staff should assist in the preparation of the budget. Student offices should help plan the activity budget. Priorities should be given to items requested so that "pruning" can be done judiciously.

The purchasing procedure initiates with a request from the teacher on the appropriate form. The principal completes a purchase order if the cost is to be charged against a high school account. The school treasurer receives and disburses all high school money. The principal fills out a district requisition if the goods are to be charged against the district budget. The district makes out the purchase order and is responsible for the disbursement of funds. The time to order most of the equipment and supplies is in the late spring or early summer so that materials will be available when school commences.

Books, equipment, and supplies must be properly received and stored. Inventories must be kept on all items to more effectively plan educational programs and budgets and to guard against loss and theft.

The school bookstore is both convenient and necessary, yet it is controversial because it is often seen as competition by some community businessmen.

The principal should spend more time analyzing the operation of the bookstore and all phases of the business process so that students enrolled in business classes can be provided with practical on-the-job training.

SUGGESTED PROJECTS AND ACTIVITIES

1. Visit the nearby school districts and gather samples of all forms used in the business operation. Compare and evaluate the forms.
2. Visit the district business office and have demonstrated procedures for handling requisitions, purchase orders, approval of invoices by the board of education for payment, checks for warrant system, filing of invoices or vouchers for future reference, budget accounting system, encumbrance versus nonencumbrance of funds.
3. Obtain a year end or a monthly report from a high school treasurer. Discuss the reasons for the various accounts and indicate which ones would probably be "clearing accounts" and why.

4. Find out from the schools, banks, and other financial institutions how the surplus school funds could and should be invested.
5. Visit school treasurers and be present while accounts are balanced at the end of the month.

REVIEW AND DISCUSSION QUESTIONS

1. What justification can be given in support of the statement, "Education is big business"?
2. What are the important considerations in budget determination?
3. Why should a secondary school principal be concerned with the district budget and the budget divisions?
4. What principle in the chapter on theory of leadership is given consideration when the faculty and staff are involved in budget making?
5. What are the advantages and disadvantages of centralized and decentralized purchasing?
6. Why should teachers and departmental chairmen initiate most requests for equipment and supplies rather than the principal?
7. What is the difference between calling for a bid and calling for a quotation?
8. When should equipment and supplies be ordered?
9. What are the purposes of maintaining inventories?
10. What are the advantages and disadvantages of maintaining a bookstore?
11. What procedures should be maintained when receiving money? In the disbursement of funds?
12. What are the purposes of a monthly report on student activity funds? A year-end report? An annual audit? Bonding of the treasurer? Issuing receipts?
13. How can the business management functions be used to improve curriculum programs?

SELECTED BIBLIOGRAPHY

Anderson, Lester W., and Lauren A. Van Dyke. *Secondary School Administration*. Boston: Houghton Mifflin Company, 1963.

Association of School Business Officials of the United States and Canada. *A Manual of Accounting Principles and Procedures for Student Activity Funds*. Bulletin No. 17. Evanston, Ill. 1957.

Burrup, Percy E. *Modern High School Administration*. New York: Harper and Brothers, 1962.

Hamilton, R. R. "The Legal Status, Control and Use of Athletic and Other Extra-curricular Funds," *The Bi-weekly School Law Letter*, September 1953.

Hill, Frederick W., and James W. Colmey. *School Business Administration in the Smaller Community*. Minneapolis: T. S. Denison and Company, Inc., 1965.

"How Much Should You Spend for Instruction and Administration," *School Management*, January 1965, pp. 116–28 (complete issue on business management problems).

Knezevich, Stephen J., and John Guy Fowlkes. *Business Management of Local School Systems*. New York: Harper and Brothers, 1960.

Mort, Paul R., Walter C. Reusser, and John W. Polley. *Public School Finance*. New York: McGraw-Hill Book Company, Inc., 1960.

Reason, Paul L., and Alpheus L. White. *Financial Accounting for Local and State School Systems*. Bulletin 22. Washington, D.C.: Government Printing Office, 1959.

Roe, William H. *School Business Management*. New York: McGraw-Hill Book Company, Inc., 1961.

U.S. Office of Education. *Financial Accounting for School Activities*. Washington, D.C.: Government Printing Office, 1959.

CHAPTER 15

Administration of the Office

There can be little question that the central administrative offices of the secondary school are the center of activity in our modern high schools. The office is the school control center. Except in small schools where the principal is still a teacher in a classroom, almost all of the basic deciding factors of organization and administration of schools take place within the central office area. Administrative decisions are centered here. Teachers receive communication instructions, absentee forms, and excuses from the office. Parents must call at the office. Records are kept here. Whatever viewpoint one takes, the central office is indeed the center of all the school activities. Therefore, a most important function of the school principal is to understand what takes place in the office and how it might be better organized for greater efficiency and effectiveness.

The Principal and the Office

The Principal's Responsibility.   It is obvious that if the administrative area is the hub of the school, the principal is the key person in the total over-all operation of the school program. He is the generator and the power source from which the activities flow. Because there are so many functions that must be performed in the office, the principal must be a good organizer and the office must be a smoothly functioning operation. The principal will know when the office is running efficiently because it runs as if no one were doing anything. The smoothness required is

377

achieved by setting to routine the many tasks that have to be performed, yet recognizing that there will always be the unusual, the different, and the emergency. The daily activities at the office can be committed to a routine and effectively handled. One primary responsibility of the principal is to so organize the office that the office routine is functioning as if the principal were not needed. Indeed, when such an organization is achieved, the principal can leave his school—as he will frequently—without fear that the school will become a mass of confusion or fall apart at the seams.

The Goal of Efficient Operation.   Although it is desirable to have an office function efficiently, the goal should not be efficiency for the sake of efficiency. The principal should have some particular goal in mind as he continually strives to implement more effective office procedures. A table in Chapter 1 entitled "Comparison of Time Spent with Principals and Authorities' Opinions As to How Time Should Be Spent in the Secondary Principalship"[1] showed that principals spend far too much time on office routine. Approximately 22.5 per cent of the principal's time was spent administering and taking care of the office or in routine office work. The principals who responded to this study felt they should be spending only 12.9 per cent of their time in this work, while authorities in school administration thought principals should only be spending 9.7 per cent of their time in office routine. In other words, the principal spends nearly one fourth of his time in office routine work, whereas authorities thought he should only be spending about 10 per cent of his time and the principal thought he should be spending just slightly more than 10 per cent of his time. There is a great gap between both the principals' and the authorities' desire and actual practice. The goal for which a principal should be working is to reduce the amount of time he spends in office and routine work so that he may spend more of his time in the supervision and improvement of instruction. The study also showed that the principal should be spending somewhere between 22 and 31 per cent of his time in the supervision and curriculum areas, whereas he is spending only about 12 per cent of his time in these areas. Since office routine occupies about 23 per cent of the principal's time, it is in this area where most of the additional time for curriculum work should be found. There are many ways that time spent on office routine could be lowered. A few specific suggestions are provided.

1. Additional secretarial or clerical help could and should be added to most secondary schools. Many of the routine duties could be delegated to a clerk. It cannot be emphasized too strongly that a principal who

---

[1] McAbee, *op. cit.*, p. 41.

spends nearly one fourth of his time in office routine is an expensive substitute for a clerk.

2. In many schools the great portion of the secretaries' time is spent taking and receiving school lunch money and doing other jobs for which less expensive clerks could be employed. The employment of clerks would provide the principal greater use of his secretary for managing and operating the office.

3. The principal and his staff and their office practice routine could be brought up to date with some of the latest business techniques and devices. Principals' offices should have the latest business equipment and communications system. The use of an intercom system greatly saves the amount of time needed in going to and fro in the school building on menial errands. Modern dictation equipment saves the time of the secretary and lets a principal have a secretary available at all times. Modern machines for duplicating correspondence, records, etc., are available and should be brought into the school office. Data-processing and computer services should be initiated.

4. The principal could have an outside group study the efficiency of his office—the tasks to be performed, the manner in which the tasks are being performed, and the changes that would make the office more effective and thus reduce his office time; thereby he might be able to spend more time in instructional programs.

Office Functions

General Office Functions. The office functions are many and varied and depend to some extent on the size of the school and the total organization of the school program. The following functions, as given by Anderson and Van Dyke, are found in most school administration centers:

1. Communicating—exchanging information by such means as intercom systems, bulletins, telephone, correspondence, and face-to-face conferences.
2. Processing materials—typing, duplicating, etc.
3. Handling correspondence and mail—preparing and filing letters for professional staff and processing staff mail.
4. Procuring supplies and equipment—for both the professional and non-professional staffs.
5. Administering attendance—checking, recording, and clearing student attendance.
6. Directing the daily program—control and necessary adjustments in the daily schedule and movement of students.
7. Administering records—maintaining, storing, summarizing and supplying information.

8. Preparing reports—the principal's annual report, reports to the state, reports to accrediting agencies, financial summaries, and the like.

9. Serving as control center for the operation of the physical plant—making certain that heat, ventilation, lights, cleaning, and other services are functioning.

10. Implementing relations with the public—conducting business with lay visitors and providing information.

11. Trouble shooting—meeting emergency situations that call for on-the-spot action.[2]

Organizing and Delegating Office Functions. The ideal is for the principal to delegate to the secretaries, clerks, and assistants as many of these functions as possible. As can be seen, many of these functions involve typing, duplicating, filing, classifying, recording, storing, summarizing, and collecting information. These functions can be handled by a secretary or clerk just as efficiently as by the principal, and in many cases more efficiently. The principal's role should be one of delegating these activities to the proper person, indicating the source from which the information should be obtained, and describing the procedures to be used. Working with his secretary, he will establish an effective filing system and will review basic procedures that should be used in recording, checking, and summarizing data. Once the basic principles and practices have been defined, the secretary can handle the routine requirements of the job. With a minimum of direction from the principal, the procuring of supplies and equipment is another function that can be turned over to the secretary or clerks. As described in the chapter on business administration, the principal should work with the staff to determine program, budget, equipment, and supplies. Once these items have been determined, except for checking the requested items against the budget and giving official approval, the principal may turn the remaining tasks over to the secretary. The secretary can complete the purchase orders or requisitions, check with the district office, inventory the materials as they arrive, and supply the teachers from the bookstore or central office.

Vital functions involving the operation of the physical plant and maintenance of the building can be handled by the custodian. The principal's prime responsibility is to serve as a clearing agent so that he is the person directing the work for the custodian. The custodian in this way receives delegated tasks from the principal.

Of the remaining office functions, the principal will need to exercise more personal attention to each individual item. Even so, delegation to assistant principals where they are available should be planned. The

[2] Lester W. Anderson and Lauren A. Van Dyke, *Secondary School Administration* (Boston: Houghton Mifflin Co., 1963), p. 531.

principal should be sure that the school functions properly with reference to the movement of students, scheduling of classes, assemblies, activities, etc. Someone must make the decisions regarding which classes are to be omitted and which facilities can best be utilized. The principal or his delegated assistant should review items that are to be announced through the intercom system or placed in the daily bulletin. Otherwise there can be misuse of important communication instruments. The principal must also be involved in aiding parents and community members on school problems. He must work closely with his faculty and staff and assist them with their problems. Much of the principal's time will be spent in conferences and in communications. Finally, the principal is usually the one person in the school to whom emergency situations that require on-the-spot decisions can be referred.

The Principal and Communications

Oral Communications. After the office is properly organized and responsibilities are delegated, one of the primary functions left to the principal is that of communications. Most of the principal's time in the office is spent in one phase or another of communications, and oral communications occupy the major portion of the principal's time. Such communications are face-to-face communications with students, parents, teachers, community representatives, salesmen, and district personnel.

About 40 per cent of the principal's communications time is spent in conferences—with individuals or groups. The principal should understand how to use group dynamics effectively. A discussion on the effective use of group dynamics is given in Chapter 2. Aside from knowledge of group dynamics, the principal should be an effective speaker and should be able to communicate ideas effectively. He must be a sympathetic listener. Frequently, the conferences involve emotional-type problems. He must be sympathetic, understanding, yet firm in administering school policy and explaining school procedures. The faculty meeting is one type of group conference in which the principal must be effective in his communications. A full discussion of the faculty meeting is given elsewhere in the text.

In addition to the face-to-face communications with groups, the principal will have many individual conferences, especially conferences with staff members. In addition to the suggestions given above regarding listening and communicating, the principal should recognize that he is working with professional individuals. The principal should try to create a tone that will be a morale booster for the faculty member after he leaves the conference. Even though the principal must sometimes refuse requests of a faculty member, the faculty member should leave the office feeling that the principal was concerned and that his decision was in the best interest of the staff member as well as the school.

Another means of oral communications is the telephone. The telephone is used very frequently by the principal in initiating and receiving calls. The secretary should be given adequate instructions on handling all the principal's incoming calls. The secretary, in the absence of the principal, should be given special instructions on handling calls to the principal so that the person making the call will understand that the principal is not able to respond at the moment but will do so just as soon as it is possible. The secretary should not say, "Mr. Jones is busy and can't speak to you," but "Mr. Jones is in a conference, may I take a message?" or "Mr. Jones is in a meeting with the superintendent. May I have him call you when he returns?"

Still another important medium in daily oral communications is the school intercom. An intercommunications system is now planned in most modern school buildings, and many older buildings are adding these useful units. The system is designed so the principal can reach any portion of his school simply by pushing the proper switch. Immediately two-way communications can be established. The time of the secretary, principal, and teacher is saved through such a system. In addition to the timesaving factor, the intercommunications system makes it possible for general information, school schedules, and emergency information to be transmitted at once to any or all rooms within the building, with assurance that the information provided will be the same in all rooms. However, a problem can be created if the intercommunications system is not controlled effectively by the principal. There should be a general understanding that only approved messages are to be given on the intercom system and that these messages are to be controlled and approved by the responsible agent in the principal's office. Because there are many business matters in a school, it is advisable to set a certain time during the school day when these messages will be delivered. With the exception of calls to students and teachers for business or emergency functions, the intercom should not be available to everyone all through the day for routine business. Where a set time for announcements and business is established, both students and teachers, as well as the principal, will begin to plan the day's business communications so they will not unduly affect the curriculum and instruction program. A communications system used in this positive manner is an important adjunct to the principal's office.

Written Communications. The principal should be able to communicate information, messages, personal greetings, and routine business effectively in written form. During the school year large folders of correspondence will be accumulated. All letters should be in duplicate. Occasionally additional copies are needed to inform other interested individuals about the nature of the communications. The secretary should file the letters properly for easy reference.

The daily bulletin or circular letter is another type of written communication. Such a bulletin is usually printed in the principal's office and circulated to the various rooms. The bulletin usually contains two types of items: items to be read to students and items for faculty and staff information only. The principal must learn to convey the necessary information in a concise, readable form. These daily bulletins can be dated, numbered, and kept on file and can be used as a matter of record for substantiating statements or interpretations of policy, procedures, and instructions. Periodically, a summary of policies and information that will be used for future reference should be prepared and placed in the teachers' handbooks.

Secretarial and Clerical Assistance

Secretarial and Clerical Functions. It should be obvious from what has already been said that the principal should be provided with adequate secretarial assistance for routine jobs and tasks. Clerical assistants should perform all duties that can be effectively delegated to them. Such delegation will provide both efficiency and economy. Whenever possible, tasks that can be performed by a person on a lower salary schedule should be assigned to assistants. Secretaries and clerks normally perform such tasks as typing, filing, handling routine correspondence, making telephone communications, doing errands around the building, providing information for teachers, students, and public, handling school mail, receiving visitors, operating office machines, receiving, tabulating, and preparing reports, arranging appointments, and other such duties. In many of the larger schools the duties of secretaries and clerks also extend to handling of data-processing machines and other such technical equipment. Given proper instructions and supervision, secretaries and clerks can inventory supplies and equipment, carry out routine ordering and purchasing, issue lockers and locker keys, open lockers as needed during the day, sell tickets, and perform many other duties.

The secretary is responsible first to the principal, and he should arrange her work duties in order that all of the work that comes to the central office may be adequately handled. The secretary in turn will outline the work for assistants, either students or full-time personnel.

In addition to the work assigned to the secretary by the principal, the teachers must also be served. The teachers in carrying out their responsibilities are much like the principal as he carries out his responsibility. There are many things that lower-salaried persons can do just as efficiently as the teacher. Prime among these tasks are typing, duplication of tests and other instructional materials to be used in class, correction and tabulation of tests, and other such tasks. Most of these tasks can be adequately performed by the clerical personnel that should be available at the central office. The head secretary should receive these requests from the teachers, organize them into priorities, and distribute them to the clerical help. In large schools clerical help may be decentralized in departmental areas. In small schools where additional help is not available, the school secretary should aid the teachers directly. The principal should serve as the person for clearance and priorities if more requests are made of the secretary than her time permits.

Student Clerks. In many schools today the curriculum program is arranged so that students can receive actual secretarial and clerical practice in the central school office. Students may register for classes in office practice and work with the principal and the secretary in carrying out the duties. Such programs, when organized and planned, are very effective and serve as excellent learning experiences for students. The school also benefits in that additional secretarial and clerical help can be made available. However, the principal must not exploit the student. He must see that these students receive a range of clerical and secretarial duties during the school year so that the time they invest will be valuable to them as well as to the school. The principal and the secretary should organize the tasks into groups, and each student should be given a checklist of functions with which they should become acquainted before the year is over. The assignments of the student secretaries should be revolved at periodic intervals to assure experiences in all facets of office instruction.

Training the Secretary. Because the secretary is in the central clearinghouse of all activities for the school, she must meet all groups concerned with school operation—students, teachers, nonteaching personnel, parents, interested community members, salesmen, board members, and district office personnel. The secretary meets all these individuals in face-to-face encounter and through media such as the telephone and correspondence. The principal should make sure that the secretary is presenting a true image of the principal and the school. Too often negative first impressions received from a secretary create ill will and misunderstanding. On the other hand, the secretary may be a most effective public relations agent for the school. Because of their important role, the principal should hold periodic training meetings for the secretarial and clerical help. Especially, new secretaries must be instructed to understand how to handle the many demands made on them. Since the secretary is the receiving agent for the principal, she must be trained to be courteous in her dealings with all individuals with whom she comes in contact. She must know more than who should receive a visitor; she should make the visitor feel that he has already been well received. Frequently those persons who are irritated over some incongruity in the school program create problems in the office; the secretary, by a proper, polite referral to the principal, can handle most of these situations.

Probably more people receive their impressions through the telephone than by any other single means of communication. The school receives many calls every day, and the person who responds on the telephone should be trained in telephone courtesy so that the callers receive a pleasant, businesslike response to their messages. The secretary should never give the impression that the school staff is unwilling or too busy to discuss any item with the person making the call. If the business cannot be handled by the secretary, a proper, courteous referral is in order.

An area where most secretaries have difficulty is the area of student relationships. The secretary must be firm so that students understand that the office is not a play area, yet polite and considerate of each individual who enters.

Finally, the secretary should be trained to hear much, see much, and tell nothing. In every organization there are problems which are internal in nature and which do not necessarily affect the adequacy or the efficiency of a given program. Schools are no exception. Whenever hundreds or thousands of students congregate in a public high school, whenever teachers of varying personalities must work cooperatively together, and whenever facilities must be planned and shared as they are in school operations, there are bound to be some interpersonal clashes. In most of these instances the principal is the one person who is involved in hearing, arbitrating, and counseling with the staff members. The secretary should be instructed that these problems are to remain at the school and are not to be carried out as gossip to the community. The principal, the secretary, and all members of the staff should make sure that their interpersonal problems are not held up to public view for ridicule, gossip, and attack.

Office Facilities and Equipment

General Facilities. The facilities needed in the high school are dependent on the size of the school. In very small high schools only a single central office may be needed. Even here it would be far better to have a receiving office separate from the principal's office because of the personal nature of many conferences. In schools that are slightly larger, a receiving room or waiting room and the principal's office are the primary office facilities. In a school building that attempts to carry out most of the modern programs the facilities must be greatly enlarged from the old-style office. In addition to the principal's office and the secretary's office, there should be a waiting room connected to the secretary's office with a counter or a closed partition with an appropriate window. Other facilities might include a vault room with appropriate shelves, rooms for whatever assistant principals and administrative personnel are required, a conference room for guidance and counseling personnel, a student council room, a nursing office, boys' and girls' sick rooms, toilet rooms, a student supply center, a faculty conference and workroom, and storage rooms. Figure 15.1 shows a floor plan of the central office of a school.

These office facilities are centrally located in this award-winning senior high school at White Bear Lake, Minnesota. The school is of revolutionary

Figure 15.1

Central Office and General Floor Plan, White Bear Lake Senior High School

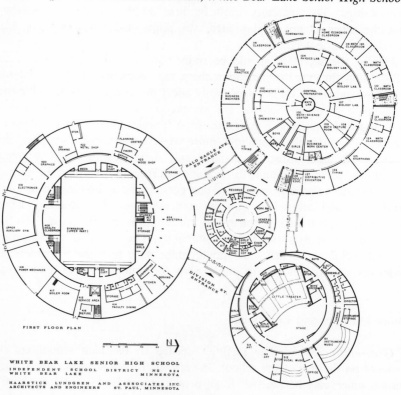

SOURCE: White Bear Lake Senior High School, White Bear Lake, Minnesota. Reprinted by permission of White Bear Lake School District and Architects Haarstick, Lundgren and Associates, Inc.

but functional design. A basement level with a second gymnasium is located under the one level shown, while a second-story library and related rooms are above the other classroom section, as shown in Figure 15.2. Figure 15.3 shows how the centrally located office serves all areas of the school. The easy accessibility of the office to patrons as well as students and teachers can also be seen as a strong feature of this unusual high school.

Figure 15.2

White Bear Lake Senior High School Floor Plan

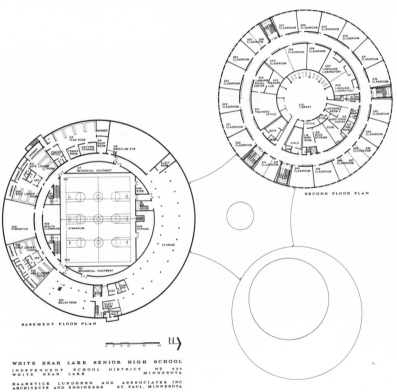

SOURCE: White Bear Lake Senior High School, White Bear Lake, Minnesota. Reprinted by permission of White Bear Lake School District and Architects Haarstick, Lundgren and Associates, Inc.

Since the facilities for each school will vary greatly depending on the size, it is suggested that the principal be involved directly in planning secondary school buildings that may be built in any community. Procedures and suggestion for such planning are given in a later chapter on planning the secondary school building.

Figure 15.3

White Bear Lake Senior High School

SOURCE: White Bear Lake Senior High School, White Bear Lake, Minnesota. Reprinted by permission of White Bear Lake School District and Architects Haarstick, Lundgren and Associates, Inc.

Office Equipment.   In addition to the general space facilities mentioned above, many equipment items should be planned for each of the rooms to make them functional in terms of the activities that are to take place. The plans should include all the types of modern office equipment for the principal, secretary, clerks, and other personnel. Besides the usual equipment large schools might include card-punching, card-sorting, and other data-processing equipment. Special consideration should be given to machines that are a major part of the production of materials for students and faculty members, such as, spirit duplicators and mimeograph and offset machines. Adequate storage units, which are necessary to file and store all the various types of forms, reports, and records, should be provided. A "work organizer," desk calendar, activity calendar, "in" and "out" basket, along with minor items are important equipment for the principal's desk. In good school planning each function that must be carried out in the school should be itemized and detailed lists of all of the equipment made. Through this type of planning, the proper facilities can be made available for the most efficient operation of the office.

Organization of Office Materials.   In addition to the general facilities, space arrangements, and office equipment, an additional element is necessary to make the office an effective and efficient operations center. A smooth office operation requires a well-organized, systematic office procedure. Fundamental to such a procedure are the organization and placement of office materials.

Perhaps more than most business offices, the public school office must have an adequate filing system to take care of the business operation, records of students, reports, and general correspondence. Much time can be wasted in locating and filing materials. To promote efficiency some districts have adopted standardized systems; however, most schools develop their own independent systems. Where such latitude is given, the principal might develop a filing system of his own. He may desire to set up the following file drawers with some of the separate sections or folders indicated below:

General school operation
    Correspondence
    Daily bulletins
    Student accounting
    Student handbook
    Teacher handbook
    Custodian's schedule
    Assignment of teachers
    Supervision assignments

Business operations
    Budgets
    Invoices
    Requisitions
    Purchase orders
    Monthly expenditure reports
    Equipment inventory
    Supply inventory

Reports
    District office—general
    Principal's annual report
    Annual financial report
    State department reports
    Regional accrediting reports

High school activities
    School clubs and organizations
    District activities association
    Regional activities association
    State activities association
    Eligibility lists
    Activity schedules

Student records
    Permanent records
    Cumulative records
    Daily register

Summary

The central administration offices are the center of all school functions. All administrative decisions are centered here. It is through the office that teachers and students receive communications, instructions, and information necessary for the ongoing school program. Students must report here for proper clearance regarding absences from school. Parents and community citizens call at the office for whatever business they may have with the school. The principal is the director of all these central functions, and he must organize the office so that it will be efficient and effective.

A well-organized office should appear, to the casual visitor, as if no one were really running it. By such planning, all details would have been worked into an efficient, smooth-functioning, organizational pattern. The goal for promoting such an efficient office procedure is to allow the principal more time for the curriculum and instructional phase of his school program. Authorities and principals alike recommend that the amount of time spent in office routine should be reduced and the amount of time spent in curriculum and instruction increased. The principal must constantly be working to find ways by which he may spend less time on routine and thereby provide more time for the truly important functions of the secondary schools. The general functions that are performed in the office are usually as follows: Communicating face to face in individual and group conferences through telephone calls and intercom; communicating through written media, such as correspondence and bulletins; typing materials, such as records, reports, and curriculum and instructional materials; processing business requisitions for supplies and equipment; carrying out the attendance program; and deciding on daily schedule and other routine matters of the school.

The principal should have an efficient secretary and other clerical assistants as needed so that all the routine functions can be promoted efficiently. The secretary and clerk would perform such tasks as typing; filing; handling routine correspondence; making telephone communications; doing errands around the building; providing information for teachers, students, and public; handling school mail; receiving visitors; operating machines; receiving and tabulating material for reports; arranging appointments; and performing other such duties as assigned by the principal. Many schools have student secretaries or clerks who register for courses in office practice as part of their curriculum work. Student secretaries spend a block of time in the office learning the required tasks and duties of the secretary. These students should be given a good, rich office practice program. The students would come under the jurisdiction of the secretary. Both the secretary and the clerks have a major responsibility in creating good will and understanding on behalf of the principal and the school generally. All first impressions are generally gathered from telephone conversations or the first face-to-face greetings that are part of the school reception. It is very important that the secretary leave a favorable impression on all callers. The secretary also has the responsibility to see that problems of school concern are not broadcast to the community and that matters of private, personal nature are held in the strictest confidence.

The principal will spend most of his routine office time in the area of communications either oral or written. Therefore, he should be an effective speaker. He should be able to present ideas clearly, effectively, and concisely. He should be a sympathetic listener but firm in administering school policy.

The office facilities and equipment should be planned for the size of the school and for the functions that will be performed in the school. The modern school should allow for office space for the principal, waiting room, secretarial or clerical room, bookstore, vault, student council, administrative assistant and counseling personnel, school nurse, sick rooms, and other general administrative offices. The office should be equipped with the latest and most modern business machines so that it can operate efficiently and effectively.

SUGGESTED PROJECTS AND ACTIVITIES

1. Spend a morning or part of the morning in an office of a high school and observe and tabulate the various functions that take place during that time. Indicate the number of persons who appear, the nature of their requests, and the procedure used to handle their requests.
2. Collect a folder of all the forms used in the central office of a school.
3. Role-play a situation in which the principal is instructing the secretary in the proper procedure for using the telephone as the receiving agent of the school.
4. Visit a business supply house and determine the types of office equipment that might be added to the school office to promote greater efficiency in operation.
5. Make a list of all the functions you believe a principal could effectively delegate to (1) a secretary, (2) other clerical assistants, (3) vice-principals, (4) attendance counselors, (5) school nurse, (6) custodians.
6. Plan a curriculum program for student secretaries in which a student would have opportunity to participate in the full range of responsibilities and duties that would be part of the school office. Work out a plan whereby curriculum units with rotation time periods are established.

7. Review the educational specifications for the central administration offices of a newly planned or completed high school.

REVIEW AND DISCUSSION QUESTIONS

1. What is the high school principal's major responsibility in regard to the functions that take place in the central administration office?
2. Why do principals spend more time in the office than either the principals or authorities recommend?
3. Name some specific ways in which a principal might find more time to spend on curriculum and instruction as a result of more efficient organization of his office staff.
4. Which is the most important function for the principal in his communication pattern—face-to-face communications or written communications? Describe and explain.
5. What functions could a principal most effectively delegate to a vice-principal and other members of his staff?
6. What duties could be assigned to a secretary or a clerk?
7. How could a principal exploit the use of student secretaries?
8. What must the principal do to assure the student secretary that she will receive meaningful experiences?
9. What are some important suggestions for a secretary?
10. What procedures should be used to plan the central administrative office in the secondary school?

SELECTED BIBLIOGRAPHY

Anderson, Lester W., and Lauren A. Van Dyke. *Secondary School Administration*. Boston: Houghton Mifflin Co., 1963.

Crew, A. B. "Secretarial Work Experiences Within the School," *Bulletin of N.A.S.S.P.*, March 1960, pp. 143–49.

Douglass, Harl R. *Modern Administration of Secondary Schools*, 2nd ed. Boston: Ginn and Company, 1963.

Fitch, M. "Developing a Student Secretary Program," *Education*, March 1949, pp. 17–18.

Jacobsen, Paul B., William C. Reavis, and James D. Logsdon. *The Effective School Principal*. Englewood Cliffs, N.J.: Prentice-Hall Company, 1963.

McCleary, Lloyd E., and Stephen P. Hencley. *Secondary School Administration: Theoretical Bases of Professional Practice*. New York: Dodd, Mead and Company, 1965.

Yeager, William A. *Administration of the Non-instructional Personnel and Services*. New York: Harper and Brothers, 1959.

CHAPTER **16**

Administration of
Auxiliary Services

In this fast-changing society, in which the school plays a significant role, there are many services expected of the school and its leaders. The principal must provide leadership in many areas that are auxiliary in nature to the primary purpose for which the school was organized. In carrying out the roles expected of him, the principal sometimes sees himself as a cross between a custodian, a bus driver, a cook, a nurse, a fire marshal, a social worker, a nursing mother, and a civil defense officer. He is expected to *know all* about these services, *see all* areas where correction is needed, and *tell all* that is needed to parents, school personnel, civil officers, child guidance clinics, and mental health associations.

The administration of auxiliary services involves the library and instructional materials center, the school plant, the school health and safety programs, the school lunch program, and the transportation program. Although the principal shares the responsibilities of these services with the superintendent and the supervisors in the district office, the principal does have a function that must be carried out in these areas in order to promote the efficient operation of the school. In carrying out his responsibilities in these areas the principal must work with the school lunch personnel, bus drivers, custodians, nurses, civil defense officials, fire marshals, and many other individuals within the school system and throughout the community generally. The degree to which these services function smoothly and operate efficiently will influence the degree to which the

393

curriculum and instructional phase of the high school program can adequately be carried out.

Administration of the Library (Instructional Materials Center)

The Library—A Center of Learning. The importance of the library, or the instructional materials center, as it is called in many modern secondary schools, has increased markedly in the past decade. The emphasis given to critical thinking, creativity, continuous progress, individualized instruction, independent study, experimentation, and the discovery approach to teaching has stimulated a renewed need for improved library services. The importance of the library to the continuous progress plan where students progress at their own rate is indicated by the following statement:

> The instructional materials center is essential to the CP school because a wide variety of materials are needed by different students at different times and they must be kept in a convenient central location. Our IMC has virtually the same definition as that given in AASL *Standards for School Library Programs,* and it embodies almost every recommendation of the *Standards.* Indeed, it adds others, for it contains not only all the materials found in good school libraries, but the equipment and supplies offered in audio-visual centers, and the materials being used in the curriculum laboratories that are sprinkled across the nation. It also provides space and guidance for using these materials.[1]

The Role of the Principal. The libraries and the library programs have long been neglected by school administrators.[2] A study of libraries in the junior high schools of the 50 states showed no evidence of planning for the unique needs of junior high school libraries.[3] In this period of educational change, when the new programs call for extensive library use, the principal must be oriented to both the functions and the needs of the library. His responsibilities are to provide a well-trained staff, adequate physical facilities, and an appropriate budget of books, magazines, supplies, and materials, to assist in the development of policies, and to encourage faculty and students to make maximum use of all library services.

In the determination of adequate standards for the library, the principal

---

[1] June Berry, "The IMC in the Continuous Progress School," *School Library Journal,* November 1964, pp. 25–28.

[2] Emily A. Copeland and Leander J. Shaw, "The Library as Presented in Selected Textbooks of Secondary School Administration and Supervision," *Bulletin of N.A.S.S.P.,* March 1957, pp. 81–92. National Education Association, Research Division, "Library Services," *Research Bulletin,* October 1958, pp. 76–81.

[3] Silvanus H. Sisson, "Planning the Junior High School Library Program," *Bulletin of N.A.S.S.P.,* February 1962, pp. 197–98.

should look beyond the minimum standards of his accreditation association to those of the American Library Association.

Providing a Well-trained Staff. The librarians perform many functions. They work with students and teachers in implementing the instructional program; they help guide the learning of students; they order, catalogue, file and provide students and teachers with instructional and resource materials and equipment as needed and desired; and they provide a learning environment where creativity, critical analysis, and continuous progress can take place. The librarian is both a teacher and a technician. The minimum qualifications, as set forth in the *Evaluative Criteria,* are as follows:

1. Broad general background equivalent to the baccalaureate degree.
2. Professional courses in education which are required for a certificate.
3. Successful teaching experience or an internship in an organized program.
4. Advanced preparation in such fields as reading instruction, curriculum development, mass communication, guidance services and research.[4]

The size of the school will determine in large part the size of the library staff. The American Library Association recommends the following as basic standards: One librarian for each 300 students or major fraction thereof up to 900 students and an additional librarian for each 400 students or major fraction thereof for enrollments over 900. The basic standard is increased by 25 per cent if the librarian has partial responsibility for audiovisual aids and by 50 per cent if the librarian assumes full responsibility.[5]

In addition to the regular staff, student assistants may be trained in library services and receive credit for such experiences. Under a qualified librarian, the student receives excellent training, and the school benefits from the student's services.

Providing Adequate Budget. Next to selecting qualified personnel, the securing of an adequate library budget is the principal's most important function relating to library services. The following standards of the American Library Association will serve as a guide to the principal:

1. $1,000 to $1,500 for library books in schools with 200–249 students. Four dollars to six dollars per student for schools over 250 enrollments.

[4] National Study of Secondary School Evaluation, *Evaluative Criteria* (Washington, D.C.: The Study, 1960), p. 259.
[5] American Library Association, *Standards for School Libraries* (Chicago: The Association, 1960), pp. 54–55.

2. Additional funds for reference books, dictionaries, magazines, news-papers, pamphlets and repair materials.

3. $200 to $800 for a professional collection for the faculty.

4. Not less than 1 per cent of the total per pupil instructional cost for the acquisition of audio-visual materials.[6]

The budget standards recommended by the American Library Associa-tion are higher than those of the accreditation associations. However, if the total number of volumes recommended by the American Library As-sociation were reached, a reduction in budget might be considered. The recommended standards, exclusive of reference books, pamphlets, news-papers, etc., are as follows:[7]

Enrollments	Books	Magazines
200 or less	6,000	10–15 titles
200–999	6,000–10,000	
1,000 or more	10 books per student	120 titles

Providing Adequate Facilities. The size of the library will depend on the philosophy of the district and school, the size of the school, and the types of programs envisioned. In the new programs such as the nongraded, multiphase Melbourne High School, the library is advertised as "bigger than the gym."[8] In the Continuous Progress Program at the Brigham Young Laboratory School, there exists a library, a branch instructional materials center, and an area of individual carrels, or study stations.[9]

Each school may need to adapt the size and number of facilities to its own needs. However, some of the following basic areas are needed: read-ing and circulation area, book storage area, magazine area, workroom, conference rooms, typing room, listening room, office, audiovisual storage area, materials storage area, and individual carrels.

Administration of the School Plant

The Principal's Role.[10] Among the many responsibilities that the board of education and the superintendent turn over to the principal is that of supervising and maintaining the school plant. This does not mean that the principal is a highly paid custodian. Nor does it mean that in districts

[6] *Ibid.*, p. 25.

[7] *Ibid.*, p. 25.

[8] Melbourne High School, Melbourne, Florida.

[9] Brigham Young Laboratory School, Provo, Utah. Also June Berry, *op. cit.*, pp. 25–28.

[10] For additional background and more technical treatment the student is referred to the following source: Emery Stoops and M. L. Rafferty, Jr., *Practices and Trends in School Administration* (New York: Ginn and Company, 1961), pp. 244–76.

where there is an efficient supervisory maintenance staff at the central office, the principal supersedes the district building-and-grounds supervisor. The principal is given the responsibility of looking after the building and its care is entrusted to him. The role of the principal in honoring this responsibility is one of scheduling activities within the building, planning the total utilization of the building, and working with the custodian to maintain the building in the best possible manner. The principal, of course, cannot perform all these duties. In addition to the custodians who will be on duty, the principal will have other staff members who will be involved in helping to care for the building. All the teachers have as their responsibilities both instructing and helping to preserve the equipment, supplies, and the building itself. In the larger schools an assistant principal will assume major responsibilities in scheduling and looking after the building. The principal should see that a planned program of plant management, by all who use and who have responsibility for use of the building, is set forth and properly administered.

One of the more consistent problems of a principal is student use of the physical plant. Students can be very careless unless they have pride in the building. Some new buildings appear to be many years old, while there are many old buildings that are attractive. The manner in which the building is maintained is usually consistent with the efforts of the principal to create an attitude of pride in the school and its traditions. A major responsibility of the principal is to help students feel the pride that can come from a building that is clean, neat, and attractive.

Utilization of the Building. In recent years much has been written and said about the utilization of our public school buildings. Great criticism has come because the buildings are in operation for only nine months of the year, five days of the week, and for a limited number of hours (six or eight) per day. Some of this criticism is true and some of it arises from the organizational pattern of schools. Yet much of the criticism is unwarranted.

The principal has the responsibility of defining the usability and utilization of his building, within the policy and organizational structure set by the board of education. To more fully take advantage of the opportunities that the building presents, the principal should see that the building is utilized to its maximum during the school year, that proper summer school courses are maintained, and that the community as well as private groups has an opportunity to schedule the building and use it within the limits that have been defined by the board of education.

Effective Building Utilization During the School Year. In an age when there is a demand for great numbers of new public high schools to take care of the increasing enrollment, principals should see that buildings under their jurisdiction receive maximum utilization. Maximum utilization should especially be obtained in communities that are contemplating new buildings and in communities in which population explosions or anticipated population explosions will require the construction of new facilities. There are principals who indicate they have adequate space for all the activities that are to be carried on within the building. A more common complaint, however, is that the school building is crowded and that more space and a new building are needed. Certainly at different times during the day a school building will have an extremely high utilization.

Part of the plan for more efficient operation comes through planned scheduling of students within the classrooms and of classroom facilities. In the discussion on scheduling in an earlier chapter a room utilization form was discussed. The principal should see that each room is scheduled on a master sheet. By glancing at the master schedule the principal can quickly determine what rooms are in use at any given time of day. He can also see the number of students who are using the facilities at any given time. Proper scheduling of classes as shown earlier along with a consistent study of master plan room utilization would aid the principal in scheduling his classes to a greater advantage. It should not be inferred that the curriculum program must fit into any facilities that might be available. The program should be designed first and the facilities scheduled to the program. The following chapter is concerned wholly with planning of facilities.

There are many times when the only difference between whether a class is scheduled at one hour or an alternate hour is simply a matter of careful planning. The program is not affected by such changes. One of the principal's earliest tasks is to determine the number of student stations that can be placed within any given room. Through such a study the principal will know when classes have reached the maximum capacity and when there is still room for "one more student." When principals make an intensive study of the student space utilization, most schools that claim to be overcrowded can indeed house more students. The principal should exhaust every means under his direction to more adequately balance loads and to house the increasing student enrollments. Some of the special considerations that the principal may have overlooked in previous utilizations would be the more adequate use of the auditorium, the cafeteria, the little theater, classrooms in connection with shop facilities, and other similar facilities.

Community Utilization of School Facilities. The community school has long been a goal in educational philosophy. Too many school systems are still far from achieving this goal. In some communities the school is more like a castle with a moat and a drawbridge around it. The drawbridge is down at nine o'clock in the morning to permit the students to enter, and it is lowered again at four in the afternoon for them to depart. After four o'clock the school remains isolated until nine the next morning. Such a concept of school building utilization is archaic and wasteful. The school should be used as much as possible by the community. The community should have access to auditoriums, gyms, lunchrooms, libraries, typing rooms, classrooms, and other facilities. There are many organizations and agencies within the community that are educational in nature. There are many other civic and community organizational groups that could profit by using school facilities. The school should be available to young and old as long as distinct policies of supervision are maintained.

Rental Policies for School Facilities. The use of the school by community organizations is determined in large part by board policy. The principal should acquaint himself with such policy and see that proper procedures are developed to carry out the policy. One major aspect of board policy involves financial consideration for use of the facilities. There is no uniformity from state to state or district to district concerning board policy in this matter. Generally, boards assume that there should be a charge, depending on the activity and the nature of the request. For example, in response to requests made by other educational agencies in the community in which fees are not charged nor is profit anticipated, boards often permit the utilization of the building without cost or for cost of custodial services only. On the other hand, if these activities involve extensive use of lights and special equipment, such as the gyms and the sewing and cooking rooms, a minimum fee is charged per hour or per night. Such a fee usually takes care of the actual costs of operating the building for the given activity. A third consideration is usually involved when some outside agency desires the use of the building for profit making. Under these conditions the building is often rented at a much higher rate but one that is still reasonable and in keeping with charges for such facilities in other places within the community or nearby communities. Whatever the financial policy of the board, the principal must carry out the policy fairly and equitably for all groups, whether they be political, religious, racial, or civic.

Scheduling of Plant Facilities. During the school day and after school hours the school plant will be used by many school and community groups. Scheduling becomes a major concern of the principal. The facilities must be properly scheduled so that all groups may know that when they have an activity scheduled, their activity will not be spoiled by other groups superimposing themselves in the facilities. Either the principal, his clerk, the assistant principal, or some designated person within the office should be responsible for scheduling the school facilities, and all requests should be channeled through this one responsible person. Some policy priorities should be established. First, it should be recognized that major school events have first priority. Therefore, dates for these events should be set early in the year and placed on the calendar. Such events might well include: graduation, state and regional activities, divisional athletic meets, and other interschool activities. Second, the intraschool program should be given the next consideration. This schedule should center around the student-body officers and their planned activities for the year. All classes and clubs should review their programs and calendar them on the master schedule. Third, once a school has scheduled all its known activities, then the building should be available to the community at large for the opportunity to schedule their events. If these priorities are followed, the school facilities will be made available first to the students and the educational program and then to the community at large.

Scheduling and the Community Calendar. In many communities a community calendar is maintained. Such a calendar is an attempt by members representing the total community to schedule all the activities of major import through a centralized agency. The purpose of the community calendar is similar to that of the high school calendar. Where a community calendar is maintained, the school should cooperate with the community and make arrangements whereby the school activities can be placed on the calendar early. Such action will avoid serious conflict at a later date with the major activities in the community. There are major functions held in the school in which the public would participate and that should take precedence over any other community activity. Therefore, the community calendar can and should aid and serve both the school and the community in a more organized manner of scheduling the total activities within the school and community.

Building Use and Summer Programs. The demands for more and better education are bringing major changes in building utilization during the summer period.

The demand for more and better education is being found in the lengthened school year. Many states and districts have increased the traditional operational year by at least ten school days, or one half a month. A second way in which the building has received greater summer use is in the increased number of summer programs. The traditional summer music, agriculture, and home economics programs have been extended to include remedial and enrichment courses in nearly every subject area. A third attempt to provide greater building utilization is found in the year-round school programs in which the buildings would be used to their maximum capacity all year. The arguments for such a program are as follows:

1. The school plant already exists, fully equipped and ready to use.
2. The overhead costs of administration continue to be approximately the same in many communities whether the schools are open or closed during the summer months.
3. Fixed charges such as insurance, interest, and capital outlay costs remain fairly constant whether the schools are in operation or shut down.
4. The teaching staff—the community's most important educational asset—is, in considerable measure, already mobilized.
5. A large percentage of the children of school age, particularly in towns and cities, is left without any constructive developmental programs during the three summer months.[11]

The Custodian's Role.   The custodian is the principal's right-hand man in school plant management and should be accorded all the dignity and recognition that can be given to a person who plays such a vital role in creating the proper atmosphere for school instruction. The position of a custodian in most school systems is recognized as one of major importance. He should no longer be considered and talked about as the janitor. The principal should make every effort to dignify his position along with that of the nonprofessional staff. Efforts should be made to encourage the custodian to belong to his associations. There is a national association of engineers and custodians. There is also a state association for these individuals. In most districts the custodians belong to local associations just as teachers belong to their professional affiliations. In attempts to provide more dignity for the custodians, some districts have provided and helped to adopt a code of ethics, systematic procedure of work instructions, and suggestions for good relationships with other people. Some districts have provided uniforms as well as other encouragements to upgrade the appearance of the custodian. In many districts pension and retirement benefits have been provided.

The custodian's main function in the school is to keep the building clean, repaired, and preserved in good state. He is often responsible for the safety and health of students and teachers. Reeder lists five major functions of the custodian:

1. Seen in the light of the modern school's place as a community and civic center, the custodian becomes more than a servant of the teachers

---

[11] American Association of School Administrators, *Year-Round School*. (Washington, D.C.: The Association, 1960), p. 3. Reprinted by permission of the American Association of School Administrators.

and pupils; he is a servant of the whole community. Often he is deputized by the civil authorities to enable him to preserve the peace at public functions held on the school grounds.

2. He is a major user of expensive supplies and equipment. He often helps to select the items which he uses in his daily work, and must know such pertinent facts as price and quality.

3. He largely determines the housekeeping standards of the school building, and thus sets the tone of the entire school program, insofar as physical environment is concerned.

4. He has the responsibility for keeping the school building in such condition that the health and safety of the pupils and teachers will not be placed in jeopardy.

5. He exerts a great moral and educational influence upon the children of the school with whom he comes in daily contact.[12]

Since the principal is given the responsibility of maintaining the school plant, the custodian should come under his jurisdiction in the same manner that the professional staff would come under his direction. The principal should organize the custodian's work schedule for the best possible utility. The principal should have a friendly relationship with him and frequently compliment him on his good work. The custodian does have a responsibility to his building-and-grounds supervisor at the district level and receives much of his instruction through this office. However, it should be the principal's responsibility to see that there is no misunderstanding regarding the function of the custodian in his building and that a proper working relationship exists with the building-and-grounds supervisor. The custodian should not be placed in the embarrassing position of having two bosses giving contrary instructions.

The following suggestions will aid the principal in his relationships with his custodians:

1. Refer to them as custodians or building engineers rather than janitors. Address them with respect and encourage teachers to do so.

2. Develop with them a reasonable work schedule for the building so that all facilities will receive regular cleaning.

3. With their help, develop a division of labor that is efficient and at the same time satisfactory to them.

4. Provide an atmosphere and working relationship so that two-way communication exists. Welcome ideas and suggestions for improvement of the building and school operations.

5. Order the work of the custodian so that all work orders are routed through principals. Teachers should especially be informed of this routing so that the custodian will not have a "boss in every room." The principal,

---

[12] W. G. Reeder, *Fundamentals of Public School Administration*, 4th ed. (New York: The Macmillan Company, 1958), pp. 249–51.

with the head custodian, should determine the order of priority for all repair and emergency needs.

6. Cultivate in the custodians a feeling of pride in their work. Compliment them on jobs well done. Help them understand the wholesome relationship between physical plant and teaching.

School Building Inspection. Although the custodian has the primary responsibility for maintaining the school plant and seeing that repairs and replacements are in order, the school principal must supervise the custodian's work. Therefore, it is important to the principal to know the physical state of the building at all times. In most cases the principal will be aware of the condition of the building because of his frequent trips to different parts of the school plant for various reasons in the course of his daily duties. However, there are many things that will escape his attention unless he periodically plans into his schedule a building and maintenance evaluation. Periodically during the year, the principal and the custodian should tour the school plant and make note of the repair items, both small and great, that should be handled. Those items which are routine in nature should be listed and turned over to the custodian for his care. Other items of more serious consequence may require financial considerations or additional labor far beyond that which is in the budget or which the custodian can provide. The principal should list these and make proper recommendations to the district office for such maintenance care as is needed. If the item is of major extent, the principal should plan to have it repaired during the summer months and therefore may need to place it in the district budget.

It is highly important that most irregularities and repairs be handled as soon as possible. The students will maintain greater pride in their building, and therefore exercise greater care, when the building is in good repair and when they can observe the well-kept appearance. Such minor things as writing on desks and walls should be corrected immediately to discourage further extension of such action.

Whenever breakage is involved, items should be repaired at once. If students are responsible for damage, and payment by the student is requested, the item should be repaired or replaced without loss of time. In the meantime proper procedures may be initiated to assure financial restitution.

Administration of Health and Safety Programs

Good physical health has always been done of the important goals of American public education. During certain periods of early colonial history, "beating the devil" out of children was used for their spiritual development. Such a practice has long been outlawed in the United States, and the emphasis has now been toward creating better health and a better physical environment for the learning process. The school has introduced programs of physical education and health, school health services, and programs of mental health, and in many other ways has worked to promote better health programs in the American schools.

The principal is concerned with school health because all the students are under his jurisdiction from six to eight hours a day. It is obvious that illnesses and accidents will arise. The principal should understand how these problem occasions should be handled.

School Health Services. The school health services have been established (1) to determine the health status of students, (2) to apprise parents regarding the findings of health examinations and other health evaluations, (3) to encourage the correction of remedial defects, (4) to aid in the development of programs for handicapped children, (5) to prevent and control disease, and (6) to provide emergency care for the sick and injured.[13] The principal must assume responsibility for the general supervision of these services in his school. The district may employ or make arrangements for others to actually carry out the program, such as nurses, hearing specialists, eye specialists, physicians, psychologists, and psychiatrists.

School Examinations. In order to be informed properly of the general health of students, most school districts require a physical examination for students. These physical examinations are often conducted by the school physician when the district has employed such a person.

In other districts a cooperative arrangement is made with the community physicians. Special reduced rates for students are given for the school physical examination, and a report is sent to the school and to the student's parents. Many problems that are unknown to the student and his parents are discovered from these examinations. The correction of the defects that are found is usually started immediately.

Where school examinations are required, the school district usually schedules them at periodic intervals, such as, kindergarten, grade three, grade seven, and grade eleven. There are some districts that require an examination every year.

In addition to the general examination given by a physician, other specific examinations are conducted by the school system. Such examina-

---

[13] National Education Association, National Association of Secondary-School Principals, *Administration of Health, Physical Education and Recreation Programs in Secondary Schools*. Bulletin 195 (Washington, D.C.: The Association, 1953), p. 3.

tions might include (1) an eye examination, (2) a hearing examination, and (3) a dental examination. Many school districts have the personnel and facilities to conduct all of these examinations, while in other districts examinations are held in cooperation with the local community agencies.

When defects, diseases, or other weaknesses are found through these examinations, a written report is usually mailed to the home of the student in whom the defect was discovered and the parents are encouraged to consult their physician. The school usually desires to know that the action recommended by the doctor was taken; therefore, some form of reporting system is usually established. Such a form is shown in Figure 16.1.

Figure 16.1

Health Examination Report to Parents

HEALTH EXAMINATION REPORT TO PARENTS

Dear _____

    Recently _____ was given a school _____
examination. The examination indicated:

        ☐ There seemed to be no problems
        ☐ There may be a problem as described below:

_____

_____

_____

    We feel that in the interest of the health of your son–daughter you will want to
investigate the matter further.   So that we can also be of help would you report to
us what action you have taken.

                         _____
                            Principal

Teacher Referrals. In addition to the examinations that are given to students, the teachers, school nurses, and other educators often are able to discover health problems of students. Typical examples of a teacher discovering student health problems might be: a teacher discovers that a student is holding a book too close to his eyes, a girl refuses to shower in the physical education program, a student is flushed and seemingly feverish, and a student does not respond to questions raised by teachers or other students. In all these examples the teacher makes a referral to the appropriate correcting agency. In most school systems this referral is channeled to the school nurse assigned to the school. The school nurse makes a more thorough investigation, administers whatever temporary measures are required, and refers the student to the other health agencies. The principal must see that this system of referrals is properly organized and functions smoothly. A referral form is often used both as a procedural technique and as a matter of record when such defects, diseases, or weaknesses are discovered. Figure 16.2 is a typical referral form used for these purposes.

Figure 16.2

Teacher's Referral to the Public Health Nurse

TEACHER'S REFERRAL TO THE PUBLIC HEALTH NURSE

Student's Name _____ School _____ Grade _____

Address _____ Parent _____ Phone _____

Date of referral: _____

Reason for referral:

_____

_____

_____

Teacher: _____

Date of report: _____

Nurse's report:

_____

_____

_____

School Sick Room. Because students are subject to illness while they are in school as well as while they are in their homes, it is necessary to provide a sick room. A sick room is a temporary location where emergency first aid can be given and where students can be housed while other arrangements are made. In many communities parents can call at the school and pick up the student who becomes ill during the school day. However, parents are not always available, and in many of the rural and outlying communities, bus transportation is a major problem. The availability of a school sick room is of paramount importance.

The sick room should be located where supervision can be easily maintained. Therefore, it is usually placed within the health service suite, which is usually within the administration portion of the building. The school nurse facilities are located within easy access of the sick room.

Administering First Aid. The school should not look upon itself as the students' physician but should be in a position to administer first aid when such action is required. In addition to the school nurse, the physical education directors are usually qualified to provide a limited amount of first aid. Most minor accidents occur in the school corridors and during the physical education and intramural activities. When these accidents do occur, the student should be referred to the school nurse, to the home, or to the physician. In case of serious accidents, the principal should require an accident report from the teacher to protect both the teacher and the principal against the event of further legal action.

Immunization. As part of the general health program, one of the most frequently used programs of school health, the immunization against contagious diseases, is included in almost all school programs. Immunization clinics are normally conducted in cooperation with the local medical associations, and usually the county physician or his representative is present during the immunization periods. The school should require a consent form to be signed by the parents for student participation in the immunization. Such a consent form assures the principal that the parents desire to have their children participate in the immunization program. The consent form can also be used as a written record in situations where student reactions to the immunization take place. An immunization consent form is shown in Figure 16.3.

Mental Health Service. The importance of good mental health cannot be overestimated in the promotion of a sound school health program. In recent years state and local mental health associations have been increasing. The principal should cooperate with these associations. Within the school, the principal will usually have counseling services. Counselors should be available to students who desire to discuss special personal problems. In addition to the counselor, the district psychologist and psychiatrist may be available. Where districts do not have these services, proper referrals to parents of appropriate community agencies should be utilized.

Accidents and Emergencies. Just as illness can be expected in the school, so can accidents and other emergencies. The school principal is responsible for the total welfare of the student in the school and as such should be prepared for any emergency that arises. Such emergencies will

Figure 16.3

Immunization Consent Form

IMMUNIZATION CONSENT FORM

Student's Name _____ Grade _____ Date _____

Home Room Teacher _____ School _____

Immunization clinics are being scheduled for high school students. Please check the immunizations you need, have your parents sign this form and return it to your home room teacher at once.

☐ ☐ ☐   Typhoid Series   Series of three shots one week apart.
                  $1.00   Booster one year after series and then
☐   Typhoid Booster   every 2 – 3 years.
                  $ .50

☐ ☐   D.T. Series   Series of 2 shots 4 weeks apart. Booster
                  $1.00   every 4 years following D.P.T. or 1 year
☐   D.T. Booster   after series, then every 4 years for any
                  $ .75   one 8 years and over.

☐ ☐   Tetanus Series   Tetanus series is not necessary if D.P.T.
                  $1.00   or D.T. series have been taken and boosters
☐   Tetanus Booster   given at proper intervals. Tetanus should
                  $ .75   be given following injury.

☐ ☐ ☐   Polio Series   Series of 3 shots 4 weeks apart, followed
                  $1.00 (per shot)   by a 4th shot 4 – 8 months later. A booster
☐   Polio Booster   1 year after the 4th shot then every 2 years.
                  $1.00

☐   Smallpox   Everyone should have a smallpox vaccination
                  $ .50   every 5 – 6 years.

Parent's Signature _____ Phone _____

It is wise to carry a record of your immunizations, especially tetanus, with you at all times. If you have a record, bring it to the clinic and have it kept up to date.

(Do not write below this line)

	B	1	2	3	Paid
Typhoid					
D.T.					
Tetanus					
Polio					
Smallpox					

extend from minor types, such as sprained ankles and wrists, to serious types, involving both mental as well as physical health, such as attempted suicide. The principal has three major responsibilities. First, it is his responsibility to instruct the teachers about the procedure to follow when

Figure 16.4

Accident Report

ACCIDENT REPORT

Date _____

Name _____ Grade _____

Parent's Name _____ Address _____

Phone _____

Accident Details:

Time accident occured: _____

Place accident occured: _____

Cause of accident: _____

Type of accident: _____

    Were parents notified? _____

    Was student taken to doctor? _____

    Other information _____

_____

_____

                    Person reporting accident _____

Subsequent action of principal and other personnel _____

_____

_____

_____

_____

---

accidents occur. Such procedure would involve providing immediate care of the student, administering first aid if necessary, and making proper referrals to the school health authorities. The principal must also instruct the teachers about their legal responsibilities. He must provide adequate instruction concerning supervision of activities. Second, when an accident occurs, the principal should see that an accident report is completed and filed for future use. Figure 16.4 is an example of a typical accident report form. The third responsibility of the principal is to see that the student is referred for the proper medical treatment. In this regard, the principal must have some record that tells who is the student's attending physician. The home should be contacted whenever possible prior to taking the student to a physician for medical treatment.

Fire and Emergency Evacuation. Seldom does a principal have a fire in his building or the need to use emergency evacuation procedures, but the possibility is always present. The principal cannot gamble with the lives of students. Therefore, he must make plans for emergency evacuation of the school building. The plans should be detailed enough so that adequate instruction can be given to students about emergency evacuation regardless of their location within the school at the time of the emergency. Periodic fire or emergency drills should be scheduled so that the signal or alarm given will immediately set into motion a rapid evacuation of all students.

Civil Defense. Civil defense is planning for coordinated use of existing governmental services and community resources in periods of emergency. Civil defense is based on the principle of self-protection extended to include groups and communities. To be effective, advanced planning at local, state, and national governmental levels is necessary. A key element of civil defense planning for a nuclear age is the provision of shelters to protect people from radioactive fallout.

The school's immediate civil defense concern is to plan for the safety and sheltering of students in an emergency and to provide for their care until they can return home. In the event of a disaster, the school facilities and personnel might also be called upon to provide emergency shelter and care for adults as well as the students. No single plan can be established for all schools. Each school district and each school within the district must devise its own plan. The school plan must be specific enough to provide for immediate action yet flexible enough to allow for adjustments as unexpected situations arise.

The National Education Association, in a pamphlet entitled, *You and*

Civil Defense—A Guide for Teachers, Administrators, and School Board Members, makes the following specific suggestions:

TEACHER

Helping to plan your own school's defense program

Participating in the Civil Defense Adult Education Program of the U.S. Office of Education

Participating in the university or college extension program

Preparing yourself in the skills of administering first aid and in other skills needed to cope with an emergency or disaster

Serving on a faculty committee to plan for civil defense instruction in appropriate parts of the curriculum

Putting to use the knowledge of civil defense you have acquired, by familiarizing pupils and parents with the procedures to follow in event of an emergency or disaster

Providing practice for pupils in safety and emergency procedures

PRINCIPAL

Initiating and supervising your own school's civil defense planning

Assigning staff responsibilities for civil defense

Obtaining civil defense materials for distribution in the school

Maintaining regular evaluation of the operational readiness of your civil defense plans and procedures

Keeping parents informed of current school civil defense plans

SUPERINTENDENT

Assisting the board of education in developing civil defense policies

Administering, coordinating, and evaluating the school system's civil defense program

Organizing needed curriculum planning to include civil defense teachings

Establishing an in-service civil defense training program for teachers and for other school personnel

SCHOOL BOARD MEMBER

Issuing a clear statement of policy regarding school-community cooperation in civil defense

Authorizing the superintendent to delegate staff responsibility for civil defense

Entering into shelter-licensing agreements through local civil defense officials.[14]

In Figure 16.5 a suggested organization plan for civil defense is presented.

[14] National Education Association, *You and Civil Defense* (Washington, D.C.: The Association, 1963). Reprinted by permission of the National Education Association.

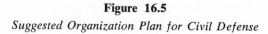

Figure 16.5

Suggested Organization Plan for Civil Defense

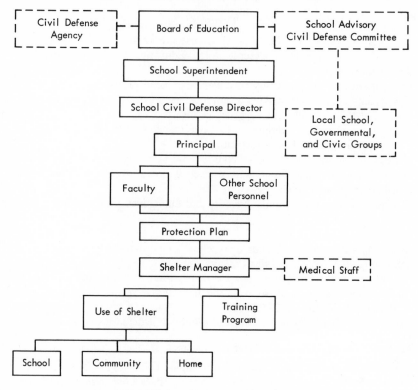

SOURCE: National Education Association, *You and Civil Defense* (Washington, D.C.: The Association, 1963). Reprinted by permission of the National Education Association.

Administration of School Lunch Services

Although school cafeterias have been in existence for many years and extend back to nearly 1853, the school lunch program as it is now known is primarily a product of recent vintage. In this program a well-balanced diet is served to the student at approximately one half the cost of the lunch. The remaining portion of the cost is paid for by local, state, and federal funds. Most of the federal funds come from surplus food programs. One has only to participate in a sack lunch and then participate in the hot lunch program to recognize both the nutritional as well as the educational advantages of such a program. However, the program is not without its problems, especially for the principal who is in the position of administering the school lunch program within the school. His problems are several. First, he must adequately supervise the personnel who prepare the lunch, the school lunch workers. He must work with the school lunch manager and with other help that is provided. In most districts there is a school lunch supervisor who works directly with the lunch managers in setting up menus, ordering and distributing food, etc. The principal, however, must still see that the program is in operation and implemented in his school. Second, there is a problem involving the financial arrangement—the matter of keeping the funds. In most school systems the principal is involved in one pattern of financial accounting or another—either in receiving money directly from students or in receiving it from lunch workers or other personnel, properly receipting it, running it through the school account, and furnishing the proper reports to the district at the end of the month. The principal may and should have supervisory help in this responsibility. He may appoint teachers, students, lunch workers, or others to actually take the tickets and to make change during the lunch period. However, most principals have the responsibility of accounting for the money.

A third important responsibility of the principal is to see that the lunchroom and its facilities are properly supervised during the lunch period. The school lunch program should not be a problem-creating situation. Educational talks must be given by teachers, principals, and others to assure acceptable behavior during the lunch period. In many schools the teachers must be assigned to help in the supervision. Students may also be used. When a positive attitude has been developed, students may need little or no supervision.

A fourth and important function of the principal in regard to the school lunch services is to schedule the students so that they may participate in the program. In some schools, scheduling is no problem because all of the student body can be out at the same time, eat their lunch, and still go back to afternoon classes in a reasonable period of time. However, in large school systems a staggered lunch period is usually needed. If a lunch period is half an hour, one half the students eat the first one-half hour and the remaining students eat the second one-half hour. At times it is desirable to have a short intervening period between scheduled lunch periods for cleaning up and preparing for the next group. The principal must arrange his curriculum program so that lunch period schedules will correspond to class periods. Further discussion is provided in the chapter on scheduling.

Administration of Transportation

Most of the problems related to pupil transportation are handled through the district-wide transportation program. Under this program the district usually maintains a bus supervisor who schedules, services, and maintains the buses. However, the principal is not completely divorced from the pupil transportation services. He has among his responsibilities the following:

1. He must arrange his school schedule to conform to the arrival and departure of the district buses.

2. Discipline problems that occur on the bus are referred to the principal. Of course the driver handles some problems himself, but basically his responsibility is to see that the students are delivered to and from school in safety. The principal is given the responsibility for proper pupil behavior and control while they are riding to and from school as well as while they are in school.

In some of the larger cities where city bus lines are in operation, the school does not operate its own bus system. In these areas the principal's responsibilities for administering transportation services are greatly lessened.

Another problem involving transportation, which has increased in recent years, is that of student transportation through the use of private automobiles. Modern schools must be planned with a large acreage devoted to parking. In older schools where student parking was not provided, the principal is constantly faced with the problems thus created. The problem of student control is also greatly increased because of the greater mobility of students. In one suburban high school of 2,000 students, over 65 per cent owned their own cars. In a matter of minutes students who care to leave the school can be literally miles away. The problems created for the principal have been increased to such a point that many schools have initiated "closed campuses." A closed campus is one where students are not permitted to leave the school once they have arrived until the close of school. Another procedure that is used is to have the parking lot be a closed portion of the campus. Once a car is parked within the parking lot, it cannot be taken out until the end of the day. Some principals have even found it wise to issue parking spaces in the same manner as lockers are issued. Parking permits are then required of students who bring cars to school.

Summary

Administration of auxiliary services involves the administration of the library and instructional materials center, the school plant, the school health and safety program, the school lunch program, and the transportation program. The district office usually has a supervisory staff that has responsibility for each of these areas and as such provides training, leadership, and supervision. However, the principal's responsibility extends throughout his own school. Each of the personnel in these areas is under the principal's jurisdiction and as such he must see that their work is properly scheduled and regulated and that problems of an emergency nature are handled. To carry out his responsibility the principal must work with librarians, school lunch personnel, bus drivers, custodians, nurses, civil defense personnel, fire marshals, and many other individuals in the community. All these services greatly enhance and affect teaching performance and, therefore, the quality of instruction.

The library should be a focal center of the school for learning activities. The principal should provide a well-trained and adequate staff and adequate budget and physical facilities.

The principal must work with the custodian to maintain the school building in the best possible manner; therefore, the principal has the responsibility of organizing the work of the custodian and seeing that it is properly carried out. In addition to the regular cleaning responsibilities, the principal should periodically make a building inspection with the custodian to see that all of the necessary repair items are found and steps taken to correct them. Aside from the custodial functions, the principal also has a responsibility for the total utilization of the building. The principal should do everything in his power to schedule the building for the greatest utilization possible, and in this regard he should work with the school and the community. In addition to scheduling activities on his own calendar, the principal should see that his activities are scheduled on the community calendar, where such a calendar is in operation. Such foresight will avoid many conflicts in the total activities that take place within a community.

The principal is also responsible for the health and safety program within a school. This program involves general health programs, immunizations, examinations, special tests, and services of nurses, doctors, dentists, psychologists, and psychiatrists. Not all districts will have the same type of program or the same number of personnel, but most districts try to have these services available in some form or another. In general, the school health services have been established to determine the health status of students, to apprise parents regarding the findings of health examinations and evaluations, to encourage the correction of remedial defects, to aid in the development of programs for handicapped children, to prevent and control disease, and to provide emergency care for the sick and the injured.

The principal should do everything in his power to maintain a building that is safe from fire and other hazards. However, in addition to the prevention program, the principal has the responsibility to have an orderly evacuation program in the event of emergency situations. The safety program should also provide procedures by which both teachers and administrators can handle the many accidents that take place in a school building and on the school grounds. Such accidents may range from bruises to deaths. The principal should be ready to handle any emergency situation.

The principal has responsibility in the school lunch service to supervise the school lunch workers, to handle the financing, to arrange schedules for student lunch dismissal, and to supervise properly the school lunch facilities.

The principal's responsibility in transportation services extends primarily to the students. The school schedule must be correlated with the arrival and departure time of buses. The principal must see that proper order and control are maintained on the buses and must effectively correct misdemeanors that occur. The students may also arrive at school in private automobiles. Special facilities for parking are required, and many other problems are created because of the great use of the automobile by students. Many schools have resorted to closed campuses and partly closed campuses in order to retain greater control over the behavior of all the students.

SUGGESTED PROJECTS AND ACTIVITIES

1. Select nonteaching personnel staff members in the university or within a school system and discuss with them how they feel about the educational program within their school and education generally. Draw them out to discuss items about themselves and prepare a report that would be interesting for you as a principal so that you could be more effective in working with this person as a nonteaching personnel staff member.

2. Work with a principal or check with the person responsible for scheduling the university buildings to find out what procedure he uses in scheduling classrooms and other facilities to receive the greatest utilization possible. Collect forms used and any other data that would be useful.

3. Review the menus for a week in a school lunch program. Determine the number of students who participate in the program for that time and the number of personnel within the school who are involved to assure the successful operation of the school lunch service. Find out from a principal how the school lunch money is managed.

4. Study a school district's transportation problems and especially those problems which are related to the high school operation. Report on the effect of the transportation system on the curriculum program.

5. In the building in which your class is being held, plan an orderly evacuation schedule program for the greatest efficiency and one that would cover all types of emergencies.

6. With the consent of a school principal, secure an Inspection Blank

for Schools, prepared by the National Board of Fire Underwriters and approved and adopted by the National Association of Public School Business Officials, and inspect and evaluate the school for fire protection.

7. Compare the standards of the American Library Association with those of your regional accreditation association. Discuss the differences, strengths, and weaknesses.

REVIEW AND DISCUSSION QUESTIONS

1. Why should the principal know such district school personnel as the lunch manager and bus supervisor.
2. Why should the principal have administrative jurisdiction over the custodian in the school rather than the district building supervisor?
3. Why should the principal organize the custodian's work rather than have each individual teacher report his needs to the custodian?
4. In what ways can the principal secure a greater utilization of the school building?
5. Why should the community be permitted to use the school facilities?
6. On what basis should the facilities be extended for community use?
7. What justification can be given for a rental policy in which different prices are based on the nature of the activity?
8. What should be the role of relationship between the teacher, the principal, the nurse, and the physician if a student falls and breaks an arm or some other accident occurs?
9. Since the principal's time is always at a premium, how may the school lunch services be organized so that the principal can secure the maximum use of his own and his faculty's time?
10. What arguments can be advanced in support of the principal's responsibility for maintaining discipline on school buses when he or his faculty members are not actually on the bus?
11. What are the principal's responsibilities in such emergencies as fire, explosion, and other general alarms, such as civil defense?
12. What are the principal's primary roles as related to the library services?

SELECTED BIBLIOGRAPHY

American Association of School Administrators. *Staff Relations in School Administration*. Washington, D.C.: The Association, 1955.
———. *Year-Round School*. Washington, D.C.: The Association, 1960.

American Library Association. *Standards for School Library Programs*. Chicago: The Association, 1960.

Ayars, Albert L. *Administering the People's Schools*. New York: McGraw-Hill Book Company, Inc. 1957.

Berry, June. "The IMC in the Continuous Progress School," *School Library Journal*, November 1964, pp. 25–28.

Biles, N. E. *Improving School Custodial Service*. Bulletin No. 13. Washington, D.C.: Superintendent of Documents, U.S. Office of Education, 1949.

Lamers, William M. *School Boards Plan for Disaster Problems*. Chicago, Illinois: National School Boards Association, Inc. Reprinted by Office of Civil and Defense Mobilization.

National Education Association. "You and Civil Defense." Washington, D.C.: The Association, 1963.

National Education Association, National Association of Secondary School Principals. *Administration of Health, Physical Education, and Recreation Programs in Secondary Schools*. Bulletin 195. Washington, D.C.: The Association, 1953.

National School Public Relations Association. "The Hip Pocket Library," *The Shape of Education for 1964*. Washington, D.C.: The Association, 1964.

National Study of Secondary School Evaluation. *Evaluative Criteria*. Washington, D.C.: The Study, 1960.

Office of Civil and Defense Mobilization. *School Shelter—An Approach to Fallout Protection*. TR–12. Washington, D.C.: Office of Civil and Defense Mobilization, 1960.

Sisson, Silvanus H. "Planning the Junior High School Library Program," *Bulletin of N.A.S.S.P.*, February 1962, pp. 197–98.

Stoops, Emery, and M. L. Rafferty, Jr. *Practices and Trends in School Administration*. Boston: Ginn and Company, 1961.

CHAPTER 17

Planning the Secondary School Plant

An old adage that "the only things certain in life are death and taxes" is not inclusive enough for the modern school administrator. Children, school buildings, and taxes are more predictable than death. The past decade has been one of increased school enrollments on all levels of education, and school buildings have arisen like mushrooms after a rainstorm. Some of these schools have been well planned for curriculum programing. Others only house students.

During the past decade there has been a great population explosion at the secondary level, which will continue for some time. Immediately following World War II the big push was to house adequately the elementary students. As the years passed and as the students progressed upward through the grades, the need for great numbers of high schools became apparent. School planners, school administrators, boards of education, and architects asked the basic question, "What should these schools be like?" Answers were not readily available. Most buildings were planned similar to those that were currently in use. However, as the need increased, school planners and architects planned new and better buildings. The total emphasis in school planning shifted to more functional school buildings designed for new programs.

With the shift from brick and mortar to describing programs, the principal became involved in school planning to a greater extent than he had ever been before. Modern school planning required that the program be established and the building planned to fit the program. Today the principal is an active agent in aiding in the development of school plant facilities.

Planning Is Necessary

Build the Building Three Times. School buildings are no longer built simply to house a given number of students. Schools are planned according to the functions that are to take place within the structure provided. If the quality of planning is poor, one should not expect maximum returns for the funds expended. Each new plant should be built several times: first, by the educators in terms of the educational specifications that describe the educational program; second, by the architect in terms of architectural specifications and working drawings that interpret the educational program; and third, by the contractor and the craftsmen engaged to complete the basic structure based on the architectural specifications.

Plan for the Educational Programs. There are times in the planning world when the educators fail to accomplish that which is their responsibility and they leave to the architect the responsibility for planning the building. Regardless of the quality of the architect, such action is like turning over a blank check to a person who does not know the amount of money in the bank. The educators at this point are abdicating their responsibility. The educators should plan the building since the building shapes and limits the types of activities that can be carried out. On the other hand, educators are not perfect. Sometimes they are blinded by certain aspects of the curriculum. Each has his own bent. Too often an educator is interested in the athletic program, or the music program, or the shop, or a single phase of the total school's curriculum. A good example of this type of planning is provided in the presentation that follows:

PLANNING BY HALVES

Recently a small community approved a bond issue for the construction of a new high school. The superintendent was desirous of providing a good functional building. He called upon all the teachers to submit suggestions for their proposed teaching areas. The teachers spent a considerable amount of time and effort to assemble data which would provide adequate and functional facilities. The suggestions which were made by teachers in certain special areas of music, art, industrial arts, home economics, physical education, athletics, agriculture and trades and industries were considered and in large part adopted into the plans for the school. These plans were based upon the needs of the students and the functions to be performed.

The suggestions which were made by teachers in language arts, social studies, science, and mathematics were rejected. Of course, the word "reject" was not used. The teachers were told, "You have certainly done a lot of work, and you have some fine suggestions, BUT. . ." One social studies teacher continued to push for facilities which would permit him to carry out a better program and was told, "Of course these facilities would lend themselves to better teaching, but who else could teach like you. . ." The argument by the teacher that this was the way teachers were trained in the universities was to no avail. When the building was completed all academic classrooms were identical, identical in size, shape, space, and facilities. All were equal—equally non-functional.[1]

The above instance is not unique. In community after community new school buildings can be found. In many of these buildings the facilities have not been planned to meet the educational program and are therefore inadequate even though they may be newly completed. Schools are constructed for the purpose of teaching the children in the community. For most communities, building the school is a once-in-a-lifetime opportunity. It is important that the structure easily house and provide for the needs of the educational program. Planning is necessary to make the school plant more functional for the teaching-learning process. If the quality of planning is poor, nonfunctional facilities are likely to result. Poor planning is a waste of money.

Who Should Do the Planning

Planning by Individuals. As has already been indicated, the board of education, the superintendent, and the principal should be involved in school planning. However, it should not be assumed that within this limited number of individuals the total knowledge needed to plan a school facility based on both the best in current practices and the needed programs for the future can be found. Examples of what happens when a single individual assumes responsibility for all planning are given below.

POOR FACILITIES PLANNED BY INDIVIDUALS

School A was planned by the superintendent. It was his school and he was proud of it. No one questioned the amount of time spent and his dedication to the planning. But when the building was completed the music department had no storage space for the many instruments. The agricultural program was planned for the early 1900's instead of present.

School B was planned by the principal, who was a former athletic coach. At the time of construction the science facilities were inadequate and obsolete and there were no modern facilities or equipment plans in the commercial area.

The language art department at School C was planned by the chairman. He did not involve other staff members. However, prior to the construction

[1] Glen F. Ovard, "It's Time to Plan Academic Classrooms," *American School Board Journal*, January 1962.

period he left the school. The next chairman of the department requested many changes. These changes were difficult to obtain and questionable in terms of the previous school program that had been set up by the first department chairman.

Obviously the above examples indicate the need for cooperative, perceptive, and detailed planning.

Planning by Committees.   School planning requires carefully directed and coordinated teamwork of various groups each with its own interests and abilities. The group should consist of professional, technical, and lay citizens who have knowledge that will contribute toward better planned facilities.[2] When they work together as a team, the school facilities will more often reflect the total needs of the local community as well as the society in general. There are many groups that should participate in the team-planning approach: the board of education, superintendent, general steering committee, principal, departmental chairman, teachers, lay citizens, and consultants in specialized areas. Figure 17.1 shows how one might

Figure 17.1

District-wide School Planning Committee[3]

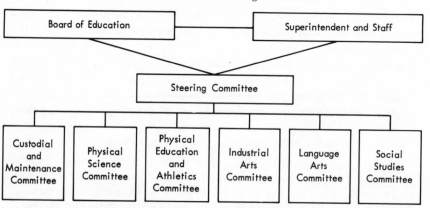

visualize the role relationship of these various groups. Not all of the areas within a high school are listed here. These are only samples of the type of committees and areas that should be represented. The principal will usually be a member of the steering committee, and is frequently an *ex officio* member of all departmental or area committees.

---

[2] A book on school planning written for the layman and which could be used effectively by this committee is: Walter McQuade, *Schoolhouse* (New York: Simon and Schuster, 1958).

[3] Only a few of the many subcommittees are shown in this illustration.

Role Functions of Committee Members. To illustrate how a committee of a certain area might be established and its role relationships established, one might consider the physical science committee as an example. The physical science committee should be composed of individuals whose major responsibility is the physical science education, i.e., teachers, department chairmen, supervisors, and science education consultants. The committee should be supplemented by interested lay citizens, such as members of the interested civic groups, a representative from one of the major industries of the community, a member from the medical profession, a geologist from a local oil firm, and other such interested citizens.

The teachers, department chairmen, and supervisors should be concerned with the educational aims and objectives, the curriculum, and the activities used in teaching and learning. The educational consultant should be a specialist in the physical science field. He is usually from a university or the state department, although this is not always true. The consultant should have the most current knowledge in the subject field and should be the best person available to aid in the identification of potential trends and teacher activities. In this regard he should have a knowledge of latest developments in planning of facilities for the specialized field. The consultant's major function is primarily one of advisement and guidance. The lay citizens will contribute attitudes and values held in common by the members of society and participate in evaluation of curriculum programs and facilities needed. Since lay citizens represent specialized areas of interest, they will also have good suggestions in regard to the latest developments in their particular areas and what the current needs in the professional fields are. Insofar as he has knowledge of the particular area, the lay citizen can make a valuable contribution. Although students are not part of the formal committee, it is usually advisable for teachers also to let students participate in sharing of ideas. Especially is this true in areas such as student government, student publications, and other student activities. Participation of students in the initial planning often leads to more functional facilities as well as a greater respect for the care of the facilities and their construction.

Define the Committee Assignment. In setting forth the task for a special committee, the principal and the chairman of the committee should set forth in detail the goals to be accomplished by the committee. The committee members should understand that their work must fit into the total program and that some modification may be needed. The committee members should further understand that their departmental planning area is only one and that there must be harmonious relationships with other departments and areas to be planned. There are always some compromises that must be made. The need for compromise receives momentum when financial conditions do not permit the construction of every facility required or suggested by all of the committees.

It should be clearly understood that neither the planning director, the steering committee, the principal, the superintendent, nor the board of education should make arbitrary compromises of the facilities that have been cooperatively planned by the various committees. If changes are necessary in order to conform to the total school plan, the subcommittees should be informed and consulted regarding the changes and allowed to discuss or present their case as necessary. Figure 17.2 shows how a committee might be set up in terms of its organizational membership.

Figure 17.2

Area Planning Committee

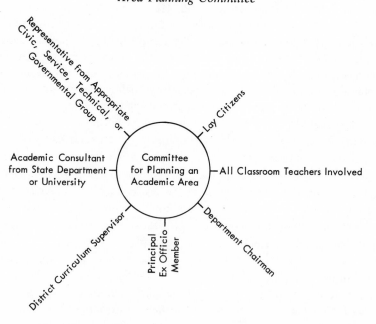

Study Group Organization and Administration.   As indicated previously, the participants of study groups should be selected because of unique contributions that they can make. These groups should be given adequate authority to carry out their assigned responsibility. Since the committees should be study groups and not decision-making groups, the committees might well be named or designated by school board endorsement on recommendation of the superintendent and principal. The size of the group should be from approximately three to seven members to allow for both cooperation and efficiency. The following specific suggestions are offered to aid the study group in its organization and administration.

1. Get started in time to complete studies before crises develop and force premature decisions.

2. Make sponsorship clear—as broad and as strong as possible.

3. Utilize as much group representation as possible, but not on every study team: church, clubs, business, professional, housewives, public officers, working groups, and minority groups whether they represent religious, racial, or national elements.

4. Define the geographical area each subcommittee is to cover. If community life is closely related to other areas, investigate the feasibility of including all of the interdependent units. This will require negotiation with independent governing bodies.

5. Set up "central steering committee" as the planning agency to develop the study plan, make subcommittee assignments, direct the fact-finding activities, and for review and final recommendations.

6. In large communities, employ a study administrator or coordinator.

7. Welcome volunteers, but do not depend entirely upon volunteer offers; ask groups to nominate their representatives.

8. Make it clear and mandatory that participants serve as individual citizens, not as spokesmen or lobbyists for their organizations.

9. Use as subcommittee chairmen men and women who have previously evidenced leadership traits and genuine interest in the problem.

10. Consider the availability of professional planners and community relations specialists as consultants.

11. Ask groups to "get the facts" and to be honest in reporting both good and bad.

12. Encourage community interest with effective news media support.

13. Use state and national data sparingly, local data to the maximum.

14. Carefully avoid premature publicity on facts, discussions, and findings.

15. Plan thoroughly for dissemination of reports when completed; consider the organization of public forums throughout the area.

16. Keep subcommittees meeting regularly, and be available to help iron out difficulties that seem to impede forward progress.

17. Create a "follow-up committee" to function after the studies are completed, constituting it with those who proved to be most active and capable during the study.

18. Encourage each subcommittee to refine its own study outline.

19. Assist subcommittees in identifying formal groups already active in the assigned area.

20. Obtain from organized professional and technical groups the criteria of adequacy, standards, or yardsticks of service to be applied to programs, facts, staff rules of thumb, budget support, etc.

21. Plan sufficient general sessions and meetings for each subcommittee to understand what other groups are studying.

22. Make arrangements for suitable physical facilities for groups, and see that their convenience is planned for in advance.

23. Prepare a basic study outline so subcommittees will have some uni-

formity or consistency, and so their reporting will conform to a general pattern without rewrite.

24. See that each subcommittee concentrates on the definition of its study problem. Try to phrase the problem as a question to be answered by facts, breaking the general question into a number of related, subordinate questions.

25. Help the "central steering committee" develop selected reading and study bibliographies for subcommittee members who wish to study, and provide means for obtaining and circulating materials for such use.[4]

Procedures for Good Planning

Good school buildings that are well planned involve some of the following basic procedures: evaluate the present program, find the best in current practice, study the trends, determine the type and number of classrooms to be utilized, determine the specific facilities that are needed to carry out the formulated educational program, prepare and interpret the educational specifications, check the architect's preliminary drawings to see that the specifications have been interpreted adequately. Each of these procedures is discussed below.

Evaluate the Present Program. The most important phase of planning involves a look at the basic program. Since the school is to be constructed to promote specific learning, it is important to consider (1) WHY—aims and objectives, (2) WHAT—curriculum content, and (3) HOW—learning activities. It is assumed that the present program exists because it fulfills basic needs of the students. However, not everything that is taught is of equal importance. Therefore, one of the most important phases of planning involves an evaluation of the basic school program.

1. WHY—The Aims and Objectives. The subject of what should be learned is based on the premise that the content is for some good purpose. Therefore, the specific purposes of the subject area should be explored and evaluated. The community lay personnel in the study committee should be encouraged to participate very actively in evaluating and stating new aims and objectives.

2. WHAT—The Curriculum Content. On the basis of the statement of the aims and objectives, an examination of the curriculum should be initiated. In some subject areas the curriculum has become unduly scripturalized. There are other areas as outmoded as the Ptolemaic theory of astronomy and Aristotelian physics. There are many specific facts that are not consistent with the findings of modern science. There are duplications

[4] W. D. McClurkin, *School Building Planning* (New York: The Macmillan Company, 1964), pp. 18–20. © Copyright, W. D. McClurkin, 1964. Reprinted by permission of The Macmillan Company.

between subject areas that should be more closely coordinated or eliminated. And finally, changes have occurred in our society which would indicate that some phases of a subject should be moved to lesser positions of importance and still other areas of the curriculum should be dropped entirely. The new curriculum should reflect the changes that have occurred in our society. This evaluation helps guarantee that the facilities are not constructed for an obsolete curriculum. The principal should play a major role in evaluation of the curriculum.

3. HOW—The Teaching and Learning Activities. Curriculum content does not pass from the mind of the teacher to the mind of the student through telepathic osmosis. Specific procedures and activities are used by the teacher for the transmission of this knowledge. Thus, the type of teaching and learning activities must be evaluated. If the activities call for a display, display space must be provided. If construction of posters, graphs, maps, etc., is indicated, appropriate space and facilities should be furnished. Demonstrations by the teacher call for certain facility requirements, while student experimentations call for other requirements.

Find the Best in Current Practice. In addition to the intensive analysis of the school curriculum, there is a need to examine carefully the educational program of other school districts throughout the state and nation. Some districts have already been through intensive evaluation and have developed operational programs consistent with their findings. Research from state and national agencies provides many suggestions that improve the local program. In addition to the purposes and curriculum, the teaching and learning activities must be considered. There have been many changes in recent years in the nature and type of teaching-learning activities. It should no longer be assumed that the changing objectives and programs can be carried out in the traditional question-answer technique. Activities are many and varied, and further improvements in science and technology will increase the number of activities. Facilities should be provided so that many activities can be utilized. Planning for the best in current practice would provide for the advancement that has been made in both theory and practice of pedagogy. Classroom planning should be consistent with these modern practices.

Study the Trends. The construction of a new school building involves a major investment by the community, and the school must be planned for many years into the future. An evaluation of the present or even the best in current practice is insufficient by itself to meet the needs of the future. Changes will occur. It is desirable to look at the trends in aims and objectives, curriculum, teaching methods, and teaching equipment and supplies in order to keep the classroom functional for the future.

The trends in aims and objectives and curriculum are best related to the specific curricular areas and will not be discussed here. However, there are certain trends in organization, activities, and facilities that are important in all the areas. MacConnell and Ovard listed some of the following trends:[5]

1. Trends in Organization. The secondary school has been under study for many years. Experiments on utilization of the staff have been sponsored throughout the nation by the National Association of Secondary School Principals. Two important generalizations can be made based on these studies:

a. Educators and lay citizens are ready for changes in the organization of schools.

b. Many different types of organizations are both feasible and practical.

Some of the experimental programs involve large- and small-group instruction, grouping of teachers for better utilization, lengthened class periods, complete reorganization of the Schedule by the week rather than a daily report of the previous day, and continuous progress school (ungraded structure, advancement depends on mastering curriculum).

2. Trends in Activities. There is such a variety of activities used in the modern classroom that a statement on trends would undoubtedly miss some important activities. However, the following activities are either prominent today or are inherent in the experimental programs:

a. Activities that bring the student in close contact with the current events, discoveries, relationships of people, and developments of science throughout the world.

b. Activities involving critical-thinking techniques, problem-solving skills, and use of community resources.

c. Activities that provide for the widespread physical and intellectual capacity of all students.

d. Activities that place greater emphasis on student initiative, creativity, originality, and self-direction.

e. Activities that teach the democratic process through pupil-teacher planning and cooperative group activity.

f. Activities that utilize the total range of audiovisual services.

g. Activities involving construction and the creation of materials by students.

h. Activities that promote a wise use of leisure time.

3. Trends in Facilities. The following are some of the trends that are taking place in classroom facilities:

a. Greater flexibility and portability of all room furnishings including: student desks, storage cabinets, book trucks, magazine racks, folding stages, and audiovisual equipment. Such flexibility extends to more permanent fixtures through removable and interchangeable tackboard-chalkboard and other wall surfaces.

b. Expanded use of audiovisual equipment.

---

[5] Taken from the *American School Board Journal*, February 1962, "General Procedures in Planning Academic Classrooms," p. 36, James D. MacConnell and Glen F. Ovard.

c. Expanded use of television as a major teaching device or tool to be used in large- and small-group instruction. Facilities for eventual use of commercial, community educational, and closed-circuit television should be planned.

d. Greater flexibility in classroom space. This flexibility may be provided through:

(1) Extension. The physical facilities may be extended by utilizing other existing areas, such as, library, projection rooms, and materials work centers. Proper orientation to these other facilities becomes a major consideration.

(2) Convertibility. Convertibility for interior flexibility involves plans for instant, overnight, semester, or summer changes.

(3) Expansibility. Plans for exterior flexibility suggest the need for facilities that permit expansion of construction in room size as needs change. Providing rooms with movable partitions so classrooms can be adjusted to various sizes from year to year must be given serious consideration. Hillsdale High School is a good example of such planning.[6]

(4) Versatility. The need for versatility is made mandatory with the great variety of teaching and learning activities employed in modern instruction. Versatility in classroom design can be achieved in many ways. However, adequate space is fundamental. The larger the classroom, the more flexibility there is inherently in the structure. A large room can accommodate more people, more groups working independently, more activities, and more equipment and supplies. Historically, classroom sizes in the United States have varied from 1,200 to 1,400 square feet in 1890 to 660 square feet in 1920. More recent trends emphasize classrooms with floor areas of up to 1,000 to 1,200 square feet.

e. Completely controlled environment. There is no longer a need for dependence upon natural light. The thermal and visual environment may be completely controlled by mechanical and electrical means. The age-old question of the ratio between windows and room size is no longer a determining criteria. Control of internal and external noises is obtained through proper orientation and acoustical treatment.[7]

Determine the Type and Number of Classrooms to be Utilized. The type of classrooms to be constructed should be determined by the curriculum as it has been revised and projected into the future by the analysis of trends. The local and state curriculum requirements also determine the kinds and number of classrooms to be constructed. Is the course to be required of all students or at certain grade levels or is the course optional?

[6] Evan Clinchy, *Profiles of Significant Schools, Hillsdale High School, San Mateo, California* (New York: Educational Facilities Laboratories, Inc., 1960).

[7] Other additional sources for flexibility and versatility may be found in Harold Silverthorn, "Flexibility, A Fact or an Illusion?" *The American School Board Journal*, January 1965, pp. 19–22. "The Supermarket School," *School Management*, August 1964, pp. 48–51.

If the state or local district requires every student to take American history, the school must plan facilities accordingly. If the state does not require a class in chemistry and the school offers the class as an elective, adequate plans require an estimate of the extent of student participation. Hence, the type of facilities is dependent on the curriculum and anticipated enrollment in the courses.

In the determination of the number of each type of facilities to be included, two major considerations are: (1) Will the educational program be organized in the conventional pattern? (2) Will newer types of organization be utilized? Anticipation of requirements under each program is discussed below.

1. Conventional.   Under the traditional program there are some basic questions to be answered. First, how many students are anticipated in each grade—anticipated by student projections and board decision of ultimate student capacity of the school? Second, what are the required and elective subjects in each grade level? Third, what is to be the policy of the number of students to be enrolled in each class? Fourth, what is the history of enrollments in elective classes? Fifth, how many class periods will there be in each day?

When the above information is known, the number of each type of facility may be computed. There are many ways to determine the exact facilities from the data. Two very simple formulas are given below.

Formula for Required Classes

Total students anticipated $\div$ in the grade	Policy of number of students in a class	$=$	Number of required sections for that subject in that grade	Number of periods $\div$ in a day	$=$	Number of rooms needed

Formula for Elective Classes

Average of history of enroll- $\div$ ments for past 5 years in elective classes	Policy of number of students in a class for that subject	$=$	Number of periods needed for each elective class	Number of periods $\div$ per day	$=$	Number of rooms needed for each elective class

2. Experimental programs.   There are numerous educational programs that are departing from the traditional approaches. These new programs include such things as team teaching, large- and small-group instruction,

individualized instruction, ungraded programs, television teaching, and programed learning. In these programs, the organization of the school day and week departs from the six or seven classes each and every day. The length of time in class depends on the needs within the curriculum area. Such a program calls for flexible class schedules. There can be many different types of program organization. The ideal plan that is best for each school can best be achieved when every student's individualized program can be master-planned through machine processing. Such scheduling is now possible.

These new educational programs require a different type of facility. A variety of instructional and resource areas will be needed. Classrooms for large- and/or small-group instruction must be provided. Individual study stations must be considered. Greater utilization of all the audiovisual aids must be attained.

However, the principles of flexibility described previously are important and necessary considerations for this type of planning. The facilities must be planned for the educational program. Some examples of planning for experimental programs are provided later.

Determining Specific Facilities. When the number and kinds of rooms that are needed have been determined, the specific facilities that should be included in each area can be listed. Facilities should be based on the teaching and learning activities that are to take place. The following examples will illustrate how activities determine the specific facilities:

Slide Rule Demonstration—
 Large slide rule, 6 to 8 feet long, mounted above chalkboard.
Students to work math problems on chalkboard—
 Chalkboard with enough linear feet to accommodate size of group involved in such activity.
Construction of posters, charts, time lines, and other graphic materials—
 Counter space, sink and water, all types of construction and drawing paper, drawing and coloring equipment and supplies, lockable cabinets, basic area separate from other instructional area. Size to be determined by number of students involved at one time. Bulletin board space to handle different projects which are going on concurrently.
Listen to foreign language instruction—
 Recording booths separate from primary instruction area, recording and listening equipment.
Student experimentation with chemical elements—
 Laboratory space, equipment and supplies. Lockable storage cabinets for chemicals and other supplies. Space needs depend on policy regarding number to do experiment at any one time.

Students to plant seeds to study growth, comparisons, etc.—
Planter boxes, located for proper light, watering, etc. Number and size to be determined by extent of projects to be going on simultaneously.
Collect and exhibit objects and artifacts of historical consequence—
Display space. Large tables with adequate space for proper viewing. Lockable display area for valuable objects and artifacts which would not be forthcoming without this type of protection.
Diagraming Sentences—
Chalkboard to accommodate size of class.
Show films—
Provisions for screen, darkening facilities or adequate equipment in lieu of darkening facilities, handy electrical outlets, audio-visual equipment, provisions for storage of equipment and supplies.[8]

In addition to the general information needed, the architect should be supplied with sufficient detail to guarantee facilities for a planned program. A sample of the detail needed can be seen in the following example for storage description for social studies classrooms:

The lockable teaching storage area should be located toward the front of the room and should provide for the following items:

Item	Number Required	Size in Inches (Inside Dimensions)
Coat closet (ventilated)	1	$8 \times 24 \times 72$
Four-drawer legal file	1	$18 \times 24 \times 52$
Drawers for posters, documents, flat maps, oversized pictures, etc.	4	$38 \times 25 \times 3$
Audiovisual projectors and equipment (temporary storage—adjustable shelf)	2	$18 \times 24 \times 24$
Shelves—adjustable for paper, models, artifacts, projects, etc.	3	$36 \times 24 \times 11$
Compartments for outline maps and paper	12	$18 \times 24 \times 2\frac{1}{4}$
Drawers for glass slides with removable tray	1 2	$18 \times 24 \times 4$ $18 \times 24 \times 3$
Drawers for filmstrips	2	$18 \times 24 \times 3$
Drawer for miscellaneous forms, supplies, with many compartments	1	$18 \times 24 \times 4$
Drawer for tape recordings	1	$18 \times 24 \times 6$
Compartments for records (vertical)	6	$3 \times 24 \times 18$
Drawer for miscellaneous	1	Space filler

Total space requirements: 14 square feet

---

[8] MacConnell and Ovard, *op. cit.*, p. 37.

Write the Educational Specifications. Unless some procedure is used to systematically put in writing the information that has thus been obtained through the items listed above, the information will not adequately be conveyed to the architect. Educational specifications should indicate to the architect the needs of the programs and facilities desired. The principal should always play a vital role in helping to plan the educational specifications so that classrooms and school facilities will be functional. Examples of educational specifications for specific subjects or areas may be found in current journals.[9]

The following outline of educational specifications by McClurkin provides in topic form specific items whereby detailed information would greatly aid in planning functional buildings.[10]

OUTLINE OF EDUCATIONAL SPECIFICATIONS

I. Community Personality Traits
   A. Public conception of educational program
   B. Related community programs
      1. Health; libraries; playground; welfare
      2. Relationships with public schools
   C. Population characteristics
      1. Census data and trends
      2. Educational characteristics
      3. Trends in school-age population
II. School System Features
   A. Status and future of the school district
      1. Relation to adjacent administrative units
      2. Relation to other governmental subdivisions
   B. Educational philosophy and goals
   C. School board policies
      1. School organization—size, travel times, grade groupings, school term, etc.
      2. Personnel policies—certificated employees, teacher load, noncertificated employees, staff ratios, off-duty hours
      3. Instructional policies—attendance, promotion, rate of survival trends, curriculum goals, standardized practices
      4. Holding power; follow-up studies; job permit policies
III. Local School Characteristics
   A. Attendance area to be served
      1. School location, size, summary of rooms

[9] Glen F. Ovard (ed.), *On Planning Academic Classrooms*. Reprints from *The American School Board Journal* (Milwaukee, Wisconsin: The Bruce Publishing Company, 1962). Separate articles are found in *The American School Board Journal* beginning January 1962 and ending October 1962.

[10] Another excellent form, along with sample detail forms, may be found in the book: James D. MacConnell, *Planning for School Buildings* (Englewood Cliffs, N.J.: Prentice-Hall, Inc., 1957), pp. 156–65.

    2. Age and grade groups to be accommodated
    3. Scope of services to be provided
    4. Enrollments anticipated by age/grade
  B. Organization plans
    1. Subject offerings, required and elective
    2. Sectioning practices; course election patterns
    3. Zoning separation of groups
    4. Graduation requirements
    5. Tentative daily-weekly schedule
  C. Utilization plans
    1. Night-Adult-Summer uses
    2. Stipulations regarding gross structure
      a. Height, layout, materials, special features

IV. Departmental Requirements
  A. Purposes, discernible trends, courses offered
  B. Number, age, grade level, sex of occupants by classes
  C. Activities in each area by class or subject
    1. Learner activities
    2. Teacher activities
    3. Traffic; internal movement; groupings
  D. Area or space requirements and layout
    1. For activities
    2. For furniture, equipment, supplies
    3. Preferred location and arrangements
      a. Orientation to other areas
      b. Internal arrangement and work areas
      c. Shared or multiple use capability
  E. List of room furnishings needed
    1. Quantities, dimensions, particular specifications
  F. Special utilities and service facilities needed
    1. Unique environmental features (heating, ventilating, lighting, humidity control, acoustical, color, electrical, plumbing, etc.)
  G. Storage requirements
    1. Items to be stored regularly and occasionally
    2. Area locations, quantity and dimensions, space arrangement, design suggestions

V. General Area Requirements (for each area—purposes, activities, occupants, location, equipment, space layout, utilities, storage, and special needs)
  A. Administration   E. Multipurpose combination areas
  B. Assembly   F. Recreation and outdoor
  C. Food service   G. Resources center
  D. Gymnasium   H. Stores and books

VI. Service System Stipulations
  A. Custodial and housekeeping
  B. Delivery

    C. Mechanical systems
    D. Parking service
    E. Sanitation
    F. Utilities
VII. Specific considerations for all
    A. Acoustical
    B. Bus loading
    C. Ceiling materials
    D. Clock system
    E. Cleaning systems
    F. Clothing storage
    G. Colors, signal code, etc.
    H. Display
    I. Exits
    J. Fencing
    K. Fire protection
    L. Floor markings
    M. Floor surfaces
    N. Hardware
    O. Intercom
    P. Outdoor facilities, lighting, paving, etc.
    Q. Plantings and landscaping
    R. Plumbing
    S. Program signals
    T. Public conveniences
    U. Safety
    V. Security
    W. Storage
    X. Traffic
    Y. Wall surfaces
    Z. Zone controls[11]

Check the Architectural Drawing. School people cannot assume that, because information is presented to the architect, all details of importance will be worked into the building drawings. Great detail is required in planning the total structure, and items of significance to particular departments could be unintentionally omitted. The only guarantee that the final building will conform to the educational program is for those individuals who worked and developed the educational specifications to review the architectural drawings to make sure that there are no omissions and that the architect has interpreted properly the intent of the educational specifications. The final check should be made prior to the letting of bids for construction. From this point on, the building is basically in the hands of the architect and building contractors. Of course, the school superintendent and board will need to maintain a continuous check, but the basic work

[11] McClurkin, *op. cit.*, pp. 77–80.

of the school principal will have been completed until such time as he or another principal is ready to move into the facilities and try to put the planned program into operation.

Examples of New School Designs

The many new programs, experiments, and innovations have affected the design of secondary schools. The new schools are planned to make changes in organization, curriculum, and teaching methods easy.[12] The pictures and floor plans of a few significant schools are presented to show new and experimental organization and to show how programs and activities are translated into brick and mortar.

1. Newton South High School.[13] Newton South High School, as shown in Figures 17.3 and 17.4, was designed around a program plan called the

Figure 17.3
Newton South High School

SOURCE: Newton South High School, Newton, Massachusetts. Reprinted by permission of Newton School District and Architects Korslund, LeNormand and Quann, Inc.

[12] Educational Facilities Laboratories, Profiles of Significant Schools, "How Award Winning Schools Compare," *Nation's Schools*, January 1965, pp. 45–78.

[13] Newton South High School, Newton, Massachusetts.

Figure 11.4

Newton South High School Floor Plan

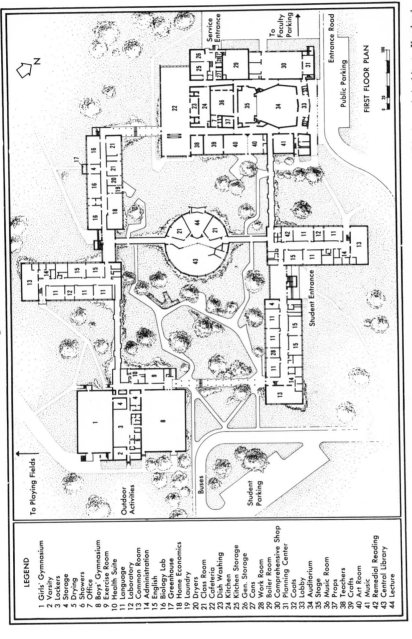

SOURCE: Newton South High School, Newton, Massachusetts. Reprinted by permission of Newton School District and Architects Korslund, LeNormand and Quann, Inc.

LEGEND

1 Girls' Gymnasium
2 Varsity
3 Lockers
4 Storage
5 Drying
6 Showers
7 Office
8 Boys' Gymnasium
9 Exercise Room
10 Health Suite
11 Language
12 Laboratory
13 Common Room
14 Administration
15 English
16 Biology Lab
17 Greenhouse
18 Home Economics
19 Laundry
20 Dryers
21 Class Room
22 Cafeteria
23 Dish Washing
24 Kitchen
25 Kitchen Storage
26 Gen. Storage
27 Cans
28 Work Room
29 Boiler Room
30 Comprehensive Shop
31 Planning Center
32 Coats
33 Lobby
34 Auditorium
35 Stage
36 Music Room
37 Props
38 Teachers
39 Crafts
40 Art Room
41 Music
42 Remedial Reading
43 Central Library
44 Lecture

FIRST FLOOR PLAN

0 20 100

To Playing Fields

Outdoor Activities

Buses

Student Parking

Student Entrance

Service Entrance

To Faculty Parking

Entrance Road

Public Parking

"house plan." The house plan retains the advantages of a large school, such as availability of highly specialized facilities and staff, while eliminating some of the disadvantages of massiveness and impersonality. Students are clustered in groups of 450 to 500 for at least part of their academic instruction and social life. Each unit or house has an administrative head who is partly autonomous in operation. Since about 80 per cent of the students go to college, the curriculum calls for various types of instructional areas. The "house plan" was designed to help solve the following problems: (1) How to communicate with the student as a whole, yet how to communicate with individuals and small groups. (2) How to divide the student body into units that are natural for the student, yet efficient for instruction, and keep administration manageable. (3) How to extend and scatter the stations to which pupils will report in the morning so that traffic is not concentrated at a single entrance. (4) How to avoid congestion of the student body at lunch time and at the close of school. (5) How to organize the extracurricular program to afford opportunities for participation for all in clubs and athletics, and not confine participation to those of outstanding talents. (6) How to give parents the assurance that they, as individual families, are not lost in the impersonal machinery of the school and that their child is known intimately and well by someone in an administrative post.

In architectural design Newton South High School has all the elements of informality and friendliness implied by the word "house" without losing any of the functional aspects needed for instruction in academic subjects.

2. Cedar City High School.[14] Cedar City High School was planned by the School Planning Laboratory of Stanford University, which is the western center for Educational Facilities Laboratory. The faculty, administrators, and consultants analyzed the high school's program and incorporated the philosophy of individualizing instruction. The building was so uniquely adapted for individualized programs that a display of it was exhibited at the American Association of School Administrator's Convention in 1964. There are six separate buildings, five of which are under one roof and appear as one building. Two areas are connected with overhead covered passageways. The auditorium will seat 982; the largest classroom, 150; the next largest, 93. There are 42 classrooms, ten small-group seminar rooms, and 340 individual study stations (carrels). A four-room arrangement in adjoining English and social science departments can be used by either department for team teaching. Two of the rooms have an acoustical curtain

[14] Cedar City High School, Cedar City, Utah.

separating them. The curtain can be opened to make one large classroom. Through scheduling, the rooms can be exchanged by the department wishing to use the team teaching facility. The school and the floor plan are shown in Figures 17.5 and 17.6. Other pictures of this school are shown elsewhere in this book.

Figure 17.5

Cedar City High School

SOURCE: Cedar City High School, Iron County School District, Cedar City, Utah. Reprinted by permission of Iron County School District and Architect L. Robert Gardner.

3. Troy High School.[15] Troy High School is planned for team teaching and flexibility. The flexible interior design permits walls to be changed as space needs change. Because team teaching with large groups of students and several teachers is planned within complexes, much of the school is carpeted. Acoustical control, interior beauty, and outstanding flexibility are designed into this high school, which was selected as one of the nation's award-winning schools.[16] Figure 17.7 provides a complete view of the school, while Figure 17.8 shows graphically the team teaching complexes as well as other portions of the school.

[15] Troy High School, Fullerton Union High School and Junior College Districts, Fullerton, California.

[16] "How Award Winning Schools Compare," *Nation's Schools*, January 1965, pp. 47–78.

Figure 17.6 *Cedar City High School Floor Plan*

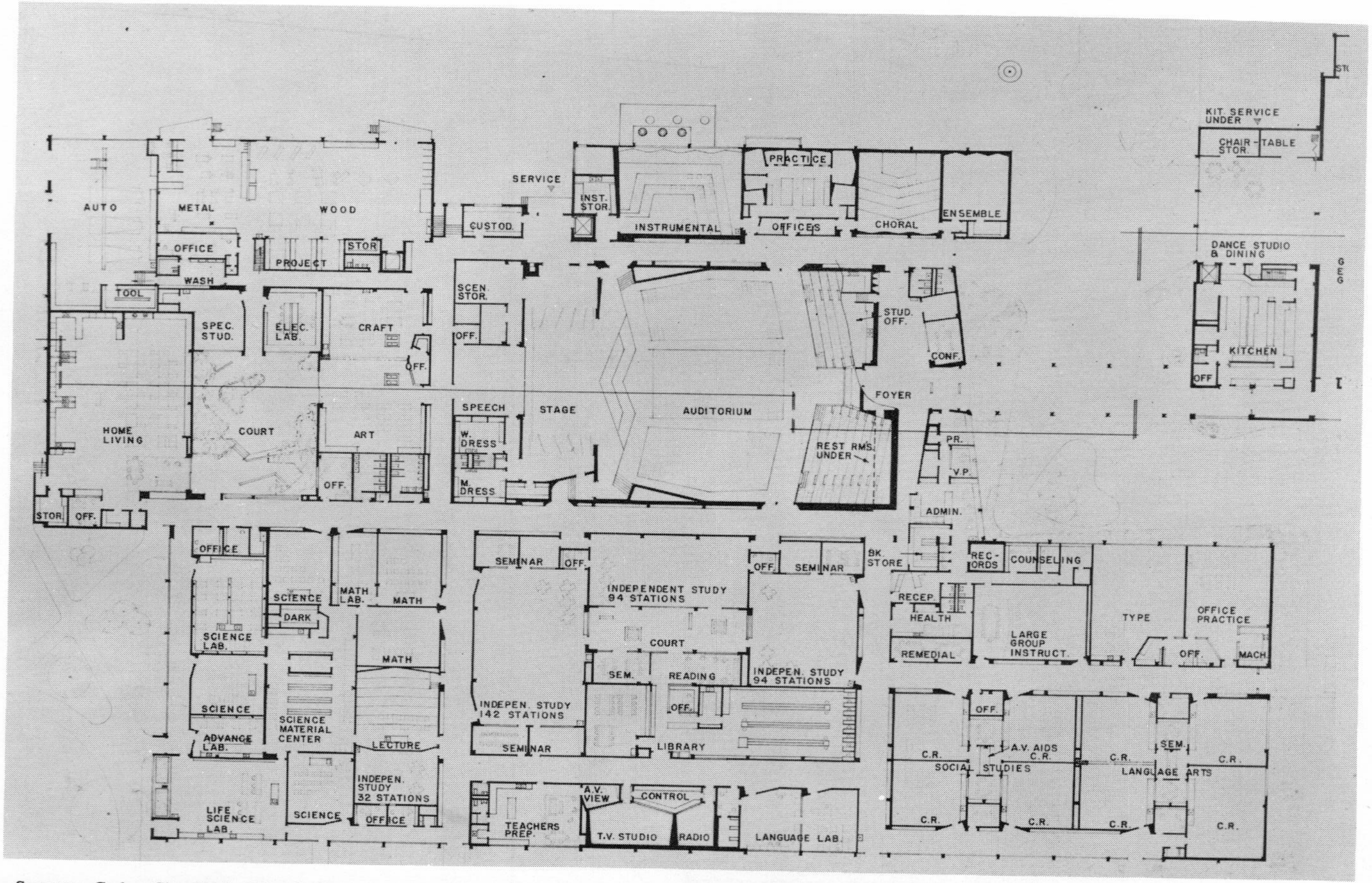

440

Figure 17.7

Troy High School

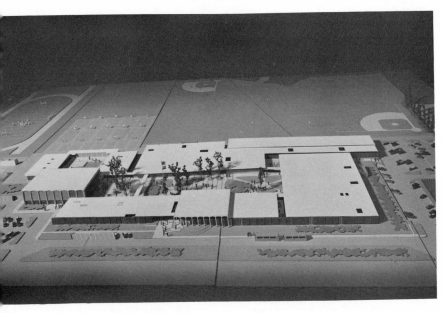

SOURCE: Troy High School, Fullerton Union High School and Junior College Districts, Fullerton, California. Reprinted by permission of Fullerton Union High School and Junior College Districts and Architect W. E. Blurock and associates of Corona del Mar.

Summary

There are many new secondary schools being constructed today due to the expanding number of student enrollments and the need to replace obsolete buildings. Secondary schools should be more adequately planned for the educational functions that are to be performed within.

The board of education and superintendent have the major role in regard to financial and legal aspects of school construction. The principal is usually involved in developing the program to be housed in the new building and in developing the educational specifications. Because no one individual has the knowledge necessary to adequately plan all areas of the secondary school program for a particular community, numerous study committees are organized. The membership of these committees should consist of a departmental chairman, members of the department, lay citizens, district supervisors, and consultants from the universities and state departments of education. The committee members should be given specific assignments in their areas of responsibility. The work of all committees should be coordinated by a central steering committee.

Figure 17.8 *Troy High School Floor Plan*

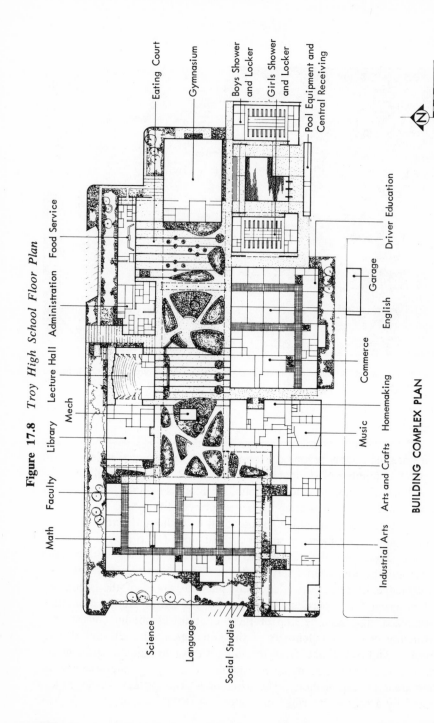

BUILDING COMPLEX PLAN

Source: Troy High School, Fullerton Union High School and Junior College Districts, Fullerton, California. Reprinted by permission of Fullerton Union High School and Junior College Districts and Architect W. E. Blurock and associates of Carros del Mar.

442

There are many procedures that school planners should use as they plan school buildings. Some general procedures for good planning are to evaluate the present program, find the best in current practice, study the trends, determine the type and number of classrooms to be utilized, determine the specific facilities, write the educational specifications, and check the architectural drawings.

The educational specifications are the written plans that describe the educational program and the facilities needed to carry out the program. The architect uses these educational specifications to formulate his designs from which the building is constructed.

SUGGESTED PROJECTS AND ACTIVITIES

1. Evaluate the educational specifications used in the construction of a new school in the community.
2. In the area of the student's teaching major, develop a set of educational specifications.
3. Visit several new schools. Discuss strengths to be found in the school plants.
4. Invite a school district's school planner or a professor of school planning to review the need for educational program prior to the construction of a building.
5. Determine the number of English classrooms needed in the following example:

    Washington High School has a student enrollment of 857 students. English is required every year.

REVIEW AND DISCUSSION QUESTIONS

1. In what way should a building be "built three times"?
2. If an architect plans and has constructed a nonfunctional school building, who is at fault?
3. Why should boards of education and the superintendent involve the principal in planning a secondary school.
4. What is a steering committee? A study committee?
5. Who should be involved in study committees?
6. What should be the role relationships of the various members of the committee?
7. Why should the assignment and responsibility of the committee be closely defined?

8. What specific suggestions could be given to the study group to aid in its organization and administration?
9. What general procedures should be followed for good school planning?
10. What are the significant considerations in the evaluation of a current program?
11. How can the significant trends be determined?
12. What are the different factors that must be considered in determining the number of classrooms in required or elective subjects?
13. In what ways would planning for experimental programs be different than for conventional programs? How would the planning be similar?
14. What are educational specifications?
15. Why should architectural drawings be evaluated against the educational specifications?

SELECTED BIBLIOGRAPHY

Educational Facilities Laboratory, Inc. *Profiles of Significant Schools.* New York: Educational Facilities Laboratory.

————. *Relocatable School Facilities.* New York: Educational Facilities Laboratory, 1964.

————. *The Things of Education.* New York: Educational Facilities Laboratory, 1961.

Engelhardt, N. L., N. L. Engelhardt, Jr., and Stanton Leggett. *School Planning and Building Handbook.* New York: F. W. Dodge Corporation, 1956.

Gores, Harold, and Jonathan King. "9 New Things in School Building," *School Management,* July 1964, pp. 129–43.

Herrick, John H., Ralph D. McLeary, Wilfred F. Clapp, and Walter F. Bogner. *From School Program to School Plant.* New York: Henry Holt and Company, 1956.

"How Award Winning Schools Compare," *Nation's Schools,* January 1965, pp. 47–78.

McClurkin, W. D. *School Building Planning.* New York: The Macmillan Company, 1964.

MacConnell, James D. *Planning for School Buildings.* Englewood Cliffs, N.J.: Prentice-Hall, Inc., 1957.

McLeod, John W. *New Ideas in School Construction; A.I.A. School Plant Studies.* Washington, D.C.: The American Institute of Architects, 1962.

McQuade, Walter (ed.). *Schoolhouse.* New York: Simon and Schuster, 1958.

Ovard, Glen F. (ed.). *On Planning Academic Classrooms—A Guide for Secondary School Planners.* American School Board Journal. Milwaukee, Wisconsin: The Bruce Publishing Company, 1962. (This publication is a collection of articles on planning academic classrooms published in *American School Board Journal,* January 1962 through October 1962.

"Significant Schools You Should See," *School Management*, July 1964, pp. 45–53.

"The Supermarket School," *School Management*, August 1964, pp. 48–51.

Trump, Lloyd. *Images of the Future*. Washington, D.C.: National Education Association, Department of Secondary School Principals, 1962.

CHAPTER 18

School Community Relations

During the past decade the American public has become very vocal in its criticism of public schools. This criticism ranges from the broad question, "What should our schools accomplish?" to the specific question, "Is this teacher or administrator doing a good job?" Some of the criticism is justified because of the weaknesses that do exist in the public school program. However, much of the criticism could be avoided if there were a better understanding and mutual cooperation between the school and the community. "A school system has public relations whether it tries to or not. Unavoidably, the public holds certain convictions about the schools, believes certain things to be true, and when the word 'school' is pronounced, conjures up a particular mental picture. These convictions, opinions, and mental images are the product of public relations, planned or otherwise."[1]

The increased criticism is not due to lack of interest in the child, but occurs because uncertainties arise regarding the progress of the child and the school in general.

"Parents are naturally interested in the education of their children. They want to know who is doing the teaching, what is being taught, and how well it is being taught. As long as they assume that all is going well, parents have little to say. But when uncertainties arise about the progress of their children or about the public school in general, their anxiety is

[1] Gloria Dapper, *Public Relations for Educators* (New York: The Macmillan Company, 1964), p. 1.

usually freely expressed, and there can be no doubt about their interest."[2] This interest of active citizens and active organizations can be put to work positively for education. More of the responsible citizens from every walk of life are joining together to work for the good of the schools. This spirit of community cooperation and participation is an exciting thing to see, and it is producing exciting results for the community as a whole as well as for the schools. The principal is usually in the center of these school community activities. His role is most important in the creation of good or poor public relations.

Definition and Importance of School Community Relations

Definition. Public relations has been defined many different ways, depending on the business or organization making the definition. Some individuals have said the phrase *public relations* has no meaning. However, the primary difficulty is that it means too many different things. Some definitions that have been used are: "public relations is whatever the individual practitioner thinks it is"; "public relations is a combination of philosophy, sociology, economics, language, psychology, journalism, communication, and other knowledges into a system of human understanding"; "public relations is merely human decency which flows from a good heart"; "public relations is just plain good human relations."

A good working definition was made by the American Association of School Administrators when public relations was defined as the cooperative development and maintenance of efficient two-way channels of information and understanding between the school, its personnel, and the community.[3] An important concept of this definition is that there is no "one" public in our communities. The solution of every new problem affects a different public. The public affected is the one that has the common problem or situation. The American Association of School Administrators stated it this way: "Strictly speaking, neither the public nor the average man are realities. They are statistical concepts only. There is no one public. There is virtually an infinite number of publics, each one to be identified with the situation or problem which is common to the individuals whose interests and welfare are commingled therein."[4]

Importance of Good Public Relations. The importance of a good school-community program of public relations can be shown in many

[2] National Society for the Study of Education, *Citizen Cooperation for Better Schools*, 1953 Yearbook (Chicago: The University of Chicago Press, 1954), p. 3.

[3] American Association of School Administrators, *Public Relations for America's Schools*, 28th Yearbook (Washington, D.C.: The Association, 1950), p. 14.

[4] *Ibid.*, p. 15.

ways. The increased criticism of public schools, which has already been indicated, is one evidence of the need for a good public relations program. Most of the criticism is due to misunderstandings that have arisen regarding the school program. These misunderstandings can usually be avoided if a proper spirit of cooperation and an attitude of understanding have been the practice in the schools. The need for a good, sound program of public relations is evidenced by the number of bond and leeway elections that are voted down by citizens of communities. Perhaps one of the most interesting examples of the need for a good public relations program was evidenced at an open meeting of educators and citizens on public relations, at which the press, including photographers, were confined to the balcony so they would not disturb the progress of the discussions.

A formal public relations program is a relatively new area for schools, and there are many people, including principals, who do not understand the importance of a good, sound public relations program. It is difficult for board members to justify the expenditures of money taken from the public to advertise to the public what is being done with the money that the public supplied. Others believe that an expenditure for public relations is simply a waste of public funds. With the growing complexity of school organization, the increased curriculum programs, and the increase in the many services necessary to adequately carry out the public school program today, the expenditure of funds to provide understanding and cooperation is not only justifiable but greatly needed. Neither the school district nor the secondary schools can afford to neglect their public relations program. This program should not be a hit-or-miss arrangement but should be well planned and effectively executed.

Purposes and Principles for Public Relations Programs

Purposes. The need for an effective public relations program has already been indicated; however, the organization of such a program should start with some definite purposes in mind. What is to be accomplished? What are the purposes of a good program? The following are some suggested purposes. Each school should add to these as their individual school-communities would indicate: (1) to develop common understandings about the aims and objectives of the schools, (2) to evaluate offerings of the school in terms of the needs filled, (3) to unite parents and teachers to meet the needs of the students, (4) to develop awareness of the importance of education in a democracy, (5) to establish confidence in the school, (6) to inform the public about the work of the school, and (7) to rally support for the maintenance of the school program.

Principles of a Good Public Relations Program. There are certain principles that should serve as guidelines for teachers and principals as they work in their communities. Adherence to these principles will aid greatly in promoting good school-community relations.

The following principles were given by the Commission on Public Relations of the American Association of School Administrators:

1. School public relations must be honest in intent and execution.
2. School public relations must be intrinsic.
3. School public relations must be continuous.
4. School public relations must be positive in approach.
5. School public relations should be comprehensive.
6. School public relations should be sensitive to its public.
7. The ideas communicated must be simple.[5]

Organizing a Public Relations Program

Know Your Community. In the definition of public relations it was stressed that there was no "one" public or community, but that there were virtually an infinite number of publics. The members of each public were identified with a common situation or problem. When one speaks of a community, it should be recognized that a community also consists of many smaller groups loosely knitted together to carry out the purposes for which they have a common interest. The administrator should remember that no community, nor the groups within it, stand willing to carry out a public school program. The school must work with these groups to help them arrive at a common goal. The following analysis by Austin, French, and Hull is helpful in understanding this concept:

> There is no ready-made school public willing to understand, to approve and to have a public opinion on school affairs. There are only loosely constructed social groups, some of which are interested in education. Out of these groups a school-public can be built through cooperative action, and in the process a public opinion develops on school affairs. But this public tends to keep falling apart and back into its several groups unless it is continuously used in the process of developing a constantly improving school.
>
> Anyone who works with a community as if it were a rather stable, unified, enduring entity needs to make a thorough study of the anatomy of democratic communities. They are dynamic, changing, loosely knit aggregates of other smaller groups that are largely free agents. They form and dissolve, split up and reunite in an unending process and in a changing pattern. They are capable of joining in unifying thought and organized

[5] *Ibid.*, pp. 17–33.

action, but it does not come naturally to them. The school administrator can best capitalize on these possibilities by providing plenty of opportunity for responsible participation in the processes by which a better school is built. If he continually does this he finds that he has helped the community build a school-public, and that there is a public opinion or mind about the school and its affairs that carries it forward from year to year.[6]

If all of these community groups must be linked together, and if the school is to be effective with them, it is important for the principal to know and to understand his community. The American Association of School Administrators provides the following study list, which may be used by the secondary school principal in obtaining information for better understanding of his community.

Steps in Developing a Public Relations Program. There are certain basic features that must be considered if an effective program is to be organized. The answers to these questions must be provided at the local level and by the personnel concerned. Other questions might be added to the list. The basic questions that principals must ask are as follows:

1. What does the public already know about the school?
2. What does the public want to know about the school?
3. What do the schools want the public to know about the school?
4. What training in public relations should a teacher be given and who should provide the training?
5. How can students be instructed so they will give proper interpretation to parents and the public?
6. Is the school's program helped or hindered by the active participation of teachers, principals, and organized groups in the state and local political campaigns, public sanctions on education, and other programs in which the school's personnel takes an active role?
7. How can the schools maintain the good will of certain pressure groups without becoming pawns of these pressure groups?
8. How can the school program and the financial considerations needed to sponsor the program be more effectively explained to the citizens?
9. How can a public relations program be interpreted as in the interests of the children rather than in the interests of the teaching profession?

After these basic questions have been resolved to the satisfaction of the principal, a list of steps necessary to formalize the program should be enumerated. In planning a program for the entire school, the principal should consider the following steps. First, the school should develop a

---

[6] David B. Austin, Will French, and J. Dan Hull, *American High School Administration*, 3rd ed. (New York: Holt, Rinehart and Winston, 1962), pp. 575–76.

clear-cut and inspiring statement of the objectives of the institution. Second, there must be an analysis and a written description of the needs that must be met to attain these objectives. The needs must be described and agreement reached before work is started. All school personnel should understand these needs and evaluate them and be ready to support and interpret them to the public. Third, there must be a thorough analysis of the means required and available to meet the needs to attain the objective. An analysis, motivation, and work with three kinds of people are needed to analyze the means: power groups and power individuals, influence groups and individuals, and money groups and individuals. Fourth, a prescription must be written for the approach to each key person or group who will contribute time, money, or influence. Fifth, there must be developed a coordinated, effective opening program to implement these prescriptions. Sixth, every member of the faculty and personnel of the school must be willing to participate wholeheartedly in the program of public relations. Seventh, an adequate follow-up, feedback, analysis, and evaluation of the actions taken must be provided. Eighth, an analysis of the media to be used in the informational phase of the program should be made.

In organizing the public relations program it would be well to remember that the emphasis in the past has been to sell the people on how good the schools are. A newer emphasis is the presentation of the schools as they might be, the kind of education that could be secured if our schools were as good as they ought to be.

Communications and Public Relations

Personal Communication. The first impression of a school received by a parent or citizen is often a lasting impression; therefore, it is necessary to do everything possible to make these impressions pleasant and favorable. Teachers and administrators should be friendly and understanding even though there may be reason for disagreement.

Because the principal is not always available, each school should have a secretary-receptionist so every person can be greeted pleasantly when he enters the school and be assured that there is someone there to help him with his problems.

Telephone courtesy is most important for establishing good first impressions. A "Good morning, may I help you?" or "Good afternoon, Hillcrest High School," lets the individual on the other end know that you are willing to talk with him about his ideas and/or problems.

The impression left by a well-organized, well-presented speech also establishes faith in the principal and in the high school.

The Press. The newspaper is a civic report card for the schools. It can tell the story about school accomplishments in an exciting way, or it can never reach the home either because the principal did not want it to or because he put the item in the pocket of his mind and forgot that it was news. Another problem exists—the principal often does not know what is "news" and how to get the news to the reporter. Dapper indicated that "the reporter assigned to the schools sees his job as informing the public fully about what is going on in education in his community. The school man sees part of his own job in precisely the same terms. And yet, they often treat each other as natural enemies."[7]

What is news? News, by definition, is something out of the ordinary. There are countless interesting stories that never get told because the teacher or the principal does not recognize a good news story. Teachers do so many unique and different things as part of their everyday experience that they frequently cannot see what would be interesting to the parents.

A few examples of news items of significance that were never published because "it was all in the teacher's day" are presented below to help the principal sharpen his "news perception."

A seventh-grade class took a field trip to the state's first capitol building, long since abandoned.

An eighth-grade teacher taught elements of the economic free-enterprise system. The students organized a store, borrowed money from a bank, signed a promissory note, made articles to sell, paid back the note, and made a profit.

A junior student won the "science fair" award. A press release was made indicating that he won, but it did not describe the project, the teacher who assisted, or other classroom competing projects.

The senior class carried out an intensive study of political parties and voting. The students spent part of their day at the polls, visited with registration officials and judges, and walked through the mechanics of voting. While at the polls, a student asked the teacher if he wasn't going to vote. His answer was, "I'm not old enough." A newspaper headline the next day might have read, "Teacher can't vote, but teaches students how . . ." How interesting a routine question can make a news story.

The civics class organized a town clean-up, paint-up project.

A unit in tenth-grade composition ended by students writing a short story. Several stories could have been printed with an accompanying brief of the elements of a short story.

Ninety per cent of the graduating class entered a college, university, or some type of advanced vocational school.

A teacher presented a paper at a state convention. His presence and purpose at the convention were sent to the press, but not what he said.

---

[7] Gloria Dapper, *op. cit.*, p. 32.

"Buses circle the world seven times" might be a headline about school bus transportation, which is so routinely scheduled every day. The total miles for the year? Personnel? Gallons of gas used?

These are only a few of the interesting, everyday occurrences that are worthy of press releases. Both the teacher and the principal should be taught to look for and report the pressworthy happenings.

As has been previously indicated, publicity does not assure good public relations. No one will deny, however, that publicity which is selective, is organized, and fills a need can do much in moving a good public relations program. The press can promote good or bad impressions of the schools.

The school principal should evaluate his present publicity releases in relationship to the general principles listed above. Parents are vitally interested in the progress and accomplishments of their children. The question might be asked, "Are we providing the right type of publicity?" The answer is generally, "No." Thirteen topics of school news were ranked by the author according to the expressed interests of school patrons and compared with the space devoted to these topics by leading newspapers as shown below.

Topics of School News	Rank According to Patron's Interests	Space in News
Pupil progress and achievement	1	4
Method of instruction	2	10
Curriculum	3	6
Health of pupils	4	9
Value of education	5	12
Discipline and behavior of pupils	6	11
Teachers and school officials	7	2
Attendance	8	13
Building and building program	9	8
Business management and finance	10	7
Board of education and administration	11	5
P.T.A.	12	3
Extracurricular activities	13	1

It can be seen from this comparison that although student progress and achievement was ranked first by the patrons according to their interests, it was ranked fourth according to the space devoted to it by the newspaper. Method of instruction is ranked second by interest, but tenth according to the space devoted it. Conversely, extracurricular activities were ranked thirteenth according to interest, but first according to the space devoted to these activities in the news.

Another study reported in the Education Supplement of the *Saturday Review* was concerned with 19 leading newspapers from all sections of the country that had full-time education editors. During the month of September all articles about education were clipped. There were 4,000 stories about schools, good in quantity but poor in quality. Over 95 per cent of the stories covered "trivia." Most of the 95 per cent concerned extracurricular activities. (This did not encircle sports. The sports were so well covered that they were not clipped as part of the 4,000 articles.) The next biggest category was about teachers giving speeches. However, these were primarily announcements about speeches; seldom was the essence of the speech given. The remaining 5 per cent of the articles were good news articles.[8]

The Public Information Department of Port Jefferson, New York, schools distributes the following instructions on how to write a news release to all members of the staff.[9]

How To Write a News Release

News writing is an art but it is also a skill that can be learned. Most school publicists can be assumed to have had a good basic training in the use of English. The fundamentals of composition learned in the usual school courses apply here. To write a good news release you need an outline, an introduction, a body and a conclusion. The essence of good writing for the press is brevity and conciseness. Read the stories in any good newspaper—particularly the papers published in your own town. Note how they put the meat of the story in the opening paragraph and follow it with less important details. Note the economy of words with which the stories are written. See how a general style of writing seems to be common to the better papers.

RULES FOR EDITORIAL CONTENT
1. Keep the story simple—don't try to *pad* it.
2. Use short sentences and short paragraphs.
3. Try to write as though you were talking to a single person.
4. Use only the ideas and the vocabulary that will be understood by the average newspaper reader. Keep away from professional terms such as "frame of reference," "core curriculum," "implementation," "homogeneous grouping" and similar phrases.
5. Stick to facts—don't editorialize. If you must have an opinion expressed, quote somebody in direct authority.
6. Avoid "a spokesman for the board" or "an informed source." Use names.

[8] Gloria Dapper and Barbara Carter, "Is Education News?" *Saturday Review,* May 17, 1962, p. 84.
[9] Reprinted with permission of The Macmillan Company from *Public Relations for Educators* by Gloria Dapper. Copyright © Gloria Dapper, 1964, pp. 59-60. Also reprinted with permission of Port Jefferson Public Schools.

7. Use specific dates, not "yesterday," "today," or "tomorrow."

8. Avoid glowing adjectives and superlatives. They belong to the commercial advertisers.

9. Check your story to see if it answers the editor's inevitable questions, "who, what, when, where, how and why."

10. Read your story again. Can you cut it?

11. The first paragraph should focus attention on the time, nature, and extent of the event.

MECHANICAL STANDARDS

1. Use department stationery for all copies on letter size paper (8½ × 11).

2. Use one side only.

3. Type your release, using double spacing to provide room for editorial changes.

4. Start your story about one third of the way down the page to leave room for the editor to write in a headline or other directions; include your own descriptive headline above the article.

5. Leave a fair margin on each side of the copy.

6. Number each page, if more than one is used.

7. Don't break a paragraph at the bottom of a page.

8. At the end of each page of a multiple-page story type "MORE." At the end of the story type —30—. All newspaper offices know what these symbols mean.

9. Type an original and three copies of each page used.

10. Staple each complete article together; submit all three to the Department Chairman.

Since newspapers are a civic report card, they are responsive to public opinion. The editors print news that patrons want to read, and like politicians, they use letters of criticism and commendation as a public barometer. The principal should not only write letters of thanks himself, but should also encourage teachers, students, parents, P.T.A. officers, and others to do the same.

Radio and Television. There are many opportunities to get news items about the school on the radio. Newscasts are frequent. "Spots," short news items, are given hourly. Spots in the public interest are often free. Such a policy is a boon to schools because a radio station's existence is through selling advertising time. The school will also want to pay for some news items. It should be remembered that time is of high priority and what is said must be short, clear, and understandable.

In addition to the short news items, some schools have regular programs and/or school reports, in which the events of the week are given or special activities are highlighted. Schools can often get on-the-spot coverage of special events or can have events and conversations recorded and then broadcast. Editing can make these types of presentations very effective.

Television is more costly, and the secondary school principal will have less opportunity to use this media. Most television programs should be visual stories with action, rather than the panel discussion variety. An interesting back-to-school day, special events days, or an unusual curriculum project may warrant the use of television. Sponsors can be found if the program is good enough.

News items can be put on television more readily. Pictures and drawings are usually needed in addition to the script. These spots are much like radio spots in the element of time. They should be short, with several varieties of script covering the same message if repetition is desired.

Many school districts now have their own educational television channel. Many programs can reach every home when proper arrangements and adapters are available. Curriculum instruction as well as information becomes available in the home by the flick of a switch.

Other Mass Communication Media.   Other means of mass communication are available to the principal. Within the city are many business, professional, and service organizations that have house reports, bulletins, and newspapers. Items of school news are usually welcome, especially if appropriate to a theme, a business event, or a special time of year affecting their business, such as back-to-school time. The principal should have a list of all these community publications along with the name of the editor and the date of publication.

State, regional, and national magazines can frequently be used for worthy school releases.

The school has its own mass media—the school newspaper, radio station, yearbook, and other special publications. Attempts to upgrade these media to present more than the trivia and gossip column would significantly improve the principal's public relation program. The principal's annual report can be printed and circulated as well as news items taken from it.

Improved Public Relations Through Individuals and Groups

Citizen Cooperation.   The area of public relations that seems to be gathering momentum, if the amount of space in professional journals can be used as an indication, is citizen cooperation. The establishment of citizen committees has gone beyond the area of school buildings. Citizen committees are being used as advisory groups for more effective solutions of all school problems. It is interesting to note the areas or levels of activity that are open to citizen cooperation, as indicated by Kenneth E. Oberholtzer. He states that, in general, there are six principal levels: studying (including assembling of data), planning, interpreting, deciding, executing, and evaluating.[10]

Citizen cooperation can be a time-consuming way to solve a problem. This question should be answered prior to establishing a committee, "Is cooperative action worthwhile in terms of the time consumed?" If the answer is "yes," procedures for initiating this type of committee should be commenced. If the answer is "no," some other technique or communication medium should be used.

Parent-Teachers' Association. One of the most consistent supporters of the school is the Parent-Teachers' Association (P.T.A.). It was organized in 1897 as the National Congress of Mothers. In 1924 it became the Congress of Parents and Teachers. The objectives of the P.T.A. are: (1) to promote the welfare of children and youth in home, school, church, and community; (2) to raise the standards of home life; (3) to secure adequate laws for the care and protection of children and youth; (4) to bring into closer relationship the home and the school, so that parents and teachers may cooperate intelligently in the training of the child; and (5) to develop between educators and the general public such united efforts as will secure for every child the highest advantage in physical, mental, social, and spiritual education.

The P.T.A. is organized at the following levels: national, state, regional, district, and school. The principal has an effective organization with national influence ready to help him with his problems. Too frequently the principal regards the P.T.A. as an organization that has as its goal "four meetings a year." The P.T.A., used effectively, can provide excellent two-way communication between the schools and its most important patrons—the parents. Under a principal who conceives his role as second vice-president in the organization to be one of dynamic leadership, mutual trust, understanding, and cooperation for the improvement of the school and the children can result.

Teacher Relations with Parent and Student. An important agent for promoting good school-community relations is the teacher. Because parents are most interested in the progress and achievement of their child, it is obvious that the key person in the program is the teacher. Actually, the root of all public relations is in the classroom. This statement by the National School Public Relations Association, a department of the National Education Association, indicates the importance of the teacher: "Because of their preparation and contacts classroom teachers have a strategic role in interpreting the schools to the people. They are familiar with the history, philosophy, purposes, and methods of education. They

---

[10] National Society for the Study of Education, *op. cit.*, p. 63.

are informed about psychology, child nature, and social processes. These talents can and have been used to develop the public relations programs of school systems in many communities."[11]

It is the teacher's responsibility to impress upon the student and thus upon the parents the favorable aspects of the school program. Teachers must be educated as to the importance of their role in public relations. This need is emphasized in the presentation "Public Relations Is for the Birds."

Public Relations Is for the Birds

If I were planning a local-association meeting on public relations, I'd call it "Public Relations Is for the Birds," and build a program around the classroom teacher's four major "publics": pupils, parents, colleagues, and the community. And I'd give teachers ample opportunity to discuss the various problems.

I'd start with a panel to introduce the birds I have in mind.

The first bird is the Frostbitten Scoff. He regards democratic classroom procedures darkly, relies on a substantial arsenal of homework and heavy-handed discipline, considers it a sign of weakness to smile.

The second bird is the Double-throated Pedagoose. Fond of multisyllabic words, the Pedagoose uses them freely on bewildered parents, often looks down his long beak at folks whose clothes and grammar don't meet his own exacting standards. He often gets support from the Speckled Buck-Passer, who blames all shortcomings of his students on their home training and doesn't mind saying so loudly and often.

Third to be introduced would be the Twitter-Pated Blush, forever apologizing that he's "just" a teacher. He might be accompanied by the Mud-slinging Splutter who enjoys a little back-of-the-hand gossip about other teachers, other schools.

Fourth to be introduced might be the Back-pedaling Hibernator, who resists all efforts to draw him into community activity. He is obviously saving himself for something. His favorite saying: "You've got to draw the line somewhere!"

Following the introductions, the group would divide into four sections for discussions of the four categories.

Later, the entire group would come together for a "quickie" panel with two participants from each group discussion. One of these would outline in two minutes the specific public-relations technique or idea an individual classroom teacher could concentrate on in the coming year. The other would give the group's consensus on one public-relations project the local association could carry on in the coming year.[12]

---

[11] National School Public Relations Association, *It Starts in the Classroom* (Washington, D.C.: National Education Association, 1951), p. 5. This association has a monthly bulletin entitled *It Starts in the Classroom*, to which every principal should subscribe.

[12] Beatrice M. Gudridge, "If I Were Planning a Local Meeting," *N.E.A. Journal*, March 1956, p. 172.

The Student as Public Relations Agent. There is no one, absolutely no one, who can build up the image of a school or tear it down faster than the student. At dinner tables across the land, this question is asked, "What did you do in school today?" The answers range from "We had beans again" to lively discussions of teachers—their peculiarities—and the instruction of the day. Nor is the principal left out of the descriptive commentary. The student who comments favorably about some aspect of the school program creates more good will toward the school than most informational publicity sent home to the parents. Teachers and principals should capitalize on the opportunity to have a public relations agent in every home.

Nonteaching Personnel as Public Relations Agents. Far too frequently the public relations program overlooks personnel who have considerable influence in a community. The nonteaching personnel in the auxiliary services—cooks, bus drivers, custodians, nurses—are usually neglected. Since they are associated with the schools but not teaching, these individuals are frequently asked—or give their opinion without being asked—about needs, programs, and the behavior of the teachers and principal. Their interest in schools should be channeled to good advantage by actively involving them in a sound public relations program.

The Administrator and Public Relations. As the teacher and the students are the most important figures in the school for promulgating good relations, the administrator is the key person in organizing, activating, and establishing the tone and structure of the public relations program. When the administrator fails in setting the proper tone and structure, criticism often becomes severe.

If the principal does not plan the long-range program and organize the structure to achieve both the long- and short-range objectives, the job will not get done. As in all phases of the school program, the principal is the key figure in the success or failure of the school's public relations program. He should encourage all members of the staff in more effective relationships, train them in the "hows" of good public relations, work with them on newspaper and other releases, and see that they receive praise for work well done. All teachers like to be recognized orally and in print for their accomplishments, but few will sound their own trumpet. The principal must appoint and delegate effective communication personnel to search out and write the stories where necessary.

Effective Communication with Words

In the final analysis, good public opinion is built on action and words. The desired actions have been described in the role relationships of the individuals and their part in a public relations program. The other means of communication, which also is part of action, is words—spoken and written. The words themselves play an important part in effective communication.

"To influence people to act for a worthy cause we must first have an easy entrance to their minds. We should use MIND-OPENING words rather than MIND-CLOSING words. People act only when they feel that it is the thing to do. They will never feel the incentive to act until they have considered the facts. They will not consider the facts until the truth can enter their minds—so why not open the mind's door rather than try to enter through the keyhole?"[13] The National School Service Institute suggests that words be given the following test:[14]

1. Will the word or phrase appeal to the self-interest of the reader or listener? If so, USE it!

2. Will it cause him to instinctively think of the cost to him? If so, DON'T use it!

3. Will it stir up an argumentative impulse? If so, DON'T use it!

4. Will it enter the experience of the reader? If so, USE it!

5. Will it arouse antagonism? If so, DON'T use it!

6. Is it beyond the experience of the reader? If so, DON'T use it!

7. Will the reader see immediately how he will benefit? If so, USE it!

8. Will it excite the natural curiosity of the reader? If so, USE it!

9. Will the reader immediately think of YOUR self-interest? If so, DON'T use it!

10. If it will cause a positive reaction—USE it! If a negative one— AVOID it!

The National School Service Institute suggests the following mind-opening and mind-closing words.[15]

MIND-CLOSING WORDS	MIND-OPENING WORDS
NEEDS	*Opportunity*
	Should or *Must Have*
	The Situation Is

The word "needy" is *seedy*. No one is interested in the other fellow's or an institution's needs. Everyone tries to button his pocket as well as his mind because it immediately suggests that he is going to be "touched" for

[13] Lew Parmenter, *No! Yes! Words Make the Difference* (Chicago: National School Service Institute), p. 3. Reprinted by permission of the National School Service Institute.

[14] *Ibid.*, p. 3.

[15] *Ibid.*, pp. 4–9.

| MIND-CLOSING | MIND-OPENING |
| WORDS | WORDS |

a contribution. Needs can usually be turned into "opportunities." A situation can be described as inadequate, then describe the desired situation which may be had with just a little greater investment.

SUPPORT   *Invest Working Capital*
                     Buy Dividend-Paying Stocks
                     Champion, Endorse

This overworked word sounds like a prop to hold up an old barn. It *asks for help.* Beggars are never popular. Education is no object of pity.

AID   *Improve*
                     Invest
                     Benefits

"Aid" is another begging word. Accent what you're *giving*—never what you want to *get.* "Bread cast upon the waters."

BETTER   *Improved*

"Better" is a comparative. You can never be sure with what the reader or listeners are comparing it.

RIGHTS   *Privileges* and *Responsibilities*

Most people think of rights as licenses.

ASSESSMENT   *Investment*

Assessment takes something away by force. Investment pays dividends.

FREEDOM   *Personal Liberty*

Freedom suggests *en masse*; personal liberty makes it individual.

TOLERANCE   *Friendliness, Appreciation*

Sometimes we tolerate what we don't like.

STATISTICS   *Facts*

Facts are stubborn things; statistics are more pliable—they are like witnesses; they can testify for either side.

HELP   *Cooperation*

A drowning man cries for help. A going enterprise seeks cooperation.

ASSISTANCE   *Participation*

Make them a partner in the enterprise.

OBJECTIVE   *Ideal, Purpose*

There are devious objectives. Ideals are worthy things.

DONATE   *Share in*

Again make partners.

TAXES   *Assure Your Future Investment*

Here supplant the idea of force with the idea of opportunity.

GET   *Give*

Never let the idea of "getting something" loose; always show how much you are giving.

MIND-CLOSING WORDS	MIND-OPENING WORDS

THINKING   *Conviction*

Thinking is when a man holds an idea; conviction is when an idea holds the man.

I   *You*

WE   *You*

The greatest bore in the world is the man, who, when you ask him how he feels, tells you.

TEACHER   *Professional Educator*

Let's glorify and justify him as the world's greatest benefactor.

STUDY   *Fun or Thrill of Learning*

EQUIPMENT   *Teaching Tools*

SUPPLIES   *Learning Tools*

Tools have made our great American production and civilization possible. Everyone understands that.

SCHOOL HOUSE   *Educational Plant*

Raise the sights to loftier heights.

PUBLIC RELATIONS   *In the Public Interest*

Many still think of Public Relations as publicity advertising and even propaganda. You are seeking understanding and appreciation.

DISAGREE   *Yes, But—*

Pause and Praise

One who makes a statement is apt to be more firmly convinced he is right when you flatly disagree. Just give him credit and see why he believes as he does BUT—then—"Have you ever thought of this, etc."

TELL   *Ask*

Provoke Thought

"Tell" has "I" as the implied subject. "Asking" places the emphasis on "you."

SHAME   *Pride, Glory*

Shame degrades; pride and glory inspire.

SELLING   *Buying*

The sale is always made in the Buyer's mind—never in the salesman's. Therefore, speak in the Buyer's language.

FREE ENTERPRISE   *Individual Opportunity*

Go *from* the generalization *to* the personal adaptation.

CALAMITY   *Lost Opportunity*

Calamity is hopeless; from Lost Opportunity we rise again.

SOCIAL SCIENCE   *The Art of Living*

Art implies truth and refreshment of the soul.

TRY   *Do*

Leave no doubt about it.

MIND-CLOSING WORDS	MIND-OPENING WORDS

DESPAIR — *Faith*
Substitute the good for the bad.

SAVE — *Safeguard*
Save implies despair; safeguard implies hope and faith.

WHAT — *Why*
What implies an idea only; Why implies a conviction.

CRITICIZE — *Laud, Praise*
No one enjoys being criticized; but he glows at being praised.

COMPARE — *Improve*
Comparisons are odious; improvements are hopeful.

IMPOSSIBLE — *Just a Little Longer, One Obstacle at a Time*
Never admit the futile. Be hopeful.

PUBLICITY — *Information*
Publicity can be bad as well as good; get people to think through the truth.

WANT — *Deserve*
Desire
Require
Want is needy, seedy—Deserve is worthy.

PUBLIC — *Individual Citizen*
Personalize the man.

DEMOCRACY — *Representative Government*
The word, "Democracy," has many interpretations. The Russians use it for their brand of totalitarianism.

SALARY — *Earned Income*
PAY
Many are receiving salaries without effort. The teacher is earning much more than her salary.

POOR — *Handicapped*
Poor is indigent—the handicap often makes the man.

GOOD — *Expert, Superior*
There are so many "good" things—a good meal, a good time, a good jag; an expert teacher is distinctive.

EXCELLENT — *Proficient*
From general to individual.

DISINTERESTED — *Complacent,*
Not Aware
The complacent knows better and can be aroused.

TEACHER TRAINING — *Professional Development* or *Growth*
You can train a dog or a moron. Development approaches the ideal.

MIND-CLOSING WORDS	MIND-OPENING WORDS

DUTY   *Exciting, Adventure, Opportunity*
Duty is oftimes onerous. Adventure is romance.

DISCIPLINE   *Inspired Desire to Be Liked*
Idea of punishment versus inspiration.

OUR SCHOOLS   *Your Schools*
The public furnishes the kids and the cash.

PROPAGANDA   *Militant Truth*
                             Facts
Propaganda has bad connotations.

CHARITY   *Enterprise, Love*
Despair versus Hope.

EXPENSE   *Investment*
Expense is a thing of the past for which we must pay. Investment is advancing money with the hope of dividend returns. Prisons are an expense—Education is an investment which gives the greatest returns of all enterprise.

PROFITS   *Earned Returns*
                             Left Over
Profits are a red flag to some. All agree that we have a right to what we earn.

INCOME   *Returns on Investment* or *on Work Performed*
Income suggests just money; returns is pay for services rendered.

COST   *Benefits*
We shy away from costs; we desire benefits.

APPROPRIATIONS   *Conversions into*
                             Benefits
                             Investment
Again Cost versus Hope.

FINANCING   *Profitable Enterprise*
Again Cost versus Hope.

PROVIDE FUNDS   *Capital Investment*
Provide is giving. Investment gives returns.

CONTRIBUTE TO   *Invest In*
Asking for contributions is begging. Asking for investments implies returns.

IN ANNUAL REPORTS

RECEIPTS   *We Took in*
EXPENDITURES   *We Paid out*
CAPITAL COST   *Investment in Buildings*
NEGATIVES   *Positives*
Accentuate the positive.

MIND-CLOSING	MIND-OPENING
WORDS	WORDS

EDUCATORS' TERMS   *Vernacular of Layman*

Too academic phraseology finds a closed door. Talking to a farmer, use agricultural illustrations—to a plumber, in terms of pipes, sinks, drains, etc.

LOWER GRADES   *Important Habit-Forming Grades*

Lower can mean inferior. We must glorify this most important first step to success, both for the pupil and the teacher.

IF YOU WANT ACTION—USE WORDS OF ACTION—VERBS— VERBS. GLOWING ADJECTIVES AND ADVERBS SLOW DOWN THE TRAIN. USE MOVING WORDS TO MOVE FORWARD TO SUCCESS.

Evaluating the Public Relations Program

In business, good public relations can be measured by the sale or purchase of an article. The volume of the sales of a business in a competitive market is a public relations barometer to the businessman. In the medical profession, the barometer of good public relations is the return of a former patient for a new or recurring illness. In the clergy, the extent of good public relations can be observed by the size of the congregation.

What is the barometer of public relations for public education? The sale of an idea or thought or plan of action, the acceptance of which may not be determined for years hence? The size of a class or the return of a student, who under present law is obligated to be in attendance for 10 to 12 years? Since the state and local boards of education have the right of a legal monopoly over the articles sold, the curriculum; the duration of exposure, school attendance laws; place of exposure, school boundary lines; and the salesman, a proper interpretation and mutual understanding of the publics of the community and the schools are essential for smooth working relations.

But how can the principal determine if his program of public relations is functional? The following modified check list published by the American Association of School Administrators can be used as a guide in evaluation:[16]

---

[16] Modified from American Association of School Administrators, *A.B.C.'s of School Public Relations* (Washington, D.C.: The Association, 1959), pp. 5–16. Reprinted by permission of the American Association of School Administrators.

Public Relations Checklist

_____Regard public relations as a two-way process—as a cooperative search for mutual understanding and effective teamwork between community and school?

_____Seek to establish favorable attitudes as well as opinions, and take into account the influence of both emotions and intellect?

_____Keep in mind the fact that there are many "publics"?

_____Derive your public relations program from the day-to-day work of the schools?

_____Know and serve the interests of the various publics in your community?

_____Maintain a continuous program of interpretation and cooperation?

_____Check the accuracy and honesty of interpretation of the information which goes out about the school?

_____Emphasize the positive approach in public relations?

_____Have a comprehensive and well-balanced program of school public relations?

_____Present your ideas in simple, understandable, and accurate form?

_____Have a curriculum which meets the needs of your community?

_____Give attention, through a carefully planned program of pupil guidance, to the problems and needs of every child?

_____Have the kind of school program which develops in the pupils a wholesome pride and sense of responsibility as members of a school community?

_____Have a friendly school, in which the public regularly finds a cordial welcome?

_____Have a student body comprised, for the most part, of enthusiastic boosters of the school?

_____Direct attention to the outstanding successes of pupils and former pupils?

_____Keep adequate records of pupils' abilities, achievements, interests, and experiences?

_____Issue to parents the kinds of progress reports which they can understand and appreciate?

_____Conduct a continuous self-survey of the school program as a basis for educational planning with the help of consultants on occasion?

_____Bring in all interested lay groups in the community to help with school plans—relying especially on the unique services of the parent-teacher association?

_____Include pupils among those who participate in cooperative planning?

_____Provide teachers with adequate time, materials, and professional leadership for effective planning?

_____Use the planning sessions, at least in part, to acquaint the participants (a) with the newer trends in education? (b) with the basic processes of democracy?

_____Strive to plan in terms of ideas and principles, arriving at evaluations and decisions apart from the persons who proposed them?

_____Evaluate the quality of school and community relations at regular intervals?

_____Maintain working conditions and relationships that attract and hold competent school employees?

_____Keep the public well informed through administrative reports?

_____Have an adequate statement on public relations in the school handbook, with provisions for carrying it out?

_____Manage the business affairs of the school in a way that commands the respect of responsible business men?

_____Publish regularly and distribute widely a series of financial reports that are attractive, interesting, and easy to understand?

_____Encourage teachers to take an active part in community affairs?

_____Direct public attention to this human interest activities and the achievements of teachers?

_____Stress the importance of every member of the staff in the public relations field?

_____Have an effective program of inservice training in school public relations for all school employees: professional staff, custodians, cafeteria workers, bus drivers, and others?

_____Have a policy of honesty, courtesy, and forthrightness in dealing with the press and the public?

_____Take the representatives of the press into your confidence and communicate with them regularly?

_____Interpret education as an investment in people?

_____Encourage the study and discussion of school needs as a point of departure in school public relations?

_____Focus attention on such basic needs as: extended educational opportunities? improved curriculum programs? additional school services? improved administrative structure? more competent teachers? better school environment? increased financial support?

_____Look upon school buildings as expressions of educational functions and purposes?

_____Strive to bring about greater recognition of the individual needs of children?

_____Make it a point to be the first to call the newspaper and report unfavorable incidents?

_____Try to be simple, honest, direct, and punctual in the use of all media?

_____Always select the best media for the specific purpose to be achieved?

_____Balance your program so that all types of media and all staff members are used in public relations?

_____Distribute information throughout the year, with a few good stories each week?

_____Release information to the public while it is still news? Publicize some of the "little things" around the school? Give space in publications to the work and accomplishments of many teachers, many departments, and many students?

_____Start planning early so that you have time to turn out a good job?

_____Give every item for publication one last check by a second staff member before its release?

_____Listen to complaints carefully, investigate the facts objectively, and seek to use them constructively?

_____Have reasonable and well-understood policies with respect to pupil conduct and disciplinary procedures?

_____Provide instructional materials that are up to date, authentic, and appropriate for the uses made of them?

_____Maintain a work space in the school for your parent-teacher association president?

_____Delegate the proper public relations functions, and commensurate authority, to staff assistants without relinquishing your own responsibility for the total program?

_____Assign responsibility to some one person for news coverage? radio programs? research? evaluation? official reports? liaison with community organizations?

_____Engage regularly in inservice activities to improve your skills in school public relations?

_____Merit community recognition and acceptance because of your professional competence and educational statesmanship?

_____Participate in the broader field of public relations by exchanging information and maintaining broad professional contacts outside your own school?

_____Invite the non-teaching personnel to attend selected staff meetings?

_____Solicit the support of professional organizations in the development of projects which will strengthen public education in the local community?

_____Assist professional organizations by suggesting areas for emphasis by these groups, and by inviting them to render services in particular areas of needs?

_____Keep professional organizations informed regarding administrative policies and basic problems relating to the educational program?

_____Coordinate the work of professional organizations with that of all other agencies in the community interested in education?

_____Give public recognition to outstanding service on behalf of public education by individuals and by professional groups?

_____Systematically appraise the schools' public relations program?

_____Take occasional polls of the opinions of pupils, teachers, and various groups of laymen with respect to items that reflect school public relations?

_____Adapt the practices followed in evaluation to the essential purposes of your own program and to the local situation in which it operates?

_____Regard evaluation as a highly important and necessary phase of the public relations program?

Summary

Public relations is defined as the cooperative development and maintenance of an efficient two-way channel of information and understanding between the school, its personnel, and the community. The school has more than one public. The public is, in effect, small groups of publics having common problems and interests.

The need for public relations is expressed in many ways—through public participation in school events, voting on bond and leeway elections, criticisms of the schools, and discussions in P.T.A. and other meetings about school problems. A good, sound program of school community relations must be devised. This program should be based on the purposes of the school. These purposes should be supported by sound principles. In this regard the public relations program should be: honest in intent and execution, intrinsic, continuous, positive in approach, comprehensive, sensitive to the public, and communicated in simple, understandable form.

The principal, as the responsible agent of the school, must organize and administer the program. In the practical aspects of the program he will want to consider (1) first impressions that are made on visiting personnel, (2) the press, (3) radio and television, (4) other mass communication media, (5) the Parent-Teachers' Association, (6) citizen cooperation, (7) teacher relations with parents and students, (8) the student as a public relations agent, (9) the principal's role in public relations, (10) nonteaching personnel as public relations agents, and (11) effective communication patterns and techniques. All these practices should be carefully developed into an effective comprehensive program.

Once the principal has a long-range, continuous program in operation, he should evaluate it for its effectiveness and improvement.

SUGGESTED PROJECTS AND ACTIVITIES

1. Examine the newspapers for a period of a week. Clip out all articles that have reference to the public school. Classify these articles as to their public relations value.
2. Visit a public relations coordinator for a school district or a high school and examine the program that is in operation. Discuss the immediate and long-range plans.
3. Write a publicity release using mind-opening words and compare this release to one you would write using mind-closing words.

4. Discuss first impressions that have been made on you in visiting schools and universities. What factors did you consider to have a good influence on you and what factors affected you negatively?
5. Using your newspaper clipping file, classify the number of articles that you have clipped on the basis of space in the news and compare with the rank of patrons' interest as shown in this chapter.
6. Discuss citizens or organizational representatives whom you would place on an advisory committee in a given curriculum area.
7. Collect comments from parents regarding the student's response to the question, "What did you do in school today?"

REVIEW AND DISCUSSION QUESTIONS

1. Which of the definitions of public relations do you believe best fits the school situation? Why?
2. How is it possible to discuss the "publics" rather than a single public?
3. What should be some of the primary purposes of a public relations program?
4. What are some basic principles in establishment of a school-community relations program? Which of the public relations media would you consider to be most effective? Why?
5. At which times would you prefer to use the press, the radio, television, consultant groups, etc.?
6. Why is more space in the newspaper related to the extracurricular activity program than to pupil progress, improvement, and achievement?
7. What can teachers do to become more effective public relations agents?
8. Why are the students considered to be the most important public relations agents?
9. What should be the place of the custodian, the school bus driver, the cooks, the nurses, and other nonteaching personnel in the public relations program?
10. Discuss some mind-opening and some mind-closing words. Essentially what is the psychological difference in these approaches?
11. What would be some effective evaluation techniques that could be used to evaluate the public relations program?

SELECTED BIBLIOGRAPHY

American Association of School Administrators. *A.B.C.'s of School Public Relations*. Washington, D.C.: The Association, 1959.

————. *Educational Administration in a Changing Community*, 37th Yearbook. Washington, D.C.: The Association, 1959.

Arend, Paul J. "The Supervisor, the School Newspaper, and Public Relations," *Bulletin of N.A.S.S.P.*, December 1961, pp. 101–5.

Campbell, Roald, and John A. Ramseyer. *Dynamics of School-Community Relations*. Boston: Allyn and Bacon, 1955.

Congreve, Willard J. "The Role of the Principal in School Improvement," *Bulletin of N.A.S.S.P.*, March 1964, pp. 3–10.

Cronin, Joseph M. "The Principal's Role in Change," *Bulletin of N.A.S.S.P.*, May 1963, pp. 29–32.

Dapper, Gloria. *Public Relations for Educators*. New York: The Macmillan Company, 1964.

Dapper, Gloria, and Barbara Carter. "Is Education News?" *Saturday Review*, May 17, 1962, p. 84.

Fox, Willard, and Glenn Gardiner. "Selling Your Ideas," *Bulletin of N.A.S.S.P.*, March 1964, pp. 72–79.

Kindred, Leslie W. *School Public Relations*. Englewood Cliffs, N.J.: Prentice-Hall, Inc., 1957.

Morris, J. R. "The Administrator and Public Relations," *Bulletin of N.A.S.S.P.*, March 1960, pp. 25–28.

National Association of Secondary-School Principals. "Public Relations for the American High School," *Bulletin of N.A.S.S.P.*, September 1960. The complete issue is devoted to public relations.

National School Public Relations Association. *It Starts in the Classroom*. Washington, D.C.: National Education Association, 1965. (A monthly bulletin.)

————. *Public Relations Gold Mine*, Volume 6. Washington, D.C.: The National Education Association, 1964.

————. *Trends in School Public Relations*. Washington, D.C.: The National Education Association, 1965. (A monthly bulletin.)

National Schools Service Institute. *No! Yes! Words Make the Difference.* Chicago: National Schools Service Institute.

National Society for the Study of Education. *Citizen Cooperation for Better Schools*, 1953 Yearbook. Chicago: University of Chicago Press, 1954.

PART V

*The changes—in curriculum, methodology, technology,
school scheduling, and staff development—are more
sweeping than the change from sailing ship to steamship,
or train to plane. Our passengers are not casual
and our freight is precious. The principal who
would move to change a school program to
prepare for the last third of this century must
move boldly yet gently, courageously yet courteously.*
    —JOSEPH M. CRONIN, "The Principal's Role in Change,"
    Bulletin of N.A.S.S.P., May 1963, p. 29.

THE PRINCIPALSHIP
AND THE
CHANGING SCHOOLS

CHAPTER 19

The Challenge of the Future

It has been shown that we are living in a revolutionary period of time. There is evidence that we may be witnessing and participating in one of the tidal waves of human thought and action that periodically sweeps over the world and changes the direction of human endeavor. Change and the need for change can be seen in all aspects of life. Long-established social values have been rejected and new ones adopted. Moral values of past generations have been set aside. Science has replaced many aspects of religious dogma. Long-established beliefs and practices have been challenged, disproved, and changed. Man has been forced to adjust to the dynamic forces of revolution.

Role of Education in a Revolutionary Period

During a revolutionary period the need for education is greater than at any other time. When the moorings of man are pulled out from under him, some new foundation must be substituted. Education is the process by which the new values, philosophy, facts, and knowledge give positive direction to future actions.

To find solutions to the population boom, the explosion in knowledge, the science-oriented, automated society of the future demands a new education. What the nature of this education will be cannot be fully visualized at this time, for the period of adjustment is just commencing. There are

475

some indications of the directions in which the new education will move. Some of these educational needs and indicators are presented below.

Education for Change. The youth of the nation, in fact individuals of all ages, must be taught the dynamics of change. This new education will teach about change in all facets of the society. It will condition the youth for the continual change that must take place. But more important, it will teach them how to change. Teaching people how to change and adjust to the cultural, technological revolution is a new, unexplored frontier in public education. The need for such an education becomes increasingly evident each day.[1]

Education for All. The people of our nation have taken pride in the fact that our educational system is planned for "All-American youth." Our youth are encouraged to go to school and, in fact, are forced to go to school. Such action has been justified on the grounds that education is good for both the welfare of the individual and the welfare of the society.

In recent years the emphasis has been on quality education because the "problem of quantity has been solved." However, making education available and even requiring children to attend school has not provided an education for all our youth. Approximately one fourth of the students of the nation do not graduate from high school. Although education is available to all, it should not be concluded that all youth are receiving an education. Certainly the dropout is not receiving an education. The school principal cannot be content because he offers a standard program available to all. In the immediate future he must find the programs and create the motivational factors that will keep all students in school.

The principal might well ask, "Why the concern for the dropout and the disadvantaged students?" The answer lies in the changing nature of the society. The War on Poverty program has shown that the "poor" are usually the parents, the youth, the disadvantaged students who lack enough education to be productive in the technological society. The U.S. Department of Labor estimates that each year automation eliminates 200,000 jobs for factory workers alone. Some estimates place the total figure as high as 40,000 jobs a week. At the same time that the jobs are decreasing for those less skilled, a larger number of youth are entering the labor market age. During the 1950's unemployment of youth became a problem. During the 1960's, 26 million young people will be entering the labor market, or 40 per cent more than in the 1950's.

The National Education Association Project on the Educational Impli-

---

[1] The May 1963 issue of the *Bulletin of N.A.S.S.P.* is devoted completely to the nature of change and examples of changing schools.

cations of Automation indicated that the undereducated and unskilled are doomed to learn the hard way that there is no room at the bottom of the ladder. The youth who are not left by the wayside are those who can demonstrate their ability to learn new skills and adapt to new situations. George Arnstein, the associate director of the project, indicates that the reluctant learners are our concern and that we must provide a place for them in the world of technology. A curriculum must be developed that is relevant to the present life and interests of the student.[2] Students among the disadvantaged and culturally deprived must have programs that teach basic skills, relate school experience to work experience, provide on-the-job training, and help make up cultural deficiencies. The challenge to the principal is to develop the curriculum that will indeed make education for all an actuality rather than a glowing generality.

Education for Individual Excellence. In addition to providing an education for all youth, the principal must be concerned about the quality of the education that they receive. An education that promotes individual excellence implies that each individual student will receive an education commensurate with his ability. Therefore, the challenge is not only to provide broad programs for all, but also to adjust these programs to the individual capacities of all students. Such programs will allow students to progress at their own best rate but, at the same time, will maintain quality levels of achievement for each student.

Some of the experimental continuous progress programs are currently meeting both of these requirements. In these programs, the student, parents, and teachers set the following goals for the student on the basis of all information available: (1) the rate of achievement—how far the student will progress through the curriculum, and (2) the level of quality—how well the student achieves. Both the rate and quality levels are different for each individual student.[3] The principal must organize his school, facilities, and staff to make this type of learning possible.

Education to Promote Exploration, Discovery, and Creativity. The problem of deciding what to teach is a most difficult one for the principal and teacher. The explosion of knowledge has been previously referred to as a force that has greatly affected our educational program. The acceleration of growth in the accumulation of knowledge has been prodigious. If plotted on a time line ranging from the birth of Christ to the present, the first doubling of knowledge would have occurred in 1750, the second in

[2] National Education Association, Project on the Educational Implications of Automation, *No Room at the Bottom: Automation and the Reluctant Learner* (Washington, D.C.: The Association, 1963), 102 pp.

[3] The Continuous Progress School at the Brigham Young University Laboratory School, Provo, Utah, has led out in this practice.

1900, the third in 1950, and the fourth in 1960.[4] The curriculum of the schools has not adjusted to such an explosion in knowledge. In most programs more pages are added to the textbook than the teacher is already unable to finish.

There is so much to be learned that students cannot possibly learn the basic body of facts in each area. It can also be assumed that in addition to the increased amount of knowledge, the body of knowledge will be radically reorganized several times during the rest of this century.

Since students will not be able to learn all the facts and since the facts will change, the emphasis of the future should be on learning techniques of exploration, discovery, analysis, and creativity. These skills and techniques can be used in all educational fields and they can be used to further expand the bodies of knowledge in each area.

Education for Social Responsibility. If a nation cannot expect to be free and ignorant at the same time, the education must provide for social awareness and responsibility. "The American way of life requires the development of a society of free men devoted to individual liberty and to the concern for public welfare. A free society must rely heavily, if its values are to be defended and realized, on the voluntary action of its citizens contributing to the public good."[5]

The Educational Policies Commission has indicated that social responsibility is not adequately developed in the American people, as evidenced by the indifference that many citizens have for the well-being of others, the racial and religious prejudices that persist, the millions of disadvantaged Americans who are still in poor housing and poor schools, and the evident lack of desire of many responsible leaders to try to improve these conditions.[6]

To help promote social responsibility, the schools must help students develop a respect for other people, toleration of their views, observance of laws, and a constant desire to improve conditions and solve the many problems that will always exist.

The Principal's Role in the Future Education

One might ask the following questions: Who will provide an education for change? Who will be concerned about an education for all youth—

[4] National Education Association, Project on Instruction, *Schools for the Sixties* (New York: McGraw-Hill Book Company, Inc., 1963), 146 pp.

[5] Editors of Education, U.S.A., *The Shape of Education for 1964* (Washington, D.C.: National School Public Relations Association, National Education Association, 1964), p. 5.

[6] Educational Policies Commission, National Education Association and American Association of School Administrators, *Social Responsibility in a Free Society* (Washington, D.C.: The Commission, 1963), 33 pp.

including those who have dropped out of our conventional programs? Who will initiate programs for individual excellence so that each student may achieve at a rate and quality level commensurate with his abilities? Who will initiate a curriculum where antiquated facts are replaced by exploration, discovery, and creative techniques to finding knowledge? Who will provide the opportunities to teach social responsibility in an age when the promotion of individual liberty is dependent on all people having equality of opportunity in social, legal, and moral settings? Who will make the school adjustable to the needs of the individual and society?

The answer to these questions is "the principal!"—if not the principal of today, then the one who will soon replace him, for the principal must also change. The society is changing. Secondary education must change to meet the changing needs of society. The principal must provide the thrust to put into orbit the new organizations, programs, and staff changes.

What, then, is the principal's role in the education of the future? He will be the innovator in curriculum and learning improvements. To accomplish these goals he will change the organization of the school, the organization and administration of his staff, and the "do-it-by-hand" operations to which he is accustomed.

Organizing the Schools of the Future. The organization of the future secondary schools must be based on the needs expressed in the changing society. The proved innovations of today will probably be the standard practice of tomorrow. Therefore, as shown in the chapter on organization, the nongraded school, large-group instruction, small-group instruction, and individualized instruction will become the traditional programs. Variations of these patterns will be numerous as programs are adapted to meet the unique needs within communities.

The emphasis will probably shift toward individualized and small-group instruction as technology for individualizing instruction becomes more commonplace. Flexible scheduling in its many forms will probably be a standard practice in the future.

However, the principal must make the changes that are in evident need today. Then he must be flexible so that changing structure can result as future needs dictate. The principal might well adopt these mottos: "If it works, it's obsolete!" and "If I'm satisfied, I had better retire!"

Organizing and Administering the Staff in Schools of the Future. Like school organization, the organization and administration of the staff are in need of change in most schools today. Large- and small-group instruction and individualized instruction require that the faculty be organized differently. Team teaching in a common subject area and in combined subject areas will also become standard practice if the present trends are any indication.

The role of a teacher will not be the same. If the new structures are to be effective, the principal must retread faculty members for the new types of teaching. This retreading will be done in summer workshops, college course, institutes, and all manner of in-service work. A common preparation period for teaching teams will improve the team teaching coordination and efforts. The principal will provide time and organize and encourage faculty members to make the adjustments needed.

Another change in the staff will be in the quality of preparation of the teacher. Master and doctoral degrees will become commonplace among the secondary school teachers. Teachers will be more specialized. The trend toward greater specialization will probably be an encouraging factor in the movement toward team teaching.

Utilizing New Media and Improved Technology. The use of new media has previously been discussed in other chapters. A brief summary of most of the newer media will suffice at this point. Programed materials have greatly aided and expanded the approaches to individualized instruction. As more self-teaching materials and devices such as microfilms, filmstrips, videotapes, and individualized television receivers are made available, this type of education will increase. Overhead projection, 8 mm. films, television—open and closed circuit—and other audiovisual aids will improve teaching.

Further automation will reduce the many hand operations of principals and teachers. The first electronic brain, Univac I, went into retirement at the Smithsonian Institute after only 12 years of operation. Its successor works 100 times faster than Univac I, and a million times faster than a human clerk. Where Univac I could remember only 1,000 words, its replacement stores 65,000 without effort.

The future school will probably have an instructional computer center or computers in every classroom. "What is it that talks to a student, guides him forward or backward through subject materials, changes his attitudes, collects his lunch money and assigns his homework? If you say a 'teacher', you are wrong. The correct answer is a digital computer. At least, this may be the answer for the advanced school system of the 1970's when computer-based classroom learning will become feasible both technically and economically."[7]

Computers are already being used to schedule students, store data, and make reports. Currently programs of instruction are being adapted to the computer. This technique is called C.A.I.—computer-assimilated instruction. A computer is more than an advanced teaching machine. It is flexible. It can change the mode of instruction during a lesson to adequately adjust

[7] Editors of Education, U.S.A., *op. cit.*, p. 28.

to the responses of the students. It may send him ahead or backward in the program.

The principal, librarian, and guidance personnel, as well as teachers, will profit through the computer's ability to classify and store material and retrieve and disseminate it on demand. The "information retrieval (I.R.) system" will do some of the following in the schools of the 1970's:

> Universities and secondary schools will be linked by data transmission lines to regional information centers. These central archives will gather, index, and store information from all sources—reports of experiments and tests, technical publications, doctoral dissertations, government reports, etc. "They will put the major catalogues of the world at the command of the local school library," and can supply pertinent information to school administrators; e.g., population trends, predictions on proposed bond elections based on previous voting trends.
>
> Optical scanners coupled to digital computers will make these information centers possible. They will scan printed and handwritten texts from around the country, simplify them, and catalogue them by author, concepts, or key words.
>
> The IR system of the future school will direct information to a person "who has not yet asked a question, but who does have a need for the answer." For example, the IR system would index the content of a new document and select the students or educators whose "information-need profiles" indicate that the content would be relevant to them.
>
> Computer-based independent study cubicles will line the halls of the advanced school system in 1970. They will combine automated teaching equipment with an IR system, aiding the student in preparing essays, and providing him with learning material graded to his level. The teaching machine will direct the student to material he should review, new areas of knowledge, and give him alternate solutions to problems. "Once the student was generally oriented to the subject under study, he might explore the area with a subject-matter expert via a two-way TV hookup."
>
> The same equipment will enable teachers continually to update their curriculum. For the counselor, student personnel records on magnetic tape will be updated by the daily progress of each student; and by monitoring this progress, the counselor can apply preventive measures before a student has developed a serious educational problem.[8]

The Future in Secondary School Administration

For the person who likes to work with adults and students, who can exercise leadership in a positive constructive way, who enjoys challenging

[8] *Ibid.*, pp. 29–30, as taken from Donald D. Bushnell, *The Role of the Computer in Future Instructional Systems*, AV Communication Review, Supplement 7 (Washington, D.C.: Department of Audiovisual Instruction, National Education Association, 1963), 70 pp.

problems and situations, and who is flexible in his ability to adjust and change, secondary school administration is a rewarding profession. Unlike the dropout who has no room at the bottom, there is room for a good principal at both the bottom and the top.

The wide range and types of schools, the growing number of schools, the increase in the need for assistant principals—these and many other factors all argue the fact that the future is promising in secondary school administration.

Not only are positions available, but also the status and financial rewards have been greatly improved. Principals are regarded highly by the members of a community, and the principal has ample opportunity to be active in leadership roles in community activities and organizations. The salary schedules are improving. Principals usually receive higher salaries than the teachers. In recent years the administrators' salaries have frequently been placed on some type of a ratio with teachers' salaries. As teachers' salaries go up, the administrators' salaries advance accordingly.

The area of school administration is fast becoming a profession. By the criteria for a profession as set forth by the Educational Policies Commission, the profession of school administration has a basic body of specialized knowledge identified, it seeks competence in its membership, it serves the needs of its members, and it has ethical standards. It promotes group solidarity and influences public policy in areas affecting school administration. However, there are still many problems to be solved before complete professional status can be achieved.

What of the future in secondary school administration? It couldn't be better! Although considerable knowledge has been obtained toward the improvement of education, the challenges are bigger and more important than ever before in history. A principal could ask for nothing more stimulating than the opportunity to be in a leadership position where he can help solve the challenging educational problems in the changing society.

SELECTED BIBLIOGRAPHY

Brown, B. Frank. *The Nongraded High School.* Englewood Cliffs, N.J.: Prentice-Hall, Inc., 1963.

Brown, James W., and James W. Thornton, Jr. (eds.). *New Media in Higher Education.* Washington, D.C.: Association for Higher Education and Division of Audiovisual Instructional Service, National Education Association, 1963.

Bush, Robert N., and Dwight W. Allen. *A New Design for High School Education.* New York: McGraw-Hill Book Company, Inc., 1964.

Bushnell, Donald D. *The Role of the Computer in Future Instructional Systems.* A V Communications Review, Supplement 7. Washington, D.C.: Department of Audiovisual Instruction, National Education Association, 1963.

Coleman, James S. "Social Change—Impact on the Adolescent," *Bulletin of N.A.S.S.P.* April 1965, pp. 11–15.

Editors of Education, U.S.A. *The Shape of Education for 1964.* Washington, D.C.: National School Public Relations Association, National Education Association, 1964.

Gardner, John W. "Innovation and Leadership in American Education," *Bulletin of N.A.S.S.P.*, March 1965, pp. 36–43.

Hemphill, J. K. "Progress Report: A Study of the Secondary School Principalship, Part II," *Bulletin of N.A.S.S.P.*, April 1964, pp. 215–33.

Kourmadas, John F. "Schools That Are Changing," *Bulletin of N.A.S.S.P.*, May 1963, pp. 33–36.

Kraft, Ivor. "The Coming Crisis in Secondary Education," *Bulletin of N.A.S.S.P.*, February 1965, pp. 5–45.

Leu, Donald J., and Herbert C. Rudman (eds.). *Preparation Programs for School Administrators—Common and Specialized Learnings.* Seventh U.C.E.A Career Development Seminar. East Lansing, Mich.: Michigan State University, 1963.

National Association of Secondary-School Principals. *N.A.S.S.P., Internship Project, News Report.* Washington, D.C.: The Association, Spring 1965.

———. "Nature of Change, Part I, Some Examples of Change, Part II," *Bulletin of N.A.S.S.P.*, May 1963. Complete issue is devoted to this topic.

National Education Association. Project on the Educational Implications of Automation. *No Room at the Bottom: Automation and the Reluctant Learner.* Washington, D.C.: The Association, 1963.

———. Project on Instruction. *Schools for the Sixties.* New York: McGraw-Hill Book Company, Inc., 1963.

National Education Association and American Association of School Administrators and Educational Policies Commission. *Social Responsibility in a Free Society.* Washington, D.C.: The Commission, 1963.

Richards, J. M. "Progress Report: A Study of the Secondary School Principalship, Part I," *Bulletin of N.A.S.S.P.*, April 1964, pp. 211–15.

Trump, J. Lloyd, and Dorsey Baynham. *Focus on Change—Guide to Better Schools.* Chicago: Rand McNally and Company, 1961.

Trump, J. Lloyd, and Lois S. Karasik. *Focus on the Individual—A Leadership Responsibility.* Washington, D.C.: The National Association of Secondary-School Principals, 1965.

Wells, Phillip C., Robert H. Nelson, and Earl M. Johnsen. "The Assistant Secondary School Principal," *Bulletin of N.A.S.S.P.*, January 1965, pp. 15–25.

APPENDIX

The Code of Ethics of the Education Profession

Administrator Ethics in Personnel Matters

Research Plan for School Leavers

Constitution and By-Laws of the Utah High School Activities Association

A Broad-Base Intramural Program

The Code of Ethics of the Education Profession[1]

PREAMBLE

We, professional educators of the United States of America, affirm our belief in the worth and dignity of man. We recognize the supreme importance of the pursuit of truth, the encouragement of scholarship, and the promotion of democratic citizenship. We regard as essential to these goals the protection of freedom to learn and to teach and the guarantee of equal educational opportunity for all. We affirm and accept our responsibility to practice our profession according to the highest ethical standards.

We acknowledge the magnitude of the profession we have chosen, and engage ourselves, individually and collectively, to judge our colleagues and to be judged by them in accordance with the applicable provisions of this code.

PRINCIPLE I

Commitment to the Student

We measure success by the progress of each student toward achievement of his maximum potential. We therefore work to stimulate the spirit of inquiry, the acquisition of knowledge and understanding, and the thoughtful formulation of worthy goals. We recognize the importance of cooperative relationships with other community institutions, especially the home.

[1] A uniform code of ethics for the entire profession adopted by the N.E.A. Representative Assembly in July, 1963. Reprinted by permission of the National Education Association.

In fulfilling our obligations to the student, we—

1. Deal justly and considerately with each student.
2. Encourage the student to study varying points of view and respect his right to form his own judgment.
3. Withhold confidential information about a student or his home unless we deem that its release serves professional purposes, benefits the student, or is required by law.
4. Make discreet use of available information about the student.
5. Conduct conferences with or concerning students in an appropriate place and manner.
6. Refrain from commenting unprofessionally about a student or his home.
7. Avoid exploiting our professional relationship with any student.
8. Tutor only in accordance with officially approved policies.
9. Inform appropriate individuals and agencies of the student's educational needs and assist in providing an understanding of his educational experiences.
10. Seek constantly to improve learning facilities and opportunities.

PRINCIPLE II

Commitment to the Community

We believe that patriotism in its highest form requires dedication to the principles of our democratic heritage. We share with all other citizens the responsibility for the development of sound public policy. As educators, we are particularly accountable for participating in the development of educational programs and policies and for interpreting them to the public.

In fulfilling our obligations to the community, we—

1. Share the responsibility for improving the educational opportunities for all.
2. Recognize that each educational institution may have a person authorized to interpret its official policies.
3. Acknowledge the right and responsibility of the public to participate in the formulation of educational policy.
4. Evaluate through appropriate professional procedures conditions within a district or institution of learning, make known serious deficiencies, and take any action deemed necessary and proper.
5. Use educational facilities for intended purposes consistent with applicable policy, law, and regulation.
6. Assume full political and citizenship responsibilities, but refrain from exploiting the institutional privileges of our professional positions to promote political candidates or partisan activities.
7. Protect the educational program against undesirable infringement.

PRINCIPLE III

Commitment to the Profession

We believe that the quality of the services of the education profession directly influences the future of the nation and its citizens. We therefore exert every effort to raise educational standards, to improve our service, to promote a climate in which the exercise of professional judgment is encouraged, and to achieve conditions which attract persons worthy of the trust to careers in education. Aware of the value of united effort, we contribute actively to the support, planning, and programs of our professional organizations.

In fulfilling our obligations to the profession, we—

1. Recognize that a profession must accept responsibility for the conduct of its members and understand that our own conduct may be regarded as representative.
2. Participate and conduct ourselves in a responsible manner in the development and implementation of policies affecting education.
3. Cooperate in the selective recruitment of prospective teachers and in the orientation of student teachers, interns, and those colleagues new to their positions.
4. Accord just and equitable treatment to all members of the profession in the exercise of their professional rights and responsibilities, and support them when unjustly accused or mistreated.
5. Refrain from assigning professional duties to non-professional personnel when such assignment is not in the best interest of the student.
6. Provide, upon request, a statement of specific reason for administrative recommendations that lead to the denial of increments, significant changes in employment, or termination of employment.
7. Refrain from exerting undue influence based on the authority of our positions in the determination of professional decisions by colleagues.
8. Keep the trust under which confidential information is exchanged.
9. Make appropriate use of time granted for professional purposes.
10. Interpret and use the writings of others and the findings of educational research with intellectual honesty.
11. Maintain our integrity when dissenting by basing our public criticism of education on valid assumptions as established by careful evaluation of facts or hypotheses.
12. Represent honestly our professional qualifications and identify ourselves only with reputable educational institutions.
13. Respond accurately to requests for evaluations of colleagues seeking professional positions.
14. Provide applicants seeking information about a position with an honest description of the assignment, the conditions of work, and related matters.

PRINCIPLE IV

Commitment to Professional Employment Practices

We regard the employment agreement as a solemn pledge to be executed both in spirit and in fact in a manner consistent with the highest ideals of professional service. Sound professional personnel relationships with governing boards are built upon personal integrity, dignity, and mutual respect.

In fulfilling our obligations to professional employment practices, we—

1. Apply for or offer a position on the basis of professional and legal qualifications.
2. Apply for a specific position only when it is known to be vacant and refrain from such practices as underbidding or commenting adversely about other candidates.
3. Fill no vacancy except where the terms, conditions, policies, and practices permit the exercise of our professional judgment and skill, and where a climate conducive to professional service exists.
4. Adhere to the conditions of a contract or to the terms of an appointment until either has been terminated legally or by mutual consent.
5. Give prompt notice of any change in availability of service, in status of applications, or in change of position.
6. Conduct professional business through the recognized educational and professional channels.
7. Accept no gratuities or gifts of significance that might influence our judgment in the exercise of our professional duties.
8. Engage in no outside employment that will impair the effectiveness of our professional service and permit no commercial exploitation of our professional position.

Administrator Ethics in Personnel Matters[2]

A Statement of Principles Amplifying the Code of Ethics for California Teachers

To fulfill his special responsibilities to pupils, parents, the community, and the profession as an executor of board policies, as adviser to the board on policies and procedures, and as a professional leader in the school district, the teacher employed in an administrative position recognizes and adheres to these standards of personnel administration:

A. In the selection and employment of new personnel. . . . .
   1. Sparing no effort to maintain and increase professional standards, he utilizes all professional placement agencies. to obtain properly qualified teachers and administrators.
   2. He attempts to make vacancies known to present employees so that they may apply for preferred positions.
   3. He considers no position vacant and seeks no applicants for it before the present employee has resigned or has been notified that he will not be re-employed.

[2] California Association of School Administrators, California Association of Secondary School Administrators, California Elementary School Administrators' Association, and Personnel Standards Commission of the California Teachers' Association and the State Council of Education, *Administrator Ethics in Personnel Matters* (California: The Associations, April 1956). Reprinted by permission of the California Teachers' Association.

491

4. He adheres strictly to adopted salary schedules in employing new personnel.

5. Insofar as possible, he describes accurately the employment policies and educational philosophy of the district, the salary schedule, and the grade level, subject areas, or other assignment for which the candidate is being considered.

6. In interviewing out-of-state candidates, he informs them clearly regarding the loss of service credits toward retirement which they may incur by changing states and advises them to consider this factor in arriving at their decision.

7. He makes no offer of employment effective while the candidate is known to be under contract to another district unless that district has first notified him of its willingness to release the employee.

8. He confers with the superintendent of the district in which a candidate is currently employed regarding the effect on that district if the employee should be released to accept a position constituting an advancement.

9. He accepts no remuneration from commercial placement agencies whose candidates he interviews or employs.

B. In the supervision and leadership of his staff. . . . .

1. He assumes responsibility for the success of all employees, realizing that failure of an employee is at least partially an administrative failure—in selection, in supervision, or in assignment.

2. He makes sure that observed weaknesses are called to the attention of the employee, and that assistance toward their correction is extended.

3. He reports no negative criticism of any employee to the board without having first discussed this criticism with the employee involved.

4. He informs the board about the good performance and contributions of employees.

5. He is alert to opportunities to further the advancement of each employee.

6. He values the professional suggestions and criticisms of staff members, according to each the recognition to which he is entitled as a fellow professional in the field of education.

7. He provides opportunity for employees to discuss their problems or complaints freely with him and assists in the cooperative development of systematic channels for reporting and discussing employee grievances and suggestions.

C. In recommending re-employment or dismissal of employees. . . . .

1. Except under extraordinary circumstances, he notifies the employee by March 15 if he is not to be recommended for re-employment. This notice is given before final board action.

2. He utilizes evaluation reports as a basis for verbal or written information to the employee regarding reasons for non-reemployment.

3. He recommends that an employee be rehired unless the employee has been notified regarding his weaknesses and has been given time for, and assistance toward their correction.

4. He does not jeopardize the educational welfare of children in order to avoid an unpleasant dismissal relationship.

D. In respect to recommendations for former employees. . . . .
  1. He states accurately his appraisal of the strengths and weaknesses of the employee.
  2. Neither by implication nor by direct statement does he suggest to an employee that a letter of recommendation will be affected by submission of a resignation or failure to resign.
  3. He records no negative criticism in a letter of reference or in direct conversation with potential employers except those which have been called to the employee's attention during appraisal conferences.
  4. When requested to supply a letter of recommendation, he complies with the request within a reasonable time.
  5. He keeps confidential the content of confidential professional papers.

Research Plan for School Leavers

A SCHEDULE FOR
A FOLLOW-UP STUDY OF SCHOOL LEAVERS[3]

What year did you leave _____ High School? _____

Name: Mr.
     Mrs. _____   Present Address _____
          Optional   Optional

     Miss

Married
Girls _____   _____
    Write maiden name here — optional City   State

Phone _____   Date _____

1. What is your present employment status?
   a. ___ Employed for wages, full time.
   b. ___ Employed for wages, part time.
   c. ___ Unemployed and seeking work.
   d. ___ In armed forces.
   e. ___ Housewife.
   f. ___ In school full time.

   _____
           Name of School   Location

   How long after leaving high school did you enter present school? _____
                                            Months

2. If you are now employed, give
   a. Name of employer _____
   b. Business or product _____
   c. Kind of work you do: (Describe briefly)
      (1) ___ Executive _____
      (2) ___ Professional _____
      (3) ___ Managerial _____
      (4) ___ Clerical _____
      (5) ___ Skilled labor _____
      (6) ___ Semiskilled labor _____
      (7) ___ Other _____
   d. How long a period of time elapsed between the end of your high school education and your first job?
      (1) ___ 0 to 3 months.
      (2) ___ 4 to 6 months.
      (3) ___ 12 to 18 months.
      (4) ___ Months.

3. How did you obtain your first job after leaving high school?
   a. ___ Through family or friend.
   b. ___ Public employment agency.
          Where located? _____
   c. ___ Private employment agency.
   d. ___ Newspaper advertisement.
   e. ___ Through the school.
          What person in school? _____
   f. ___ Found it yourself.

[3] Glenn E. Smith, *Principles and Practices of the Guidance Program* (New York: The Macmillan Company, 1951), pp. 326–330. Reprinted with permission of The Macmillan Company.

4. If employed full time, what is your weekly wage range?

    a. ___ $21 to $30   c. ___ $41 to $50

    b. ___ $31 to $40   d. ___ $51 to $60   e. ___ over $60

5. List the jobs you have held since leaving school:

Employer	Kind of Work	Length of Employment

6. To what extent is your present job like the type of work you hoped you would follow when you left high school?

    a. ___ Didn't have any definite ideas about work while in high school.

    b. ___ Not related at all.

    c. ___ Is somewhat related.

    d. ___ Closely related, but not what I expected.

    e. ___ Exactly the kind of job I hoped I would get.

7. What is the relation of your high-school training to your present job?

    a. ___ No relation at all.

    b. ___ Gave me a general background.

    c. ___ Gave me a specific preparation.

8. What subjects taken in high school have been most helpful to you in your present job?

_____

9. What subjects taken in high school have been least helpful to you in your present job?

_____

10. How well satisfied are you with your present job?

    a. ___ Highly satisfied.

    b. ___ Reasonably well satisfied.

    c. ___ Indifferent.

    d. ___ Somewhat dissatisfied.

    e. ___ Very dissatisfied.

11. To what extent has the counseling you received been helpful to you? (Counseling here means individual help by teachers, counselors, and principal with educational, vocational, social, and other similar problems.)

    a. ___ Didn't receive counseling in high school.

    b. ___ It wasn't helpful at all.

    c. ___ Very little help.

    d. ___ Some help.

    e. ___ Extremely helpful.

12. To what extent do you feel a high school should attempt to help pupils solve their educational, vocational, and personal problems?

    a. ___ Very much

    b. ___ Much.

    c. ___ Some.

    d. ___ Very little.

    e. ___ None.

13. How much help did you receive from your high-school teachers in choosing and planning for an occupation?
    a. ____ None.
    b. ____ Very little.
    c. ____ Some.
    d. ____ Much.
    e. ____ Very much.

14. What were the outstanding qualities of the teacher you remember as having been most helpful to you while in high school?
    a. ____ Fairness.
    b. ____ Sense of humor.
    c. ____ Presentation of subject matter.
    d. ____ Personal appearance.
    e. ____ Pleasing personality.
    f. ____ Made you work hard.
    g. ____ Attempted to make class work fit the abilities and interests of each individual pupil.
    h. ____ Other _____

15. If you are employed in some community away from here, give your reason for leaving.
    a. ____ No opportunity in what I wanted to do.
    b. ____ Left because my family moved away.
    c. ____ Didn't like the community where I went to school.
    d. ____ Wanted to live where I am now.
    e. ____ Other reason.

16. If you attended college after leaving high school, which of your high-school experiences do you feel were most helpful to you?
    a. ____ College preparatory courses.
    b. ____ Extracurricular activities.
    c. ____ Learning to get along with others.
    d. ____ Counseling by faculty members.
    e. ____ Personal associations with teachers.
    f. ____ Other _____

17. If you attended school after leaving high school, give the following information:
    a. How long did you go? _____
       Months
    b. Degrees or diplomas received _____
    c. Do you think the high school should have provided the kind of training you have taken since leaving school? _____
       Yes   No
    d. Give types and names of schools you have attended:
       College _____
       Trade school _____
       Business school _____
       Evening school _____
       Employer's training program _____
       Correspondence course _____
       Other _____

18. List the social, civic, religious, and other community activities in which you now regularly participate. Indicate offices you hold or have held in each group.
    _____
    _____

19. List your present hobby or hobbies.
    _____
    _____

Constitution of the Utah High School Activities Association[4]

PREAMBLE

Recognizing the growing need for a cooperative agency, established by authority of the boards of education of the State of Utah, to plan, supervise, and administer activities in which schools and students thereof participate on an interdistrict basis, we, the Board of Education whose official endorsements are attached hereto approve this Constitution establishing the Utah High School Activities Association.

ARTICLE I

Name

The name of this Association shall be the Utah High School Activities Association (herein referred to in brief as "This Association" or "Activities Association.")

ARTICLE II

Purposes

Section 1: This Association, through the employment of the instrumentalities hereinafter set up, shall:

[4] Reprinted by permission of the Utah High School Activities Association, a member of the National Federation of High School Athletic Associations.

(a) Plan, supervise, control and administer all of the interscholastic activities in which its member schools may engage on an interdistrict basis as enumerated herein.

(b) Plan and administer such activities or have them planned and administered under its own officers or by committees or institutions appointed by them.

Section 2: In the performance of the functions, it shall be the aim of the Association to:

(a) Stress the cultural values, the appreciations and skills involved in all competitive activities and to promote cooperation and friendship.

(b) Encourage those interdistrict programs of activities which may be looked upon as promoting the general accepted objectives of secondary education.

ARTICLE III

Membership

Section 1: This Association shall consist of the following classifications of high schools in the State of Utah whose governing boards shall by official resolution approve and adopt this Constitution:

(a) Public High Schools
(b) High Schools conducted by colleges and universities for the purpose of practice teaching or educational research
(c) Private secondary schools
(d) Other secondary schools not enumerated herein
(e) All school memberships shall be approved by the Board of Directors of this association.

Section 2: Application for membership in this Association shall be signed by the principal of the high school and the official representative of the governing board of the school.

ARTICLE IV

Organization

Section 1: This Association shall function through:

(a) Regional Boards of Managers
(b) A Legislative Council
(c) A Board of Directors
(d) The executive officers who shall be:
    (1) A President
    (2) A Vice-president
    (3) An Executive Secretary-Treasurer

Section 2: (a) The state shall be divided into whatever number of regions the Legislative Council deems necessary.

(b) Each member high school shall be placed in one of these regions under the direction of the Legislative Council. (At present the Regions are constituted as follows:)

Region One

Division One—Bear River, Box Elder, Logan, Sky View.

Division Two—Ben Lomond, Bonneville, Ogden, Weber.

Region Two

Division One—Bountiful, Clearfield, Davis, Viewmont.

Division Two—East, Highland, South, West.

Region Three

Division One—Cyprus, Granger, Granite, Olympus, Skyline.

Division Two—Bingham, Hillcrest, Jordan, Judge Memorial, Murray, Tooele.

Region Four

Division One—American Fork, B. Y. High, Lehi, Pleasant Grove, Orem.

Division Two—Carbon, Payson, Provo, Spanish Fork, Springville.

Region Five

Dugway, Grantsville, Morgan, North Rich, North Summit, Park City, Rowland Hall - St. Mark's, South Rich, South Summit, Saint Francis, Saint Joseph, Tintic, Utah School For The Deaf, Wasatch.

Region Six

Altamont, Duchesne, East Carbon, Grand, Green River, Manila, Monticello, Notre Dame, San Juan, Tabiona, Uintah, Union.

Region Seven

Bryce Valley, Emery County, Escalante, Gunnison, Juab, Manti, North Sanpete, North Sevier, Panguitch, Piute, Richfield, South Sevier, Valley, Wasatch Academy, Wayne.

Region Eight

Beaver, Cedar City, Delta, Dixie, Enterprise, Hurricane, Kanab, Milford, Millard, Parowan.

(c) Each region shall divide itself into four legislative districts. For purposes of identification and voting these legislative districts shall be numbered and placed by regions as follows:

Region One Legislative District 1, 2, 3, 4

Region Two Legislative District 5, 6, 7, 8

Region Three Legislative District 9, 10, 11, 12

(and so on)

Section 3: (a) The management of the affairs of each region shall be vested in a Regional Board of Managers.

(b) Each Regional Board of Managers shall consist of at least one representative from each school district within said region. Any school board member, superintendent of schools, or senior high school principal is eligible to serve as a member of the Regional Board of Managers.

(c) The members constituting each Regional Board of Managers shall be elected at an annual meeting of the region to be held not later than May 15th. The meeting shall be called by the Regional Chairman and shall consist of one representative of each school district Board of Education, all superintendents, and all high school principals. The term of office shall be for one year, this term to begin July 1 and to end June 30th following, or until his successor has been duly elected and qualified.

(d) The member of the State Board of Directors from each region shall be a member of the Regional Board of Managers and shall be elected at the aforesaid annual meeting of the Region to be held not later than the first week in May. Those eligible to vote for the Directors from any region shall be one representative of each school district Board of Education, all superintendents of schools, and all senior high school principals within said region, provided the schools over which these representatives preside are member schools of this Association.

(e) Each Regional Board of Managers shall meet at such time and place as it may determine. A meeting may be called at any time upon the request of a majority of the Regional Board.

(f) The Regional Board of Managers shall have power to formulate its own organization.

(g) The Regional Board of Managers shall have general supervision over all activity contests held in its region or district, and shall have jurisdiction over questions arising therefrom, including eligibility. An appeal from its decisions on all matters involving interpretation of the Constitution may be made to the Board of Directors.

(h) The accounts of each region shall be audited annually by a Certified Public Accountant or a bonded employee of any member school district other than the Secretary-treasurer of the Region, and a copy of the audit shall be sent to each member school of the Region and to the Executive Secretary of the Association.

(i) All regional contests which have been approved by the Utah High School Activities Association shall be under the direction of the Board of that region.

(j) A school may be charged by any member school with violating the rules of the Association or with unsportsmanlike conduct. The Regional Board of Managers, after sending a copy of the charges to the responsible officials of the school concerned and giving due notice of the time and place of the meeting, shall consider the charges promptly. The Board may temporarily suspend a school.

ARTICLE V

Legislative Council

Section 1:(a) A Legislative Council, one member from each of the Legislative Districts within the Association provided for in Article IV, Section 2 (c) above, shall be the legislative, policy making body of this Association.

(b) The members of the Legislative Council shall be nominated and elected as follows:

(1) Candidates in each Legislative District shall be nominated and elected by the school representatives of each Legislative District.

(2) The election shall be held at the same time as the annual meeting of the region.

(c) The president, vice-president and secretary of the Association shall be president, vice-president and secretary respectively of the Legislative Council. The Council shall select such other officers as it deems advisable.

Section 2: (a) All proposed amendments to the Constitution shall be submitted to the Executive Secretary not later than December 31st preceding the date of the annual meeting of the Legislative Council. The Executive Secretary shall submit all such proposed amendments in writing to all member schools and to all superintendents of member schools not later than January 20th following.

(b) All proposed amendments to this Constitution and By-Laws and all other proposed legislation of a permanent character shall be referred to this Council for consideration. In considering such proposals, the Council shall permit any school authority, public or private to appear and promote or oppose any proposal or to counsel or advise the Council regarding any proposed modifications or proposals.

(c) Amendments to this Constitution having been presented to this Council for consideration and approved by the Council as provided for in the preceding paragraph must then be presented by mail ballot to all voting members of the Association, and if accepted by a two-thirds majority vote of the votes cast by the voting members of the Association, be a valid part of the Constitution. Those eligible to vote shall be one board member from each district, the district superintendent of schools, and the principals of member schools.

(d) Proposals in harmony with this Constitution and Amendments to the By-Laws accepted by a majority vote of this Council at meetings called in accordance with this Constitution, shall be the policy of this Association.

Section 3: (a) In initiating this organization representatives from districts 1, 4, 5, 9, 13, 16, 17, 21, 25, 28, 29 shall be elected for one year; representatives from districts 2, 6, 8, 10, 14, 18, 20, 22, 26, 30, 32 shall be elected for a two-year term; representatives from districts 3, 7, 11, 12, 15, 19, 23, 24, 27, 31 shall be elected for three years. In the event more than thirty-two legislative districts are created by the Legislative Council, one third of the new districts so created shall elect a member of the Legislative Council for one year term, one third for a two year term, and one third for a three year term. The Legislative Council shall designate the term for candidates from each newly created district. Present members of the Legislative Council may be re-elected for one term to initiate this amendment.

(b) In case of vacancy due to any cause, other than the expiration of a term, the chairman of the regional board of managers of the region whose member is causing the vacancy, shall appoint a representative to serve until the time of the next regular election. The representative must be appointed from the district in which the vacancy occurs. If the vacancy is not filled in 60 days the president of the Association shall fill such vacancy.

ARTICLE VI

Board of Directors

Section 1: The administration of the affairs of this Association shall be vested in a Board of Directors whose members are elected for a period of three years, except as hereinafter provided in Section 2, one from each of the administrative regions of the State as provided in Article IV, Section 2, the president and the vice-president of the Association, and the Director of Secondary Education of the State Department of Education, and one member appointed by the State School Boards Association.

Section 2: The present Regional representatives shall complete the terms for which they have been elected and will represent the new regions to which they have been assigned, with the exception of the Region IV. The Board of Directors will select one of the two representatives from Region IV to complete the term. Any new regions created shall choose representatives for a period of three years beginning with July 1 of the year in which their organization becomes effective or as directed by the Board of Directors.

Section 3: (a) The manner of election of the members of the Board of Directors shall be as provided in Article IV, Section 3, Paragraph D. Newly elected members of the Board of Directors shall take office July 1 following their election and shall hold office until their successors are elected and qualified.

(b) No member of the Board of Directors shall be eligible to succeed himself to this office.

(c) No Regional Division shall be permitted to have a member on the Board of Directors for two successive terms.

Section 4: The officers of the Board of Directors shall be president, vice-president, and executive secretary-treasurer. The president of the Association shall be president of the Board of Directors. The vice-president shall preside in the absence of the president. The executive secretary-treasurer shall be chosen by the Board of Directors, but shall not be a member of said board.

Section 5: Two candidates for president and vice-president shall be chosen by the Legislative Council at a regular meeting of the Council held on or before March 15 of each Election year. Starting with 1955, candidates for the office of president shall be from schools of the "A" classification and the candidates for vice-president are to be from the "B" classification. The names of the candidates are to be submitted by mail to each eligible voter as defined in Article XII, Sections 1 and 2. As president and vice-president of the Association, these elected members shall serve as chairman and vice-chairman respectively of the Board of Directors. Each shall take office July 1, following his election and shall hold office for two years and until a new vice-president is elected from the classification not represented by the vice-president. The vice-president automatically becomes president of the Association and president of the Board of Directors and Legislative Council at the close of his term as vice-president.

Section 6: The officers and members of the Board of Directors of this Association are hereby authorized to act as an administrative board in the interpretation and final decisions on all questions arising within the scope of this organization as determined by the Legislative Council, or the Constitution, from the directing of interscholastic activities, from protection of interests of member schools, from promotion of welfare of students who participate in interschool activities as conducted by the various districts and regions of which this Association is composed, and from the integration of the activities program with the school curriculum.

Section 7: The majority of the Board shall constitute a quorum for the transaction of business.

Section 8: The Board of Directors shall have power to fill vacancies arising within the Board, to serve until the next regular annual meeting of the Region or until the successor has been chosen and qualified.

Section 9: In case of controversy from any cause relative to violation of the Constitution or By-Laws of this Association, the Board of Directors shall constitute a Board of Appeals which shall hear all complaints, decide protests, and interpret the Constitution and By-Laws. In case any one of the Board of Directors is directly interested in the controversy, the President shall appoint a disinterested person to take the place of such member while deciding the case.

Section 10: The Board of Directors shall be responsible for carrying out the policies and conducting the business of the Association and shall be empowered to provide office facilities and employees for the proper conduct of such business. Special committees may be appointed by the Board of Directors to administer activities of this Association.

Section 11: The Board of Directors shall receive and hold title to all funds transferred to this Association by the Utah High School Athletic Association and shall manage such funds solely in the interest of the activity to which such funds originally belonged, and no funds shall be diverted therefrom except by the following method: A recommendation supported by a two-thirds vote of those in attendance at any annual meeting and a majority vote of those eligible voters in a state-wide referendum to be taken by the Board of Directors following such recommendation at the annual meeting.

Section 12: The Board of Directors shall each year prepare or cause to be prepared a budget for the operation of the Association, which budget shall indicate a proposed schedule of dues from members and shall include anticipated revenues, and proposed expenditures for each activity in which this Association participates. Any transfer of surplus funds from one activity to another which are included in this budget must be approved by a majority vote of the Legislative Council. This budget shall be presented to the Legislative Council for approval. Within the total budget, the Board of Directors may transfer funds from one item to another as circumstances make such action necessary to carry on the program for which this Association is organized, provided that such transfer shall be reported to the Legislative Council at its annual meeting.

ARTICLE VII

Funds, Fees and Expenses

Section 1: The annual dues of member schools shall be determined by the Board of Directors.

Note: In schools of more than four grades enrollment shall include those grades nine to twelve inclusive which participate in the state senior high school program of activities.

Section 2: The dues shall be for the school year and are due and payable on or before October 1 and must be paid on or before January 1. In case a school has allowed its membership to lapse, it cannot regain membership until it has paid into the treasury the current dues plus a penalty amounting to one-third of the annual dues for that school for each year lapsed. The penalty payment shall not exceed one full year's dues.

Section 3: All membership dues collected shall be considered Association funds and shall be applied to the payment of expenses involved in conducting the business of the association.

Section 4: The Board of Directors is hereby authorized to levy entry fees and such other assessments upon all schools participating in any interscholastic activity as shall be adequate to meet the total expenses involved in the conduct of such activity and such proportionate share of overhead as is deemed necessary.

Section 5: The determination of additional activity fees, receipts of contests, their collection and distribution shall be left to the discretion of the Board of Directors.

ARTICLE VIII

The Executive Secretary-Treasurer

Section 1: The Executive Secretary-treasurer is an officer of the Association and of the Board of Directors, and shall be selected by the Board for a two year term starting with 1956. He shall have no vote on the board.

Section 2: The executive secretary-treasurer shall furnish a bond, the amount of which shall be determined by the Board of Directors.

Section 3: The executive secretary-treasurer shall receive for deposit all funds belonging to the Association. He shall pay out money from funds belonging to this Association in the payment of bills only upon order of the Board of Directors. The President of the Association shall countersign all checks. The Board of Directors shall establish a procedure for payment of bills which shall expedite the business of the Association in accordance with budget limitations of the Association and in harmony with good budgetary procedure.

Section 4: The Executive Secretary-treasurer shall make a complete financial statement to the Association annually. His accounts shall be audited annually by a Certified Public Accountant approved by the Board of Directors.

Section 5: The executive secretary-treasurer shall keep separate and complete bookkeeping records of all receipts and expenditures relating to all the various activities of this Association.

Section 6: It shall be the duty of the executive secretary-treasurer within fifteen days after January 1st of each year to furnish the members of this Association with an official list of all schools belonging to this Association.

Section 7: When directed by the Board of Directors, the executive secretary-treasurer shall submit questions to the members by mail, but no binding vote shall be taken except as otherwise provided in this Constitution.

ARTICLE IX

Meetings

Section 1: There may be an annual meeting of this Association to which all those eligible to vote are invited. The time and place of such meeting, if called, shall be set by the Board of Directors.

Section 2: Special meetings of the whole membership may be called by the President when directed by action of the Legislative Council and must be called by the Secretary upon the written request of twenty per cent of the member schools.

Section 3: Representatives of the majority of the member schools shall constitute a quorum for the transaction of business.

Section 4: The officers of the Legislative Council shall determine the time and place for the annual meeting of the Council. Special meetings may be called by the President and must be called by the secretary upon the written request of a majority of the Council.

Section 5: The principal of each member school, or someone delegated by him in writing, shall represent such school in all matters involving the relationship of his school with other schools under the rules of this Association.

ARTICLE X

Miscellaneous

Section 1: The officers of the Utah High School Athletic Association holding office at the time this Constitution becomes effective shall be accepted as officers of the Utah High School Activities Association, and shall continue to serve in their respective capacities as officers of this Association until their terms shall expire or as new officers shall be elected to take their place according to the regular procedure as outlined in this Constitution.

Section 2: Any office in the Association shall become vacant if the incumbent ceases to be a high school principal, superintendent, or a school board member in the district from which he was elected, except that any member of the Council removed from his district through redistricting of the State shall continue to represent his organized district until the expiration of his term.

ARTICLE XI

The interscholastic activities within the jurisdiction of this Association are:
1. Athletics, including dancing and marching

2. Music
3. Speech activities, including debate and drama
4. Commercial activities, including typing and shorthand
5. Such other activities not enumerated above as may be approved by the Board of Directors.

ARTICLE XII

Elections

Section 1: The vote for proposed amendments to the Constitution and the election for the vice-president shall be conducted by mail ballot during the month of April. The election of the president in 1955 shall be conducted in the same manner as is the vice-president.

Section 2: Those eligible to vote on proposed amendments to the Constitution and for vice-president (and for president in 1955) are one board member for each school district whose schools are members of the Association, all superintendents with at least one member school in the Association, and the principal of each member school.

Section 3: The Legislative Council shall appoint an election committee of three members to conduct each election and count the ballots.

Constitution and By-Laws of the Utah High School Activities Association [5]

ELIGIBILITY OF PLAYERS

ARTICLE I

19 Year Age Rule

Section 1. No student shall be eligible to represent his school in any contest who has reached the age of nineteen years at the beginning of the semester in which the contest takes place.

Semester Attendance Rule

Section 2. (a)   A student shall be eligible to represent his school in interscholastic competition for as many semesters, not exceeding eight, as are regularly offered by his school to complete the necessary credits for graduation.

(b) In case a student transfers from one high school to another, the total amount of residence in high schools eligible to membership in this association, including the ninth grade, shall not exceed eight semesters.

Insofar as this rule affects eligibility in regular six or four-year high schools, students may be eligible for eight semesters; in three-year high schools they may be eligible for six semesters; and in two-year high schools they may be eligible for four semesters. In other words, a student is eligible only for as many semesters as it would normally take him to graduate.

(For example: If a student repeats the tenth grade of a three-year high

[5] Reprinted by permission of the Utah High School Activities Association.

school, thus taking four semesters to complete the tenth grade, he will be eligible for activities only two more semesters. If he should transfer to a two-year senior high school for the eleventh grade he will be eligible in that school for only two semesters. In the case of all transfers the responsibility rests with the school to which a student transfers to secure an accurate record of the previous high school attendance of a student.)

There may be a lapse in attendance between semesters without penalty, providing that the work of the last previous semester attended is completed satisfactorily.

(c) In this computation, six or more weeks attendance in any semester, without competition, shall count as a full semester but playing in a league game or taking part in any contest at any time during a semester shall count as attendance for the semester, independent of the number of days actually attended.

Six or more weeks attendance is interpreted to mean enrollment—the lapsed time from the date the student first attends school until the last day of school attendance in that semester.

Sports Season Rule

Section 3. No student shall participate in interscholastic activities during more than four seasons in any one activity. (Three seasons if three year high school; two seasons if two year high school.)

Playing on Team of Higher Institution

Section 4. No student shall be eligible to represent his school in interscholastic competition who has ever participated on the team of an institution higher than that of secondary grade.

Last Day of Enrollment

Section 5. No student shall be eligible to represent his school in interscholastic competition unless he shall have been enrolled and in full residence not later than the beginning of the eleventh school day of the first semester, with the following exceptions: If he enters the third week, he shall be in attendance one full week before he may participate in interscholastic competition; if he enters the fourth week, he shall be in attendance two full weeks before he may so participate; if he enters school later than the fourth week, he shall be ineligible to play during the semester. In the second semester, students must register within the first two weeks to be eligible.

When the Second Semester Begins

Section 6. A student ineligible for any cause during one semester of school shall not participate in the next semester until the school work of that semester shall have actually begun.

If the semester ends on Friday the student is not eligible to play until the following week.

Amateur Rule

Section 7: (a) All contestants participating in athletic activities approved and/or sponsored by the Association must be amateurs. Professionalism is defined as having accepted remuneration directly or indirectly for playing in approved Association athletic contests as an individual or team participant or playing under an assumed name. Reasonable meals, lodging and transportation charges may be accepted if accepted in service but not in any other way. Athletes may not receive donations, prizes and/or gifts for participation and any money paid for expenses must be paid to the school and not the individual. A student who becomes a professional in any Association approved and/or sponsored athletic sport is considered a professional in all approved and/or sponsored athletic sports and is barred from further high school athletics.

(b) Contestants participating in any approved and/or sponsored athletic activity of any kind during the summer, or during a season when the player is not a member of a regular high school team, shall not be considered a violation of this article, providing he does not receive money, prizes, and/or gifts for his services.

Scholastic Regulations

Section 8. No student shall be eligible to represent his school in interscholastic competition unless he is passing satisfactorily in at least five periods where the student is on a six period day, or six periods, where the student is on a seven period day, etc. Subjects once passed and accredited, but repeated for any reason in a subsequent semester, shall not be counted a second time.

Section 9. No student shall be eligible to represent his school in interscholastic competition unless he shall have passed satisfactorily in at least five periods where the student is on a six period day, or six periods where the student is on a seven period day, etc. for the previous semester the student was in school, except in the case of those who are entering upon secondary school work for the first time having been duly promoted from the grade below.

Note that this refers to the previous semester only and not to credit received during the entire previous year.

This section does not apply to students who are transferring to a four year high school from an eighth grade, to a three year high school from the ninth grade or a junior high school, or to a two year senior high school from the tenth grade of a junior high school. In case of transfer of ninth or tenth grade students from a high school in which students of those grades are eligible for competition in high school activities, the previous semester's work must be completed and all semesters of attendance in these grades are credited against the total permitted for eligibility.

It is not permissible for students to make up work in the summer or fall in order to get credit for enough work in the previous semester.

Section 10: No student shall receive credit toward eligibility in any semester unless he shall have been in attendance at least twelve weeks of that semester. (e.g. A student may not enter the first semester when it is half completed and receive credit in that semester to make him eligible the next semester.)

Any student who has received credit in the spring semester of one school year, but who is unable to enter school the next fall until six weeks or more late, will not be permitted to participate in interscholastic activities in that semester but he will have that semester's residence count as one of the total number of semesters attendance permitted for eligibility. However, he will be permitted to count the previous semester's credit toward his eligibility for the second semester of the next year.

Transfer Rule

Section 11. No student changing from one high school to another shall be eligible to represent the latter school in interscholastic competition until he shall have been in attendance one full semester and shall have passed satisfactorily in at least five periods where the student was on a six period day, or six periods where the student was on a seven period day. This rule shall not be construed to include those who are entering senior high school from junior high school or those who, having completed all the work given in one high school, are entering another school in a grade one year in advance of the work given in the first school, provided the work of the previous semester is satisfactorily passed in accordance with above requirements.

Exception—This rule shall not apply if the transfer is made necessary because of the change of residence of the parent or legal guardian.

1. A legal guardian, other than a parent, must be so declared by court action.

2. Students who transfer from one school to another school, without a change in residence, must be in attendance one full semester before being eligible for interscholastic activities. This means that students may not switch from school to school in the same school district, or adjacent school districts, without a loss in competition for one semester.

3. Students are ineligible for the first semester after leaving a private school, or any other school where they have not lived with their parents. One of the main objectives of the Transfer Rule is to discourage the "tramp athlete."

Undue Influence

Section 12. The use of undue influence by any person connected or not connected with the school to secure or to retain a student or the parents of a student shall cause the student to be ineligible and shall jeopardize the standing of the school in the Association.

Graduates Ineligible

Section 13. To be eligible for competition, a student shall not have graduated from any four year high school course or its equivalent.

May Not Play on Two Teams

Section 14. No student shall be eligible for competition in any athletic activity who, during the regular playing season or tournament seasons of that activity, plays with or is a member of any team other than his high school team.

(This prohibits boys on high school teams from playing with industrial leagues, "M" Men, or other outside teams.)

Physical Examination Required

Section 15. No student shall be eligible for competition in any athletic activity who is not able to pass a physical examination given by a practicing M.D. That such an examination has been given and successfully passed by the student shall be certified to on the eligibility application form.

ARTICLE II

Exchange of Eligibility Lists

Section 1. (a) At least five days prior to the first contest in the fall semester each high school shall submit to all scheduled opponents and the office of the secretary-treasurer a master list of all students eligible during the first semester for activities under the provisions of the By-Laws of the Constitution. Additions to the list will be certified at once to the secretary-treasurer and to the competing schools in a similar manner on an additional master list. At the beginning of the Second semester the same procedure as for the first semester shall be followed. These lists shall be certified by the principal of the competing school.

(b) Certification shall be based on complete information concerning the student's age and scholastic history. Questionable cases shall be referred to the state secretary before the privilege of competition is given.

Interpretations

The purpose of this Section is to clarify eligibility in advance of contests rather than subsequently. The State Association will expect schools to check with care all lists submitted and to report at once to the competing school any seemingly authentic information indicating the eligibility of a player and will look with disfavor on protests made after games have been played unless it can be shown that evidence of ineligibility was not in hand or available before the contest.

Schools may not waive the exchange of eligibility lists before a game.

Participation on second or reserve teams is to be considered as a season of competition and should be so included on eligibility lists under the heading "Number of Seasons of Participation in This Sport Including Present Season."

Where a change is made in the record of age, number of semesters of attendance, or seasons of competition, from that which has previously appeared on eligibility lists, and where such a change would be to the advantage of the student concerned, it shall not be made until permission has been secured from the office of the State Secretary.

Attention is called to Section (a) which provides that a copy of the Eligibility List for each activity should be sent to each scheduled opponent and the office of the executive secretary at the beginning of each season or semester.

ARTICLE III

Protests and Penalties

Section 1. All protests shall be filed in writing with the Regional Board of Managers. Protests should include all necessary information bearing on the case. All expense must be paid by the school at fault.

Section 2. All contests in which players compete whose names do not appear on eligibility lists may be declared forfeited, and the offending school, or schools pay any expense incurred by the region in the adjudication of controversies.

The offending school shall be subject to suspension.

Breach of Contract

Section 3. In case of breach of contract, the Region Board of Managers shall have authority to assess a penalty, not to exceed $25.00 against the offending school. The amount shall be sent to the secretary-treasurer, who shall remit that portion due to the offended school and deposit the balance in the Regional Treasury.

Defacement of School Property and Unsportsmanlike Conduct

Section 4. (a) Defacement or marring of school property by members of another school may subject the offending school to suspension from the Association for one year. This offense shall be understood to include disfigurement of any sort, by means of paint, kalsomine, chalk, or like material upon school property or upon any other property; also, the commission of any act by a member or members of another school which would tend to throw discredit upon the latter school.

(b) A student who has been guilty of dishonesty regarding his age shall be disqualified from further participation in contests of this Association.

(c) A student who has been guilty of using improper language in a game shall be disqualified from further participation in that contest.

(d) Betting on the part of a player shall disqualify him from participation in any athletic contest of this Association.

ARTICLE IV

Schedule

Section 1. All scheduled interscholastic contests shall be governed by this Association.

Section 2. All schedules of games shall be approved by the local Boards of Education. Contests, other than the scheduled games, shall be approved by the Regional Board of Managers at least one week before the date of competition. All games or schedules shall be so arranged as to interfere with but a minimum of school work.

Awards

Section 3. (a) No award of any kind other than medals and/or certificates shall be made to players participating in inter-school activities. Medals shall not exceed three dollars ($3.00) in value.

(b) No fabric letter of any kind shall be awarded by a school or by any other organization for activities.

(c) Any member of the Association violating this rule shall be suspended for one year.

Practice Post-season, and Pre-season Contests

Section 4. (a) The Board of Directors shall determine the time that schools shall utilize for practice in each and all activities.

(b) Pre-season games and contests, Post-season games and contests, and number of games to be played during the sport season shall be governed by the Board of Directors.

ARTICLE V

Certified Teacher Only May Coach

Section 1. Coaches other than those regularly employed by the Board of Education as certified teachers shall be prohibited.

ARTICLE VI

Contests with Non-member Schools Prohibited

Section 1. Members of the Utah High School Activities Association shall be prohibited from engaging in contests with Utah High Schools that are not members of the Utah High School Activities Association.

Section 2. Members of the Utah High School Activities Association shall be prohibited from engaging in contests with high schools outside of Utah who are not members of their respective state high school associations.

Section 3. The penalty for violation of the above sections may be suspension or expulsion from the Utah High School Activities Association for the offending school.

ELIGIBILITY AND OUT-OF-SEASON ATHLETIC ACTIVITIES

The Board of Directors have ruled that any student engaging in any out-of-season athletic activity is ineligible for the remainder of the current school year in all activities which are sponsored by this Association. A student is considered engaging in out-of-season activities when, after participating in an activity sponsored by the U.H.S.A.A., he joins a non-school group and continues competition in the same activity. A student participating with a non-school group, in league or tournament play, not completed by the end of the U.H.S.A.A. sports season, would be permitted to play with his group until the conclusion of their league or tournament. The spirit of this regulation is that varsity, second team, sophomore squad members, etc., should discontinue basketball, and all other school activities, at the conclusion of the respective U.H.S.A.A. playing seasons.

A high school athlete, who has been a member of a basketball team or squad in his school, is ineligible for the balance of the school year in all activities which are sponsored by this Association if he participates in any basketball games beyond the Regional or Divisional league season which includes his school.

You are reminded that any high school squad member is prohibited from playing with non-school squads during the regular playing season or tournament seasons of that activity.

The Board of Directors have approved of the following resolutions of the Society of State Health, Physical Education and Recreation Directors resulting from the National Conference in April, 1951, at Detroit.

We believe that:

a. Interscholastic athletic participation for girls should be an outgrowth of a broad program of physical education instruction and intramural athletics.

b. Interscholastic athletics for girls should be of the sports day or play-day type.

c. Girls' athletic teams should be coached and directed by well-qualified, professionally prepared women.

d. Rules and policies governing athletic activities for girls should be developed in accordance with the needs of girls, and should be developed by, or acceptable to, professionally qualified women physical educators.

e. Games should be officiated insofar as possible by qualified women officials.

f. We are unalterably opposed to state and regional tournaments for girls.

A Broad-Base Intramural Program

STUDENTS CODE

1. I will be on time for all activities.
2. I will play hard and fair to the end.
3. I will conduct myself as a gentleman or lady.
4. I will not alibi.
5. I will not gloat over winning.
6. I will not be a rotten loser.
7. I will not underestimate an opponent, or overestimate myself.
8. I will honor the game thou playest for he who playeth the game straight and clean and hard is a winner even tho he loses.

RULES GOVERNING I.M.A.

The intramural program for both boys and girls will be organized through the homerooms with the points of both boys and girls being credited to the homeroom for all activities. The total points of both boys and girls for all activities at the end of the year will determine the intramural champion. Each room will choose the name that it desires to go by during the year.

INTRAMURAL ACTIVITY COMMITTEE

The boy's director of P.E., the girl's director of P.E., the director of instrumental and string music, director of debating, director of vocal music, director

516

of dramatics, and any others the principal deems necessary to appoint, will form the ruling body and be known as the I.M.A. Committee. Chairman to be appointed by principal of the school and will preside at all meetings. Meetings to be held when necessary.

I. M. PRESIDENT OF (MANAGER) (GIRL & BOY)

To be chosen, after application, by the directors of boys' and girls' intramural. Each to be responsible for respective activities.

ACTIVITY MANAGER

To be chosen by the I.M.A. Committee to manage each activity sponsored by the committee. It shall be the duty of this manager to attend to all details connected with the management of the activity.
1. Advertise starting date ten days in advance.
2. Have all entries in four days before activity starts. If not in, check with homeroom managers.
3. Post complete tournament bracket and first day's schedule three days before starting date. Post all schedules three days ahead if possible.
4. Line up officials for all contests and make sure they will be there.
5. Have all equipment needed by officials and players on hand before activity time.
6. Be at contest to see everything goes as planned.
7. Take all of the day's schedule down at the end of the day and put up the results.
8. Keep participation records of individuals in the activity.
9. When activity is complete, give to I.M. president. Each activity manager will receive student body points for successfully managing an activity.

HOMEROOM MANAGER

Each homeroom will elect one boy and one girl I.M. manager to manage their homeroom in all activities. It will be their duty to get their entries into the I.M. activity manager three days before the activity starts. Must keep home active in all activities. They will keep a record of all points earned by each individual in their homeroom and turn the record into the I.M.A. Committee when asked for.

BULLETIN BOARD

There is an I.M. bulletin board in the halls, near the school office, also on the left side of the trophy case as one enters the gym.

ELIGIBILITY

Every boy and girl registered in school is eligible to participate in any activity. Must have a good physical rating and suggested school insurance or a plan of insurance. During football and basketball the boys on the "A" team will not be eligible to play in that sport. (B Basketball) A list of these boys will be posted by the coach at the beginning of each sport. Must conform to school regulation.

GENERAL RULES

Activities must be run off when scheduled or the homeroom at fault will forfeit the contest. Two homerooms may be combined. However, permission of the committee should be gained when there are not enough in one homeroom to make up a unit. Any team that fails to report for the first activity contest will lose their entrance points. The team winning the event will receive the number of points list and the rest of the places will be apportioned down from that number depending on number entered.

Each homeroom may enter one team in all team activities and a double elimination tournament will be held.

Each homeroom may enter as many individuals as they wish in individual activities. Music, speech, arts, debating, only two may enter from each room. The finals in the above will not be judged in competition with each other but will stand on their own merit: 50 points for superior, 42 excellent, 34 good, 26 very promising, 18 medium, 10 fair.

AWARDS

Homeroom champions will have their picture framed and hung in the intramural case by the gym. Also in the yearbook. Teams who win each event will also have picture in yearbook.

INDIVIDUAL AWARDS

For boy and girl with most individual points—picture in yearbook, recognition given in assembly.

INDIVIDUAL POINTS

Intramural president	50
Art	5 and 1 for each degree above fair
Debating	10 or 6 and 3 for every win after first debate

Homeroom manager	25
Judge of an activity	3
Music	5 and 1 for each degree above fair
Officiating a sport	2
Playing a game	1 for each game played in
Speech arts	5 and 1 for each degree above fair
Track	3 and 1 for every event the student places in

HOMEROOM SCORING AND ACTIVITY MANAGER

EVENT	ENTRANCE POINTS	WINNERS POINTS	MANAGER POINTS
Archery	35	50	10
Art	50	100	10
Badminton (Boys)	25	25	20
" (Girls)			
" (Mixed)			
Basketball (Boys and Girls)	50	100	20
Debating	50	100	20
Dramatic Monologues	25	50	10
Instrumental Solo	25	50	10
Instrumental Duet	25	50	10
Instrumental Quartet	25	75	10
Interpretative Reading	25	50	10
Music Appreciation	25	25	10
Ping Pong (Boys and Girls)	25	25	10
Soft Ball (Mixed)	50	100	20
Speech	25	75	10
Touch Football	50	100	20
Speedball	50	100	20
Snow Sculpture			
Track	50	100	20
Wrestling	50	100	20
Vocal Solos	25	50	10
Vocal Duets	25	50	10
Vocal Trio	35	75	10
Vocal Quartettes or Larger	35	75	10
Volleyball	50	100	20
Other			

CHART FOR COMPUTING HOMEROOM POINTS

(Add entrance points to total)

	100 Points	75 Points	50 Points	25 Points		100	75	50	25
1st	100	75	50	25	Superior	100	75	50	25
2	88	66	44	22	Excellent	84	63	42	21
3	76	57	38	19	Good	68	51	34	17
4	64	48	32	16	V. P.	52	39	26	13
5	52	39	26	13	Medium	36	27	18	9
6	40	30	20	10	Fair	20	15	10	5
7	28	21	14	7					
8	19	12	8	4					

INTRAMURALS
RECORDS

NAME   ACTIVITY

TEAM POINTS

INDIVIDUAL
POINTS

INTRAMURALS
ENTRY BLANK

Enter _____ In _____
        Name of Team or Individual   Activity

To begin on _____   Following is a list of entrants:
                  Date

TOUCH FOOTBALL
(Example of Requirements)
(Presented for Each Activity)

ENTRANCE POINTS 50   WINNERS POINTS 100

<u>RULES</u>

1. All games should be played at time scheduled, on high school playing field and on the space assigned for the different games.
2. The game shall consist of four five-minute quarters with a three minute rest between halves, and one minute rest between quarters. Change goals only at half time. Three downs for touchdown or lose the ball.
3. In case of a tie game, three downs will be given each team from the center of the field and the score or total yardage will then win the game.
4. Eight players shall represent or comprise a team. No team may participate that does not have at least five men there.
5. A team that is not present and ready to play 10 minutes after game time shall lose the game by forfeit.
6. The ball shall be put in play at the beginning of each half and after each score by a kickoff from 12 yards in front of the kickers goal. The kickoff may be run back by the offensive team whether they catch it or not. Out of bounds will be played where it leaves the playing area. A kick over the goal line will be placed on the 12 yard line to be put into play.
7. The team scored on will have the choice of kicking or receiving. A team may try a drop kick or a field goal when forced to kick. The ball must go between the goal posts, field goal counts three points, extra point one. Time is out on extra point try.
8. After a touchdown the ball will be kicked, run or passed from the five yard line when trying for extra point.
9. Offside penalty is 5 yards. Unnecessary roughness 25 yards and the person ejected from the game. Only brush blocking on the line and two hand touch below the belt to halt the player advancing the ball. Other rules have the same interpretation as regular football rules.

Play Hard   Play Clean   Have Fun   Enjoy Intramurals

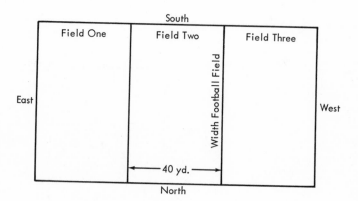

South

| Field One | Field Two | Field Three |

Width Football Field

East

West

←—— 40 yd. ——→

North

Index of Names

Index of Subjects

525